YEARLY

CURRENT AFFAIRS

2025

01 JANUARY TO 31 DECEMBER

EDITION: First

Published By: Physicswallah Private Limited

Physics Wallah Publication

ISBN: 978-93-6897-469-7

MRP: 199/-

Mobile App: Physics Wallah (Available on Play Store)

Website: **www.pw.live**

Youtube Channels: Physics Wallah - Alakh Pandey
SSC Wallah,
Defence Wallah,
Banking Wallah

Email: publication@pw.live

SKU Code: 50e30731-7a00-4c53-a62e-02dad2caca63

Printed By Utility Forms Pvt. Ltd.

PREFACE

Dear Aspirants,

Introducing the **Yearly Current Affairs Magazine**, a comprehensive compilation of the most significant events, National news, International news, Banking and Economy, Schemes, Sports, Developments, Science and technology updates, Appointments and Resignation, and Summits and Conference etc. that have taken place in the past twelve months (January to December 2024).

Our highly skilled professional team at **Physics Wallah (PW)** diligently ensures that aspirants receive the best chapter-wise current affairs spanning from January to December 2024. This includes Upcoming Exam Notification 2025, Union Budget 2024-25, Nobel Prize & Bharat Ratna 2024, Lok Sabha & States Election 2024,G20 & G7 Summit 2024,51st Chief Justice Of India, India's 1st Reusable Hybrid Rocket 'RHUMI-1',Pager, Walkie-Talkie Blasts in Lebanon, 1000+ Current Affairs Questions, 1000+ One Liner Current Affairs, Games and Puzzle, and Previous Year Question Paper designed for various competitive exams like Banking, SSC, Railway, Defence, Teaching, and Other Government Exams.

By reading the current affairs, attempting the 1000+ One Liner Current Affairs blaster, and engaging with the Games and Puzzles provided in the book, aspirants can assess their progress and enhance their preparedness for upcoming competitive exams. Mastering the Physics Wallah (PW) Yearly Current Affairs magazine, curated by Aasim Sir and PW team, will undoubtedly increase the aspirants' chances of qualifying for the exam with the highest possible score.

We sincerely hope that this Yearly Current Affairs magazine proves to be valuable study material, assisting you in preparing for your upcoming competitive exams.

The Book Features:

- Upcoming Exam Notification to Pull Your Socks up
- Coverage of last 12 months current affairs across 21 chapters
- 1000+ One Liner Current Affairs Questions
- Infographics Form Content For a better understanding
- 1000+ CA Questions for your Last Step Towards Exam
- Games and Puzzles related to Current Affairs to boost your Mind
- Past Year Question Paper to Understand the Label and Type of Questions
- Monthly current affairs magazine through QR code

Current Affairs Trend Analysis 2024 Exams

Chapters Name	SSC CHSL (5 Shifts)	SSC MTS (5 Shifts)	SSC CGL (5Shifts)	NDA	CDS	AFCAT	IBPS PO	SBI PO
National Affairs	2	3	4	2	2		3	5
International Affairs	2			2	1	1	1	2
Banking and Economy			1				8	8
State Affairs	3	3	3			2		2
Ranking and Reports	1	2		1			1	
MoU and Agreements			1	2	2			2
Science and Tech	1					1	1	3
Defence and Securities	1		1		2	1	1	1
Schemes and Projects	3	1	3	1			4	2
Summit and Conference		1						
Environment and Ecology			2		1			1
Sports Affairs	5	3	4		1		1	1
Awards and Honours	2	6	2		1	1	1	1
Appointments and Resignations	4	2	1				2	
Obituaries								
Important Days								
Books and Authors	1		1					
Total Questions	25	21	23	8	10	7	23	28
Average questions per paper	5	4-5	4-5	8	10	7	23	28

CONTENTS

UPCOMING EXAMS NOTIFICATION

Upcoming SSC Exams 2025

Staff Selection Commission (SSC) tentative calendar of examinations for the year 2025-2026:

S. No.	Name of Examination	Tier/ Phase	Date of Advt.	Closing date	Date/ Month of Exam
1	JSA/ LDC Grade Limited Departmental Competitive Examination, 2024 (only for DoPT)	Paper-I (CBE)*	28-Feb-2025 (Friday)	20-Mar-2025 (Thursday)	Apr-May, 2025
2	SSA/ UDC Grade Limited Departmental Competitive Examination, 2024 (only for DoPT)	Paper-I (CBE)*	06-Mar-2025 (Thursday)	26-Mar-2025 (Wednesday)	Apr-May, 2025
3	ASO Grade Limited Departmental Competitive Examination, 2022- 2024	Paper-I (CBE)*	20-Mar-2025 (Thursday)	09-Apr-2025 (Wednesday)	Apr-May, 2025
4	Selection Post Examination, Phase- XIII, 2025	CBE*	16-Apr-2025 (Wednesday)	15-May-2025 (Thursday)	Jun-Jul, 2025
5	Combined Graduate Level Examination, 2025	Tier-I (CBE)*	22-Apr-2025 (Tuesday)	21-May-2025 (Wednesday)	Jun-Jul, 2025
6	Sub-Inspector in Delhi Police and Central Armed Police Forces Examination, 2025	Paper-I (CBE)*	16-May-2025 (Friday)	14-Jun-2025 (Saturday)	Jul-Aug, 2025
7	Combined Higher Secondary (10+2) Level Examination, 2025	Tier-I (CBE)*	27-May-2025 (Tuesday)	25-Jun-2025 (Wednesday)	Jul-Aug, 2025
8	Multi Tasking (Non- Technical) Staff, and Havaldar (CBIC & CBN) Examination-2025	CBE*	26-Jun-2025 (Thursday)	25-Jul-2025 (Friday)	Sep-Oct, 2025
9	Stenographer Grade 'C' & 'D' Examination, 2025	CBE*	29-Jul-2025 (Tuesday)	21-Aug-2025 (Thursday)	Oct-Nov, 2025
10	Junior Engineer (Civil, Mechanical, Electrical) Examination, 2025	Paper-I (CBE)*	05-Aug-2025 (Tuesday)	28-Aug-2025 (Thursday)	Oct-Nov, 2025
11	Combined Hindi Translators Examination, 2025	Paper-I (CBE)*	26-Aug-2025 (Tuesday)	18-Sep-2025 (Thursday)	Oct-Nov, 2025
12	Constable (Executive) Male and Female in Delhi Police Examination, 2025	CBE*	02-Sep-2025 (Tuesday)	01-Oct-2025 (Wednesday)	Nov-Dec, 2025
13	Constable (Driver)-Male in Delhi Police Examination, 2025	CBE*	19-Sep-2025 (Friday)	12-Oct-2025 (Sunday)	Nov-Dec, 2025
14	Head Constable (Ministerial) in Delhi Police Examination, 2025	CBE*	07-Oct-2025 (Tuesday)	05-Nov-2025 (Wednesday)	Dec, 2025 -Jan, 2026
15	Head Constable {Assistant Wireless Operator (AWO)/Tele-Printer Operator (TPO)} in Delhi Police Examination, 2025	CBE*	14-Oct-2025 (Tuesday)	06-Nov-2025 (Thursday)	Dec, 2025 -Jan, 2026
16	Grade 'C' Stenographer Limited Departmental Competitive Examination, 2025	Paper-I (CBE)*	30-Oct-2025 (Thursday)	19-Nov-2025 (Wednesday)	Jan-Feb, 2026
17	Constables (GD) in Central Armed Police Forces (CAPFs), NIA, SSF and Rifleman (GD) in Assam Rifles Examination, 2026	CBE*	11-Nov-2025 (Tuesday)	15-Dec-2025 (Monday)	Mar-Apr, 2026
18	JSA/ LDC Grade Limited Departmental Competitive Examination, 2025	Paper-I (CBE)*	16-Dec-2025 (Tuesday)	05-Jan-2026 (Monday)	Jan-Feb, 2026
19	SSA/ UDC Grade Limited Departmental Competitive Examination, 2025	Paper-I (CBE)*	23-Dec-2025 (Tuesday)	12-Jan-2026 (Monday)	Jan-Feb, 2026
20	ASO Grade Limited Departmental Competitive Examination, 2025	Paper-I (CBE)*	15-Jan-2026 (Thursday)	04-Feb-2026 (Wednesday)	Mar-Apr, 2026

***CBE- Computer Based Examination**

Upcoming Bank Exams 2025

The tentative schedule of IBPS RRB, IBPS Clerk, IBPS PO, IBPS SO, and SBI PO & Clerk exams in 2025-26:

Exam	Notification	Online Application Dates	Prelims Exam Date	Mains Exam Date
IBPS RRB 2025	June 2025	June 2025	August 2025	-
IBPS Clerk 2025	August 2025	September 2025	-	-
IBPS PO 2025	August/September 2025	October 2025	-	-
IBPS SO 2025	September 2025	December 2025	-	-
SBI Clerk 2024	16 December 2024	17 December 2024	February 2025	March–April 2025
SBI PO 2024	-	-	-	-

Upcoming Defence Exams 2025

The tentative schedule of Defence Exams including NDA, CDS, CAPF, AFCAT and Other Exams:

Exam	Notification	Exam Date
NDA 1 2025	11 Dec 2024	13 Apr 2025
CDS 1 2025	11 Dec 2024	13 Apr 2025
CAPF 2025	5 March 2025	03 August 2025
AFCAT 2025	February 2025	August 2025

Upcoming Railway Exams 2025

The tentative schedule of Railway Exams including RRB ALP, Technician, NTPC, Group -D Level 1 and RPF Exams:

Exam	Notification	Exam Date
RRB Group D Level 1	January 2025	As per Schedule
Assistant Loco Pilot (ALP)	January-March 2025	As per Schedule
Technician	April-June 2025	As per Schedule
Non-Technical Popular Categories	July-September 2025	As per Schedule
Junior Engineer	July-September 2025	As per Schedule

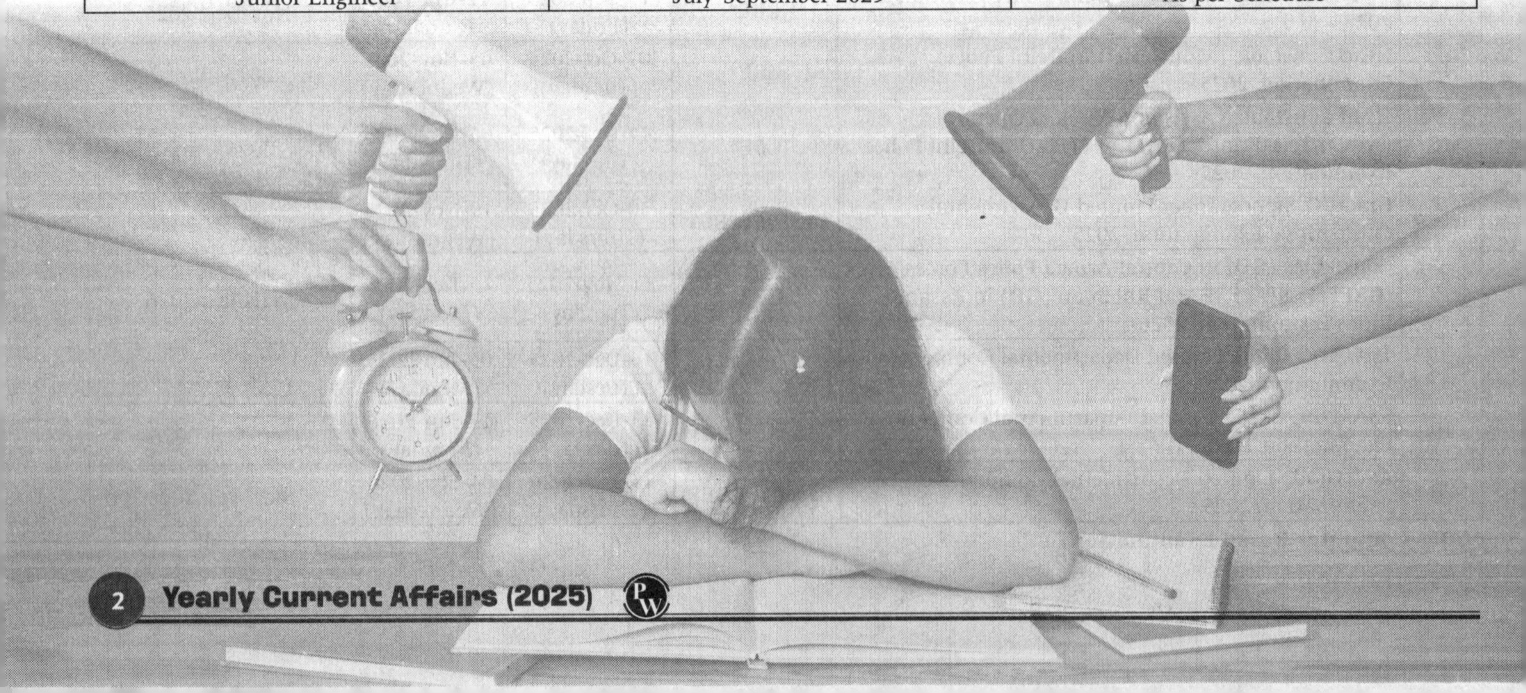

LOK SABHA & STATE ELECTION 2024 HIGHLIGHTS

18TH LOKSABHA ELECTION

ELECTION TIMELINE

- **Election Period:** Held over seven phases from **19 April to 1 June 2024**.
- **Total Constituencies: 543** Lok Sabha seats contested.
- **Vote Counting and Results Declaration:** 4 June 2024.
- **Government Formation:** Narendra Modi sworn in as Prime Minister on June 9, 2024.

MAJOR PARTIES

Bharatiya Janata Party (BJP): Won 240 seats (plurality).
Indian National Congress (INC): Secured 99 seats.

MAJOR PARTIES

Uttar Pradesh: Samajwadi Party (SP) victory
West Bengal: Trinamool Congress (AITC) victory
Maharashtra: Shiv Sena (SS-UBT), INC, and NCP-SP victories

SEAT DISTRIBUTION IN THE 543-SEAT LOK SABHA

- **Required Absolute Majority:** 272 seats.
- **National Democratic Alliance (NDA):** 293 seats
- **Bharatiya Janata Party (BJP):** 240 seats **(Lost 63 seats from previous 303)**
- **Allied Parties:**
  - Telugu Desam Party (TDP): **13 seats (Gained 13)**
  - Janata Dal (United) (JD(U)): **2.95% seat share (Won 12 Seats, Lost 4 seats)**
- **Indian National Developmental Inclusive Alliance (I.N.D.I.A.):** 235 seats
  - **Indian National Congress (INC):** 99 seats **(Gained 47 seats)**
  - **Samajwadi Party (SP):** 37 seats **(Gained 32 seats)**
  - **Trinamool Congress (AITC):** 29 seats **(Gained 7 seats)**
  - **Other Allied Parties:**
  - Shiv Sena (SS-UBT): **1.66% seat share**
  - Nationalist Congress Party (NCP-SP): **1.48% seat share**

MAJOR MILESTONES

Narendra Modi re-elected for a third consecutive term as Prime Minister.
Modi becomes the second Indian Prime Minister to be re-elected for a third term since Jawaharlal Nehru (1962).
Second BJP leader after Atal Bihari Vajpayee to lead the party to the single largest party in the Lok Sabha thrice.

SPEAKER OF THE LOK SABHA

- **Election Date:** 26 June 2024
- **Elected Speaker:** Om Birla
- **Defeated Opponent:** Kodikunnil Suresh (opposition candidate) in a voice vote.

CONSECUTIVE TERMS

- Om Birla became the 5th Speaker to retain the position for two consecutive terms.
- Previous Speakers with Consecutive Terms:
  - G. M. C. Balayogi
  - Balram Jakhar
  - G. S. Dhillon
  - M. A. Ayyangar

NOTABLE FACTS ABOUT 18TH LOKSABHA ELECTION

- Candidates from 41 parties have been elected. National parties have won 346 seats (64%).
- Parties recognised as state parties in at least one state have won 179 seats (33%).
- 11 seats have been won by unrecognised parties, and seven by independents.
- 262 MPs elected to the 18th Lok Sabha have previously served as members of Lok Sabha.
- Two MPs have served seven terms in Lok Sabha.
- The average age of MPs elected to the 18th Lok Sabha is 56 years.
- The oldest MP is 82 years old was T. R. Baalu. Three MPs elected to the 18th Lok Sabha are 25 years old.
- 74 MPs (14%) elected to the 18th Lok Sabha are women. 41% of women MPs (30 MPs) have previously been members of Lok Sabha.
- Over 2 lakh NOTA votes were cast in Indore, the highest ever for any constituency.

HISTORICAL CONTEXT

- **Fourth Speaker Election:** Only the fourth election for the Lok Sabha Speaker in India's history.
- **Previous Speaker Election:** Last held in 1976 during the 5th Lok Sabha.
- **1976 Result:** Baliram Bhagat (INC-R) defeated Jagannathrao Joshi (BJS).

OTHER IMPORTANT FACTS

- The vote-from-home option is available for the first time for people above 85 years of age and those with over 40% disability.
- 18.2 million voters exercised their voting rights for the first time in the 2024 general elections.

List of Cabinet Ministers of India 2024

The Modi Cabinet 3.0 consists of 72 ministers, including 36 ministers of state in total, 5 ministers of state with independent responsibility, and 30 cabinet ministers. Eleven members of the NDA have been elected to the Modi Cabinet 2024 and are listed as Cabinet Ministers in 2024.

The below table is the List of Cabinet Ministers of Modi 3.0 cabinet:

S.No	Minister Name	Minister Portfolio	Party	Elected State
1	Rajnath Singh	Defence	BJP	Uttar Pradesh
2	Amit Shah	Home Affairs and Cooperation	BJP	Gujarat
3	Nitin Gadkari	Road Transport and Highways	BJP	Maharashtra
4	Jagat Prakash Nadda	Health and Family Welfare and Minister of Chemicals and Fertilizers	BJP	Himachal Pradesh
5	Shivraj Singh Chouhan	Agriculture, Farmers Welfare and Rural Development	BJP	Madhya Pradesh
6	Nirmala Sitharaman	Finance and Corporate Affairs	BJP	Karnataka
7	S Jaishankar	External Affairs	BJP	Gujarat
8	Manohar Lal Khattar	Housing, Urban Affairs and Power	BJP	Haryana
9	HD Kumaraswamy	Ministry of Heavy Industries and Steel	Janata Dal Secular	Karnataka
10	Piyush Goyal	Commerce and Industry	BJP	Maharashtra
11	Dharmendra Pradhan	Education	BJP	Odisha
12	Jitan Ram Manjhi	Micro, Small and Medium Enterprises	Hindustani Awam Morcha (Secular)	Bihar
13	Rajiv Ranjan Singh/Lallan Singh	Panchayati Raj; and Fisheries, Animal Husbandry and Dairying	Janata Dal United	Bihar
14	Sarbananda Sonowal	Ports, Shipping and Waterways	BJP	Assam
15	Virendra Kumar	Social Justice and Empowerment	BJP	Madhya Pradesh

S.No	Minister Name	Minister Portfolio	Party	Elected State
16	Ram Mohan Naidu	Civil Aviation	Telugu Desam Party	Andhra Pradesh
17	Pralhad Joshi	Consumer Affairs, Food and Public Distribution; and New and Renewable Energy	BJP	Karnataka
18	Jual Oram	Tribal Affairs	BJP	Jharkhand
19	Giriraj Singh	Textiles	BJP	Bihar
20	Ashwini Vaishnaw	Railways; Information and Broadcasting; and Electronics and Information Technology	BJP	Odisha
21	Jyotiraditya Scindia	Communications; and Development of the North Eastern Region	BJP	Madhya Pradesh
22	Bhupender Yadav	Environment, Forest and Climate Change	BJP	Rajasthan
23	Gajendra Singh Shekhawat	Culture; and Tourism	BJP	Rajasthan
24	Annapurna Devi	Women and Child Development	BJP	Jharkhand
25	Kiren Rijiju	Parliamentary Affairs; and Minority Affairs	BJP	Arunachal Pradesh
26	Hardeep Singh Puri	Petroleum and Natural Gas	BJP	Uttar Pradesh
27	Mansukh Mandaviya	Labour and Employment; and Youth Affairs and Sports	BJP	Gujarat
28	G Kishan Reddy	Coal and Mines	BJP	Telangana
29	Chirag Paswan	Food Processing Industries	LJP	Bihar
30	CR Patil	Jal Shakti	BJP	Gujarat

STATE ASSEMBLY ELECTION, 2024

MAHARASHTRA ASSEMBLY ELECTIONS 2024

Chief Minister	Devendra Fadnavis
Total Seats	288
Majority Mark	145
Main Parties	NDA (BJP, Eknath Shinde's Shiv Sena, Ajit Pawar's NCP), INDIA Alliance (INC, Sharad Pawar's NCP, UBT's Shiv Sena
Governor	C. P. Radhakrishnan
Key Winners	Devendra Fadnavis, Eknath Shinde, Ajit Pawar
Voter Turnout	66.05%

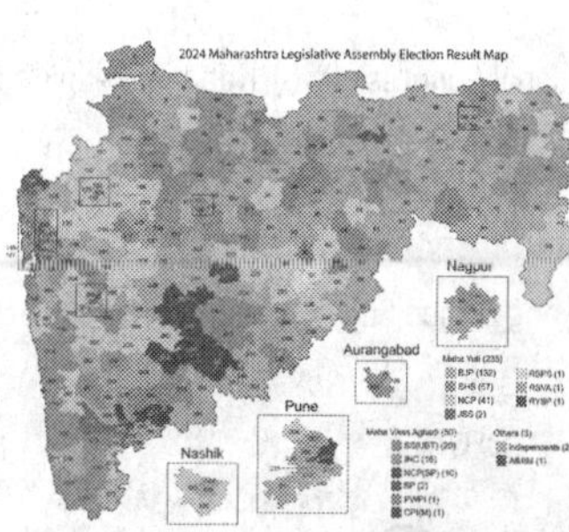

JHARKHAND ASSEMBLY ELECTIONS 2024

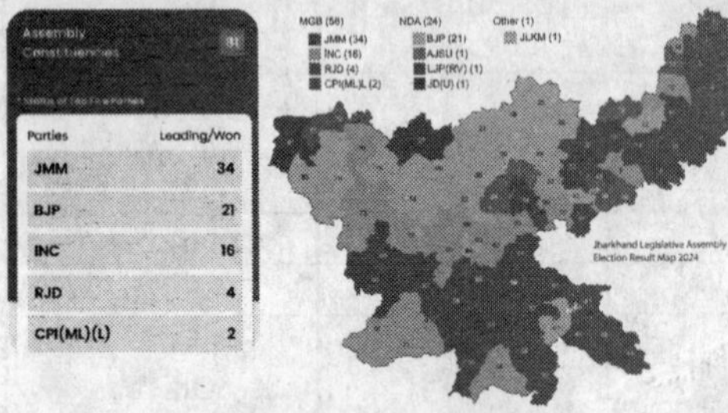

Chief Minister	Hemant Soren
Total Seats	81
Majority Mark	41
Main Parties	JMM, BJP, INC, RJD
Governor	Santosh Gangwar
Key Winners	Hemant Soren
Voter Turnout	67.74%
Notable Point	The voting percentage was 67.74%, the highest since the formation of the state in 2000. This is the fourth term of Jharkhand Mukti Morcha (JMM) leader Hemant Soren.

HARYANA ASSEMBLY ELECTIONS 2024

Chief Minister	Nayab Singh Saini
Total Seats	90
Majority Mark	46
Main Parties	BJP, INC, IND
Governor	Bandaru Dattatreya
Key Winners	Nayab Singh Saini
Voter Turnout	67.90%
Notable Point	The Bharatiya Janata Party (BJP) secured victory for the third consecutive time.

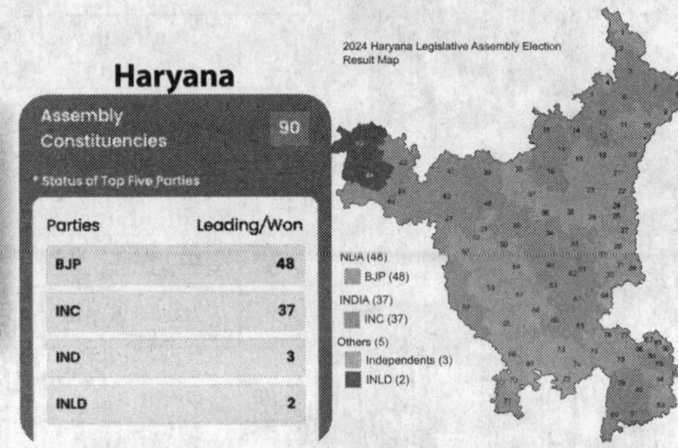

JAMMU & KASHMIR ASSEMBLY ELECTIONS 2024

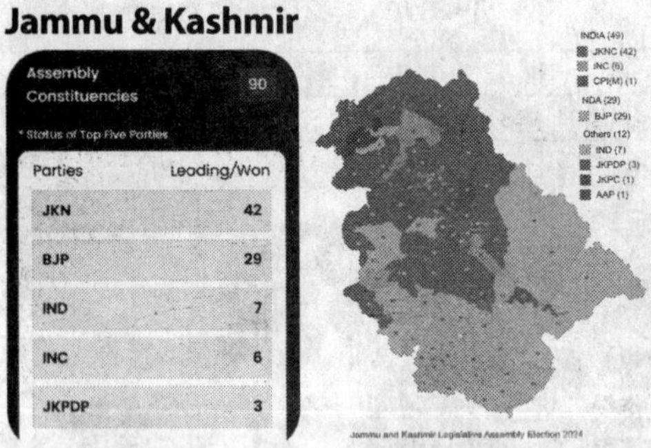

Chief Minister	Omar Abdullah
Total Seats	90
Majority Mark	46
Main Parties	JKN, BJP, IND
Governor	Manoj Sinha
Key Winners	Omar Abdullah
Voter Turnout	63.88%
Notable Point	The Jammu and Kashmir Assembly elections, to be held in 2024, were the first elections to be held after the abrogation of Article 370 in 2019.

ARUNACHAL PRADESH ASSEMBLY ELECTIONS 2024

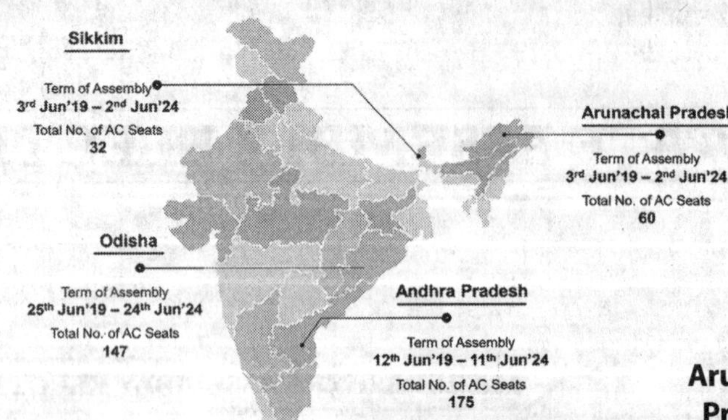

Chief Minister	Pema Khandu (BJP)
Total Seats	60
Majority Mark	31
Main Parties	Bharatiya Janata Party (BJP), Indian National Congress (INC), National People's Party (NPP), others
BJP Seats	46 (including 10 unopposed)
Governor	Lt. Gen. Kaiwalya Trivikram Parnaik (Retd)
Key Winners	Pema Khandu (Mukto, unopposed), Pasang Dorjee Sona (Mechuka), Kamlung Mossang (Miao)
Voter Turnout	82.95%
Opposition Role	Limited, with NPP as the main opposition party

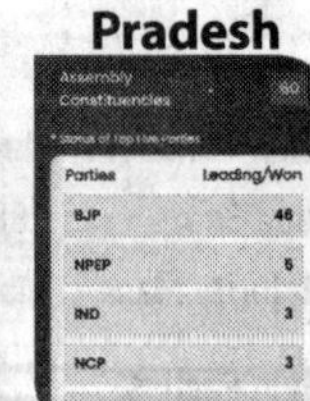

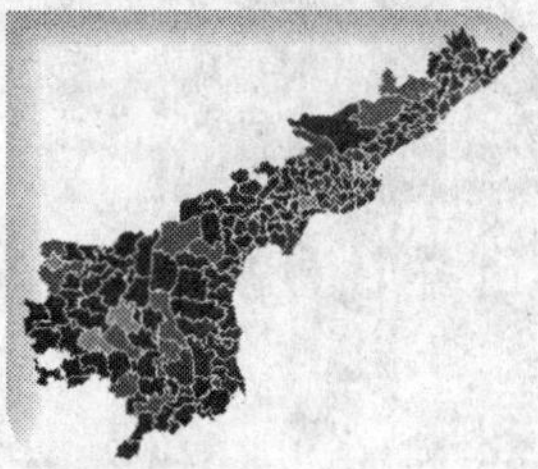

ANDHRA PRADESH ASSEMBLY ELECTIONS 2024

Andhra Pradesh

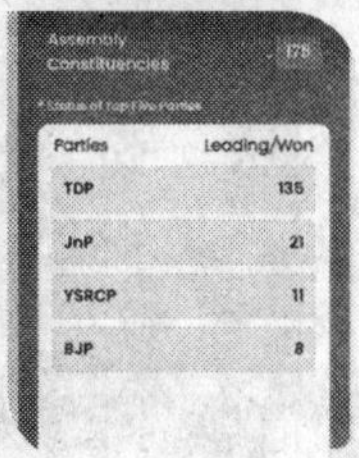

Chief Minister	N. Chandrababu Naidu (TDP)
Total Seats	175
Majority Mark	88
Main Parties	Yuvajana Sramika Rythu Congress Party (YSRCP), Telugu Desam Party (TDP), Jana Sena Party (JSP), Bharatiya Janata Party (BJP), Indian National Congress (INC), others
Governor	S. Abdul Nazeer
Key Winners	• N. Chandrababu Naidu (Kuppam) • Pawan Kalyan (Bhimavaram) • Daggubati Purandeswari (Visakhapatnam)
Voter Turnout	80.39%
Campaign Focus	Development, governance, anti-incumbency
Opposition Role	YSRCP, led by Y. S. Jagan Mohan Reddy, significantly lost ground
Notable Trends	TDP's major comeback with a strong alliance with JSP and BJP

SIKKIM ASSEMBLY ELECTIONS 2024

Chief Minister	Prem Singh Tamang (SKM)
Total Seats	32
Majority Mark	17
Main Parties	Sikkim Krantikari Morcha (SKM), Sikkim Democratic Front (SDF), Bharatiya Janata Party (BJP), others
Governor	Om Prakash Mathur
Key Winners	Prem Singh Tamang (Rhenock), Bedu Singh Panth (Temi- Namphing), Delay Namgyal Barfungpa (Gangtok)
Voter Turnout	79.88%
Notable Trends	SKM's overwhelming victory indicates strong public support and effective governance strategies

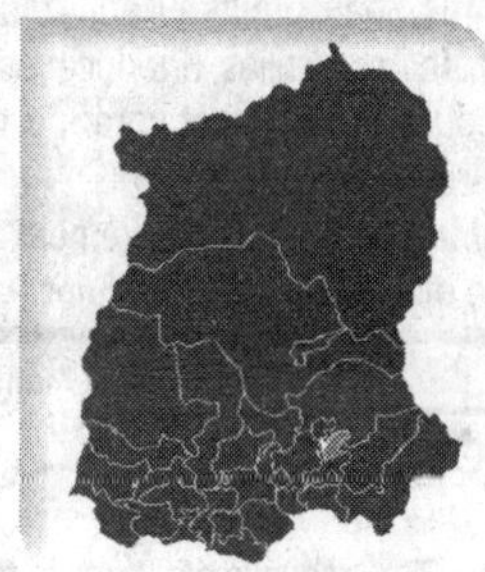

Sikkim

ODISHA ASSEMBLY ELECTIONS 2024

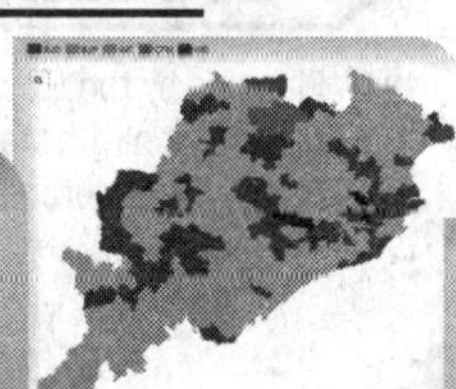

Odisha

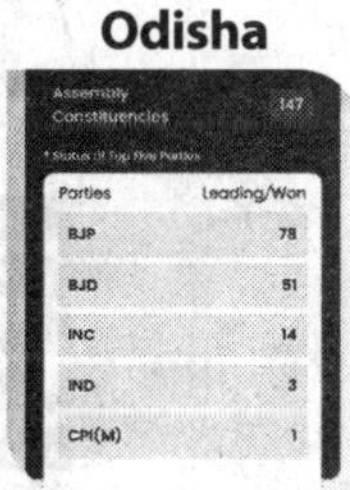

Chief Minister	Mohan Charan Majhi (BJP)
Total Seats	147
Majority Mark	74
Main Parties	Bharatiya Janata Party (BJP), Biju Janata Dal (BJD), indian National Congress (INC), others
Governor	Dr. Kambhampati Hari Babu
Voter Turnout	74.51%
Campaign Focus	Development, anti-incumbency, governance issues
Opposition Role	BJD, led by Naveen Patnaik, faces significant loss, marking end of 24-year rule
Notable Trends	BJP's historic win, BJD's significant decline in seats

ONE NATION, ONE ELECTION: A STEP TOWARDS SIMULTANEITY

The High-level Committee (HLC), chaired by former President Ram Nath Kovind, recently submitted its report on "One Nation, One Election."

Focus: "One Nation, One Election" concept
Other Members of Committee: Amit Shah, Ghulam Nabi Azad, N. K Singh, Dr. Subhash C. Kashyap, Shri Harish Salve, Sanjay Kothari, Arjun Ram Meghwal.
Scope: Synchronize Lok Sabha, State Assemblies, and local body elections (Exclusions: Panchayats, State Municipalities, and By-elections)
Benefits: Improve governance, reduce costs, boost voter participation
Report Submitted To: President Draupadi Murmu
Note: The **central government tabled two bills in Parliament** to push the 'One Nation, One Election' proposal in Winter session 2024.
- After a heated debate, the bills were sent to **a Joint Parliamentary Committee** for further scrutiny.

TWO-STEP ELECTION PROCESS

- **Lok Sabha and State Assemblies:** Simultaneous elections in the first phase.
- **Local Bodies:** Elections to municipalities and panchayats synchronized within 100 days of state and national elections.

CONSTITUTIONAL AMENDMENTS

Amendments to Articles 83, 85, 172, 174, and 356 to enable simultaneous elections.

GLOBAL EXAMPLES

- **South Africa:** Elections for national, provincial, and municipal levels in a 5-year cycle.
- **Sweden:** National and local elections are held simultaneously every five years.
- While these examples provide insights, India's scale and diversity present unique challenges.

UNIFIED ELECTORAL ROLL AND ID

- An amendment is required to article 325.
- It requires ratification from states.

ADDRESSING HUNG HOUSES

- Fresh elections for incomplete terms, with the new House continuing only till the term of the previous one.

LOGISTICAL PLANNING

- Planning by the Election Commission of India (ECI) in collaboration with state commissions for personnel, security, and resources.

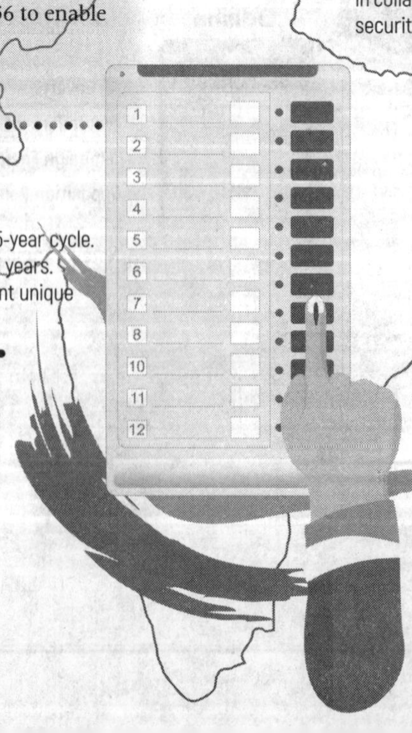

ANDHRA PRADESH ASSEMBLY ELECTIONS 2024

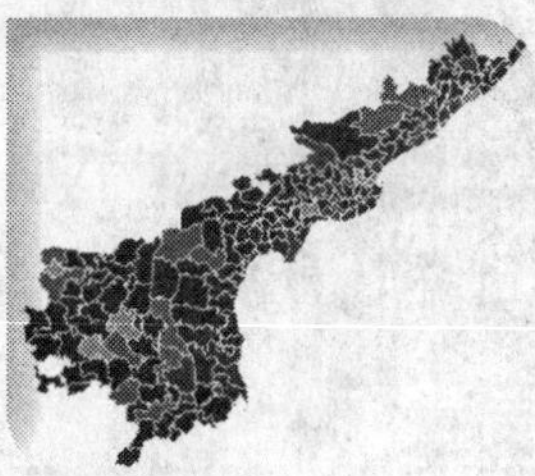

Andhra Pradesh

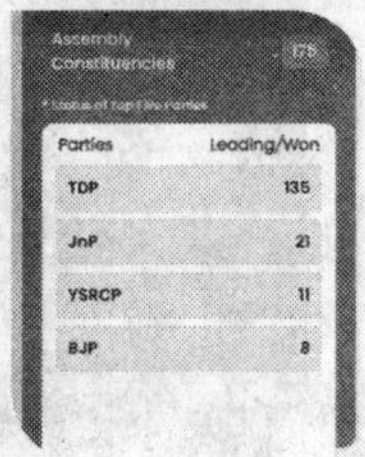

Chief Minister	N. Chandrababu Naidu (TDP)
Total Seats	175
Majority Mark	88
Main Parties	Yuvajana Sramika Rythu Congress Party (YSRCP), Telugu Desam Party (TDP), Jana Sena Party (JSP), Bharatiya Janata Party (BJP), Indian National Congress (INC), others
Governor	S. Abdul Nazeer
Key Winners	• N. Chandrababu Naidu (Kuppam) • Pawan Kalyan (Bhimavaram) • Daggubati Purandeswari (Visakhapatnam)
Voter Turnout	80.39%
Campaign Focus	Development, governance, anti-incumbency
Opposition Role	YSRCP, led by Y. S. Jagan Mohan Reddy, significantly lost ground
Notable Trends	TDP's major comeback with a strong alliance with JSP and BJP

SIKKIM ASSEMBLY ELECTIONS 2024

Chief Minister	Prem Singh Tamang (SKM)
Total Seats	32
Majority Mark	17
Main Parties	Sikkim Krantikari Morcha (SKM), Sikkim Democratic Front (SDF), Bharatiya Janata Party (BJP), others
Governor	Om Prakash Mathur
Key Winners	Prem Singh Tamang (Rhenock), Bedu Singh Panth (Temi- Namphing), Delay Namgyal Barfungpa (Gangtok)
Voter Turnout	79.88%
Notable Trends	SKM's overwhelming victory indicates strong public support and effective governance strategies

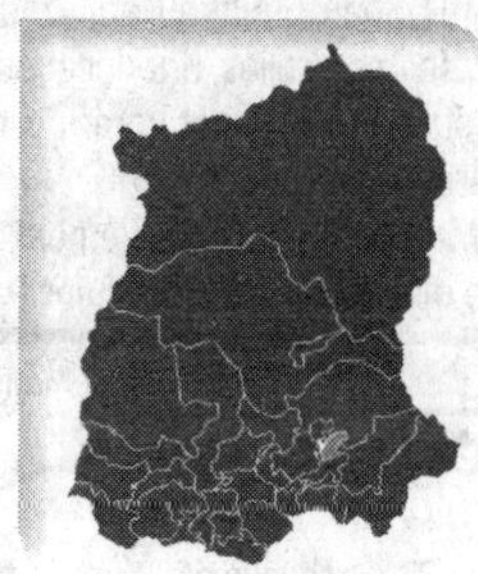

Sikkim

ODISHA ASSEMBLY ELECTIONS 2024

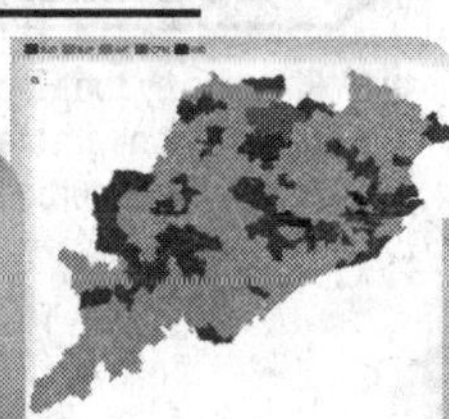

Odisha

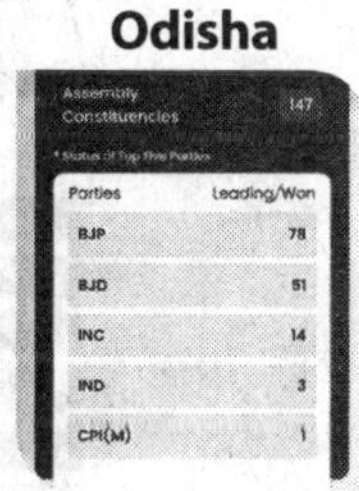

Chief Minister	Mohan Charan Majhi (BJP)
Total Seats	147
Majority Mark	74
Main Parties	Bharatiya Janata Party (BJP), Biju Janata Dal (BJD), indian National Congress (INC), others
Governor	Dr. Kambhampati Hari Babu
Voter Turnout	74.51%
Campaign Focus	Development, anti-incumbency, governance issues
Opposition Role	BJD, led by Naveen Patnaik, faces significant loss, marking end of 24-year rule
Notable Trends	BJP's historic win, BJD's significant decline in seats

NATIONAL AFFAIRS

ONE NATION, ONE ELECTION: A STEP TOWARDS SIMULTANEITY

The High-level Committee (HLC), chaired by former President Ram Nath Kovind, recently submitted its report on "One Nation, One Election."

Focus: "One Nation, One Election" concept
Other Members of Committee: Amit Shah, Ghulam Nabi Azad, N. K Singh, Dr. Subhash C. Kashyap, Shri Harish Salve, Sanjay Kothari, Arjun Ram Meghwal.
Scope: Synchronize Lok Sabha, State Assemblies, and local body elections (Exclusions: Panchayats, State Municipalities, and By-elections)
Benefits: Improve governance, reduce costs, boost voter participation
Report Submitted To: President Draupadi Murmu
Note: The **central government tabled two bills in Parliament** to push the 'One Nation, One Election' proposal in Winter session 2024.
- After a heated debate, the bills were sent to **a Joint Parliamentary Committee** for further scrutiny.

TWO-STEP ELECTION PROCESS

- **Lok Sabha and State Assemblies:** Simultaneous elections in the first phase.
- **Local Bodies:** Elections to municipalities and panchayats synchronized within 100 days of state and national elections.

CONSTITUTIONAL AMENDMENTS

Amendments to Articles 83, 85, 172, 174, and 356 to enable simultaneous elections.

GLOBAL EXAMPLES

- **South Africa:** Elections for national, provincial, and municipal levels in a 5-year cycle.
- **Sweden:** National and local elections are held simultaneously every five years.
- While these examples provide insights, India's scale and diversity present unique challenges.

UNIFIED ELECTORAL ROLL AND ID

- An amendment is required to article 325.
- It requires ratification from states.

ADDRESSING HUNG HOUSES

- Fresh elections for incomplete terms, with the new House continuing only till the term of the previous one.

LOGISTICAL PLANNING

- Planning by the Election Commission of India (ECI) in collaboration with state commissions for personnel, security, and resources.

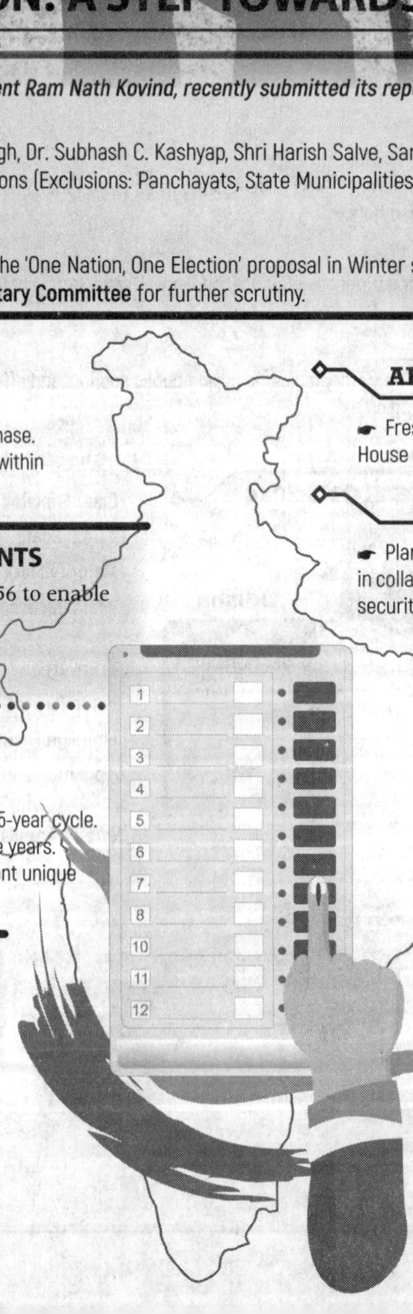

ONE NATION ONE ELECTION

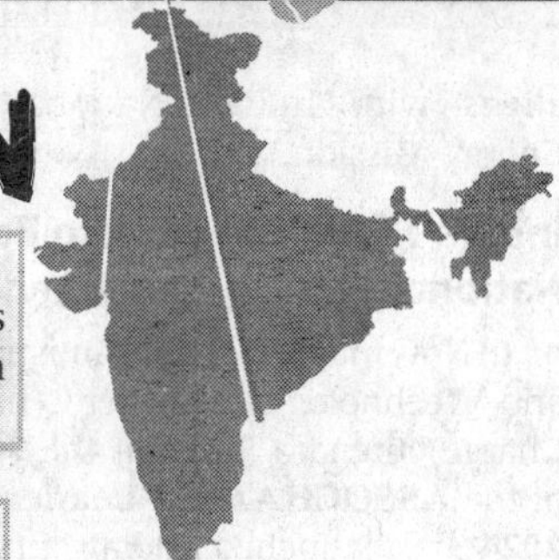

Election for
LOK SABHA + ALL STATE ASSEMBLIES
Together

VOTE
Voters will vote for LS and the state assemblies elections on a single day, simultaneously (or in a phased manner, as the case may be).

Present status of elections in India

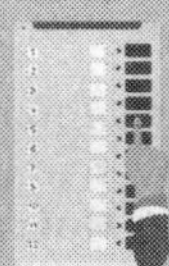

5 YEARS

Elections Year 1 — Elections Year 2

- Elections for the Lok Sabha and state assemblies are conducted separately.
- These elections occur either after the current government's five-year term ends or the government is dissolved for various reasons.

History of simultaneous elections in India

1952

1957

1959: The synchronized election cycle was first disrupted in kerala in July 1959 due to president's Rule.

1962

1967

1968-1969: The premature dissolution of some LAs in 1968 and 1969 again disrupted the cycle of simultaneous election cycle.

Arguments in Favour of simultaneous elections

- **Reduces** costs of holding separate elections.
- Boosts **Voter turnout** due to convenience.
- Allows ruling parties to focus on **Governance.**
- Enhances **administrative efficiency.**
- **Minimizes** governance **disruptions** from the model code of conduct.

Arguments in Against of simultaneous elections

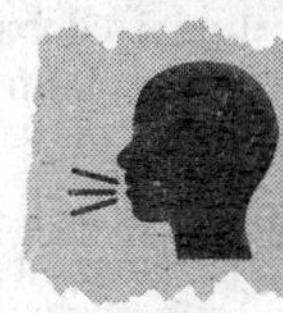

- **Limits accountability** by merging elections for different governance levels.
- ONOE contradicts India's **federalism.**
- **Reduces government accountability** with elections only every five years.
- **Disadvantages regional parties** in terms of strategy and expenditure.
- **Creates complications** if a government collapses or parliament dissolves early.

Proposed Two Bills

1st Bill

Holding simultaneous elections of the **Lok Sabha and Assembly elections.**

Constitutional Amendment (According to Ram Nath Kovind Panel)

1. This bill will require a **'Special majority'** of the Lok Sabha and Rajya Sabha.
2. It can be passed by Parliament **without the ratification by state assemblies.**

2nd Bill

Holding Local body elections within 100 days.

Constitutional Amendment (According to Ram Nath Kovind Panel)

1. This bill will require a **'Special majority'** of both the Lok Sabha and Rajya Sabha.
2. It also requires the approval or **ratification of more than half of India's states.**

Newly Launched/ Inaugurated

India's First Bio-Bitumen National Highway Inaugurated

- Union Minister Shri Nitin Gadkari inaugurated India's First National Highway constructed using bio-bitumen material in the Nagpur-Mansar Bypass project of National Highway 44 in Nagpur District.
- This is the first national highway in the country built using bitumen made from crop residues -lignin.
- This road is constructed by joint collaboration of Central Road Research Institute -CRRI and Pune-based biotech firm- Praj Industries.

India's First Green Hydrogen Fueling Station in Leh Commissioned

- In November, Amara Raja Infra commissioned **'India's first green hydrogen fuelling station'** in Leh, Ladakh, for NTPC Ltd.
- It was inaugurated by Union Minister for Power and Housing and Urban Affairs Shri Manohar Lal.
- The station, built at an altitude of 3,400 meters, can produce 80 kg of green hydrogen daily and powers five hydrogen fuel cell buses.
- This project, completed in two years under extreme conditions with temperatures varying between –25°Celsius to 30°Celsius, marks a significant step towards sustainable transportation and

aligns with India's National Hydrogen Energy Mission.

India's 1st AI Data Bank to Boost National Security Launched

- In November 2024, the Ministry of Science and Technology Minister (Independent Charge) Jitendra Singh at the **7th Edition** of the **ASSOCHAM AI Leadership Meet 2024** has launched India's first Artificial Intelligence (AI) data bank
- **Purpose:** The initiative aims to drive innovation and enhance national security.
- **Support Provided:** It will grant researchers, startups, and developers access to high-quality, diverse datasets.
- **Outcome:** These resources are essential for creating scalable and inclusive AI solutions.
- The event, themed **"AI for India: Advancing India's AI Development – Innovation, Ethics, and Governance".**

India's first Constitution Museum inaugurated at OP Jindal University

- In November 2024, India's first Constitution Museum was inaugurated at the O P Jindal Global University by Law Minister Arjun Ram Meghwal and Lok Sabha Speaker Om Birla.
- The museum will educate current and future generations about our constitution, its formation, and the discussions and debates that occurred during its creation.

India launched first Indigenous antibiotic 'Nafithromycin'

- In December 2024, the Union Minister Dr Jitendra Singh formally launched the first indigenous antibiotic 'Nafithromycin' for drug-resistant infections.
- The antibiotic "Naphithromycin" has been developed in collaboration with the "Biotechnology Industry Research Assistance Council" (BIRAC), a unit of the Department of Biotechnology.
- It is the country's first indigenously developed antibiotic that aims to tackle antimicrobial resistance (AMR).

PM Modi launched India's 1st Free Air Ambulance Service at AIIMS Rishikesh

- In October 2024, the Prime Minister Narendra Modi virtually inaugurated the country's first government helicopter ambulance service at AIIMS Rishikesh.
- The service will operate like 108 ambulances, transporting patients from across the state to AIIMS, free of charge.

SUPREME COURT UNVEILS NEW JUSTICE STATUE

- **Location & Presenter:** The then Chief Justice of India, DY Chandrachud, unveiled a new Lady Justice statue at the Supreme Court.
- **Symbolism Changes:** The statue does not wear a blindfold, emphasizing that justice in India is informed rather than impartial.
- Instead of a sword, the statue holds the Constitution, highlighting a focus on constitutional values over punishment.
- **New Attire:** The statue is dressed in a saree instead of a robe, reflecting a move away from colonial influences.
- **Colonial Departure:** The new design symbolizes the replacement of colonial-era laws such as the IPC (Indian Penal Code) and CrPC (Code of Criminal Procedure).

Union Minister Piyush Goyal inaugurated 'One District One Product' wall

- In October 2024, Union Minister Piyush Goyal inaugurated the "One District One Product" (ODOP) Wall at the Indian Embassy in Riyadh, Saudi Arabia.
- With ODOP, the government aims to spotlight local products on international platforms, transforming various districts across India into "Made in India" hubs.
- ODOP was launched by the Ministry of Food Processing Industries in 2018.

Uttarakhand CM Inaugurated Jauljibi Mela 2024 in Pithoragarh

- In November 2024, Uttarakhand CM Pushkar Singh Dhami inaugurated the Jauljibi Mela 2024 in Pithoragarh.
- The festival previously ranked amongst North India's largest trade fairs, and attracts merchants from Tibet, Nepal, and India.
- The fair was first organised by the zamindar of Askot in 1914, with the zamindar family maintaining the tradition annually until 1948, when Askot principality was annexed into India.

'TULIP' brand launched to promote Products of Disadvantaged Artisans

- In November 2024, the government of India has launched the TULIP (Traditional Artisans' Upliftment Livelihood Programme) brand to provide a platform for the marginalised artisan communities to sell their products.
- The TULIP brand was launched by the Union Ministry of Social Justice and Empowerment at the opening of the 'Shilp Samagam Mela 2024'.
- The TULIP(Traditional Artisans' Upliftment Livelihood Programme) is an e-marketplace where artisans from Scheduled Castes, Other Backward Classes, sanitation workers, and persons with disabilities can sell their products in India and abroad.

India's first International Centre for Audit of Local Governance (iCAL) inaugurated in Gujarat

- In July 2024, India's first International Centre for Audit of Local Governance (iCAL) was inaugurated in **Rajkot, Gujarat.**
- It aims to improve local governance audits, set global standards, and enhance financial management and service delivery.
- iCAL will serve as a collaborative platform for policymakers, administrators, and auditors linked with local governments.
- It aligns India's auditing practices with 40 countries that have **Supreme Audit Institutions (SAI).**

'Hamara Samvidhan, Hamara Samman' Portal

- The Department of Justice is implementing a pan-India, year-long nationwide campaign titled **'Hamara Samvidhan Hamara Samman'** to celebrate the **75th year** of India as a Republic and the adoption of India's Constitution.
- The campaign was **launched on January 24, 2024, by the Hon'ble Vice-President of India**.
- The 'Hamara Samvidhan Hamara Samman Portal' which was launched during the 2nd regional event at Prayagraj on 16th July, 2024 serves as a knowledge repository to enhance public awareness about the Constitution and their legal rights.

PM LAUNCHED 'DHARTI AABA JANJATIYA GRAM UTKARSH ABHIYAN (DAJGUA)'

- On October 2, 2024, PM Modi launched the **Dharti Aaba Janjatiya Gram Utkarsh Abhiyan (DAJGUA)** in **Hazaribagh, Jharkhand**.
- The scheme's total expenditure is Rs 79,150 crore. The Abhiyan will cover around 63,000 villages in 549 districts and 2,740 blocks across 30 States and Union Territories.
- On 15th November 2024, Janjati Gaurav Diwas, India, celebrated the first anniversary of the Pradhan Mantri Janjati Adivasi Nyaya Maha Abhiyan (PM-JANMAN).

Mumbai's First Underground Metro Inaugurated

- On October 5, 2024, PM Modi launched Mumbai's first underground Metro Line 3. It connects Colaba, Bandra, and SEEPZ.
- He also introduced the Metro Connect 3 app.

Asia's first Pre-Clinical Network Facility launched

- On 16 July 2024, the Minister of State (IC) for Science, Technology, and Earth Sciences Dr. Jitendra Singh inaugurated CEPI's first "Pre-clinical Network Facility" in Asia at **BRIC-THSTI, Faridabad, Haryana.**
- BRIC-THSTI is the first CEPI-accredited laboratory in Asia and the **9th in the world,** with other labs located in Europe, Australia, and the USA.
- It was chosen for its ability **to handle high-risk Biosafety Level-3 pathogens** like COVID-19 and tuberculosis and has one of India's largest animal research facilities.

iBRIC

- **The Biotechnology Research and Innovation Council (BRIC) -Translational Health Science and Technology Institute (THSTI)** was set up in 2009, under the Department of Biotechnology, It uses science, medicine, and technology to improve public health.
- **The Coalition of Epidemic Preparedness Innovations (CEPI)** was founded in 2017 in Davos, Switzerland, develops vaccines for diseases like Ebola and Nipah, and works on creating a vaccine library for future epidemics.

PM Inaugurated India's Longest Urban Tunnel

- On 13 July 2024, Prime Minister Narendra Modi inaugurated India's longest and largest urban tunnel project **'the Thane Borivali Twin Tunnel'.**
- The Mumbai Metropolitan Region Development Authority (MMRDA) has built an 11.8 km direct subway line connecting Thane and Borivali, cutting 12 km of distance and reducing travel time to just 12 minutes.
- The estimated cost for this project is Rs. 16,600 crores.
- The project avoids harming the Sanjay Gandhi National Park and will cut carbon emissions by 1,50,000 MT annually.

SEHER Launched to Boost Financial Literacy for Women

- In July 2024, the Women Entrepreneurship Platform (WEP) and TransUnion CIBIL launched 'SEHER,' a program to educate and empower women entrepreneurs in India.
- It focuses on financial literacy and business skills to help women access financial tools for growth and job creation.

Manohar Khattar launched Three Power Sector Portals

- On 20 August 2024, Union Minister Manohar Lal Khattar launched three online platforms: **PROMPT, DRIPS, and JAL VIDYUT DPR** —to improve efficiency, transparency, and effectiveness in the power sector.
- Purpose of Portals:
- **PROMPT (Portal for Online Monitoring of Projects—Thermal)** tracks thermal power projects to address delays.
- **JAL VIDYUT DPR (Monitoring Survey and Investigation Activities of Hydroelectric Projects and Pumped Storage Projects)** monitors hydroelectric and pumped storage projects for better management.
- **DRIPS (Disaster Resource Inventory for Power Sector)** connects officials to restore power quickly during disasters like floods and cyclones.
- These platforms were **developed by the Central Electricity Authority (CEA)** under the Ministry of Power, with NTPC assisting in PROMPT's development.

President Droupadi Murmu inaugurated Swami Vivekananda Vidya Mandir in Silvassa

- The President of India, Smt Droupadi Murmu inaugurated Swami Vivekananda Vidya Mandir at Silvassa, Dadra and Nagar Haveli and Daman and Diu on 13th November 2024.
- The opening of this school will offer students a great learning environment and boost the region's development in higher education.

Union Minister inaugurated India's First Biomanufacturing Institute in Mohali

- On 28th October 2024, Union Minister Dr. Jitendra Singh inaugurated India's first Biomanufacturing Institute, **BRIC-National Agri-Food Bio-Manufacturing Institute (BRIC-NABI),** in Mohali.
- This institute aims to transform the agri-food sector using advanced biotechnology, supporting Prime Minister Narendra Modi's vision of a "Developed India."
- The BRIC-NABI was formed through the merger of the National Agri-Food Biotechnology Institute (NABI) and the Centre of Innovative and Applied Bioprocessing (CIAB).

Shivraj S Chouhan launched Nayi Chetna 3.0

- In November 2024, the Union Minister Shivraj Singh Chouhan has launched the third edition of **Nayi Chetna – Pahal Badlaav Ki,** a national campaign against gender-based violence in Rang Bhawan Auditorium, New Delhi.
- The month-long campaign, organized by the **Deendayal Antyodaya Yojana – National Rural Livelihoods Mission (DAY-NRLM)** under the aegis of the Ministry of Rural Development.
- It aims to amplify awareness and drive informed action against gender-based violence through grassroots initiatives.
- The campaign's slogan is "**Ek Saath, Ek Awaaz, Hinsa Ke Khilaaf**".

PM launched 'Karmayogi Saptah' – National Learning Week

- In October 2024, Prime Minister Narendra Modi launched the week-long **Karmayogi Saptah (19th-25th October)** in New Delhi to improve civil servants' skills through workshops and learning modules.
- As part of **Mission Karmayogi** (started in September 2020), the program encourages lifelong learning, preparing civil servants for future challenges.
- It aims to build an efficient, citizen-focused government and support India's vision for **Viksit Bharat by 2047.**

Union Minister C.R. Paatil launched the Bhu-Neer portal

- On 20th November 2024, Union Minister of Jal Shakti, C.R. Paatil, launched the Bhu-Neer portal during the concluding ceremony of India Water Week 2024.
- Developed by the Central Ground Water Authority (CGWA) in collaboration with the National Informatics Centre (NIC), the portal aims to enhance transparency, efficiency, and sustainability in groundwater usage.
- It replaces the older NOCAP system and features a PAN-based single ID system, QR-coded NOCs, and a user-friendly interface.

Government Launched Training Program on Chemical and Petrochemical Industrial Safety

- Under the Viksit Bharat@2047 initiative, the Department of Chemicals and Petrochemicals has introduced its first training program on "Chemical and Petrochemical Industrial Safety" in Ahmedabad, Gujarat.
- The program, themed "Safety First, Sustainability Always: Protecting People and Planet," was held at the Central Institute of Petrochemical Engineering & Technology (CIPET): Institute of Petrochemicals Technology (IPT).

Centre launched 'Prashasan Gaon Ki Ore' Campaign for Improving Service Delivery

- The Centre recently launched "Prashasan Gaon Ki Ore", a nation-wide campaign to redress public grievances and improve service delivery, during the good governance week from December 19 to 24.
- In this campaign, over 700 district collectors will be participating and officials will be visiting tehsils and panchayat samiti headquarters.
- Prashasan Gaon Ki Ore is a decentralised version of special campaign 4.0 conducted in central ministries and departments and public sector undertakings (PSUs) from October 2 to 31, 2024.

Nitin Gadkari launched Humsafar Policy

- On 7 October 2024, Union Minister Nitin Gadkari launched the 'Humsafar Policy' in New Delhi to provide world-class amenities along India's National Highways and Expressways.
- The policy aims to provide clean toilets, baby care rooms, wheelchair access, EV charging stations, parking, and dormitories at fuel stations to make travel easier and support local businesses.
- Commuters will be able to find details of relevant service providers near their location instantly on the NHAI's 'Rajmarg Yatra app.

Prasar Bharati launched OTT Platform 'Waves'

- On 21st November 2024, Prasar Bharati, India's public broadcaster, launched its OTT platform "Waves" during the 55th International Film Festival of India (IFFI) in Goa.
- "Waves" offers live TV, movies, games, and events in over 12 languages.
- The platform combines nostalgia with modern trends, featuring classics like Ramayan alongside contemporary shows.

EAM Jaishankar inaugurated India's new consulate in Brisbane

- External Affairs Minister S Jaishankar inaugurated the new Consulate General of India in Brisbane on 4th November 2024.
- This consulate will strengthen ties with Queensland state (Australia), promote trade, foster educational linkages, and serve the Indian diaspora.
- This is India's fourth consulate in Australia, following Sydney, Melbourne, and Perth.

Ministry of Power launched CSIRT-Power for cybersecurity

- In September 2024, Ministry of Power launched 'CSIRT-Power', a specialized Computer Security Incident Response Team, to protect its power sector from cyber threats.
- Inaugurated by Union Minister Manohar Lal, this initiative aims to enhance cybersecurity resilience amid the sector's digital transformation.
- Equipped with advanced tools and a dedicated team, CSIRT-Power will coordinate incident responses, analyze sector-specific threats, and implement proactive measures.

DAE launched 'One DAE One Subscription'

- On 29 July 2024, the **Department of Atomic Energy (DAE)** launched the 'One DAE One Subscription' (ODOS) program at **Tata Memorial Hospital, Mumbai**, to give its 60+ units easy access to national and international research papers.
- Under ODOS, DAE partnered with **Wiley and Springer publishers** to provide access to over 4,000 journals, including many open-access titles, and support free publishing for researchers without extra fees.
- This initiative, **part of the larger One Nation One Subscription (ONOS) program**, aims to boost research, collaboration, and knowledge-sharing for thousands of researchers and students across India.

Shri Ashwini Vaishnaw inaugurated India's 500th Community Radio Station

- Union Minister Ashwini Vaishnaw launched India's **500th community radio station**, 'Apna Radio 90.0 FM,' in **Aizawl, Mizoram**, on 25th July 2024. The station will focus on local issues, especially helping Mizoram's farming community.
- The government also announced the winners of the **10th National Community Radio Awards**, which honor creative, sustainable, and culture-promoting radio programs.
- Award-winning stations include **Radio Mayur (Bihar)** for its tech programs, **Radio Brahmaputra (Assam)** for promoting local culture, and **Radio Benziger (Kerala)** for its sustainable practices.

India Launches First Grain ATM in Odisha

- India's First Grain ATM, **'Annapurti,' was** launched on 9 August 2024 in Bhubaneswar, Odisha.
- This 24/7 machine provides food grains (wheat, rice, millet) quickly and easily using biometric verification under the National Food Security Act (NFSA).
- Key features of the Grain ATM include: 24/7 Access, Universal Access, Fast Dispensing, Modular Design, and Energy Efficiency.

India's First Fashion Forecasting Initiative 'VisioNxt'

- Union Minister of Textiles Shri Giriraj Singh launched VisioNxt, a bilingual web portal, and India-specific Fashion Trend Book Paridhi 24x25 on September 5, 2024.

- **VisioNxt**, India's first fashion forecasting initiative by **NIFT** and the Ministry of Textiles, uses **AI** and **Emotional Intelligence** to predict fashion trends unique to India's culture.
- It offers **trend mapping**, consultancy, and courses, supported by the bilingual portal **www.visionxt.in**. It also introduced India's first inclusive trend book, **Paridhi 24×25.**

PM Modi launched Namo Bharat Rail

- PM Modi launched the Namo Bharat Rapid Rail (earlier called Vande Metro) and the new Vande Bharat trains on September 16, 2024.
- The Rapid Rail runs between Bhuj and Ahmedabad, covering 360 km in 5 hours 45 minutes with 9 stops.
- The train has advanced safety systems, such as KAVACH to prevent collisions and fire detection, and a seating capacity of 1,150 passengers.

President inaugurated Vishwashanti Buddha Vihara

- On 4 September 2024, President Droupadi Murmu inaugurated the 'Vishwashanti Buddha Vihara' in Udgir, Maharashtra's Latur district.
- The event featured the unveiling of a 520 kg, 10.5-feet statue of Lord Buddha.
- The Vihara, built on 1.15 hectares, can accommodate 1,200 people and features an entry gate modeled after the Sanchi Stupa.

Abu Dhabi Opens IIT Delhi Campus

- On 4 September 2024, Sheikh Khaled bin Mohamed bin Zayed Al Nahyan, Crown Prince of Abu Dhabi, inaugurated the first international campus of the Indian Institute of Technology Delhi (IIT-Delhi) in Abu Dhabi.

- Strategic partnerships were announced with leading Abu Dhabi institutions, including Khalifa University, Sorbonne University Abu Dhabi, and Mohamed bin Zayed University of Artificial Intelligence.
- Earlier, in January 2024, IIT Delhi - Abu Dhabi launched its first Master of Technology (M.Tech.) in Energy Transition and Sustainability.

National Importance

Delhi Airport became India's First Airport to Connect 150 Destinations

- In December 2024, Delhi's Indira Gandhi International (IGI) Airport has become the first airport in India to connect 150 destinations. Notably, Delhi International Airport Limited (DIAL), operates and manages the IGI Airport in New Delhi.
- This major achievement was marked by the launch of Thai AirAsia X's direct flights between Delhi and Bangkok-Don Mueang.

PM Modi attended Quad Summit

- On 21 September 2024, Prime Minister Narendra Modi attended the sixth Quad Leaders' Summit in Wilmington, Delaware.
- Hosted by US President Joe Biden, the summit also included Japanese Prime Minister Fumio Kishida and Australian Prime Minister Anthony Albanese.
- The leaders discussed various global issues, including regional conflicts, maritime security, technology, and clean energy.
- They released the **"Wilmington Declaration,"** reaffirming their commitment to a free and open Indo-Pacific.

India-Spain decide to celebrate 2026 as India-Spain Year of Culture, Tourism and AI

- India and Spain have agreed to observe 2026 as the Year of Culture, Tourism, and Artificial Intelligence (AI).
- An MoU was signed to enhance cooperation in rail transport.
- An agreement was finalized for mutual assistance in customs matters.
- Cultural exchange programs were agreed upon for 2024-2028.
- Spain will open a Consulate in Bengaluru, while India will operationalize its Consulate in Barcelona.
- A Fast Track mechanism will be established to boost Indian investments in Spain and Spanish investments in India, under respective trade departments.
- A Joint Commission will be formed under the Audio Visual Co-Production Agreement.

Supreme Court sets target of eliminating child marriage in Rajasthan by 2030

- The Supreme Court of India has set a target to eliminate child marriage in Rajasthan by 2030. Announced on October 18, 2024, the court's guidelines emphasize a "prevention, protection, and prosecution" model.
- Local authorities, including panchayats, school officials, and child protection officers, are held accountable.
- The court also ruled that the Prohibition of Child Marriage Act, 2006, supersedes personal laws.

India Re-Elected to UN Peacebuilding Commission for 2025-2026

- India has secured its re-election to the United Nations Peacebuilding Commission (PBC) for the 2025-2026 term.
- The Commission advises the UN General Assembly and Security Council on peacebuilding and sustaining peace efforts
- The UN Peacebuilding Commission, established in December 2005, is an advisory body that supports and strengthens peace efforts in conflict-affected countries.

SC allowed sub-classification of SCs, STs

- On 1 August 2024, the Supreme Court allowed dividing Scheduled Castes (SCs) and Scheduled Tribes (STs) into sub-groups to ensure fair reservation benefits.
- This 6-1 majority decision overturns the 2004 ruling in E.V. Chinnaiah vs. State of Andhra Pradesh, fundamentally altering the landscape of reservation policies in India.
- The Supreme Court has **extended the 'creamy layer' principle**, previously applicable to OBCs (Indra Sawhney Case), to also include SCs and STs.

PM Modi addressed UN Assembly

- Prime Minister Narendra Modi addressed at the 79th U.N. General Assembly session, themed **"Summit of the Future"**, held in New York on September 22, 2024.
- He emphasized the need for global action against terrorism and emerging threats in cyber, maritime, and space domains.
- Modi also called for reforms in global governance institutions to maintain their relevance and effectiveness.

23rd Law Commission formed for reforms

- The Ministry of Law and Justice set up the 23rd Law Commission for a **three-year term,** from 1st September 2024 to 31st August 2027.
- The Law Commission of India is a **non-statutory advisory** body that reviews and recommends legal reforms to ensure justice and promote good governance.

India Joined US-Led Minerals Security Finance Network

- In September 2024, India officially became part of the Minerals Security Finance Network (MSFN), a group led by the United States.
- The network now includes 14 countries and the European Union.
- The MSFN is linked to the Minerals Security Partnership (MSP), which was started by the US in 2022. India joined the MSP in June 2023, showing its growing role in securing important minerals globally.
- The MSFN focuses on reducing dependence on specific countries, especially China.

2nd India-UK 2+2 Foreign and Defence Dialogue held in New Delhi

- The second India and the United Kingdom 2+2 Foreign and Defence Dialogue was held in **New Delhi.**
- The first was held in New Delhi in October 2023, and both countries have agreed to hold their third Dialogue next year in the United Kingdom.
- The 2+2 Foreign and Defence dialogue is a **Senior official-level mechanism** for discussing and reviewing all aspects of the India-UK Comprehensive Strategic Partnership.

India and Japan hold 3rd 2+2 Dialogue in New Delhi

- In August 2024, India and Japan held their third 2+2 meeting in **New Delhi.** The discussion was focused on **Free and Open Indo-Pacific** and emphasized a rules-based regional order.
- Both countries reaffirmed their support for the QUAD and joint military exercises like Malabar.
- This dialogue aims to deepen the **"Special Strategic and Global Partnership"** between the two nations.
- Japan introduced its Unified Complex Radio Antenna (UNICORN) system to enhance warship detection and discussed updating defense agreements to address new security challenges.
- The first India-Japan 2+2 Ministerial Dialogue was held in New Delhi in November 2019.
- The second India-Japan 2+2 Ministerial Dialogue was held in Tokyo, Japan in September 2022.

CABINET APPROVALS

Cabinet approved One Nation One Subscription (ONOS)

- In November 2024, the Union Cabinet, chaired by Prime Minister Shri Narendra Modi, has approved One Nation One Subscription, a new Central Sector Scheme for providing country-wide access to scholarly research articles and journal publications.
- Under this Central Sector Scheme, Rs 6,000 crore has been allocated for three calendar years: 2025, 2026, and 2027.
- The One Nation One Subscription scheme aligns with the National Education Policy (NEP) 2020, Anusandhan National Research Foundation (ANRF), and the government's Viksit Bharat@2047 vision.

Cabinet approved National Mission on Natural Farming

- In November 2024, the Union Cabinet chaired by Prime Minister Narendra Modi has approved the launching of the 'National Mission on Natural Farming (NMNF)' as a standalone Centrally Sponsored Scheme under the **Ministry of Agriculture & Farmers' Welfare.**
- The scheme has a total outlay of Rs.2481 crore (Government of India share – Rs.1584 crore; State share – Rs.897 crore) till the 15th Finance Commission (2025-26).
- **Objective** – To promote natural farming in mission mode across the country.

Cabinet approved development of National Maritime Heritage Complex (NMHC) in Lothal

- On 9th October 2024, the Union Cabinet, led by Prime Minister Narendra Modi, approved the development of the **National Maritime Heritage Complex (NMHC)** at **Lothal, Gujarat.**
- This complex aims to showcase India's 4,500-year-old maritime heritage.
- To be developed by the **Ministry of Ports, Shipping & Waterways (MoPSW),** the project features a 77-meter lighthouse museum, set to be the tallest in the world. It is funded by the Directorate General of Lighthouses and Lightships (DGLL).
- Lothal, located in the Bhal region of Gujarat, is a Harappan site dating back to 2,200 BC and was discovered in 1954 by S.R. Rao.

Classical Status Granted To Five Languages

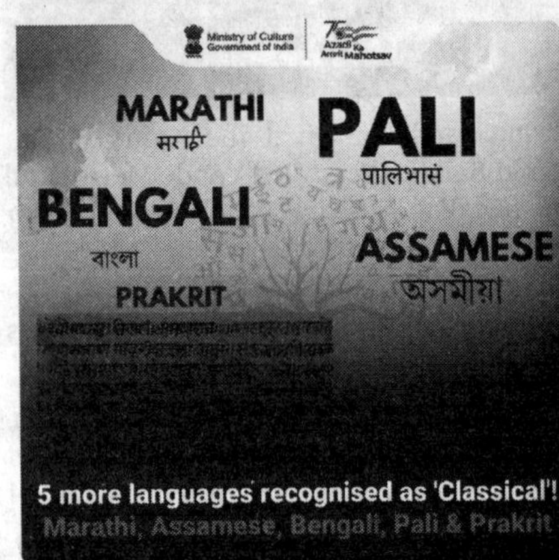

- On 3 October 2024, the Union Cabinet, led by Prime Minister Narendra Modi, declared **Marathi, Bengali, Pali, Prakrit, and Assamese** as Classical Languages. This brings the total number of Classical Languages in India to 11.
- These languages joined **Tamil, Sanskrit, Telugu, Kannada, Malayalam, and Odia** in this prestigious category.
- To be recognized as a Classical Language, a language must be over 1500 years old, have ancient texts considered a heritage, and show distinct development from its modern form.
- The latest additions were approved after recommendations by the Linguistic Experts Committee (LEC) under Sahitya Akademi in 2024.

Cabinet approved Gujarat semiconductor unit

- On 2nd September 2024, the Union Cabinet, led by PM Narendra Modi, approved a ₹3,300 crore semiconductor plant by Kaynes Semicon Pvt Ltd in Sanand, Gujarat.
- The plant will produce 60 lakh chips daily by mid-2025 for use in cars, mobiles, and electronics.
- Four more semiconductor plants have been approved under India's Semiconductor Mission (2022), with a ₹76,000 crore budget to attract investments.
- The total investment of ₹1.5 lakh crore aims to produce 7 crore chips daily.

OTHER SEMICONDUCTOR PLANTS

- Micron Technology (USA): Sanand (Gujarat)
- Tata Electronics plants: Dholera (Gujarat),
- Tata Electronics plants: Morigaon(Assam), and
- CG Power (Murugappa Group): Sanand (Gujarat)

Cabinet approved Eight High-Speed Road Corridors

- The government approved 8 high-speed road projects, including Agra-Gwalior and Kharagpur-Moregram, covering 936 km at a cost of ₹50,655 crore.
- These projects will use PPP models like BOT, HAM, and EPC.
- Over the past decade (2014-2024), India's national highways expanded from 91,000 km to 1.46 lakh km.
- Investments in highways increased from ₹50,000 crore to ₹3.1 lakh crore, following a corridor-based development approach.

PM Modi's Historic Visit to Brunei

- Prime Minister Narendra Modi became the first Indian PM to visit Brunei, marking 40 years of diplomatic ties.
- Brunei is key to India's 'Act East' Policy due to its South China Sea location, ASEAN membership, and economic ties.
- PM Modi inaugurated a new Indian Chancery, discussed defense and space cooperation, and explored LNG supply agreements.

India joined GloBE anti-corruption committee

- India has been elected to the 15-member Steering Committee of the GlobE Network, a global anti-corruption body.
- Led by the Ministry of Home Affairs, with the CBI and ED as key members, India will contribute to shaping international anti-corruption efforts and asset recovery strategies.
- Launched in 2021 by the G20, the GlobE Network now includes 121 countries, supporting global cooperation against corruption.
- India enhanced its role in the network during its 2023 G20 Presidency.

GLOBE NETWORK
(GLOBAL OPERATIONAL NETWORK OF ANTI-CORRUPTION LAW ENFORCEMENT AUTHORITIES)

Initiative	G-20 initiative, supported by India since 2020
Established	2021 during UN General Assembly Special Session on Corruption
Membership	121 countries and 219 authorities
Governance	1 Chairman, 1 Vice-Chairman, and 13 Steering Committee Members
Purpose	Sharing intelligence and best practices to combat global corruption
India's Role	Led by the Ministry of Home Affairs with CBI and ED as members

India, China Reach Deal on Easing Lac Tensions

- In October 2024, India and China have agreed on new patrolling arrangements to resolve the military stand-off at the Line of Actual Control (LAC).
- The agreement addresses issues from 2020 and aims to reduce military presence.
- It also brings changes to the status quo, particularly in the "Y junction" area of the Depsang Plains.

India Provided Hemodialysis Machines to PNG and Medicines to Lebanon

- In November 2024, India sent 12 Haemo-Dialysis machines and portable water purification units to Papua New Guinea, fulfilling a promise made at the FIPIC III Summit.
- This support aims to improve healthcare in Papua New Guinea, for patients with kidney problems.
- India also sent 11 tons of medicines, including antibiotics and cardiovascular drugs, to Lebanon. This is part of a 33-ton aid package to help Lebanon during ongoing violence near its southern border.

Hizb-Ut-Tahrir was Declared a Terrorist Group in India

- In October 2024, the Union Ministry of Home Affairs (MHA) declared Hizb-ut-Tahrir (HuT) a terrorist organization under the Unlawful Activities (Prevention) Act (UAPA) to counter radicalism and terrorism.
- On October 9, 2024, NIA arrested Faizul Rahman, HuT's Tamil Nadu and Puducherry leader, for promoting separatism and disaffection.
- Hizb-ut-Tahrir (HuT) was founded in 1953 in Jerusalem. It works in over 40 countries, promoting strict Islamic ideas but denies any links to extremists.

Missions/Campaigns/ Projects

India Conduct First-ever Ganges River Dolphin Tagging in Assam

- In December 2024, India conducted the First-ever Ganges River Dolphin satellite tagging in Assam.
- The tagging of India's national aquatic animal, the Gangetic River Dolphin, is part of **'Project Dolphin'** of the Union Ministry of Environment, Forest and Climate Change to track the movement pattern of the highly endangered species.
- This initiative was implemented by Wildlife Institute of India (WII) and conducted by the Union Environment Ministry in collaboration with the Assam Forest Department.

- This is the first tagging, not only in India but also for the species.
- The Ganges River Dolphin is distributed across the Ganga-Brahmaputra-Meghna and Karnaphuli river systems.

3 Years of PM GatiShakti National Master Plan

- On 13th October 2024, PM Modi celebrated three years of the PM Gati Shakti initiative.
- The initiative, launched in October 2021 with a ₹100 lakh crore budget, aims to transform infrastructure development.
- It integrates 16 ministries on a GIS platform, promoting faster project completion, multi-sector collaboration, and enhanced economic zones.

Electricity Plan Targets 500 Gw Renewables By 2030

- India's National Electricity Plan (2024) aims for over 500 GW of renewable energy by 2030, which includes 47 GW of battery storage and 31 GW of pumped storage.
- The plan will involve building 191,000 km of new transmission lines to support this growth in energy capacity.
- It focuses on powering Green Hydrogen and Ammonia hubs, increasing inter-regional power capacity to 168 GW, and improving cross-border connections.
- The plan offers investment opportunities worth around INR 9.15 lakh crore (~$110 billion) by 2032, with new transmission projects available for investors over the next decade.

10 Years of Swachh Bharat Mission

- Swachh Bharat Mission completed the 10 years of implementation on 2nd October 2024.
- This year's theme, **'Swabhav Swachhata, Sanskaar Swachhata,'** emphasises the importance of cleanliness and environmental well-being.
- The Swachh Bharat (Clean India) Mission (SBM) was launched in 2014 with the goal of achieving universal sanitation coverage by 2019, as a tribute to the 150th Birth Anniversary of Mahatma Gandhi.

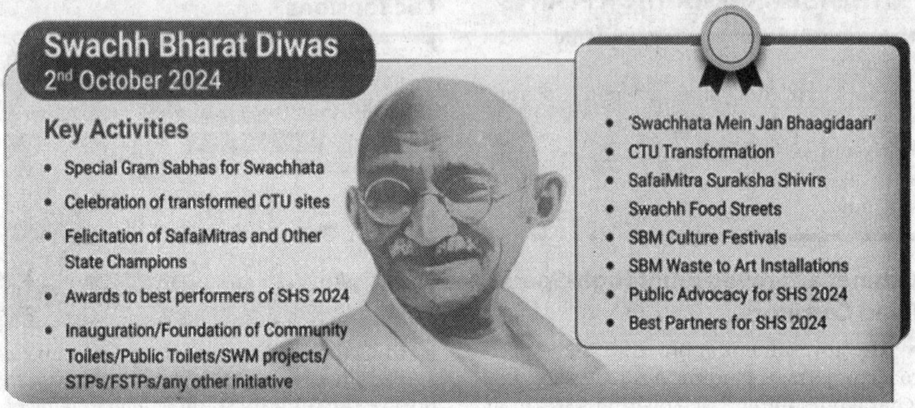

THE SWACHH BHARAT MISSION (SBM)

- The Swachh Bharat Mission (SBM) was launched on 2nd October 2014, Mahatma Gandhi's birthday, as a national movement to prioritize sanitation and achieve universal sanitation coverage across India.
- It includes two centrally sponsored sub-missions:
  - **SBM (Gramin)** under the Ministry of Jal Shakti, currently in Phase II (2020-2025),
  - **SBM (Urban)** under the Ministry of Housing and Urban Affairs, in Phase II until 2026.
- SBM uses a **"Whole of Government approach"** to improve water, sanitation, and hygiene **(WASH)** in India, significantly enhancing health, social well-being, and environmental outcomes.

Miscellaneous

PM Modi Laid Foundation Stone of Ken-Betwa Project

- In Khajuraho, Madhya Pradesh, Prime Minister Narendra Modi laid the foundation stone of the project to integrate Ken and Betwa rivers on December 25.
- The Ken-Betwa national river interlinking project is the first of the 30 rivers to be interlinked under the central government's 'Interlinking of Rivers under the National Perspective Plan".
- This project includes the construction of the Dhaudhan Dam, which is 77 meters long and 2 kilometers wide, as well as a 230-kilometer-long canal.
- The total cost of the project is Rs 44 thousand 605 crores.
- In this project of Rs 44,605 crore, 90 percent contribution will be made by the Center and the remaining 10 percent amount will be borne by the state government.

Madhya Pradesh to translocate 14 Tigers to Gujarat, Chhattisgarh, Odisha

- The Madhya Pradesh government will translocate 14 tigers to Rajasthan, Odisha and Chhattisgarh under the animal exchange programme.
- These will be transferred from tiger reserves in Madhya Pradesh's Bandhavgarh, Panna, Kanha, and Pench.
- Six tigresses and two tigers will be moved to Chhattisgarh, four tigresses to Rajasthan, and one tiger with two tigresses to Odisha.
- MP accounted for the highest number of 785 striped animals in the country, followed by Karnataka (563) and Uttarakhand (560).

15 States, 11 Ministries to showcase Tableaux at Republic Day 2025

- The Ministry of Defence recently announced the theme for the Republic Day 2025 tableaux is "Swarnim Bharat: Virasat aur Vikas" (Golden India: Heritage and Development).
- This year the expert committee of the Union Defence Ministry has selected 15 states, 11 ministries to display their tableaux on Kartavya Path on 26 January 2025.
- These states and UTs are Andhra Pradesh, Bihar, Chandigarh, Dadar Nagar Haveli & Daman and Diu, Goa, Gujarat, Haryana, Jharkhand, Karnataka, Madhya Pradesh, Punjab, Tripura, Uttarakhand, Uttar Pradesh and West Bengal.

Defence Ministry Launches 'Rashtraparv' Website and App

- On December 25, 2024, Defence Secretary Rajesh Kumar Singh launched the 'Rashtraparv' website and mobile app.
- It features live-streaming, ticket purchasing options, seating arrangement details, and route maps for attendees.
- This initiative promotes citizen-centric governance and serves as a tribute to Vajpayee's legacy on Good Governance Day.

Railways Conducts Trial Run of Electric Engine on India's First Cable-Stayed Rail Bridge

- The Indian Railways has successfully completed a trial run of an electric engine on Anji Khad Bridge, India's first cable-stayed rail bridge, in Reasi district of Jammu and Kashmir.

- This bridge is part of the Udhampur-Srinagar-Baramulla Railway Link Project.
- The bridge has a single pylon that stands 331 metres above the riverbed.
- It has a total length of 473.25 metres, with the viaduct measuring 120 metres and the central embankment 94.25 metres.
- It is the world's second-highest railway bridge.
- The highest railway bridge is the Chenab arch bridge at Kauri, which stands 359 metres above the riverbed.

Uber launched women-only bike taxi service 'Moto Women' in Bengaluru

- Uber India has introduced **'Uber Moto Women'** in Bengaluru, marking its first women-exclusive bike taxi service globally.
- The initiative aims to address women's safety and mobility needs while creating flexible earning opportunities for female drivers.
- Uber Moto Women drivers will have the option to switch between accepting only female riders or all passengers.

India names underwater structures in the Indian Ocean

- On 9 August 2024, India named three underwater structures in the Indian Ocean: **Ashoka Seamount, Chandragupta Ridge, and Kalpataru Ridge.**
- These names were approved by international bodies like the International Hydrographic Organisation (IHO) and UNESCO's Intergovernmental Oceanographic Commission (IOC).
- Ashoka Seamount and Kalpataru Ridge were found in 2012 by a Russian ship, and Chandragupta Ridge was discovered in 2020 by an Indian research vessel. These structures are large, unique, and important for marine biodiversity.
- The names honor Chandragupta Maurya, Ashoka (great rulers of ancient India), and "Kalpataru," a mythical wish-fulfilling tree symbolizing abundance and prosperity.

IRCTC upgraded to 'Schedule A' CPSE

- **The Indian Railway Catering and Tourism Corporation (IRCTC)**, a Mini-Ratna PSU, has been promoted from **'Schedule B' to 'Schedule A' CPSE** by the Ministry of Railways.
- This promotion highlights IRCTC's strong performance and its important role in the hospitality, travel, and tourism sectors.
- IRCTC has shown **impressive financial growth,** with its income increasing by 50.63% over three years, from ₹1954.48 crore in FY 2021-22 to ₹4434.66 crore in FY 2023-24.
- CPSEs are categorized into **four schedules (A, B, C, D)**. Being in 'Schedule A' means IRCTC has higher recognition, more independence, and is eligible for higher status like Maharatna.

Right to Information (RTI) museum to be set up in Rajasthan's Beawar

- In October 2024, the foundation stone for the Right to Information Museum was laid in Beawar, Rajasthan, the birthplace of the RTI movement.
- A stone slab with the Constitution's Preamble inscribed in Hindi and English was placed on the museum's site.
- The museum would act as a resource centre for reference and learning on rights-based movements.

Goa assembly bill for ST reservation

- On 5 August 2024, the Lok Sabha introduced the Readjustment of Representation of Scheduled Tribes in Assembly Constituencies of the State of Goa Bill, 2024.
- It was debated in the Lok Sabha in the current Winter Session (December 2024).
- This bill aims to reserve seats for Scheduled Tribes (STs) in the Goa Legislative Assembly, addressing the lack of representation despite a significant ST population.

Telangana becomes first state to get NITI Aayog's WEP

- Telangana has become the first State, in the country, to get a chapter of NITI Aayog's Women Entrepreneurship Platform (WEP).
- It was done in collaboration with WE Hub and the state government.
- Telangana was selected for its robust entrepreneurial ecosystem and emphasis on women-led businesses.
- The state supports women from underserved areas through funding, technology access, and support networks.

First Integrated Check Post along India-Bhutan opened in Assam

- The first Integrated Check Post (ICP) along the India-Bhutan border was inaugurated at Darranga in Assam in November 2024.
- ICP Darranga covers 14.5 acres and is situated about 700 meters from the India-Bhutan border.
- Earlier, third-country nationals were permitted to enter/exit Bhutan only via the Paro International Airport or the Jaigaon-Phuentsholing land border.

Arunachal's Tawang hosts world's highest Enduro Mountain Biking Race: Monduro 4.0

- Monduro 4.0, the world's highest enduro mountain biking race, has begun in Tawang, Arunachal Pradesh. It is part of the Asia Enduro Series (AES).
- Organized by the Tawang Cycling Association and the Department of Tourism, it starts at 14,400 feet and descends to 8,000 feet.
- Participants include bikers from across India and eight other countries.

Gujarat becomes India's first state to implement a dedicated semiconductor policy

- Gujarat government introduced India's first Gujarat Semiconductor Policy 2022-2027.
- Gujarat State Electronics Mission (GSEM) is focused on creating a dynamic

ecosystem for Electronics, Semiconductor, Display, Design, and Innovation.

- Tata Electronics is establishing India's first high-tech chip manufacturing plant at Dholera's special industrial region, in collaboration with Taiwan's Powerchip Semiconductor Manufacturing Corp.

RSS Celebrates 100 Years of Service

- The Rashtriya Swayamsevak Sangh (RSS) celebrated its 100th anniversary on 12th October 2024, marking its founding by Keshav Baliram Hedgewar on Vijayadashami in 1925.
- RSS is now the world's largest voluntary organization, promoting Hindu interests and shaping India's socio-political landscape.

Pune to Host Historic Army Day Parade 2025

- The Army Day Parade will be held on January 15, 2025, in Pune. This is the first time the event will take place in Pune, moving from its traditional venue in Delhi.
- The Army Day Parade commemorates Field Marshal K.M. Cariappa's appointment as the first Indian Commander-in-Chief of the Indian Army in 1949.

PM Lays The Foundation for Textile Park (PM MITRA)

- On September 20, 2024, PM Narendra Modi laid the foundation for the PM MITRA Textile Park in Amravati, Maharashtra.
- The park will cover 1,000 acres and is part of a plan to build seven such parks across India.
- The PM MITRA Park project, launched in 2021, aims to create modern textile hubs in seven states: Maharashtra, Tamil Nadu, Telangana, Gujarat, Karnataka, Madhya Pradesh, and Uttar Pradesh.

Indian Constitution's original manuscript replica showcased at Sharjah International Book Fair 2024

- The National Book Trust (NBT) of India showcased a certified A3-sized replica of the original handwritten Indian Constitution at the 43rd Sharjah International Book Fair (SIBF).

- The replica displayed Acts and Stanzas with exceptional clarity.
- SIBF 2024, themed "It Starts with a Book," features over 400 authors, 600 workshops, and exclusive sessions led by global creative writing experts.

55th International Film Festival of India

- The 55th International Film Festival of India (IFFI) took place in Panaji, Goa from November 20-28, 2024.
- This prestigious festival showcased over 180 films from 81 countries, including 15 world premieres.
- The theme for this year was "Young Filmmakers – The Future is Now", highlighting emerging talent.

First International Solar Festival (ISF)

- On 5 September 2024, Prime Minister Narendra Modi hailed India's remarkable solar growth at the first International Solar Festival.
- International Solar Alliance (ISA) guided by 'Towards 1000' strategy, i.e., mobilize USD 1,000 billion investments in solar energy solutions by 2030.
- It was conceptualized by India and France at the CoP21 (Paris, 2015) of UNFCCC.

PM Modi inaugurated 1st Bodoland Mahotsav

- Prime Minister Narendra Modi inaugurated the first Bodoland Mahotsav in New Delhi.
- The two-day event focuses on language, literature, and culture to promote peace and build a vibrant Bodo society.
- The Mahotsav aims to unite the indigenous Bodo people from Bodoland, Assam, West Bengal, Nepal, and other border areas of the Northeast.
- The theme for the Mahotsav is **'Peace and Harmony for Prosperous Bharat'**.

First Goan Gains Indian Citizenship via CAA

- On 28 August 2024, Joseph Francis Pereira, a 78-year-old Pakistani Christian, became the first Goan to receive Indian citizenship under the Citizenship Amendment Act (CAA).
- Pereira, originally from Paroda village in South Goa, moved to Pakistan for studies before Goa's liberation. He later settled in Karachi. He returned to India in 2013 after retirement.

Sarai Kale Khan ISBT Chowk in Delhi renamed after Birsa Munda

- In November 2024, Housing and Urban Affairs Minister Manohar Lal Khattar announced the renaming of the chowk outside Sarai Kale Khan ISBT in Delhi after Bhagwan Birsa Munda.
- The announcement was made on Bhagwan Birsa Munda's 150th birth anniversary.
- Union Home Minister Amit Shah, Manohar Lal Khattar, and Delhi LG VK Saxena unveiled a statue of Bhagwan Birsa Munda in the national capital on the same occasion.

Delhi Road Renamed 'Jamaica Marg' for Ties

- PM Modi renamed the road outside the Jamaica High Commission in Delhi as 'Jamaica Marg' during a press conference with Jamaican PM Andrew Holness.
- Modi appreciated Jamaica's care for its 70,000-strong Indian community, residing there for 180 years.
- The leaders discussed enhancing sports, cultural exchanges, and cooperation during Holness's historic visit.

Maldives First Lady Visits India's FSSAI

- On 7 October 2024, the First Lady of the Maldives, Sajidha Mohamed, visited the Food Safety and Standards Authority of India (FSSAI) headquarters in New Delhi.
- The visit included discussions on food safety regulations and a demonstration of the Food Safety on Wheels initiative, a mobile food testing laboratory.

Rights of Detenu in Preventive Detention

- In the **Jaseela Shaji vs Union of India (2024) case**, the Supreme Court ruled that a detained person must be given all reasons and documents for their detention to make a proper appeal.
- Preventive detention allows authorities to detain someone without trial for public order or national security, but safeguards include giving reasons and a chance to appeal quickly.
- If reasons or documents are delayed, it violates Article 22(5).

PM Modi lays the foundation for Vadhvan Port

- On 30th August 2024, PM Modi laid the foundation for Vadhvan Port in Palghar, Maharashtra, India's largest deep-water container port.
- The port, with a ₹76,220 crore investment, will handle 254 million tonnes of cargo annually and support ultra-large container ships with a 20-meter natural draft.
- Developed by Vadhvan Port Project Limited, a joint venture of Jawaharlal Nehru Port Authority and Maharashtra Maritime Board, it aims to become a global maritime hub by 2030.

Stamp commemorates singer Mukesh's 100th birthday

- On 24 July 2024, the Ministry of Culture issued a commemorative stamp in honor of the legendary singer Mukesh, marking his 100th birth anniversary.

- The unveiling ceremony took place at the Akashwani Bhawan in New Delhi.
- The stamp symbolizes Mukesh's remarkable career and enduring legacy, celebrating his centenary and immortalizing his profound impact on the music industry.

Ayodhya's Ram Mandir

- **Opening Date:** January 22, 2024, inaugurated by PM Narendra Modi.
- **Foundation Stone:** Bhumi Poojan on August 5, 2020.
- **Construction:** No steel or iron; materials include pink sandstone, granite, white Makrana marble, colored marble, and teakwood.
- **Temple Area:** 54,700 sq ft; entire complex over 70 acres.
- **Construction Supervision:** Shri Ram Janmabhoomi Teerth Kshetra Trust.
- **Consecration Ritual:** "Pran Pratistha" ceremony.
- **Complex Features:**
  - A well, shrines to other deities, a museum, and a time capsule.
  - The main structure is on a 14-meter-thick concrete layer with a 21-foot granite plinth.
  - Surrounded by a 732-meter long, 14-foot wide rectangular wall (Parkota).

Farsi Added to India's Classical Languages

- The Government of India has decided to include **Farsi (Persian)** as one of the nine classical languages in India under the **New Education Policy.**
- **Tamil was the first language in India to be accorded classical language status in 2004.**
- **The National Education Policy 2020 states the importance of preserving Pali, Persian, and Prakrit languages** and their works of literature.

Controversy Over Katchatheevu Island Resurfaced

- The Katchatheevu Island controversy became a major political issue in Tamil Nadu during the 2024 Lok Sabha elections.
- Katchatheevu is a 285-acre island in the Palk Strait that was **transferred to Sri Lanka under the 1974 Indo-Sri Lankan Maritime Agreement** signed by then Prime Minister Indira Gandhi.
- In recent years, Katchatheevu gained importance due to China's growing influence over Sri Lanka, **raising concerns about India's maritime security.**

Om Birla Re-elected as Lok Sabha Speaker

- Om Birla, a Bharatiya Janata Party (BJP) MP from Rajasthan's Kota constituency, has been re-elected as the Speaker of the **18th Lok Sabha** through a voice vote.
- This yearLok Sabha witnessed **contested election** for Lok Sabha Speaker post **between Om Birla and the INDIA bloc's nominee Kodikunnil Suresh.**

Vice President inaugurated Prerna Sthal

- Vice President Jagdeep Dhankar inaugurated the **'Prerna Sthal' on the Parliament House** premises, where **15 statues of prominent freedom fighters and historical icons,** including Mahatma Gandhi and B.R. Ambedkar, have been relocated to a single site.
- The event was attended by key government officials, including Lok Sabha Speaker Om Birla, Deputy Chairperson of the Rajya Sabha Harivansh, and several ministers such as Kiren Rijiju, L. Murugan, Arjun Ram Meghwal, and Ashwini Vaishnaw.

DGCA Issues Circular to Promote Gender Equality in Aviation

- **India's Directorate General of Civil Aviation (DGCA)** issued an advisory circular titled "**Gender Equality in Civil Aviation Sector,**" aiming to achieve **25% representation of women** in the aviation workforce **by 2025.**

- The circular aligns with the **gender equality** principles of the Indian Constitution and the International Civil Aviation Organization (ICAO), emphasizing equal opportunities in aviation.

India's Project ISHAN

- India has embarked on a huge initiative called **ISHAN (Indian Single Sky Harmonized Air Traffic Management),** which is a historic step toward revolutionizing air transport.
- This project, which promises several advantages for both airlines and travelers, attempts **to unify the nation's dispersed airspace into a single entity.**

Government Raises Retirement & Death Gratuity Limits

- The Indian government has raised the maximum limit of retirement and death gratuity **from Rs 20 lakh to Rs 25 lakh** for Central government **employees, effective January 1, 2024.**
- **Ministry of Personnel, Public Grievances and Pensions** has issued an official memorandum in this regard.

Road Safety Conclave in Delhi

- The **Confederation of Indian Industry (CII)** hosted the National Conclave on Road Safety in New Delhi on January 16, 2024. The theme of the conclave was **"Indian Roads@2030 – Raising the Bar of Safety".** Union Minister for Road Transport and Highways, Shri Nitin Gadkari, inaugurated the conclave.
- The Indian government planned **to halve the number of accidental deaths by 2030.**
- Shri Nitin Gadkari emphasized the importance of focusing on strengthening the **'4Es of Road Safety'** - Engineering (Road & Vehicle Engineering), Enforcement, Education, and Emergency Medical Service.

Govt Forms Dispute Resolution Panel for Solar/ Wind sector

- **The Ministry of New & Renewable Energy (MNRE)** has established a **three-member committee** to resolve unforeseen disputes between solar and wind power developers, EPC contractors, and **Renewable Energy Implementing Agencies (REIAs)** such as NTPC, SECI, SJVN, etc.
- The committee will examine cases in a time-bound manner, submitting recommendations to the Ministry of New & Renewable Energy (MNRE).

Cabinet approves Ayodhya Airport as an International Airport

- The Union Cabinet, chaired by Prime Minister Shri Narendra Modi, approved the proposal to declare Ayodhya Airport as an International Airport and name it **"Maharishi Valmiki International Airport, Ayodhyadham."**
- The airport's name, "Maharishi Valmiki International Airport, Ayodhyadham," paid homage to **Maharishi Valmiki, the sage attributed with composing the epic Ramayana,** adding a cultural touch to the airport's identity.

India's First Hygienic Food Street 'Prasadam' inaugurated in Ujjain

- Dr. Mansukh Mandaviya, Union Minister for Health & Family Welfare inaugurated the country's **1st Healthy & Hygienic Food Street, 'PRASADAM,' at Neelkanth Van, Mahakal Lok, in Ujjain, Madhya Pradesh.**
- This food street is **the first of 100 planned food streets across various districts** in the country, following guidelines set by the Food Safety and Standards Authority of India (FSSAI).

27th National Youth Festival

- Prime Minister Narendra Modi inaugurated the **27th National Youth Festival in Nashik, Maharashtra.**
- The theme of the five-day festival is **"MYBharat-VixitBharat@2047- By the youth, for the youth".**

PM Inaugurated Bharat Ratna Mega Common Facility Centre (CFC)

- Prime Minister Narendra Modi inaugurated the **Bharat Ratnam Mega CFC at the SEEPZ SEZ in Mumbai.**
- The Mega CFC will provide **infrastructure, equipment, and training** for the gems and jewellery manufacturing industry.
- It aims to create a supportive environment for entrepreneurs, MSMEs, and small businesses in the industry to grow and thrive.

India's Longest Sea Bridge Opened

- **Prime Minister Narendra Modi** inaugurated **Mumbai Trans Harbour Link (MTHL),** India's longest sea bridge.
- The MTHL spanning **21.8 km, with 16.5 km over** the sea is projected to support over 70,000 vehicles daily.
- Named the **Atal Bihari Vajpayee Sewri-Nhava Sheva Atal Setu**, a six-lane engineering marvel has been built at a cost of **Rs 17,840 crore** with the financial assistance from Japan.

India's First Dark Sky Park in Maharashtra

- **Pench Tiger Reserve (PTR)** in **Maharashtra** is recognized as **India's first Dark Sky Park** and the **fifth in Asia,** aimed at preserving the night sky and preventing light pollution, appealing to astronomy enthusiasts.
- The **International Union for Conservation of Nature (IUCN)** emphasizes the intrinsic value of the night sky as a natural, cultural, and historical resource.
- The **Dark and Quiet Skies for Science and Society Working Group**, led by the International Astronomical Union, recommends the creation of **'Dark Sky Oases'** by governments.

Project for Artificial Reefs in Vizhinjam

- **Union Minister of Fisheries Sri. Parshotham Rupala** launched a project to deposit artificial reefs in the seabed **in Vizhinjam, Thiruvananthapuram.**
- It is being implemented under the **Pradhan Mantri Matsya Sampada Yojana** with a total outlay of **13.02 crore.**
- In the first phase, 6,300 artificial reefs will be laid in **42 fishing villages from Pozhiyur to Varkala in Thiruvananthapuram district.**

Successful Trial Run on World's Highest Railway Bridge

- The Indian Railway conducted a successful trial run on the newly constructed world's highest railway bridge, Chenab Rail Bridge, **in Jammu and Kashmir.**
- The Chenab Rail Bridge in Jammu and Kashmir, **part of the Udhampur-Srinagar-Baramulla Rail Link,** is the **world's highest single-arch railway bridge at 359 meters above the Chenab riverbed and 1.3 km long.**

NCP-Sharad Pawar Faction Gets ECI Recognition

- The Election Commission of India (ECI) has recently recognized the **Nationalist Congress Party (NCP) faction led by Sharad Pawar** and allotted a new party symbol.
- The new party symbol given to them is a **'man blowing turha'.**

● The ECI had allotted the NCP's symbol **'Wall Clock'** to the Ajit Pawar faction of the party on February 6.

India's Longest Transportation Tunnel Inaugurated in Jammu

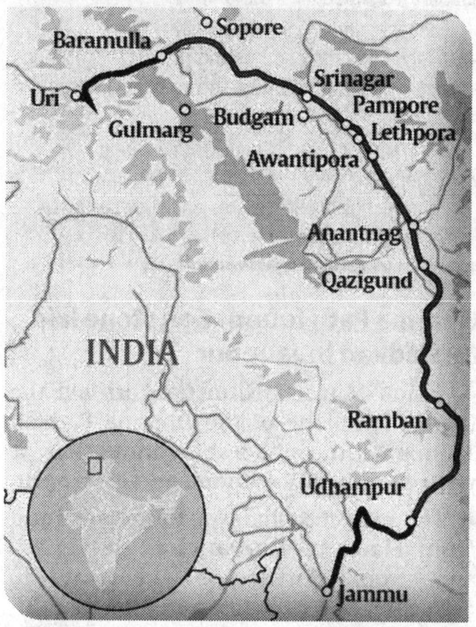

● Prime Minister Narendra Modi inaugurated India's longest railway tunnel on the **Udhampur-Srinagar-Baramulla Rail Link.**

● The tunnel is **12.77 km long** and known as **T-50**, falls between the **Khari-**Sumber section, Trains can now run from Baramulla to Sangaldan via Banihal.

● The prime minister also inaugurated the **48.1-km-long Banihal-Khari-Sumber-Sangaldan section.**

Government Forms Committee to Stop Unwanted Marketing Calls

● **The Department of Consumer Affairs, along with DoT, DFS, TRAI,** and other regulatory bodies, has formed a committee to draft guidelines to tackle pesky, promotional, and unsolicited commercial calls.

● The first meeting was led by **Shri Rohit Kumar Singh, Secretary of DoCA,** on February 14, 2024, focusing on protecting people's privacy, especially from calls made by financial and real estate companies.

● The committee discussed about using a special technology (DLT) to register telemarketers and making these callers use a **specific number series (140)** so people can identify them easily.

Sugar Subsidy Extended for Antyodya Anna Yojna

● The **Union Cabinet** has given its approval to extend the sugar subsidy scheme for Antyodya Anna Yojna families distributed through the Public Distribution Scheme (PDS) for **an additional two years, extending until March 2026.**

● Additionally, the Cabinet has sanctioned the continuation of the Animal Husbandry Infrastructure Development Fund, allocating over 29,610 crore rupees for an additional three years, up to 2025-26.

● **Antyodaya Anna Yojana (AAY)** was launched in December 2000, **this scheme aims to provide highly subsidized food to the poorest families in India.**

Dras Winter Carnival, 2024

● The Dras Winter Carnival-2024 kicked off **in Ladakh** with grandeur, under the theme **"Celebrating Life in the Second Coldest Inhabited Place in the World."**

● Carnival was jointly organized by the **Indian Army and local communities.**

Diamond Jubilee Celebration of Supreme Court

● Prime Minister Shri Narendra Modi inaugurated the Diamond Jubilee celebration of the Supreme Court of India **on 28 January** at the Supreme Court auditorium.

● In celebration of the Supreme Court's **seventy-fifth anniversary,** the Prime Minister launched citizen-centric information and technology initiatives, including **Digital Supreme Court Reports (Digi SCR), Digital Courts 2.0**, and a new website for the Supreme Court.

● **The Digital Courts 2.0 application** is a recent initiative under the e-Courts **project to make court records available to the Judges of the district courts in electronic form.**

National Arogya Fair, 2024

● At the inauguration of the National Arogya Fair 2024 at **Jawaharlal Nehru Stadium in New Delhi**.

● With a theme of **'Har din Har Ghar AYUSH' campaign,** it aims to impart the benefits of Indian traditional medicine systems to the people.

Talabira Thermal Power Project

● Prime Minister Narendra Modi inaugurated the Talabira Thermal Power Project **by Neyveli Lignite Corporation India Limited in Odisha.**

● Valued at over 27,000 crore rupees, the project focused on generating electricity at a rate of 3.65 rupees per unit.

● The Ministry highlighted the plant's emphasis on higher efficiency, reduced carbon emissions, and a notable **10 percent commitment to eco-friendly biomass co-firing.**

'Great Indian Board Reboot' in Mumbai

● The Indian Institute of Corporate Affairs **(IICA)**, the leading think tank under the Ministry of Corporate Affairs, Government of India, organized the **first-ever 'The Great Indian Board Reboot: Roadshow 2024'** at the **NSE Headquarters in Mumbai** on January 31, 2024.

● This inaugural event, held in collaboration with the National Stock Exchange (NSE) India and the Bombay Stock Exchange (BSE).

"SUFALAM" Inaugurated

● Union Minister Shri Pashupati Kumar Paras launched the **"SUFALAM: Start-Up Forum for Aspiring Leaders and Mentors Startup Conclave 2024,"** emphasizing the role of startups in the food processing sector.

First CDS Gen. Bipin Rawat's Statue Unveiled

● Defence Minister Rajnath Singh unveiled a life-size statue of the late General Bipin Rawat, the nation's first Chief of Defence Staff (CDS), **at TonsBridge School in Dehradun** on 12 February 2024.

● The ceremony was attended by Uttarakhand Chief Minister Pushkar Singh Dhami.

President murmu's Life Journey on Radio

● President Droupadi Murmu discussed her life experiences in an exclusive conversation with Union Minister Smriti Irani on the radio show **'Nai Soch Nai Kahani - A Radio Journey with Smriti Irani.'**

● This episode, recorded at Rashtrapati Bhawan, aired on **World Radio Day, February 13, 2024.**

● During the hour-long interaction, President **Murmu shared stories from her childhood and public life,** highlighting her journey from a small village to becoming India's President.

Kilkari programme & Mobile Health Academy Launched

● Union Ministers of State for Health and Family Welfare, Prof. S P Singh Baghel (Former) and Dr. Bharati Pravin Pawar, virtually launched the Kilkari programme and Mobile Academy on February 7, 2024.

- **The Kilkari programme,** a mobile health initiative, **aims to deliver 72 weekly audio messages via IVRS** on reproductive, maternal, neonatal, and child health to registered beneficiaries' mobile phones.
- **The Mobile Academy,** also launched during this event, **provides a free audio training course for Accredited Social Health Activists (ASHAs)** to enhance their knowledge and communication skills via mobile phones. This initiative is cost-effective and efficient, allowing simultaneous training of thousands of ASHAs.
- **Both programs are hosted by the Ministry of Health and Family Welfare.**

First Green Hydrogen Plant at Cochin Airport

- Cochin International Airport Ltd **(CIAL) in Kerala has partnered with Bharat Petroleum Corporation Ltd (BPCL)** to establish the **world's first green hydrogen plant** at an airport, aiming to produce **1000 KW** of power.
- CIAL will provide land, water, and green energy resources, while BPCL will oversee the plant's setup and operation. The project, expected to be completed by next year, will initially power airport vehicles.
- The MOU was signed in the presence of Chief Minister Pinarayi Vijayan, who also chairs CIAL. CIAL is known for its commitment to green energy, being **the world's first fully solar-powered airport with a capacity of 50 MW.**

PM Modi Inaugurates Five New AIIMS

- Prime Minister Narendra Modi recently inaugurated five new All India Institute of Medical Sciences (AIIMS) facilities on **February 25, 2024.** The newly inaugurated AIIMS are located in **Rajkot** (Gujarat), **Bathinda** (Punjab), **Raebareli** (Uttar Pradesh), **Kalyani** (West Bengal), and **Mangalagiri** (Andhra Pradesh).
- PM Modi **also launched over 200 healthcare infrastructure projects** worth more than ₹11,700 crore across 23 states and union territories.
- These projects include the establishment of new medical and nursing colleges, **under the Pradhan Mantri - Ayushman Bharat Health Infrastructure Mission (PM-ABHIM).**

'Sagar Aankalan' Port Efficiency Guidelines Launched

- Union Minister Sarbananda Sonowal recently launched the 'Sagar Aankalan' **guidelines for the Indian port performance index.** These guidelines aim to enhance the efficiency and competitiveness of Indian ports by benchmarking their logistics performance and **harmonizing standards with global benchmarks.**
- The initiative was announced at a stakeholders' meeting focused on implementing agreements from the **Global Maritime India Summit (GMIS) 2023.**
- The 'Sagar Aankalan' guidelines are part of a broader strategic effort to modernize India's maritime infrastructure, aligning with the **Maritime Amrit Kaal Vision 2047.**

EC launches CVIGIL app for election supervision

- The Election Commission launched the cVIGIL app **to keep a close watch on the election process.**
- It is a **single app** for recording, reporting, and resolving violations of the model code of conduct.
- Through this app, online complaints regarding violations of the model code of conduct can be made by capturing photos, videos, etc. **Citizens can report Model Code of Conduct and expenditure violations** through the cVIGIL app.

BhashaNet portal unveiled by MeitY/ NIXI

- The Ministry of Electronics and Information Technology (MeitY) and National Internet Exchange of India (NIXI) have announced the **launch of the BhashaNet portal at the Universal Acceptance Day** event on March 21, 2024.
- The event was held with the active support of the Internet Corporation for Assigned Names and Numbers (ICANN).
- The event marked a significant milestone in **advancing digital inclusion and promoting Universal Acceptance across India.**
- The theme of the event was "BhashaNet: Impetus Towards Universal Acceptance".

GLOBAL UNIVERSAL ACCEPTANCE DAY

- Event Date and Location: Held on March 28, 2024, at Crowne Plaza in Belgrade, Serbia
- Organizers: Organized by ICANN and UASG with support from global partners
- Focus: Promoted digital inclusivity and a multilingual internet, addressing technical challenges to ensure all domain names and email addresses are supported.
- Program: Included plenary sessions and workshops on integrating Universal Acceptance (UA) into technical curriculums and showcasing UA implementation.

Dharma Path foundation stone laid by Gadkari in Jaunpur

- Union Minister Nitin Gadkari laid the foundation stone of the Dharma Path in Jaunpur, Uttar Pradesh, **connecting it with Ayodhya, Varanasi, and Mirzapur.**
- The project includes a **four-lane road from Hauz to Purvanchal University** and from Purvanchal University to Shahganj, costing 3,405 crore rupees.

'Eat Right Station' certification to 150 railway stations

- **The Food Safety and Standards Authority of India (FSSAI)** has granted the 'Eat Right Station' certification to 150 railway stations.
- Prominent stations that received this certification include New Delhi, Varanasi, Kolkata, Hyderabad, Chandigarh, Kozhikode, Guwahati, Visakhapatnam, and Chennai among others. Additionally, **six metro stations**, including those in Noida and Kolkata, were also accredited as 'Eat Right Stations'.
- This initiative is **part of the broader Eat Right India movement** aimed at promoting informed food choices and ensuring food safety across India's vast railway network

Union Minister Pralhad Joshi launches "Coal Logistics Plan and Policy"

- Union Minister Pralhad Joshi has launched the Coal Logistics Plan and Policy, aiming to modernize coal transportation in India.
- The plan proposes a shift to a railway-based system in FMCs projects, **targeting a 14% reduction in rail logistic costs** and an annual saving of Rs 21,000 Crore.
- This initiative aims to meet rising energy demand, reduce air pollution,

traffic congestion, and carbon emissions. Additionally, it anticipates a **10% saving in the average turnaround time of wagons nationwide.**

'Birth Defects Awareness Month' launched by NITI Aayog

- Dr. V K Paul of NITI Aayog launched the National Birth Defects Awareness Month 2024 in New Delhi. The theme is **"Breaking barriers: inclusive support for children with birth defects."**
- This campaign is an effort for observing Birth defect day, which is observed on 3rd of March every year and it is an initiative in raising awareness for all birth defects.
- The campaign will focus on early identification of birth defects such as clubfoot, hearing impairments, retinal defects, and cleft lips, and **will maintain a registry of birth defects through the Ayushman Bharat Health Account (ABHA)** to facilitate effective tracking and treatment.

Amit Shah inaugurated NUCFDC Limited in New Delhi

- Union Home and Cooperation Minister Amit Shah launched the **National Urban Co-operative Finance and Development Corporation Limited (NUCFDC)** in New Delhi.
- This initiative aims to modernize and strengthen the Urban Cooperative Banking Sector under the goal of **'Sahakar se Samriddhi'** for **'Aatma Nirbhar Bharat'.**
- NUCFDC has received a Certificate of Registration from the RBI to operate as a **Non-Banking Finance Company and serve as the umbrella organization for urban cooperative banks.**

PM Modi launches India's first hydrogen fuel cell ferry

- India's first indigenously developed hydrogen fuel cell ferry, **constructed by Cochin Shipyard Limited (CSL),** is part of the **Harit Nauka initiative**. The initiative aims to demonstrate the viability of hydrogen as a maritime fuel. The ferry is set to **operate in Varanasi, Uttar Pradesh.**
- The vessel's development included collaboration between **KPIT Technologies, Pune, and the Council of Scientific and Industrial Research (CSIR) labs,** under the Union Ministry of Science and Technology.

India's 1st green hydrogen plant in Hisar

- Union Steel Minister Jyotiraditya Scindia (Former) inaugurated India's 1st Green Hydrogen Plant **at Jindal Stainless Limited, Hisar.**
- This off-grid plant is a milestone in the stainless steel sector, featuring rooftop and floating solar panels. It will **slash carbon emissions by 2,700 Metric Tonnes** annually and 54,000 tons over two decades.

India's first underwater metro in Kolkata

- Prime Minister Narendra Modi inaugurated India's first underwater metro rail service in Kolkata on Mar 6, 2024.
- This historic project, **part of the East-West Metro corridor,** includes a tunnel that runs beneath the River Hooghly, **connecting Howrah Maidan and Esplanade.**
- The tunnel is a marvel of engineering, with trains traveling **16 meters below the river's** surface.

Postal voting age raised to 85 years

- The Indian government, in consultation with the Election Commission, recently **amended the Conduct of Election Rules, 1961,** raising the minimum age for senior citizens eligible to vote by postal ballot **from 80 to 85 years.**
- This change was made because statistics showed that 97-98% of senior citizens aged above 80 years preferred to vote in person rather than using the postal ballot facility in the past 11 assembly polls since 2020.

India's first National Speed Breeding Crop Facility

- Union Minister of Science & Technology, Dr. Jitendra Singh, inaugurated the first-of-its-kind "National Speed Breeding Crop Facility" at the **premier National Agri-Food Biotechnology Institute (NABI) in Mohali.**
- This facility, **developed under the Atal Jai Anusandhan Biotech Mission,** aims to accelerate the breeding of crop varieties by using a controlled environment to achieve more than four generations of a crop per year.

Vaishnaw Launches 'Niti For States' Platform

- Minister of Railways and IT, Ashwini Vaishnaw, launched NITI Aayog's **'NITI For States'** platform on March 7 in New Delhi.
- This platform serves as a cross-sectoral knowledge platform aimed at becoming a Digital Public Infrastructure for Policy and Good Governance.
- The "NITI For States" platform is expected **to strengthen cooperative federalism and empower data-driven governance** by equipping officials with actionable knowledge and insights.

Vaishnaw Launches India's Fastest Router

- Union Minister for Communications, Electronics and Information Technology, and Railways Ashwini Vaishnaw launched India's fastest and **indigenously developed IP/MPLS (Multiprotocol Label Switching) router in Bengaluru.**
- The router was developed by the collaboration of the government's **Department of Telecom, CDOT, and Nivetti.**
- The indigenously developed router has a speed of **2.4 terabytes per second (tbps).** Terabytes per second (TBps) is the rate of data transmission.

Two National Centres of Excellence for women announced

- On the occasion of **International Women's Day on March 8, 2024,** Union Minister of Sports and Youth Affairs announced the establishment of two National Centres of Excellence, exclusively for women.
- NCOEs cover **23 focused/priority disciplines** where Indian athletes have a chance to win medals in global competitions like the Asian Games and the Olympics.

Cabinet approved ambitious IndiaAI Mission to strengthen the AI Innovation Ecosystem

- The Union Cabinet approved the ambitious IndiaAI Mission to strengthen the AI Innovation Ecosystem with a budgetary outlay of Rs. 10,371.92 crore to be spent on **creating AI infrastructure, AI skillsets, AI startups to AI applications during the next five years** of the mission duration.
- The mission aims to build a high-end scalable AI computing ecosystem with 10,000 or more GPUs **through a public-private partnerships.**

MSP for Raw Jute 2024-25 season

- **The Cabinet Committee on Economic Affairs** chaired by Prime Minister Shri Narendra Modi, has given its approval for the Minimum Support Prices (MSP) for Raw Jute for the 2024-25 season.

- MSP is set at **Rs. 5,335 per quintal,** ensuring a 64.8% return over the all-India weighted average cost of production.

National Cooperative Database inaugurated by Amit Shah

- Union Home Minister and Minister of Cooperation, Shri Amit Shah, inaugurated the National Cooperative Database and released the **'National Cooperative Database 2023: A Report' in New Delhi.**
- The program is aimed at the expansion of the cooperative sector and providing momentum to it.

Agriculture Integrated Command and Control Center inaugurated

- Union Minister of Agriculture & Farmers' Welfare and Tribal Affairs, Shri Arjun Munda, inaugurated the Agriculture Integrated Command and Control Center **at Krishi Bhawan, Delhi.**
- The initiative **aims to empower farmers with information, services, and facilities using digital technology.**

Jal Shakti Abhiyan: Catch The Rain-2024 campaign launch

- The Union Minister for Jal Shakti, launched the nationwide **'Jal Shakti Abhiyan: Catch the Rain-2024' campaign on March 9, 2024, from New Delhi.**
- **The fifth edition** of the campaign was **themed 'Nari Shakti se Jal Shakti'** to recognize the crucial role played by women in water management, conservation, and sustainability.
- The campaign run from March 9, 2024, to November 30, 2024, focusing on water conservation and rainwater harvesting in both urban and rural areas across all districts in the nation.

Foundation stone for MSME-Tech Center in Sindhudurg

- Union Minister Narayan Rane inaugurated the **MSME-Technology Centre in Sindhudurg, Maharashtra,** along with the **Sindhudurg Audyogik Mahotsav** and Self Employment Conclave.
- The government aims to expand technology access for MSMEs nationwide. The project cost was 182 Crore rupees, **focusing on general engineering and food processing.**

Citizenship Amendment Act (CAA) implementation notified

- In March 2024, the Indian government notified the Rules for the Citizenship Amendment Act (CAA), setting the stage for implementing the law more than four years after its passage in Parliament in December 2019.
- It aims to **provide Indian citizenship to persecuted minority communities,** including Hindus, Sikhs, Buddhists, Jains, Parsis, and Christians, who migrated to India from Afghanistan, Bangladesh, and Pakistan **on or before December 31, 2014.**

Credit Assistance Program for Jan Aushadhi Kendras launched

- Dr. Mansukh Mandaviya, the then Union Minister for Chemicals & Fertilizers and Health & Family Welfare, inaugurated a credit assistance program for Jan Aushadhi Kendras.
- He presided over the exchange of an **MoU between Small Industries Development Bank of India (SIDBI) and Pharmaceuticals and Medical Devices Bureau of India (PMBI).**

Amit Shah launches NIA's Digital CCMS

- Union Home Minister Amit Shah inaugurated **a digital Criminal Case Management System (CCMS)** by the NIA, along with two new branch offices in Jammu and Kochi and a residential complex in Raipur.
- The CCMS will enhance coordination in counterterrorism and organized crime cases, while the **Sankalan app by NCRB** aids in navigating new criminal laws.

100 jails certified as Eat Right Campus by FSSAI

- Around 100 jails across India have been certified as Eat Right Campuses by FSSAI.
- **Uttar Pradesh has the highest number** of certified jails, **followed by Punjab, Bihar, and Madhya Pradesh.**
- Notable facilities include Tihar Prison in Delhi, Central Jail Gaya in Bihar, Modern Central Jail in Punjab, and Central Jail Rewa in Madhya Pradesh.

Financial upgradation scheme for 'Gramin Dak Sevaks' unveiled

- The then Union Minister Shri Ashwini Vaishnaw unveiled a financial upgradation scheme **for over 2.56 lakhs Gramin Dak Sevaks (GDSs)** in the Department of Posts.
- Every Gramin Dak Sevak will get **three financial upgrades on completion of 12, 24, and 36 years of service** amounting to Rs 4,320/-, Rs. 5,520/-, and Rs 7,200/- per annum respectively.

India's First Integrated Oil Palm Processing Unit by 3F Oil Palm Inaugurated

- Prime Minister Narendra Modi virtually inaugurated India's first integrated oil palm processing unit, operated by 3F Oil Palm **in Roing, Arunachal Pradesh.**
- The project, led by **3F Oil Palm,** features cutting-edge facilities including a Palm Oil Processing and Refinery, a zero-discharge effluent plant, and a palm waste-based power plant.

Election Commission launched 'Know Your Candidate' app

- The Election Commission of India, led by Chief Election Commissioner Rajiv Kumar, unveiled the Know Your Candidate **(KYC) mobile application.**
- This app empowers voters to verify if any candidate contesting elections in their constituency has a criminal background.
- Available for both Android and iOS platforms, the app **aims to promote transparency and accountability in the electoral process.**

Shipping Ministry approves Rs 645 crore for Brahmaputra waterways

- Union Minister of Ports, Shipping & Waterways and Ayush, Shri Sarbananda Sonowal, announced **an investment of over ₹645 crores for 10 waterways projects** under the **Sagarmala programme in Assam.**
- The projects aim to develop terminals and riverine infrastructure along the river Brahmaputra (National Waterways 2) to enhance connectivity and spur economic growth.
- Each project will receive 100% financial assistance from the central government.

Telangana's first NIELIT plaque unveiled

- The then Union Tourism Minister G. Kishan Reddy inaugurated **Telangana's first National Institute of Electronics and Information Technology (NIELIT) in Secunderabad.**
- The institute **aims to address the shortage of skilled workforce in the local sector** by training 5,000 people over the next three years.

- The center, operating from an 11,000 sq.ft. facility, will enhance skills and training in electronics and IT sectors to meet international standards.
- The quick establishment of the center demonstrates the government's commitment to creating better opportunities for youth.

Railways on track for 100% electrification by Early 2025

- Indian Railways is advancing rapidly in electrifying its Broad Gauge railway lines. In 2024, approximately 97% of the network is electrified.
- **As of the end of June, over 90% electrification was achieved** on broad-gauge routes. Railway Electrification Directorate data: 59,096 of total 65,350 RKM electrified, accounting for 90.43% of total network.

myCGHS App Launched by Health Ministry

- **Ministry of Health and Family Welfare,** launched the myCGHS app for iOS devices.
- The app is specifically designed **to improve access to Electronic Health Records (EHR), information, and resources for Central Government Health Scheme (CGHS) beneficiaries.**

DD Kisan embraces AI with 'Krish and Bhoomi'

- On May 26, 2024, DD Kisan launched two AI anchors: AI Krish and AI Bhoomi.
- These **computer-based news anchors** function like humans, tirelessly **delivering news 24/7.**
- They will provide essential information about agricultural research, trends in mandis, weather changes, and government schemes in **fifty languages across India.**

WCD ministry 'officially' dissolves Food and Nutrition Board

- The **Women and Child Development (WCD) Ministry** in New Delhi has officially dissolved the **Food and Nutrition Board (FNB)** as part of a plan to rationalize government bodies.
- The FNB was a technical wing of the ministry, responsible for providing technical and logistical support for community nutrition programs.

IndiaSkills 2024 competition

- IndiaSkills 2024, the **nation's largest skill competition organized by NSDC,** in New Delhi, testing 900 students across 61 categories.
- The IndiaSkills National Competition 2024 was held from **15th to 19th May at Yashobhoomi, Dwarka,** featuring over 900 participants from more than 30 states and Union Territories, competing in **61 skills.**
- **Odisha** emerged as the top state with 17 Gold, 13 Silver, 9 Bronze, and 12 Medallions for Excellence, followed by Karnataka, Tamil Nadu, Maharashtra, and Uttar Pradesh.

Licenses of 14 Patanjali products suspended

- Following an affidavit submitted by the **Uttarakhand government** to the **Supreme Court**, the licenses for **14 products** sold by **Patanjali Ayurved** and **Divya Pharmacy** have been suspended.
- This action stems from allegations of misleading advertisements, which have violated the **Drugs and Magic Remedies (Objectionable Advertisements) Act, 1954**.
- The **State Licensing Authority** issued the suspension order on MoU and Agreements, citing repeated violations of advertising laws.

'Anuvadini' App Launched by GoI

- Anuvadini is a **web-based platform** that offered voice, document, and image translation services **in 22 regional Bharatlya and foreign languages.**
- The initiative aimed to make study material for all school and higher **education courses available in digital form,** specifically in Indian languages listed in the 8th Schedule of the Indian Constitution.
- This step aligned with the **National Education Policy (NEP) 2020** recommendations, emphasizing the importance of studying in one's mother tongue.

'Panchayat se Parliament Tak' Programme Launched

- The Parliament hosted a program called **'Panchayat Se Parliament Tak'** for over **500 women representatives** from Panchayats and urban local bodies.
- The program aimed to empower and support women's grassroots leaders by providing them with essential training and resources.
- It was organized by the **Institute of Constitutional Parliamentary Studies (ICPS)** in coordination with the National Commission for Women.
- Lok Sabha Speaker Om Birla inaugurated the program in the Central Hall of Samvidhan Sadan.

Indian Institute of Mass Communication gets Deemed University Status

- The Indian Institute of Mass Communication **(IIMC),** a prominent institution for Journalism and Mass Communication, was declared **a deemed-to-be University under a 'distinct category' by the Education Ministry,** following the recommendations of the University Grants Commission (UGC).

EdCIL Vidyanjali Scholarship Programme Launched

- On **6th February 2024,** Union Minister Dharmendra Pradhan launched the EdCIL **Vidyanjali Scholarship Programme** in New Delhi.
- Nearly **14,000 Navodaya Vidyalaya students** have secured admissions to prestigious institutes like IITs and NITs without coaching, with 70 students receiving scholarships totaling Rs. 5 crore.
- The Vidyanjali Fintech Platform was **inaugurated to streamline financial support,** with scholarship letters presented to six meritorious Navodaya Vidyalaya.

SWATI Portal Launched

- The **"Science for Women-A Technology & Innovation (SWATI)"** Portal, launched by Principal Scientific Advisor Prof Ajay Kumar Sood, is a pioneering initiative aimed at **showcasing Indian women and girls in STEM fields.**
- Developed and maintained by the **National Institute of Plant Genome Research (NIPGR), New Delhi,** it is an interactive database intended to address gender disparity in various sectors.

National Conference on APAAR

- On February 13, 2024, Education Minister Dharmendra Pradhan inaugurated the National Conference on APAAR, marking the creation of 25 crore **Automated Permanent Academic Account Registry (APAAR) IDs.**
- This initiative, **aligned with the National Education Policy (NEP) 2020,** aims to provide a prestigious and internationally recognized record for Indian students.

Digital Launch of PM-USHA at Mumbai University

- Prime Minister Narendra Modi digitally launched the **Pradhan Mantri Uchchatar Shiksha Abhiyan (PM-USHA)** via video conferencing at **Mumbai University's Sir Kawasji Jahangir Convocation Hall.**
- Mumbai University received a **grant of 20 crore rupees** for infrastructure and educational development.

Kerala's first generative AI teacher 'Iris' introduced

- Kerala recently introduced its **first generative AI teacher** named **Iris** at KTCT Higher Secondary School in Thiruvananthapuram.
- This initiative, developed in collaboration with **Makerlabs Edutech Private Limited,** is part of the **Atal Tinkering Lab (ATL)** project by NITI Aayog.
- Iris **can speak three languages**, answer complex questions, and features voice assistance, interactive learning modules, and mobility capabilities.

SheRNI platform for female scientists launched

- The UGC's INFLIBNET Centre launched **SheRNI** to connect Indian women scientists, promote collaboration, and recognize their contributions.
- UGC Chairman M Jagadesh Kumar stressed the significance of acknowledging women scientists as key contributors to India's development.
- SheRNI aims **to foster scientific advancement and innovation** through collaboration.

Gujarat Sets Surya Namaskar Record

- **Gujarat** set a Guinness record for performing mass **Surya Namaskar simultaneously at 108 places** in the state on the **first day of the new year.** The locations included **51 historic sites** of the state.
- **More than 2500 people** performed Surya Namaskar at the state-level function held **at the iconic Modhera Sun Temple.**

125-Foot Bir Lachit Borphukan Statue Unveils

- Prime Minister Narendra Modi recently unveiled a monumental **125-foot statue of Bir Lachit Borphukan at Lahdoigarh, Holongapar in Jorhat, Assam.** The statue, known as the **"Statue of Valour,"** was inaugurated during a ceremony attended by Chief Minister Himanta Biswa Sarma and other dignitaries.
- Lachit Borphukan was a legendary **army commander of the Ahom kingdom** (1228-1826).

Andaman's vulnerable Shompen tribe votes for the first time

- First time in **Andaman and Nicobar Islands,** seven members of the **Shompen tribe,** a particularly vulnerable tribal group (PVTGs) of Great Nicobar Islands exercised their **voting rights for the lone Lok Sabha seat** in the union territory.
- Not only Shompen tribe members exercised their voting rights at polling station 411 named as **'Shompen Hut'** built inside the forest staff quarters.

Sahityotsav marks Sahitya Akademi's 70-year journey

- Sahitya Akademi organized **"Sahityotsav,"** the **world's largest literature festival,** to mark its 70-year journey.
- Inaugurated by **Arjun Ram Meghwal,** the event hosts over 1100 writers and scholars celebrating **India's literary diversity** with 190 sessions.
- It emphasizes post-independence India's literary richness and inclusion of underrepresented communities.

Miraj's sitars and tanpuras get GI tags

- **Miraj,** a town in **Maharashtra's Sangli district,** renowned for its craftsmanship in musical instruments, has been awarded Geographical Indication (GI) tags **for its sitars and tanpuras.**
- The GI tags signify that these instruments originate from Miraj, enhancing their commercial value and authenticity.
- **Sitars and tanpuras made in Miraj** are highly sought after by prominent artists, both in classical music and the film industry.

PRAGATI-2024 for Ayurveda research unveiled by CCRAS

- The **Central Council for Research in Ayurvedic Sciences (CCRAS)** has launched the Pharma Research in AyurGyan and Techno Innovation **(PRAGATI-2024)** initiative to promote research and innovation in the field of Ayurveda.
- This program aims to foster collaborative research between **CCRAS and the Ayurveda drug industry.**

Country's First Digital Museum of Epigraphy In Hyderabad

- The then Union Culture Minister, **G Kishan Reddy,** inaugurated the construction of **India's inaugural digital National Museum of Epigraphy** at the **Salar Jung Museum in Hyderabad.**
- The Archaeological Survey of India is overseeing the establishment of this museum, which will house approximately **one lakh ancient inscriptions in various languages** and from different historical periods.
- Last year, Union Finance Minister Nirmala Sitharaman had announced the creation of the **Bharat Shared Repository of Inscriptions (BharatSHRI),** involving the digitization of these inscriptions.

India's first Ayurvedic cafe opens in Delhi

- **Soma - The Ayurvedic Kitchen,** situated within the premises of **Maharishi Ayurveda Hospital in Shalimar Bagh, Delhi,** offers a unique dining experience rooted in Ayurvedic principles.
- The Ayurvedic Kitchen aims to showcase the benefits of Ayurvedic cuisine and promote a holistic approach to dining and wellness.

Major archaeological discovery at Phanigiri

- Officials of the **Department of Archaeology and Museums** in Telangana have made a significant discovery at the **Phanigiri Buddhist site** in **Suryapet district.**
- The team **found an earthen pot with a diameter of 16.7 cm** and a height of 15 cm on 29 March.
- Inside the pot, they discovered **3,730 lead coins.** Each coin bears an **elephant symbol** on one side and a **Ujjain symbol** on the other.

Republic day, 2024

- **Occasion:** 75th Anniversary
- **Chief Guest:** Emmanuel Macron, President of France
- **Theme:** Bharat - The Mother of Democracy
- **Presentations:** Showcased by 16 states and union territories along with 9 ministries/departments.

Overview @ Parade 2024

- **First Time Events:**
  - An all-women tri-service contingent marched at the border for the first time.
  - The Delhi Police women's band and 1500 women members from various states participated in the march.
  - Display of bravery by NSG Commandos along with new weapons.
  - Performance by 1000 NCC cadets.
  - The first, about 1,500 farmers and their spouses have been invited as special guests for the Republic Day Parade 2024.

Award Winner of Republic Day 2024

Best Marching Contingents

- **Among the Three Services:** Sikh Regiment Contingent.
- **Among CAPF/Other Auxiliary Forces:** Delhi Police Women Marching Contingent.

Best Tableaux States/UTs Category:

- **First**: Odisha's tableau, themed "Woman Empowerment in Viksit Bharat,"
- **Second:** Gujarat's "Dhordo: A Global Icon of Gujarat's Border Tourism"
- **Third**: Tamil Nadu's "Kudavolai System in Ancient Tamil Nadu – Mother of Democracy"
- **Ministries/Departments Category:** The Ministry of Culture won with their tableau "Bharat: Mother of Democracy,"

Awards by Public Choice

An online poll on the MyGov platform allowed citizens to vote for their favorite tableaux and marching contingents. The results were:

Best Marching Contingents

- **Among the Three Services:** Rajputana Rifles Regimental Marching Contingent.
- **Among CAPF/Other Auxiliary Forces:** The CRPF Woman Marching Contingent.

Best Tableaux States/UTs Category:

First: Gujarat's "Dhordo: A Global Icon of Gujarat's Border Tourism" tableau.

Second: Uttar Pradesh's "Viksit Bharat Samradh Virasat" tableau.

Third: Andhra Pradesh's "Transforming School Education in Andhra Pradesh – Making Students Globally Competitive" tableau.

Central Ministries/Departments Category: The "Vibrant Villages" tableau by the Ministry of Home Affairs.

Commemorative Coin & Stamp

- The Ministry of Defense released a commemorative coin and stamp for the Republic Day Celebrations 2024.

National School Band Competition

- A nationwide school band competition was held to foster patriotism and unity among students.

Vande Bharatam 3.0

- Selected women artists from the third edition of the Vande Bharatam dance competition performed at Kartavya Path during the Republic Day Parade.

Veer Gatha 3.0

- The third edition of Project Veer Gatha declared 100 school students as winners, who attended the 75th Republic Day Parade.

Bharat Parv

- The Ministry of Tourism organized 'Bharat Parv' at the Red Fort, featuring cultural performances, military bands, a Crafts Bazaar, and diverse food courts.

Parakram Diwas

- The Ministry of Culture celebrated Parakram Diwas at Red Fort, highlighting the life of Netaji Subhash Chandra Bose with 3-D projection mapping and performances.

Beating the Retreat ceremony

- The Republic Day 2024 celebrations concluded with the Beating the Retreat ceremony **held at Vijay Chowk in New Delhi on January 29, 2024.**
- This historic event marked the end of the Republic Day festivities and **featured a splendid display of military bands from the Indian Army, Navy, Air Force, and Central Armed Police Forces (CAPF),** performing a total of 31 Indian tunes.
- The ceremony began with the bands playing the National Anthem.
- This year's ceremony was attended by President Droupadi Murmu, Prime Minister Narendra Modi, and Defence Minister Rajnath Singh

GAME AND PUZZLE

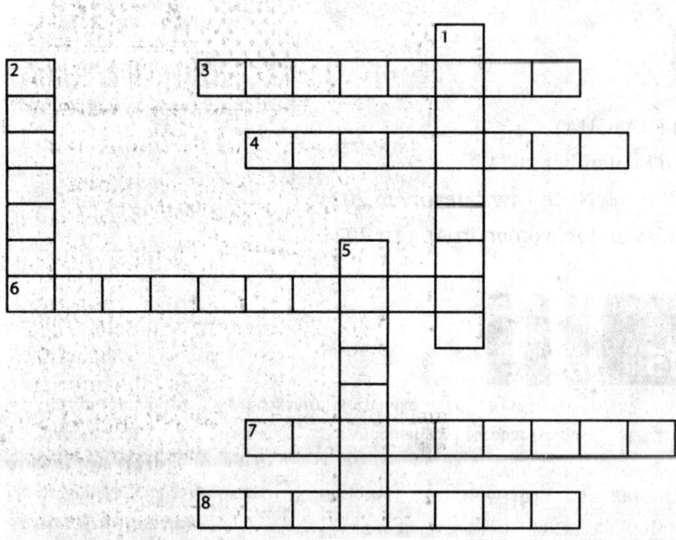

Across

3. AI platform for fashion forecasting in India
4. Policy focused on upgrading amenities along India's highways
6. Rapid Rail launched by PM Modi in September 2024
7. Hackathon launched by NITI Aayog in 2024 to promote zero-emission trucks
8. Fund for agricultural startups and rural enterprises

Down

1. First grain ATM launched in Bhubaneswar, Odisha
2. Recently PM Modi laid the foundation Of this Largest deep-water container port in India
5. India's first Biomanufacturing Institute, located in Mohali

LEARN THROUGH MAP

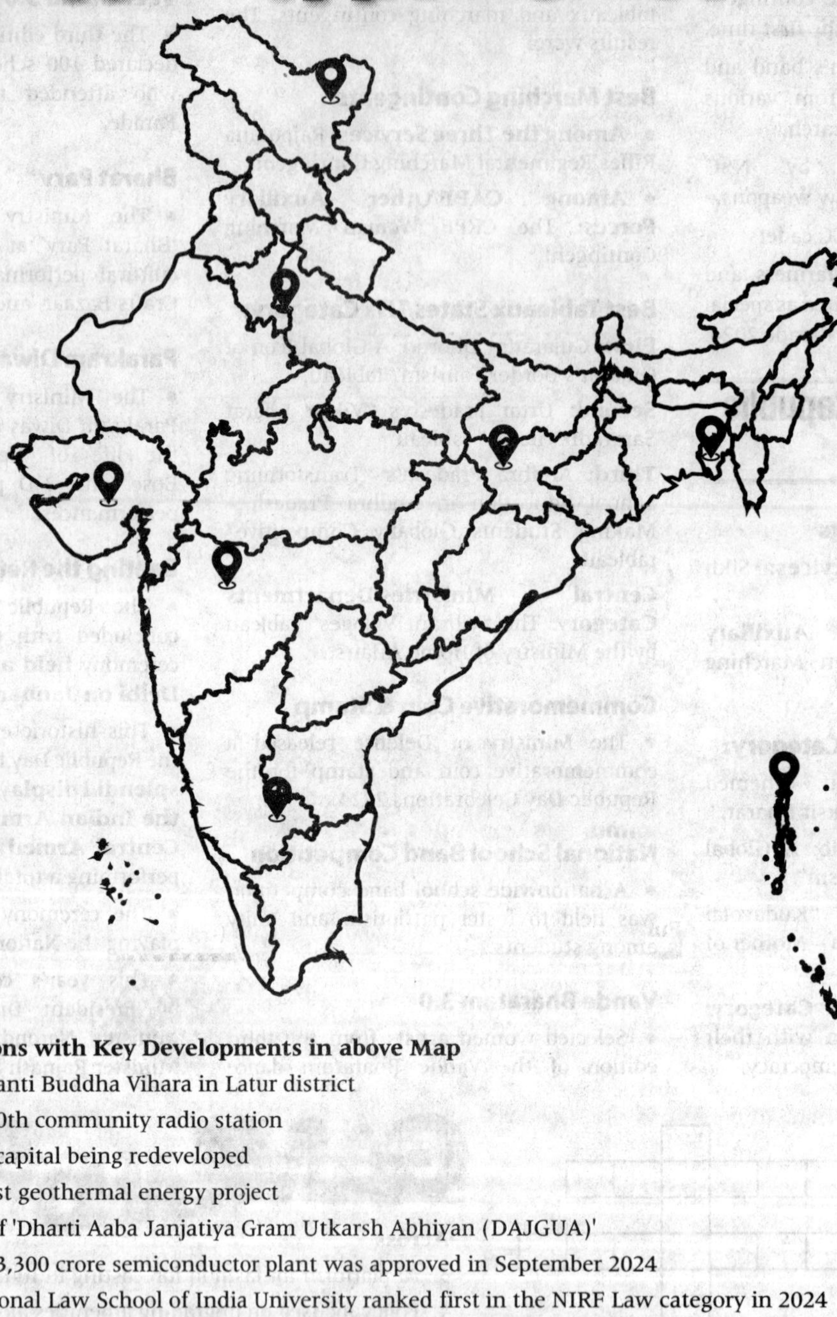

Mark the States/Regions with Key Developments in above Map

1. Location of Vishwashanti Buddha Vihara in Latur district
2. Location of India's 500th community radio station
3. Union Territory with capital being redeveloped
4. Location of India's first geothermal energy project
5. State for the launch of 'Dharti Aaba Janjatiya Gram Utkarsh Abhiyan (DAJGUA)'
6. The state site of the ₹3,300 crore semiconductor plant was approved in September 2024
7. City home to the National Law School of India University ranked first in the NIRF Law category in 2024
8. City for the launch of the Digital Shakti Center by the National Commission for Women in August 2024

SCAN TO GET MULTIPLE CHOICE QUESTIONS

Scan Me

Answer Key (Puzzle):

1. Annapurti 2. Vadhvan 3. VisionXt 4. Humsafar 5. BRIC-NABI 6. Namo Bharat 7. GearShift 8. AgriSURE

Answer Key (Map):

1. Maharashtra 2. Mizoram 3. Andaman and Nicobar Islands 4. Ladakh 5. Jharkhand (Hazaribagh) 6. Gujarat (Sanand) 7. Bengaluru, Karnataka 8. New Delhi

PAGER, WALKIE-TALKIE BLASTS IN LEBANON

What Happened?

In September 2024, Several fatalities and injuries occurred in Lebanon due to explosions caused by hand-held radios like walkie-talkies and pagers modified with Pentaerythritol tetranitrate (PETN). Hezbollah reportedly used these devices to evade detection, marking a new trend in modern warfare technology.

Walkie-Talkies

- Portable two-way communication devices using radio waves.
- Invented in 1937 by Don Hings for pilots, later widely used in military operations.
- Components include a transmitter-receiver unit, antenna, speaker-microphone, and push-to-talk button.
- Used extensively in emergency services, military operations, and industries like construction.

Communication Modes

Simplex: One-way communication (e.g., pagers).

Half-Duplex: Alternating communication (e.g., walkie-talkies).

Full-Duplex: Simultaneous communication (e.g., telephones).

PAGERS

- Wireless devices for receiving and displaying messages.
- Popular in the 1980s, still used in healthcare and emergency services for their reliability in low-signal areas.

COVERT USES

- Difficult to track due to lack of GPS and internet connectivity.
- Can be modified for remote detonation or as triggers in covert operations.

GEOPOLITICAL SIGNIFICANCE OF LEBANON

- Located in the Levant region (a region in the eastern Mediterranean Basin) of West Asia, bordered by Syria, Israel, and the Mediterranean Sea.
- Beirut, the capital, remains a focal point of Middle Eastern geopolitics.

MODERN WARFARE IMPLICATIONS

Devices like walkie-talkies and pagers, modified for covert purposes, have become integral to asymmetric warfare. Hezbollah's adaptation of such devices highlights evolving challenges in surveillance and regulation.

ABOUT HEZBOLLAH

- A Shia militia and political party in Lebanon, formed during the Lebanese Civil War (1975-1990).
- Strongly influenced by Iran's 1979 Islamic Revolution, receiving support from Iran and the Islamic Revolutionary Guard Corps (IRGC).
- Designated a terrorist organization by nations like the US and Israel.

International Affairs

Moldova Joins International Solar Alliance (ISA)

- Moldova became the 105th full member of the International Solar Alliance (ISA).
- The agreement was signed in New Delhi by India's Minister of External Affairs, S. Jaishankar, and Moldovan Deputy Prime Minister Mihai Popsoi.
- The ISA, co-founded by India and France in 2015, aims to mobilize USD 1,000 billion for solar energy by 2030.
- Last month, Armenia became the 104th full member of the International Solar Alliance (ISA).

Britain Becomes First European Nation to Join CPTPP

- Britain has become the first European Nation to join the Comprehensive and Progressive Agreement for Trans-Pacific Partnership (CPTPP).
- Britain becomes the 12th member of the trade club, which comprises Australia, Brunei, Canada, Chile, Japan, Malaysia, Mexico, New Zealand, Peru, Singapore and Vietnam.
- This is Britain's largest trade deal since leaving the European Union (Brexit) in 2020.

John Dramani Mahama Wins Ghana Presidential Election

- Ghana's former President John Dramani Mahama won the country's presidential election in December 2024.
- National Democratic Congress (NDC) candidate Mahama beat Ruling-party presidential candidate Mahamudu Bawumia.
- Mahama was first elected to parliament in 1996 and served as communications minister from 1998 to 2001. He was appointed as vice president in 2009.

India and France Collaborate to Establish World's Largest Museum

- India has partnered with France Museums Développement to develop the 'Yuga Yugeen Bharat National Museum', which aims to become the world's largest cultural center.
- The museum is part of the Central Vista Redevelopment Project. It will cover about 155,000 square meters across the North and South Blocks in Delhi and will have eight sections that display 10,000 years of India's history.
- Prime Minister Narendra Modi first introduced the Yuga Yugeen Bharat National Museum during the International Museum Expo in May 2023.

Belarus joins SCO as 10th member

- The Eurasian Country of Belarus was Joins as the 10th full member of the SCO.
- The Indian Prime Minister skipped the meeting, and India was represented by the External Affairs Minister Dr. S Jaishankar in Kazakhstan in July 2024.
- China will host the 25th SCO Council of Heads of State Meeting in 2025, after taking over the rotating presidency from Kazakhstan.
- The organization now has 10 members, two observer states and 14 dialogue partners.

China's First Atmospheric Monitoring Station in Antarctica Begins Operations

- China has officially inaugurated its first overseas atmospheric background station in Antarctica.
- The "Zhongshan National Atmospheric Background Station" is located in the Larsemann Hills in East Antarctica.
- It will conduct continuous, long-term monitoring of atmospheric components in the Antarctic.
- It is China's ninth operational atmospheric monitoring station and its first overseas.
- India has two active research stations - "Maitri and Bharti" - in Antarctica.

Iraq Conducts First National Census in Nearly 40 Years

- Iraq conducted its first nationwide census since 1987, during Saddam Hussein's regime.
- Authorities partnered with the United Nations Population Fund (UNFPA) to organize the census and collect accurate population data to support effective policies and promote inclusive growth.
- The last nationwide census in Iraq was held in 1987. Another one held in 1997 excluded the Kurdish region.

Australia Proposes Ban on Social Media for Children Under 16

- The Australian government will legislate for a ban on social media for children under the age of 16 soon.
- Australia is trialing an age-verification system to assist in blocking children from accessing social media platforms.
- France last year proposed a ban on social media for those under 15.
- The United States has for decades required technology companies to seek parental consent to access the data of children under 13.

South Africa Launches Trusted Tour Operator Scheme to Boost Tourism From India

- South Africa has introduced a new scheme called the 'Trusted Tour Operator Scheme' (TTOS) to boost tourism from India and China in November 2024.
- The scheme aims to promote tourism by making it faster and easier to obtain visas.
- Currently, Indians make up about 3% of South Africa's international tourists.
- TTOS is an initiative of the Department of Home Affairs, South Africa.

EAM Jaishankar Inaugurates India's New Consulate in Brisbane

- External Affairs Minister S Jaishankar has inaugurated the new Consulate General of India in Brisbane in November 2024.
- Besides Brisbane, India has consulates in Melbourne, Perth and Sydney.
- The consulate in Brisbane will be headed by consul general Neetu Bhagotia.

UK became First Country to Stop Electricity Production From Coal

- In October 2024, Britain became the first G7 country to stop using coal for power by closing its last coal plant, Uniper's Ratcliffe-on-Soar, in the Midlands.
- The first coal-powered plant globally began operation in London (UK) in 1882, while India commissioned its first significant thermal power station, the Hussain Sagar Thermal Power Station in Hyderabad, in 1920.
- Britain, which has a target to reach net zero emissions by 2050, also plans to decarbonise the electricity sector by 2030.
- India aims to achieve Net Zero by 2070.

UN Chief Guterres Banned to Enter in Israel

- In October 2024, Israel banned UN Chief Antonio Guterres from entering the country, accusing him of not condemning Iran's missile attacks on Israel.
- The UN chief criticized the recent rocket attacks in the Middle East without mentioning any specific countries.
- Antonio Guterres became the ninth secretary-general of the United Nations on January 1, 2017.

UAE Launches Global Energy Efficiency Alliance at COP29

- The UAE has unveiled an ambitious initiative to establish the 'Global Energy Efficiency Alliance' during COP29, hosted in Azerbaijan.
- The Alliance aims to double annual global energy efficiency rates by 2030 and reduce carbon emissions.
- This initiative aligns with the UAE's historic 'UAE Consensus' from COP28.

Celebration of Rosh Hashanah Festival

- Rosh Hashanah is the New Year in Judaism. The biblical name for this holiday is 'Yom Teruah'.
- Rosh Hashanah marks the beginning of the civil year, according to the teachings of Judaism, and is the traditional anniversary of the creation of Adam and Eve, the first man and woman according to the Hebrew Bible.
- In 2024, Rosh Hashana began at sundown on October 2 and ended at nightfall on October 4.

World Agrees on USD 300 Billion Climate Aid for Developing Nations

- In November 2024, Countries at the COP29 summit in Azerbaijan's capital Baku adopted a $300 billion a year global finance target to help poorer nations cope with impacts of climate change.
- The agreement was meant to provide momentum for international efforts to curb global warming in a year destined to be the hottest on record.
- The agreement would provide $300 billion annually by 2035.
- The deal also lays the groundwork for next year's climate summit, to be held in the Amazon rainforest of Brazil.

UK agrees to give sovereignty of Chagos Islands to Mauritius

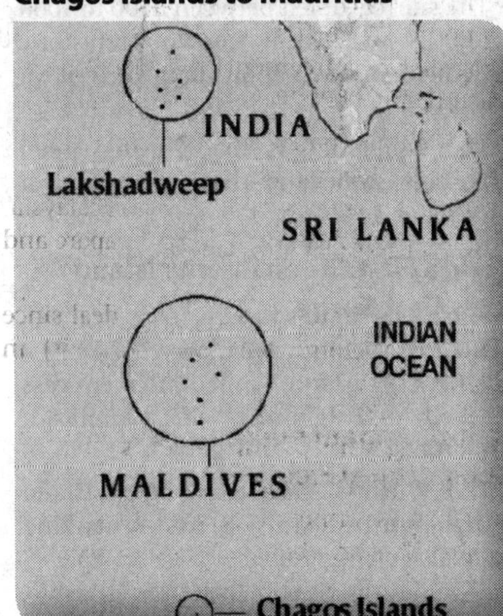

- In October 2024, Britain agreed to transfer sovereignty of the Chagos Islands to Mauritius.
- The Chagos Islands are a group of more than 60 islands in the Indian Ocean.
- The agreement ensures that the UK-US military base on Diego Garcia, the main island, will continue to operate and have a clear legal status for the first time in over fifty years.
- In 1814, the island was ceded to Britain by France.

ASIAN DEVELOPMENT BANK

Israel Joins Asian Development Bank (ADB) as 69th Member Country

- Israel officially joined the Asian Development Bank (ADB) as its 69th member and 20th non-regional member, after fulfilling all necessary membership requirements in October 2024.
- Israel formally submitted its application for ADB membership in January 2022.

Headquarters in 2011

Abbreviation	ADB
Formation	19 December 1966
Purpose	Social and Economic Development
Headquarters	Manila, Philippines
Region served	Indo-Pacific
Membership	69 countries
President	Masatsugu Asakawa

Egypt becomes 2nd country in 2024 to be declared 'Malaria-Free'

- Egypt was officially declared 'malaria-free' by the World Health Organization (WHO) on October 20, 2024.
- Egypt is the third country to be awarded a malaria-free certification in the WHO Eastern Mediterranean Region following the United Arab Emirates and Morocco, and the first since 2010.
- Globally, a total of 44 countries and 1 territory have reached this milestone.

8,200-Year-Old Eyeliner Discovered At Yesilova Mound In Turkey

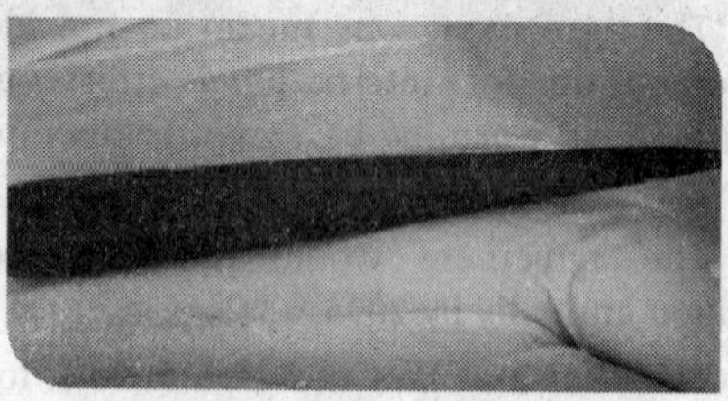

- Archaeologists have discovered a 8,200 Year-old Kohl pen, believed to be word's oldest example of eyeliner in October 2024 in prehistoric city in Turkey.
- The site, occupied between 6500 to 4000 B.C.E., is the oldest known prehistoric settlement in the region, named Yeşilova Hoyuk.
- The kohl stick is made using green serpentine stone and there are traces of black paint on its tip.

World's First Green Energy Island Faces Cost Surge

- On 29th October 2024, the world's first green energy island, named after Princess Elisabeth of Belgium, faced a significant cost surge.
- The Princess Elisabeth Energy Island in the North Sea is a first-of-its-kind renewable energy hub.
- The island will distribute power to multiple countries, support marine biodiversity with eco-friendly designs, and generate 3.5 GW of wind energy.

Nepal Announces Free Cancer Care for Kids

- On 28th October 2024, the Ministry of Health and Population in Nepal announced that children under the age of 14 will receive free cancer treatment at designated public hospitals.
- This initiative aims to alleviate the financial burden on families and ensure timely medical intervention.
- This initiative is effective from November 16 and aims to ease the financial burden on parents.

USA, Japan, and South Korea launched the DiGi Framework

- The United States, Japan, and South Korea have signed the Digital Infrastructure Growth Initiative for India Framework (DiGi Framework) to support the development of India's digital infrastructure.
- The DiGi Framework will be supported by the U.S. International Development Finance Corporation, the Export-Import Bank of Korea (Korea Eximbank) and the Japan Bank for International Cooperation (JBIC).
- The U.S. International Development Finance Corporation (DFC) was set up by the United States government in 2019. Its headquarters is in Washington, D.C.

Brazil Rejects China's Belt and Road Plan

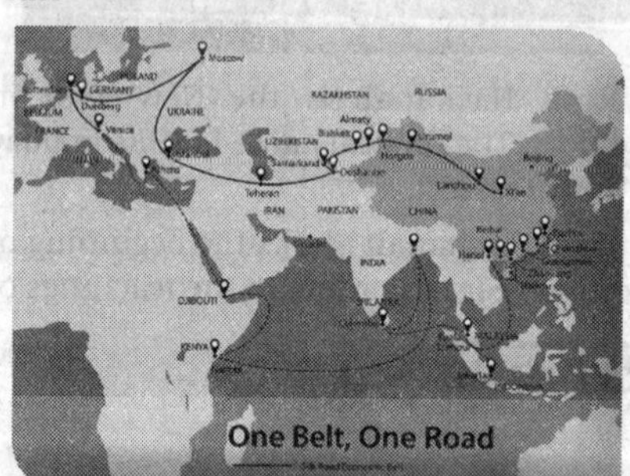

- Brazil has decided to leave China's Belt and Road Initiative (BRI).
- This makes it the second BRICS country, after India, to not support the multi-billion-dollar project.
- China proposed the BRI in 2013 with the purpose of restoring the ancient Silk Route.
- So far, China has signed BRI cooperation agreements with more than 150 countries and 30 international organisations.

Rome Declaration Addresses Water Scarcity In Agriculture

- On October 17, 2024, member countries of the Food and Agriculture Organization (FAO) adopted the Rome Declaration on Water Scarcity in Agriculture (WASAG).
- The declaration was launched on the occasion of the High-level Rome Water Dialogue, took place on the sidelines of FAO's annual World Food Forum (WFF).
- The WASAG initiative was launched at the United Nations Climate Conference in Marrakesh in 2016 to support countries in addressing water scarcity challenges.

Saudi Arabia denied seat on UN Human Rights Council

- Saudi Arabia lost its bid for a seat on the UN Human Rights Council (UNHRC), finishing sixth in a competitive Asia-Pacific vote.
- Countries like Cyprus, the Marshall Islands, Qatar, South Korea, and Thailand secured the seats.
- The 193-member General Assembly elected 18 new members to serve on the 47-nation Human Rights Council, which allocates seats to regional groups to ensure geographical representation.

India launches 'Study in India' campaign at UAE Education Show

- On 9th October 2024, India officially launched the "Study in India" campaign at the 20th International Education Show in Sharjah, UAE.
- The campaign highlights over 590 Indian institutions offering diverse courses and benefits like fee waivers and scholarships.
- The Compain was organized by EdCIL, a Miniratna company under the Ministry of Education.

IIT Madras To Open Its First Innovation Hub In Dubai

- The Indian Institute of Technology Madras (IITM) announced the launch of its first international flagship centre in Dubai, the IITM Global Dubai Centre, in early 2025.
- The Centre is a result of a collaboration between IIT Madras and the Dubai Department of Economy and Tourism (DET).

Route of the Turkmenistan-Afghanistan -Pakistan-India (TAPI) natural gas pipeline

TAPI Gas Pipeline Project

- In October 2024, Afghanistan and Turkmenistan officials jointly inaugurated the Turkmenistan-Afghanistan-Pakistan-India (TAPI) gas pipeline project on the Turkmenistan side.
- The pipeline originates at the Galkynysh Gas Field in Turkmenistan, passes through Afghanistan (including cities like Herat and Kandahar), continues into Pakistan through Quetta and Multan, and terminates at Fazilka in India.
- TAPI Pipeline, emerged in the mid-1990s, is designed to transport natural gas extracted from the Galkynysh gas field in southeastern Turkmenistan.

CALIFORNIA ENACTS LAW TO RESTRICT STUDENT SMARTPHONE USE

- On 23 September 2024, California Governor Gavin Newsom signed Assembly Bill 3216, known as the Phone-Free School Act.
- This law mandates that by 1 July 2026, all school districts, charter schools, and county education offices must develop policies to limit or prohibit smartphone use during school hours.

Jordan Declared World's First Leprosy-Free Nation

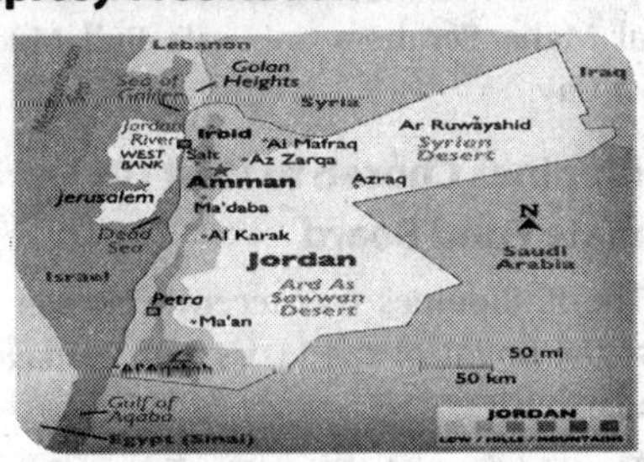

- Jordan becomes first country in the world to be declared free from leprosy by the World Health Organization.
- Leprosy is a slow disease affecting skin, nerves, and eyes, spread through long-term contact with droplets, not casual touch. Symptoms include numbness, blisters, and muscle weakness.

Sharjah Unveils World's First AI-Powered Business Licensing

- In September 2024, the Sharjah Investment Forum (SIF 2024) unveiled the world's first AI-powered trade licence service.
- This innovative system, developed in collaboration with Microsoft and the Sharjah Publishing City Free Zone, allows entrepreneurs and investors to complete the licensing process in under five minutes.

Algeria Joins BRICS New Development Bank

- Algeria has been officially authorized to join the BRICS New Development Bank (NDB), as announced by the bank's president, Dilma Rousseff.
- The NDB, established by the BRICS countries (Brazil, Russia, India, China, and South Africa) in 2015, aims to support infrastructure and sustainable development projects in emerging economies and developing nations

UAE Completes Arab World's First Nuclear Plant

- The United Arab Emirates has successfully completed the Arab world's first nuclear power plant, the 'Barakah Nuclear Energy Plant'.
- It is situated in Al Dhafra, within the Emirate of Abu Dhabi, UAE.
- Construction of the plant commenced in July 2012. It started operations in 2020.

Nepal became 101st Member of ISA

- Nepal has become the 101st country to join the International Solar Alliance (ISA) as a full member.
- The ISA is a collaborative initiative between India and France aimed at uniting efforts to combat climate change by implementing solar energy solutions.
- It was conceptualized on the side lines of COP21 in Paris in 2015.

Paetongtarn Shinawatra becomes Thailand's Youngest Prime Minister

- Thailand's Parliament elected Paetongtarn Shinawatra as their youngest Prime Minister, days after her father Thaksin Shinawatra was removed by a court order in August 2024.
- The 37-year-old Shinawatra received 319 votes, which is nearly two-thirds of the house.
- With this victory, she became the second female to hold the prime ministerial position after her aunt Yingluck Shinawatra.

RUSSIA'S SHIVELUCH VOLCANO ERUPTS AFTER POWERFUL 7.0 EARTHQUAKE

- One of Russia's most active volcanoes, 'Shiveluch volcano' has erupted on the far eastern Kamchatka Peninsula.
- It spewed out an ash cloud over an area of 108,000sq km (41,700sq miles), according to the Kamchatka branch of the Geophysical Survey of the Russian Academy of Sciences.

Croatia to Reintroduces Compulsory Military Service

- Croatia will reintroduce compulsory two-month military service starting in 2025.
- From January 1, 2026, Croatians will be required to serve in the army amid growing international tensions.
- The country had abolished conscription in 2008, transitioning to a volunteer-based system.

Dhulikhel: Nepal's First WHO-Recognized Healthy City

- Dhulikhel, a town in Nepal's Kavrepalanchok district, has been named the country's first "healthy city" and the second healthiest in Asia by the World Health Organisation (WHO) after years of health-focused efforts starting in 2014.
- The town scored 65.48 points for health-related efforts like healthcare access and nutrition programs.
- It earned a $5,000 reward from the WHO.

Operation Herof by Baloch Liberation Army group

- On August 25-26, the Baloch Liberation Army (BLA) launched coordinated attacks across Balochistan.
- Hundreds of fighters from BLA's Majeed Brigade, STOS, and Fatah Squad participated in the attacks.

- They challenged the state for 20 hours and briefly took control of Balochistan
- The BLA named this operation 'Herof.' Herof is a word from the Balochi and Brahui languages, meaning 'Black Storm'.

Australia Enforces 'Right to Disconnect' Law

- On 26 August 2024, Australia's 'Right to Disconnect' law came into effect.
- This law allows employees to ignore work-related communications outside of working hours without fear of repercussions.

Indian Prime Minister visits Ukraine

- India's Prime Minister visited Ukraine for the first time since 1992, signing agreements in agriculture, healthcare, and culture, and providing Four Portable hospitals (BHISHM cubes) for emergency medical aid.
- Each BHISHM((Bharat Health Initiative for Sahyog Hita & Maitri) Cube consists of medicines and equipment for the first line of care for all kinds of injuries and medical situations.

World's Second Largest Diamond Unearthed in Botswana

- In August 2024, a massive 2,492-carat diamond was unearthed at the Karowe mine in Botswana.
- Lucara Diamond discovered the second-largest diamond ever, after the 3,106-carat Cullinan diamond found in South Africa in 1905.
- The previous biggest discovery in Botswana was a 1,758-carat stone found at the same mine in 2019.

India-Israel Launch Water Innovation Hub at IIT Madras

- In August 2024, India and Israel launched a new Water Technology Center, named 'India - Israel Center of Water Technology' (CoWT) at IIT-Madras. This initiative aims to enhance sustainable water management practices in India.
- The center will serve as a hub for innovation, research, and capacity-building in water technologies, focusing on urban water supply solutions.
- A Joint Statement of Intent was signed by the Embassy of Israel, IIT Madras, and the AMRUT mission of the Ministry of Housing and Urban Affairs.

Curacao Becomes Associate Member of Caribbean Community

- The Dutch Caribbean island of Curacao became the newest associate member of the Caribbean Community (CARICOM).
- CARICOM comprises 15 Member States and six Associate Members, mostly island states in the Caribbean.

- Secretary-General – Carla Barnett
- Seat of Secretariat – Georgetown, Guyana
- Chairman – Dickon Mitchell
- Establishment – 4 July 1973

Cote d'Ivoire makes history as first nation to deploy R21/Matrix-M™ Malaria Vaccine

- In a historic step in the battle to beat malaria, the first official vaccination is due to take place in Abidjan, Cote d'Ivoire and will be subsequently rolled-out in 38 districts across the country.

KEYNOTES

BANGLADESH CRISIS

- **Event Date:** August 2024
- **Incident:** Over 130 people died during a student protest against quotas in government jobs, which escalated into a major crisis for Bangladesh.
- **Political Outcome:**
  - Sheikh Hasina resigned in August 2024 and was ousted from power.
  - Ended her rule since January 2009.
- **Interim Government:**
  - Nobel laureate Muhammad Yunus is heading Bangladesh's interim government.
  - Decision made in a meeting involving President Mohammed Shahabuddin, military leaders, and student leaders.
- **Post-Resignation Unrest:**
  - Reports from the Office of the High Commissioner for Human Rights (OHCHR) and media sources indicate continuous attacks on Hindus and their temples in Bangladesh following Sheikh Hasina's resignation.

- The new vaccine has been authorised by Ghana, Nigeria, Burkina Faso and the Central African Republic, and many others are preparing to receive shipments.
- R21/Matrix-M™ is a low-dose, highly effective and affordable vaccine which can be manufactured at speed and scale. With the Serum Institute of India committed to producing 100 million vaccines.

Israeli labels UNRWA a Terrorist Organization

- Israel labels UN Relief and Works Agency for Palestine Refugees (UNRWA) a terror group and votes to ban it, ending nearly eight decades of services for Palestinian refugees.
- The Knesset passed two bills: one banning UNRWA's activities in Israel, and another prohibiting Israeli authorities from contacting UNRWA, canceling the 1967 treaty.
- UNRWA was founded by the United Nations in 1949.

Sri Lanka celebrates annual Kataragama Esala Festival

- The annual Kataragama Esala festival was celebrated in Sri Lanka.
- Spanning fifteen days from 6 July to 21 July 2024, this festival culminates in the final Maha Perahera on Esala Full Moon Poya Day.

Philippines Chosen to Host UN Climate Fund Board

- The Philippines was recently chosen to host the board of the "Loss and Damage" fund.
- The Loss and Damage Fund Board comprises 26 members from Parties to the Convention and Paris Agreement, with 12 members from developed country Parties and 14 members from developing country Parties.
- The "Loss and Damage" fund was set up at the COP27 UN Climate Change Conference in 2022 to help countries that are weak and have been hit by natural disasters.

Romania, Bulgaria, Greece Boost NATO Eastern Flank Mobility

- In July 2024, Romania, Bulgaria, and Greece signed a significant deal to enhance cross-border military mobility on NATO's eastern flank.

- This agreement aims to expedite the movement of troops and weapons, ensuring swift response capabilities.
- The urgency stems from Russia's 2022 invasion of Ukraine, prompting NATO and the European Union to streamline preparations for potential conflicts with Moscow.

179 Dead In South Korea's Worst Plane Crash in Decades

Keynotes:

- **Incident**: A Jeju Air Boeing 737-800 crashed in Muan, South Korea, on December 29, killing 179 people with only two survivors.
- **Flight Details**: The 15-year-old plane was arriving from Bangkok; its front landing gear was not deployed during landing.
- **Government Action**: Acting President Choi Sang-mok ordered a full airline safety inspection.
- **Black Box**: Both the Flight Data Recorder (FDR) and Cockpit Voice Recorder (CVR) were retrieved for investigation.
- **More about Black Box**: Black boxes, actually orange, record flight data (FDR) and cockpit audio (CVR) to reconstruct crash events. Developed in the 1950s by Australian scientist David Warren, black boxes are installed in the aircraft's tail for crash survivability.

China Approves World's Largest, $137-Billion Dam on the Brahmaputra River

- China has approved the construction of the world's largest hydropower dam on the lower reaches of the Yarlung Zangbo River, the Tibetan name for the Brahmaputra, near the Indian border.
- The project might cost over one trillion yuan or $137 billion.
- The project is part of China's 14th Five-Year Plan (2021–2025) and its long-term goals until 2035.
- It aims to use the river's hydropower by taking advantage of a 2,000-meter vertical drop over 50 kilometers.

Bald Eagle Officially Declared National Bird of the United States

- The 'Bald Eagle' has been officially designated as the national bird of the United States.
- The bird has been a national emblem in the US for years, appearing on the Great Seal of the US used on US documents since 1782.
- 242 years ago, in 1782, it was declared a national symbol by the Congress. However, it has now also received legislative recognition.

Rwanda Declares end of Marburg Virus Disease (MVD)

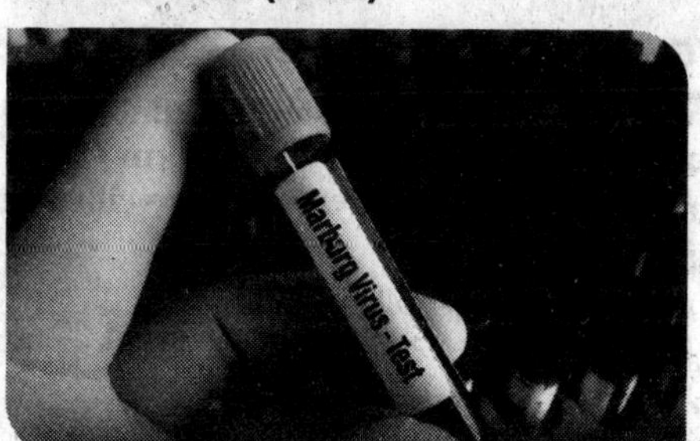

- The World Health Organisation (WHO) and the Rwandan Government declared the end of its Marburg Virus Disease (MVD) outbreak.
- East African country, Rwanda, first declared the Marburg Virus Disease outbreak on September 27, 2024.
- Marburg virus disease (MVD), earlier known as Marburg haemorrhagic fever, is a severe and often fatal haemorrhagic fever caused by the Marburg virus (MARV).
- The virus was first identified in 1967 during simultaneous outbreaks in Marburg and Frankfurt, Germany, and Belgrade, Serbia.

Bangladesh Joins Colombo Security Conclave

- On July 10, 2024, Bangladesh officially joined the Colombo Security Conclave (CSC) as its fifth member during the 8th Deputy National Security Adviser meeting in Mauritius.
- The CSC was created in 2020 by India, Sri Lanka, and the Maldives as starting members.
- Mauritius joined the conclave in 2022 while. Seychelles is an observer state.

Finland passed law to block asylum seekers crossing from Russia

- In July 2024, Finland's parliament approved a controversial law granting border guards the authority to refuse entry to asylum seekers crossing over from Russia.
- The move comes after an increase in asylum seekers from Russia, which led Finland to close its border with its eastern neighbor.
- Finland shut its land borders with Russia late last year.

Essar Launches Europe's Hydrogen-Ready Power Plant

- Essar Energy Transition (EET) launched Europe's first hydrogen-ready combined heat and power (CHP) plant.
- The project at the Stanlow refinery in the UK aims to be completed by 2027.
- EET Hydrogen Power will replace old boilers, providing 125 MW of power and 6,000 tonnes of steam daily.

Japan Introduces Holographic Banknotes

- Japan has introduced new banknotes featuring cutting-edge holography to combat counterfeiting.
- The 10,000 yen bill features Shibusawa Eiichi, known as the "father of Japanese capitalism."
- These banknotes, issued for the first time in 20 years, include denominations of 10,000 yen, 5,000 yen, and 1,000 yen. Each note showcases a holographic portrait of a historical figure, creating the illusion of rotation in 3D.

Nordic-Baltic Participation in Raisina Dialogue

- The eight Nordic-Baltic countries participated in the Raisina Dialogue in New Delhi.
- Cooperation between India and NB8 includes innovation, green transition, maritime affairs, health, IP rights, new technologies, space, AI, student exchanges, culture, and tourism.

India Elected to Key UN Bodies

- India successfully secured the **re-election of Jagjit Pavadia for a third term** on the International Narcotics Control Board **(INCB) from March 2025 to 2030**.
- India was elected to the **Commission on the Status of Women** for the term 2025-2029, showing its commitment to gender equality and women's empowerment.
- India gained seats on the Executive Boards of **UNICEF, UNDP, UNFPA, UNOPS, and WFP** for the term 2025-2027.

India Amends DTAA with Mauritius to Prevent Tax Evasion

- India signed a protocol to amend the Double Taxation Avoidance Agreement (DTAA) with Mauritius to prevent misuse of the treaty for tax evasion or avoidance.
- **Mauritius is India's fourth largest source of Foreign Portfolio Investments (FPI),** with investments amounting to ₹4.19 lakh crore as of March 2024.
- A **DTAA is a bilateral agreement designed to prevent international double taxation,** promoting economic activities like capital investment and trade between two nations.

UPI Services Launched in Sri Lanka and Mauritius

India's UPI services were launched in Sri Lanka and Mauritius, along **with RuPay card services in Mauritius.**

- UPI was **launched in 2016 by the National Payment Corporation of India (NPCI).**
- Countries accepting UPI include Bhutan, UAE, Singapore, Nepal, Oman, France, Sri Lanka, and Mauritius.

SQUAD Institutionalized in Indo-Pacific

- A new security group called SQUAD was formed in the Indo-Pacific **to improve regional security and cooperation.**
- **SQUAD includes the USA, Australia, the Philippines, and Japan,** creating a four-way security group to tackle regional challenges.
- SQUAD aims to strengthen ties among its members and counter China's dominant actions in the South China Sea, supporting a rules-based order in the Indo-Pacific.

G7 to Shut Down Coal-Fired Power Plants by 2035

- The energy ministers from the Group of Seven (G7) countries have agreed to shut down their coal-fired power plants by 2035.
- This decision is part of the G7's larger **goal to limit global temperature rise to 1.5°C and achieve net-zero emissions.**
- The G7 includes seven advanced economies: Canada, France, Germany, Italy, Japan, the United Kingdom, and the United States, along with the European Union.

WTO and ITC Launch WEIDE Fund

- On February 25, the WTO and International Trade Centre (ITC) launched the USD 50 million Women Exporters in the Digital Economy (WEIDE) Fund at the 13th Ministerial Conference in Abu Dhabi.
- The fund aims to help women-led businesses and entrepreneurs in developing and least-developed countries adopt digital technologies and expand their online presence.

Hungary Introduced Bridge of National Unity

- Hungary has introduced the 'Bridge of National Unity,' a striking 700-meter-long pedestrian bridge that spans the majestic Danube River in Budapest.
- Representing a symbol of unity, this architectural marvel stands as a testament to Hungary's rich heritage and progressive vision.

Govt to Fence Indo-Myanmar Border

- The Indian government has announced plans to **fence the entire 1,643 km Indo-Myanmar border** to enhance surveillance and security.
- The decision follows ethnic conflict in Manipur, which shares nearly 400 km of this border.
- **The construction aims to put an end to the Free Movement Regime (FMR),** which allowed border residents to travel up to 16 km into the neighboring country without a visa.

India Secures Operation of Sittwe Port in Myanmar

- India has secured operational rights to the Sittwe Port in Myanmar, marking its second overseas port acquisition after Chabahar Port in Iran.
- **About Sittwe Port Agreement:**
  - **Port Name:** Sittwe
  - **Location:** Myanmar
  - **Operator:** India Ports Global Limited (IPGL)
  - **Project Context:** The Sittwe Port is an integral part of the Kaladan multi-modal transit transport project.
  - **Objective:** To establish a sea route connecting Kolkata, with Sittwe seaport in Myanmar.

France Enshrines Abortion Rights in Constitution

- French lawmakers approved a bill to enshrine the right to abortion in the Constitution of France during a joint session of Parliament at the Palace of Versailles.
- The bill was approved in an overwhelming 780-72 vote.
- The move makes France the first country in the world to **offer explicit protection for terminating a pregnancy in its basic law.**

India Launches UPI at Eiffel Tower

- India launched the Unified Payments Interface (UPI) at the Eiffel Tower in Paris during France's Republic Day reception.
- Developed by the National Payments Corporation of India in 2016, UPI allows 24/7 payments via a virtual payment address.
- In July 2023, Prime Minister Modi had revealed the agreement between India and France to implement the UPI payment mechanism.

France Leads EU with Digital Visas

- From January 1, 2024, France has taken the lead in introducing **Digital Schengen visas,** making it the inaugural country within the European Union to implement these visas.
- This initiative is a precursor to the anticipated **complete digitization of Schengen visa processes scheduled for 2026.**
- This strategic step aligns with the broader goal of embracing digital advancements in visa procedures.

Spain Joins International Solar Alliance

- Spain joined the International Solar Alliance (ISA) as its **99th member.**
- **Launched by France and India during COP21 in Paris,** the ISA intends to use a large-scale solar energy deployment to carry out the Paris Climate Agreement.
- It acts as a platform for member nations to work together to advance the global energy transition, improve energy access, guarantee energy security.

India-China Trade Hits Record High

- Chinese envoy Ma Jia announced that India-China trade hit a record $136.2 billion in 2023, surpassing $135.98 billion in 2022, despite a mid-year slowdown.
- She credited the growth to improved bilateral ties, including an informal meeting between PM Modi and President Xi Jinping in August.

- The trade deficit in 2022 had exceeded $100 billion in China's favor.

Shanghai Proposes 'One Person, One File' Surveillance

- The Shanghai government has proposed the "One Person, One File" (OPOF) program to expand digital surveillance and censorship in China.
- The plan involves tripling facial recognition cameras and creating detailed personal data files for all residents.
- It aims to establish comprehensive technology-driven social control.

China's New Territorial Sea Baseline Raises Concerns

- China's recent announcement of a **new territorial sea baseline in the northern part of the Gulf of Tonkin,** which it shares with Vietnam, has raised concerns about potential impacts on existing agreements and regional stability.
- The Gulf of Tonkin, **also known as Beibu Gulf**, holds historical significance for maritime demarcation between China and Vietnam in the South China Sea.
- China's disclosure of seven base points forming the baseline for its sovereignty claims in this area has sparked concerns among neighboring countries and the international community.
- China recently announced a new territorial sea baseline in the northern Gulf of Tonkin, shared with Vietnam, raising concerns about regional stability and existing agreements.
- The Gulf of Tonkin, or Beibu Gulf, is historically significant for maritime boundaries between China and Vietnam in the South China Sea.
- China's identification of seven base points for its sovereignty claims has alarmed neighboring countries and the global community.

India, Moldova Sign Diplomatic Visa Waiver

- With the signing of a visa waiver agreement, **citizens of Moldova and India are able to travel without a visa** for diplomatic and official purposes.
- The deal was inked in New Delhi by Moldovan ambassador Ana Taban and Ministry of External Affairs (MEA) secretary Pavan Kapoor (West).
- After establishing diplomatic relations in 1992, India and Moldova have enjoyed cordial and amicable relations, which will be further strengthened by the pact.

EU Approves First Global AI Rules

- The European Union (EU) has given the final approval to the **world's first comprehensive rules on Artificial Intelligence (AI),** known as the Artificial Intelligence Act.
- This groundbreaking legislation follows a **'risk-based' approach,** meaning the higher the risk an AI system poses to society, the stricter the rules.
- The Act categorizes different types of AI according to risk, with high-risk AI systems subject to stringent requirements and obligations.

EU's New Visa Rules for Indian Travellers

- European Union (EU) has adopted new visa rules that will allow frequent travellers from India to apply for **multiple-entry Schengen visas with longer validity,** easing travel to **29 European countries.**
- Indian nationals can now be issued long-term, multi-entry Schengen visas **valid for two years after having obtained and lawfully used two visas** within the previous three years.
- The two-year visa will normally be followed by a five-year visa, if the passport has sufficient validity remaining.

EU-India Collaboration on EV Battery Recycling

- The European Union (EU) and India launched an **Expression of Interest (EoI)** for startups working in Battery Recycling Technologies for Electric Vehicles (EVs) for a matchmaking event.
- The matchmaking aims **to enhance the cooperation between European and Indian Small and Medium-sized Enterprises (SMEs)** and startups in the clean and green technologies sector.

EU Law Adopted to Restore Degraded Ecosystems

- The European Parliament adopted the **EU's first law aimed at restoring degraded ecosystems,** initially proposed by the European Commission in June 2022, with 336 votes in favor.
- The law mandates **EU countries to restore at least 20% of their land and sea areas by 2030,** with all ecosystems in need of restoration to be addressed by 2050.

EU Launches Red Sea Naval Mission

- The European Union launched a naval mission **to protect cargo ships in the Red Sea from attacks from Yemen's Houthi rebels** on 19 February.
- The mission aimed to ensure freedom of navigation and will work alongside the US-led naval coalition.

Maldives Adopts India's RuPay Service

- The Maldives aim to strengthen its own currency, the Maldivian Rufiyaa (MVR), by accepting India's RuPay payment service.
- Despite recent turbulence in bilateral relations, the Maldives is set to launch RuPay, a product of the National Payments Corporation of India (NPCI).

PNC Wins Maldives Parliamentary Elections

- In Maldives, the People's National Congress (PNC) secured a landslide win in the parliamentary elections held on 21 April 2024.
- The PNC clinched over 66 seats, solidifying its position in the political landscape of the nation.
- **Dr. Mohammed Muizzu had won the Presidential election** as a PPM-PNC candidate last year.

UAE Introduces Long-Term Residency Visa for Indians

- Dubai's Department of Economy and Tourism (DET) has introduced a **five-year multiple-entry visa for Indian tourists.**
- This visa is issued within two to five working days upon receiving and accepting the service request. It permits the holder to stay in the country for 90 days.
- The Blue Residency Visa joins existing long-term residency programs like the Golden Visa for investors and specialists and the Green Visa for skilled professionals and business owners.

Abu Dhabi Hosts Electric Vehicle Innovation Summit

- **The third Electric Vehicle Innovation Summit (EVIS)** was hosted at the Abu Dhabi National Exhibition Centre, highlighting the **MENA region's shift towards sustainable transportation.**
- The summit reflects growing consumer interest in electric mobility in the Middle East, supported by collaborative efforts despite challenges like charging infrastructure and costs.
- EVIS underscores the region's commitment to achieving **net-zero emissions by 2050.**

Dubai to Launch World's First Electric Air Taxi Service

- Dubai's Road and Transport Authority has **signed an agreement with Joby Aviation** to introduce **world's first air taxi service** in Dubai.

- The agreement gives Joby Aviation the **rights to operate the air taxi service in Dubai for a period of six years.**
- The agreement is expected to position Dubai as a world leader in proving clean, fast air travel in the megapolis.

UAE Launches Falcon Foundation for AI

- The United Arab Emirates has initiated the Falcon Foundation, a non-profit organization dedicated to advancing open-source generative AI models.
- With a 300-million-dollar investment led by Abu Dhabi's Advanced Technology Research Council, the **aim is to democratize AI development and foster collaboration.**

Indian PM Visits UAE to Strengthen Bilateral Relations

- This is Prime Minister Narendra Modi's **seventh visit to the UAE since 2015** and his third in the past eight months, highlighting the importance of bilateral relations.
- During this visit, the Prime Minister Inaugurates the **Bochasanwasi Shri Akshar Purushottam Swaminarayan Sanstha (BAPS) temple,** the **first Hindu temple in Abu Dhabi.**
- Several key agreements were signed, including a Memorandum of Understanding **(MoU) for using local currencies (INR-AED)** for transactions and another for **establishing an Indian Institute of Technology (IIT) in Abu Dhabi.**

Dubai Launches 'India by the Creek' Festival

- Dubai launched the inaugural "India by the Creek" festival, **showcasing Indian culture at Al Seef Park** from March 8th to 10th.
- The event celebrated the historical and cultural ties between India and Dubai, offering diverse programs including music, literature, and workshops.
- The festival took place at **Al Seef Park, a historic trade hub on the Dubai Creek.**

Mahalaxmi Jatra Celebrated in Kathmandu

- The Mahalaxmi Jatra in Kathmandu Valley, **celebrated on Akshaya Tritiya of Baisakh month,** honors the **goddess Mahalaxmi.**
- In **places like Banepa and Panauti** in Nepal, devotees construct chariots for the goddess and other deities, take them around the village, and engage in festive activities like playing with vermillion.

Kathmandu Ranks Highest for Unhealthy Air

- Kathmandu has been experiencing significant air quality issues. **The Air Quality Index (AQI)** in Kathmandu has reached unhealthy levels.
- The main pollutant contributing to the poor air quality is PM2.5. PM2.5 refers to atmospheric particulate matter (PM) that has a diameter of less than 2.5 micrometers, which is about 3% the diameter of a human hair.
- The PM2.5 concentration in Kathmandu was **18.4 times** the World Health Organization's annual air quality guideline value.

Nepal Includes Disputed Map on Rs 100 Currency Note

- Nepal decided to include a map on its Rs 100 currency note depicting areas administered by India in Uttarakhand, such as **Limpiadhura, Lipulekh, and Kalapani, as part of its territory.**
- India asserted that Nepal's unilateral measures would not alter the ground reality.
- The **dispute centers on a 372-sq-km area at the India-Nepal-China trijunction in Uttarakhand's** Pithoragarh district.

Nepal's Parliament Approves BIMSTEC Charter

- Nepal's parliament approved the BIMSTEC Charter, solidifying the country's commitment to the regional group.
- **The BIMSTEC Charter, signed during the Fifth BIMSTEC Summit** in Colombo on March 30, 2022, outlines principles and structures for cooperation among member states.

Nepal Declares Pokhara as Tourism Capital

- On March 17, the government of Nepal formally declared Pokhara as the nation's tourism capital during a ceremony held at Barahi Ghat.
- Prime Minister of Nepal presided over the event, which featured musical performances by renowned artists, showcasing the cultural vibrancy of the region.

US and India Audit Kolkata Port for MSRA

- The US and India audited Kolkata Port to evaluate its potential for a new **Master Ship Repair Agreement (MSRA), aiming to enhance naval maintenance and repair capabilities in the Indo-Pacific region.**
- In April 2024, Cochin Shipyard Ltd signed a similar MSRA deal.
- The MSRA aims to establish India as a major hub for US Navy ship maintenance, allowing US warships to access critical repair services at Indian ports.

US 2024 Special 301 Report: India on Priority Watch List

- **The United States Trade Representative (USTR) released its 2024 Special 301 Report,** which **placed India on the Priority Watch List** due to ongoing issues related to intellectual property (IP) protection and enforcement.
- The report emphasized the need for collaborative efforts and ongoing dialogue between the US and India to address complex IP issues in the coming year.

US and UK Agreement on AI Safety Testing

- The **US and UK have signed a landmark agreement on artificial intelligence (AI),** as the allies become the first countries to formally co-operate on how to test and assess risks from emerging AI models.
- The agreement will see both countries work together to develop "robust" methods for evaluating the safety of AI tools and its systems.

Alabama Executes Inmate Using Nitrogen Gas

- **Alabama** has carried out the **first known execution using nitrogen gas** in the **United States**. The inmate, **Kenneth Smith,** was put to death by **nitrogen hypoxia.**
- This method is designed to replace oxygen in the body with a high concentration of nitrogen, causing death.

Japan Inaugurates Kohima Peace Memorial

- On May 8, 2024, Nagaland Chief Minister Neiphiu Rio and Japanese Ambassador to India Hiroshi Suzuki jointly dedicated the **Kohima Peace Memorial and lay the groundwork for Eco Park Kohima.**
- Because it honors the cooperative efforts of the Government of Japan and the Japanese International Corporation Agency with the Government of Nagaland, the Kohima Peace Memorial and Eco Park is very meaningful.

10th India-Japan Disarmament Consultations in Tokyo

- On 24th April 2024, the 10th Round of **India-Japan Consultations on Disarmament, Non-Proliferation and Export Control was held in Tokyo.**

- The two sides exchanged views on developments in the areas of disarmament and non-proliferation relating to nuclear, chemical and biological domains, outer space security, non-proliferation issues, conventional weapons and export control.
- The Indian delegation was led by the Joint Secretary (Disarmament and International Security Affairs), Ministry of External Affairs, **Muanpuii Saiawi.**

16th India-Japan Foreign Ministers' Strategic Dialogue in Tokyo

- Japan's involvement in India's Northeast **aims to transform connectivity and the industrial landscape,** benefiting neighboring countries through enhanced linkages. Both nations have agreed on the need to enhance economic stability and supply chain resilience by strategically improving trade and technology ties.
- The dialogue emphasized preparing bilateral relations to respond to emerging geopolitical, geoeconomic, and technological trends, advancing the India-Japan Special Strategic Global Partnership.

Sri Lanka Signs 20-Year Deal with Adani Green

- The Sri Lankan cabinet approved the agreement on 7 May 2024.
- According to the agreement, which spans 20 years, **Adani Green Energy will receive payment of 8.26 cents per kilowatt-hour (kWh)** for the electricity produced by the two wind power stations.

Sri Lanka Approves Kankesanthurai Port Renovation

- The Sri Lankan Cabinet has approved the renovation of the Kankesanthurai Port in the Northern Province of Sri Lanka.
- The entire cost of the project, which is USD 61.5 million, will be **granted by India.**
- The Kankesanthurai Port, also known as the KKS Port, is located in the northern region of Sri Lanka.

Indo-Bangla Baul Music Festival in Dhaka

- A nine-day Indo-Bangla Baul music festival **commenced in Dhaka,** celebrating the **250th birth anniversary of mystic saint and bard Fakir Lalan Shah.**
- Organized by Lalon Biswasangha, with support from the Indian High Commission and Bangladesh's Ministry of Cultural Affairs, the **festival honors Lalan Shah's humanist teachings.**
- Baul singer Farida Parveen highlighted Lalan's role as a mystic, philosopher, and social reformer, whose songs blended various religious elements.

Bangladesh Faces Issues Repaying Chinese Loans

- In **Bangladesh, public sector power companies are facing trouble** in loan repayment to their Chinese creditors amid the forex crisis.
- The public sector power producer **B-R Powergen Ltd** signed an agreement with the Industrial and **Commercial Bank of China (ICBC) and EXIM Bank of China** for buyer's credit in a $129 million syndicated loan.

Chad's Mahamat Deby Wins Presidential Election

- Mahamat Deby Itno, **Chad's military leader, has won the presidential election.**
- His main rival, Prime Minister Succès Masra, contested.

World's Highest Observatory Opens in Chile

- The University of Tokyo has inaugurated the **world's highest observatory, the Atacama Observatory (TAO),** on 30 April, 2024.
- Located at an altitude of 5,640 meters on the summit of Cerro Chajnantor in northern Chile, **TAO houses a 6.5-meter optical-infrared telescope.**
- The observatory aims to unravel mysteries of the universe, such as dark energy and primordial first stars.

Nigeria Implements WHO-Recommended Men5CV Vaccine

- Nigeria has taken a step forward in global health by being the **first country to implement a new World Health Organization (WHO)-recommended vaccine, Men5CV, targeting 5 strains of the meningococcus bacteria.**
- This initiative is part of a broader effort to combat meningitis, particularly in **Africa's "Meningitis Belt,"** where Nigeria is among the 26 hyper-endemic countries.
- The vaccine campaign targets over a million people aged 1-29 in the affected regions.

Zimbabwe Introduces Gold-Backed Currency

- Zimbabwe replaced **its collapsing local currency** with a new one backed by gold and foreign currencies that **it hopes will be more stable and help bring down inflation.**
- The Southern African country relaunched its own currency in 2019 after a decade of dollarisation, but it struggled to win public trust and more than 80% of domestic transactions are now conducted in foreign currency.
- **The new currency - called Zimbabwe Gold (ZiG)** - will circulate alongside foreign currencies.

UK Warns Against Travel to Pakistan

- The Foreign, Commonwealth & Development Office (FCDO) of the United Kingdom has named Pakistan in its list of countries that are 'too dangerous' for UK citizens to travel to.
- The total number of destinations banned by FCDO stands at 24.
- The list is based on potential risks, including crime, war, terrorism, disease, weather conditions, natural disasters, and other threats to visitor safety.
- The countries newly added to the list are Russia, Ukraine, Israel, Iran, Sudan, Lebanon, Belarus, and the Palestinian territories.

India Abstains on Pakistan's Islamophobia Resolution at UNGA

- The UN General Assembly adopted a resolution titled **'Measures to Combat Islamophobia,'** introduced by Pakistan and co-sponsored by China, with 115 votes in favor and 44 abstentions, including India.
- **The resolution aims to combat discrimination against Muslims,** citing incidents like Quran desecration, mosque attacks, and religious intolerance.
- **India emphasized the need to address all forms of religious discrimination,** including anti-Hindu, anti-Buddhist, and anti-Sikh sentiments, for a more inclusive approach.

Iran's President Ebrahim Raisi Dies in Helicopter Crash

- Iranian President Ebrahim Raisi died in a helicopter crash in the Dizmar forest in East Azarbaijan Province.
- Following Raisi's death, Iran's First Vice President Mohammad Mokhber was appointed acting President by Iran's Supreme leader Ali Khamenei.

Iran Announces Visa-Free Travel for Indian Tourists

- The Iranian government has approved a visa-free policy for Indian nationals. This policy will be only valid for tourism purposes.
- With this exemption, Indian citizens holding ordinary passports can enter Iran without a visa once every six months for a maximum stay of 15 days.
- Currently, 48 countries provide visa-free entry to Indian citizens. These countries include Malaysia, Indonesia, Thailand, and others.

World Bank Allocates $16 Million for Afghan Women-Led Businesses

- The World Bank allocates USD 16 million to support small businesses in Afghanistan, particularly those owned and operated by women.
- The funding will be managed by the Aga Khan Foundation in the United States and channeled through the Afghanistan Reconstruction Trust Fund (ARTF).
- The project aims to strengthen Afghanistan's small financial sector, enabling small business owners and women-led enterprises to access credit, rebuild their businesses.

UK Passes Rwanda Asylum Law

- The UK parliament has passed Rwanda asylum law that will allow the government to send asylum seekers to Rwanda for their claims to be considered by the East African nation.
- The then British Prime Minister Rishi Sunak promised to start sending asylum seekers to Rwanda within 10 to 12 weeks as the upper house of the parliament finally passed the required legislation.
- The government had booked commercial charter planes and trained staff to take migrants to Rwanda.

King Charles III Receives New Banknotes

- Britain's King Charles III was presented with the first set of banknotes bearing his portrait by Bank of England representatives at Buckingham Palace in London.
- It is the first time the Bank of England has changed the image of the British monarch on a banknote, as King Charles' late mother, Queen Elizabeth II, was the first monarch to appear on a Bank of England note in 1960.

UK and Ukraine Sign Security Agreement

- A security agreement has been signed between Ukraine and the United Kingdom.
- The UK promised to provide £2.5 billion for Ukraine's defense in 2024.
- The agreement is valid for ten years and will expire if Ukraine becomes a NATO member.

Iran Launches Airstrikes on Israel

- On April 13, 2024, Iran launched airstrikes on Israel using 200-300 drones and ballistic missiles in response to an Israeli airstrike on an Iranian consulate in Syria.
- The Iranian Revolutionary Guard Corps (IRGC) conducted these attacks, calling the operation "Operation True Promise," in retaliation for Israel's actions.

India Votes for Palestine's Full UN Membership

- India voted in favor of a draft UN General Assembly resolution supporting Palestine's bid for full membership in the United Nations.
- The resolution, presented by the United Arab Emirates as Chair of the Arab Group, garnered 143 votes in favor, 9 against, and 25 abstentions.
- This vote underscores India's continued commitment to Palestine's full membership in the UN and its longstanding support for Palestinian self-determination.

Frederik X Becomes King of Denmark

- Frederik X became the new king of Denmark after his mother, Queen Margrethe II, abdicated.
- This marks the first voluntary relinquishment of the Danish throne in nearly 900 years.
- Margrethe signed her abdication at Christiansborg Palace in Copenhagen.

President Murmu Visits Mauritius for National Day

- President Droupadi Murmu visited Mauritius as the Chief Guest for their National Day celebrations.
- The visit aimed to strengthen the close historical, cultural, and economic ties between India and Mauritius, particularly in maritime security and capacity building.

S. Jaishankar's official visit to Philippines

- Indian External Affairs Minister (EAM) S. Jaishankar had an official visit to the Philippines amid rising tensions between the Philippines and Chinese naval forces over the Second Thomas Shoal.
- Mr. Jaishankar reaffirmed India's support for Philippine sovereignty in its dispute with China.
- He also stressed the need to follow international maritime law, including the 1982 UNCLOS.

Sweden Joined NATO

- Sweden officially became the 32nd member of NATO after completing its accession process in Washington.
- Sweden's strategic location enhances NATO's control over the Baltic Sea and reinforces NATO's northern flank alongside Norway and Finland.
- NATO operates on the principle of collective defense, where an attack on one member is considered an attack on all, as per Article 5 of the Washington Treaty.

Slovenia and Sweden Sign Artemis Accords

- Slovenia signed the Artemis Accords on April 19, 2024, during a U.S.-Slovenia Strategic Dialogue in Ljubljana, while Sweden signed on April 16, 2024, in Stockholm.
- Both countries have committed to best practices for space exploration, aligning with the principles of the 1967 Outer Space Treaty.
- With Slovenia becoming the 39th and Sweden the 38th signatories, the Artemis Accords continue to expand, promoting international collaboration in space.

Yaoundé Declaration to End Malaria Deaths Signed by 11 African Countries

- The declaration was signed by the health ministers of 11 African countries with the highest burden of malaria, committing to accelerated action to end malaria deaths.
- It was signed at the Yaoundé conference, co-hosted by the World Health Organization and the Government of Cameroon.
- The signatories include Burkina Faso, Cameroon, the Democratic Republic of the Congo, Ghana, Mali, Mozambique, Niger, Nigeria, Sudan, Uganda, and Tanzania.

37th African Union Summit in Addis Ababa

- The 37th African Union Summit was held in Addis Ababa, focusing on education, development, and priorities for 2024 and beyond.
- During the summit, the Africa Club was launched.
- The Africa Club aims to strengthen Africa's role in the global financial system by aligning its efforts with the Sustainable Development Goals (SDGs) and the African Union's Agenda 2063.
- The African Union has recently joined the G-20 group, marking a significant step in enhancing its global influence and integration.

Algeria Inaugurates Africa's Largest Mosque

- Algeria inaugurated Africa's biggest mosque" and the third-biggest mosque in the world, following over a decade of construction and preparation marred by controversy.

- The Great Mosque of Algiers is situated in the capital, with a minaret towering 265 meters (869 feet) high and a large prayer room.

Greece Legalizes Same-Sex Marriage

- Greece has become the world's first Christian Orthodox nation to legalise same-sex marriage after the Athens parliament passed the landmark reform.
- The decision, supported by 176 out of 300 lawmakers in parliament and with 76 against, follows months of polarized political and public discourse, and has been welcomed as a long-awaited vindication by the country's LGBTQ+ couples.

UNDP and EU Fund PNG Climate Initiatives

- The United Nations Development Programme (UNDP) and the European Union (EU) have allocated grants totaling over US$420,000 (approximately 1.6 million PGK) to support initiatives aimed at combating deforestation, improving food and nutrition security, and adapting to the impacts of climate change.
- These grants are set to benefit communities across in Enga Province, Papua New Guinea.

Saudi Arabia Unveils 3D Printed Mosque

- The Kingdom of Saudi Arabia is now home to the world's first 3D-printed mosque, spanning an area of 5,600 sqm.
- Located within the Al-Jawhara suburb of Jeddah, the mosque stands as a tribute to the late equestrian Abdulaziz Abdullah Sharbatly.
- The project by Forsan Real Estate utilizes cutting-edge 3D printing technology from Guanli.

Mexico Overtakes China as Top US Import Source

- Mexico surpassed China as the leading source of goods imported to the United States for the first time in over two decades.
- U.S. Commerce Department figures show a nearly 5% increase in the value of goods imported from Mexico to over $475 billion in 2023.
- In contrast, the value of Chinese imports fell by 20% to $427 billion during the same period.

Qatar Releases Eight Indian Navy Veterans

- Eight Indian nationals working for Dahra Global detained in Qatar were released, with seven returning to India.
- The Ministry of External Affairs thanked Qatar's Amir for facilitating their release.
- Additionally, eight Indian Navy veterans, initially sentenced to death in Qatar for alleged espionage while overseeing submarine induction, had their punishment commuted to extended prison terms after diplomatic efforts by India.

PM Modi Meets Emir of Qatar

- Prime Minister Narendra Modi and the Emir of Qatar, Sheikh Tamim bin Hamad al-Thani, held a bilateral meeting in Doha.
- They discussed various avenues to boost both economies and strengthen India-Qatar ties.
- Talks covered economic cooperation, investments, energy, space collaboration, infrastructure, cultural bonds, and regional issues.

Junta-led Burkina Faso, Mali, Niger Exit ECOWAS

- The junta-led governments of Burkina Faso, Mali, and Niger have declared their immediate withdrawal from the Economic Community of West African States (ECOWAS).
- These countries accused ECOWAS of deviating from its founding principles and Pan-African ideals, claiming it is influenced by foreign powers.
- All three nations are facing escalating jihadist insurgencies and widespread poverty.

North Korea Demolishes Reunification Monument

- North Korea has demolished a major monument known informally as the Arch of Reunification, in its capital that symbolized the goal of reconciliation with South Korea on the orders of the leader Kim Jong Un.
- The arch, formally known as the Monument to the Three Charters for National Reunification, stood 30 meters tall and was symbolic of the three charters.

Egypt Inaugurates Solar Stations At Heritage Sites

- Solar power stations have been set up at five world heritage sites and museums in Egypt.
- The solar power stations were inaugurated at the Giza Plateau's Visitor Centre, Manial Palace in Cairo, Sharm El Sheikh Museum, and two museums in Alexandria (The National and the Royal Jewelry Museums).
- Collectively, they have a total capacity of 325kW of solar PV systems generating 520MWh/year. This is estimated to reduce approximately 295 tons/year of carbon dioxide equivalent.

India And Dominican Republic To Establish JETCO

- The Union Cabinet has approved the protocol for establishing a Joint Economic and Trade Committee (JETCO) between India and the Dominican Republic.
- JETCO is a bilateral mechanism designed to promote economic cooperation and commercial relations.
- The committee aims to expand commerce and industry, address challenges in the export and import of goods and services, and provide a gateway to Latin American and Caribbean markets.
- India has similar JETCO agreements with the UK, Singapore, Thailand, Indonesia, Malaysia, Vietnam, South Korea, Canada, Mauritius, and Oman.

Singapore Joined Vibrant Gujarat Summit

- Singapore will participate as a partner country at the Vibrant Gujarat Global Summit (VGGS).
- It announced an investment worth over ₹2,300 crore.
- This was through expanded investments in Gujarat's green economy and sustainability sector.
- Vibrant Gujarat Global Summit was organized in Gandhi Nagar.

IPEF To Host Clean Economy Investor Forum in Singapore

- The Indo-Pacific Economic Framework for Prosperity (IPEF) held its first Clean Economy Investor Forum in Singapore on June 5-6, 2024.
- The forum aimed to attract investments for sustainable infrastructure, climate technology, and renewable energy projects.
- Partner Countries: The IPEF includes 14 partner countries, such as Australia, India, Japan, and the United States.
- Focus Areas: The IPEF's cooperation focuses on four main areas: Trade, Supply Chain, Clean Economy, and Fair Economy.

Argentina Withdraw From BRICS

- The newly elected President of Argentina, Javier Milei, had decided to pull out of plans to join the BRICS bloc. Argentina had been set to join on January 1, 2024.
- The four new candidates formally became members on January 1, 2024.
- New Members. Egypt, Ethiopia, Iran, and the United Arab Emirates.
- BRICS Summit 2024: Scheduled to be held in Russia in October 2024.

Australia Pledges $3bn for AUKUS Submarines

- Australia has announced a contribution of $3 billion for the construction of nuclear-powered submarines under the AUKUS partnership.
- AUKUS It aims to bolster defense capabilities and counter China's assertiveness in the Indo-Pacific region.
- The program involves building nuclear reactors for the submarines in Derby, UK, and constructing the submarines in Adelaide, Australia, with BAE Systems.

NZ Bans Disposable E-Cigarettes

- New Zealand banned disposable e-cigarettes, or vapes, and raised financial penalties for those who sell such products to minors.
- Recently, the government repealed a unique law enacted by the previous left-leaning government to phase out tobacco smoking by imposing a lifetime ban on young people buying cigarettes.
- Under the new laws, retailers that sell vapes to children under 18 years of age will face fines of up to 100,000 New Zealand dollars ($60,000), while individuals will be fined 1,000 New Zealand dollars ($600).

FILL IN THE BLANKS

1. The Rome Declaration on Water Scarcity in Agriculture was adopted by ________ and WASAG.
2. Nepal's electricity will be transmitted to Bangladesh through the ________ transmission line.
3. The first Goan to receive Indian citizenship under the Citizenship Amendment Act (CAA) in August 2024 was ________.
4. South Africa launched the ________ to facilitate faster visa processing for Indian and Chinese tourists.

MATCHING GAME

Column A	Column B
1. World's first green energy island	A. Sharjah
2. Study In India Campaign launched in	B. Brisbane
3. India-Singapore Link Real Time Retail Payment Systems	C. UPI-Pay Now
4. India's new consulate	D. Manila
5. Headquarters of Asian Development Bank	E. Princess Elisabeth Energy Island

SCAN TO GET MULTIPLE CHOICE QUESTIONS

Scan Me

Answer Key (Fill In The Blanks):

1. FAO 2. 400 KV Dhalkebar-Muzaffarpur 3. Joseph Francis Pereira 4. Trusted Tour Operator Scheme (TTOS)

Answer Key (Matching Game):

1→E 2→A 3→C 4→B 5→D

UNION BUDGET 2024-25

- The Union Budget was presented by Finance Minister Nirmala Sitharaman on 23 July 2024. As per the budget, the fiscal Deficit Target has been reduced to 4.9% for FY25.
- The focus of the budget is on Employment, Skilling, MSMEs, and the Middle Class.

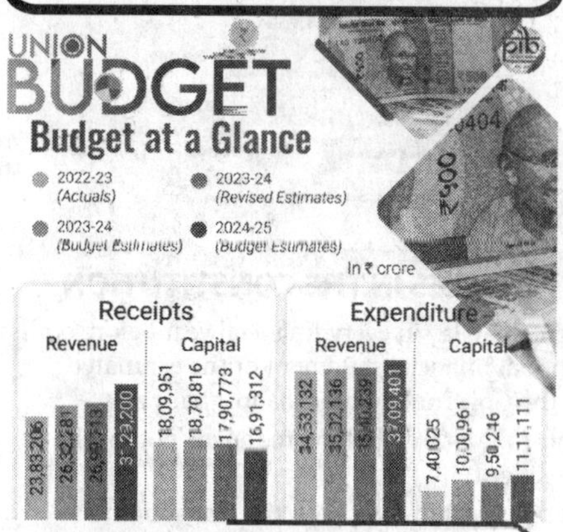

BUDGET ESTIMATES 2024-25

- **Total receipts other than borrowings:** ₹32.07 lakh crore.
- **Total expenditure:** ₹48.21 lakh crore.
- **Net tax receipt:** ₹25.83 lakh crore.
- **Fiscal deficit:** 4.9 per cent of GDP.

AGRICULTURE & RESILIENCE

- Allocation of ₹1.52 lakh crore for agriculture and allied sectors.
- Introduction of 109 high-yielding and climate-resilient crop varieties.
- Natural farming initiatives for 1 crore farmers.

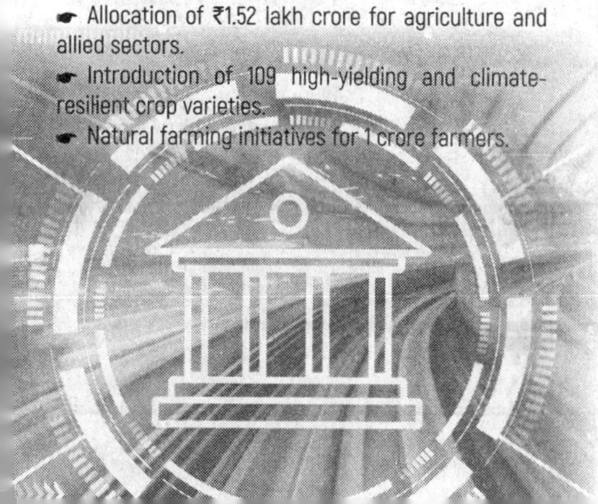

NINE BUDGET PRIORITIES IN PURSUIT OF 'VIKSIT BHARAT'

- Productivity and resilience in Agriculture
- Employment & Skilling
- Inclusive Human Resource Development and Social Justice
- Manufacturing & Services
- Urban Development
- Energy Security
- Infrastructure
- Innovation, Research & Development
- Next Generation Reforms

UNION BUDGET

Key Numbers

In ₹ crore

	2022-23 (Actuals)	2023-24 (Budget Estimates)	2023-24 (Revised Estimates)	2024-25 (Budget Estimates)
Revenue Receipts	23,83,206	26,32,281	26,99,713	31,29,200
Capital Receipts	18,09,951	18,70,816	17,90,773	16,91,312
Total Receipts	41,93,157	45,03,097	44,90,486	48,20,512
Total Expenditure	41,93,157	45,03,097	44,90,486	48,20,512
Effective Capital Expenditure	10,46,289	13,70,949	12,71,436	15,01,889
Revenue Deficit	10,69,926	8,69,855	8,40,527	5,80,201
Effective Revenue Deficit	7,63,662	4,99,867	5,19,337	1,89,423
Fiscal Deficit	17,37,755	17,86,816	17,34,773	16,13,312
Primary Deficit	8,09,238	7,06,845	6,79,346	4,50,372

EMPLOYMENT SKILLING INITIATIVES

- The Union Govt.'s Package of 5 schemes to provide jobs, skill development, and opportunities for 4.1 crore youth over the next 5 years.
- New centrally sponsored scheme for skilling 20 lakh youth over 5 years.
- Upgrading 1,000 Industrial Training Institutes for skill development.
- Three New Schemes:
  - **Scheme A:** Direct benefit transfer of 1-month salary in 3 installments up to ₹15,000 for first-time employees registered in EPFO.
  - **Scheme B:** Incentives for job creation in manufacturing, directly benefiting both employee and employer.
  - **Scheme C:** Reimbursement to employers up to ₹3,000 per month for 2 years for each additional employee.

REVENUE GENERATION

- **Securities Transaction Tax:** Increased on F&O transactions.
- **Customs Duty Changes:** Aimed to enhance domestic value addition in precious metals.
- **Income Tax Act Review:** Comprehensive review to simplify and reduce litigation.

MSMEs

- Support Mechanisms: To facilitate credit continuation for stressed MSMEs.
- Mudra Loan Limit: Increased to ₹20 lakh from ₹10 lakh.
- Credit Guarantee Scheme: For MSMEs in manufacturing with a guarantee cover of up to ₹100 crore.

Infrastructure and Housing

- Urban Housing: ₹10 lakh crore for 1 crore urban poor and middle-class families.
- Pradhan Mantri Gram Sadak Yojana: Fourth phase to connect 25,000 rural habitations with all-weather roads.
- Investment in Infrastructure: Promoted through viability gap funding and enabling policies.
- Capital expenditure of ₹11.11 lakh crore.
- ₹1.5 lakh crore for long-term interest-free loans to state governments for infrastructure investment.

INCOME TAX AND CAPITAL GAINS

Category	Details
Standard Deduction	Increased from ₹50,000 to ₹75,000
Family Pension Deduction	Raised from ₹15,000 to ₹25,000
Tax Slabs	₹0-3 lakh: NIL
	₹3-7 lakh: 5%
	₹7-10 lakh: 10%
	₹10-12 lakh: 15%
	₹12-15 lakh: 20%
	Above ₹15 lakh: 30%
Capital Gains Tax	STCG: Increased to 20% on certain assets
	LTCG: Raised to 12.5% (With an exemption of ₹ 1.25 lakh per financial year)
Angel Tax	Abolished
Foreign Companies Tax Rate	Reduced from 40% to 35%

ADDITIONAL HIGHLIGHTS

- GIS mapping and IT-based system for urban property records management.
- Govt. aimed to reach a deficit below 4.5 percent by FY 2025-26.
- Chief Economic Advisor projects growth at 6.5-7% for FY25.
- ₹11.5k crore for flood control in Bihar, Assam, Himachal Pradesh, Uttarakhand, and Sikkim.
- Government to incentivize 30 lakh youth entering the job market by providing one month PF contribution.
- Over ₹3 lakh crore allocated for schemes benefiting women and girls.

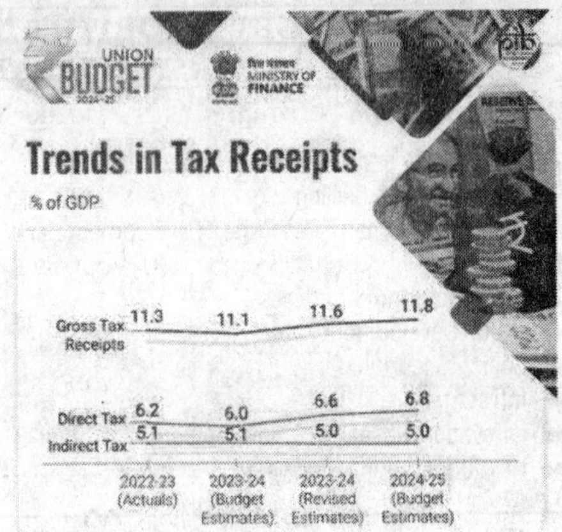

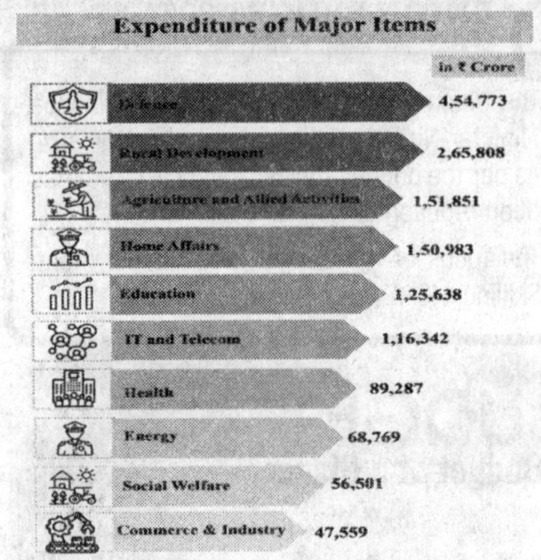

WHAT IS BUDGET

- According to Article 112 of the Indian Constitution, the Union Budget for a year is called the Annual Financial Statement (AFS).
- It is a statement of the estimated receipts and expenditure of the government in a financial year (which begins on 1st April of the current year and ends on 31 March of the following year).
- The term 'Budget' is not mentioned in the Constitution of India.
- The Department of Economic Affairs (DEA) in the Ministry of Finance is responsible for preparing the Union Budget.
- Interim Budget is a short term financial plan that covers government expenses until the elections.

SOME IMPORTANT ARTICLES IN THE CONSTITUTION

- **Article 112:** The President shall lay in every financial year before both Houses of Parliament the annual financial statement of the estimated receipts and expenditure of the Government of India for that year.
- **Article 113:** No demand for a grant shall be made except on the recommendation of the President.
- **Article 114:** No sum can be withdrawn from the Consolidated Fund of India (CFI) without the permission of Parliament.
- **Article 266:** All revenues received by the Government shall be credited to the "Consolidated Fund of India". All other public moneys, such as provident funds, postal insurance, etc., shall be credited to the Public Account of India.
- **Article 267:** Parliament may by law establish a Contingency Fund of India to meet unforeseen or unexpected expenditure.

HISTORY OF BUDGET

- India's first budget was presented on April 7, 1860 by the then Finance Minister of British India James Wilson.
- Mr Liaquat Ali Khan, member of the interim Government presented the budget of 1947-48.
- The first Union Budget of Independent India was presented by the first Finance Minister of Independent India, Sir R.K. Shanmukham Chetty, on November 26, 1947.
- John Mathai presented the subsequent Union Budgets of 1949-50 and 1950-51.
- The budget of 1949-50 was the first instance of a budget being prepared for a United India, including all princely states.
- In the year 2017, the Railway Budget was merged with the Union Budget.
- Indira Gandhi was the only woman Finance Minister who was also the Prime Minister while presenting the budget.

Banking

ADB approves $788 million loan for Amaravati in AP

- Asian Development Bank (ADB) approved a results-based loan of 788.8 million dollars (about Rs 6,620 crore) to Andhra Pradesh to develop Amaravati as a green and smart capital city that offers world-class infrastructure.
- The loan will be provided in Japanese yen, amounting to 121.97 billion yen.
- The Amaravati Inclusive and Sustainable Capital City Development Programme is meant to make Amaravati a growth center for the region, increase economic opportunities, create jobs, and improve the residents' lives.

Reserve Bank of India (RBI) gets its New Governor, as Shaktikanta Das Quits

- 26th Governor of Reserve Bank of India
- Tenure- three-year
- **Assumed office:** 11 December 2024
- **Prior to this post:** Worked as Revenue Secretary of India
- **Salary:** ₹250,000
- **Deputy Governors:** 4 (M. Rajeshwar Rao, Swaminathan J, T. Rabi Sankar, Dr. M.D. Patra)

Previous RBI Governor:
Shaktikanta Das
1st RBI Governor:
Sir Osborne Smith
1st Indian RBI Governor:
C. D. Deshmukh

SBI named as the Best Bank in India for 2024

- On 27th October 2024, the State Bank of India (SBI) was named as the Best Bank in India for 2024 by **Global Finance Magazine.**
- The award was presented at the 31st Annual Best Bank Awards held in Washington, DC, during the IMF and World Bank Annual Meetings.

SBI raises ₹50,000 crore via bonds in FY25

- As per data released in November 2024, State Bank of India (SBI), the country's largest lender, has raised ₹50,000 crore through domestic bonds in the financial year 2025.
- This amount includes ₹30,000 crore in long-term bonds, ₹15,000 crore in Tier 2 bonds, and ₹5,000 crore in AT1 bonds.
- These bonds are of 15-year tenor except for the AT1 Bonds which are perpetual.
- Earlier in November, SBI also raised ₹10,000 crore through its seventh infrastructure bond issuance.

SBI Empowers Rural Youth Entrepreneurs Through Jagriti Yatra 2024 to Boost 'Viksit Bharat'

- State Bank of India (SBI) has partnered with Jagriti Yatra 2024, a transformative 8,000-km, 15-day entrepreneurial journey across India's Tier 2 and Tier 3 regions.
- This initiative will help 500 young people explore entrepreneurship, get expert guidance, and gain hands-on learning experience.
- Through this collaboration, SBI aims to nurture future innovators, advancing India's vision of a 'Viksit Bharat' by 2047.

SBI launched 'MSME Sahaj' for Instant Digital Invoice Financing

- In July 2024, the State Bank of India (SBI) launched MSME Sahaj, a digital platform to speed up invoice financing for MSMEs.
- It enables loans of up to ₹1 lakh against GST-registered invoices to be approved within 15 minutes through a fully digital process.

SBI and APIX team launches SBI Innovation Hub for Fintechs

- In November 2024, the State Bank of India (SBI) has launched the 'SBI Innovation Hub' in partnership with APIX, a global innovation platform for financial institutions and FinTechs.
- The hub offers a space for startups and innovators to create advanced financial solutions for SBI's digital customers.
- It provides participants with access to over 250 financial service APIs from SBI.

IDFC FIRST Bank launches real-time tracking for international money

- IDFC FIRST Bank has become the first Indian bank to offer real-time tracking for money sent abroad.
- This service, developed in partnership with SWIFT (Society for Worldwide Interbank Financial Telecommunication), is accessible through the bank's mobile app and internet banking platforms.
- The SWIFT GPI tracking plugin provides real-time updates on fund status, showing if the money is in transit or credited to the recipient's account.

EIB funds ₹2,800 Cr for Bengaluru Suburban Railway

- On 25th October 2024, the European Investment Bank (EIB) Global announced a ₹300 million (approximately ₹2,800 crore) loan to develop a new suburban railway network in Bengaluru.
- This project aims to enhance urban mobility by constructing four dedicated rail corridors, covering a total length of 149 km with 58 stations.

EUROPEAN INVESTMENT BANK

- Founded - 1958
- Location - Kirchberg, Luxembourg
- President - Nadia Calviño
- Vice President - Ambroise Fayolle
- Member state - 27

PNB becomes a PCAF signatory, strengthening its commitment to climate responsibility

- Punjab National Bank (PNB), India's second-largest public sector bank, has joined the global Partnership for Carbon Accounting Financials (PCAF).
- This aligns with the Reserve Bank of India's (RBI) draft framework on climate-related financial risk disclosures.
- Starting 2025-26, banks must report on governance, strategy, and risk management for climate risks.
- From 2027-28, they will also report on metrics and targets for these risks and opportunities.

BoB introduces special 'bob Utsav Deposit Scheme' for the Festive Season

- On 14th October 2024, the Bank of Baroda (BoB) introduced the BOB Utsav Deposit Scheme for the festive season.
- This special scheme offers a 400-day term deposit with an interest rate of 7.30% for general citizens, 7.80% for senior citizens (60-80 years), and 7.90% for super senior citizens (80+ years).

YES BANK and Paisabazaar launched the PaisaSave Cashback Credit Card

- In September 2024, YES BANK and Paisabazaar launched the PaisaSave Cashback Credit Card.
- This co-branded card offers 3% cashback on online purchases from popular platforms like Amazon and Flipkart, and 1.5% cashback on offline transactions. It also includes a 1% fuel surcharge waiver.

Banks and Fis to Invest Rs 32.5 Trillion in Renewable Energy by 2030

- On 16th September 2024, banks and financial institutions pledged ₹32.5 trillion ($386 billion) for renewable energy projects by 2030 at the 4th RE-Invest Summit, organized by the Ministry of New and Renewable Energy (MNRE).
- The investment aims to add 570 GW of renewable energy capacity, supporting India's goal of 500 GW by 2030.

PNB launches 'Safety Ring' to enhance internet and Mobile Banking Security

- On 9th July 2024, Punjab National Bank (PNB) introduced the 'Safety Ring' within its internet and mobile banking systems.
- This optional security feature empowers customers to set daily transaction limits for term deposits (TDs).
- By doing so, it prevents unauthorized closure, withdrawal, or overdraft beyond the defined limit, bolstering security against cyber frauds.

Union Bank of India becomes 1st Major Indian Bank to join PCAF

- On 9th September 2024, Union Bank of India became the first major Indian bank to join the Partnership for Carbon Accounting Financials (PCAF).
- This step aligns with global focus on climate risk management and the RBI's recent draft guidelines on climate risk disclosures.

Piramal Finance and Central Bank of India Partner to Reach Underserved Markets

- On 23rd August 2024, Piramal Capital and Housing Finance Limited (Piramal Finance), a wholly owned subsidiary of Piramal Enterprises Limited (PEL), announced a strategic co-lending partnership with the Central Bank of India.
- Leveraging Central Bank of India's extensive branch network and Piramal Finance's "High Tech + High Touch" strategy, the partnership will offer competitive interest rates and customized credit solutions.

Bandhan Bank Launched 'Avni' Savings Account for Women

- On 26th August 2024, Bandhan Bank has launched the 'Avni' savings account, tailored specifically for women.
- This account offers a range of benefits, including free airport lounge access, personal accident insurance of ₹10 lakh, and lost card liability of ₹3.5 lakh.
- It provides flexibility in maintaining a monthly average balance and includes a free cash deposit limit of ₹5,00,000 per month.

FM unveils specially minted ₹100 commemorative coin to mark centenary of SBI's Horniman Circle Branch

- In November 2024, Finance Minister Nirmala Sitharaman unveiled a specially minted ₹100 commemorative coin to mark the centenary of SBI's iconic Horniman Circle Branch.
- Alongside the coin launch, she also unveiled the 5th edition of **The Evolution of the State Bank of India,** chronicling a transformative era in the bank's journey between 1981 and 1996.

Paytm receives NPCI Nod to onboard new UPI users

- On 22nd October 2024, Paytm received approval from the National Payments Corporation of India (NPCI) to onboard new Unified Payments Interface (UPI) users, following a nine-month ban imposed by the Reserve Bank of India (RBI).
- This decision allows Paytm to resume adding new users under NPCI's guidelines, aiming to increase its UPI transaction volumes and improve its market position.

ABOUT PAYTM

- **Founded:** August 2010
- **Founder:** Vijay Shekhar Sharma
- **Headquarters:** Noida, Uttar Pradesh
- **Parent company:** One 97 Communications

UPI rule changes: UPI Lite transaction, wallet limit hiked

- The Reserve Bank of India (RBI) has hiked the per-transaction limits on UPI Lite from Rs 500 to Rs 1,000. The overall wallet limit of UPI Lite has also been raised from Rs 2,000 to Rs 5,000 in December 2024.
- The framework, introduced in January 2022 and updated in August 2023, aims to simplify small-value offline digital payments.

UPI transaction value crosses Rs 20 lakh crore mark for third month in a row

- On 1st August 2024, the National Payments Corporation of India (NPCI) reported that UPI transaction values exceeded ₹20 lakh crore for the third consecutive month in July.
- November 2024 witnessed a remarkable surge in UPI transactions in India, reaching 15.48 billion, a 38% year-on-year increase.
- The total transaction value via UPI stood at Rs 21.55 lakh crore, a 24 per cent surge as compared to November 2023.

Razorpay Partners with MHA to Fortify India's Digital Payments Ecosystem

- Razorpay, India's top omnichannel payments and banking platform, has partnered with the Ministry of Home Affairs (MHA) and the Indian Cyber Crime Coordination Centre (I4C).
- The goal of this collaboration is to improve the security of the country's growing digital payments system.
- India contributes 46% of the global digital payment volume.
- This highlights the urgent need for strong cybersecurity measures to protect businesses and consumers.

PhonePe launches 'Credit Line on UPI' for enhanced flexibility

- On 22nd August 2024, PhonePe launched the 'Credit Line on UPI' feature.
- Users can link pre-approved bank credit lines to UPI on the PhonePe app for easy payments to merchants.

Airtel Payments Bank enhances security with AI-Powered Face Match

- On 21st August 2024, Airtel Payments Bank introduced the AI-powered Face Match feature to enhance account security.
- This advanced security measure uses machine learning algorithms to analyze user behavior, transaction patterns, and location data.

NCLT approves Slice and North East Small Finance Bank merger

- On 19th August 2024, the National Company Law Tribunal (NCLT) approved the merger of Bengaluru-based Slice (a consumer payments and lending company) with Guwahati-headquartered North East Small Finance Bank (NESFB).

PNB launches ANTAH DRISHTI Braille Debit Card for visually impaired customers

- On 12th August 2024, Punjab National Bank (PNB) launched the PNB ANTAH DRISHTI Braille Debit Card, designed specifically for visually impaired customers.
- This contactless National Common Mobility Card (NCMC) is available on the RuPay network.
- The card features raised Braille dots, a rounded notch for easy orientation, Glossy Spot UV Lamination and Contrasting Colours.

IndusInd Bank and BFIL partnered with Ministry of Agriculture to Empower Farmer Producer Organizations

- In November 2024, IndusInd Bank Limited (IBL) and its subsidiary Bharat Financial Inclusion Limited (BFIL) signed an MoU with the Ministry of Agriculture and Farmers Welfare to launch the Bharat Sanjeevani Krishi Utthan initiative.
- The initiative supports the government's program to promote 10,000 Farmer Producer Organizations (FPOs).
- It aims to empower FPOs across India with a strong framework.

Pine Labs-owned Setu Launches UPISetu in Partnership with Axis Bank

- Setu, a Pine Labs-owned API infrastructure provider, has launched UPISetu in collaboration with Axis Bank in August 2024.
- UPISetu offers various UPI services including QR code payments, Autopay, EMI options, and Third-Party Validation.

Axis Bank and Visa launch exclusive 'PRIMUS' credit card for India's elite

- On 12th August 2024, Axis Bank, in partnership with Visa, launched the exclusive 'PRIMUS' credit card, tailored for India's ultra-high-net-worth individuals (UHNWIs).
- Offered by invitation only, this ultra-premium card provides bespoke privileges and benefits under the Visa Infinite Privilege offering.

RBL Bank launches RuPay Credit Cards with UPI and NCMC functionalities

- On 1st August 2024, RBL Bank launched new RuPay credit cards integrated with Unified Payments Interface (UPI) and National Common Mobility Card (NCMC) functionalities.
- This innovative offering allows users to perform seamless and secure UPI transactions, while the NCMC feature facilitates hassle-free travel payments on public transport.

Paytm partnered with Axis Bank to offer POS solutions

- On 23rd July 2024, Paytm partnered with Axis Bank to provide point-of-sale (POS) solutions and electronic data capture (EDC) devices to merchants.
- Paytm's EDC devices come with integrated software offering inventory management, invoice generation, promotions, sales tracking, and customer relationship management (CRM).

Punjab & Sind Bank launches e-bank guarantee facility

- In November 2024, Punjab & Sind Bank (PSB), a public sector bank, launched an e-Bank Guarantee (e-BG) facility in partnership with National e-Governance Services Ltd (NeSL).
- This new facility replaces the paper-based BG issuance process with stamping and signatures.
- With the secured transmission and enhanced transparency, beneficiaries will save efforts and time in the verification of physical BGs.

SBI MF becomes first to surpass ₹10 lakh crore AUM, outpacing ICICI and HDFC

- In November 2024, SBI Mutual Fund, the country's largest asset management company (AMC), has achieved a record average asset under management (AAUM) of ₹10.99 lakh crore in the September quarter (Q2 FY25), according to data from the Association of Mutual Funds in India (AMFI).
- The fund house had concluded FY24 with an AAUM of ₹9.14 lakh crore.

Insolvency and Bankruptcy Board of India in association with INSOL India organizes International Conclave 2024

- The Insolvency and Bankruptcy Board of India (IBBI) in association with INSOL India organized an International Conclave focusing on **"Insolvency Resolution: Evolution & Global Perspective"**.

RBI

RBI keeps rates unchanged, cuts CRR by 50 bps to 4% – MPC December 2024 review

- The Reserve Bank of India's (RBI's) six-member monetary policy committee (MPC) has decided to keep the policy repo rate unchanged at 6.5 percent — the status quo for an 11th straight time — maintaining a "neutral" stance.
- Even as it reduced the cash reserve ratio (CRR) by 50 basis points to 4 percent to boost liquidity in the system, it lowered the 2024-25 gross domestic product (GDP) growth projection to 6.6 per cent from 7.2 percent earlier.
- The inflation projection for this financial year, meanwhile, was increased by 30 bps to 4.8 percent.
- Repo rate is the rate at which the RBI lends to commercial banks, while CRR is the proportion of deposits that banks must keep with the central bank. One basis point is the hundredth of a percentage point.

RBI CURRENT POLICY RATE

- **Policy Repo Rate:** 6.50%
- **Standing Deposit Facility (SDF):** 6.25%
- **Marginal Standing Facility (MSF):** 6.75%
- **Bank Rate:** 6.75%
- **Reverse Repo Rate:** 3.35%
- **Cash Reserve Ratio (CRR):** 4.00%
- **Statutory Liquidity Ratio (SLR):** 18%

SWFI's Top 100 Largest Central Bank Rankings by Total Assets 2024: RBI Ranked 12 Globally

- The Reserve Bank of India (RBI) has been ranked 12th globally in the **Sovereign Wealth Fund Institute's** (SWFI) Top 100 Largest Central Bank Rankings by Total Assets for 2024, announced on August 1st, 2024.
- RBI's balance sheet grew by 11.08% to ₹70.47 trillion as of March 31, 2024.
- The U.S. Federal Reserve topped the list with assets exceeding $8 trillion.

RBI Governor Shaktikanta Das Rated 'A+' In Global Finance Central Banker Report 2024

- The then Governor of the Reserve Bank of India (RBI) Shaktikanta Das received an 'A+' rating for the second consecutive year.
- He was ranked among the top three central bankers in the 2024 Global Finance Central Banker Report Card.
- The Central Banker Report, published annually by Global Finance since 1994, assesses central bank governors from 101 countries.
- He was awarded this recognition with Christian Kettel Thomsen (Denmark) and Thomas Jordan (Switzerland).

RBI raises collateral-free agriculture loan limit to Rs 2 lakh per borrower from 1.6 lakh

- The Reserve Bank of India enhanced the collateral-free agriculture loans limit to Rs 2 lakh per borrower from the existing Rs 1.6 lakh.
- This will enhance coverage of small and marginal farmers in the formal credit system.

RBI's High-Level Policy Conference of Central Banks from Global South

- The Reserve Bank of India (RBI) organised a two-day "High-Level Policy Conference of Central Banks from the Global South" in Mumbai, Maharashtra in November 2024.
- This was the third international conference to be organised by the Reserve Bank of India under its RBI@90 celebration.
- The High-Level Policy Conference of Central Banks from the Global South had the theme **"Building Synergies"**.
- RBI's first international conference, on **"Digital Public Infrastructure and Emerging Technologies"**, was held in Bengaluru in August 2024.
- The second conference, themed **"Central Banking at Crossroads"**, took place in New Delhi in October 2024.

RBI allows small finance banks to offer pre-sanctioned credit via UPI

- In December 2024, the Reserve Bank of India (RBI) has decided to permit Small Finance Banks (SFBs) to extend pre-sanctioned credit lines through the UPI.
- The credit line on UPI was first introduced in September 2023 and was made available through Scheduled Commercial Banks (SCBs).
- This move aims to support underserved groups, including small businesses, micro-entrepreneurs, and individuals in rural and semi-urban regions.

RBI revokes authorisation certificate of UAE Exchange Centre

- In October 2024, the Reserve Bank has revoked the certificate of authorisation of UAE Exchange Centre LLC for non-compliance with regulatory requirements.
- Now, it cannot transact the business of cross-border in-bound money transfer.
- UAE Exchange Centre LLC (UAEEC), based in Dubai, received a Certificate of Authorisation (CoA).
- It was authorized as an "Overseas Principal" for cross-border inbound customer-to-customer money transfers.

RBI revises NPA provisioning norms for cooperative banks

- On 2nd August 2024, the Reserve Bank of India (RBI) revised the NPA provisioning norms for cooperative banks to ensure uniformity.
- The new guidelines require Urban, State, and Central Cooperative Banks to recognize provisions for NPAs as an expense in the Profit & Loss account starting FY25.

India's Forex Reserves Surpass $700 Billion Milestone for the First Time

Total Forex Reserves	$704.89 billion, a record increase of $12.58 billion.
Components of Forex Reserves	Foreign Currency Assets (FCAs): $616 billion (up by $10.4 billion) Gold Reserves: $65.7 billion (up by $2 billion) Special Drawing Rights (SDRs): $18.547 billion (up by $8 million) IMF Reserve Position: $4.387 billion (down by $71 million)
Key Global Standing	India joins China, Japan, and Switzerland in having forex reserves surpassing $700 billion.
RBI's Market Interventions	Surge attributed to RBI's dollar purchases and favorable valuation adjustments. Data as of 1st week of November 2024.

RBI, Maldives Monetary Authority sign pact to promote use of local currencies

- In November 2024, the Reserve Bank of India (RBI) and the Maldives Monetary Authority (MMA) signed a Memorandum of Understanding (MoU).
- The MoU aims to create a framework to promote the use of local currencies, the Indian Rupee (INR) and the Maldivian Rufiyaa (MVR), for cross-border transactions.
- Shaktikanta Das, the then Governor of the RBI, and Mr. Ahmed Munawar, the Governor of the MMA, signed the MoU.

Banking Laws Amendment Bill 2024

- The Lok Sabha passed the Banking Laws Amendment Bill, 2024, the first Bill of the Winter Session in December 2024.
- It aims to enhance governance and regulatory oversight in India's banking sector by amending key statutes such as the Reserve Bank of India Act (1934), the Banking Regulation Act (1949), and the State Bank of India Act (1955).
- The Banking Laws Amendment Bill, 2024, passed in Lok Sabha, proposed changes like allowing up to **four nominees for bank accounts** and redefining 'substantial interest' thresholds.

RBI announces launch of Unified Lending Interface (ULI)

- To facilitate the efficient delivery of frictionless credit, the then RBI Governor, Shri Shaktikanta Das, announced the **Unified Lending Interface (ULI) at the RBI@90 Global Conference** on August 26, 2024, in Bengaluru.
- ULI is a technology platform that provides easy access to authenticated data from multiple sources.
- It uses standardized APIs, allowing all lenders to connect seamlessly through a 'plug and play' model.

- The ULI is developed by RBIH and co-conceptualized with the Reserve Bank of India (RBI).

RBI recognized FACE as self-regulatory body for FinTech sector

- On 28th August 2024, the Reserve Bank of India (RBI) recognized the Fintech Association for Consumer Empowerment (FACE) as a Self-Regulatory Organization (SRO) for the FinTech sector.
- This recognition aims to foster a balanced approach between innovation and regulation.

RBI announces continuous clearing of cheques under CTS

- On 8th August 2024, the Reserve Bank of India (RBI) announced the implementation of Continuous Clearing of Cheques under the Cheque Truncation System (CTS).
- This new system will significantly reduce the cheque clearing time from the current two days to just a few hours.
- The initiative focuses on improving customer experience and business efficiency.
- It replaces batch processing with continuous clearing and real-time settlement to reduce risks.

RBI constitutes 10-member expert committee on benchmarking of its data

- On 12th August 2024, the Reserve Bank of India (RBI) established a 10-member Expert Committee on Benchmarking of its Statistics, chaired by Deputy Governor Michael Debabrata Patra.
- A 10-member committee will regularly assess the quality of statistics released by the RBI and offer recommendations for improvements.

Jio Financial Services gained RBI approval for CIC conversion

- On 12th July 2024, the Reserve Bank of India (RBI) granted approval for the conversion of Jio Financial Services from a Non-Banking Financial Company (NBFC) to a Core Investment Company (CIC).
- Jio Financial Services, which emerged from the conglomerate Reliance Industries Ltd (RIL), had applied for this transition as mandated by the RBI.
- As a CIC, Jio Financial Services will focus primarily on investments in and management of its subsidiary companies, enhancing value discovery for investors.
- It has obtained RBI's approval to operate as online payment aggregator in October 2024 as well.

RBI eases LRS norms for investment via GIFT IFSC

- On 10th July 2024, the Reserve Bank of India (RBI) expanded and strengthening the to International Financial Services Centres (IFSCs) under the Liberalised Remittance Scheme (LRS).
- This move aligns GIFT IFSC with global financial centers, enhancing investment and strengthening the banking ecosystem. Residents can invest up to $250,000 per year through the FCA account.

RBI sells $406 Million in bonds following Index Inclusion

- In July 2024, the Reserve Bank of India (RBI) sold ₹34 billion ($406 million) worth of bonds in the secondary market.
- This move was aimed at absorbing excess liquidity in the banking system following India's bonds inclusion in JPMorgan Chase & Co.'s emerging market bond index.

RBI introduced the Draft Foreign Exchange Management Regulations, 2024

- The Reserve Bank of India (RBI) introduced the Draft Foreign Exchange Management (Export and Import of Goods and Services) Regulations, 2024, under the Foreign Exchange Management Act (FEMA), 1999.
- These regulations aim to simplify and liberalize foreign exchange transactions, especially for small exporters and importers.
- Key changes include requiring exporters to declare the full export value and repatriate it within nine months. Authorized Dealers can extend this period for valid reasons.

RBI slaps ₹1.32 Crore Monetary Penalty on PNB

- The Reserve Bank of India (RBI) fined Punjab National Bank ₹131.80 lakh for non-compliance with rules on **'Loans and Advances'** and **'Know Your Customer (KYC)'.**
- The penalty was imposed after supervisory findings revealed the bank sanctioned loans to state government-owned corporations against receivables from the government.

NHB raises Rs 3,830 cr through 10-yr bonds at 7.14%; gets 'AAA' rating

- State-owned National Housing Bank (NHB) has raised Rs 3,830 crore through 10-year bonds in the domestic debt capital markets at a coupon rate of 7.14 percent.
- NHB, a development financial institution, was looking to raise Rs 5,000 crore, with a base issue size of Rs 2,000 crore and a green shoe option of Rs 3,000 crore. But it could not raise the full amount.
- The bonds have been rated 'AAA' by domestic credit agency CRISIL, ICRA, and CARE.

ABOUT NATIONAL HOUSING BANK (NHB)

- **Founded:** 9 July 1988
- **Headquarters:** New Delhi
- **Jurisdiction:** Ministry of Finance
- **MD:** Sanjay Shukla

Economy

Indian Economy to Grow 6.6% in FY26: Ind-Ra

- India Ratings and Research (Ind-Ra) has projected the Indian economy to grow at 6.6% in 2025-26, up from 6.4% in the current fiscal year.
- The rating agency has also forecast a 6.4% gross domestic product (GDP) growth for FY25, 20 basis points lower than the RBI's 6.6% estimates.
- Ind-Ra expects retail inflation in FY26 to average 4.4 percent, lower than the FY25 forecast of 4.9 percent.

Economic Survey of India 2023-24

Union Finance Minister Nirmala Sitharaman tabled the Economic Survey of India 2023-24 along with Statistical Appendix in both the Houses of Parliament on 22nd July 2024.

The Economic Survey 2023-24 projected the FY25 real GDP growth at 6.5-7%, lower than the India's real GDP of 8.2% in FY24

Here are some key highlights:

- **State of the Economy:** The survey indicates that India is on a "strong wicket and stable footing."
- **Monetary Management and Financial Intermediation:** Stability remains a priority.
- **Prices and Inflation:** Inflation is under control.
- **External Sector:** Despite challenges, stability prevails.
- **Medium-Term Outlook:** A growth strategy for "New India."
- **Climate Change and Energy Transition:** Balancing trade-offs.

- **Social Sector:** Emphasizes benefits that empower citizens.
- **Employment and Skill Development**: Focusing on quality.
- **Agriculture and Food Management:** Opportunities for improvement.
- **Industry and Services:** Addressing small and medium matters.
- **Infrastructure:** Unlocking potential growth.
- **Climate Change and India:** A lens on environmental challenges.

Economy growth rate dips to 5.4% during July-September Quarter 2024

- India's real GDP growth rate fell to 5.4% in the July-September 2024 quarter, compared to 8.1% in the same period in 2023, according to National Statistics Office (NSO).
- The manufacturing sector grew modestly by 2.2%, while the mining and quarrying sector declined slightly by 0.1%.
- Despite this, the real GVA showed positive growth of 6.2% in the first half (April-September) of FY 2024-25.

Retail inflation at a 14-month high, rises to 6.21% in October 2024

- India's retail inflation, based on the Consumer Price Index (CPI), surged to a 14-month high of 6.21% in October 2024 due to rising food prices, data released by the Ministry of Statistics & Programme Implementation (MoSPI).
- The data shows higher inflation in rural areas at 6.68% compared to 5.62% in urban regions.
- The Reserve Bank of India (RBI) aims to keep inflation within a range of 2-6 %, with a medium-term target of 4%.

WPI Inflation Eases in November 2024, After Hitting a 4-Month High in October

- According to latest govt. data, Wholesale Price Inflation (WPI) eased to 1.89% in November 2024 due to cheaper food prices, especially vegetables.
- In October 2024, WPI had risen to a 4-month high of 2.36%.
- In November 2023, WPI was much lower at 0.39%.
- The fuel and power category saw a deflation of 5.83% in November, slightly higher than 5.79% in October.

NHPC, SECI, Railtel, and SJVN Gain Navratna Status

- Finance Minister Nirmala Sitharaman granted **'Navratna'** status to four Central Public Sector Enterprises (CPSEs): NHPC, Solar Energy Corporation of India (SECI), Railtel Corporation of India (RCIL), and Satluj Jal Vidyut Nigam (SJVN). This brings the total number of Navratna CPSEs in India to **25**.
- The Navratna status is awarded based on criteria including excellent performance ratings, a composite score of 60 or above in selected performance indicators, and the CPSEs' status as Miniratna I and Schedule 'A'.

ABOUT HINDUSTAN AERONAUTICS LIMITED (HAL)

- HAL was founded in 1940 in Bangalore as Hindustan Aircraft Limited, which was merged with Aeronautics India Limited in 1964 to form HAL.
- It is a government-owned company under the Ministry of Defence.
- It is headquartered in Bengaluru, Karnataka.
- It operates 20 production and R&D centres across India.
- It manufactures fighter aircraft such as Tejas LCA, Sukhoi Su-30MKI, Jaguar and Hawk. It manufactures helicopters including Dhruv ALH, Rudra, Cheetah, Chetak and LCH.

Hindustan Aeronautics becomes 14th Maharatna CPSE

- On 12th October 2024, Hindustan Aeronautics Limited (HAL) was elevated to Maharatna CPSE status, becoming the 14th such enterprise in India.

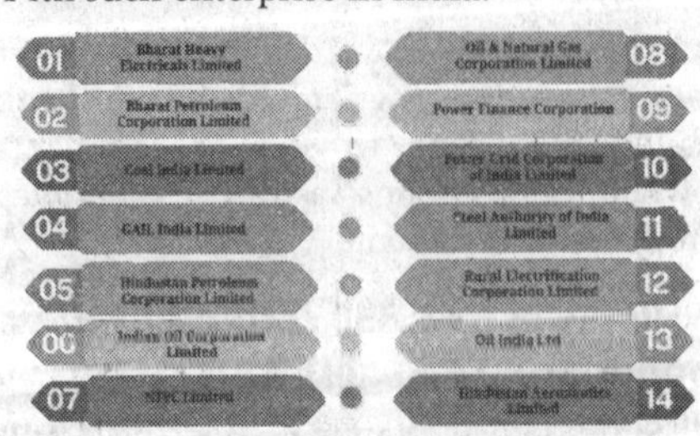

- It is a key player in India's defense sector, manufacturing aircraft, helicopters, and aerospace components.

Union Government Releases XV Finance Commission Grants for Rural Local Bodies

- On 12th October 2024, the Centre released the first installment of the Fifteenth Finance Commission grants for 2024-25 to Rural Local Bodies (RLBs) in Andhra Pradesh and Rajasthan.
- Andhra Pradesh received ₹395.50 crore in untied grants and ₹593.26 crore in tied grants. Rajasthan received ₹507.11 crore in untied grants and ₹760.67 crore in tied grants.

FCI launched ANNA DARPAN to revolutionize supply chain

- On 3rd October 2024, the Food Corporation of India (FCI) launched ANNA DARPAN, a digital transformation initiative aimed at revolutionizing its supply chain management system.
- This new micro services-based integrated system is designed to enhance operational efficiency, improve user experience, and facilitate data-driven decision-making across various levels, including Mandis, Mills, and Depots.

Commercial Cultivation of HT Basmati Rice

- In July 2024, the Indian government for the first time allowed the commercial cultivation of two non-transgenic varieties of herbicide-tolerant (HT) basmati rice: Pusa Basmati 1979 and Pusa Basmati 1985.
- It has been developed by the Indian Council of Agricultural Research (ICAR) to promote sustainable paddy cultivation practices that conserve water and reduce carbon emissions.
- India is the second-largest producer of rice after China.

Government removes Floor Price on Basmati Rice

- On 13th September 2024, the Indian government removed the $950 per tonne minimum export price (MEP) on basmati rice.
- The Agricultural and Processed Food Products Export Development Authority (APEDA) monitors export contracts to prevent unrealistic pricing.
- The MEP was initially set at $1,200 per tonne in August 2023 to curb misclassification of non-basmati rice.

GST collection rises 8.5% to Rs 1.82 lakh cr in November 2024

- The total gross Goods and Services Tax (GST) revenue grew 8.5 per cent to over

Rs 1.82 lakh crore in November 2024 as compared to Rs 1.68 lakh crore in November 2023.

- The Central GST collection stood at Rs 34,141 crore, State GST at Rs 43,047 crore, Integrated IGST at Rs 91,828 crore and cess at Rs 13,253 crore.

GST Collection of Previous Months

July 2024 – 1.82 lakh crore
August 2024 – 1.75 lakh crore
September 2024 – 1.73 lakh crore
October 2024 – 1.87 lakh crore

CBDT launches campaign to inform taxpayers on undeclared foreign assets

- In November 2024, the Central Board of Direct Taxes (CBDT) has launched a Compliance-Cum-Awareness Campaign for Assessment Year 2024-25 to assist taxpayers in accurately completing Schedule Foreign Assets (Schedule FA) and reporting income from foreign sources (Schedule FSI) in their income tax returns (ITR).
- Informational messages will be sent via SMS and email to resident taxpayers who have already submitted their ITRs for Assessment Year 2024-25.
- These messages are intended for individuals who may have foreign accounts or assets or received income from foreign jurisdictions.

CBDT formed an internal committee to comprehensively review

- On 7th October 2024, the Central Board of Direct Taxes (CBDT) formed an internal committee to comprehensively review the Income-tax Act, 1961.
- This initiative, announced in the Union Budget 2024-25 by Finance Minister Nirmala Sitharaman, aims to simplify the Act, reduce litigation, and improve taxpayer experience.

Corporate Social Responsibility (CSR) Expenditure 2023

- In August 2024, government data revealed that education received the highest share of corporate social responsibility (CSR) expenditure in FY23, with Rs 10,085 crore allocated.
- Total CSR expenditure increased from Rs 26,579.78 crore in FY22 to Rs 29,986.92 crore in FY23. The number of CSR projects rose from 44,425 to 51,966.
- Companies outside the public sector contributed 84% of the total CSR spend.
- Maharashtra, Karnataka, Gujarat received the most CSR spends while North East states, Lakshadweep and Leh and Ladakh received the least CSR spendings.

MoSPI restructured to enhance survey frequency and data quality

- On 19st August 2024, the Ministry of Statistics and Programme Implementation (MoSPI) restructured to improve survey frequency and data quality.
- The reorganization created two new divisions: Household Survey Division and Enterprise Survey Division.

India creates 46.7 million jobs in fiscal 2023-24

- In the fiscal year 2023-24, India generated 46.7 million jobs, bringing the total employment to 643.3 million.
- This significant growth reflects an employment growth rate of 6%, surpassing the 3.2% from the previous fiscal year. The data, released by the Reserve Bank of India (RBI), counters concerns about jobless growth.
- Notably, India's GDP grew at 8.2% in FY24, exceeding estimates, while RBI projected a 7.2% GDP growth for FY25.

India's Manufacturing sector witnesses 7.4% employment growth in fiscal 2022-23

- India's total estimated employment in manufacturing industries showed a robust growth of 7.4 percent in the fiscal 2022-23 over the previous year.
- According to the latest data by the Ministry of Statistics and Programme Implementation (MoSPI), employment rose to 1.84 crore in 2022-23 from 1.72 crore in 2021-22 highest-ever increase in the sector in more than a decade.
- The top five states employing the highest number of persons in this sector were Tamil Nadu, Maharashtra, Gujarat, Uttar Pradesh and Karnataka.

Government withdraws windfall tax on Oil Product

- In December 2024, the Indian government declared the removal of the windfall tax on crude oil, aviation turbine fuel (ATF), petrol, and diesel exports.
- This tax, introduced in July 2022 in response to soaring global crude prices, was withdrawn after global oil prices stabilized at approximately $70-$75 per barrel.

Union Minister Piyush Goyal inaugurates Invest India's new office in Singapore

- On 22nd September 2024, Union Minister of Commerce & Industry Piyush Goyal inaugurated Invest India's first overseas office in Singapore.
- This office aims to facilitate regional investments into India, serving as a dedicated point of contact for companies from the ASEAN region and beyond.

India Targets $500 Billion in Electronics Manufacturing by 2030

- According to a report by NITI Aayog, India aims to achieve $500 billion in domestic electronics manufacturing by 2030.
- Growth in electronics manufacturing could create approximately 6 million jobs. The report emphasizes the importance of Global Value Chains (GVCs), which account for 70% of international trade.
- India's electronics sector has seen significant growth, reaching $155 billion in FY23, with production of $101 billion.

Financial Affairs

India Became 2nd Largest Smartphone Market Globally

- According to Counterpoint Research, India's smartphone market has emerged as the second largest globally by unit volume and third largest by value in the third quarter of 2024.
- India accounted for 15.5% of global smartphone shipments, following China with a 22% share.
- Apple leads the used smartphone market with a 25% share, followed by Xiaomi and Samsung.

RBI, SEBI unveil rules for converting excess investment by FPIs into FDI

- Reserve Bank of India and the Securities and Exchange Board of India introduced new guidelines requiring foreign portfolio investors (FPIs) to get government approval and investee company consent for equity stakes exceeding prescribed limits.
- Under the Foreign Exchange Management Act (FEMA), FPIs are allowed to hold up to 10 percent of a company's total paid-up equity capital.
- Any FPI breaching this limit now has the option to divest holdings or reclassify such holdings as FDI, subject to several conditions.

SEBI announces new framework to curb excessive speculation in stock market

- On 1st October 2024, the Securities and Exchange Board of India (SEBI) announced a new framework to curb excessive speculation in the stock market.
- The measures, effective from November 20, 2024, include increasing the contract size from ₹5 lakh to ₹15 lakh, raising margin requirements, and mandating upfront collection of option premiums.

About SEBI

- Establishment: 1988
- Type: Non-statutory body to regulate the securities market
- Autonomous Status: 30 January 1992
- Headquarters: Mumbai
- Regional offices: New Delhi, Kolkata, Chennai and Ahmedabad

SEBI imposes Rs 9 lakh fine on Reliance Securities for 'flouting market norms'

- The Securities and Exchange Board of India (SEBI) has imposed a Rs.9 lakh monetary penalty on Reliance Securities for "flouting market norms" and stock broker rules in December 2024.
- The market regulator's order came after National Stock Exchange (NSE) and Bombay Stock Exchange (BSE) carried out a thematic onsite inspection of the books of accounts, records and other documents of authorised persons (APs) of Reliance Securities Ltd (RSL).

SEBI required UPI for debt security bids up to ₹5 Lakh

- On 24th September 2024, SEBI mandated that individual investors applying for public issues of debt securities through intermediaries must use UPI for amounts up to ₹5 lakh, effective from 1st November 2024.
- Investors must provide their bank account-linked UPI ID in the bid-cum-application form.

SEBI Imposes ₹1 Crore Fine on Jai Anmol in Reliance Home Finance case

- On 24th September 2024, the Securities and Exchange Board of India (SEBI) imposed a ₹1 crore fine on Jai Anmol Ambani, son of Anil Ambani, for alleged irregularities in Reliance Home Finance.
- SEBI found that Jai Anmol failed to exercise due diligence in lending practices and approved unsecured loans.
- This penalty follows SEBI's earlier action in August 2024, where Anil Ambani and 24 others were barred from the securities market for five years for fund diversion.

New Asset Class approved by SEBI

- On 30th September 2024, the Securities and Exchange Board of India (SEBI) approved a new asset class positioned between mutual funds (MFs) and portfolio management services (PMS).
- Investors can participate with a minimum investment of Rs 10 lakh across all strategies within a specific Asset Management Company (AMC).

SEBI Launches AI Chatbot 'SEVA' for Investors

- On July 29, the Securities and Exchange Board of India (SEBI) introduced 'SEVA,' an AI-powered chatbot designed to assist investors with a range of functions.
- This initiative aims to enhance investor experience and accessibility to crucial market information.
- A chatbot, such as SEVA, is a computer program designed to simulate human conversation.

NSE LAUNCHES MOBILE APP & WEBSITES IN 8 ADDITIONAL LANGUAGES

- In November 2024, the National Stock Exchange of India (NSE) launched a mobile app as well as websites in eight additional languages to commemorate 30 years of operations.
- Trading in the equities market commenced on the NSE on 3rd November 1994.
- MD and CEO of NSE – Ashishkumar Chauhan
- Total number of languages supported by the NSE – 12

SEBI study reveals individual traders face severe losses in Equity F&O Segment

- A SEBI study, released on 23 September 2024, revealed that **93%** of individual traders in the equity futures and options (F&O) segment incurred significant losses between FY22 and FY24.
- The combined net loss for these traders exceeded ₹1.8 lakh crore.
- The study highlighted that only 7.2% of traders made profits, with just **1% earning over ₹1 lakh** after transaction costs. Despite consecutive losses, 75% of traders continued trading.

Government Launches 'Agri Fund for Start-Ups & Rural Enterprises' (AgriSURE)

- The Government of India launched the 'Agri Fund for Start-Ups & Rural Enterprises' (AgriSURE) to support start-ups and agripreneurs through investments in sector-specific, sector-agnostic, and debt Alternative Investment Funds (AIFs), as well as direct equity support to start-ups working in agriculture and allied sectors.
- This initiative aims to foster innovation and sustainability in India's agricultural sector through the establishment of a Rs 750 crore Category-II Alternative Investment Fund (AIF).
- The fund will be set up with an initial corpus of ₹750 crore, with ₹250 crore each from NABARD and the Ministry of Agriculture, and ₹250 crore from other institutions.

NABARD : KEY POINTS

- **Full Name:** National Bank for Agriculture and Rural Development
- **Established:** 1982
- **Headquarters:** Mumbai

Star Health's introducing Braille Insurance Policies for the Visually Impaired

- On 4th September 2024, Star Health and Allied Insurance launched "Special Care Gold," **India's first insurance policy in Braille.**
- This policy is tailored for individuals with 40% or more disability, ensuring visually impaired individuals can access health insurance information independently.
- The initiative promotes inclusivity and economic empowerment, aligning with **IRDAI's "Insurance for All" vision.**

Bajaj Capital Insurance launches Human+AI Campaign "BlessMeGanesha"

- On 23rd September 2024, Bajaj Capital Insurance launched the "BlessMeGanesha" campaign, featuring a unique Human+AI musical composition called "Ganesha Aarti".
- This innovative project involved 3,500 employees contributing their versions of Ganesha Vandana, with AI enhancing the final piece.

IndiaFirst Life became 1st insurer to launch operations in GIFT City

- On 28th August 2024, IndiaFirst Life achieved a significant milestone by becoming the first Indian life insurer to commence operations in Gujarat International Finance Tec City (GIFT City).
- IndiaFirst Life aims to cater to the global audience at GIFT City, providing a specially designed ULIP product called **India First Life Wealth Wise plan,** denominated in US dollars.

IRDAI imposes penalty of Rs 2 Cr on HDFC Life

- On 1st August 2024, the Insurance Regulatory and Development Authority of India (IRDAI) imposed a ₹2 crore penalty on HDFC Life for regulatory violations identified during an inspection covering the financial years 2017-2020.
- The penalty includes ₹1 crore for issues related to the protection of policyholders' interests and another ₹1 crore for irregularities in outsourcing services.

LIC launched agency transformation initiative 'Jeevan Samarth'

- Life Insurance Corporation (LIC) has introduced the 'Jeevan Samarth' initiative to transform its agency ecosystem. In collaboration with a global consulting firm, LIC will comprehensively review and revamp its existing agency framework at the branch, division, and zonal levels.
- The goal is to align with industry changes, enhance agent skills, and provide suitable long-term savings, protection, health insurance, ULIP, and pension solutions.

IRDAI revised guidelines on Long-Term Motor Insurance Commissions

- On 19th July 2024, the Insurance Regulatory and Development Authority of India (IRDAI) revised its guidelines on commissions for long-term motor insurance policies.
- The new guidelines align these policies with standard one-year motor insurance policies, allowing insurers to set commission rates within their expense management framework.

ICICI Lombard introduces 'Elevate': Revolutionizing Health Insurance with AI

- On 9th July 2024, ICICI Lombard, a leading private general insurer in India, launched 'Elevate', a revolutionary health insurance product powered by AI.
- This innovative offering is designed to meet the diverse needs of modern lifestyles and unforeseen medical emergencies, emphasizing personalized solutions and comprehensive coverage.

TCS launches Pace Studio in Philippines

- On 27th August 2024, Tata Consultancy Services (TCS) unveiled its cutting-edge TCS Pace Studio in Manila, Philippines.
- This state-of-the-art facility aims to co-innovate with clients, fostering tailored solutions for their unique business needs and driving digital innovation across the Asia Pacific region.
- Equipped with interactive screens, audio-video systems, and virtual reality headsets, the studio showcases TCS' innovative platforms like TCS AI WisdomNext, TCS TwinX, and TCS Zero Carbon Platform.

Zomato acquired Paytm Insider for Rs 2,048 Crore

- On 22nd August 2024, Zomato announced its acquisition of Paytm Insider, the entertainment and events ticketing arm of One 97 Communications Limited, for ₹2,048 crore.
- This strategic move allows Zomato to enter the entertainment ticketing sector, complementing its existing dining and food delivery services.

Hindustan Zinc launches EcoZen, Asia's first low carbon ₹green' zinc

- Vedanta-owned Hindustan Zinc (HZL), India's largest zinc producer, has launched EcoZen, Asia's first low-carbon green zinc brand in July 2024.
- This initiative aligns with HZL's goal of achieving net-zero emissions by 2050.
- The use of EcoZen in galvanising one tonne of steel is expected to avoid around 400 kilograms of carbon emissions.
- The primary application of zinc is for galvanization of steel to protect it from corrosion.

HDFC Securities launched "Brokerage as a Service" for partners

- On 19th August 2024, HDFC Securities launched "Brokerage as a Service" (BaaS) to empower institutions and fintech companies.
- This service allows partners to integrate HDFC Securities' advanced trading platform, HDFC SKY, into their applications and websites.
- BaaS offers multiple integration options, including SDK and Open API, enabling seamless order placement and management.

SIDBI secured USD 215.6 Million from Green Climate Fund

- On 22nd July 2024, the Small Industries Development Bank of India (SIDBI) secured a $215.6 million loan from the Green Climate Fund (GCF) to support the Financing Mitigation and Adaptation Projects (FMAP) initiative.
- The FMAP program aims to reduce greenhouse gas emissions by 35.3 million tonnes and benefit over 10.8 million people through water savings and community resilience.

NI-MSME Hyderabad earned 3-Star 'UTKRISHT' Accreditation

- The National Institute for MSME (NI-MSME), Hyderabad, received a 3-Star "UTKRISHT" Accreditation from the Capacity Building Commission on 12th August 2024.
- This recognition was awarded for NI-MSME's excellence in promoting and developing MSMEs, adhering to national standards, and its significant role in entrepreneurship and skill development.

Fast tracking BIMSTEC Free Trade Agreement

- On 8th August 2024, the Indian Minister of Commerce & Industry called for expedited negotiations of the BIMSTEC Free Trade Agreement (FTA) at the BIMSTEC Business Summit in New Delhi.
- The minister emphasized the need for a preferential trade agreement to enhance intra-regional trade and investment.
- The BIMSTEC FTA, initially signed in 2004, aims to reduce tariffs, promote investment, and foster economic cooperation among member countries.

World Bank approves $188 million loan to Maharashtra to stimulate growth in backward districts

- In December 2024, the World Bank approved a $188.28-million loan to stimulate economic growth in Maharashtra, especially in the lagging districts.
- **Aim-** To enhance district-level planning and growth strategies.
- The loan, provided by the International Bank for Reconstruction and Development (IBRD) has a final maturity of 15 years, including a grace period of 5 years.

India's external debt rises by $31 bn to $647 bn in 2023: World Bank report

- India's total external debt has increased by $ 31 billion to $ 646.79 billion in 2023, according to the World Bank International Debt Report released in December 2024.
- The report stated that interest payment increased from $ 15.08 billion in 2022 to $ 22.54 billion in 2023.
- Long-term debt stocks have risen 7 per cent to $ 498 billion in 2023, while short-term debt stocks declined marginally to $ 126.32 billion in 2023.

India signs $98 million loan agreement with ADB to boost horticulture productivity

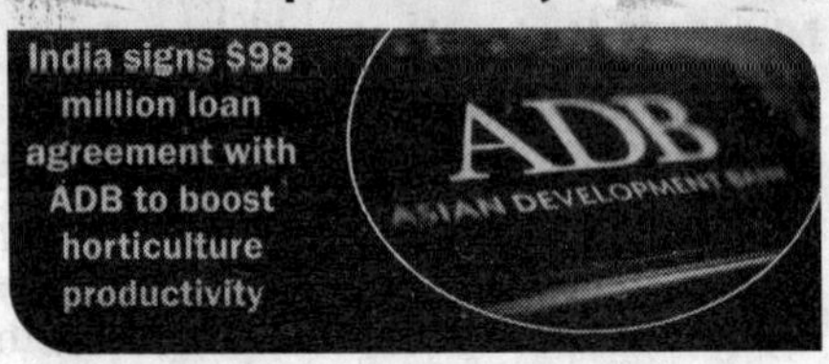

- In November 2024, India and the Asian Development Bank (ADB) have signed a $98 million loan agreement to enhance horticulture crop productivity in the country.
- The funding will support the establishment of disease-free planting material systems, boosting crop yields, quality, and resilience to climate change.

About Asian Development Bank (ADB)

- ADB was established in 1966.
- It is owned by members – 69 nations 49 from the region.
- It aims to promote social and economic development in Asia and the Pacific.
- It is headquartered in Manila, Philippines.
- The bank also maintains 31 field offices around the world to promote social and economic development in Asia.

India, ADB sign $50 million loan for climate-resilient water security in Meghalaya

- The Government of India signed a $50 million loan agreement with the Asian Development Bank (ADB) in December 2024.
- The loan will improve water security in Meghalaya by building climate-adaptive water harvesting systems.
- The project is in line with the Meghalaya State Water Policy (MSWP) 2019.
- It aims to achieve sustainable development, manage, and use the state's water resources through a participatory approach.

ADB approves $200 million for Uttarakhand Livability Improvement Project

- The Asian Development Bank (ADB) approved a $200 million loan for Uttarakhand's Livability Improvement Project to upgrade urban infrastructure and improve climate resilience.
- The project costs $465.9 million, funded by ADB ($200 million), the European Investment Bank ($191 million), and the Uttarakhand government ($74.9 million).
- The project focuses on improving water supply, sanitation, drainage, flood management, urban mobility, and other services to enhance quality of life.

ADB approved $200M for Nagpur Metro Expansion

- On 24th July 2024, the Asian Development Bank (ADB) approved a $200 million loan to support the expansion of the Nagpur Metro.
- This project aims to extend four metro rail corridors, adding 43.8 kilometers of elevated tracks and 32 stations.

ADB to build 400 MW Solar Power Plant in Gujarat

- In July 2024, the Asian Development Bank (ADB) arranged a ₹1,460 crore loan for the ENGIE group to construct a 400-megawatt solar photovoltaic power plant in Surendranagar, Gujarat.
- ADB and the Asian Infrastructure Investment Bank (AIIB) will each provide ₹7.3 billion, totaling approximately USD 175.9 million.
- This project aligns with India's goal of achieving 500 gigawatts of non-fossil fuel energy capacity by 2030.

India becomes 3rd largest supplier of health & nutrition support to UNICEF

- On 11th October 2024, India was recognized as the third-largest supplier of health and nutrition support to UNICEF.
- From 2016 to 2023, Indian businesses provided nearly $6 billion worth of goods and services, including vaccines, pharmaceuticals, and nutrition supplies.
- UNICEF, established in 1946, continues to partner with India to enhance child health, education, and protection.

IFC to partner with Bajaj Finance to invest $400 mn for climate finance

- In November 2024, the International Finance Corporation (IFC) announced to partner with Bajaj Finance to invest $400 million out of the $1 billion fundraising to aid in the expansion of the latter's EV fleet, energy-efficient consumer goods (EECG), and women empowerment.
- The partnership will also boost Bajaj Finance's ability to fund and support more women-owned micro-enterprises and women micro-borrowers.
- IFC is a member of the World Bank Group with focus on the private sector in the emerging market.

IFC Partners with Axis Bank for India's First Blue Loan of $500 Million

- In October 2024, the International Finance Corporation (IFC) partnered with Axis Bank to provide a $500 million loan aimed at scaling up blue finance and green projects in India.
- Blue loans focus on funding water and wastewater management, reducing ocean plastic pollution, restoring marine ecosystems, and promoting offshore renewable energy, among others.
- India has immense potential for water efficiency, wastewater treatment, and green infrastructure, projected to grow into a $3 billion market by 2029.

Jio Financial Services launched SmartGold

- On 29th October 2024, Jio Financial Services launched SmartGold, a digital gold investment platform accessible through the JioFinance app.
- SmartGold allows customers to invest in 24-karat gold starting from as low as ₹10.

RIL jumped 2 places in Fortune's Global 500 list for 2024

- On 5th August 2024, Reliance Industries Limited (RIL) climbed two spots to rank 86th on the Fortune Global 500 list.
- RIL remains the highest-ranked Indian firm on the list, with revenues of $108.8 billion and a profit of $8.4 billion in the last fiscal year.
- The company has advanced 69 places over the past three years, from 155th in 2021.

Tata Group unveils ₹27,000 Crore Semiconductor facility in Assam

- On 3rd August 2024, Tata Group held the Bhumi Pujan ceremony for its ₹27,000 crore semiconductor assembly and test facility in Jagiroad, Assam.
- This state-of-the-art plant will produce 4.83 crore chips per day, focusing on applications in automotive, mobile devices, and AI.
- The facility is expected to become operational by mid-2025, creating 27,000 jobs.

Nvidia overtook Apple to become the most valuable company

- In October 2024, Nvidia overtook Apple to become the world's most valuable company. Nvidia's market value briefly reached $3.53 trillion, surpassing Apple's $3.52 trillion.
- Nvidia's stock has seen significant gains throughout 2024, reflecting the growing importance of AI technology in various industries.

Airbus launches State-of-the-Art Headquarters and Training Centre in Delhi

- On 24th October 2024, Airbus inaugurated its new India and South Asia Headquarters and Training Centre in New Delhi.
- The state-of-the-art facility, located at Indira Gandhi International Airport, will house all three of Airbus's business units: Commercial Aircraft, Helicopters, and Defence & Space.
- The centre will also feature four A320neo Full Flight Simulators (FFS) and aims to train 800 pilots and 200 technicians annually.

India's first integrated Agri-Export Facility at Jawaharlal Nehru Port

- On 27th July 2024, India approved its first integrated agri-export facility at Jawaharlal Nehru Port, Mumbai.
- This ₹284 crore public-private partnership (PPP) project aims to streamline agri-logistics, reduce wastage, and extend the shelf life of agricultural products.

RBI Permit UPI Payments Via Third-Party Apps for PPI Holders

- In December 2024, the Reserve Bank of India (RBI) allowed full-KYC prepaid payment instruments (PPIs) like wallets and gift cards to make and receive UPI payments via third-party apps like Google Pay and PhonePe.
- This aligns with **RBI's Payments Vision 2025**, promoting interoperability and digital payment adoption.
- Earlier, UPI payments with PPIs **were limited to the issuer's app**.
- Unified Payments Interface (UPI) was developed by National Payments Corporation of India (NPCI) in 2016.

55th GST Council Meeting Concludes in Jaisalmer

- The 55th meeting of India's Goods and Services Tax (GST) Council was held in Jaisalmer, Rajasthan.
- It was Chaired by Union Minister for Finance & Corporate Affairs Smt. Nirmala Sitharaman.
- The Council approved raising the GST rate on old and used electric vehicles from 12 per cent to 18 per cent. This move aims to align the tax structure of used EVs with that of new EVs, which are currently taxed at 5 per cent.
- Caramel popcorn will have an 18% GST.
- GST council also recommended fully exempting GST on 'Gene Therapy'.

Aditya Birla Capital Becomes First to Integrate Financial Services on ONDC

- Aditya Birla Capital becomes first BFSI(Banking, Financial Services, and Insurance) company to offer all three main financial services on the Open Network for Digital Commerce (ONDC) platform.
- These services include lending, insurance, and mutual fund investments.
- Through ONDC Network, various live buyer apps will be able to offer Aditya Birla Capital's personal loans, health insurance, and mutual funds to their customers.

Banking and Economy

Govt to get Rs 3,662 crore from LIC

- **State-run Life Insurance Corporation of India (LIC)** will provide a dividend of ₹3,662 crore to the Government of India, which is the largest shareholder in the company.
- LIC declared a final dividend of ₹6 per share for the financial year ended March 31, 2024.
- The government currently holds 96.50% stake in LIC, accounting for 6,10,36,22,781 shares out of 6,32,49,97,701 fully paid-up equity shares.

RBI launches "PRAVAAH" portal

- The **PRAVAAH (Platform for Regulatory Application, Validation, and Authorization)** portal is a centralized **web-based platform** designed **to simplify the process of applying for various regulatory approvals** from the RBI.
- This secure portal allows individuals and entities to:
  - Submit applications online
  - Track the status of their applications
  - Respond to queries from the RBI
  - Receive timely decisions
- Currently, the PRAVAAH portal hosts 60 different application forms covering various regulatory and supervisory departments of the RBI, with plans to add more as needed.

Poonawalla Fincorp and IndusInd Bank launch RuPay Credit Card

- Poonawalla Fincorp Limited announced the launch of a **co-branded credit card** in collaboration with IndusInd Bank on 28 May 2024.
- The IndusInd Bank Poonawalla Fincorp eLITE RuPay Platinum Credit Card is aimed **at redefining and elevating the banking experience for customers.**

Bank of Maharashtra leads PSU Banks in FY24 growth

- Bank of Maharashtra recorded a 15.94% rise in total business (domestic), **leading the pack among public sector banks.** State Bank of India (SBI) followed with a 13.12% growth.
- Bank of Maharashtra **maintained its top spot in terms of growth in deposit mobilization,** achieving a 15.66% rise in deposits. SBI, Bank of India, and Canara

Bank also achieved double-digit growth in deposits.

- Bank of Maharashtra continued to top the chart with a 52.73% growth in low-cost Current Account and Savings Account (CASA) deposits.
- Bank of Maharashtra reported the lowest gross non-performing assets (NPAs) at 1.88% and net NPAs at 0.2% as of 31 March 2024.
- Bank of Maharashtra led PSBs with a 17.38% capital adequacy ratio at the end of FY24.

SBI General Launches 'Surety Bond Bima'

- **SBI General Insurance, the non-life insurance arm of State Bank of India** (SBI), has launched the General Surety Bond Bima (Conditional & Unconditional) insurance product.
- The Surety Bond Insurance **acts as a security arrangement for infrastructure projects,** benefiting both contractors and the principal (contract awarding authority).
- It includes various bonds such as bid bonds, advance payment bonds, performance bonds, and retention money bonds.

IRDAI Issues New Corporate Governance Rules

- The **Insurance Regulatory and Development Authority of India (IRDAI)** has issued new regulations titled **"Corporate Governance for Insurers,"** effective from 20 March 2024.
- These new corporate governance regulations were notified under the Insurance Regulatory and Development Authority of India (Corporate Governance for Insurers) Regulations, 2024 ("the Regulations").
- These regulations **aim to enhance governance structures within insurance companies** to safeguard the interests of stakeholders, including policyholders.

IREDA Gets Navratna Status

- **The Indian Renewable Energy Development Agency (IREDA)** has been granted 'Navratna' status **by the Department of Public Enterprises,** reflecting its improved financial performance and strategic importance.
- Year-on-year, IREDA saw a 32% rise in net profit, maintaining a consistent quarterly profit of ₹337 crore.
- Navratna **status allows IREDA to execute investments** of up to ₹1,000 crore without central approval, allocate up to 30% of their net worth annually (up to ₹1,000 crore), and participate in joint ventures, partnerships, and set up overseas subsidiaries

RBI Approves Rs 2.11 Lakh Cr Surplus Transfer To Government

- The Reserve Bank of India (RBI) has approved **a record surplus transfer of ₹2.11 lakh crore to the Central Government** for the financial year 2023-24.
- This substantial surplus payment marks a **141% increase compared to the previous year's** dividend of Rs 87,416 crore.
- The surplus transfer is for the financial year 2023-2024, but it will reflect in the government account in the financial year 2024-25.

India Registers Record $778 Billion Export In 2023-24

- In the financial year 2023-24, India achieved a historic milestone by registering record exports totaling $778 billion.
- This impressive figure **combines both goods (merchandise) exports and services exports.**
- While services exports increased from $325.3 billion to $341.1 billion, merchandise exports experienced a marginal decline from $451.1 billion to $437.1 billion.

Phonepe Starts Cross-Border Upi In Sri Lanka

- PhonePe announced a partnership with LankaPay to enable UPI payments acceptance at LankaQR merchant points in Sri Lanka.
- Under this, any UPI or PhonePe app user in Sri Lanka can scan any LankaQR code placed at the merchant's location to transact. The merchant will receive settlement in Lankan rupees.

Zomato to surrender RBI payment aggregator license

- In May 2024, Zomato Payment Pvt Ltd (ZPPL) has decided to voluntarily surrender the certificate of authorisation it obtained from the Reserve Bank to operate as an online payment aggregator.
- Zomato announced the formation of ZPPL as a wholly owned subsidiary in 2021 to carry out the business of aggregating payments and issuing prepaid payment instruments.

SAIL-Bhilai to set up 15-MW floating solar plant

- Bhilai Steel Plant (BSP), a subsidiary of Steel Authority of India (SAIL), will set up Chhattisgarh's first 15 megawatt (MW) floating solar project at its Maroda-1 reservoir.
- The Maroda reservoir is spread across 2.1 square kilometers with a water storage capacity of 19 cubic milimetres (MM3).
- The project is anticipated to generate approximately 34.26 million units of green power annually, which will be utilised by BSP as captive power.

IRDAI mandates rural insurance coverage

- IRDAI has mandated life and general insurers **to provide insurance coverage to specific Gram Panchayats,** aiming to extend insurance services to rural areas.
- The Life Insurance Council, in consultation with the **Ministry of Panchayat Raj,** will determine the minimum number of Gram Panchayats for each insurer based on parameters like market share.

ICICI Bank enables UPI for NRIs

- ICICI Bank has enabled UPI payments for NRIs using their international mobile numbers.
- This service, available through the iMobile Pay app, allows NRIs to make payments in India by scanning QR codes, sending money to UPI IDs, or directly to Indian mobile numbers and bank accounts.
- The facility is supported in countries like Australia, Canada, Hong Kong, Oman, Qatar, Saudi Arabia, Singapore, UAE, UK, and USA.

FPSB India, IFSCA to promote GIFT IFSC

- Financial Planning Standards Board India (FPSB India) announced a collaboration with the International Financial Services Centres Authority (IFSCA) located in GIFT City, Gandhinagar.
- The partnership aims **to position GIFT IFSC as a 'Global Finance Hub' by enhancing the financial market ecosystem** and fostering skilled professionals.
- The Memorandum of Understanding (MoU) includes provisions for talent pipeline support, ecosystem development, promotional activities, and research collaboration.

Former BharatPe COO launches Eternal Capital

- Former BharatPe COO Dhruv Dhanraj Bahl has launched Eternal Capital, a **venture capital fund aiming to raise Rs 120 crore** with a greenshoe option to increase by another Rs 120 crore.
- The fund plans to support 40 early-stage startups across various sectors over the next three years.

Adani Green secures $400M for solar projects

- Adani Green Energy Ltd has secured a $400 million green loan for its ongoing solar projects **in Gujarat and Rajasthan.**
- The lenders involved are DBS Bank, Intesa Sanpaolo, MUFG Bank, Rabobank, and Sumitomo Mitsui Banking.

RBI fines three co-op banks

- In May 2024, the Reserve Bank of India (RBI) imposed **monetary penalties on three co-operative banks for rule violations.**
- These banks are **Lokmangal Co-operative Bank, The Udgir Urban Co-operative Bank, and The Satara Sahakari Bank.**
- The central bank imposed Rs 5 lakh penalty on Lokmangal Co-operative Bank, Rs 2 lakh on The Satara Sahakari Bank, and Rs 1 lakh on The Udgir Urban Co-operative Bank.

NPCI To Develop UPI-Like System In Namibia

- The NPCI's overseas arm has struck an agreement with the Bank of Namibia (BoN) to build a UPI-like quick payment system for Namibia.
- The alliance aims to assist Namibia modernize its financial ecosystem by leveraging India's UPI technology and experience.
- This partnership marks NPCI's **first-ever collaboration with a central bank to deploy the UPI stack in an international market.**

India Becomes Third Largest Producer of Solar Power

- According to the Global Electricity Review 2024 by Ember, India overtook Japan to become the world's third- highest producer of solar power in 2023.
- In 2023, India produced 113 billion units (BU) of solar power, more than Japan, which produced 110 BU.
- China remains the leading producer of solar power globally, producing 584 BU in 2024, followed by the United States.
- India ranks fifth globally in installed power capacity, with 73 gigawatts (GW) of solar power capacity.

RBI cancels Acemoney NBFC license

- The Reserve Bank of India (RBI) cancelled the Certificate of Registration (CoR) of Acemoney (India) Ltd, a Delhi-based non-banking financial company (NBFC), due to irregular lending practices.
- The company was found to be non-compliant with RBI guidelines on risk management, code of conduct in outsourcing financial services, and charging excessive interest rates.

India's E-Commerce To Be 3rd Largest By 2030

- India's e-commerce market is projected to become the third largest globally by 2030, with an estimated market value of $300 billion.
- This rapid growth is driven by increasing internet penetration, affordable smartphones, and a growing middle class.
- The market is expected to grow at a CAGR of 21.5% from 2024 to 2030.

India's Services Sector Growth and Challenges

- **A report titled "India's rise as the emerging services factory of the world"** has been released **by Goldman Sachs,** highlighting the country's significant growth in services exports.
- **India's services exports reached $340 billion in 2023** and are expected to grow to $800 billion by 2030.
- By 2030, these exports are predicted to make up 11% of India's total GDP, an increase from 9.7% in 2023, showing how important the services sector is becoming for the economy.

Airtel Payments Bank's new NCMC-enabled debit, prepaid cards

- Airtel Payments Bank has launched new debit and prepaid cards that are designed to be more convenient and environmentally friendly for their customers in India.
- National Common Mobility Card **(NCMC) allows these cards to be used for various purposes beyond traditional debit/prepaid cards.**
- This card is linked to a savings account and allows debit transactions like purchases and ATM withdrawals.

Bandhan Life Insurance unveils new identity and growth strategy

- Bandhan Life Insurance, **formerly known as Aegon Life Insurance,** has rebranded itself with the **tagline 'Bharat Ki Udaan, Bandhan Se',** reflecting its commitment to empowering the aspirations of India.
- Under the ownership of Bandhan Financial Holdings, the company is embarking on an aggressive growth strategy, aiming to recruit 1,000 new employees and expand its customer base.

SBI Life launched ideationX

- SBI Life Insurance has inaugurated IdeationX, a groundbreaking initiative **aimed at fostering life insurance innovation.**
- This initiative encourages future leaders from top B-Schools to devise unconventional solutions that cater to evolving consumer needs in the insurance sector.
- IdeationX targets students from prestigious B-Schools nationwide, urging them to think creatively and present innovative life insurance solutions.

Govt Launched Initiative To Combat OTP Frauds

- The Indian government, in collaboration with SBI Cards and Payment Services Ltd and telecom operators, launched an initiative to combat OTP frauds.
- The solution involves tracking the geolocation of customers to ensure OTPs are delivered securely.
- This initiative aims to enhance digital payment security and reduce cyber fraud, which has siphoned off Rs 10,319 crore between April 2021 and December 2023.

NBBL partners with SBI to introduce NCMC recharge category

- NPCIBharat BillPay Limited (NBBL) in collaboration with State Bank of India (SBI) has onboarded SBI NCMC cards on its Bharat BillPay platform.
- Enabling the SBI National Common Mobility Card on Bharat BillPay tries to provide a seamless experience for consumers.

Vedanta's Hindustan Zinc becomes 3rd largest silver producer globally

- In April 2024, Vedanta's company Hindustan Zinc Limited has become the third largest silver producer globally according to the 2024 World Silver Survey conducted by 'The Silver Institute' of the US.
- As per a survey, **its Sindesar Khurd Mine in Rajasthan now stands as the world's second-largest silver-producing mine,** moving up from last year's fourth spot.
- The company has a market share of 75 per cent of the growing zinc market in India.

RBI to offer CBDC-R to non-bank payment operators

- The Reserve Bank of India (RBI) proposed to make CBDC-R (CBDC-Retail) accessible to a broader population **by allowing non-bank payment system operators to offer CBDC wallets.**

- Non-bank payment system operators include third-party payment applications like Phone Pe, Google Pay, etc.

General Insurance industry premium grows 12.78% in FY24

- According to data released by the General Insurance Council (GIC), non-life insurance companies experienced a growth of 12.78% in financial year 2023-24 (FY24) to reach Rs 2.89 trillion, compared to 16.4 percent in the previous fiscal.
- The premium of general insurance companies grew by 14.24% year-on-year in FY24 to Rs 2.45 trillion. But, the FY24 growth is lower than the 16% achieved in FY23.
- The premiums of public sector general insurers increased by 8.99% to Rs 90,344.49 crore, while those of their private sector counterparts increased by 17.53% to Rs 1.55 trillion.

Govt launched CDP-SURAKSHA platform For Horticulture Farmers

- The Indian government has launched the CDP-SURAKSHA platform to provide subsidies to horticulture farmers under the Cluster Development Programme (CDP).
- SURAKSHA stands for "System for Unified Resource Allocation, Knowledge, and Secure Horticulture Assistance."
- This digital platform ensures instant subsidy disbursement using e-RUPI vouchers from the National Payments Corporation of India (NPCI).
- Key features of CDP-SURAKSHA include integration with PM-KISAN, cloud-based server space from NIC, UIDAI validation, e-RUPI integration, local government directory (LGD), content management system, geotagging, and geo-fencing.

WTO's "Global Trade Outlook and Statistics" Report

- **The WTO's "Global Trade Outlook and Statistics" report** projects world merchandise trade volume to grow by 2.6% in 2024 and 3.3% in 2025, following a decline of -1.2% in 2023.
- India's share of global goods exports was 1.8% and imports were 2.8% in 2023.
- World real GDP growth slowed from 3.1% in 2022 to 2.7% in 2023, and is expected to remain stable at 2.6% in 2024 and 2.7% in 2025.
- **India became the 4th largest exporter of digitally delivered services,** with its share rising to 6% in 2023 from 4.4% in 2019, reaching $257 billion, marking a 17% increase from the previous year, surpassing Germany and China's 4% growth.

Air India, BIAL sign deal to develop Bengaluru airport as hub

- In April 2024, Air India and Bangalore International Airport Limited (BIAL) announced a partnership aimed at transforming the Bengaluru airport into an aviation hub.
- The agreement includes plans for the development of a dedicated domestic lounge, expansion of international services, and establishment of a maintenance, repair, and overhaul (MRO) facility.
- According to a joint statement, Air India, along with other Tata Group airlines – AIX Connect and Vistara, will collaborate with BIAL **to improve international connectivity, operational efficiency, and passenger experience** over the next five years.

Mobile wallet payments in India to surpass Rs 531 trillion in 2028

- **According to GlobalData,** a leading data and analytics company based in London, **payments made via mobile wallets in India are expected to exceed Rs 531.8 trillion by 2028.**
- The value of mobile wallet transactions in India, as reported by GlobalData, experienced a significant increase, reaching Rs 202.8 trillion ($2.5 trillion) in 2023, with a CAGR of 72.1% between 2019 and 2023.

Regulatory Sandbox by TRAI

- The Telecom Regulatory Authority of India **(TRAI) has proposed a Regulatory Sandbox** to encourage innovative technologies, services, use cases, and business models in the digital communication sector.
- **A Regulatory Sandbox is a live testing environment for new telecom products,** services, and business models under the Telecommunication Act 2023.
- It involves a limited user base for a specific duration with certain regulatory relaxations.

SBI, Standard Chartered embrace new RBI norms

- On 4th April 2024, The State Bank of India (SBI) and Standard Chartered Bank India carried out a Credit Default Swap (CDS) trade worth ₹25 crore.
- This was the first such transaction after the Reserve Bank of India (RBI) issued new guidelines for this instrument.
- The trade involved a 1-year rupee CDS featuring REC, according to senior executives at Standard Chartered Bank.

IPPB Introduces Aeps Service Charges

- In order to control and maintain the operational expenses related to offering AePS services, India Post Payments Bank (IPPB) has implemented service fees for AePS transactions.
- Customers will initially be eligible for three complimentary AePS issuer transactions per month, including mini statements, cash withdrawals, and cash deposits.
- Mini statements will cost ₹5 plus GST every transaction, while cash withdrawals and deposits will cost ₹20 plus GST per transaction.

RBI to set up Digital India Trust Agency

- As a new tool against cybercrime, the Reserve Bank of India (RBI) is thinking of creating the Digital India Trust Agency (DIGITA).
- The approval of legitimate applications and the rise in unlawful loan applications that are registered with the public are the main objectives of this planned agency.
- The planned organization will make it possible for digital lending applications to be validated and keep a list of verified apps available to the public.

AAI to post record ₹5,000-crore profit in FY24

- **AAI reported a record profit of around ₹5,000 crore in the fiscal year 2023-24,** marking the highest profit in its history.
- AAI is projected to achieve a turnover of more than ₹15,000 crore in 2023-24, also marking the highest turnover in its history.
- In the previous fiscal year (FY23), AAI reported a profit before tax of ₹3,963.75 crore and a profit after tax of ₹2,972 crore. The total revenue for FY23 stood at ₹12,172.35 crore.

SEBI Launches New Version of SCORES

- The Securities and Exchange Board of India **(SEBI) introduced an upgraded version of its complaint redressal system, called SEBI Complaint Redressal System (SCORES 2.0),** effective from April 1.
- Enhancements in the new SCORES system **focus on improving user**

experience and expediting investor complaint resolution across the securities market.

- Key features of SCORES 2.0 include the establishment of standardized timelines for complaint resolution, set at 21 calendar days from the complaint's receipt date.

Yes Bank and IDFC First Bank announce surcharge on utility payments

- Yes Bank and IDFC First Bank have announced the introduction of a surcharge on utility transactions, effective from 1st May 2024.
- The surcharge is applied to various utility expenses, including telecommunications, electricity, gas, water, internet services, and cable services.
- The introduction of a surcharge on utility transactions by Yes Bank and IDFC First Bank implies potential increased costs for credit card users when paying for essential services.

AU Small Finance Bank merges with Fincare SFB

- AU Small Finance Bank merges with Fincare Small Finance Bank, signaling a significant consolidation within the banking sector.
- **The merger, completed on April 1, 2024, via an all-stock transaction, bolsters AU SFB's footprint in South India** while expanding its customer base and distribution network.
- Merger details include Fincare SFB shareholders receiving 579 equity shares in AU SFB for every 2,000 equity shares held.

Indirect Tax Collection For Fy24 Exceeds Estimates

- Indirect tax collection for the financial year 2023-24 has surpassed the revised estimates (RE) of Rs 14.84 trillion by a significant margin, primarily driven by record GST collections.
- **The gross GST collection for 2023-24 reached Rs 20.18 trillion, which includes state GST, Central GST,** integrated GST, and compensation cess, marking an impressive **11.7% increase from the previous year.**
- The revised estimates for central GST, including compensation cess, stood at Rs 9.57 trillion, while for excise duty it was Rs 3.08 trillion, and customs Rs 2.19 trillion.

NHAI capex increases by 20% to Rs 2.07 trillion

- The National Highways Authority of India **(NHAI) recorded a capital expenditure of Rs 2.07 trillion in FY24,** marking a 20% increase compared to expenditures in both FY22 and FY23.
- NHAI **accomplished the construction of 6,644 km of national highways in FY24,** slightly exceeding the target of 6,544 km.
- This represents a 20% increase over the 5,544 km constructed in FY23 and a significant 53% increase over the 4,331 km constructed in FY22.

RBI fines IDFC First Bank, LIC Housing Finance

- The Reserve Bank of India (RBI) has imposed **a monetary penalty of Rs 1 crore on IDFC First Bank,** a private sector lender, for non-compliance with certain directions related to Loans and Advances.

India's forex reserves hit new high of $645.6 billion

- India's foreign exchange reserves surged to a **record high for the third consecutive week, reaching $645.58 billion by the week ended March 29,** according to data from the Reserve Bank of India (RBI).
- This marks an increase of $2.95 billion in the reserves from the previous week.
- The latest data on external vulnerability indicators suggest enhanced resilience of India's external sector, according to Governor Das.

Bandhan Mutual Fund launches Innovation Fund

- Bandhan Mutual Fund has announced the launch of the Bandhan Innovation Fund, **an open-ended equity thematic** scheme.
- **The fund's investment strategy includes:** Allocating 35-45% to leading innovators with substantial industry R&D investments.
- Allocating 35-45% to rising innovators who use innovation for competitive advantage. Allocating 10-15% to emerging innovators.

India Plans To Replace Minimum Wage With Living Wage System By 2025

- India plans to replace its minimum wage system with a living wage system by 2025, with assistance from the International Labour Organisation (ILO) to develop the framework.
- A living wage, as defined by the ILO, ensures workers can afford a decent standard of living, covering essentials like food, housing, education, and healthcare.
- The shift aims to alleviate poverty, reduce wage discrepancies, and support the achievement of Sustainable Development Goals (SDGs) by 2030.

RBI Issues Framework For Recognising SROs

- The Reserve Bank of India (RBI) has come up with a final omnibus framework for self-regulatory organisations mandating them to set up grievance redressal mechanisms for members and a non-discriminatory fee structure, among others.
- The omnibus framework prescribes the broad objectives, functions, eligibility criteria and governance standards.
- The dispute resolution process should consistently use efficient, fair and transparent policies and procedures that are in line with the regulatory and statutory requirements.

RBI fines Tamilnad Mercantile Bank Rs 1.31 crore

- The Reserve Bank of India (RBI) has imposed penalties on **DCB Bank and Tamilnad Mercantile Bank** for non-compliance with certain directions related to 'interest rate on advances'.
- A monetary penalty of Rs 63.6 lakh has been imposed on DCB Bank.
- The central bank informed that a penalty of Rs 1.31 crore has been imposed on Tamilnad Mercantile Bank for non-compliance.

Net FDI in India down 38.4% in April-January

- The net foreign direct investment (FDI) in India, **inflows minus outflows, declined 38.4 per cent year-on-year to $15.41 billion in the first 10 months of this financial year.**
- According to the Reserve Bank of India's data in the March 2024 bulletin, FDI in India was $25.53 billion and outflows were $10.11 billion in April 2023-January 2024.
- In the same period last year, FDI inflows stood at $36.75 billion, while outflows reached $11.75 billion.

IndusInd Bank launches All-in-1 Payment Wearables

- In March 2024, IndusInd Bank launched Indus PayWear, India's first all-in-one payment wearables.
- These stylish accessories allow users to make contactless payments by simply tapping them on NFC-enabled terminals.
- The wearables tokenize IndusInd Bank debit or credit cards, ensuring secure transactions.

Razorpay Surpasses $150 Billion In TPV

- Fintech major Razorpay announced it has achieved an annualised total payment volume (TPV) of $150 billion, and unveiled several new features including an AI chatbot.

- The company also launched 'Payment Gateway 3.0', making it India's only payment gateway that solves not just the payment journey but the whole buyer journey.
- Powered by its proprietary AI engine called 'AI Nucleus', the checkout option will help businesses expect more than 30 per cent higher conversions, translating to higher revenues.

RBI bans JM Financial from lending against shares

- On 5th March 2024, the Reserve Bank of India (RBI) banned JM Financial Products Ltd from lending against shares and debentures.
- This action was due to regulatory and governance lapses, including deficiencies in loans for IPO financing and NCD subscriptions.
- JM Financial can continue servicing existing loans but must halt new financing activities immediately.

GoI allocates Rs 6200 crore to boost RRBs

- The central government has allocated Rs 6212.03 crore to Regional Rural Banks (RRBs) as part of the recapitalization scheme.
- **It aimed at supporting RRBs to maintain the minimum prescribed capital-to-risk (Weighted) assets ratio** of 9 percent.
- The performance of RRBs has improved significantly, with a consolidated CRAR (Capital to Risk-weighted Assets Ratio) at an all-time high of 13.83 per cent as of December 31, 2023.

Noise, Airtel Payments Bank, and Mastercard launch smartwatch for payments

- Airtel Payments Bank collaborated with Noise, a smartwatch brand, and Mastercard, a global technology company in the payments space, to unveil A New Way to Pay.
- Customers who have a savings account with Airtel Payments Bank can purchase this smart watch from the Airtel Thanks App.
- A customer would be able to make payments between Rs 1 to Rs 25,000 per day using the Airtel Payments Bank Smart Watch.

Paytm Payments Bank fined Rs 5.49 crore for money laundering violations

- This penalty follows a review initiated by FIU-IND based on specific information from law enforcement agencies regarding illegal activities, including online gambling, facilitated by entities linked to the bank.
- The money from these activities was routed through accounts maintained with Paytm Payments Bank Ltd.
- Despite a compliance Show Cause Notice, the violations were found substantiated, leading to the imposition of the penalty by the Director of FIU-IND under Section 13 of PMLA.

RBI revamps BBPS norms for efficiency

- The Reserve Bank of India (RBI) has announced a revised regulatory framework for the Bharat Bill Payment Systems (BBPS), which will come into effect on April 1, 2024.
- The updated framework aims to streamline bill payments, promote broader participation, and enhance consumer protection measures in response to the changing dynamics of the payment landscape.

RBI to launch Interoperable Payment System for Internet Banking

- In March 2024, the Reserve Bank of India (RBI) announced the launch of an interoperable payment system for internet banking transactions.
- This system, facilitated by NPCI Bharat BillPay Ltd, aims to streamline digital payments by allowing customers to make payments through their bank accounts to any merchant.

30 banks join RBI UDGAM for unclaimed deposits

- In March 2024, the Reserve Bank of India (RBI) announced that 30 banks have joined the UDGAM portal to help individuals search for unclaimed deposits.
- These banks cover around 90% of unclaimed deposits in value terms under the Depositor Education and Awareness (DEA) Fund.
- The UDGAM portal allows users to search for unclaimed deposits across multiple banks with a single query, providing a centralized and efficient way to reclaim forgotten funds.

RBI directs card issuers to offer network choice

- The Reserve Bank of India (RBI) has directed card issuers not to enter into agreements with card networks that restrict them from using other networks' services.
- This move aims to give customers more choice. Card issuers must offer customers the option to choose from multiple networks when issuing cards or during renewal.
- The authorized networks include American Express, Diners Club, MasterCard, RuPay, and Visa.

RBI, Bank Indonesia sign currency agreement

- RBI signed an agreement with Bank Indonesia to promote the use of local currencies for cross-border transactions.
- Aim of the MoU is to promote the use of Indian Rupee (INR) and Indonesian Rupiah (IDR) bilaterally.
- Covers all current account transactions, permissible capital account transactions, and other economic and financial transactions as agreed upon by both countries.

SBI partners with Aurionpro for banking platform

- Aurionpro Solutions has secured a ₹100 crore contract from the State Bank of India (SBI) to provide its cash management and transaction banking platform, 'iCashpro+'.
- The implementation will occur over the next 12 months, with an additional six years allocated for maintenance and support services.
- This move will help SBI upgrade its current Cash Management Product (CMP) platform and establish 'iCashpro+' as a preferred solution for banks.

RBI fines Bank of India, Bandhan Bank

- The Reserve Bank of India (RBI) imposed monetary penalties on two banks, Bandhan Bank and Bank of India, and one non-banking finance company, Indostar Capital Finance, for rule violations.
- Bank of India was fined around Rs 1.41 crore for various violations including not paying interest on certain term deposit accounts.
- Bandhan Bank and Indostar Capital Finance were fined Rs 29.55 lakh and Rs 13.60 lakh respectively for rule breaches.

Insurance sector attracts Rs 54,000 crore FDI in 9 years

- Over the last nine years, the Indian insurance sector has attracted approximately Rs 54,000 crore in foreign direct investment (FDI), largely due to increased FDI limits.
- The government's policies progressively raised the permissible FDI limit from 26%

in 2014 to 49% in 2015, and further to 74% in 2021.

- Insurance penetration in India increased slightly from 3.9% to 4%, while insurance density saw a significant jump from USD 52 to USD 92.

Japan Loses Spot As 3rd Largest Economy

- Japan has lost its position as the world's third-largest economy, falling to fourth place after its economy contracted by 0.4% in the last quarter of 2023.
- **This recession followed a 3.3% shrinkage in the previous quarter,** marking two consecutive quarters of negative growth.
- Germany has now overtaken Japan, with its economy valued at approximately \$4.4 trillion compared to Japan's \$4.2 trillion in 2023 .

IRDAI issues draft regulations for Bima Sugam

- Insurance Regulatory and Development Authority of India (IRDAI) has issued draft regulations for "Bima Sugam - Insurance Electronic Marketplace" on 13 February 2024.
- The key objectives of Bima Sugam are **to empower and protect the interest of policyholders,** increase the penetration of insurance in India, and enhance accessibility.

Wipro acquires insurtech firm Aggne for $66M

- Wipro, the Indian IT services firm, has acquired a 60% stake in the US-based insurtech company Aggne Global for \$66 million.
- The deal is an all-cash transaction, with an option for Wipro to purchase the remaining stake over time.

India Surpasses China as HSBC's 3rd Largest Profit Hub

- In February 2024, India surpassed China as HSBC's third-largest profit hub.
- HSBC's profit before tax in India rose by 19% to \$1.51 billion in 2023. In contrast, China's profit plummeted by 89% due to losses in various sectors.
- India has secured its position as the third most profitable region for The Hongkong and Shanghai Banking Corporation Limited (HSBC) in 2023.

PayPal Registers With India's Financial Intelligence Unit

- Payment gateway platform PayPal has registered with the Finance Ministry's Financial Intelligence Unit- India (FIU-IND), according to a report by Inc42.
- The FIU-IND is a government organization that collects financial intelligence about offenses under the Prevention of Money Laundering Act (PMLA), 2002.
- PayPal has also appointed a principal officer to communicate with the FIU, as required by PMLA.

RBI Grants Payment Aggregator Licence To Mswipe

- In February 2024, the Reserve Bank of India (RBI) granted a payment aggregator (PA) licence to Mswipe Technologies. This follows an in-principle approval received in August 2022.
- The licence allows Mswipe to offer full-stack payment solutions, including offline and online payment acceptance for merchants.

India approves 100% FDI in space sector

- The Indian government has recently approved an amendment to the Foreign Direct Investment (FDI) policy for the space sector.
- The new policy allows up to 100% FDI under the automatic route for the manufacturing of components, systems, and sub-systems for satellites, ground segments, and user segments.
- Up to 74% investment will be allowed under the automatic route for manufacturing and operating an entire satellite.
- For launch vehicles and their systems and subsystems or the creation of a spaceport, up to 49% FDI will be allowed under the automatic route.

Amul celebrates golden jubilee

- Gujarat Cooperative Milk Marketing Federation (GCMMF), which owns the 'Amul' brand, celebrated its Golden Jubilee on February 22, 2024.
- Prime Minister Narendra Modi attended the celebration and inaugurated five projects worth Rs 1,200 crore.
- More than 1.25 lakh dairy farmers, with representatives from around 18,600 villages in Gujarat, attended the programme.

Japan to invest Rs 12,800 crore in India

- Japanese government has committed a loan of 232.209 billion yen (about Rs 12,800 crore) for nine projects related to various sectors in India.
- The projects included North East Road Network Connectivity, Project for Promoting Start-up and Innovation in Telangana, Project for the Construction of Chennai Peripheral Ring Road, Project for Promoting Sustainable Horticulture in Haryana and Project for Climate Change Response and ecosystem Services Enhancement in Rajasthan.

IOB joins Rs 1-lakh-crore market cap league

- In February 2024, Indian Overseas Bank (IOB) joined the elite Rs 1-lakh-crore market cap league, becoming the fifth public sector lender to achieve this milestone.
- This achievement follows strong quarterly earnings, with a 30% YoY increase in net profit to Rs 723 crore for Q3 FY24.
- The State Bank of India holds the top position in market capitalization, standing at approximately Rs 5.8 lakh crore, followed by Bank of Baroda and Punjab National Bank, both with a market capitalization of Rs 1.33 lakh crore.

NTPC Green Energy signs Rs 80,000 Cr MoU with Maharashtra

- On 29th January 2024, NTPC Green Energy Limited (NGEL) signed an MoU with the Government of Maharashtra for developing green hydr[illegible], green ammonia, and green methanol [illegible]ojects.
- The MoU, valued at ₹80,000 crore, includes pumped storage projects of 2 GW and renewable energy projects up to 5 GW.

ICICI Prudential launches Gold Pension Savings plan

- ICICI Prudential Life Insurance launched a new pension product called ICICI Pru Gold Pension Savings.
- The product aims to assist individuals in building a significant retirement corpus through systematic contributions.
- One feature allows customers to withdraw up to 25% of their contributions after three years, providing flexibility for addressing liquidity needs.

SEBI proposes ways for offshore funds to dispose securities

- SEBI proposes methods for offshore funds with expired India licences to dispose of securities they hold through a discussion paper.
- Discussion papers are the initial step SEBI takes before making rule changes for market entities.
- 55 offshore funds with expired India licences hold securities worth 3.3 billion Indian rupees (\$39.77 million), according to SEBI.

ADB, GoI sign $200M loan for Brahmaputra Project

- The Government of India and the Asian Development Bank (ADB) have signed a $200 million loan to enhance flood and riverbank erosion management along the Brahmaputra River in Assam.
- The project aims to stabilize the river in flood-prone areas and improve the state's disaster resilience.

PayU, NPCI introduce credit lines on UPI

- PayU has partnered with NPCI to enable merchants to accept digital payments via credit lines, anticipating significant growth in credit-based digital transactions.
- PayU aims to offer valuable insights to merchants regarding consumer credit types, facilitating tailored growth strategies and enhanced customer experiences. This initiative reflects PayU's commitment to innovation and enhancing financial flexibility for customers.

LIC launches 'Amritbaal' insurance for children

- The Life Insurance Corporation of India (LIC) has announced the launch of a new non-participating product called 'Amritbaal', specifically designed for children.
- 'Amritbaal' is a Non-Linked, Non-Participating, Individual, Savings, Life Insurance Plan.
- It aims to cater to the financial needs of children, particularly for their higher education and other requirements.

SBI launches digital enrolment for PMJJBY and PMSBY schemes

- The State Bank of India (SBI) has announced that individuals can now use the self-subscribing route to enroll in the Pradhan Mantri Jeevan Jyoti Bima Yojana (PMJJBY) and Pradhan Mantri Suraksha Bima Yojana (PMSBY) schemes.
- PMJJBY provides a death coverage of Rs 2,00,000 to the beneficiary of the policy in the event of the insured person's sudden demise.
- On the other hand, PMSBY is an accident insurance scheme that offers coverage for accidental death and disability resulting from an accident.
- These schemes are part of the government's initiatives to provide affordable insurance coverage to citizens, particularly those in the economically vulnerable segments of society.

SIDBI Releases Impact Study 'Prabhaav' on startup fund

- The Small Industries Development Bank of India (SIDBI) recently revealed the impact assessment report of the Fund of Funds for Startups (FFS).
- This assessment was conducted by CRISIL, a leading analytics company in India known for its expertise in Alternative Investment Fund (AIF) benchmarking.
- The report, named Prabhaav, was unveiled by SIDBI. The Fund of Funds for Startups (FFS) is a vital component of the Startup India Action Plan initiated by Prime Minister Narendra Modi in 2016.

Yes Bank conducts first export finance transaction on ITFS platform

- Yes Bank became the first Indian bank to execute an export finance transaction on the International Trade Financing Services Platform (ITFS) of RXIL Global IFSC Limited (RXIL).
- This strategic partnership facilitates arranging credit for exporters and importers from both Indian and Global Institutions through Factoring, Forfaiting, and other trade financing services at competitive pricing with quick turnaround using a digital platform.
- This is the first transaction on the ITFS platform in collaboration with any bank in India.

ICICI Bank Canada launches 'Money2India (Canada)' app

- ICICI Bank Canada announces the launch of its mobile banking app, 'Money2India (Canada)'.
- The app enables customers of any bank in Canada to send money instantly and round the clock to any bank in India without opening an account with ICICI Bank Canada.
- The launch of 'Money2India (Canada)' app marks ICICI Bank Canada's foray into Canada's remittance market.

DLabs at ISB launches 'Build for Billions'

- Hyderabad Based DLabs at the Indian School of Business (ISB) launched 'Build for Billions' in partnership with Reserve Bank Innovation Hub (RBIH) and Union Bank of India.
- It aims to address livelihood issues for gig workers, migrant workers, domestic workers, street vendors, carpenters, plumbers, electricians, and construction laborers.

SBI Introduced Green Term Deposits Denominated In Rupees

- State Bank of India (SBI) has launched SBI Green Rupee Term Deposit (SGRTD) in an effort to raise money for projects and activities that promote the environment and help India's green finance ecosystem flourish.
- Green term deposits are open to resident individuals, non-individuals and non-resident Indians as well, through a branch network.
- SBI's green offering has tenors of 111 days, 1,777 days and 2,222 days.

AI startup Krutrim became India's first unicorn in 2024

- Krutrim, an AI startup founded by Bhavish Aggarwal, the CEO of Ola, has indeed become India's first AI unicorn in 2024.
- Krutrim secured $50 million in funding. Matrix Partners India and other notable investors led the investment.
- This funding round valued Krutrim at an impressive $1 billion, making it India's first AI unicorn.

LIC unveiled 'Jeevan Dhara II' deferred annuity plan

- LIC has launched a new plan named "Jeevan Dhara II". It is a non-linked, non-participating, individual, savings, deferred annuity plan.
- The policyholder has the option to choose the mode of premium payment, deferment period, annuity option, and mode of annuity payment.
- Annuity rates are guaranteed at the inception of the policy and annuities are payable post Deferment Period in arrears throughout the lifetime of Annuitant(s) as per the Annuity Option chosen.

NSE retains position as the world's largest exchange in 2023

- The National Stock Exchange of India (NSE) retained its position as the world's largest derivatives exchange for the fifth consecutive year in 2023.
- NSE is ranked 3rd in the world in the equity segment by the number of trades (electronic order book) in 2023, as per the statistics maintained by the World Federation of Exchanges (WFE).
- The year also saw record high turnover on a single day in the equity segment of Rs 167,942.47 crores on November 30, 2023, and Rs 381,623.12 crores on December 2, 2023, in the equity derivatives segment.

Centre forms 16th Finance Commission with Dr. Panagariya

- In January 2024, the Indian government formed the 16th Finance Commission under the chairmanship of Dr. Arvind Panagariya, former Vice Chairman of NITI Aayog.
- Key members include Ajay Narayan Jha, Annie George Mathew, Dr. Niranjan Rajadhyaksha, and Dr. Soumya Kanti Ghosh.
- The Finance Commission has been requested to make its report available by 31st of October, 2025 covering five years commencing on the 1st of April, 2026.

Ola Electric first EV company to get PLI approval

- Ola Electric becomes the first Indian e-scooter company to be eligible for the government's production-linked incentive (PLI) scheme.
- The PLI certification is expected to provide financial benefits of INR 15,000 to 18,000 per unit, potentially enhancing the affordability of electric vehicles.
- The Ministry of Heavy Industries has approved Ola Electric's eligibility after a four-month-long process.

India's GDP growth seen at 6.2% in '24: UN report

- The United Nations has released a new report World Economic Situation and Prospects 2024 which states that India's gross domestic product (GDP) growth for the 2024 calendar year will remain at 6.2 per cent, compared to 6.7 per cent earlier.
- Key finding of the report: The reports project a lower global GDP growth rate of an estimated 2.4 percent in 2024, down from 2.7 percent in 2023.
- This is attributed to lingering risks and uncertainties surrounding the Russia-Ukraine war, the conflict in Palestine, and the decisions of several developed economies to keep interest rates higher for longer.

SEBI allows short-selling by all investors

- Securities and Exchange Board of India (SEBI) allows short-selling for all investor categories but prohibits naked short-selling
- All stocks in the futures and options segment are eligible for short-selling
- Institutional investors cannot engage in day trading and all transactions will be grossed at the custodian level
- Securities Lending and Borrowing (SLB) scheme will be implemented simultaneously with institutional investor short selling

PFC gets RBI nod for GIFT City finance firm

- Power Finance Corporation (PFC) has received approval from the Reserve Bank of India (RBI) to set up a wholly-owned finance company in the GIFT City in Gujarat.
- The new entity at the International Financial Services Centre (IFSC) is expected to offer new business opportunities for PFC and contribute to the growth of the country's power sector.
- PFC aims to leverage the conducive environment for international lending activities and world-class infrastructure provided by GIFT City to establish its global presence and expand its business opportunities.

DPIIT organises Startup India Innovation Week

- The Department for Promotion of Industry and Internal Trade (DPIIT) is organising the Startup India Innovation Week 2024 from 10th to 18th January 2024.
- The aim of the event is to bring together the country's startups, entrepreneurs, investors, policymakers, and other stakeholders.

Institutional investments in Indian real estate hit 5-year low

- According to data released by workplace solutions firm Vestian, Institutional investments in the Indian real estate sector fell to $4.3 billion in 2023, a 12% decrease from 2022 and the lowest since 2019.
- Foreign investments dropped by 30% to $2.7 billion, with their share in total investment falling from 79% to 65%.
- Domestic investments more than doubled to $1.5 billion, with their share increasing to 35% in 2023.

Paytm to invest Rs 100 cr in GIFT City

- One97 Communications, the parent company of Paytm, plans to invest Rs 100 crore in Gujarat International Finance Tec-City (GIFT City).
- The development center aims to build an artificial intelligence (AI)-driven cross-border remittance and payments technology system.

Govt announces ₹45,000 crore for river cruise tourism

- The ministry of ports, shipping, and waterways has announced a ₹45,000 crore investment to develop river cruise tourism.
- This investment includes ₹35,000 crore for cruise vessels and ₹10,000 crore for cruise terminal infrastructure by 2047.
- To enhance inland waterways for cargo trade, a ₹15,200 crore investment was agreed upon at the Global Maritime India Summit (GMIS), held in Mumbai in October last year.
- Sonowal launched the 'Harit Nauka' guidelines and 'River Cruise Tourism Roadmap, 2047' at the IWDC.

Indian Bank launches a co-branded credit card

- Indian Bank has partnered with FPL Technologies to launch the Indian Bank One co-branded credit card.
- The card utilizes both Visa and RuPay platforms, issued by Indian Bank and managed by FPL Technologies.
- It features international validity with a 1% forex fee, catering to digitally savvy Indian consumers.

USIDFC and NIIF to set up $1 billion renewable energy fund

- In January 2024, the United States International Development Finance Corporation (USIDFC) and India's National Investment and Infrastructure Fund (NIIF) announced a joint initiative to set up a $1 billion fund for renewable energy projects in India.
- USIDFC committed $500 million to First Solar's 3.5 GW solar module plant and $425 million to Tata Power's upcoming solar module plant in Tamil Nadu.
- NIIF is an investment platform for international and Indian investors managed by the Government of India, with over $44.9 billion of equity capital commitments across its four funds.

Simmtech to set up ₹1,250 crore semiconductor unit

- South Korea-based Simmtech has signed an MoU with the Gujarat Government to invest over Rs 1,250 crore in the state, aiming to support Micron's semiconductor plant.
- The MoU was exchanged in the presence of Union Minister of IT and Electronics Ashwini Vaishnaw and Gujarat Chief Minister Bhupendra Patel.

ONGC Videsh and IOC launch Global Treasury Centres

- Public Sector Companies like ONGC Videsh Ltd and Indian Oil Corporation have launched their respective Global Treasury Centres at GIFT City to manage international assets and raise funds.
- The ONGC Videsh Ltd treasury centre will manage operations of over 25 subsidiaries and raise close to $4 billion, while the Indian Oil Corporation is expected to raise over $5 billion from the GIFT IFSC.

Digital Connexion launches MAA10 data centre in Chennai

- Digital Connexion, a joint venture involving Reliance Industries Ltd, Canada's Brookfield Asset Management, and Digital Realty, has unveiled its first data centre campus in Chennai.
- The data centre, MAA10, offers 20 Mw of IT load in its first phase and is designed for scalable growth, catering to various customer needs.
- The company has already begun work on the second phase of the Chennai data centre and has also purchased land in Mumbai for a 40 Mw facility.

NDB provides $500 million loan to Gujarat

- Shanghai-headquartered New Development Bank (NDB) signed an agreement for providing a $500-million loan to the Gujarat government.
- The funds will be utilized for the construction of approximately 1,200 kilometers of roads, enhancing connectivity and accessibility in Gujarat.

L&T wins Mumbai-Ahmedabad high-speed rail project

- In January 2024, Larsen & Toubro (L&T) won a significant contract to build the electrification system for the Mumbai-Ahmedabad High-Speed Rail (MAHSR) project.
- This project, also known as the Bullet Train Project, involves constructing a 508 km route with trains running at speeds up to 320 km/h.
- The contract, awarded by the National High-Speed Rail Corporation Limited (NHSRCL), includes design, supply, and installation of a 25 kV power supply system.
- This project is funded by the Japan International Cooperation Agency (JICA).

Gujarat, Kerala, Karnataka best in startup ecosystems

- The Department for Promotion of Industry and Internal Trade (DPIIT) released the States' startup ranking for 2022.
- According to the ranking Gujarat, Kerala and Karnataka have emerged as the best-performing States in developing startup ecosystems for budding entrepreneurs.
- Tamil Nadu, Himachal Pradesh, Maharashtra, Odisha, and Telangana are also categorized as top performers.

GIFT City, IGX, GSPC collaborate on hydrogen trading

- The International Financial Services Centre (IFSC) at GIFT City has announced a strategic collaboration with the Indian Gas Exchange (IGX) and Gujarat State Petroleum Corporation (GSPC).
- This initiative, set to be the second of its kind in the world, positions GIFT City as a leader in the emerging green hydrogen economy.
- The collaboration aims to create a global hydrogen price index to enhance transparency, bolster investor confidence, and facilitate the global growth of the green hydrogen market.

Tata retains IPL title sponsorship for 5 more years

- Tata Sons retains IPL title sponsorship rights from 2024 to 2028 by matching Aditya Birla Group's bid of Rs 2500 crores, i.e. Rs 500 crore per year
- Board of Control for Cricket in India (BCCI) released the tender for title sponsorship rights for IPL seasons 2024-2028 and set the base price at Rs 1,750 crore over five years, or Rs 350 crore per year for 74 matches.
- BCCI recommends bidders apply for 84 and 94 matches at base prices of Rs 375 crore and Rs 400 crore, respectively

TCS is world's 2nd most valuable IT brand

- According to the Brand Finance 2024 research, Accenture, Tata Consultancy Services (TCS), and Infosys have the highest brand values in the IT sector.
- With a noteworthy 11% increase in brand value, reaching $19.2 billion, TCS takes second place.
- Out of all worldwide IT giants, TCS has experienced the largest absolute gain in brand value, increasing by about $2 billion over the previous year's $17.2 billion.

RBI fines Dhanlaxmi Bank, ESAF, Punjab and Sind Bank

- On 12 January 2024, The Reserve Bank of India (RBI) imposed monetary penalties against ESAF Small Finance Bank, Dhanlaxmi Bank, and Punjab and Sind Bank over various non-compliances.
- It has levied Rs 1.2 crore on private sector Dhankaxmi Bank for three violations.
- The central bank has imposed Rs 1 crore on state-owned Punjab & Sind Bank for violating lending rules.
- ESAF Small Finance Bank will have to pay Rs 30 lakh for deficiencies in customer service.

Major UPI apps enabled for Singapore remittances

- Indians can now receive remittances from Singapore directly into their bank accounts on a real-time basis through major UPI and bank apps, like SBI, Axis Bank, and ICICI Bank, the National Payments Corporation of India (NPCI).
- This facility can be accessed by users of BHIM, PhonePe, and Paytm apps.
- The new functionality is set to enable Indians to receive remittances from Singapore-based Indian diaspora directly into their bank accounts.

IndusInd Bank launches 'Samman RuPay Credit Card'

- On 9 January 2024, IndusInd Bank announced the launch of the UPI-enabled 'IndusInd Bank Samman RuPay Credit Card', in collaboration with National Payments Corporation of India (NPCI).
- This credit card is specially designed for government sector employees.

FILL IN THE BLANKS

1. In July 2024, __________ launched the 'Union Premier' branches for high-value customers in rural and semi-urban markets.
2. In July 2024, __________ raised India's growth forecast to 7% for 2024-25.
3. Recently, __________ launched the Amrit Vrishti 444 Day Term Deposit with a 25% interest rate.
4. __________ approved loans worth $240.5 million for rooftop solar systems in India.
5. __________ partnered with IDFC First Bank recently to boost bancassurance in India.
6. India signed a $500 million agreement with __________ for the Green National Highway Corridor project.
7. __________ is appointed as the new MD of SBI.
8. __________ was recently declared the best bank of India for 2024 by Global Finance Magazine.

GAME AND PUZZLE

Across

1. RBI's quarterly survey for manufacturing policy input
4. City where the 31st Annual Best Bank Awards were held on 27th October 2024
6. Association recognized by the RBI as a Self-Regulatory Organization for the FinTech sector
8. Company approved by NPCI to onboard new UPI users after a nine-month ban by RBI

Down

2. Bank that introduced the "Avni" savings account for women
3. First digital solution for MSME instant financing, launched by SBI
5. Company that overtook Apple to become the world's most valuable company in October 2024
7. ICICI Lombard's AI-powered health insurance product launched in 2024

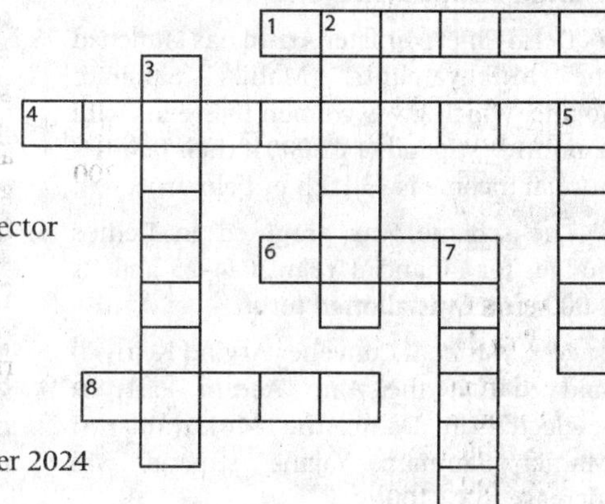

SCAN TO GET MULTIPLE CHOICE QUESTIONS

Scan Me

Answer Key (Fill In The Blanks):

1. Union Bank of India 2. IMF (International Monetary Fund) 3. State Bank of India (SBI) 4. Asian Development Bank (ADB) 5. LIC (Life Insurance Corporation) 6. World Bank 7. Rama Mohan Rao Amara 8. State Bank of India (SBI)

Answer Key (Game and Puzzle):

1. OBICUS 2. Bandhan 3. MSME Sahaj 4. Washington 5. Nvidia 6. FACE 7. Elevate 8. Paytm

Delhi CM launched 'Mukhyamantri Mahila Samman Yojana'

- Delhi Chief Minister Atishi has launched the Mukhyamantri Mahila Samman Yojana, which gives women living in Delhi a monthly stipend of ₹1,000 if their family's annual income is ₹3 lakh or below.
- The scheme was proposed in Delhi's budget for Financial Year 2024-25 and Rs 2,000 crore was allotted for it.
- AAP National Convener Arvind Kejriwal said that if the Aam Aadmi Party is re-elected in Delhi, the Mukhyamantri Mahila Samman Yojana stipend will increase to ₹2,100.

Kejriwal launches 'Sanjeevani Yojana' for free elderly healthcare in Delhi

- AAP National Convener Arvind Kejriwal announced the 'Sanjeevani Yojana', which will cater to all senior citizens in the national capital.
- The scheme is designed to provide free treatment to Delhi's elderly residents aged 60 and above.
- There is no upper limit on the treatment amount under Sanjeevani Yojana.

Assam CM attends Bhutan's 117th National Day

- Assam Chief Minister Himanta Biswa Sarma attended Bhutan's 117th National Day celebration on 17 December 2024 at Thimphu, the capital of Bhutan.
- This day marks the coronation of the first King of Bhutan, Druk Gyalpo Ugyen Wangchuck, on December 17, 1907.
- In Bhutan, the official title of the King is Druk Gyalpo, which means Dragon King in Dzongkha.
- Assam, Arunachal Pradesh, West Bengal and Sikkim share a land border with Bhutan.

West Bengal CM launched "Banglar Bari" scheme

- West Bengal Chief Minister Mamata Banerjee has launched the "Banglar Bari" scheme to provide houses for the state's rural poor.
- Ms. Banerjee distributed funds to 42 beneficiaries in 21 districts, and over 1.2 million people in the state are eligible for the first installment.
- Under the scheme, each family will receive a total of ₹1.20 lakh for building a house, with ₹60,000 given in the first installment. However, beneficiaries in some areas of Jangalmahal and the Darjeeling hills will receive ₹1.30 lakh.

Uttarakhand to implement Uniform Civil Code from January 2025

- Uttarakhand Chief Minister Pushkar Singh Dhami announced that the state will implement the Uniform Civil Code (UCC) in January 2025.
- Uttarakhand will be first state in the country to implement the UCC since Independence.
- For this, a five-member expert committee was formed under the chairmanship of retired judge Ranjana Prakash Desai.

Google To Set Up Its India's First Safety Engineering Centre In Hyderabad

- On 4th December 2024, Google announced the launch of its first Safety Engineering Centre (GSEC) in Hyderabad.
- GSEC in Hyderabad would be the first of its kind in the APAC region, after Tokyo, and only the fifth in the world, with similar facilities in Dublin, Munich, and Malaga.
- It will focus on cutting-edge research, AI-driven security solutions, and fostering collaboration among cybersecurity experts.

Devendra Fadnavis sworn in as 18th of Maharashtra

- On 5th December 2024, Governor C.P. Radhakrishnan administered the oath of office and secrecy to Devendra Fadnavis in the presence of Prime Minister Narendra Modi, several Union Ministers, and Chief Ministers and Deputy Chief Ministers of NDA-ruled States.
- Eknath Shinde and Ajit Pawar were sworn in as Deputy Chief Ministers, underscoring the balance of power within the alliance.
- The Mahayuti alliance, comprising the BJP, Shiv Sena (led by Eknath Shinde), and Ajit Pawar's faction of the NCP, has won 235 out of 288 seats.
- The BJP emerged as the single largest party with 132 seats, followed by Shiv Sena with 57 seats, and NCP with 41 seats.

Odisha govt approved Rs 1.36 lakh Cr investment projects

- On 29th November 2024, the Odisha government approved 20 investment projects worth Rs 1.36 lakh crore.
- These projects, spanning sectors like steel, chemicals, green energy, and textiles, are expected to generate 74,350 jobs.

GEOGRAPHICAL INDICATION TAG 2024 LIST IN INDIA

GI Tagged Product	Type	State/UTs
Kutch Rogan Craft	Handicraft	Gujarat
Ambaji White Marble	Natural	Gujarat
Kutch Bandhani	Handicraft	Gujarat
Gharchola Craft of Gujarat	Handicraft	Gujarat
Gujarat Soof Embroidery	Handicraft	Gujarat
Ahmedabad Sodagari Block Print	Handicraft	Gujarat
Surat Sadeli Craft	Handicraft	Gujarat
Bharuch Sujani Weaving	Handicraft	Gujarat
Kutch Ajrakh	Handicraft	Gujarat
Arunachal Pradesh Apatani Textile	Handicraft	Arunachal Pradesh
Arunachal Pradesh Monpa Textile	Handicraft	Arunachal Pradesh
Arunachal Pradesh Nyishi Textile	Handicraft	Arunachal Pradesh
Arunachal Pradesh Monpa Handmade Paper	Handicraft	Arunachal Pradesh
Arunachal Pradesh Adi Textile	Handicraft	Arunachal Pradesh
Arunachal Pradesh Singpho Phalap (Singpho Tea)	Agricultural	Arunachal Pradesh and Assam
Arunachal Pradesh Galo Textile	Handicraft	Arunachal Pradesh
Arunachal Pradesh Adi Apong	Manufactured	Arunachal Pradesh
Arunachal Pradesh Dao (Sword)	Manufactured	Arunachal Pradesh
Arunachal Pradesh Angnyat Millet	Agricultural	Arunachal Pradesh
Arunachal Pradesh Marua Apo (Marua Millet Beverage)	Manufactured	Arunachal Pradesh
Arunachal Pradesh Tai Khamti Textile	Handicraft	Arunachal Pradesh
Narasapur Crochet Lace Products	Handicraft	Andhra Pradesh
Ratlam Riyawan Lahsun (Garlic)	Agricultural	Madhya Pradesh
Sawantwadi Ganjifa Cards	Handicraft	Maharashtra
Vasmat Haldi (Turmeric)	Agricultural	Maharashtra
Nandurbar Amchur	Agricultural	Maharashtra
Nandurbar Mirchi	Agricultural	Maharashtra
Miraj Tanpura	Handicraft	Maharashtra
Hupari Silver Craft	Handicraft	Maharashtra
Miraj Sitar	Handicraft	Maharashtra
Sawantwadi Wooden Craft	Handicraft	Maharashtra
Majuli Mask of Assam	Handicraft	Assam

GI Tagged Product	Type	State/UTs
Assam Majuli Manuscript Painting	Handicraft	Assam
Bodo Dokhona	Handicraft	Assam
Bodo Eri Silk	Handicraft	Assam
Bodo Jwmgra	Handicraft	Assam
Bodo Gamsa	Handicraft	Assam
Bodo Keradapini	Agricultural	Assam
Bodo Thorkha	Handicraft	Assam
Bodo Gongar Dunjia	Agricultural	Assam
Bodo Kham	Handicraft	Assam
Bodo Serja	Handicraft	Assam
Bodo Sifung	Handicraft	Assam
Bodo Khardwi	Agricultural	Assam
Bodo Gongona	Handicraft	Assam
Bodo Jotha	Handicraft	Assam
Assam Jaapi	Handicraft	Assam
Assam Asharikandi Terracotta Craft	Handicraft	Assam
Assam Bihu Dhol	Handicraft	Assam
Assam Pani Meteka Craft	Handicraft	Assam
Sarthebari Metal Craft	Handicraft	Assam
Patchwork of Rampur	Handicraft	Uttar Pradesh
Mathura Sanjhi Craft	Handicraft	Uttar Pradesh
Bundelkhand Kathiya Gehu (Wheat)	Agricultural	Uttar Pradesh and Madhya Pradesh
Banaras Tabla	Handicraft	Uttar Pradesh
Banaras Lal Bharwamirch	Agricultural	Uttar Pradesh
Pilibhit Bansuri	Handicraft	Uttar Pradesh
Chiraigaon Karonda of Varanasi	Agricultural	Uttar Pradesh
Banaras Mural Painting	Handicraft	Uttar Pradesh
Banaras Lal Peda	Foodstuff	Uttar Pradesh
Banaras Shehnai	Handicraft	Uttar Pradesh
Sambhal Bone Craft	Handicraft	Uttar Pradesh
Moonj Craft of Uttar Pradesh	Handicraft	Uttar Pradesh
Chitrakoot Wooden Crafts & Toys	Handicraft	Uttar Pradesh
Jaunpur Imarti	Foodstuff	Uttar Pradesh
Banaras Thandai	Foodstuff	Uttar Pradesh
Pilkhuwa Hand Block Print Textile	Handicraft	Uttar Pradesh
Banaras Metal Casting Craft	Handicraft	Uttar Pradesh
Bareilly Cane & Bamboo Craft	Handicraft	Uttar Pradesh

GI Tagged Product	Type	State/UTs
Tharu Embroidery of Uttar Pradesh	Handicraft	Uttar Pradesh
Bareilly Zari Zardoji	Handicraft	Uttar Pradesh
Banaras Tirangi Barfi	Food Stuff	Uttar Pradesh
Tripura Risa Textile	Handicraft	Tripura
Tripura Pachra-Rignai	Handicraft	Tripura
Tripura Matabari Peda (Sweet)	Foodstuff	Tripura

GI Tagged Product	Type	State/UTs
Lakadong Turmeric	Agricultural	Meghalaya
Meghalaya Garo Textile	Handicraft	Meghalaya
Meghalaya Lyrnai Pottery	Handicraft	Meghalaya
Meghalaya Chubitchi	Manufactured	Meghalaya
Banglar Muslin	Handicraft	West Bengal
Cuttack Rupa Tarakasi (Silver Filigree)	Handicraft	Odisha
Hyderabad Lac Bangles	Handicraft	Telangana

Gujarat's traditional handicraft Gharchola received GI tag

- On 29th November 2024, Gujarat's traditional handicraft Gharchola received the Geographical Indication (GI) tag from the Union government.
- This recognition took Gujarat's total GI tags to 27, with 23 in the handicraft sector.
- The GI tag was presented at the **"GI and Beyond - Virasat Se Vikas Tak"** program in New Delhi.

Hemant Soren took oath as the 14th CM of Jharkhand

- On 28th November 2024, Hemant Soren took the oath as the 14th Chief Minister of Jharkhand at Ranchi's Morabadi Ground.
- The ceremony, administered by Governor Santosh Kumar Gangwar, was attended by key leaders from the INDIA bloc, including Rahul Gandhi and Mamata Banerjee.
- Soren's JMM-led alliance secured 56 out of 81 seats in the assembly, marking his fourth term as Chief Minister.

Nayab Singh Saini sworn in as 11th CM of Haryana

- On 17th October 2024, Nayab Singh Saini was sworn in as the Chief Minister of Haryana for the second time, following the BJP's historic third consecutive term win in the state elections. The BJP secured 48 out of 90 seats.

- Nayab Singh Saini took oath for the first time as the Chief Minister of Haryana in March 2024.

Omar Abdullah sworn in as Chief Minister of Jammu and Kashmir

- On 16th October 2024, Omar Abdullah took the oath of office as the Chief Minister of Jammu and Kashmir at the Sher-i-Kashmir International Convention Centre (SKICC) in Srinagar.
- This marks his second term as Chief Minister, following his previous tenure from 2009 to 2015.
- Omar Abdullah, a prominent leader of the National Conference (NC), was elected after the NC secured a majority in the recent assembly elections.

Gujarat launched its new Cottage and Rural Industries Policy 2024-29

- On 27th November 2024, Gujarat launched its new Cottage and Rural Industries Policy 2024-29 in Gandhinagar.
- The policy aims to create 12 lakh jobs over the next five years by providing increased loans up to Rs 25 lakh and subsidies up to Rs 3.75 lakh for artisans and entrepreneurs.

Delhi govt launched portal for Old-Age Pension Scheme

- On 26th November 2024, the Delhi government launched a dedicated portal for its Old-Age Pension Scheme to streamline applications for senior citizens.
- The scheme provides ₹2,000/month for individuals aged 60-69 and ₹2,500/month for those aged 70+ or SC/ST/minorities beneficiaries aged 60-69.

Andhra Pradesh govt abolished the garbage tax

- In November 2024, the Andhra Pradesh government abolished the garbage tax, following a bill introduced by Municipal Administration Minister P. Narayana.
- It was initially introduced by the YSRCP government to fund waste collection services. The tax faced criticism for lack of public consultation.

Jammu and Kashmir celebrated its 1st Constitution Day

- On 26th November 2024, Jammu & Kashmir celebrated its first Constitution Day since 1950.
- This historic event followed the abrogation of Article 370 in 2019, integrating the region fully into India.

Tamil Nadu reported a 20.12% growth in SGST collections

- In November 2024, Tamil Nadu reported a 20.12% growth in State Goods and Services Tax (SGST) collections for the fiscal year 2024-25.
- Provisional figures from the Comptroller and Auditor-General of India (CAG) indicate collections reached ₹35,414.05 crore, up from ₹29,481.97 crore the previous year.

Telangana to establish Joint Consultative Committee with CII

- On 22nd November 2024, the Telangana government announced the formation of a Joint Consultative Committee with the Confederation of Indian Industry (CII).
- The committee aims to address industrial challenges in the state. It includes the Special Chief Secretary for Industries and CII leaders.

UP govt unveiled plans for Lucknow's 1st night safari

- In November 2024, the Uttar Pradesh government unveiled plans for Lucknow's first night safari, set to open by December 2026.
- The safari, spanning 900 acres in the Kukrail forest, will feature themed sections like Indian Walking Trail and African Wetland. Attractions include sky cycling, a 5.5-km tramway, and a 7D theatre.

Telangana govt announced 100% tax exemption for EVs

- On 18th November 2024, the Telangana government announced a 100% tax exemption on road tax and registration fees for electric vehicles (EVs) until December 31, 2026.
- This policy covers two-wheelers, four-wheelers, three-wheelers, and electric buses, aiming to boost EV adoption and reduce air pollution, especially in urban areas like Hyderabad.
- The initiative is part of Telangana's broader Electric Vehicle and Energy Storage Policy 2020-2030.

Gujarat launched its 1st dedicated Semiconductor Policy (2022-27)

- On 8th November 2024, Gujarat launched its first dedicated Semiconductor Policy (2022-2027) to boost economic growth.
- Key projects include Micron's Rs 22,500 crore ATMP plant in Sanand and Tata Electronics' Rs 91,000 crore AI-enabled fabrication facility in Dholera.

Uttarakhand CM unveiled new sports initiatives

- On 12th November 2024, Uttarakhand Chief Minister Pushkar Singh Dhami unveiled new sports initiatives worth ₹13.78 crore.
- The projects include the development of the Panna Lal Bhalla Cricket Stadium (₹9.05 crore), electrical facade beautification of Dam Kothi and Chandi Devi Bridges (₹1.43 crore and ₹3.30 crore respectively).

Bengaluru Unveiled Its First Digital Population Clock

- On 8th November 2024, Bengaluru unveiled its first digital population clock at the Institute for Social and Economic Change (ISEC). It was developed in collaboration with the Union Ministry of Health and Family Welfare (MoHFW).
- This initiative aims to enhance awareness of population dynamics.

Telangana launched statewide caste census

- The Telangana government launched a statewide caste census on 6th November 2024.
- This comprehensive survey, the first since 1931, aims to collect data on social, educational, economic, employment, political, and caste dynamics across 1.17 crore households.

UP govt to boost veterinary services with New Policy

- The Uttar Pradesh government introduced a new policy on 4th November 2024, to enhance veterinary services in rural areas.
- The policy will be implemented in both government and private institutions, with support from key veterinary colleges in the state.

Madhya Pradesh cabinet approved 35% job reservation for women in state services

- The Madhya Pradesh cabinet, led by Chief Minister Mohan Yadav, approved a 35% job reservation for women in state services on 5th November 2024.
- This decision, increasing the previous 33% quota, aims to promote gender equality and empower women.

Zero Waste initiative started in Rajasthan Village

- On 29th October 2024, the village of Aandhi in Jaipur, Rajasthan, launched a pioneering zero-waste initiative using green technology.
- The project includes an Organic Waste Bio-Methanation Plant, Vermifiltration Technology, Constructed Wetlands, and a Resource Recovery Center.

Kaziranga National Park declared India's 2nd butterfly diversity hub

- In October 2024, Kaziranga National Park was declared India's second butterfly diversity hub with over 446 species recorded.
- This achievement follows years of research by Dr. Monsoon Jyoti Gogoi, who highlighted the park's rich butterfly diversity during the first-ever Butterfly Conservation Meet-2024.
- The park now ranks second in butterfly species diversity among India's protected areas, after Namdapha National Park.

Barda Wildlife Sanctuary inaugurated in Gujarat

- In October 2024, the Barda Wildlife Sanctuary and the Barda Jungle Safari were inaugurated in Gujarat.
- The sanctuary spans approximately 192 square kilometers and features diverse flora and fauna, including 368 plant species and 22 mammal species.

Bihar's first Inland Container Depot Inaugurated in Bihta

- In October 2024, Bihar's first Inland Container Depot (ICD) was inaugurated in Bihta by Bihar Industries Minister Nitish Mishra.
- The facility, developed by Pristine Magadh Infrastructure, aims to boost logistics through warehousing, customs services, and multi-modal transport.

Haryana: 1st state to implement Dalit sub-quotas

- In October 2024, Haryana became the first state to implement Dalit sub-quotas.
- Following a Supreme Court ruling, the state government divided Scheduled Castes (SCs) into two groups: Deprived Scheduled Castes (DSC) and Other Scheduled Castes (OSC).
- Each group will now receive 50% of the 20% SC quota in government jobs, aiming to better represent disadvantaged communities.

Saharanpur, Rewa, and Ambikapur Airports launched by PM Modi

- On 20th October 2024, Prime Minister Narendra Modi inaugurated three new airports in Saharanpur (Uttar Pradesh), Rewa (Madhya Pradesh), and Ambikapur (Chhattisgarh) under the Regional Connectivity Scheme (RCS) – UDAN.
- The RCS-UDAN initiative, launched in 2016, focuses on improving infrastructure and connectivity in underserved regions of India.

Sanskrit to become Mandatory in 416 Uttarakhand Madrasas

- In November 2024, the Uttarakhand Madrasa Education Board (UMEB) proposed to make Sanskrit a mandatory subject in 416 registered madrassas across the state.

- The initiative, part of a broader effort to modernize madrasa education, aims to introduce Sanskrit for students from Classes 5 to 8.

Telangana appoints commission for SC Sub Classification

- On 12th October 2024, the Telangana government appointed a one-man commission, headed by retired Justice Shameem Akhtar, to study the sub-classification of Scheduled Castes (SCs) for reservation benefits.
- This move follows a Supreme Court ruling and aims to ensure fair distribution of reservation benefits among different SC sub-groups.

Bihar gets approval for 2nd Tiger Reserve in Kaimur

- In November 2024, the central government has given its in-principle approval for Bihar's second tiger reserve in Kaimur district.
- It symbolizes the state's commitment to protecting biodiversity and supporting the growing tiger population.
- Kaimur's forests cover an area of 1,134 square kilometers, making them the largest in Bihar.

PM Modi inaugurated the Banjara Virasat Museum

- On 5th October 2024, Prime Minister Narendra Modi inaugurated the Banjara Virasat Museum in Poharadevi, Maharashtra.
- The four-story museum has 13 galleries depicting the Banjara legacy through the portraits of Banjara community leaders and the Banjara movement.
- Sant Sevalal and Sant Ramrao Maharaj are the spiritual leaders of the Banjara community.

UP CM Unveils New Multi-Coloured Logo for Mahakumbh 2025 in Prayagraj

- On 6th October 2024, Uttar Pradesh Chief Minister Yogi Adityanath unveiled the new multi-coloured logo for Mahakumbh 2025 in Prayagraj.
- The logo symbolizes religious and economic prosperity, featuring the Amrit Kalash, a sacred vessel from the mythological ocean churning, along with a temple, a seer, an urn, the Akshayvat tree, and an image of Lord Hanuman.
- Kumbh Mela is recognised by the UNESCO as an 'Intangible Cultural Heritage of Humanity'.

Odisha conducted its first-ever leopard census

- On 3rd October 2024, Odisha conducted its first-ever leopard census, revealing a population of 696 leopards.
- The independent count, conducted by the state's Forest Department, used camera traps and other tracking methods.
- The census highlighted an increase from the previous count of 568 leopards in 2022 by the National Tiger Conservation Authority (NTCA).

Telangana CM launches 'Digital Family Cards' on pilot basis

- In October 2024, Telangana Chief Minister A. Revanth Reddy launched the Digital Family Cards on a pilot basis in Hyderabad.
- This initiative aims to digitize family records, making it easier for citizens to access and update their family information.

Prashant Kishore officially launched the Jan Suraj Party

- On 2nd October 2024, election strategist-turned-politician Prashant Kishore officially launched the Jan Suraj Party in Patna.
- Kishore appointed former diplomat Manoj Bharti as the working president. The Bihar State Assembly elections are scheduled in 2025.

CM Nitish Kumar inaugurated newly constructed Bapu Tower in Patna

- On 2nd October 2024, Bihar Chief Minister Nitish Kumar inaugurated the newly constructed Bapu Tower in Patna on Mahatma Gandhi's birth anniversary.
- The seven-storeyed, funnel-shaped building, constructed at a cost of ₹129 crore, features galleries showcasing Gandhi's life and work.

Delhi Government increases minimum wages for workers

- On 25th September 2024, the Delhi government announced an increase in minimum wages for workers, effective from 1 October.
- The new rates are ₹18,066 for unskilled workers, ₹19,929 for semi-skilled workers, and ₹21,917 for skilled workers.

West Bengal government shuts down Kolkata's iconic tram service

- On 24th September 2024, the West Bengal government announced the discontinuation of Kolkata's iconic tram service, except for a heritage route from Esplanade to Maidan.
- Introduced by the British in 1873, Kolkata's trams were the last of their kind in India.

Mankidia community becomes 6th PVTG to get Habitat Rights over forests in Odisha

- On 22nd September 2024, the Mankidia community in Odisha's Mayurbhanj district received habitat rights under the Forest Rights Act, 2006.
- This recognition makes them the sixth Particularly Vulnerable Tribal Group (PVTG) in the state to gain such rights.

Maharashtra govt renames Pune Airport as 'Jagadguru Sant Tukaram Maharaj International Airport'

- On 23rd September 2024, the Maharashtra government approved renaming Pune Airport to Jagadguru Sant Tukaram Maharaj Pune International Airport.

- This honours the 17th-century saint and poet, Sant Tukaram Maharaj, known for his contributions to the Bhakti movement through his devotional poetry, Abhanga.

Uttarakhand enacts landmark Property Damage Recovery Act

- In September 2024, Uttarakhand enacted the Public and Private Property Damage Recovery (Ordinance) Act, 2024.
- This landmark legislation aims to recover costs from individuals responsible for damaging public and private property during protests, strikes, and riots.

President Murmu Appointd Atishi as Delhi's 8th Chief Minister

- On 21st September 2024, Atishi Marlena was sworn in as the new Chief Minister of Delhi, succeeding Arvind Kejriwal.
- Atishi, a senior AAP leader and former Education and PWD Minister, is the third woman to hold this position in Delhi.

Jagdeep Dhankhar Inaugurated 'Samvidhan Mandir' in Maharashtra

- On 15th September 2024, Vice President Jagdeep Dhankhar inaugurated the "Samvidhan Mandir" at 433 Industrial Training Institutes across Maharashtra.
- This initiative, organized by the Maharashtra Skill, Employment, Entrepreneurship, and Innovation Department, aims to promote constitutional literacy among students.

Nagaland Govt approved the implementation of the Inner Line Permit system

- Nagaland State Government has approved the implementation of the Inner Line Permit (ILP) in Chumoukedima, Niuland, and Dimapur districts.
- The decision to implement ILP in these three districts was taken during a Cabinet meeting held on 11th September 2024, under the chairmanship of Chief Minister Neiphiu Rio.

MP govt constitutes delimitation commission for fresh demarcation of Divisions, Districts and Tehsils

- On 9th September 2024, the Madhya Pradesh government constituted a delimitation commission to re-examine and redraw the boundaries of Divisions, Districts, and Tehsils.
- The initiative seeks to rationalize boundaries for better governance and public convenience, particularly in large districts like Sagar, Ujjain, Indore, and Dhar.

UP govt hosted SEMICON India 2024 at India Expo Mart

- The Uttar Pradesh government hosted SEMICON India 2024 at the India Expo Mart in Greater Noida from 11th to 13th September 2024.
- Inaugurated by Prime Minister Narendra Modi, the event aimed to position India as a global semiconductor hub.
- SEMI, in collaboration with München India and with the support of the Union Ministry of Information Technology (MeitY), has organised the SEMICON India 2024 exhibition and conference.
- The theme was 'Shaping the Semiconductor Future'.

8 Railway Stations in Lucknow division renamed

- On 28th August 2024, eight railway stations in the Lucknow division of Northern Railways were officially renamed to honour saints and freedom fighters. The stations and their new names are:
  - Kasimpur Halt is now Jais City.
  - Jais is now Guru Gorakhnath Dham.
  - Misrauli is now Maa Kalikan Dham.
  - Bani is now Swami Paramhans.
  - Nihalgarh is now Maharaja Bijli Pasi.
  - Akbarganj is now Maa Ahorva Bhawani Dham.
  - Wazirganj Halt is now Amar Shaheed Bhale Sultan.
  - Fursatganj is now Tapeshwarnath Dham.

Rajasthan and Madhya Pradesh to develop 'Shri Krishna Gaman Path'

- On 26th August 2024, Rajasthan and Madhya Pradesh announced a joint initiative to develop the 'Shri Krishna Gaman Path'.
- This religious circuit will connect Krishna's birthplace, Mathura, with Ujjain, tracing the historical journey of Lord Krishna.

BPCL launched drone-based afforestation project in Bihar

- On 21th August 2024, Bharat Petroleum Corporation Limited (BPCL) launched the 'Aranya' afforestation project in Bihar to plant 100,000 seedballs over 50 hectares using drone technology.
- The project targets three key forest regions: Umga Pahadi in the Madanpur Forest of Aurangabad, the Rajauli Forest Area in Nawada, and the Brahmyoni, Dungeshwari, Pretshila, and Barabar Hills in Gaya.

Registration of temples, mutts and trusts is mandatory in Bihar

- On 8th August 2024, the Bihar government mandated the registration of all unregistered temples, mutts, and trusts.
- District magistrates were instructed to ensure compliance and submit details of immovable assets to the Bihar State Board of Religious Trusts (BSBRT) for online listing.

Himachal govt approves 'Mukhya Mantri Sukh Shiksha Yojana'

- On 25th August 2024, the Himachal Pradesh government approved the Mukhya Mantri Sukh Shiksha Yojana, allocating Rs 53.21 crore annually to support vulnerable families.
- Eligible children will receive a monthly grant of Rs 1,000 for their educational, health, and nutritional needs until they turn 18.

Odisha Chief Minister announced Subhadra scheme

- In August 2024,Odisha Chief Minister Mohan Majhi announced the Subhadra scheme, which aims to empower women in the state. Under this scheme, one crore women aged between 21 and 60 will receive Rs 50,000 in installments over the next five years.
- The total budget allocated for the scheme is Rs 55,825 crore. Payments of Rs 10,000 annually will be made in two installments each year.

Nagaland becomes 1st state to implement disaster insurance

- On 8th August 2024, Nagaland became the first Indian state to implement a disaster management insurance scheme.
- The state signed an agreement with SBI General Insurance to launch the Disaster Risk Transfer Parametric Insurance Solution (DRTPS).

Union Minister announces new Peacock Sanctuaries in Karnataka and Kerala

- In August 2024, Union Minister for Environment, Forest, and Climate Change, Bhupender Yadav, announced the creation of two new Peacock Sanctuaries in India: Adichunchanagiri in Karnataka and Choolannuar in Kerala.

Haryana becomes first state to procure all crops at MSP

- In August 2024, the Haryana state government declared its intention to purchase all crops at the Minimum Support Price (MSP). It made Haryana the first state in the country to implement such a comprehensive MSP policy.
- This initiative expands the MSP coverage from 14 to 23 crops, providing farmers with a stable income and encouraging crop diversification.

Telangana CM announces ₹309 Crore Development Package for Kalwakurthy

- On 28th July 2024, Telangana Chief Minister A. Revanth Reddy announced a ₹309 crore development package for the Kalwakurthy Assembly constituency.
- The package includes a 50-bed mother and child hospital, a skill development center, a four-lane road, an R&B guest house, Panchayat Raj roads, high-level bridges, and infrastructure for government schools.

Bihar Assembly passed Anti-Paper Leak Bill to Combat Exam Malpractices

- On 24th July 2024, the Bihar Assembly passed the Bihar Public Examinations (Prevention of Unfair Means) Bill, 2024.
- The bill stipulates severe punishments for offenders, including a prison term of three to five years and a fine of ₹10 lakh.

J&K LG Manoj Sinha launched 'Hausla 2.0' and JK Startup Portal in Srinagar

- On 20th July 2024, Lieutenant Governor Manoj Sinha launched the 'Hausla 2.0' and JK Startup Portal in Srinagar.
- Building upon the success of Hausla 1.0, this initiative aims to enhance financial inclusion among women in Jammu and Kashmir by promoting entrepreneurship and facilitating market access.

UP Tourism booth inaugurated at Korea International Tourism Fair in Seoul

- On 20th July 2024, the ninth Korea International Tourism Fair commenced at Ilsan, northwest of Seoul, shining a spotlight on India's rich history and vibrant culture.
- The UP Tourism booth showcased the state's microcosm of heritage, including 42 UNESCO World Heritage Sites, with six in Uttar Pradesh. The fair fosters tourism growth and international collaboration.

Assam Ended 1935 Muslim Marriage Act

- In August 2024, the Assam Assembly passed the **Assam Repealing Bill, 2024,** which abolished the Assam Moslem Marriages and Divorces Registration Act of 1935 and the Assam Repealing Ordinance of 2024.
- The new legislation will ensure compulsory registration of Muslim marriages and eliminate the provision allowing minors' marriages to be registered by their guardians.

World's largest Ramayan Temple in Bihar

- The Viraat Ramayan Mandir is an under-construction Hindu temple complex located in the twin villages of Kaithawalia and Bahuara near Chakia in East Champaran district, Bihar, India.
- The temple is planned to be 123 meters (405 feet) high, double the height of Cambodia's Angkor Wat Hindu Temple.
- It will be completed by 2025-end at an estimated cost of ₹500 crore.

Rajasthan became first state to adopt a Road Safety Action Plan

- In July 2024, Rajasthan has taken a significant step by becoming the first Indian state to adopt a comprehensive 10-year Road Safety Action Plan.
- The plan aims to reduce road accidents by 50% by 2030. Developed in collaboration with the World Bank, it focuses on basic safety, safety behaviors, and advanced measures.

Jharkhand Mica Mines declared Child Labour Free

- In July 2024, the National Commission for Protection of Child Rights (NCPCR) declared the mica mines in Jharkhand as 'Child Labour Free'.
- This achievement is the result of collaborative efforts by the state, district, local governing bodies, the 'Child Labour Free Mica' program, children, and communities.
- Over 20,000 children who were previously involved in mica mining are now enrolled in schools, marking a generational change and promising a brighter future for these young lives.

Bihar's first transgender Sub-Inspectors make history

- Manvi Madhu Kashyap and two other transgender individuals have made history by becoming the first transwoman sub-inspectors in Bihar Police.
- Despite facing rejection and discrimination from coaching centers, Kashyap persevered and cleared the Bihar Police Subordinate Selection Commission (BPSSC) exams.

CM Manik Saha attended Kharchi Puja celebrations in Agartala

- In July 2024, Tripura Chief Minister Manik Saha participated in the Kharchi Puja celebration in Agartala. Kharchi Puja is one of the most popular festivals in Tripura, attracting thousands of pilgrims.
- The festival lasts for seven consecutive days, during which rituals, cultural programs, and a grand fair take place at the Chaturdash Devta Temple in old Agartala.

CM Adityanath inaugurated Uttar Pradesh Mango Festival

- On 12th July 2024, Uttar Pradesh Chief Minister Yogi Adityanath inaugurated the Uttar Pradesh Mango Festival 2024 at Awadh Shilp Gram.
- The state is set to export 40 tonnes of mangoes to Japan and Malaysia this year, with the iconic Dussehri mangoes from Lucknow making their debut in the United States.
- The festival features a mango exhibition showcasing 120 varieties of special mangoes, along with a mango-eating competition and a training seminar that has drawn mango farmers from U.P., Uttarakhand, Madhya Pradesh, Rajasthan, and Chhattisgarh.

East India's first Disabled Varsity at Ranchi

- In July 2024, Jharkhand government planned to establish its first university dedicated to the education and empowerment of disabled individuals in Ranchi.
- This significant development aims to address the longstanding educational gaps and challenges faced by people with disabilities in the region.

Uttar Pradesh launches 'Mitra Van' initiative along borders

- In July 2024, the Uttar Pradesh government, led by Chief Minister Yogi Adityanath, unveiled a major environmental initiative called 'Mitra Van' (Friendship Forest) as part of the Vriksharopan Jan Abhiyan-2024.
- This ambitious project aims to enhance greenery along the borders of Uttar Pradesh, including its international border with Nepal. Locations have been selected by 35 forest divisions for this purpose.

Tata Power launched 'Ghar Ghar Solar' initiative in Uttar Pradesh

- In July 2024, Tata Power Solar Systems Limited launched the 'Ghar Ghar Solar, Tata Power ke Sang' initiative in Uttar Pradesh (UP), starting from Varanasi. This transformative rooftop solar program aims to power every home in the state with clean energy.
- Residents can avail a maximum subsidy of up to ₹1,08,000 on rooftop solar installation. The subsidy includes ₹78,000 from the Central Government for up to 3 kW, and an additional ₹30,000 (₹15,000 per kW) from the State Government.

Maharashtra won Best Agriculture State Award for 2024

- In July 2024, Maharashtra was honored with the Best Agriculture State Award for 2024 by the 15th Agriculture Leadership Awards Committee.
- Maharashtra's innovative farming projects and efforts to improve rural areas contributed to this recognition. Notably, the state's economy, which constitutes 12.92% of India's GDP, relies significantly on agriculture and related industries.

Nagaland won Best State in Horticulture Award 2024

- Nagaland was honoured with the prestigious Agriculture Leadership Award 2024 for its outstanding performance in the field of horticulture. The award ceremony took place at the 15th Agriculture Leadership Conclave held in New Delhi on 10th July 2024.
- Salhoutuonuo Kruse, Minister for Women Resource Development & Horticulture, accepted the accolade on behalf of the state.

Madhya Pradesh CM launched 'Lokpath Mobile App' for road issues

- Madhya Pradesh Chief Minister Dr. Mohan Yadav recently launched the "Lokpath Mobile App" to address road issues reported by the public.
- The Lokpath Mobile App enhances transparency and accountability by allowing citizens to report road problems directly to officials.

Chief Minister Pramod Sawant launched the 'Goem Vinamulya Vij Yevjan' in Goa

- On 26th July 2024, Chief Minister Pramod Sawant launched the 'Goem Vinamulya Vij Yevjan' at the Secretariat in Porvorim, Goa.
- This initiative, organized by the Goa Energy Development Agency (GEDA), aims to boost solar energy adoption by providing free installation of residential solar power plants up to 5 kW for consumers using 400 units or less annually.

Rajiv Gandhi Civil Abhaya Hastham Scheme launched by Telangana

- On 20th July 2024, Telangana Chief Minister Sri A. Revanth Reddy launched the "Rajiv Gandhi Civils Abhayahastam" scheme.
- This initiative aims to support poor students with 1 lakh rupees who have passed the preliminary UPSC Civil Services Examination and wish to prepare for the main examination.

Maharashtra Chief Minister announced Ladla Bhai Yojana

- On 17th July 2024, the Maharashtra Chief Minister announced the launch of the "Ladla Bhai Yojana", also known as "Maza Ladka Bhau Yojana" to provide financial assistance to the state's youth who have passed 12th grade, diploma courses, or are graduates.
- Eligible youths will receive ₹6,000, ₹8,000, or ₹10,000 every month based on their educational qualification.

Haryana launched IT Saksham Yuva Scheme 2024

- On 13th July 2024, the Haryana government launched the IT Saksham Yuva Scheme 2024, aiming to create 5,000 jobs in its first phase.
- This initiative, part of the broader 'Mission 60,000,' targets youth from underprivileged backgrounds.

Madhya Pradesh topped best performing state in SVANidhi Scheme

- Madhya Pradesh has secured the first place under the **'Best Performing State'** category in the Prime Minister SVANidhi scheme.
- Launched in 2020, SVANidhi aids urban street vendors by providing collateral-free loans up to Rs 50,000. Assam ranks second in the same category.

Kagyed Dance Festival was Celebrated in Sikkim

- **Kagyed Dance Festival:** Celebrated annually in Sikkim at Tsuklakhang Palace, Gangtok.
- **Significance:** In honour of eight tantric gods and goddesses, the Kagyed.
- **Timing:** Held on the 28th and 29th day of the 10th month of the Tibetan Lunar Calendar (usually in December).
- **Activities:** Features traditional Lama dances and songs, attracting locals and tourists.
- **Conclusion:** Ends with burning effigies, symbolizing the triumph of good over evil.

Madhya Pradesh Named "Global Destination for 2025" by the Wall Street Journal

- Madhya Pradesh has been recognised by the Wall Street Journal as one of the "Go-To Global Destinations for 2025".
- It has 14 (3 permanent and 11 tentative) UNESCO World Heritage Sites, and 9 Tiger Reserves.
- With world-renowned sites like Khajuraho, Bandhavgarh National Park, and Pachmarhi, it offers a unique blend of history and nature.

New Campus of Nalanda University's Inaugurated

- **Location:** Rajgir, Bihar
- **Distance from Nalanda University Ruins:** 12 k.m
- **Inaugurated by:** Prime Minister of India
- **Date:** 19 June 2024
- **Attendees:** Governor of Bihar, Chief Minister of Bihar, Shri Nitish Kumar, External Affairs Minister Dr. S. Jaishankar, MoS for External Affairs, Shri Pabitra Margherita and Chancellor of the University, Prof. Aravind Panagariya

World's Tallest Ambedkar Statue Unveiled

- The Andhra Pradesh government unveiled the **world's tallest statue of BR Ambedkar**, known as the architect of the Indian Constitution, **in Vijayawada**.

- Standing 206 feet from the ground, the **'Statue of Social Justice'** statue will be in the list of the top 50 tallest statues in the world, which Sardar Vallabhai Patel's 'Statue of Unity' tops.

Amaravati as sole capital city of Andhra Pradesh

- June 2024, Andhra Pradesh Chief Minister, **N. Chandrababu Naidu** made a decisive announcement that Amaravati will be the sole capital of the state.
- As the first Chief Minister of bifurcated Andhra Pradesh from 2014 to 2019, Naidu initially proposed Amaravati as the capital city.

WEF's C4IR Inaugurated in Hyderabad

- The Telangana state government announced plans for a Life Sciences GCC Consortium, aiming to foster collaboration and innovation among life sciences companies in Hyderabad.
- They also launched the Centre for Fourth Industrial Revolution in Life Sciences (C4IR) in partnership with the World Economic Forum, focusing on healthcare and life sciences.

27th district of Arunachal Pradesh

- **Bichom**, carved out of West and East Kameng, became the **27th district** of Arunachal Pradesh.
- Chief Minister Pema Khandu inaugurated the district and laid the foundation of its **headquarters at Napangphung**.
- A total of 27 villages from West Kameng and 28 from East Kameng were made part of Bichom district.

Ambubachi Mela 2024 Concluded With Record Devotee

- The 4-day-long annual menstruation cycle of Maa Kamakhya, which was magnificently celebrated as Ambubachi Mela concludes on 26 January 2024.
- The temple doors, which had been closed since the start of the event on June 22, was opened on Tuesday (June 25) for the devotees.
- According to temple secretary Jnan Nath Sarma (Gyan), last year, the temple witnessed around 22 lakh devotees from across the world, however this year, the number reached up to 30 lakh.

India's First Eco - Friendly State Government Headquarters

- The Assam Secretariat inaugurated a 2.5 MW solar power project, making it India's first green state government headquarters.
- The project was installed at a cost of Rs 12.5 crore and is expected to save Rs 30 lakh in electricity bills monthly for the Assam Secretariat.
- Chief Minister Himanta Biswa Sarma highlighted the initiative as a significant step towards achieving a Net-Zero Government, emphasizing Assam's commitment to environmental sustainability and renewable energy.

"DRIMS" Platform for Disaster Management

- Assam has taken a significant step in disaster management by launching the **Disaster Reporting and Information Management System (DRIMS).**
- Developed in collaboration with UNICEF, DRIMS is a pioneering digital platform that facilitates online reporting of disaster-induced damages.
- Its primary objectives are precise damage assessment and swift disbursal of aid to those affected.

Kaji Nemu (Citrus Limon) as the 'State Fruit'

- The Assam government has officially declared **'Kaji Nemu' (Citrus Limon),** commonly known as citrus lemon, as the **state fruit of Assam**.
- Assam Chief Minister Himanta Biswa Sarma highlighted the unique aroma and antioxidant properties of Assam lemon that enrich local cuisines.

50 MW Solar Project in Sonitpur

- Assam Chief Minister Himanta Biswa Sarma performed the Bhumi Pujan ceremony of the 50 MW Solar Project being developed in Sonitpur, Assam by SJVN Green Energy Limited (SGEL).
- The 50 MW Solar Project is being developed in Sitalmari village, in Barsola Block under Dhekiajuli Revenue Sector in Sonitpur district.

Nitish Kumar takes oath as Bihar CM

- JD(U) leader Nitish Kumar took oath of office and secrecy for the record ninth time as Chief Minister of Bihar on 28 January 2024.
- Eight other cabinet ministers also took oath at Rajbhavan with him.
- From the BJP, party's state president Samrat Choudhary, former minister Vijay Kumar Sinha had took oath as Deputy-Chief Ministers in Nitish Kumar's cabinet.

India's first Dolphin Research Centre

- **The National Dolphin Research Centre (NDRC)** is India's first-ever research facility dedicated to the study and conservation of freshwater dolphins, especially those in the Ganges River.

- The institute, located close to **Ganga river in Patna**, was inaugurated on March 4, 2024 by Bihar Chief Minister Nitish Kumar.
- The NDRC aims to assist scientists and researchers in studying **Gangetic dolphins** comprehensively.

Bihar's Shahi Litchis

- Amrapali Foods, with over 30 years of experience in processing Litchis, has proudly launched **India's first-ever Direct-to-Consumer (D2C)** delivery service for Shahi Litchis.
- These regal fruits, synonymous with the **Muzaffarpur district of Bihar**, are now available for discerning consumers nationwide.
- The Shahi Litchis, awarded the Geographical Indication (GI) Tag, offer delightful sweetness and freshness.

Punjab Police Launch 'Mission Nishchay

- Punjab Police has launched 'Mission Nishchay' in Fazilka district, in collaboration with BSF and Village Defence Committees, to combat drug trafficking along the India-Pakistan border.
- The initiative aims to gather actionable intelligence and engage local communities to tackle drug-related activities effectively.
- 'Mission Nishchay' underscores the strategic focus on enhancing border security and disrupting drug networks, emphasizing community involvement and coordinated efforts with security forces.

Sadak Surakhya Force

- In Punjab, the State government has set up the 'Sadak Surakhya Force' (SSF), the first of its kind in the country, to reduce road fatalities.
- The State Chief Minister Bhagwant Singh Mann flagged off 144 hi-tech vehicles from Jalandhar.

• Anyone in the State can get help by dialing number 112, and the vehicle will reach the spot within ten minutes of receiving the call.

• With more than 1,200 police jawans, 144 hi-tech vehicles have been flagged off and about 90 female drivers will also handle the steering of vehicles.

North India's first 'Pizza ATM'

• Chandigarh Industrial and Tourism Development Corporation (CITCO) has introduced a new pizza maker that can produce hot pizzas in just three minutes, which is a first in North India.

• It is located near calm waters, providing a tranquil atmosphere for visitors.

• This recently installed pizza vending machine is the only operational ATM of its kind in India.

211 PM SHRI schools in Chhattisgarh

• Union Minister of Education and Skill Development & Entrepreneurship, Shri Dharmendra Pradhan, along with Chief Minister of Chhattisgarh, Shri Vishnu Deo Sai, inaugurated 211 PM SHRI schools in Raipur.

• Shri Pradhan also inaugurated a Digital Library for Kendriya Vidyalaya and Virtual Reality labs for Navodaya Vidyalaya of the State.

South Eastern Coalfield Limited's Gevra Mine

• Chhattisgarh-based Coal India subsidiary South Eastern Coalfield Limited's Gevra mine is set to become the largest coal mine in Asia. The mine has been granted environmental clearance to expand production capacity to 70 million tons per annum from the current 52.5 million tons.

• The Ministry of Coal, in coordination with the Ministry of Environment, Forest, and Climate Change (MoEFCC), played a crucial role in fast-tracking the environmental clearance process.

ONGC's sea survival centre in Goa

• Prime Minister Narendra Modi inaugurated ONGC's sea survival centre in Goa on 6 February.

• It aims to advance the Indian sea survival training ecosystem to global standards as a one-of-a-kind Integrated Sea Survival Training Centre. It is expected to train 10,000-15,000 personnel annually.

• Personnel will be trained in simulated and controlled harsh weather conditions. The centre will help trainees deal with real-life disasters and enhance their sea survival skills.

Copper Unit Plant At Mundra, Gujarat

• Adani group announced the start of the first phase of the world's largest single-location copper manufacturing plant at Mundra in Gujarat.

• Kutch Copper "commissioned the first phase" of USD 1.2 billion "greenfield copper refinery by dispatching the maiden batch of cathodes to customers.

• The first phase of the facility that will produce 0.5 million tonnes a year of refined copper has started operations and full-scale 1 million tonnes capacity is expected by FY29 (March 2029).

Gujarat Minister launches Shiksha Reform

• Gujarat's Minister of State for Education, Praful Pansheriya, launched the online learning platform Shiksha Reform in Surat.

• Shiksha Reform is a collaborative effort with Microsoft and a leading Finnish university.

• Shiksha Reform offers short-term courses in cutting-edge fields like artificial intelligence and cyber security in association with Microsoft and the Finnish university.

Fabexa Fabric Sourcing Expo

• On 21 May 2024, Chief Minister Bhupendra Patel inaugurated the FABEXA Fabric Sourcing Expo 2024 in Gandhinagar, Gujarat.

• Organized by the Maskati Cloth Mahajan of Ahmedabad, this textile and readymade garments exhibition aims to showcase new technical designs and industry trends.

"Savera" Program for Early Breast Cancer Detection

• The then Haryana Chief Minister Manohar Lal Khattar inaugurated the "Savera" program, a groundbreaking initiative aimed at early detection and prevention of breast cancer in women.

• Developed in collaboration with the Medanta Foundation and the Health Department, Savera leverages the unique ability of visually impaired women to conduct breast cancer screenings.

• The launch of Savera coincides with the establishment of the National Cancer Institute at AIIMS Jhajjar, equipped with 1,000 beds.

Haryana New Chief Minister

• BJP leader Nayab Singh Saini took oath as the Chief Minister of the state in March 2024, after senior party leader Manohar Lal Khattar resigned from the post.

• Khattar's resignation came after the BJP and the Jannayak Janata Party (JJP) broke off their ruling alliance in Haryana following differences.

• Nayab Singh Saini takes oath as the Chief Minister of Haryana, by Haryana Governor Bandaru Dattatreya at the Raj Bhavan in Chandigarh.

'My School-My Pride' Campaign

• In a move aligned with the National Education Policy (NEP)-2020, Himachal Pradesh has unveiled the 'My School-My Pride' campaign under the 'Apna Vidyalay' programme.

India's First-Ever 'Hybrid Pitch'

• India's first-ever 'hybrid pitch' was unveiled at the HPCA stadium in Dharamsala.

• The hybrid pitch, which combines natural turf with synthetic fibres, promises enhanced durability and consistent playability, reducing the strain on ground staff and maintaining quality playing conditions.

Enrolling in pension scheme reduced to 50

• The Jharkhand cabinet approved the proposal of including all women, tribals and Dalits above 50 in its old-age pension scheme.

• Earlier, those above 60 years used to get the benefit of the scheme, under which Rs 1,000 is provided to each beneficiary per month.

• The cabinet also gave its nod for the appointment of Yogendra Prasad as the chairman of the State Backward Commission for three years.

Karnataka Mandates 33% Reservation for Women

• In a significant move aimed at promoting gender equality and empowering women, the Karnataka government has mandated a 33% reservation for women in government contract jobs.

• This decision was announced on May 24, 2024, by Chief Minister Siddaramaiah, and is set to be implemented across various government departments and public sector undertakings.

• The reservation applies to outsourced jobs lasting more than 45 days and employing over 20 people.

Bengaluru's First Driverless Metro Train

• The Bangalore Metro Rail Corporation Limited (BMRCL) has received its first 6-coach prototype driverless metro train supplied by a Chinese manufacturer as part of a larger deal.

India's first UNESCO City of Literature

- Kozhikode in north Kerala, known for its rich cultural heritage, was officially declared as India's first UNESCO 'City of Literature'.
- In October 2023, Kozhikode had earned a place in the 'Literature' category of the UNESCO Creative Cities Network (UCCN).

Operation 'AMRITH'

- The Kerala Drug Control Department has taken a proactive step to combat the growing threat of antimicrobial resistance (AMR) through Operation Amrith (Antimicrobial Resistance Intervention For Total Health).
- This initiative aims to curb the overuse of antibiotics in the state by conducting surprise raids in pharmacies and detecting over-the-counter (OTC) sales of antibiotics without a doctor's prescription.

GAIL's 10 MW Green Hydrogen Plant

- On 24 May 2024, GAIL (India) Limited marked a significant milestone by inaugurating its first Green Hydrogen Plant at GAIL Vijaipur in Madhya Pradesh.
- The plant, powered by a 10 MW PEM (Proton Exchange Membrane) electrolyzer, has a capacity to produce 4.3 tonnes of green hydrogen per day.

New Lokayukta of Madhya Pradesh

- Justice Satyendra Kumar Singh has been appointed as the new Lokayukta of Madhya Pradesh.
- Justice Singh was appointed as Lokayukta under the Madhya Pradesh Lokayukta and Up-Lokayukta Adhiniyam 1981.

World's First Vedic Clock

- The world's first Vedic clock has been installed in Ujjain, this clock will display the Panchang, planetary positions, and Muhurat.
- The clock time will calculate from one sunrise to another. It is located on an 85-foot-high tower in Jantar Mantar, Ujjain.

'Bag Less School' Initiative

- The Madhya Pradesh government has made a significant decision to introduce 'bag less school' once a week for students in classes 1 to 12 starting from the upcoming academic session of 2024-25.
- This initiative aims to alleviate the stress faced by students and will be implemented in both government and private schools across the state.

School On Wheels

- Manipur, Governor Sushri Anusuiya Uikey inaugurated 'School on Wheels' on 26 May 2024 at a ceremony held in Imphal.
- The initiative which is implemented by Vidya Bharati Shiksha Vikash Samiti Manipur aims to reach out to the students in the relief camps in the State.
- The school bus is equipped with a library, computers and sports items with a teacher and visits relief camps in different places in the State.

"Cherrapunji Gin" secures top honour

- "Cherrapunji Gin" has achieved top honors at the Global Spirits Competition.
- This prestigious recognition underscores the gin's exceptional quality and craftsmanship.
- While specific details about the award remain undisclosed, it's evident that "Cherrapunji Gin" has made a significant impact in the spirits industry.

Chapchar Kut Festival

- Chapchar Kut, the grandest festival in Mizoram, resonated throughout the state with vibrant traditional customs and jubilant festivities.
- Thousands of attendees converged upon the Assam Rifles Ground – Lammual – in the heart of Aizawl city, filling it to its capacity.

4th Organic Orange Festival

- Recently, the 4th edition of the two-day Organic Orange Festival was held in Rüsoma Village, Nagaland, with the intention of encouraging rural farmers to promote organic products and the opportunity for income generation.
- Rüsoma Village, also known as the 'Gardening village' is located in the Capital of Nagaland, Kohima.

4th National Chilika Birds Festival

- The then Chief minister of Odisha Naveen Patnaik inaugurated the fourth National Chilika Birds Festival at an event coordinated by the department of tourism, department of forest, and Chilika Development Authority.

Jagannath Temple Corridor Project

- The then Odisha Chief Minister Naveen Patnaik inaugurated the redeveloped Samaleswari Temple in Sambalpur district, one of the most revered shrines in the western region of the state.

Adani Ports Acquired Gopalpur Port

- The Shapoorji Pallonji Group announced the sale of its brownfield Gopalpur Port to Adani Ports and SEZ Ltd for an enterprise value of ₹ 3,350 crore, as part of its deleveraging strategy with planned asset monetisation.

Gupteswar Forest In Odisha

- The pristine Gupteswar Forest, adjacent to Gupteswar Shiva temple in Odisha's Koraput district has been declared as the fourth Biodiversity-Heritage Site (BHS) of the state.

India's First Indoor Athletics And Aquatic Centres

- Odisha Former Chief Minister Naveen Patnaik inaugurated India's first indoor athletics and aquatic centres at the Kalinga stadium in Bhubaneshwar.
- The newly developed India's first indoor athletics stadium has the facilities to host national and international athletic events.

Majestic Great Indian Bustard

- Jaisalmer, a city in the state of Rajasthan, India, is closely associated with the conservation and preservation of the critically endangered Great Indian Bustard (Ardeotis nigriceps).
- The Great Indian Bustard is primarily found in arid and semi-arid grasslands, which make up a significant portion of the Thar Desert region surrounding Jaisalmer.
- Listed as critically endangered on the International Union for Conservation of Nature (IUCN) Red List, the Great Indian Bustard faces threats such as habitat loss, fragmentation, hunting, and disturbance.

'Viksit Bharat Viksit Rajasthan' Program

- Prime Minister Shri Narendra Modi addressed the 'Viksit Bharat Viksit Rajasthan' program via video conferencing.
- These projects span across various critical sectors, including Roads, Railways, Solar Energy, Power Transmission, Drinking Water, and Petroleum & Natural Gas.

First Northeastern State to Restore Old Pension System

- Sikkim Chief Minister Prem Singh Tamang has announced the restoration of the Old Pension System (OPS) for state government employees appointed on or after April 1, 2006.
- According to the Sikkim Services Pension Rules of 1990, employees employed on or before March 31, 1990, will be eligible for the benefits of this reinstatement..

Buddhist festival Saga Dawa

- Saga Dawa, also known as the Triple Blessed Festival, is a significant and sacred celebration for followers of Mahayana Buddhism in Sikkim.

- This auspicious month commemorates three pivotal events in Lord Buddha's life: his birth, enlightenment, and liberation from the physical realm.
- During Saga Dawa, Buddhists offer prayers in various monasteries throughout the month.

Param Vir Chakra garden

- Tamil Nadu Governor R.N. Ravi inaugurated Param Vir Chakra garden and Aikyam exhibition in the Kanchi Mahaswami Vidya Mandir in Tambaram.
- This garden commemorates the gallantry and sacrifices of India's brave soldiers who have been awarded the Param Vir Chakra, the highest military decoration in the country.

Matabari Pera, Pachra from receives GI tag

- Tripura Chief Minister Manik Saha informed that two items from the state have earned the prestigious Geographical Indication (GI) tag.
- The two items that received the tag are Matabari Pera – a dairy-based confectionary item traditionally served as prasad at the Tripurasundari temple in Gomati district – and Pachra – a handwoven cloth used by the state's Indigenous communities.

World's First Asian King Vulture Conservation & Breeding Centre

- Uttar Pradesh is set to establish the world's first conservation and breeding centre for Asian king vultures or red-headed vultures in Maharajganj.
- The facility will improve the population of critically endangered species listed in the International Union for Conservation of Nature's red list since 2007.
- The centre is named Jatayu Conservation and Breeding Centre.

South Asia's largest ammunition & missiles complex

- The Adani Group has inaugurated the Ammunition & Missiles Complex in Kanpur, Uttar Pradesh.
- This Adani Defence project is the first phase of the state's defense corridor and honors the heroes of the Balakot strike.
- Uttar Pradesh Chief Minister Yogi Adityanath, along with the then Chief of Army Staff Gen Manoj Pande, inaugurated the complex.
- Spread across 500 acres, the complex is set to become one of the largest integrated ammunition manufacturing facilities in South Asia.

'Onavillu' to Ram Mandir

- On January 22, 2024, legendary Sree Padmabhaswamy temple in Thiruvananthauram, gifted traditional 'Onamvillu' (Bow of Onam season) to Ram Lalla.
- Usually, Onavillu is a special gift offered to Onathappan, the deity of Onam celebrations. It is removed from the pookkalam (flower carpet on the courtyard) on the third day of Onam.
- It is considered to be a three hundred years old tradition in Padmanabha Swamy Mandir, Thiruvananthapuram, the richest Hindu worship centre.

India's First Urban Ropeway

- Inaugurated in March 24, 2022, by Prime Minister Narendra Modi, India's first ever urban ropeway is currently in under construction. It is expected to open in May 2025.
- This is part of the Varanasi Ropeway Project which comes under the National Ropeways Development Programme, 'Parvatmala Pariyojana'.

Uttarakhand takes up Uniform Civil Code

- On February 7, 2024, the Legislative Assembly of the state of Uttarakhand in India passed the Uniform Civil Code (UCC) Bill.
- On March 13, the bill was granted assent by President Droupadi Murmu.
- The bill claims to establish a uniform and equal set of rules on personal status law, including marriage, divorce, succession, and inheritance, that applies to all citizens of the state irrespective of religion.

'Pirul Lao-Paise Pao' Campaign

- Uttarakhand Chief Minister Pushkar Singh Dhami launched the Pirul Lao-Paisa Pao in the Rudraprayag district on 8 May 2024.
- The Uttarakhand government has launched the Pirul Lao-Paise Pao campaign to contain the raging forest fire in the state.

Himalayan Basket

- Uttarakhand Chief Minister Pushkar Singh Dhami launched the 'Himalayan Basket' initiative.
- Under the Himalayan Basket, agricultural products like milk, turmeric, and mint are purchased, and different products are made from them and supplied to foreign countries.
- The 'Himalayan Basket' initiative is designed to boost local employment by capitalizing on the district's abundant agricultural resources.

India's first Astro tourism campaign - Nakshatra Sabha

- In order to boost tourism in the state, the Uttarakhand government organised a first-of-its kind Astro-tourism named 'Nakshatra Sabha' in Mussoorie.
- The first astro-tourism event was held at Mussoorie City, also famous as the Queen of the Hills, on 1 and 2 June 2024.
- The event was held at the George Everest Peak, which is popular amongst tourists as it offers spectacular views of the Doon Valley and the snow-clad Himalayan mountains.

LEARN THROUGH MAP

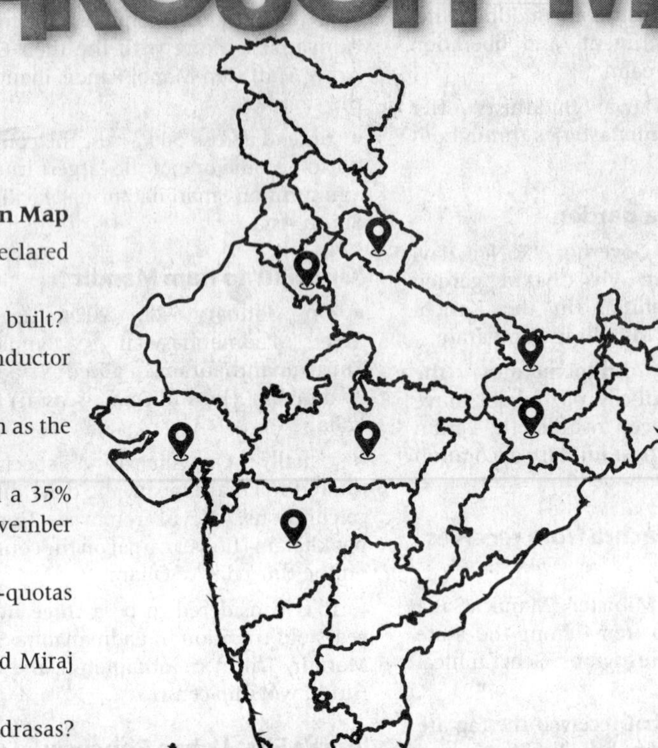

Mark the States/Regions with Key Developments in Map

1. In which state is Kaziranga National Park, now declared India's second butterfly diversity hub, located?
2. Where is the world's largest Ramayana temple being built?
3. Which state launched its first dedicated Semiconductor Policy (2022–2027) in November 2024?
4. Find the eastern state where Hemant Soren took oath as the 14th Chief Minister on 28th November 2024
5. Identify the Indian state on the map that approved a 35% job reservation for women in state services on 5th November 2024
6. Which state became the first to implement Dalit sub-quotas in government jobs in October 2024?
7. In which state were Sawantwadi Wooden Crafts and Miraj Tanpura awarded GI tags in 2024?
8. Which state has made Sanskrit mandatory in 416 madrasas?

MATCHING GAME

Initiative/Event	States
A. First-ever leopard census conducted	1. Maharashtra
B. First state to implement disaster insurance	2. Odisha
C. Location of newly inaugurated Banjara Virasat Museum	3. Nagaland
D. India's first disabled university being established	4. Jharkhand
E. State(s) developing Shri Krishna Gaman Path	5. Rajasthan
F. Approval for second tiger reserve at Kaimur	6. Bihar
G. Launch of the 'Mitra Van' initiative along borders	7. Uttar Pradesh
H. First state to adopt a comprehensive Road Safety Action Plan	8. Madhya Pradesh

Answer Key (Map):

1. Assam 2. Bihta, Bihar 3. Gujarat 4. Jharkhand 5. Madhya Pradesh 6. Haryana 7. Maharashtra 8. Uttarakhand

Answer Key (Matching Game):

A → 2 B → 3 C → 1 D → 4 E → 8 F → 6 G → 7 H → 5

RANKING AND REPORTS

SDG INDIA INDEX 2023-24

What is the SDG India Index?

The SDG India Index, developed by NITI Aayog, is a tool to measure and track India's performance across 16 of the 17 SDGs using 113 indicators aligned with the National Indicator Framework.

- **Purpose:** Encourage localization of SDGs at the state and union territory (UT) levels to inform and drive development strategies.
- **Scoring:** States and UTs are assessed on a scale of 0-100, with higher scores indicating better progress. Categories include:
  - Aspirant: 0–49
  - Front-Runner: 65–99
  - Performer: 50–64
  - Achiever: 100
- **Exclusion:** Goal 14 (Life Below Water) is excluded from the composite score as it pertains to only nine coastal states.
- **Overall Score:** India's national SDG score improved to 71 in 2023-24, up from 66 in 2020-21.
- **Top Performers:** Uttarakhand, Kerala, Tamil Nadu, Goa, and Himachal Pradesh.
- **Goal Progress:** Significant strides in Goals 1 (No Poverty), 8 (Decent Work and Economic Growth), 13 (Climate Action), and 15 (Life on Land).
- **Fastest Movers:** Uttar Pradesh, Jammu and Kashmir, Uttarakhand, Sikkim, and Haryana showed remarkable progress.
- **Lowest Performers:** Bihar Lagged behind with a score of 57, followed by Jharkhand at 62.
- India's commitment to SDGs remains strong, with concerted efforts at local levels.

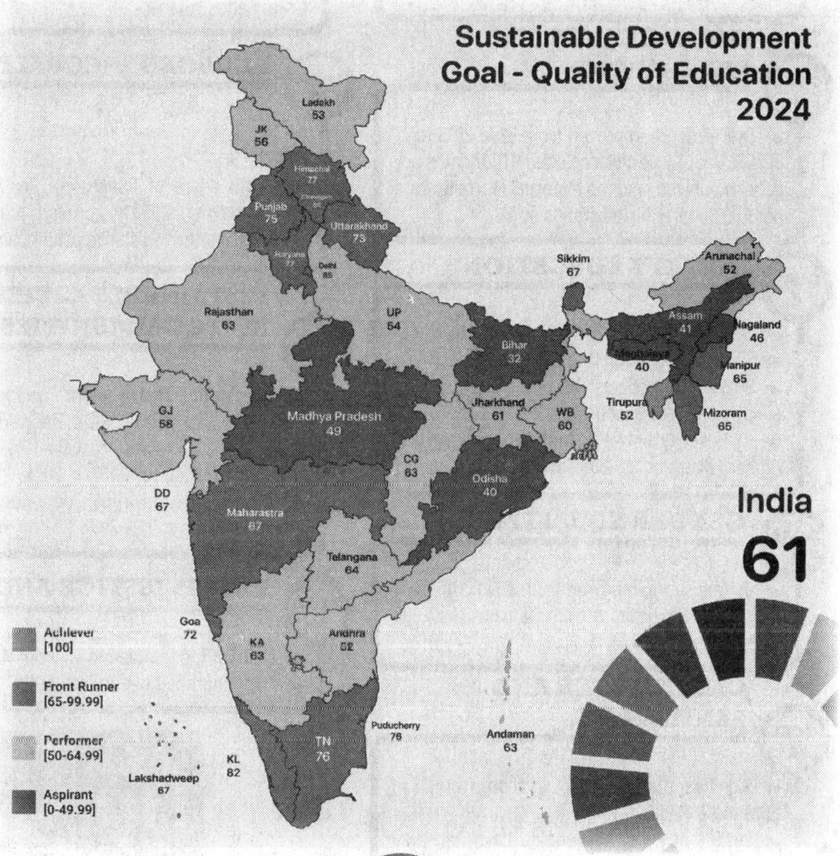

SUSTAINABLE DEVELOPMENT GOALS

SDG KEY HIGHLIGHTS

GOAL 1 NO POVERTY

- Improved score from 60 in 2020-21 to 72 in 2023-24. 99.7% of the persons demanding employment under MGNREGA were offered employment in 2023-2024.

GOAL 2 ZERO HUNGER

- Improvement in overall composite score from Aspirant to Performer category. 99.01% beneficiaries covered under National Food Security Act (NFSA), 2013.

GOAL 3 GOOD HEALTH AND WELL-BEING

- Overall score improved from 52 in 2018 to 77 in 2023-24. 93.23% children aged 9-11 months are fully immunised, and the Maternal Mortality Rate per 1,00,000 live births stands at 97.

GOAL 4 QUALITY EDUCATION

- Adjusted Net Enrolment Rate (ANER) for elementary education is 96.5% for 2021-22.
- 88.65% of schools have access to both electricity and drinking water.
- 100% parity between females and males in Higher Education (18-23 years).

GOAL 5 GENDER EQUALITY

- Overall score improved from 36 in 2018 to 49 in 2023-24. Sex ratio at birth (females per 1,000 males) stands at 929.

GOAL 6 CLEAN WATER AND SANITATION

- Significant improvement in score from 63 in 2018 to 89 in 2023-24.
- 99.29% of rural households have improved their source of drinking water.
- 94.7% of schools have functional toilets for girls.

GOAL 7 AFFORDABLE AND CLEAN ENERGY

- The highest score amongst all SDGs is also significant improvement from 51 in 2018 to 96 in 2023-24.
- 100% households have access to electricity under the Saubhagya Scheme.
- Significant improvement in households have clean cooking fuel (LPG + PNG) connections from 92.02% (2020) to 96.35% (2024).

GOAL 8 DECENT WORK AND ECONOMIC GROWTH

- 5.88% annual growth rate of India's GDP per capita at constant prices in 2022-23.
- Reduction in unemployment rate from 6.2% in 2018-19 to 3.40% in 2022-23.

GOAL 9 INDUSTRY, INNOVATION AND INFRASTRUCTURE

- Improvement in score from 41 in 2018 to 61 in 2023-24. 99.70% of targeted habitations connected with all-weather roads under PM Gram Sadak Yojana.

GOAL 10 REDUCED INEQUALITIES

- Decrease in points from 67 in 2020-21 to 65 in 2023-24.
- 45.61% seats of Panchayati Raj Institutions held by women. 28.57% representation of SC/ST persons in state legislative assemblies.

GOAL 11 SUSTAINABLE CITIES AND COMMUNITIES

- Significant improvement in score from 39 in 2018 to 83 in 2023-24. The percentage of municipal solid waste processed has increased from 68% in 2020 to 78.46% in 2024.
- 97% of wards have 100% door-to-door waste collection.

GOAL 12 RESPONSIBLE CONSUMPTION AND PRODUCTION

- 91.5% of biomedical waste generated is treated in 2022.
- 54.99% hazardous waste recycled/utilized in 2022-23.

GOAL 13 CLIMATE ACTION

- Drastic improvement from 54 (Performer category) in 2020-21 to 67 (Front Runner category) in the SDG India Index 4 (2023-24).
- Disaster preparedness score as per Disaster Resilience Index stands at 19.20.
- Improvement in electricity generation from renewable energy from 36.37% in 2020 to 43.28% in 2024.
- 94.86% of industries comply with environmental standards.

GOAL 14 LIFE BELOW WATER

- Goal 14 has not been included in the calculation of the Composite Score for the Index as it solely pertains to the nine coastal States

GOAL 15 LIFE ON LAND

- Score improved from 66 in 2020-21 to 75 in 2023-24.
- Nearly 25% of geographical area under forests and tree cover.

GOAL 16 PEACE, JUSTICE AND STRONG INSTITUTIONS

- 95.5% of the population is under Aadhaar coverage as of March 2024.
- 71.3% charge sheeting rate of IPC crimes as per NCRB 2022.

RANKING AND REPORTS

Global Patent Filing Report 2024

- According to the World Intellectual Property Organisation's (WIPO) Global Patent Filing Report, India now ranks 6th globally in terms of patent applications, with 64,480 patent filings in 2023.
- This puts India among the leading nations, including China, the United States, Japan, and South Korea, in terms of intellectual property activity.
- For the first time in history, more than half (55.2%) of India's patent applications in 2023 were filed by residents.

Inaugural Times Higher Education (THE) Interdisciplinary Science Rankings 2025

- In November 2024, KIIT University secured the 4th position in India in the inaugural Times Higher Education (THE) Interdisciplinary Science Rankings 2025.
- Globally, KIIT ranks 92nd, making it one of only four Indian universities in the top 100.
- Anna University leads among Indian institutions and has secured the 41st position globally.
- Only four Indian universities—both private and public—feature among the top 100 universities globally.

India Joined Top 50 in Network Readiness Index 2024

- Released in November 20024, the Network Readiness Index (NRI) 2024, highlighted a major achievement for India, which rose 11 spots to rank 49th globally.
- The NRI assesses 133 countries on their ability to utilize networks for economic growth, innovation, and digital transformation.
- India secured the 49th position, up from 60th in 2023, with a score of 53.63.
- The country excelled in AI scientific publications, AI talent concentration, and ICT services exports, reflecting its growing dominance in technological innovation and digital transformation.

Basic Animal Husbandry Statistics 2024

- Union Minister, Ministry of Fisheries, Animal Husbandry & Dairying Shri Rajiv Ranjan Singh alias Lalan Singh released the annual publication of 'Basic Animal Husbandry Statistics 2024'.
- The BAHS - 2024 is based on the outcomes of the Integrated Sample Survey conducted for the period from 1st March 2023 to 29th February 2024.
- The top five milk producing States during 2023-24 was Uttar Pradesh with a share of 16.21 % of total milk production followed by Rajasthan (14.51 %), Madhya Pradesh (8.91 %), Gujarat (7.65 %), and Maharashtra (6.71 %).
- The major contribution in the total Egg production comes from Andhra Pradesh with a share of 17.85 % of total Egg production followed by Tamil Nadu (15.64 %), Telangana (12.88%), West Bengal (11.37%) and Karnataka (6.63 %).
- The Major contribution in the total Wool production comes from Rajasthan with a share of 47.53% followed by Jammu & Kashmir (23.06%), Gujarat (6.18%), Maharashtra (4.75%) and Himachal Pradesh (4.22%).

U.N. Methane Monitoring Program Report 2024

- In November 2024, the United Nations Environment Programme (UNEP) released the Methane Monitoring Program Report 2024.
- The report, part of the International Methane Emissions Observatory (IMEO), provides open, reliable data to help reduce methane emissions.
- It highlights the Methane Alert and Response System (MARS), which uses satellite data to detect large emissions.
- The report emphasizes the need for urgent action to meet the Global Methane Pledge target of reducing emissions by 30% by 2030.

Climate Change Performance Index 2025

- **India's Rank:** 10th
- **Commitments:** Net-zero emissions target by 2070.
- **Aim:** To install 500 GW of renewable energy capacity by 2030.
- It Covers 63 countries + European Union, responsible for 90% of global emissions.
- The top three spots were left vacant as no country achieved a "very high" rating.
- Denmark ranks 4th, followed by the Netherlands (5th) reflecting strong performance in climate action.

QS World University Rankings: Asia 2025

- In November 2024, the QS World University Rankings: Asia 2025 were released, assessing 984 institutions across 25 countries in Eastern, Southern, Southeastern, and Central Asia.
- Peking University topped the list for the second consecutive year, with the University of Hong Kong, National University of Singapore, and Nanyang Technological University following.

Top Rankings for India

- **Top 50:** IIT Delhi (44th) and IIT Bombay (48th).
- **Top 100:** Includes IIT Madras (56), IIT Kharagpur (60), Indian Institute of Science (62), IIT Kanpur (67), and University of Delhi (81).

EdelGive Hurun India Philanthropy List 2024

- In November 2024, the EdelGive Hurun India Philanthropy List 2024 was released, identifying 203 philanthropists who collectively donated ₹8,783 crore, a 55% increase compared to two years ago.
- Shiv Nadar topped the list with a donation of ₹2,153 crore, primarily for education. Other top donors included Mukesh Ambani, the Bajaj family, Kumar Mangalam Birla, and Gautam Adani.
- Notably, 18 philanthropists donated over ₹100 crore each, with Rohini Nilekani being the most generous woman with a donation of ₹154 crore.

3rd edition of World Solar Report series

- In November 2024, the International Solar Alliance (ISA) launched the 3rd edition of the World Solar Report series at its 7th Assembly.
- The series includes four reports: World Solar Market Report, World Investment Report, World Technology Report, and Green Hydrogen Readiness Assessment for African Countries.

- The World Solar Market Report reveals exceptional solar growth, with global capacity soaring from 1.22 GW in 2000 to 1,418.97 GW in 2023.
- The latest World Investment Report highlights a global shift toward sustainable energy, with energy investments rising from $2.4 trillion in 2018 to $3.1 trillion by 2024.

London topped the list of the world's top 100 "city brands"

- In November 2024, London was named the top city brand in the world for the second consecutive year by the Brand Finance Global City Index 2024.
- London scored 90.9 out of 100, followed by New York and Paris.
- The ranking was based on a survey of 15,000 people across 20 countries, including Türkiye, the US, Germany, Australia, the UAE, Brazil, China, and others.

Global Hunger Index (GHI) 2024

- Recently, India ranked 105th out of 127 countries in the Global Hunger Index (GHI) 2024 with a score of 27.3, compared to 111th in the report of 2023.
- The 2024 GHI report is the 19th edition, published by Concern Worldwide (Ireland) and Welthungerhilfe (Germany).
- The GHI score is calculated on a 100-point scale reflecting the severity of hunger – 0 is the best score (implies no hunger) and 100 is the worst.
- India's child wasting rate is at 18.7 per cent; child stunting, is 35.5 per cent; prevalence of undernourishment, is 13.7 per cent; and under-five mortality rate, is 2.9 per cent.

Rank in 2024	Country
1	Belarus
2	Bosnia & Herzegovina
3	Chile
4	China
5	Costa Rica
6	Croatia
7	Estonia
8	Georgia
9	Hungary
10	Kuwait
105	India
109	Pakistan
116	Afghanistan
126	Yemen
127	Somalia

Henley Passport Index 2024

- Singapore topped the list with access to 195 destinations.
- Finland, France, Germany, Italy, Japan, South Korea and Spain share the second spot with access to 192 destinations.
- The Henley Passport Index involves the process of evaluating several key factors, including Visa-Free Access, Diplomatic Relations, and International Agreements.
- India has improved its ranking to 84th, allowing visa-free access to 58 destinations.
- It is released by Henley & Partners, a United Kingdom-based immigration consultancy.

World Justice Project's Rule of Law Index 2024

- On 26th October 2024, the World Justice Project (WJP) released its Rule of Law Index 2024.
- India ranks 79th out of 142 countries.
- The 2024 Rule of Law Index ranks Afghanistan 140th out of 142 countries in terms of law and order and security. The other two bottom ranked countries are: Cambodia (141) and Venezuela (142).

2024 Global Multidimensional Poverty Index

- The 2024 Global Multidimensional Poverty Index (MPI) released by the **United Nations Development Programme (UNDP) and the Oxford Poverty and Human Development Initiative (OPHI)** on 17th October 2024.
- The 2024 Global Multidimensional Poverty Index, is published with the theme of **"Poverty Amid Conflict".**
- The index reveals that 1.1 billion people across 112 countries live in acute multidimensional poverty. Over half of these individuals are children.
- The five countries with the largest number of people living in poverty are India (234 million), Pakistan (93 million), Ethiopia (86 million), Nigeria (74 million) and the Democratic Republic of the Congo (66 million).

Abu Dhabi crowned world's richest city in sovereign wealth funds

- On 8th October 2024, Abu Dhabi was crowned the world's richest city in terms of sovereign wealth fund assets.
- According to a report by Global SWF, Abu Dhabi's funds manage an impressive $1.7 trillion.

- This places Abu Dhabi slightly above Oslo, home to the world's largest SWF, the Government Pension Fund, which manages over $1.6 trillion.

India ranked 39 in Global Innovation Index list

- Recently, India climbed one place to 39th rank out of 133 economies in the Global Innovation Index (GII) 2024 rankings, according to a report by the Geneva-based World Intellectual Property Organization.
- Switzerland, Sweden, the United States, Singapore and the United Kingdom are the world's most innovative economies.
- China, Turkiye, India, Viet Nam and the Philippines are the fastest 10-year climbers, according to WIPO's Global Innovation Index (GII) 2024.

India became World's 3rd largest Producer and Consumer of Ethanol

- On 26 September 2024, India was recognized as the world's third-largest producer and consumer of ethanol.
- The country follows the United States and Brazil in ethanol production.
- Ethanol production has nearly tripled, contributing to reduced greenhouse gas emissions and greater investment opportunities.

World Talent Ranking 2024

- The recently released IMD World Talent Ranking 2024 shows the overall ranking for 67 economies.
- India is ranked 58th globally in the World Talent Ranking 2024 with a talent score of 40.47.
- Switzerland is ranked first, followed by Singapore.
- Institute for Management Development (IMD) publishes the World Talent Ranking 2024.

Hurun India Under-35 List 2024

- The recently released 2024 Hurun India Under 35 features 150 outstanding entrepreneurs under the age of 35.

- Reliance Retail's non-executive director Isha Ambani and Toddle's Parita are the youngest women to feature in the first list of 2024 Hurun India Under 35.
- The youngest person included in the 2024 Hurun India Under 35 was Ankush Sachdeva of ShareChat.
- Akash Ambani ranked 32nd on the list. Ghazala Alagh was also included in the list for her work on Mamaearth.
- Among the prominent names on the list are Ankush Sachdeva of ShareChat, Keshav Reddy, Pranav Aggarwal, Siddharth Vij, and edtech startup figures like Alakh Pandey.

Majority of Atrocities against SC from 13 States

- A recent government report, released on 22 September 2024, reveals that 97.7% of atrocities against Scheduled Castes (SCs) in 2022 were reported from 13 states.
- Uttar Pradesh, Rajasthan, and Madhya Pradesh recorded the highest numbers, with 12,287, 8,651, and 7,732 cases respectively.
- Similarly, the majority of atrocities against Scheduled Tribes (STs) were also concentrated in 13 states, which reported 98.91 per cent of all cases in 2022.

Asia Power Index 2024

Rank	Country / Territory	Score	Status
1	United States	81.7	Superpowers ≥ 70 points
2	China	72.7	
3	India	39.1	
4	Japan	38.9	
5	Australia	31.9	
6	Russia	31.1	
7	South Korea	31.0	
8	Singapore	26.4	

- India has officially surpassed Japan to become the third most powerful nation in Asia, according to the 2024 Asia Power Index released by the Lowy Institute on 25 September 2024.
- The index evaluates countries based on their resource capabilities and influence in the Asia-Pacific region.
- Japan's slower population growth and limited military expansion contributed to its decline in the rankings.

India achieves Tier 1 status in Global Cyber Security Index 2024

- On 20 September 2024, India achieved Tier 1 status in the Global Cybersecurity Index (GCI) 2024, published by the International Telecommunication Union (ITU), with a score of 98.49.
- The report places 46 countries in Tier 1, the highest of the five tiers, reserved for "role modelling" countries that demonstrate a strong commitment in all five cybersecurity pillars.
- India has been an active member of the ITU since 1869 and has been a regular member of the ITU Council since 1952.

Periodic Labour Force Survey (PLFS) Report 2023-24

- In September 2024, the National Statistical Office (NSO) released the annual Periodic Labour Force Survey (PLFS) report 2023-24, showing the unemployment rate stagnated at 3.2% that raises concerns about the inability to generate enough formal jobs.
- The unemployment rate for 2023-24 remained unchanged at 3.2%, the same as in 2022-23.
- Labour Force Participation Rate (LFPR) showed a significant increase in LFPR to 60.1% in 2023-24 from 57.9% in 2022-23 at national level. LFPR represents the share of people either working or seeking work in the population.
- Worker Population Ratio was 58.2% in the year 2023-2024. The same for male and female was 76.3% and 40.3% respectively. WPR is defined as the percentage of employed persons in the population.

Kerala Retains top spot in India Food Index 2024

- In September 2024, Kerala retained the top spot in the State Food Safety Index 2024 (SFSI) for the second consecutive year.
- Released by the Food Safety and Standards Authority of India (FSSAI) during the Global Food Regulators Summit, the index evaluates states on food safety standards.
- Tamil Nadu and Jammu & Kashmir secured the second and third positions, respectively.

India Became 6th largest market in MSCI ACWI Investable Market Index

- On 18 September 2024, India became the sixth-largest market in the MSCI All Country World Investable Market Index (ACWI IMI), surpassing China.
- India's weight in the index stood at 2.35%, just behind France.
- The MSCI ACWI Investable Market Index (IMI) tracks global capital markets, including large- and mid-cap stocks.

India Ranked 40th in World for Alcoholic Beverage Exports

- In September 2024, India ranked 40th globally in alcoholic beverage exports, with a significant export value of over ₹2,200 crore in the fiscal year 2023-24.
- Major export destinations include the UAE, Singapore, the Netherlands, Tanzania, Angola, Kenya, and Rwanda.
- The Agricultural and Processed Food Export Development Authority (APEDA) plans to promote both the Indian alcoholic and non-alcoholic beverages globally with a target of $1 billion in export revenue over the next few years.
- APEDA as part of the 'Make in India' initiative targeted to increase exports of Indian Spirits to major foreign destinations.

Amul topped Global Food Brand Rankings in 2024

- Amul was recognised as the world's strongest food brand in Brand Finance's Global Food & Drinks Report 2024.
- The report highlighted Amul's impressive Brand Strength Index (BSI) score of 91 out of 100, earning it an AAA+ rating.
- Amul's brand value saw an 11 per cent increase from 2023, reaching $3.3 billion in the latest ranking.

National Institutional Ranking Framework (NIRF): 2024

- Union Minister for Education Shri Dharmendra Pradhan on August 12, released the India Rankings 2024, which implements the National Institutional Ranking Framework (NIRF) drafted by the Ministry of Education in 2015.

- The NIRF rankings will cover 13 categories including universities, colleges, research institutions, engineering, management, pharmacy, medical, dental, law, architecture and planning, agriculture and allied sectors and innovation.

Top 3 institute in overall category

- Indian Institute of Technology Madras
- Indian Institute of Science
- Indian Institute of Technology Bombay

Top 3 institute in Universities category

- Indian Institute of Science
- Jawaharlal Nehru University
- Jamia Millia Islamia, Delhi

Hurun India Rich List 2024

- According to the Hurun India Rich List 2024, the total number of billionaires now stands at 334.
- Adani Group chairman Gautam Adani topped the 2024 Hurun India Rich List with a wealth of ₹11.6 lakh crore. In 2024, Adani's wealth increased by 95%, while Ambani's wealth grew by 25% to ₹10.15 lakh crore.

TOP 10 RICHEST INDIANS

Rank	Name	Company	Wealth (INR Crore)
1	Gautam Adani	Adani	1,161,800
2	Mukesh Ambani	Reliance Industries	1,014,700
3	Shiv Nadar	HCL	314,000
4	Cyrus S Poonawalla	Serum Institute of India	289,800
5	Dilip Shanghvi	Sun Pharmaceutical	249,900
6	Kumar Mangalam Birla	Aditya Birla	235,200
7	Gopichand Hinduja	Hinduja	192,700
8	Radhakishan Damani	Avenue Supermarts	190,900
9	Azim Premji	Wipro	190,700
10	Niraj Bajaj	Bajaj	162,800

India Retained Eighth Position in Global Agricultural Exports

- Recently, the World Trade Organization (WTO) reported that India retained its position as the eighth-largest exporter of agricultural products in 2023.
- Despite a decline in exports from $55 billion in 2022 to $51 billion in 2023, India maintained its ranking.
- Among the top ten agricultural exporters, only Brazil, the EU, and Thailand saw an increase in exports.

India ranked 2nd largest Aluminium producer

- Recently, India was confirmed as the world's second-largest aluminium producer.
- In the fiscal year 2023-24, India's primary aluminium production reached a record 41.6 lakh tonnes, up from 40.73 lakh tonnes in the previous year.
- This growth highlights India's significant role in the global aluminium market, alongside its positions as the third-largest lime producer and fourth-largest iron ore producer.

State of the World's Forests 2024 Report

- On 22 July 2024, State of the World's Forests 2024 was released by the **Food and Agriculture Organization (FAO)** of the United Nations recently.
- The report provides a comprehensive analysis of global forest conditions and trends, revealing both positive developments and ongoing challenges.
- Russia, Brazil, Canada, the United States of America, and China are the top five countries collectively accounting for 54 percent of the global forest area.
- Australia, the Democratic Republic of Congo, Indonesia, Peru, and India, among others, contribute to about two-thirds of the global forest area.

World Population Prospects 2024

- World Population Prospects 2024 is the twenty-eighth edition of the official United Nations population estimates and projections.
- It presents population estimates from the 1950s to the present for 237 countries or areas, underpinned by analyses of historical demographic trends.
- The 2024 revision also presents population projections for the year 2100 that reflect a range of plausible outcomes at the global, regional and national levels.

India ranks 5th in Global Generative AI Innovations

- According to the World Intellectual Property Organisation (WIPO), India has emerged as the fifth-biggest location for GenAI inventions. Domestic inventors have filed 1350 patents globally on generative artificial intelligence (GenAI).
- The list was led by China which filed over 38,000 GenAI patents, far outpacing inventors in the US (6,276 inventions), Republic of Korea (4,155), Japan (3,409), and India.

UNESCO introduced the New World Soil Health Index

- On 1 July 2024, UNESCO introduced the New World Soil Health Index during an international conference in Agadir, Morocco.
- In India, about 32% of land is under degradation and 25% is undergoing desertification.
- 75% of land is already degraded, directly impacting 3.2 billion people (World Atlas of Desertification). This will rise to 90% by 2050.
- The index aims to standardize soil quality assessment globally. It provides a standardized measure for analyzing and comparing soil quality across different regions and ecosystems.

18TH INDIA STATE OF FOREST REPORT (ISFR) 2023

Keynotes:

- **Forest and Tree Cover**: Covers **25.17%** of India's geographical area.
- **Forest Cover: 21.76%** of the geographical area.
- **Tree Cover: 3.41%** of the geographical area.
- **Comparison with 2021**: Increase in forest and tree cover.
- Published biennially by the **Forest Survey of India (FSI)** since 1987.
- **Top States (Increase in Forest and Tree Cover)**:
  - Chhattisgarh
  - Odisha
  - Uttar Pradesh
  - Rajasthan
- **Top States (Increase in Forest Cover)**:
  - Mizoram
  - Odisha
  - Gujarat
- **Area-wise Largest Forest and Tree Cover**:
  - Madhya Pradesh
  - Arunachal Pradesh
  - Maharashtra
- **Area-wise Largest Forest Cover**:
  - Madhya Pradesh
  - Arunachal Pradesh
  - Chhattisgarh
- **Percentage of Forest Cover (Geographical Area)**:
  - **Lakshadweep**: Highest at **91.33%**, followed by Mizoram and Andaman & Nicobar Islands.
  - **19 states/UTs**: Over **33%** forest cover.
  - **8 states/UTs**: Forest cover above **75%**:
  - Mizoram, Lakshadweep, Andaman & Nicobar Islands, Arunachal Pradesh, Nagaland, Meghalaya, Tripura, and Manipur.
- **Mangrove Cover: 4,992 sq km.**
- **Bamboo Bearing Area**: Increased since the 2021 assessment.
- **Carbon Stock**:
  - Current stock: **30.43 billion tonnes of CO2 equivalent**.
  - Target for 2030: **2.5–3.0 billion tonnes.**

Mid-Year Air Quality Assessment for India by CREA

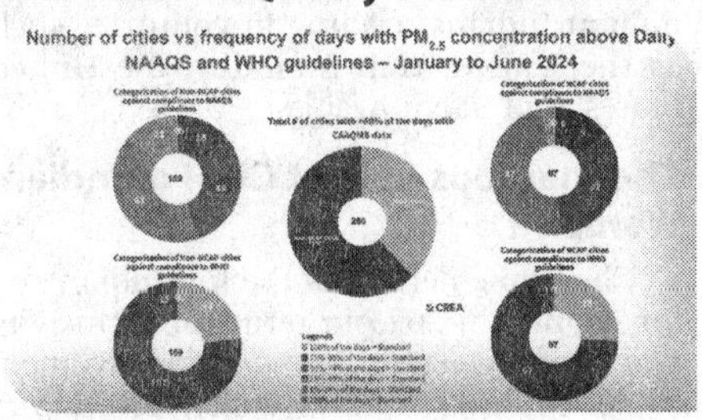

- Recently, the mid-year air quality assessment for India by the Centre for Research on Energy and Clean Air (CREA), covering the period from January to June 2024, provides a comprehensive overview of the nation's air pollution levels.
- Byrnihat, located on the Assam-Meghalaya border, emerged as the most polluted city in India, with an average PM2.5 concentration of 140 $\mu g/m^3$ (Micrograms per Cubic Metre).
- Among India's top 10 polluted cities, three were in Haryana, two each in Rajasthan and Uttar Pradesh, and one each in Delhi, Assam, and Bihar.
- Delhi ranked as the 3rd most polluted city, with PM2.5 levels at 102 $\mu g/m^3$.

Ranking and Reports

World Happiness Report 2024

- **Publisher:** United Nations Sustainable Development Solutions Network
- **Leading Country:** Finland – Celebrating its 7th consecutive year as the happiest country!
- **Dominant Region:** Nordic Countries – A beacon of joy and contentment!
- **Least Happy Country:** Afghanistan – Struggling at the bottom of the happiness scale.
- **Resilience Highlight:** Israel – Achieving a high ranking despite ongoing conflicts, showcasing incredible resilience!
- **India's Ranking:** 126th out of 143 countries – A journey of growth and potential.
- **Urgent Concern:** The report highlights a widening happiness inequality and a troubling decline in children's happiness.
- **Emphasis:** The need for policy action to enhance well-being and happiness for all. Let's work towards a happier world together!

Report of Snow Leopards Status in India

- Union Minister of Environment, Forest, and Climate Change, Shri Bhupender Yadav released the report on the Status of Snow Leopards in India during the National Board for Wildlife meeting held in New Delhi.
- The Snow Leopard Population Assessment in India (SPAI) Program is the first-ever scientific exercise that reports Snow leopard population of 718 individuals in India.
- Based on data analysis, the estimated population in different states are as follows: Ladakh (477), Uttarakhand (124), Himachal Pradesh (51), Arunachal Pradesh (36), Sikkim (21), and Jammu and Kashmir (9).

Henley Passport Index 2024

- The Henley Passport Index 2024 was released highlighting the "power" of passports of 199 countries.
- The index is created by London-based global citizenship and residence advisory firm Henley & Partners, using exclusive data from the International Air Transport Association (IATA).
- The index was topped by Singapore. Passports of this country has visa-free access to 195 destinations
- According to the latest ranking, India stands at the 81st rank in the list of most powerful passports. India shares the rank with Gabon.
- The least powerful passport in the world is Afghanistan. It ranked at 107th spot with access to 28 countries. It is followed by Syria (106), Iraq (105), Pakistan (104) and Yemen (103).

'World Employment and Social Outlook' report 2024

- The International Labour Organization (ILO) has released the 2024 'World Employment and Social Outlook' report.
- The report forecasts that the number of unemployed people will rise by 2 million, lifting the global unemployment rate to 5.2 percent from 5.1 percent in 2023.

Global Firepower's Military Strength Rankings 2024

- The United States took the first spot in Global Firepower's Military Strength Rankings 2024, followed by Russia and China.
- India clinched fourth spot, above the United Kingdom and Japan.
- Bhutan is at the bottom of the list with a power index of 6.3704.

Global Cooperation Barometer 2024

- The World Economic Forum (WEF) has released a report titled the Global Cooperation Barometer 2024.
- The report was developed in collaboration with management consultants McKinsey & Company.
- India ranked 93 out of 180 countries on the corruption perceptions index for 2023.

Electoral Democracy Index 2023

- India ranks 108th in the Electoral Democracy Index of the V-dem Democracy report 2023.
- India ranks way below countries such as Tanzania, Bolivia, Mexico, Singapore and Nigeria.

Global Brand Guardianship Index 2024

- Reliance Industries Limited (RIL) chairman and managing director Mukesh Ambani has been ranked first among all the Indians and second globally in the Brand Guardianship Index 2024 compiled by Brand Finance.

Annual NeSDA Way Forward Report for 2023

- The Department of Administrative Reforms and Public Grievances (DARPG) released a report (National e-Governance Service Delivery Assessment (NeSDA) Way Forward Annual Report 2023) showcasing efforts to improve e-Service delivery.
- Jammu and Kashmir offer the highest number of e-services (1117) among all States/UTs.
- Jammu and Kashmir, Kerala, Assam, and Odisha provide 100% of their services through their identified Single Unified Service Delivery Portal.

Global Climate Report 2023

- The World Meteorological Organization (WMO) released its State of the Global Climate Report 2023, confirming that 2023 was the warmest year on record.
- The report highlights the alarming trends in various climate indicators, including record-breaking greenhouse gas levels, surface temperatures, ocean heat and acidification, sea level rise, Antarctic sea ice cover, and glacier retreat.

All-India Consumer Price Index

- The All-India Consumer Price Index for Agricultural Laborers and Rural Laborers (Base: 1986-87=100) remained steady in February 2024, with figures of 1258 and 1269, respectively.

International IP Index 2024

- The US Chamber of Commerce released the 12th edition of its International IP (intellectual property) Index.
- India ranked at 42 out of the 55 countries in the index with an overall score of 38.64 per cent.
- The United States emerged at the top of the list followed by the United Kingdom and France.

Top Ranks of International IP Index 2024

Rank	Country
1	United States
2	United Kingdom
3	France
4	Germany
5	Sweden

India ranks in Hepatitis B and C Cases Worldwide

- In 2022, India ranked second in terms of the number of hepatitis B and C cases globally, after China, with an estimated 35 million infections, according to a report by the World Health Organization (WHO).

Global Tourism Index 2024

- India's rank on the World Economic Forum's Travel & Tourism Development Index 2024 has risen to 39th place, reflecting the resurgence of global tourism after the pandemic.
- While the United States topped the list, India stood as the highest-ranked country in South Asia and among the lower-middle-income economies.
- After the US, Spain, Japan, France and Australia figure among the top five in the 2024 list.

Global Cities Index 2024

- Delhi, the national capital of India, has secured the 350th rank in the Oxford Economics' Global Cities Index.
- The index ranks cities from 163 countries based on five categories: Economics, Human Capital, Quality of Life, Environment, and Governance.
- New York leads, followed by London, San Jose, Tokyo, and Paris.

Ronaldo tops forbes' list of Highest-Paid Athletes again

- Cristiano Ronaldo has once again secured the top spot on Forbes' list of highest-paid athletes, marking the fourth time he has achieved this distinction.

World Migration Report 2024

- The World Migration Report 2024, published by the International Organization for Migration (IOM), provides a comprehensive overview of global migration trends and challenges.
- According to the report, India has a slightly higher share of female immigrants than males.
- India is home to the world's largest number of international migrants, with 18 million Indians residing in countries such as the United Arab Emirates, the United States, and Saudi Arabia.

Chennai Tops As Best City For Indian Women

- Chennai emerged as the top Indian city for women in 2023 in terms of inclusivity and conduciveness to working women, as per findings from diversity, equity and inclusivity consultant Avtar Group's Top Cities for Women in India (TCWI) 2023.
- Tamil Nadu cities topped both categories that the study covered – 49 cities in the million-plus population category and 64 cities in the less than a million-population category.

US Leads 2024 Military Rankings

- In the 2024 Global Firepower Military Strength Rankings, the US secured the top position, with Russia and China following.
- In the global military hierarchy, India steadfastly secures its standing as the 4th most potent military force. Bhutan ranks lowest with a power index of 6.3704.
- In terms of military strength, Pakistan, secures the ninth position.

World Bank's Logistics Performance Index Report 2023

- According to the World Bank's 'Logistics Performance Index Report (2023): Connecting to Compete 2023', India ranks 38 out of 139 countries.

- India's rank has improved by six places from 44 in 2018 and sixteen places from 54 in 2014.

Hurun Global Unicorn Index 2024

- According to the Hurun Global Unicorn Index 2024, India for the first time recorded a decline in unicorn creation since 2017.
- However, India is still the third largest hub of unicorns in the world after the United States of America and China.

India's Human Development Index 2023-24

- India's ranking on the United Nations Human Development Index improved by one position in 2022 to 134 out of 193 countries ranked compared to 135 out of 192 countries ranked in 2021 on the back of a marginal increase in its HDI value to 0.644 compared to 0.633 in 2021.

UNDP Gender Inequality Index 2022

- According to the Gender Inequality Index 2022 released by the United Nations Development Programme out of 193 countries India stands at rank 108 with a score of 0.437.
- India's rank was 122 out of 191 countries with a score of 0.490 in the Gender Inequality Index 2021.
- This marks a good jump of 14 ranks on GII 2022 vis-a-vis GII 2021.

Top 3 Countries of World Press Freedom Index 2024

Rank	Country	Global Score
1	Norway	91.89
2	Denmark	89.6
3	Sweden	88.32

World Press Freedom Index 2024

- Reporters Without Borders (RSF) released the 2024 World Press Freedom Index, which ranks 180 countries based on the freedom of journalism, reporting, and media functioning.
- As per the recent index, India has been ranked in the 159th position, which is two ranks higher than last year, however, India still lags behind countries like Turkey, Pakistan, and Sri Lanka, which are ranked at 158, 152, and 150, respectively.

Environmental Performance Index 2024

- The Environmental Performance Index 2024 ranks Estonia first, highlighting global challenges in reducing emissions and protecting biodiversity.
- India ranks 176th, emphasizing the need for stronger sustainability efforts.

India ranks 63rd on Energy Transition Index

- India has been ranked 63rd on a global Energy Transition Index released on June 19 by the World Economic Forum.
- European nations dominated the top ranks with Sweden topping the index, followed by Denmark, Finland, Switzerland and France in the top five. China was ranked 20th.

FILL IN THE BLANKS

1. The Artificial Intelligence Preparedness Index 2024 was released by the ______.
2. The Climate Change Performance Index (CCPI) 2025 was jointly published by Germanwatch, the NewClimate Institute, and the ______.
3. The Global Hunger Index (GHI) 2024 was released by Concern Worldwide and ______.
4. The World Justice Project Rule of Law Index 2024 was published by the ______.
5. The Global Multidimensional Poverty Index (MPI) 2024 was released by the United Nations Development Programme (UNDP) and the ______.
6. The World Talent Ranking 2024 was published by the ______.
7. The Global Cybersecurity Index (GCI) 2024 was released by the ______.
8. The Henley Passport Index 2024 was compiled and published by ______.

MATCHING GAME

Index	Rank/Position
A. KIIT University's position in India in the Interdisciplinary Science Rankings 2025	1. 4th
B. India's position in the Network Readiness Index (NRI) 2024	2. 80th
C. India's position in the Climate Change Performance Index (CCPI) 2025	3. 39th
D. India's rank in the Global Innovation Index (GII) 2024	4. 49th
E. India's rank in the World Justice Project (WJP) Rule of Law Index 2024	5. 10th
F. India's rank in the Henley Passport Index 2024	6. 79th

Scan Me

SCAN TO GET MULTIPLE CHOICE QUESTIONS

Answer Key (Fill In The Blanks): 1. International Monetary Fund (IMF) 2. Climate Action Network 3. Welthungerhilfe 4. World Justice Project (WJP) 5. Oxford Poverty and Human Development Initiative (OPHI) 6. Institute for Management Development (IMD) 7. International Telecommunication Union (ITU) 8. Henley & Partners

Answer Key (Matching Game): A → 1 B → 4 C → 5 D → 3 E → 6 F → 2

MOU AND AGREEMENTS

AIR INDIA-VISTARA MERGER

- On 12th November 2024, Air India, the flagship airline of the Tata Group, announced the completion of the operational integration and legal merger between itself and Vistara, a joint venture between the Tata Group and Singapore Airlines.
- This is the first major expansion of codeshare arrangements between Star Alliance carriers since 2010.
- The merger also received support from other key stakeholders including the Ministry of Civil Aviation (MoCA), Bureau of Civil Aviation Security (BCAS) and several international regulators.
- In November 2022, the National Company Law Tribunal (NCLT) approved the merger of Air India and Vistara.

Air India

- Air India is the flag carrier airline of India, headquartered in Gurugram, Haryana.
- The airline is owned by Air India Limited, a subsidiary of the Tata Group and Singapore Airlines.

HISTORICAL POINTS

- Air India was founded by JRD Tata as Tata Airlines in 1932.
- Tata himself flew the first single-engine de Havilland Puss Moth, carrying air mail from Karachi to Bombay.
- In 1953, the airline was nationalized by the Government of India and renamed Air India.
- In 1960, Air India inducted its first Boeing 707, becoming the first Asian airline to use a jet aircraft.
- The airline launched its first long-haul flight from Mumbai to London in 1948.
- In 2022, Air India was privatized and returned to the Tata Group after 69 years.
- Air India became the 27th member of the Star Alliance in 2014

KEY PEOPLE

- **Chairman:** Natarajan Chandrasekaran
- **CEO & MD:** Campbell Wilson

HEADQUARTERS AND HUBS

- **Headquarters:** Gurugram, Haryana
- **Main Hub:** Indira Gandhi International Airport, Delhi
- **Fleet Expansion:** Air India announced an order for 470 aircraft from Airbus and Boeing in 2023.

KEY POINTS OF THE MERGER

- **Formation of a Full-Service Carrier:** The merger integrates Vistara's operations into Air India, creating a unified full-service carrier.
- **Expanded Network:** The new entity will operate over 5,600 weekly flights, connecting more than 90 domestic and international destinations with a fleet of 208 aircraft.
- **Enhanced Connectivity:** The combined airline will offer extended worldwide connectivity to over 800 destinations through more than 75 code share and interline partners.
- **Loyalty Program Integration:** Club Vistara members have been seamlessly transferred to Air India's Maharaja Club, preserving their benefits and points.
- **Investment by Singapore Airlines:** Singapore Airlines will invest an additional ₹3,194.5 crore in the enlarged entity.

VISTARA

- Vistara was a full-service airline based in Gurugram, Haryana, India, and a joint venture between Tata Sons and Singapore Airlines.
- It commenced operations on January 9, 2015, and ceased operations on November 12, 2024, following its merger with Air India.

HISTORICAL POINTS

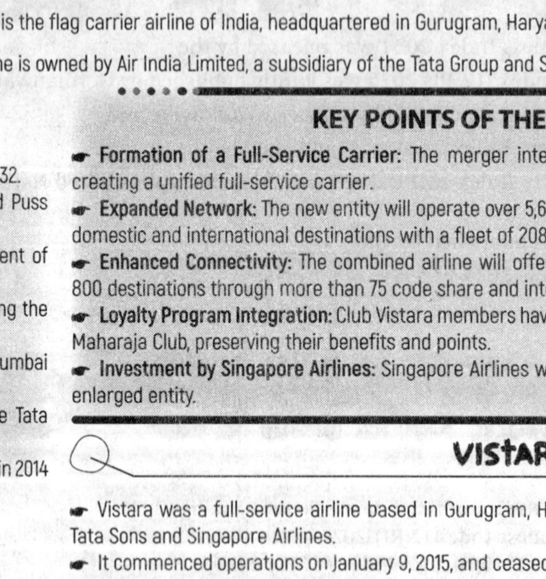

- Vistara was founded in 2013 as Tata SIA Airlines Limited, a joint venture between Tata Sons and Singapore Airlines.
- The airline commenced operations on January 9, 2015, with its inaugural flight from Delhi to Mumbai.
- The name "Vistara" was derived from the Sanskrit word "vistara," meaning "limitless expanse".
- The airline operated a fleet of Airbus A320neo, A321neo, and Boeing 787-9 Dreamliner aircraft.

MoUs and Agreements

Prasar Bharati to broadcast Hockey India League

- Prasar Bharati has signed a Memorandum of Understanding (MoU) with Hockey India to provide a live broadcast of the upcoming Hockey India League (HIL).
- With this MoU, Doordarshan has become the official broadcast partner for Hockey India League 2024-25 which commenced on December 28 in Rourkela.

EC signs electoral cooperation agreement with Uzbekistan

- In October 2024, the Election Commission of India signed an electoral cooperation agreement with Uzbekistan's central poll body.
- A four-member delegation from Uzbekistan led by Khusanova Mukhtar participated in the 2024 Lok Sabha elections in India.
- The Election Commission of India is a permanent and independent body established by the Constitution of India to ensure free and fair elections in the country.

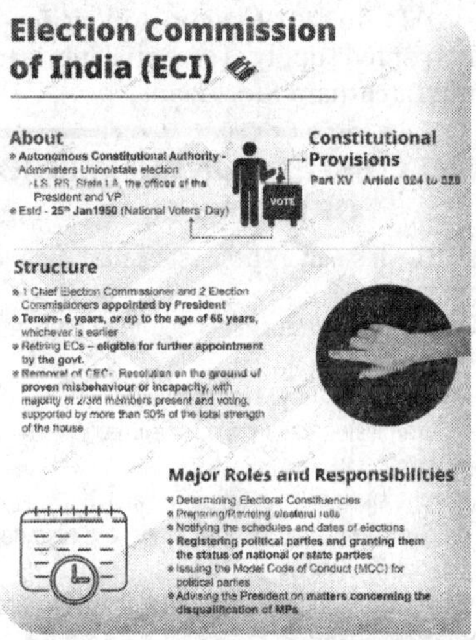

Indian Railways and Switzerland's Ministry of Transport signed an MoU for technical cooperation

- In October 2024, the Indian Railways has signed an MoU with the Federal Department of Environment, Transport, Energy and Communications (DETEC) of Switzerland to boost up Technological cooperation.
- MoU outlines a broad cooperation in many fields based on the exchange of technology, track maintenance, management and construction.

SWITZERLAND

- **Switzerland is bordered by:** Germany (north), France (west), Italy (south), Austria and Liechtenstein (east).
- **Area:** Approximately 41,290 square kilometers (15,940 square miles).
- **Lakes:** Lake Geneva, Lake Zurich, Lake Constance.
- **Rivers:** Rhine, Rhone, Aare, and Ticino.
- **Swiss National Park:** Switzerland's oldest national park.
- **Currency:** Swiss franc

ABOUT SPAIN

- **Location:** Southwestern Europe
- **Bordered by:** Portugal (west), France and Andorra (northeast), Mediterranean Sea (east and southeast), Atlantic Ocean (northwest) and Gibraltar (south, British Overseas Territory).
- **Mountain Ranges:** The Pyrenees, Sierra Nevada, and Cantabrian Mountains.
- **Rivers:** Major rivers include the Ebro, Tagus, Guadalquivir, and Douro.
- **Official Currency:** Euro (EUR)
- **Official language:** Spanish (Castilian)
- **Prime Minister:** Pedro Sánchez

GERMANY

- **Location:** Central Europe
- **North:** Denmark, North Sea, Baltic Sea
- **East:** Poland, Czech Republic
- **South:** Austria, Switzerland
- **West:** France, Luxembourg, Belgium, Netherlands
- **Area:** Approximately 357,022 square kilometers (137,847 square miles).
- **Capital:** Berlin
- **Government:** Federal parliamentary republic
- **Currency:** Euro (€).
- **Language:** German (official)
- **Population:** ~84 million (as of 2023)
- **President:** Frank-Walter Steinmeier
- **Chancellor:** Olaf Scholz

- The first version of MoU was signed on 31st August 2017 for the period of five years.

India-Spain signed MoUs in rail transport, customs & investment

- On 28th October 2024, during a bilateral meeting in Vadodara, Gujarat, India and Spain signed several Memorandums of Understanding (MoUs) to enhance cooperation in rail transport, customs, and investment.
- Both countries also announced 2026 as the India-Spain Year of Culture, Tourism, and AI.

India-Germany sign MoUs and agreements in various fields

- In October 2024, India and Germany signed a number of treaties, including the Mutual Legal Assistance Treaty in Criminal Matters and the Indo-German Green Hydrogen Road Map, during the 7th India-Germany Intergovernmental Consultations.

UNITED ARAB EMIRATES (UAE)

- UAE is a federation of seven emirates located in the southeast of the Arabian Peninsula, bordered by Saudi Arabia to the south and west, Oman to the east, and the Persian Gulf to the north.
- The country was founded on 2nd December 1971.
- **Capital:** Abu Dhabi
- **Official Language:** Arabic (English is widely spoken)
- **Ruler of Abu Dhabi & President of UAE:** Sheikh Mohamed bin Zayed Al Nahyan (as of 2024)
- **Ruler of Dubai & Prime Minister of UAE:** Sheikh Mohammed bin Rashid Al Maktoum.
- **Official languages:** Arabic
- **Total Area:** 83,600 km2 (32,300 sq mi)
- **Currency:** UAE dirham (AED)

- The India-Germany Green Hydrogen Roadmap outlines strategies to promote private sector investment, trade and export of green hydrogen to decarbonize difficult sectors such as steel, refineries and heavy-duty transport.

UPI and UAE's AANI link-up

- On 8th October 2024, India and the UAE signed a MoU to interlink India's Unified Payments Interface (UPI) with the UAE's AANI instant payment platform.
- This collaboration aims to facilitate seamless cross-border transactions, benefiting over 3 million Indians residing in the UAE.

SPORTS AUTHORITY OF INDIA (SAI)

- The Sports Authority of India (SAI) was established in 1984
- SAI is the apex sports organization under the Ministry of Youth Affairs and Sports.
- Headquarters: Lodhi Road, Delhi, India
- The two SAI Sports Academies are Netaji Subhas National Institute of Sports (NSNIS) in Patiala and Lakshmibai National College of Physical Education (LNCPE), in Thiruvananthapuram.

DEFENCE RESEARCH AND DEVELOPMENT ORGANISATION (DRDO)

- The DRDO is the premier R&D agency under the Department of Defence Research and Development in Ministry of Defence, Government of India.
- DRDO was established in 1958 after combining Technical Development Establishment (TDEs) of the Indian Army and the Directorate of Technical Development & Production (DTDP) with the Defence Science Organisation (DSO).
- It is headed by the Secretary, Department of Defence, R & D, and the Director General of DRDO.
- Project Indigo was the DRDO's first major defence project.
- Headquarters: DRDO Bhavan, New Delhi, India
- Motto: "Strength's Origin is in Science"

India & Jamaica exchange 4 MoUs on Digital Infrastructure, Cultural Exchange & Sports

- Recently, India and Jamaica signed four Memorandum of Understanding in the fields of Digital Public Infrastructure, Cultural Exchange and Sports.
- These MoUs were exchanged after delegation-level talks held between Prime Minister Narendra Modi and his visiting Jamaican counterpart Dr Andrew Holness in New Delhi.
- Prime Minister Andrew Holness is the first Jamaican Prime Minister to visit India who was on a four-day visit to India from 30 September to 3 October 2024.

Maharashtra govt, SAI sign MoU to establish National Centre of Excellence in Mumbai

- On 6th October 2024, the Government of Maharashtra and the Sports Authority of India (SAI) signed a MoU to establish a National Centre of Excellence in Kandivali, Mumbai.
- The sports complex will be developed on a 37-acre land parcel and will include modern sports infrastructure like athlete hostels, a central kitchen, a new hockey turf, a multipurpose sports hall, and a high-performance sports science center.

Rubber Research Institute signs MoU with Indian Oil

- On 25th September 2024, the Rubber Research Institute of India (RRII) signed an MoU with Indian Oil Corporation Ltd (IOCL) to enhance research on Rubber Process Oils.
- This collaboration aims to improve the performance and sustainability of both tyre and non-tyre rubber products.

ABOUT RUBBER RESEARCH INSTITUTE OF INDIA (RRII)

- RRII was established in 1955.
- RRII is a key institution under the Ministry of Commerce and Industry.
- It is dedicated to advancing rubber technology.

FSSAI and Brazil's MAPA Sign MoU to Enhance Food Safety Cooperation

- On 25th September 2024, the Food Safety and Standards Authority of India (FSSAI) signed an MoU with Brazil's Ministry of Agriculture and Livestock (MAPA) to enhance food safety cooperation.
- This agreement, formalized at the Global Food Regulators Summit 2024 in New Delhi, aims to improve food safety standards through joint projects and technical exchanges.

ADDITIONAL INFORMATION

- The United Planters Association of Southern India (UPASI) was established in 1893.
- The Rubber Board was set up in 1947 to oversee the cultivation and development of rubber.

DRDO Transferred High-Altitude Technologies to Power Grid Corporation

- Defence Institute of Physiology and Allied Sciences (DIPAS), a leading laboratory under the Defence Research and Development Organisation (DRDO), handed over high-altitude sustenance technologies to Power Grid Corporation of India Limited (PGCIL) on September 21, 2024.
- The Pang-Kaithal HVDC Project located at an altitude of 15,760 ft is a significant step towards energy security in Ladakh region and comprehensive integration of solar power into India's national grid.

UAE, India sign MoU to Strengthen Public Sector Audit Cooperation

- In September 2024, the Comptroller and Auditor General of India (CAG) has signed an MoU with the United Arab Emirates (UAE) Accountability Authority to foster collaboration between the two institutions in public sector audits.
- The CAG is the supreme audit body in India, and the UAE Accountability Authority is the supreme audit authority in the UAE.
- The Comptroller and Auditor General of India (CAG) is a constitutional body established under Article 148 of the Constitution.

RINL and IOCL sign MoU for supply of Hydraulic and Lubricating Oil

- On 28th August 2024, Rashtriya Ispat Nigam Limited (RINL) signed a Memorandum of Understanding (MoU) with Indian Oil Corporation Limited (IOCL) for the supply of hydraulic and lubricating oils and greases.
- This five-year agreement, effective from 2024 to 2029, aims to ensure an uninterrupted supply of essential lubricants to Visakhapatnam Steel Plant.

ABOUT COMPETITION COMMISSION OF INDIA (CCI)

- The CCI is a statutory body established under the Competition Act, 2002.
- CCI is responsible for enforcing the Competition Act, 2002.
- It was duly constituted in March 2009.
- The Commission consists of one Chairperson and six Members.
- The commission is a quasi-judicial body which gives opinions to statutory authorities and also deals with other cases.
- It works within the Ministry of Corporate Affairs.

India and Sri Lanka sign MoU for LNG infrastructure development

- A Memorandum of Understanding was signed between Indian company 'Petronet LNG limited' and a Sri Lanka based private company for infrastructure development and supply of Liquified Natural Gas in Colombo.
- The MoU would allow for development of LNG based power plants with capacity of over 1000 MW at Kerawalapitiya near Colombo as well as supply of the fuel from Kochi LNG Terminal.

IIT Gandhinagar & IIT Indore launched cNARMADA

- The Indian Institute of Technology Gandhinagar (IITGN) has created a new center called the Centre for Narmada River Basin Management (cNARMADA) to study the Narmada River and its surrounding areas.
- This center will work with IIT Indore and is supported by the Ministry of Jalshakti, responsible for water resources in India.

Indian Railways and NCRTC launch 'One India-One Ticket' initiative

- On 12th August 2024, Indian Railways and the National Capital Region Transport Corporation (NCRTC) launched the 'One India-One Ticket' initiative.
- It aims to simplify travel by allowing passengers to book and travel using both Indian Railways and Namo Bharat trains with a single ticket.

MEA and NSIL sign MoU for launch of Nepalese Munal Satellite

- On 10th August 2024, the Ministry of External Affairs (MEA) and NewSpace India Limited (NSIL) signed an MoU to launch Nepal's Munal satellite.
- Developed by the Nepal Academy of Science and Technology (NAST) with assistance from Antarikchya Pratishan Nepal (APN), the satellite aims to create a vegetation density database of Earth's surface.

Tata Power Solar partnered with Bank of India for Solar & EV Financing

- On 26th July 2024, Tata Power Solar Systems Ltd. partnered with Bank of India to offer easy financing options for rooftop solar installations and EV charging stations.
- This collaboration supports the government's green energy initiatives, providing loans with attractive interest rates and collateral-free options to residential users, housing societies, and MSMEs.
- Under the PM Surya Ghar Yojana, residential customers can avail loans up to ₹2 lakh for solar systems up to 3 KW at 7.10% interest per annum.

IAEA and UNOSSC strengthened South-South Cooperation

- In July 2024, the International Atomic Energy Agency (IAEA) has collaborated with the United Nations Office for South-South Cooperation (UNOSSC) to improve sustainable development through South-South and triangular cooperation, with an initial focus on climate change's effects on developing nations.
- Under the agreement, the IAEA will engage in UNOSSC programmes such as 'Data to Policy Network' and 'Solutions Lab,'.

Indian Oil Corp. and Indian Navy partnered for Hydrogen E-Mobility

- On22ndJuly2024, IndianOilCorporation Ltd. (IOCL) and the Indian Navy signed a Memorandum of Understanding (MoU) to promote hydrogen e-mobility.
- As part of this initiative, IOCL handed over a state-of-the-art green hydrogen fuel cell bus to the Indian Navy for trials and performance testing.

Airbus and Tata to launch first made-in-India H125 helicopter by 2026

- On 23rd July 2024, Airbus and Tata Advanced Systems formalized a contract to establish the first Final Assembly Line (FAL) for the H125 helicopter in India.
- This facility, set to be operational by 2026, will produce the H125 helicopter for both domestic and neighboring markets.
- The H125, known for its versatility and performance, will support various missions, including emergency medical services, law enforcement, and tourism.

RRU, NSE IX signed MoU for Economic and Financial Security Cooperation

- On 19th July 2024, Rashtriya Raksha University (RRU) and NSE International Exchange (NSE IX) signed a MoU to enhance cooperation in economic and financial security.
- The agreement aims to bridge the gap between economic stability and national security, emphasizing the crucial role of financial growth in maintaining national security.

NTPC Vidyut Vyapar Nigam Ltd and Haryana Govt Signed an Agreement to set up A Green Charcoal Plant

- In July 2024, NTPC Vidyut Vyapar Nigam Ltd and Haryana Govt sign MoU to establish green charcoal production plants from waste.
- NVVNL will set up two green charcoal plants in Gurugram and Faridabad, Haryana. These plants will convert municipal waste into charcoal or green coal.
- India's largest waste-to-charcoal plant is in Varanasi, Uttar Pradesh, and it can process 600 tonnes of waste daily.

AIM, WIPO Join Hands to Boost Innovation in Global South

- On 22 July 2024, The Atal Innovation Mission(AIM) of the NITI Aayog has signed a letter of intent with the World Intellectual Property Organisation (WIPO) to jointly build suitable programmes to promote Innovation, Entrepreneurship and Intellectual property for Global South.
- Global South refers to the underdeveloped, less developed and developing countries of Asia, Africa and Latin America.

LIC Enters Into Tie-Up With IDFC First Bank under Corporate Agency Arrangement

- Life Insurance Corporation of India (LIC) has entered into a tie-up with IDFC First Bank Ltd under a corporate agency arrangement on 16th July 2024.
- This collaboration enables more than 1 crore customers of IDFC First Bank to buy LIC policies online through the bank's website.
- The partnership leverages IDFC First Bank's significant online transaction volume, offering an end-to-end solution for diverse life insurance needs.

India-Taiwan agreement boosts Organic Product Trade

- The India-Taiwan Mutual Recognition Agreement (MRA) for organic products came into effect on 8 July 2024. This was announced at the 9th Working Group Meeting on Trade of India and Taiwan in New Delhi.
- Under the agreement, organic products from India can be exported to Taiwan after it is certified by a competent authority in India. Similarly, Taiwan's organic products can be sold in India if they are certified by a competent authority in Taiwan.

NTPC VIDYUT VYAPAR NIGAM LIMITED

- NTPC Vidyut Vyapar Nigam Limited was established in 2002 by the Central Government-owned NTPC Limited.
- It is in the business of electricity trading and has been made the nodal agency by the Government of India for cross border trading of electricity with Bangladesh, Bhutan and Nepal.
- Headquarters: New Delhi
- Chief Executive Officer (CEO): N K Sharma

China and U.S. Science Agreement Extended Until 2029

- China and the United States have agreed to extend their Science and Technology Cooperation Agreement for five more years starting August 27, 2024.
- The Agreement was established in 1979 by Chinese leader Deng Xiaoping and U.S. President Jimmy Carter.
- The Agreement encompasses 40 sub-agreements across various fields, including agriculture and nuclear fusion.

National MoU

NSDC and ILO partner for "Skill Development and Lifelong Learning"

- The National Skill Development Corporation (NSDC) and the International Labour Organization (ILO) have partnered to focus on "Skill Development and Lifelong Learning."
- The collaboration aims to address skill gaps and enhance the employability of workers.
- It will create effective training systems and promote continuous learning throughout an individual's career.

MEA, MeitY, and CSC partnered to enhance eMigrate Services

- The Ministry of External Affairs (MEA), Ministry of Electronics and Information Technology (MeitY), and CSC e-Governance Services India Limited have signed a MoU to enhance eMigrate services through Common Services Centres (CSCs).
- The eMigrate project aims to assist blue-collar workers going to Emigration Check Required (ECR) countries.

Swiggy partners with "SHIELD" for enhanced fraud prevention

- Swiggy, the popular food delivery platform, has collaborated with SHIELD, a leading fraud prevention company, to enhance security and prevent fraudulent activities.
- This partnership aims to safeguard user accounts, transactions, and sensitive data.

Airbus, SIDBI signed MoU for helicopter financing in India

- Airbus Helicopters and the Small Industries Development Bank of India (SIDBI) have signed an MoU for financing the purchase of Airbus' helicopters in India.
- Under this collaboration, both entities will identify potential civil helicopter operators in India seeking financing solutions for acquiring Airbus helicopters.
- This strategic move aims to make civil helicopters more accessible to operators in India and foster growth in the rotary wing aircraft market.

FICCI, IESA signed contract to foster innovation in semiconductor

- The Federation of Indian Chambers of Commerce and Industry (FICCI) and the India Electronics and Semiconductor Association (IESA) have signed an MoU to foster innovation in the semiconductor and electronics sector.
- The partnership aims to leverage their combined strengths to promote research and development, attract investments, and strengthen India's position in the global semiconductor supply chain.
- The MoU establishes a framework for collaboration on various initiatives, including technology roundtables, industry partnerships, and policy advocacy.

AFMS and IIT Kanpur sign MoU to develop technology to solve healthcare problems

- The Armed Forces Medical Services (AFMS) signed a Memorandum of Understanding (MoU) for collaborative research and training with the Indian Institute of Technology (IIT) Kanpur on 18 April 2024.
- Under this MoU, AFMS and IIT Kanpur will team up to undertake research and develop new technologies to address health problems faced by soldiers in difficult terrains.

Rashtriya Raksha University signs MoU with French Starburst Aerospace

- Gandhinagar-based Rashtriya Raksha University (RRU) and Starburst Aerospace of France entered into an MoU to advance aerospace, defence, and homeland security innovation.
- The MoU includes the creation of a venture capital fund of 100 million euros for aerospace, defence and security technology and provides export promotion support for Indian start-ups to explore international markets.

BEL signed MoU with IIT Mandi for co-operation in various fields

- Bharat Electronics Limited (BEL) signed an MoU with IIT Mandi for cooperation in research and technology/product development.
- The focus areas include semiconductors, quantum technologies, and drones.
- The partnership will foster innovation, enhance product quality, and expand the range of solutions provided by BEL.

ISKCON collaborates with NSDC for skill development

- ISKCON (International Society for Krishna Consciousness) has partnered with the National Skill Development Corporation (NSDC) to promote skill development across India.
- This collaboration focuses on empowering youth by offering training in various sectors, including hospitality, agriculture, and traditional arts.
- The strategic partnership will focus on skilling youth from tribal and marginalised communities in Uttar Pradesh, Maharashtra, Rajasthan, Gujarat, and Madhya Pradesh.

KABIL and CSIR-IMMT sign MoU for Technical and Knowledge cooperation for Critical Minerals

- Khanij Bidesh India Limited (KABIL) signed an MoU with CSIR-IMMT for technical and knowledge cooperation in critical minerals.
- The collaboration aims to leverage CSIR-IMMT's expertise for projects like metallurgical test work-plans, process flowsheets, and technology selection for mineral processing.
- KABIL, a JV of NALCO, HCL, and MECL, focuses on securing strategic minerals.

MoD signed contract worth over Rs. 2,890 cr with HAL

- The Ministry of Defence signed a contract with Hindustan Aeronautics Limited (HAL) on March 15, 2024, for the Mid Life Upgrade (MLU) of 25 Dornier Aircraft for the Indian Navy, valued at Rs. 2,890 crore.
- The MLU involves incorporating state-of-the-art Avionics Systems and Primary Role sensors into the Dornier Aircraft, enhancing their operational capability.

RECPDCL and BHEL to jointly develop utility-scale renewable energy projects

- REC Power Development and Consultancy and BHEL signed an MoU to form a special purpose vehicle (SPV) for developing utility-scale renewable energy projects.
- It will focus on catering to the energy requirement of commercial and industrial (C&I) segment with initial capacity of 1 GW which would be scaled further.
- This collaboration brings together our extensive experience in the renewable energy sector with BHEL's proven expertise in manufacturing and engineering.
- Renewable energy projects of 10 MW or more are referred as utility-scale projects.

Ministry of Rural Development signs an MoU with J-PAL South Asia to provide technical assistance

- The Ministry of Rural Development (MoRD) signed an MoU with J-PAL South Asia to provide technical assistance for inclusive development under the Deendayal Antyodaya Yojana - National Rural Livelihoods Mission (DAY-NRLM).
- The collaboration aims to empower rural women through the 'Samaveshi Aajeevika' program, which includes business training, life-skills coaching, and financial support.
- J-PAL South Asia will help MoRD adopt scientific evidence and data in decision-making and set up a Gender Impact Lab for new research.

AIIMS-ECHS signed MoA for health services to ex-servicemen

- AIIMS and the Ex-Servicemen Contributory Health Scheme (ECHS) signed an MoA to provide health services to ex-servicemen and their families.
- This agreement ensures free-of-cost health services, including emergency care, benefiting over 30,000 ex-servicemen and their dependents.
- The collaboration aims to reduce the patient load in army hospitals and provide cashless, cap-less specialty treatment through ECHS.

MoU signed between ICAR and Dhanuka Agritech Limited

- The Indian Council of Agricultural Research (ICAR) and Dhanuka Agritech Limited signed an MoU to enhance agricultural practices.
- The agreement aims to deliver new technology to farmers, especially those with small land holdings.
- Dhanuka Agritech will provide training in agricultural production by partnering with central institutes, ATARIs, and KVKs.

Ministry of Heavy Industries signed an MOU with IIT-Roorkee

- The Ministry of Heavy Industries (MHI) signed an MoU with IIT Roorkee to foster innovation in the automotive and electric vehicle (EV) sectors.
- It aims to establish a Centre of Excellence (CoE) and an Industry Accelerator at IIT Roorkee under the Scheme for Enhancement of Competitiveness in the Indian Capital Goods Sector Phase II.
- The total project cost is ₹24.66 crore, with MHI contributing ₹19.87 crore and industry partners adding ₹4.78 crore.

India, EFTA ink free trade agreement

- India and the European Free Trade Association (EFTA) signed a Trade and Economic Partnership Agreement (TEPA) on March 10, 2024.
- This agreement includes Iceland, Liechtenstein, Norway, and Switzerland.
- TEPA aims to boost economic growth, create job opportunities, and strengthen bilateral relations.
- EFTA committed to promoting investments worth USD 100 billion and generating 1 million jobs in India over the next 15 years.

RBI, Bank of Indonesia sign MoU promoting use of local currencies for trade

- The Reserve Bank of India (RBI) and Bank Indonesia (BI) signed an MoU to promote the use of local currencies (INR and IDR) for cross-border transactions.
- The MoU aims to facilitate bilateral trade by enabling exporters and importers to invoice and pay in their respective domestic currencies.
- The MoU covers all current account transactions, permissible capital account transactions and any other economic and financial transactions as agreed upon by both countries.

Nokia and IISc teamed up to drive 6G Research in India

- Nokia and the Indian Institute of Science (IISc) have teamed up to drive 6G research in India.
- Their collaboration focuses on 6G radio technologies, 6G architecture, and AI/ML applications.
- They aim to develop sustainable, energy-efficient communication systems, improve network resilience, and enhance transportation safety, healthcare, and education through "Network as Sensor" technologies.

SSB inks MoU for free education of 100 children of force personnel

- The Sashastra Seema Bal (SSB) signed an MoU with United World Academy, Bengaluru, to provide free education to 100 children of SSB personnel and those who sacrificed their lives in the line of duty.
- The agreement ensures free admission and academic fees, with boarding expenses around ₹1.08 lakh per annum.
- The about 80,000 personnel strong Sashastra Seema Bal (SSB) functions under the Union home ministry and is primarily tasked to guard unfenced Indian borders with Nepal and Bhutan apart from rendering a variety of duties in the internal security domain of the country.

IEPFA and DBS Bank ink MoU to spread awareness on investment and fraudulent schemes

- The Investor Education and Protection Fund Authority (IEPFA) and DBS Bank signed an MoU to spread awareness about investment and fraudulent schemes.
- DBS Bank will use its extensive network of branches, ATMs, and digital platforms to disseminate safety messages.
- The initiative will feature safety messages on ATM screens, the bank's website, WhatsApp, and social media accounts.

IREDA and PNB join hands to Co-Finance Renewable Energy Projects

- Indian Renewable Energy Development Agency Ltd. (IREDA) and Punjab National Bank (PNB) have signed an MoU aimed at advancing renewable energy initiatives across the nation.

- The MoU includes provisions for joint lending, loan syndication, underwriting, and management of Trust and Retention Accounts (TRA) for IREDA borrowers.
- This partnership aligns with India's goal to achieve 500 GW of non-fossil-based electricity generation capacity by 2030.

CIAL, BPCL to establish 1st Green Hydrogen Plant at Cochin Airport

- Cochin International Airport Ltd. (CIAL) has entered into a MoU with Bharat Petroleum Corporation Ltd. (BPCL) for setting up a green hydrogen plant on the premises of Cochin Airport.
- This plant will produce green hydrogen using renewable energy sources, aligning with CIAL's commitment to sustainable aviation.
- BPCL will oversee the plant's establishment and operations, while CIAL will provide land, water, and green energy resources.
- The initial output will power airport vehicles, aiming for carbon neutrality.

India and Colombia signed MoU on Digital Cooperation

- In February 2024, India and Colombia signed an MoU to promote digital transformation.
- The collaboration aims to share successful digital solutions, such as India Stack, to enhance digital public infrastructures in Colombia.
- The partnership includes capacity-building programs, exchange of best practices, and development of pilot solutions.

Education Ministry partners FIFA to boost Football

- The Ministry of Education has partnered with FIFA to promote football in schools across India.
- Their joint initiative aims to distribute 11 lakh footballs to more than 1.5 lakh schools, making the sport accessible to students nationwide.

IPPB enter into MoU with Hindustan Zinc to offer financial inclusion services in Rajasthan

- India Post Payments Bank (IPPB) and Hindustan Zinc Limited (HZL) have formed a transformative alliance to pioneer inclusive financial solutions in rural Rajasthan, India.
- The alliance aims to provide financial inclusion services to HZL's beneficiaries, facilitating doorstep banking service delivery to unserved and underserved populations.

International MoU

India-Iran 10-year deal to operate Chabahar Port

- In May 2024, India signed a significant 10-year agreement with Iran to operate the Chabahar Port, located on the southeastern coast of Iran along the Gulf of Oman.
- This deal signifies India's commitment to enhancing its presence in the region and fostering economic development through increased trade and infrastructure connectivity.

PhonePe partners with eSewa, HAN Pokhara to promote UPI in Nepal

- PhonePe partnered with eSewa and the Hotel Association of Nepal (HAN) Pokhara to promote UPI payments in Nepal.
- This collaboration was announced during the Fewa New Year Festival in Pokhara, aiming to popularize digital payments among local merchants and tourists.
- The initiative includes on-ground activations, digital branding, and interactive activities to demonstrate UPI's convenience.

India, Russia signed agreement to strengthen Bilateral Cooperation in Nuclear Energy

- In February 2024, India and Russia signed an agreement to strengthen bilateral cooperation in nuclear energy.
- The agreement, signed at the Kudankulam Nuclear Power Project (KKNPP) site, amends the 2008 intergovernmental agreement to build additional reactors.
- The collaboration includes constructing more reactors at KKNPP and developing Russia-designed nuclear power plants at new sites in India.

India and France ink deal on Defence Space agreement

- India and France signed a Defence Space Agreement, during French President Emmanuel Macron's visit to India for Republic Day celebrations.
- This agreement includes joint development and deployment of military satellites, bolstering both offensive and defensive capabilities.

Switzerland-India Free Trade Agreement 2024

- India and the European Free Trade Association (EFTA), which includes Switzerland, signed a Trade and Economic Partnership Agreement (TEPA) on March 10, 2024.
- EFTA committed to promoting investments worth USD 100 billion and generating 1 million direct jobs in India over the next 15 years.
- The agreement covers trade in goods, services, investment promotion, intellectual property rights, and sustainable development.

INDIA'S 1ST REUSABLE HYBRID ROCKET 'RHUMI-1'

Tamil Nadu-based startup Space Zone India launched its first reusable hybrid rocket, **RHUMI-1**, on August 24, 2024, under the **RHUMI-2024 mission.**

KEY HIGHLIGHTS

- It is the world's first mobile launch of a hybrid rocket.
- **Launch Location:** Thiruvidanthai, near Chennai, on East Coast Road.

WHAT IS AN OXIDIZERS?

Oxidizers are solids, liquids, or gases that react readily with most organic material or reducing agents with no energy input. Oxidizers are a severe fire hazard. They are not necessarily combustible, but they can intensify combustion and increase the flammable range for chemicals so they ignite more readily.

ABOUT RHUMI-1

- Powered by a hybrid motor with common fuel and an electric parachute system.
- **Size:** The rocket is 3.5 meters long.
- **Name Meaning:** Named after Rumitharan, the son of Anand Megalingam, CEO and founder of Space Zone India.
- **Development:** Built by Space Zone India with help from the Martin Group.
- **Payload:** Carries 3 Cube Satellites and 50 PICO Satellites.
- **Purpose of PICO Satellites:** To collect data on atmosphere, altitude, ozone levels, and environmental conditions.

SPECIAL FEATURES

- **Adjustable Launch Angle:** The rocket's angle can be set between 0 to 120 degrees for better control of its path.
- **Student Learning:** Free workshops on rockets and satellites were organised for students and government schools in India.
- **Eco-Friendly Parachute:** Uses a CO2-triggered parachute to safely recover rocket parts, making it cost-effective and good for the environment.
- **Other Uses:** Apart from space, it can help in farming, environmental monitoring, and disaster management.
- **Hybrid Design:** Combines solid fuel and liquid oxidiser.
- **Safety Feature:** Fuel and oxidizer are only mixed during combustion.
- **Reduced Risk:** Lowers the chance of accidental explosions.

PHASES OF THE RLV PROJECT

- RLV-TD: Tested how the RLV behaves at high speeds.
- RLV-LEX: Carried out flight tests.
- RLV Technology Demonstrator: Showcased important technologies needed for reusable rockets.

ISRO'S RLV PROJECT

The Reusable Launch Vehicle (RLV) project by ISRO to reduce the cost of space missions and make India a leader in space technology.

WHY THE RLV PROJECT IS IMPORTANT?

- **Cost Saving:** Unlike current rockets that are used once, RLVs can be reused many times, making missions cheaper.
- **Easier Access to Space:** Allows India to carry out more space missions at a lower cost.
- **New Technology:** Helps develop advanced technologies like hypersonic speed, auto-navigation, and heat protection systems.

ABOUT SPACE ZONE INDIA

Space Zone India, the private aero-technology company behind RHUMI-1, is at the forefront of innovation in India's space sector.

Chairman: K Megalingam

Headquarters: Chennai

SPACE TECH

ESA Successfully Launched Copernicus Sentinel-1C Satellite

- On 5th December 2024, the European Space Agency (ESA) successfully launched the Copernicus Sentinel-1C Satellite aboard a Vega-C rocket from Europe's Spaceport in Kourou, French Guiana.
- Sentinel-1C is part of Copernicus, the European Union's Space program Earth observation component.
- This launch is the 6th Sentinel satellite in the Copernicus program launched by Arianespace.
- Sentinel-1A was the first satellite in the series, launched in April 2014, followed by the launch of Sentinel-1B in 2016.

Chinese Astronauts Set New Record for Longest Spacewalk

- China's Shenzhou-19 crew members, Cai Xuzhe and Song Lingdong, broke a 23-year-old US record by completing a 9 hour spacewalk.
- Two astronauts aboard the Tiangong space station set a new world record for the longest spacewalk, surpassing the previous 8-hour, 56-minute mark held by US astronauts James Voss and Susan Helms on March 12, 2001.

Space X Successfully Launches Koreasat-6A

- In November 2024, SpaceX successfully launched the Koreasat-6A communications satellite for KT SAT Corporation Ltd., South Korea's national satellite operator.

- The Falcon 9 rocket lifted off from Cape Canaveral, Florida, deploying the satellite into geostationary transfer orbit 35 minutes after liftoff.
- Koreasat-6A, built by Thales Alenia Space, will enhance broadcast and fixed satellite services across South Korea, supporting the Korea Augmentation Satellite System (KASS) for improved GPS accuracy.

Zimbabwe launched its 2nd satellite ZIMSAT-2

- On 5th November 2024, Zimbabwe launched its second satellite 'ZIMSAT-2' from Russia's Vostochny Cosmodrome.
- The satellite was developed in collaboration with the Zimbabwe National Geo-Spatial and Space Agency (ZINGSA) and Southwest State University (SWSU).
- This mission follows the November 2022 deployment of Zimbabwe's inaugural satellite, ZIMSAT-1.
- ZIMSAT-2 carries a multispectral camera for agricultural monitoring, mineral prospecting, and climate change studies.

Japan and India Collaborate to Address Space Debris

- Tokyo-based Orbital Lasers and Indian robotics company InspeCity Collaborate to Address Space Debris.
- The project is the latest example of collaboration between Japan and India, whose governments are working together on the joint Lunar Polar Exploration (LUPEX) mission, which could launch as early as 2026.
- InspeCity was founded in 2022 and raised $1.5 million last year, while Orbital Lasers has raised 900 million yen ($5.8 million) since it was established in January.

SpaceX's Polaris Dawn Mission Breaks New Records in Space

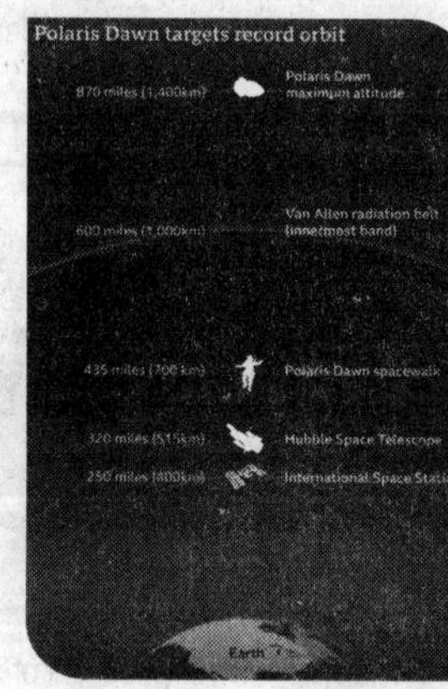

- SpaceX's Polaris Dawn mission, led by Jared Isaacman, achieved remarkable milestones in space exploration.
- The mission included the first-ever private spacewalk (Extravehicular Activity or EVA) performed by civilians.
- The crew comprised Jared Isaacman (Commander), Scott "Kidd" Poteet (Pilot), Sarah Gillis (Mission Specialist), and Anna Menon (Mission Specialist and Medical Officer).
- The crew reached an altitude of 1,408 kilometres, the highest human flight since NASA's Gemini 11 mission in 1966.

China Launches Fourth Manned Mission to Space Station Tiangong

- On October 30, 2024, China launched its fourth manned mission, Shenzhou-19, to the Tiangong space station.
- The mission included a three-member crew, featuring Wang Haoze, China's only female spaceflight engineer.

- The crew conducted 86 scientific experiments and replaced the previous team, marking another step forward in China's space exploration journey.

ESA Launches Moonlight Programme for Lunar Communications and Navigation

- The European Space Agency (ESA) launched the Moonlight Lunar Communications and Navigation Services (LCNS) programme on October 15, 2024, during the International Astronautical Congress.
- This is Europe's first satellite constellation dedicated to telecommunication and navigation for the Moon.
- The program's primary focus is to provide coverage, especially at the Moon's South Pole.

Chinese Lunar Probe Finds Water Traces in Moon's Soil

- On July 23, 2024, the Chinese lunar probe Chang'e-5 detected traces of water in soil samples collected from the Moon.
- These samples were retrieved during the Chang'e-5 mission in 2020, which marked China's first successful mission to return lunar rock and soil.

European Space Agency to Study Apophis Asteroid in 2029

- The European Space Agency (ESA) has announced a mission to study the Apophis asteroid when it approaches Earth at an extremely close distance in 2029.
- Apophis, once feared to collide with Earth, will pass within 32,000 km, providing a rare opportunity for research.
- ESA follows NASA as the second major agency to plan a mission to study the asteroid.

ABOUT ASTEROIDS

- Asteroids are small, rocky objects that orbit the Sun, primarily found in the asteroid belt between the orbits of Mars and Jupiter.
- They are remnants from the early formation of the solar system, dating back over 4.6 billion years.
- Asteroids can range in size from a few meters to several hundred kilometers in diameter.
- Some asteroids are solid, while others are rubble piles held together by gravity.
- Asteroids are classified into different types based on their composition.
- The three main types are C-type (carbonaceous), S-type (silicate or stony), and M-type (metallic). There are also other less common types, such as D-type (dark), V-type (basaltic), and P-type (primitive).

SpaceFields Tests India's First Aerospike Rocket Engine

- SpaceFields, a startup at the Indian Institute of Science Bengaluru (IISc), tested India's first aerospike rocket engine at IISc's Propulsion Test Facility in Challakere, Karnataka.
- The 168 mm aerospike engine was successfully ignited during a static test.
- SpaceFields used Titanium Grade-5 as the main material for the engine, as well as their patented thermal insulation to protect against high temperatures.

BepiColombo Sends First Images of Mercury's South Pole

- On September 8, 2024, the BepiColombo mission captured the first clear images of Mercury's South Pole.
- The images reveal cratered terrain and features like the Vivaldi and Stoddart basins.
- BepiColombo is a joint mission between the European Space Agency (ESA) and the Japan Aerospace Exploration Agency (JAXA), launched in 2018. Its main goal is to study Mercury.
- BepiColombo has two further flybys planned for December 2024 and January 2025.

Quad Nations Launch Cancer Moonshot Initiative

- The Quad Cancer Moonshot Initiative was announced by Prime Minister Modi to combat cancer in the Indo-Pacific region.
- Launched by India, the US, Australia, and Japan, the initiative focuses on innovative strategies for cancer prevention, detection, and treatment.
- It aims to reduce the burden of cancer on patients and their families in the region.

Japan Ends SLIM Moon Lander Mission

- The Japan Aerospace Exploration Agency (JAXA) has ended its Smart Lander for Investigating Moon (SLIM) mission after losing contact with the spacecraft.
- The H-IIA Launch Vehicle No.47 took SLIM into orbit on September 7, 2023, from the Tanegashima Space Centre and achieved Japan's first Moon soft landing on January 20, 2024.
- SLIM is a small-scale lunar lander designed for precise landings, reduced equipment size and weight, and investigating the Moon's origins.

SpaceX Successfully Catches Starship Booster with "Mechazilla"

- SpaceX successfully landed its Starship rocket using a new structure called "Mechazilla."
- Mechazilla is a term used to describe SpaceX's tower-based rocket-catching system designed to catch the company's reusable rocket stages, particularly the Super Heavy booster and potentially the Starship, during landing.
- The term "Mechazilla" was coined by SpaceX CEO Elon Musk, likening the tower's structure and mechanism to a robotic Godzilla.

Chinese scientists discover new pattern of solar rotation

- Using the CHASE (Chinese H-alpha Solar Explorer) satellite, Chinese researchers discovered a new pattern in the solar atmosphere's rotating dynamics.
- With a three-year operational plan, CHASE was introduced in October 2021.
- It allows for constant observation of solar phenomena because it orbits the Earth in a fixed position with respect to the sun.

South Korea launched Korea Aerospace Administration (KASA)

- South Korea launched its national space agency, Korea AeroSpace Administration (KASA), on May 27, 2024.
- Headquartered in Sacheon, South Gyeongsang Province, KASA aims to boost science and commercial space projects.
- It oversees the Korea Aerospace Research Institute and Korea Astronomy and Space Science Institute.

Oleg Kononenko become first person to spend 1,000 days in space

- Russian cosmonaut Oleg Kononenko has become the first person to spend a cumulative total of 1,000 days in space.
- He achieved this milestone on June 4, 2024, during his current mission to the International Space Station (ISS), which began on September 15, 2023.
- His cumulative time in space now totals 1,000 days, surpassing the previous record of 878 days held by fellow Russian Gennady Padalka.

Japan became 5th country to successfully land on the Moon

- Japan became the fifth country to reach the moon when one of its unmanned spacecraft successfully landed softly on the lunar surface.

- The Smart Lander for Investigating the Moon (SLIM) mission, led by the Japan Aerospace Exploration Agency (JAXA), achieved a precise landing using advanced technology.
- The SLIM spacecraft landed approximately **55 meters east of the original target landing site.**

NISAR Mission joint mission between NASA and ISRO

- The NASA-ISRO Synthetic Aperture Radar (NISAR) Mission is a groundbreaking joint Earth-observing mission between NASA and the Indian Space Research Organization (ISRO).
- Launched in March 2024, NISAR aims to measure Earth's dynamic surfaces, changing ecosystems, and ice masses.
- It uses dual radar frequencies (L-band and S-band) to map the planet every 12 days, detecting even tiny surface movements.

Axiom Mission 3

- On January 20, **Axiom Mission 3 (Ax-3)** achieved a significant milestone by successfully docking at the **International Space Station (ISS)**.
- This feat follows the launch of a SpaceX Falcon 9 rocket on January 18, carrying a cohort of European astronauts, including Turkey's first space traveler and three representatives from the European Space Agency (ESA), from NASA's Kennedy Space Center in Florida.
- The collaborative efforts of **NASA, Axiom Space, and SpaceX** are currently in full swing. This phase initiates during the spacecraft's approach to the ISS.

Second Rocket Launch Port of ISRO

- Prime Minister Modi laid the foundation stone of the **second rocket launchport of ISRO at Kulasekarapattinam,** in Tamil Nadu.
- The path taken by launches from SDSC necessitates maneuvering eastwards around Sri Lanka before embarking on a southward flight, resulting in increased fuel consumption.

Odysseus Completes First US Moon Landing in 50 Years

- The **Odysseus lunar lander** has made the **first United States landing on the moon** in more than 50 years, in what has been described as similar to a **"cargo mission".**

World's First Wooden Satellite

- Japan is planning to launch the **world's first wooden satellite in September 2024.**
- The satellite, named **"LignoSat"**, is made of magnolia wood, which has been found to be particularly stable and resistant to cracking.
- The project is a collaboration between **Kyoto University and the logging company Sumitomo Forestry.**
- The aim is to test the use of biodegradable materials like wood as environmentally friendly alternatives to the metals currently used in all satellites.

China Opens Qinling Station

- China has officially opened the **Qinling Station in Antarctica.** This significant development marks a new chapter in China's scientific exploration and research in the Antarctic region.
- The establishment of this station underscores **China's growing role in polar science**, a field that has critical implications for understanding climate change, sea-level rise, and other global environmental issues.

Prof Jayant Murthy honoured with Asteroid name

- An asteroid has been named after Indian Professor and distinguished scientist **Jayant Murthy**
- He is known for his work in space missions, ultraviolet astronomy, and interstellar medium.
- Previously cataloged as **2005 EX296,** the asteroid has now been designated as **(215884) Jayantmurthy.**

Astronomers identified two ancient star Shakti and Shiva

- Astronomers have identified Shakti and Shiva, two ancient star streams, as some of the earliest building blocks of the Milky Way galaxy.
- These streams, discovered using data from the European Space Agency's Gaia telescope, are believed to have merged with the Milky Way around 12 billion years ago.
- Each structure contains stars with similar chemical compositions, formed approximately 12-13 billion years ago.

World's 1st Rocket with fully 3D-Printed Engine

- **Agnikul Cosmos,** a start-up incubated at IIT Madras, achieved a historic milestone by launching the **world's first single-piece 3D printed rocket engine.**
- The rocket, named **Agnibaan**, was successfully test-fired from Sriharikota on 30 May 2024.
- Notably, Agnibaan is powered by the only rocket engine in India that uses both gas and liquid fuel (liquid oxygen/kerosene).

Gaia BH3: Sleeping Giant Black Hole

- Astronomers discovered a "sleeping giant" black hole named **"Gaia BH3"** in the Milky Way galaxy by **European Space Agency's Gaia mission.**
- It is the most massive stellar-mass black hole ever found in the Milky Way, with a mass 33 times greater than our Sun.

Three new moons found

- Astronomers from the **International Astronomical Union** have identified **three previously undiscovered moons** orbiting the outer planets of our solar system.
- Two were found around **Neptune**, and one around **Uranus**.

Pars-I Remote Sensing Satellite

- **Iran** declared on March 1, 2024, that it had successfully launched its domestically produced **'Pars-I' remote sensing satellite** into orbit using a **Russian Soyuz-2.1b rocket.**
- This achievement signifies increasing strategic space collaboration between the two countries amidst mutual Western sanctions.

Sub-metre Optical Satellite

- On April 8, 2024, **Tata Advanced Systems Limited (TASL)** announced the successful deployment of its sub-meter optical satellite into space.
- The satellite, assembled and tested in India, was launched from the **Kennedy Space Center in Florida, USA,** aboard SpaceX's Falcon 9 rocket **on 7 April 2024.**
- **"TASL's TSAT-1A satellite** will provide high-resolution optical satellite images, offering increased collection capacity, dynamic range, and low-latency delivery through its multispectral and hyperspectral capabilities,".

New Angara A5 heavy-lift rocket

- **Russia** conducted the inaugural test of its **Angara-A5 space rocket** on 11 April 2024, from the Vostochny Cosmodrome in the Far East.
- The 179-foot-tall (54.5 meters) rocket is produced entirely from Russian components and uses a more environmentally friendly

fuel than the nation's previous heavy-lift rocket, the Proton-M.

- This marks the **fourth time** Roscosmos has launched the Angara A5. Its first test flight took place in 2014, and its second in 2020.

Chang'e-6 mission

- **China** has landed an uncrewed spacecraft on the far side of the moon, overcoming a key hurdle in its landmark mission to retrieve the world's first rock and soil samples from the dark lunar hemisphere.
- **Chang'e-6** touched down in the **South Pole-Aitken Basin** at 6:23am Beijing time **on Sunday** after completing a multistage landing process.

ISRO

ISRO launched Spadex Mission for Space Docking

- **ISRO's SpaDeX Mission:** The Indian Space Research Organisation (ISRO) successfully launched the **Space Docking Experiment (SpaDeX)** mission on December 30, 2024.
- **Launch Details:** The **PSLV C60 rocket** carried two small satellites, **SDX01 (Chaser)** and **SDX02 (Target)**, along with **24 payloads**, from the **Satish Dhawan Space Centre, Sriharikota**.
- **Mission Objective:** Demonstrate **spacecraft rendezvous**, **docking**, and **undocking technologies**, a capability mastered by only a few nations like the **US**, **Russia**, and **China**.
- **Strategic Importance:** The mission positions **India among elite spacefaring nations** and supports future projects such as **Chandrayaan-4**, **BAS**, and **Gaganyaan**.

ISRO Successfully Launches the Proba-3 mission

- In December 2024, the Indian Space Research Organisation (ISRO) successfully launched the Proba-3 mission aboard the Polar Satellite Launch Vehicle (PSLV-C59) from the Satish Dhawan Space Centre in Sriharikota.
- Proba-3 is an In-Orbit Demonstration (IOD) mission of the European Space Agency.
- This mission, a collaboration with the European Space Agency (ESA), aims to study the Sun's corona by creating an artificial eclipse using two spacecraft flying in precise formation.

ISRO Gets Government Approval For Venus Mission "Shukrayaan"

- In November 2024, the Indian government approved ISRO's Shukrayaan Venus Orbiter Mission.
- Scheduled for launch in 2028, the mission aims to study Venus's atmosphere, surface, and subsurface.
- According to ISRO, this Mission will cost approximately Rs 1,236 crore and LVM-3 will be used as the launch vehicle.

ISRO Launches India's First Analog Space Mission In Leh, Ladakh

- In November 2024, the Indian Space Research Organization (ISRO) launched its first analog space mission in Leh, Ladakh.
- The mission, named "Hab-1", simulates life in an interplanetary habitat to study extraterrestrial conditions.
- The mission has been developed by a partnership of the Human Spaceflight Centre, ISRO, AAKA Space Studio, the University of Ladakh, and IIT Bombay.

ISRO's PSLV C-37 Upper Stage Re-Enters Earth's Atmosphere

- The upper stage of the Indian Space Research Organisation's (ISRO) PSLV C-37 mission re-entered the Earth's atmosphere in October 2024, eight years after its launch.
- This mission originally launched on February 15, 2017, setting a world record by deploying 104 satellites in a single launch.
- It was the 39th mission of the Indian Polar Satellite Launch Vehicle (PSLV) programme.

National Space Commission Approves India's Fifth Lunar Mission

- On October 9, 2024, India's National Space Commission approved the Lunar Polar Exploration Mission (LUPEX).
- This is India's fifth lunar mission, a collaboration between ISRO and Japan's space agency JAXA.
- LUPEX aims to explore water and other valuable resources at the Moon's south pole.

Cabinet Approves Chandrayaan-4 Mission

- On September 18, 2024, the Union Cabinet, led by Prime Minister Narendra Modi, approved the Chandrayaan-4 Mission.
- The mission aims to land on the Moon, collect samples, and return them to Earth.
- Chandrayaan-4 will test technologies for docking, undocking, and safe return, advancing India's lunar exploration capabilities.

ISRO'S PLANNED MISSIONS

Year	Mission name	Mission description
2024	Gaganyaan-1	The first test flight of the Gaganyaan spacecraft, designed to carry three astronauts.
2024	NISAR	A joint project with NASA to launch the first dual-band radar imaging satellite for remote sensing.
2025	Gaganyaan-2	The second test flight before the inaugural crewed mission.
2025	Venus Orbiter Mission (Shukrayaan)	An orbiter mission to study the atmosphere of Venus.
2026	Mars Orbiter Mission 2 (Mangalyaan-2)	India's second interplanetary mission to Mars is primarily an orbiter mission.
2026	Lunar Polar Exploration Mission	In collaboration with JAXA to explore the Moon's south pole region.
2026	Gaganyaan 3	The first crewed Gaganyaan mission.
2028	Chandrayaan-4	A lunar sample-return mission, the fourth in the Chandrayaan series.
2035	Bharatiya Antariksha Station	Indian space station.
TBA	AstroSat-2	A space telescope is proposed as the successor to Astrosat-1.

ISRO's Aditya-L1 Completes First Halo Orbit Around L1

- On July 2, 2024, ISRO's Aditya-L1 mission achieved its first halo orbit around the Sun-Earth L1 point.
- The Aditya-L1 mission is an Indian solar observatory located at the Lagrangian point L1, which was launched on September 2, 2023 and placed in its targeted halo orbit on January 6, 2024.
- The spacecraft takes 178 days to complete one revolution around the L1 point in its halo orbit.

India Welcomes First Civilian Space Tourist, Gopichand Thotakura

- On 26 August 2024, India welcomed its first civilian space tourist, Gopichand Thotakura, who returned from a historic space journey.
- Thotakura participated in Blue Origin's New Shepard-25 mission, making him the second Indian to travel to space after Rakesh Sharma in 1984.

India Selects Crew Members for Axiom-4 Mission

- On 2 August 2024, India selected Group Captain Shubhanshu Shukla and Group Captain Prasanth Balakrishnan Nair for the Axiom-4 mission to the International Space Station (ISS).
- Group Captain Shukla will serve as the prime mission pilot, while Group Captain Nair will be the backup. Both officers will undergo training in the U.S. starting in early August 2024.
- The Axiom-4 mission, scheduled for Spring 2025, is the fourth private astronaut mission to the ISS and aims to enhance India's human spaceflight capabilities.

ISRO to Launch Australian Spacecraft "Optimus" Aboard SSLV

- NewSpace India Limited (NSIL) and Space Machines Company have signed a Dedicated Launch Service Agreement, marking a significant milestone in space collaboration between India and Australia.
- The 450kg Optimus spacecraft, the largest Australian-designed and built spacecraft to date, will be launched on ISRO's Small Satellite Launch Vehicle (SSLV).
- This initiative, known as Space MAITRI (Mission for Australia-India's Technology, Research and Innovation), is a significant advancement in the strategic partnership between the two countries in the sector of space.

INSAT-3DS satellite (An exclusive meteorological satellite)

- **INSAT-3DS** is an exclusive meteorological satellite realized by ISRO with the primary objective to provide continuity of services to the existing in-orbit INSAT-3D and 3DR satellites.
- The Satellite had successfully completed Satellite Assembly, Integration & Testing activities at **U R Rao Satellite Centre, Bengaluru.**

XPoSat (X-ray Polarimeter Satellite)

- Indian Space Research Organisation (ISRO) has successfully launched **X-ray Polarimeter Satellite (XPoSat)** aboard Polar Satellite Launch Vehicle PSLV-C58.
- The satellite was launched from Satish Dhawan Space Centre in Sriharikota, Andhra Pradesh.
- This mission marks **India's first dedicated scientific endeavour** to study the polarisation of cosmic X-rays from celestial sources.
- The mission life of the primary payload XPoSat is **about five years**.

Woman Robot Astronaut "Vyommitra"

- Woman Robot Astronaut **"Vyommitra"** will fly into Space ahead of ISRO's ambitious "Gaganyaan" mission, which will be India's first human manned Space Flight carrying Indian Astronauts into Space.
- "Vyommitra" is a name derived from two Sanskrit words namely, **"Vyoma" (meaning Space) and "Mitra" (meaning Friend).**
- "Vyommitra" will precede India's first human-crewed spaceflight, "Gaganyaan," which aims to carry Indian astronauts into space.
- The uncrewed "Vyommitra" mission is slated for the third quarter of this year, while the manned "Gaganyaan" mission is scheduled for launch in the following year, 2025.

Next Generation Weather Satellite INSAT-3DS

- The Indian Space Research Organisation (ISRO) successfully launched **GSLV F14** from the Satish Dhawan Space Centre Sriharikota.
- The **INSAT 3DS weather satellite** was injected into its designated path around 20 minutes after lift-off. **All stages of the rocket, including the cryogenic stage, performed as expected.**

Statio Shiv Shakti

- **International Astronomical Union** has approved the name **"Statio Shiv Shakti"** for the landing site of Chandrayaan-3's Vikram lander.
- The approval was given on **March 19, 2024.**
- Prime Minister Narendra Modi declares on **August 26, 2023,** that the landing site would be named **'Shiva Shakti'**.

'Young Scientist Programme - YUVIKA

- ISRO is organising a special program called 'Young Scientist Programme- **YUva VIgyani KAryakram (YUVIKA)** starting from May 13th this year, aimed at school children.
- The primary goal is to provide foundational knowledge on Space Science, Technology, and Applications, as well as introduce emerging trends in the field.
- This two-week initiative includes classroom sessions, practical experiments, CANSAT activities, Robotic kits, Model rocketry, interactions with ISRO scientists, and field trips.

India's Second Privately Developed Rocket

- Organising a space startup launched a rocket called **Agnibaan** from the Satish Dhawan Space Centre in Sriharikota, Andhra Pradesh. .
- It's the **second time in India** that a private sector company has launched a rocket into space. They used only Indian rocket engines which used both liquid fuel and gas.

Multi-Purpose App "SAKHI"

- The Vikram Sarabhai Space Centre (VSSC) has developed a multi-purpose app **'SAKHI'** to assist Gaganyaan Crew.
- The Space-borne Assistant and Knowledge Hub for Crew Interaction (SAKHI) is equipped to monitor astronauts' health, maintain communication with Earth, and manage dietary schedules.
- It serves as an essential tool for the crew, offering real-time assistance and access to necessary data.

- It would assist astronauts during the Gaganyaan space flight mission, facilitating tasks such as accessing vital technical information and communication.

4 Astronauts For Gaganyaan

- PM Modi announced the names of the **four astronauts,** who would fly to low-Earth orbit as part of the **ISRO's Gaganyaan, the first crewed Indian space mission.**
- The selected astronauts are: **Prashanth Balakrishnan Nair, Angad Prathap, Ajit Krishnan, and Shubanshu Shukla.**
- They are all either **wing commanders or group captains** with the Indian Air Force (IAF) and have extensive experience working as test pilots.

Reusable Launch Vehicle (RLV) named "Pushpak"

- The Indian Space Research Organisation (Isro) successfully executed a landing mission for its Reusable Launch Vehicle (RLV) named **"Pushpak"** from the Aeronautical Test Range (ATR) in Karnataka's Chalakere.

Nodal centre for ISRO's START programme

- The Indian Space Research Organisation (ISRO) has designated the **Gujarat Council on Science and Technology (GUJCOST)** as the Nodal Centre for the 'Space Science and Technology Awareness Training **(START)**' program.
- This initiative aims to raise awareness and provide training in space science and technology, with GUJCOST leading efforts in this regard.

GAGANYAAN

- **Objective:** Demonstrate human spaceflight capability by launching a crew of 3 members to an orbit of 400 km for a 3-day mission and safely return to Earth.
- **Programme Launched:** In 2007 by ISRO as a part of the Indian Human Space Flight Programme (IHSP).

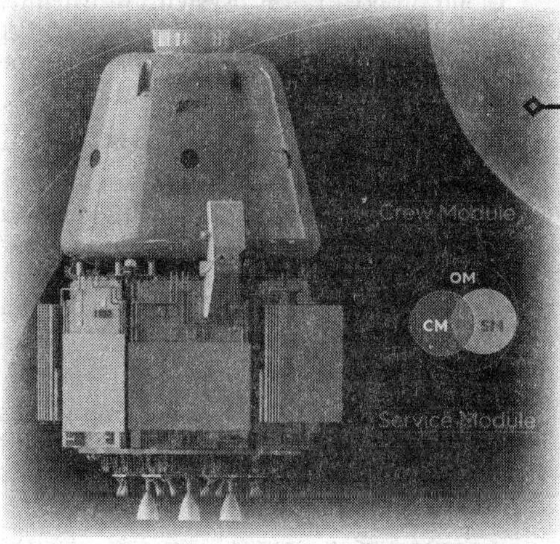

LAUNCH VEHICLE

- **Rocket:** Launch Vehicle Mark-3 (LVM3/GSLV Mk3), India's heaviest rocket.
- **Stages:** Solid stage, liquid stage, and cryogenic stage.
- **Human Rating:** Re-configured to meet human rating requirements, named Human Rated LVM3 (HLVM3).

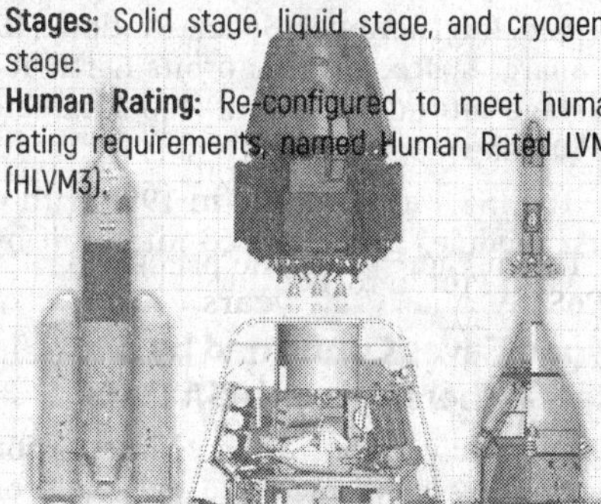

MISSION STATUS

Manned and Unmanned Missions:
Includes both types.

First Unmanned Mission:
Gaganyaan-1, a test flight to check technology readiness, scheduled for end of 2024.

Manned Mission:
Will fly a three-member crew into a low Earth orbit at 400 km for three days, scheduled later.

DEVELOPMENT AND TESTING

- **Launch Crew Module and Crew Escape System:**
  - **Life Support Systems:** Development to provide an earth-like environment in space.
  - **Crew Emergency Escape:** Provision for emergency escape.
  - **Crew Management:** Training, recovery, and rehabilitation aspects.
- **Recent Tests:**
  - **October 2023:** Successful test of a basic crew module and crew escape system (CES).
  - **CES Function:** Ensures crew safety by taking them to a safe distance during emergencies.
  - **November 2023:** Experimentation with crew module uprighting system to ensure it stays upright during sea splashdown.

KEY POINTS FOR REVISION

- **Gaganyaan Objective:** Human spaceflight capability, 400 km orbit, 3 days mission.
- **Launch Vehicle:** LVM3/GSLV Mk3, re-configured as HLVM3.
- **Mission Status:** Unmanned mission by end of 2024, manned mission later.
- **Crew Module Development:** Life support, emergency escape, training, and recovery.
- **Recent Tests:** Successful crew module and CES test, uprighting system experimentation.
- **Astronaut Training:** Completed in Russia, MOU with Glavkosmos.

ASTRONAUT TRAINING

- **Selected Astronauts:** Four astronauts completed generic training.
- **Training Location:** Russia's Yuri Gagarin Cosmonaut Training Centre.
- **Training Agreement:** MOU signed between ISRO and Glavkosmos (subsidiary of Russian space agency Roscosmos) in June 2019.

Sunita Williams' Historic Third Space Flight

- **Launch Site:** Cape Canaveral, Florida.
- **Spacecraft:** Boeing Starliner.
- **Crew Members:** Sunita Williams (pilot) and Barry "Butch" Wilmore **(Veteran of two spaceflights, totaling 178 days in space)**.
- **Significance:** Boeing joined SpaceX as the second private firm to provide crew transport to and from the ISS.
- **Objective:** Assess the spacecraft's functionalities from launch to docking and its return to Earth in the western United States.

Key Details

- **First Woman on a Maiden Mission:** Indian-origin NASA astronaut **Sunita Williams**, at 59 years old, has made history by becoming the **first woman to pilot a test spacecraft** on its maiden crewed mission. She flew aboard the **Boeing Starliner alongside astronaut Barry "Butch" Wilmore.**

- **Spacecraft:** The Boeing Starliner launched from the **Cape Canaveral Space Force Station in Florida on June 5, 2024,** using the United Launch **Alliance's Atlas V rocket.**

International Space Station

Introduction

- **Assembly:** The ISS has been assembled section by section over several years.
- **First Segment Launch: November 20, 1998,** via Russian Proton rocket named **Zarya** (meaning 'sunrise').
- **First Human Expedition:** Launched in Soyuz TM 31 rocket from Baikonur Cosmodrome, Kazakhstan.
- **Visitors: 240 individuals from 19** countries, including Malaysia and the UAE.

NASA

NASA's Crew-9 Mission Launched to Bring Astronauts Back to Earth

- NASA successfully launched the Crew-9 mission on September 28, 2024, from Cape Canaveral Space Force Station in Florida.
- The mission is focused on rescuing astronauts Sunita Williams and Barry Wilmore, who have been stranded on the International Space Station since June 6, 2024, due to issues with Boeing's Starliner spacecraft.
- This is the ninth operational mission under NASA and SpaceX's partnership program, which began in 2020.

Sunita Williams Takes Command of ISS for the Second Time

- On September 22, 2024, NASA astronaut Sunita Williams assumed command of the International Space Station for the second time.
- She previously commanded Expedition 33 in 2012.
- The International Space Station (ISS) is a large spacecraft that orbits Earth at an average altitude of about 400 kilometers (250 miles).
- The ISS was launched in 1998 with the first module, Zarya, placed into orbit by a Russian Proton rocket.

Moon Caves Confirmed by Researchers Using NASA Data

- On July 15, 2024, international researchers confirmed the existence of a cave in the Moon's Sea of Tranquility.
- The cave measures approximately 40 meters wide and extends for several yards.
- The discovery was based on data from NASA's Lunar Reconnaissance Orbiter, specifically the Miniature Radio-Frequency (Mini-RF) instrument.

NASA Sends Missy Elliott's Song to Deep Space

- On July 12, 2024, NASA transmitted the hip-hop song "The Rain (Supa Dupa Fly)" by Missy Elliott to Venus.
- The transmission was sent using NASA's Deep Space Network (DSN) from the Jet Propulsion Laboratory in Southern California.

X-59 Supersonic Jet 'Son of Concorde'

- The X-59 supersonic aircraft, or "son of Concorde," was rolled out by NASA and Lockheed Martin.
- It can travel at 925 miles per hour, producing a less disruptive sonic boom.
- The X-59 is part of NASA's Quesst mission aimed at providing data to reconsider the ban on supersonic flights.
- It features a thin, tapered nose to break up shock waves and a cockpit positioned halfway down the plane, requiring pilots to rely on camera monitors.

The PACE mission

- NASA's satellite mission to study ocean health, air quality, and the effects of a changing climate for the benefit of humanity launched successfully into orbit.
- Known as PACE (Plankton, Aerosol, Cloud, ocean Ecosystem) satellite, launched aboard a SpaceX Falcon 9 rocket from Space Launch Complex 40 at Cape Canaveral Space Force Station in Florida.

NASA discovers 'Super-Earth'

- US space agency NASA has announced the discovery of a 'super-Earth,' a planet that might support life and is located 137 light-years away.
- Dubbed 'TOI-715 b', it is said to be about one and a half times as wide as Earth.
- The planet orbits within the 'conservative' habitable zone around its parent star, which might give it the right temperature for liquid water to form on its surface.

PREFIRE (Polar Radiant Energy in the Far-InfraRed Experiment) mission

- NASA has successfully launched the first of a pair of climate satellites designed for the PREFIRE (Polar Radiant Energy in the Far-InfraRed Experiment) mission.
- The satellite, carried by Rocket Lab's Electron rocket from New Zealand, will study heat emissions at Earth's poles.
- These shoebox-size cube satellites will measure the amount of heat Earth radiates into space from the Arctic and Antarctic regions.
- PREFIRE aims to improve predictions related to sea ice loss, ice sheet melt, and sea level rise, providing crucial information for climate research and adaptation.

NASA's Advanced Composite Solar Sail System (ACS3)

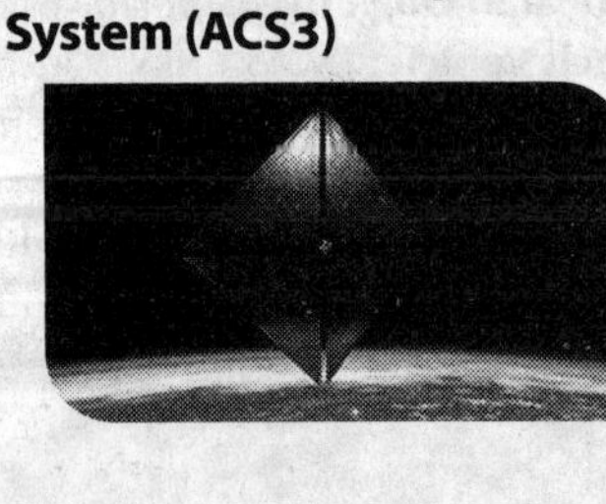

- NASA's **advanced composite solar sail system (ACS3)** was launched to space on 23 April aboard a Rocket Lab (Colorado, Colo., U.S.) composites-intensive Electron rocket from the company's Launch Complex 1 on the **Mahia Peninsula of New Zealand.**

BIO TECH and HEALTH

India Launches Its First Diabetes Biobank

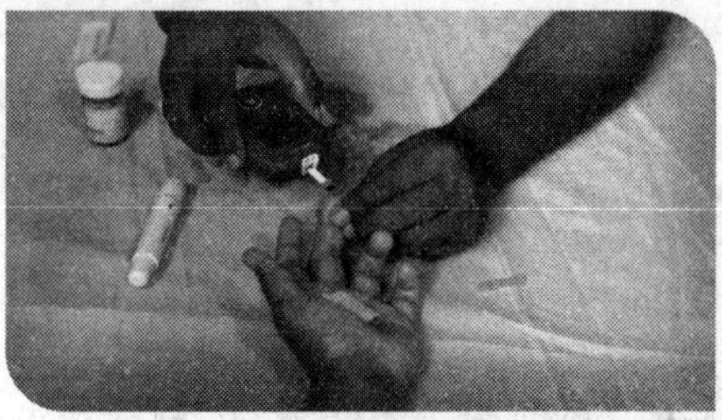

- India has launched its first-ever diabetes biobank in Chennai.
- Indian Council of Medical Research (ICMR) in collaboration with the Madras Diabetes Research Foundation (MDRF) has set up the country's first diabetes biobank.
- This biobank, located at MDRF, aims to collect, store, and distribute biological samples to support advanced scientific research on diabetes in India.

IIT MADRAS UNVEILS WORLD'S FIRST 3D HIGH-RESOLUTION HUMAN FETAL BRAIN IMAGES

- In December 2024, researchers at IIT Madras unveiled the world's most detailed 3D high-resolution images of the human foetal brain.
- The Sudha Gopalakrishnan Brain Centre digitally imaged 5,132 brain sections at cell resolution using advanced brain mapping technology.
- This dataset, named "DHARANI", is the largest publicly accessible digital dataset of the human foetal brain and aims to advance neuroscience research and fetal medicine.

RUSSIA DEVELOPS NEW MRNA VACCINE AGAINST CANCER

- General Director of the Radiology Medical Research Centre of the Russian Ministry of Health, Andrey Kaprin said that Russia has developed its own cancer vaccine.
- It will be available to patients for free from early 2025.
- The personalised vaccine, which uses genetic material derived from a patient's tumour, will cost the state approximately 300,000 rubles (USD 2,869) per dose.

Scientists develop India's First Anti-Pesticide Bodysuit

- Union Minister Jitendra Singh has unveiled "Kisan Kavach", Bharat's first-of-its-kind anti-pesticide bodysuit.
- The kit consists of a trouser, pullover, and a face-cover made of 'oxime fabric ' that can chemically breakdown any of the common pesticides that get sprayed onto cloth or body during spraying operations.
- It is Developed by the Biotechnology Research and Innovation Council (BRIC-inStem), Bangalore in collaboration with Sepio Health Pvt. Ltd.
- It is washable and reusable suit, priced at ₹4,000, can last up to a year.

Australia Creates the World's First Bionic Eye

- Researchers at Monash University in Australia have developed the world's first bionic eye, offering new hope for people with blindness.
- The innovative device, called the 'Gennaris Bionic Vision System,' is a groundbreaking technology aimed at restoring vision for those who have lost it.

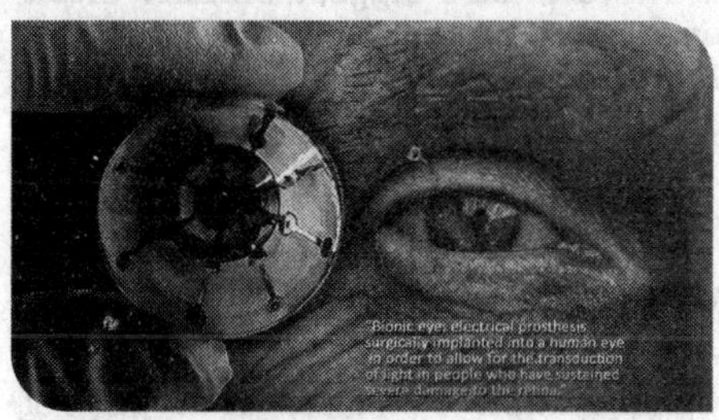

BioNTech Launches Clinical Trials for 1st Lung Cancer Vaccine

- BioNTech has initiated international trials for BNT116, an mRNA-based vaccine targeting non-small cell lung cancer (NSCLC).
- The vaccine employs mRNA technology to activate the immune system to recognize and attack lung cancer cells.
- BNT116 builds on the successful mRNA technology used in Covid-19 vaccines.

Zydus Lifesciences Gets WHO Approval for Typhoid Vaccine

- Zydus Lifesciences Ltd received in-principle acceptability from the WHO for its Typhoid Vi conjugate vaccine, ZyVac TCV.
- The vaccine, developed at the Zydus Biotech Park in Ahmedabad, offers immunization against Salmonella typhi, the bacteria causing typhoid fever.
- ZyVac TCV is suitable for people aged 6 months to 65 years and is now eligible for purchase by UN procurement agencies.

IIT Hyderabad Inaugurates New High-End Research Centre

- On September 9, 2024, IIT Hyderabad inaugurated the Centre for in-situ and Correlative Microscopy (CISCoM).
- This advanced facility will enhance scientific collaboration with real-time microscopy techniques.
- Funded with ₹60 crore by the Department of Science and Technology and ₹20 crore by academic and industrial partners, CISCoM is expected to serve as a critical resource for researchers and industries.

ICMR Develops CRISPR Cas-Based TB Detection Kit

- On July 24, 2024, ICMR introduced a CRISPR Cas-based system for TB detection, considered the "world's cheapest TB testing system."
- The kit uses saliva DNA to detect TB bacteria, even in early stages, and can test over 1,500 samples in about two hours.

India Launches First Covid Severity Biomarker Kit

- Scientists at Dr. B.R. Ambedkar Memorial Hospital in Raipur developed India's first Covid severity biomarker kit.
- The kit uses Quantitative PCR-based testing with 91% sensitivity and 94% specificity to assess the severity of infections in early stages.

Scientists Develop "Smart" Insulin for Diabetes Treatment

- On October 16, 2024, researchers developed NNC2215, a "smart" insulin designed to adjust its activity based on blood glucose levels.
- This insulin remains inactive until required, reducing risks of hyperglycemia and hypoglycemia.

First indigenously developed Hepatitis A vaccine - Havisure

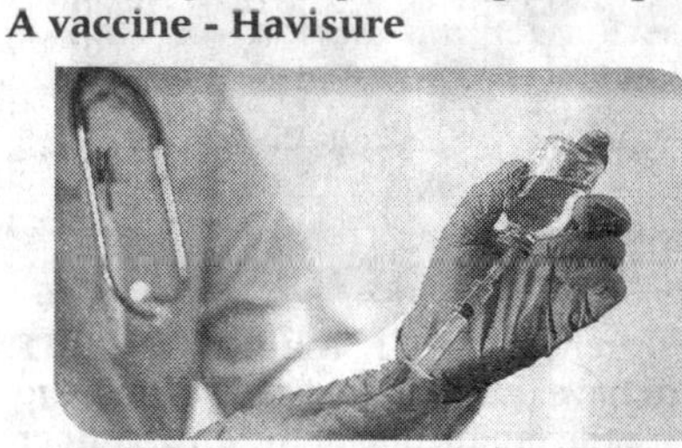

- **Indian Immunologicals Ltd (IIL)** launched India's first indigenously developed Hepatitis A vaccine, **Havisure,** demonstrating a commitment to advancing healthcare solutions for the nation.
- **Priced at ₹2,150 per dose,** Havisure is a two-dose vaccine, recommended for routine immunization of children above 12 months, individuals at risk of exposure or travel to high-prevalence regions,

occupational risk individuals, and those with chronic liver diseases.

- Indian Immunologicals Ltd (IIL) is a wholly-owned subsidiary of National Dairy Development Board (NDDB).

AI-powered model 'Garbhini-GA2'

- The Indian Institute of Technology **(IIT) Madras** and Translational Health Science and Technology Institute (THSTI), Faridabad have collaborated to develop the **first India-specific Artificial Intelligence (AI) model Garbhini-GA2** to determine the age of a foetus in a pregnant woman in the second and third trimesters precisely.
- Researchers at IIT Madras and THSTI developed the new technology as part of the Interdisciplinary Group for Advanced Research on Birth Outcomes – **DBT India Initiative' (GARBH-Ini) program.**
- The AI Model, called the **'Garbhini-GA2'** is the first late-trimester GA estimation model to be developed and validated using Indian population data.

IIT Guwahati Launches SWASTHA Project

- Secretary of the MeitY, S Krishnan, inaugurated the **SWASTHA project** and the state-of-the-art **ISO 5 and 6** clean room facilities at the Centre for Nanotechnology, IIT Guwahati.
- SWASTHA (Smart Wearable Advanced NanoSensing Technologies in Healthcare ASICs) aims to transform healthcare through cutting-edge nanoelectronic theranostic devices.
- The project is committed to delivering top-notch products and prototypes in micro/nanoelectronics and nanomaterials, with a special focus on healthcare and energy applications.

Anti-Cancer Drug 'Camptothecin'

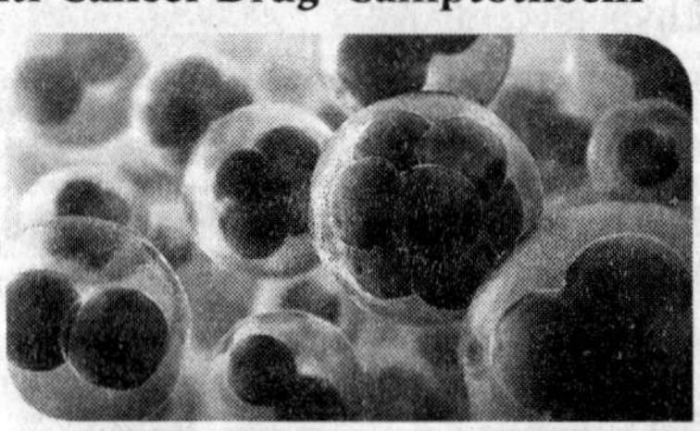

- Researchers at **IIT Madras and IIT Mandi** have used metabolic engineering to increase the production of the **anti-cancer drug camptothecin (CPT)** in plant cells.
- CPT is currently extracted from the endangered plant Nathapodytes nimmoniana, **leading to a 20% decline in its population in the last decade.**
- The research aims to provide a sustainable and high-yielding alternative source for CPT to reduce the need to harvest endangered plants.

New Malaria Vaccine MOSQUIRIX

- For the first time, an effective new **malaria vaccine Mosquirix** has rolled out in **Cameroon, Africa.**
- It is also known as **RTS,S/AS01**. In 2021, WHO licensed Mosquirix for children in sub-Saharan Africa with moderateto-high Plasmodium falciparum malaria transmission.

First recombinant vaccine for Swine Fever Virus

- Indian Institute of Technology Guwahati **(IIT Guwahati)** transferred vaccine technology to BioMed Pvt. Ltd, a vaccine manufacturing company.
- With the collaborative efforts between researchers from the Department of Biosciences and Bioengineering at IIT Guwahati, and Assam Agricultural University in Guwahati, the vaccine technology was developed.

India's biggest Climate Clock

- On 23 April 2024, **Council of Scientific & Industrial Research (CSIR)**, as a part of the Earth Day Celebrations, installed and activated **India's biggest Climate Clock** on the CSIR Headquarters Building in **Rafi Marg, New Delhi.**
- The event signifies CSIR's aim to spread awareness about climate change and its ill effects.

White Rabbit Collaboration

- **CERN** has introduced the **White Rabbit Collaboration** to promote the adoption of its White Rabbit (WR) technology, initially developed to synchronize devices in particle accelerators with sub-nanosecond precision.
- This technology has applications **beyond particle physics** and has been incorporated into the Precision Time Protocol (PTP) standard.

Ancient viral genomes discovered

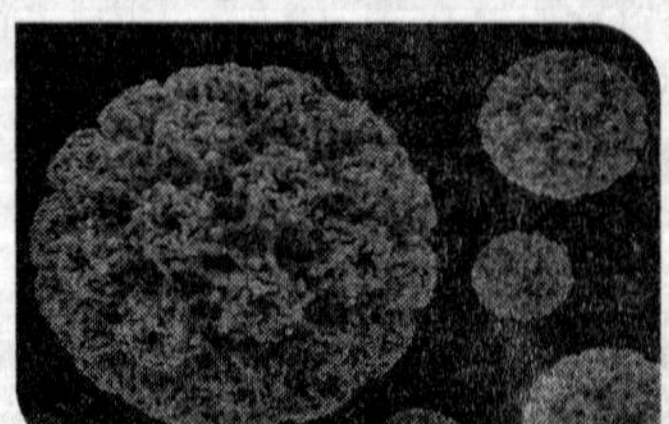

- Researchers from the Federal University of São Paulo have uncovered the **oldest known human viruses** in Neanderthal bones dating **back over 50,000 years.**
- The experiments identified two viruses, human parvovirus B19 and a human hepatitis B virus.
- These viral genomes were recovered from human remains of first-generation African people in Mexico, as well as an individual who was an Indigenous person.

New Discovery

Oldest Eyeliner in the World Found in Turkey

- Archaeologists discovered the world's oldest eyeliner in Yeşilova Höyük, an ancient settlement in western Turkey.
- The eyeliner, in the form of a kohl stick, dates back 8,200 years.
- It was likely used by dipping it into a kohl container and applying it as makeup.
- Kohl, still widely used today, remains a popular cosmetic product worldwide.

Indian Scientists Discover a New Exoplanet, TOI-6651b

- On October 28, 2024, scientists from the Physical Research Laboratory (PRL), Ahmedabad, identified a new exoplanet named TOI-6651b.
- TOI-6651b is five times larger and 60 times more massive than Earth, located 690 light-years away.
- The planet orbits a Sun-like star in just five days and is found in the rare "Neptunian desert," providing valuable insights into planetary evolution and formation.

WHAT IS AN EXOPLANET?

- An exoplanet is any planet beyond our solar system.
- Most orbit other stars, but free-floating exoplanets, called rogue planets, orbit the galactic center and are untethered to any star.

Snake Species Named After Leonardo DiCaprio Discovered

- Scientists have identified a new snake species in the Western Himalayas and named it Anguiculus dicaprioi after Leonardo DiCaprio for his contributions to wildlife conservation.
- It belongs to the Colubridae family, the largest snake family, comprising 1,938 species.
- The snake is found in Himachal Pradesh's Chamba, Kullu, and Shimla, Uttarakhand's Nainital, and Chitwan National Park in Nepal.

WHO Approves First Diagnostic Test for Mpox

- On October 4, 2024, the World Health Organization approved the Alinity m MPXV assay, the first diagnostic test for Mpox.
- Developed by Abbott Laboratories, the test uses real-time PCR to detect Mpox virus DNA from skin swabs.

Astronomers Discover Largest Black Hole Jets, "Porphyrion"

- In September 2024, astronomers identified the largest black hole jets ever observed, named "Porphyrion."
- These jets span 23 million light-years, equal to 140 Milky Way galaxies lined up.
- Emerging from a supermassive black hole 7.5 billion light-years away, the jets significantly influence surrounding cosmic structures.

New Turmeric Relative Identified in Nagaland

- Researchers have discovered a new species, Curcuma ungamensis, related to turmeric in Ungma village in Mokokchung district of Nagaland.
- It has been named Curcuma ungamensis after the village called Ungma located in Mokokchung district of Nagaland.
- This family includes about 200 species in India, such as the well-known turmeric (Curcuma longa) and black turmeric (Curcuma caesia).
- The plant grows to a height of 65-90 cm and produces attractive yellow flowers when fully grown.
- Plants in this genus are mainly found in South and Southeast Asia.

New 'Dancing Girls' Ginger Species Found in Northeast India

- Scientists identified six new species in the Globba genus, commonly called "dancing girl" or "dancing lady" ginger.
- These species are:
  - Globba corniculata, Globba paschimbengalensis, and Globba polymorpha (found in Darjeeling, West Bengal).
  - Globba tyrnaensis and Globba janakiae (discovered in Meghalaya).
  - Globba yadaviana (recorded in Mizoram).

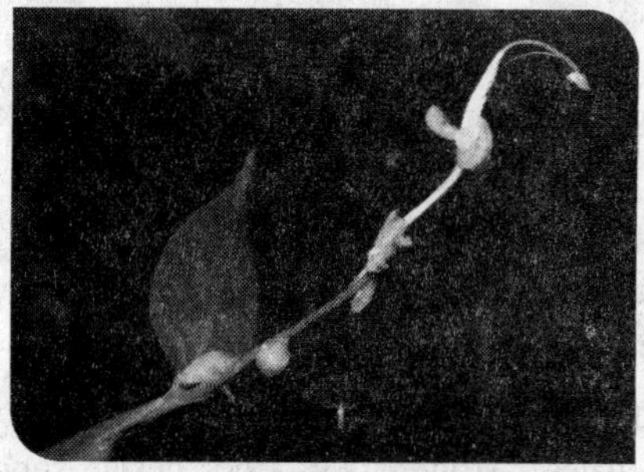

India Discovers First Methane-Eating Bacteria

- Scientists have reported the discovery of India's first indigenous methane-eating bacteria, known as methanotrophs, in rice fields and wetlands in Western India.
- The team isolated and described a novel genus and species of methanotrophs, named Methylocucumis oryzae.
- Methane, the second most important greenhouse gas, has 26 times more global warming potential than carbon dioxide.

Heaviest Antimatter Particle Discovered

- Scientists discovered the heaviest antimatter particle, named antihyperhydrogen-4, at the Relativistic Heavy Ion Collider in New York.
- Antimatter is a type of matter composed of antiparticles, which have the same mass as ordinary matter particles but possess opposite electric charges.
- A hypothetical antimatter atom composed of an antiproton and four antineutrons. It's essentially the antimatter counterpart of the helium-4 atom, which consists of two protons & two neutrons.

Miscellaneous

South Korea Successfully launches 3rd Spy Satellite into Orbit

- South Korea successfully placed its third homegrown spy satellite into orbit.
- South Korean Indigenous spy satellite was launched on a SpaceX Falcon 9 rocket from the Vandenberg Space Force Base (US).
- This is third military satellite launched by South Korea as the first one was launched in December 2023 followed by the second one in April 2024.
- South Korea plans to send two more satellites into space by 2025.

Royal Enfield launches EV brand "Flying Flea"

- Royal Enfield launched its first electric vehicle (EV) brand, 'Flying Flea', on 5th November 2024.
- The first model under the Flying Flea EV brand will arrive in 2026 and will be called the FF-C6.

IIT Kanpur Unveils Analaksya Stealth Tech To Make Objects Invisible To Radar

- In November 2024, IIT Kanpur unveiled the Analakshya Metamaterial Surface Cloaking System (MSCS), a groundbreaking stealth technology designed to make objects almost invisible to radar.
- Developed by a team of researchers and students from IIT Kanpur, the Analakshya MSCS is a textile-based broadband metamaterial microwave absorber.
- It has been licensed to Meta Tattva Systems Pvt. Ltd. for manufacturing, marking a critical step towards its deployment by the Indian Armed Forces.

GoI launched India's first Artificial Intelligence data bank

- On 20th November 2024, the Ministry of Science and Technology launched India's first practical Artificial Intelligence (AI) Data Bank, to boost national security.
- Minister Jitendra Singh announced the initiative at the 7th ASSOCHAM AI Leadership Meet 2024.
- The event is themed "AI for India: Advancing India's AI Development—Innovation, Ethics, and Governance."

Clean Ganga Mission Introduces 'Dolphin Ambulance'

- In November 2024, the National Mission for Clean Ganga (NMCG) announced to launch 'Dolphin Ambulance' initiative to rescue injured Ganga dolphins.
- The Dolphin Ambulance initiative, officially named Advancing Rescue System for the Protection of Stranded Ganges River Dolphins, has been allocated a budget of Rs 1 crore.
- Dolphin is already declared as the national aquatic animal of India, Ganga

Dolphin is also found in the river system of India, Bangladesh and Nepal.

India's First Electric Microcar "Robin" Set for 2025 Launch

- On 16 August 2024, Wings EV announced the launch of Robin, India's first electric microcar, set for April 2025.
- Robin, a two-seater EV, aims to ease urban commuting with zero emissions and reduced congestion.
- It will be available in three variants: a basic model with a 65 km range priced at ₹2 lakh, a mid variant with a 90 km range at ₹2.5 lakh, and a premium variant with additional safety features at ₹3 lakh.

China Builds World's First High-Temperature Superconducting Tokamak

- China-based fusion energy company 'Energy Singularity' has made the world's first high-temperature superconducting tokamak device.
- China witnessed completion and operation of the world's f irst fully high-temperature superconducting tokamak device, named HH70, in its eastern Municipality of Shanghai.
- The term "tokamak" comes to us from a Russian acronym that stands for "toroidal chamber with magnetic coils", which is an experimental machine designed to harness the energy of fusion.

Indian Railways Develops Master Clock System

- On 20 August 2024, Indian Railways announced the development of a Master Clock System to synchronize time across its entire network.
- This system will replace the current manual time-keeping method, where station masters set time based on instructions from section controllers.
- The new system will source time from reliable sources like NAVIC or the National Physical Laboratory (NPL) and integrate it across various railway applications and systems.

China to Build Thorium Molten Salt Nuclear Reactor by 2025

- China plans to create the world's first nuclear power plant based on molten thorium salt in the Gobi Desert by 2025.
- China's molten thorium salt nuclear power plant will be the first and only molten salt nuclear reactor since the United States shut down its test reactor in 1969.
- Thorium-232, the only naturally occurring isotope of thorium, is considered 'fertile' for fission.

India to Assist Nepal's Munal Satellite Launch

- The Ministry of External Affairs and New Space India Limited has recently signed an agreement to assist launch of the Nepal-built Munal satellite.
- Munal is an indigenous satellite developed in Nepal under the aegis of the Nepal Academy of Science and Technology (NAST).
- Antarikchya Pratishan Nepal (APN), a Nepalese space startup, has assisted Nepalese students in the design and fabrication of this satellite.

India to Launch First Quantum Computer Under National Quantum Mission

- India set to become the seventh country to launch a dedicated quantum mission after the US, Austria, Finland, France, Canada, and China.
- The mission has been allocated nearly ₹6,000 crore, with plans to establish four Section 8 companies under the aegis of premier institutions like IITs and IISc.
- India's first quantum computer, after its launch, is expected to achieve computation of 6 qubits over the next few months.

Cabinet Approves ₹1236 Crore Venus Orbiter Mission (VOM)

- Recently, the Union Cabinet chaired by the Prime Minister Shri Narendra Modi has approved the development of Venus Orbiter Mission (VOM).
- The 'Venus Orbiter Mission' is envisaged to place a scientific spacecraft in orbit around the planet Venus to better understand the Venusian surface and subsurface, atmospheric processes, and the influence of the Sun on the Venusian atmosphere.
- The Venus Orbiter Mission is scheduled to be launched in March 2028, costing around Rs 1236 crore, of which Rs 824 crore will be spent on the spacecraft.
- The VOM will be India's second interplanetary mission after the Mars Orbiter Mission that was launched on November 5, 2013, and entered the Martian orbit on September 24, 2014.

Asia's Largest Cherenkov Telescope Inaugurated in Ladakh

- Dr. Ajit Kumar Mohanty, Secretary DAE & Chairman of the Atomic Energy Commission, inaugurated the Major Atmospheric Cherenkov Experiment (MACE) Observatory at Hanle, Ladakh, on 4th October 2024.
- MACE is the largest imaging Cherenkov telescope in Asia.
- Located at an altitude of ~4,300 m, it is also the highest of its kind in the world. The telescope is indigenously built by BARC with support from ECIL and other Indian industry partners.

CCS Approves New Missile Testing Range in Andhra Pradesh

- The Cabinet Committee on Security (CCS), led by Prime Minister Narendra Modi, has approved the establishment of a new missile testing range in Nagayalanka, Andhra Pradesh.
- The facility will be designed to support testing of a wide range of missile systems, including surface-to-air missiles and anti-tank missiles.

India's first Demonstration Facility for Biopolymers Inaugurated

- Dr Jitendra Singh inaugurated India's first Demonstration Facility for Biopolymers at Jejuri in Pune in October 2024.
- This facility focuses on developing technology for producing Polylactic Acid (PLA) bioplastic.
- Biopolymers are made from biological sources such as fats, vegetable oils, and sugars.

Mukesh Ambani Unveils AI Suite "Jio Brain"

- Reliance Industries Limited (RIL) Chairman Mukesh Ambani introduced a new AI initiative called "Jio Brain.
- Jio Brain is a comprehensive set of AI tools developed to enhance efficiency and engagement within Reliance and its various businesses.

Cabinet Approves Bharatiya Antariksh Station (BAS)

- The Union Cabinet, led by Prime Minister Narendra Modi, has approved the construction of the first unit of the Bharatiya Antariksh Station (BAS) under the Gaganyaan program.
- ISRO aims to establish India's own space station, BAS, by 2035, with its assembly taking place in phases.
- A budget of ₹20,193 crore has been allocated for the continuation of the Gaganyaan mission and the development of BAS.

IIT Indore Unveils TENG Technology Shoes

- In 2024, IIT Indore has created advanced shoes using a special technology called Tribo-Electric Nanogenerator (TENG).
- These shoes, are designed to harness energy from human motion, providing a sustainable power source for electronic devices.

- These shoes utilize advanced tribo-pairs, specifically Fluorinated Ethylene Propylene (FEP) and Aluminium, to generate power with each step.

Country's lightest bulletproof jacket

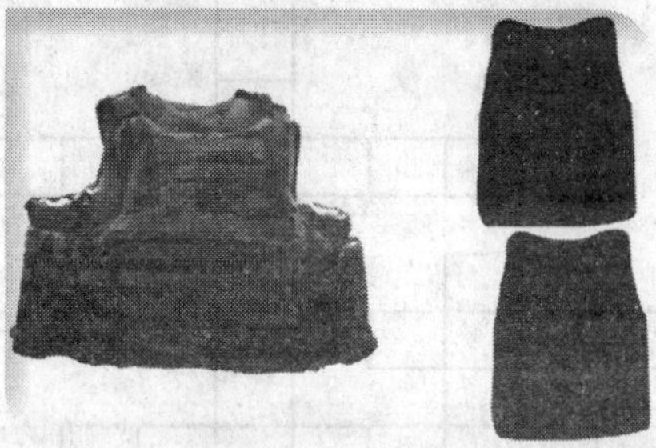

- **DRDO's Defence Materials and Stores Research and Development Establishment (DMSRDE), Kanpur** has successfully developed the lightest bulletproof jacket in the country for protection against **7.62 x 54 R API (level 6 of BIS 17051) ammunition.**
- This jacket is based on a new design approach where novel material along with new processes has been used.
- Recently, this bulletproof jacket was **successfully tested at TBRL, Chandigarh** as per BIS 17051-2018.
- The front hard armour panel (HAP) of this jacket defeats multiple hits (six shots) of 7.62x54 R API (sniper rounds) in both ICW (in-conjunction with) and standalone design.

India's first mobile Medical Devices Calibration Facility

- Indian Institute of Technology Madras **(IIT Madras)** has launched **India's First 'medical devices calibration facility on wheels'.**
- This has been developed by IIT Madras under its **'Anaivarukkum IITM'** (IITM for all) Initiatives.
- This mobile facility will ensure pervasive quality healthcare irrespective of geographical locations across the country.

World's first 100% biodegradable pen

- The world's first 100% biodegradable pen was launched in India **by entrepreneur Saurabh H Mehta.**
- This innovative pen is made entirely without plastic and features a recycled paper refill, non-toxic ink, and options for a metal, paper, or bamboo exterior.
- Saurabh's mission was to prove that the 95% plastic content in pens is avoidable, and it can be replaced with sustainable materials.

Supercontinent Sahul

- Archeologists discover ancient supercontinent **Sahul linked Asia to Australia**
- During the last ice age, approximately 70,000 years ago, a prehistoric supercontinent called **Sahul** existed.
- It connected present-day **Australia with Papua New Guinea** to the north and Tasmania to the south.

World's first 6G device

- A Japanese consortium has unveiled the **world's first high-speed 6G prototype device.**
- This groundbreaking device can transmit data at an impressive rate of **100 gigabits per second (Gbps),** covering a distance of over 300 feet.
- This represents a remarkable **20-fold improvement** compared to the current 5G technology.

Pasqal to deploy 1st Quantum Computer

- **Pasqal,** a French quantum computing company, has signed an **agreement with Aramco,** one of the world's leading integrated energy and chemicals companies, to install the **first quantum computer in the Kingdom of Saudi Arabia.**
- The agreement, announced on May 20, 2024, will see Pasqal install, maintain, and operate a **200-qubit quantum computer,** scheduled for deployment in the second half of 2025.

First space tourist from India

- **Gopi Thotakura,** an India-born aviator and commercial pilot based in the United States, recently became the first space tourist from India.

First Indigenous Bomber UAV

- Bengaluru's Flying **Wedge Defence** unveiled India's first indigenous bomber unmanned aircraft, **the FWD-200B.**
- Prioritizing cost-effectiveness and self-reliance, the firm aims to establish India as a pioneer in cutting-edge defense solutions.
- The FWD-200B has a **payload capacity of 100 kgs** and is classified as a **MALE Unmanned Combat Aerial Vehicle (medium-altitude, long-endurance).**

India's First Graphene Centre

- The Union government recently launched India's first graphene centre (IICG) **in Kerala.**
- The centre was established to foster research and development, product innovation and capacity building **in the area of graphene and 2D material systems.**

PHI-3-MINI

- Microsoft unveiled the latest version of its **'lightweight' AI model – the Phi-3-Mini.**
- It is the **smallest AI model** developed by **Microsoft.** It is believed to be the first in a series of three smaller models planned by Microsoft.
- **Phi-2 was introduced in December 2023** and reportedly equaled models like **Meta's Llama 2.**
- Phi-3 models significantly outperformed several models of the same size or even larger ones, including Gemma 7B and Mistral 7B, in key areas.

3D Printed Brain Tissue

- Researchers have created the **world's first 3D-printed brain tissue** that behaves like natural brain tissue.
- It refers to **bioprinting techniques** that generate structures resembling real brain tissue.

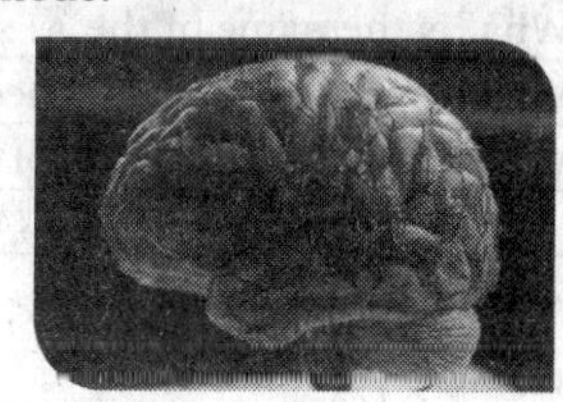

- It is a low-cost medical technology that could help with brain damage. The technology **uses human induced pluripotent stem cells (hiPSC)** to create young neurons of the cerebral cortex.

India Joins World's Largest Radio Telescope

- The government of India has formally signed up to join the Square Kilometer Array Observatory (SKAO). The Government has approved India's participation in the Rs 1250 crore international mega-science project, the Square Kilometer Array (SKA).
- SKAO is an ambitious multinational initiative to build the world's largest radio telescope spanning one square kilometre.
- The Council approved the installation of the Square Kilometer Array Observatory, the world's largest radio telescope, in February 2021.

GAME AND PUZZLE

Across

3. What is the name of the world's first bionic eye developed in Australia?
5. What is the name of India's fifth lunar mission approved in October 2024?
6. Who was India's first civilian space tourist?
7. What is the name of India's first electric microcar?

Down

1. Which SpaceX mission included the first-ever private spacewalk?
2. Which mission does the European Space Agency (ESA) focus on for lunar communications?
4. Which space mission captured the first images of Mercury's South Pole?
8. Which country launched the Aditya-L1 mission to study the Sun?

MATCHING GAME

S.No.	Questions	Answer
1	Which type of fusion reactor is being developed in China using high-temperature superconductivity?	A. Rufus
2	Which telescope in Ladakh holds the title of the largest imaging Cherenkov telescope in Asia?	B. Shukrayaan
3	What is the name of the AI shopping assistant Amazon launched in India in 2024?	C. Tokamak
4	Which space mission is scheduled by India to explore Venus in 2025?	D. BAS
5	Which spacecraft is ISRO planning to launch in 2024 as part of a collaboration with Australia?	E. MACE
6	What is the name of India's upcoming space station?	F. Optimus

SCAN TO GET MULTIPLE CHOICE QUESTIONS

Scan Me

Answer Key (Matching Game):

1. C. Tokamak 2. E. MACE 3. A. Rufus 4. B. Shukrayaan 5. F. Optimus 6. D. BAS

Answer Key (Game and Puzzle):

1. OBICUS 2. Bandhan 3. MSME Sahaj 4. Washington 5. Nvidia 6. FACE 7. Elevate 8. Paytm

DEFENCE AND SECURITIES

INDIA'S FIRST SPACE EXERCISE 'ANTARIKSHA ABHYAS'

What Happened?

- India hosted the First Space Exercise **Antariksha Abhyas 2024**, a military exercise designed to combat **space-based threats** and protect the country's vital **space assets**.
- **Dates:** 11–13 November 2024
- **Organised By:** Defence Space Agency (DSA) under the **Headquarters Integrated Defence Staff**
- **Inaugurated By:** Chief of Defence Staff, **General Anil Chauhan**

Why is this Exercise Important?

- **Global Trends in Space Warfare:** Countries like the **USA, Russia, and China** already have dedicated aerospace commands. India is preparing to match their capabilities.
- **Modern Threats:** Space is increasingly **congested, contested, and competitive**. Threats include anti-satellite weapons, cyber-attacks, and space debris.

What Are India's Space Assets?

- India relies on **over 100 satellites** for:
- Communication
- Weather Forecasting
- Earth Observation
- Navigation
- Scientific Research
- Defence
- **Key Tools:** Rockets are used for launching these satellites!

Technological Focus

1 Anti-Satellite (ASAT) Weapons:

- India's **Mission Shakti** in March 2019 showcased its ability to destroy hostile satellites.
- The exercise tests **ASAT systems** and their role in space defense.

2 Cybersecurity in Space:

- Protecting satellites from **cyber-attacks** and ensuring secure communication during conflicts.

3 Space Debris Management:

- Addressing risks from space debris in orbit, a growing global concern.

Mission Shakti: India's Space Shield

- **Mission Shakti** is India's anti-satellite weapon program led by DRDO.
- **March 27, 2019:** Successfully destroyed a satellite in space, making India one of the few countries with this capability!

Key Objectives of Antariksha Abhyas 2024

1 Strengthen India's Space Defense:

- Build resilience against disruptions to space-based services critical for military operations.
- Enhance **Space Domain Awareness** to monitor and track objects in space.

2 Foster Innovation:

- Collaborate with **DRDO, ISRO, and academia** to develop advanced space technologies.

3 Prepare for Future Conflicts:

- Test India's readiness to counter space-based threats and secure its strategic assets.

Who's Participating?

- **Defence Space Agency** and allied units
- Indian Army, Navy, Air Force
- **Defence Cyber Agency**, Intelligence Agency, and Strategic Forces Command
- **ISRO** and **DRDO**

What's Next? Aerospace Command!

- India is planning to set up an Aerospace Command, like the USA, Russia, and China, to handle space warfare.
- **Fun Fact:** The idea was recommended by the **Naresh Chandra Committee**, which reviewed the **Kargil Review Committee's** findings.
- **First Step:** In 2019, India established the Defence Space Agency and Defence Space Research Organisation.

Do you know?

- On 27 March 2019, India successfully conducted Mission Shakti (an anti-satellite missile test) and demonstrated its capability to intercept and destroy a satellite in outer space based on complete indigenous technology.
- With this test, India joined an exclusive group of space-faring nations consisting of the USA, Russia and China.
- Prime Minister Narendra Modi approved the establishment of the Defence Space Agency during the Combined Commanders' Conference at Air Force Station, Jodhpur, in September 2018 as a first step towards establishing the aerospace command.
- The Kármán line, 100 kilometres above mean sea level, is considered the boundary where Earth ends and outer space begins.

Military Exercises

Exercise SURYA KIRAN 2024

- **Event:** The 18th Joint Military Exercise SURYA KIRAN.
- **Dates:** Scheduled from December 31, 2024, to January 13, 2025, in Saljhandi, Nepal.
- **Objective:** Strengthen cooperation in jungle warfare, counter-terrorism in mountains, and disaster relief as per UN guidelines.
- **Frequency:** Annual exercise, alternate hosting between India and Nepal.
- **Leadership:** Indian Army contingent led by 11th Gorkha Rifles; Nepal Army represented by Srijung Battalion.
- **Indian Contingent:** 334 soldiers

India, Sri Lanka Joint Naval Exercise 'SLINEX 2024' Concluded

- The bilateral naval exercise SLINEX 2024 (Sri Lanka–India Exercise) conducted from 17 to 20 Dec 2024 at Visakhapatnam under the aegis of the Eastern Naval Command.
- The exercise was held in two phases – the Harbour Phase from 17 to 18 December and the Sea Phase from 19 to 20 December..
- In this edition, India deployed INS Sumitra with a Special Forces unit, while Sri Lanka participated with SLNS Sayura and its own Special Forces team.

4th edition of Exercise 'HARIMAU SHAKTI' Concluded

- The 4th edition of Exercise HARIMAU SHAKTI commenced at Bentong Camp, Pahang district, Malaysia.
- The Exercise was conducted from 2nd to 15th December 2024.
- The Indian contingent, consisting of 78 personnel, was represented by a Battalion of the MAHAR Regiment in this Edition.
- Last edition was conducted in Nov 2023 at Umroi Cantonment in Meghalaya, India.

Exercise 'Sanyukt Vimochan' 2024 Concluded

- On 18th and 19th November 2024, the Indian Army conducted the 'Sanyukt Vimochan 2024' Humanitarian Assistance and Disaster Relief (HADR) exercise in Ahmedabad and Porbandar, Gujarat.
- It focussed on the theme of 'Cyclone in Coastal Region of Gujarat'.
- The event included a Tabletop Exercise on cyclone management and a Multi-Agency Capability Demonstration with participation from the Indian Army, Navy, Air Force, Coast Guard, and National Disaster Response Force (NDRF).

INS Tabar Participated in Indo-French 'VARUNA' Naval Exercise

- The 22nd Indo-French 'Exercise VARUNA' was held from 2nd to 4th September 2024 in the Mediterranean Sea.
- INS Tabar participated in the 22nd Indo-French Exercise VARUNA.
- The Indian Navy was represented by a shipborne helicopter and a P8I aircraft.
- The French Navy was represented by the FS Provence ship, Suffren Submarine, Atlantique 2 aircraft, and NH90 and Dauphin helicopters.
- This exercise started in 2001 to strengthen the relationship between India and France.

Indian Navy in Exercise 'Kakadu 2024'

- The Indian Navy took part in Exercise Kakadu 2024, led by Captain Ajay Kanwar.
- Exercise Kakadu 2024 took place from

12th July to 2nd August 2024 in Darwin, Australia.

- This exercise is Australia's largest maritime warfare exercise.
- It aims to build strong defence partnerships among countries in the Indo-Pacific region.

Indian Air Force Participated in Exercise 'Eastern Bridge VII'

- The Indian Air Force successfully participated in Exercise Eastern Bridge VII at the RAFO airbase in Masirah, Oman from 11th to 22nd September 2024.
- Advanced aircraft like MiG-29 and Jaguar from the Indian Air Force (IAF) and F-16 and Hawk from Oman's Royal Air Force of Oman (RAFO) took part.
- The exercise focused on enhancing cooperation between the two air forces.

Exercise 'Udara Shakti 2024'

- The Indian Air Force and the Royal Malaysian Air Force conducted Exercise 'Udara Shakti 2024' from 5th to 9th August 2024.
- This exercise took place at Kuantan Air Base in Malaysia.
- Indian Su-30MKI jets and Malaysian Su-30MKM jets participated in various air combat scenarios.

'Nomadic Elephant 2024'

- The 16th edition of the Nomadic Elephant exercise was held in Umroi, Meghalaya, from 3rd to 16th July 2024.
- This joint exercise between the Indian Army and the Mongolian Army focused on training for UN peacekeeping missions.
- The training was designed for semi-urban and mountainous terrains.

Exercise 'MAITREE 2024'

- The 13th edition of Exercise MAITREE was conducted in Tak Province, Thailand, from 1st to 15th July 2024.
- It is a joint military exercise between the Indian Army and the Royal Thai Army.
- The focus of this exercise was on counter-insurgency and counter-terrorism operations in urban and jungle environments.

Exercise 'KAZIND-2024'

- The 8th edition of Exercise KAZIND was held in Auli, Uttarakhand, from 30th September to 13th October 2024.
- It is a joint military exercise between India and Kazakhstan that started in 2016 as 'Exercise PRABAL DOSTYK.'
- After the second edition, it was renamed 'KAZIND' and upgraded to a company-level exercise.

BILATERAL MILITARY EXERCISES

Participating Countries	Army/Navy/Air Force	Exercise Name
India and Australia	Army	AUSTRA HIND
	Navy	AUSINDEX
India and Bangladesh	Army	SAMPRITI
	Navy	IN-BN CORPAT
	Air Force	Table Top Ex
India and China	Army	HAND IN HAND
India and France	Army	SHAKTI
	Navy	VARUNA
	Air Force	GARUDA
India and Indonesia	Army	GARUDA SHAKTI
	Navy	IND-INDO CORPAT
India and Japan	Army	DHARMA GUARDIAN
	Navy	JIMEX
India and Kazakhstan	Army	PRABAL DOSTYK
India and Kyrgyzstan	Army	KHANJAR
India and Maldives	Army	EKUVERIN
India and Mongolia	Army	NOMADIC ELEPHANT
India and Myanmar	Army	IMBEX
	Navy	IMCOR
India and Nepal	Army	SURYA KIRAN
India and Oman	Army	AL NAGAH
	Navy	Naseem-al-Bahr
	Air Force	EASTERN BRIDGE-IV
India and Russia	Army	INDRA
	Navy	INDRA NAVY
	Air Force	INDRA
India and Seychelles	Army	LAMITIYE
India and Sri Lanka	Army	MITRA SHAKTI
	Navy	SLINEX
India and Thailand	Army	MAITREE
	Navy	INDO-THAI CORPAT
	Air Force	SIAM BHARAT
India and the United Kingdom	Army	AJEYA WARRIOR
	Navy	KONKAN
	Air Force	INDRADHANUSH-IV
India and USA	Army	YUDHABHAYAS & VAJRA PRAHAR
	Navy	MALABAR (Multilateral)
	Army	YUDH ABHYAS
	Air Force	RED FLAG 16-1
India and Vietnam	Army	VINBAX

'Parvat Prahaar' in Ladakh

- The Indian Army conducted Exercise Parvat Prahaar in the Ladakh region near the India-China border in August 2024.
- The name Parvat Prahaar means "Mountain Strike," and it focuses on operations in the Himalayan regions.
- The Mountain Strike Corps of the Northern Command, which is responsible for operations in this sensitive region along the Line of Actual Control (LAC), is involved in the exercise.

'Khaan Quest 2024'

- The 21st edition of Exercise 'Khaan Quest' was held in Ulaanbaatar, Mongolia, from 27th July to 9th August 2024.
- Indian forces participated in this multinational peacekeeping exercise, which prepares soldiers for UN peacekeeping missions.

- It started as a bilateral exercise in 2003 and became a multinational exercise in 2006.

IAF in 'Pitch Black 2024'

- The Indian Air Force took part in Exercise Pitch Black 2024, a biennial exercise hosted by Australia.
- Exercise Pitch Black 2024 occurred from 12th July to 2nd August 2024 at the RAAF Base in Darwin, Australia.
- This was the largest edition in its 43-year history, with 20 nations participating.
- The IAF's Su-30 MKI fighter jets represented India in this multinational exercise.

Russia Concludes Largest Naval Exercise Ocean-24

- Russia and China conducted a joint naval exercise called 'Ocean-24' in the Sea of Japan from 10 to 16 September 2024.
- The exercise demonstrated their combined military strength to Western nations.

IAF Successfully Completes 'Exercise Eastern Bridge VII' with Oman

- On 21 September 2024, the Indian Air Force completed Exercise 'Eastern Bridge VII' with Oman's Royal Air Force (RAFO) at the Masirah Airbase.
- Aircraft involved included the IAF's MiG-29 and Jaguar and RAFO's F-16 and Hawk.
- The exercise aimed to improve tactical skills and military coordination.

Exercise RED FLAG 2024

- An Indian Air Force (IAF) contingent participated in the Exercise Red Flag 2024 conducted at Eielson Air Force Base, Alaska of the United States Air Force, from 04 Jun to 14 Jun 24.
- This was the second edition of Ex Red Flag 2024, which is an advanced aerial combat training exercise, held four times in a year by the US Air Force.
- The exercise witnessed participation of the Indian Air Force along with Republic of Singapore Air Force (RSAF), Royal Air Force (RAF) of the United Kingdom, Royal Netherlands Air Force (RNLAF), German Luftwaffe, and the US Air Force (USAF).

India-France joint military exercise SHAKTI commenced in Meghalaya

- The 7th edition of the joint military exercise 'Shakti' between India and France commenced in Umroi, Meghalaya from May 13 to 26, 2024.
- Exercise "Shakti" is a biennial training event conducted alternatively in India and France. The last edition took place in France in November 2021.
- The exercise focuses on multi-domain operations in semi-urban and mountainous terrain, enhancing joint military capabilities and fostering defense cooperation between the two nations.

Indian Navy conducted Exercise Poorvi Lehar on East Coast

- The Indian Navy conducted a Military Exercise named "Poorvi Lehar" on the Eastern Coast of India from April 20-26, 2024.
- The exercise aimed to assess the Indian Navy's preparedness to meet Maritime Security challenges in the region.
- It involved ships, submarines, aircraft, and special forces from the Eastern Naval Command, IAF, Andaman & Nicobar Command, and Coast Guard.

India-Uzbekistan joint military exercise DUSTLIK 2024

- The fifth edition of the India and Uzbekistan joint military exercise Dustlik was held from 15th to 28th April 2024 in Termez, Uzbekistan.
- The aim of Exercise DUSTLIK is to foster military cooperation and enhance combined capabilities to execute joint operations in mountainous as well as semi urban terrain.
- The first edition of the exercise was held in Uzbekistan in November 2019. The last edition was conducted in Pithoragarh in February 2023.

India, Maldives & Sri Lanka's Dosti-16' Kicks off in Maldives

- Indian and Sri Lankan coast guard ships joined the Dosti 16 exercise held in the Maldives from February 22-25.
- The exercise brought together the coast guards of Maldives, India, and Sri Lanka to address shared maritime security concerns through collaboration and interoperability.
- It aimed to enhance cooperation, strengthen friendship, and develop mutual operational capability among the participating countries.

10th edition of Joint Military Exercise 'LAMITIYE-2024' in Seychelles

- The Tenth Edition of Joint Military Exercise 'LAMITIYE', between Indian Army & Seychelles Defence Forces, commenced at Seychelles Defence Academy.
- The Exercise aims to achieve cohesion, jointness and interoperability between both the Defence Forces during Peacekeeping Operations.
- The exercise 'LAMITIYE', meaning 'Friendship' in the Creole language, has been conducted in Seychelles since 2001.

Exercise Tiger Triumph – 2024

- India and the US conducted a bilateral tri-Service Humanitarian Assistance and Disaster Relief (HADR) Exercise named Tiger Triumph – 24 from 18 to 31 March 2024.
- The exercise aims to enhance interoperability and refine Standard Operating Procedures for conducting HADR operations.
- It involves the Indian Navy, Army, and Air Force along with the US Navy, Marine Corps, and Army.

India, Mozambique and Tanzania trilateral exercise IMT Trilat - 2024

- INS Tir and INS Sujata participated in the second edition of India Mozambique Tanzania (IMT) TriLateral (TRILAT) Exercise, a joint maritime exercise that was held from 21 to 29 March 2024.
- **INS Tir and INS Sujata** engaged with the respective Navies at the ports of Zanzibar (Tanzania and Maputo (Mozambique).
- The first edition of IMT TRILAT exercise conducted **on October 2022,** saw participation of **INS Tarkash** with the Tanzanian and Mozambique Navies.

Indian-Thai Navy first bilateral exercise "Ex-Ayutthaya" connects to Ayodhya

- The Indian Navy and Royal Thai Navy (RTN) conducted a maiden bilateral exercise named 'Ex-Ayutthaya.'
- The 'Ex-Ayutthaya' translates to 'The Invincible One' or 'Undefeatable', and "symbolizes the significance of two of the oldest cities, Ayodhya in India and Ayutthaya in Thailand.
- The exercise highlights their ancient cities, rich cultural connections, and shared historical narratives spanning centuries.

12th Edition of MILAN Naval Exercise

- MILAN 2024 is the 12th edition of the biennial Multilateral Naval Exercise held at Visakhapatnam, under the aegis of Eastern Naval Command.
- It includes ships and aircraft from various countries, focusing on air defense, anti-submarine, and anti-surface warfare drills.
- MILAN enhances maritime security and promotes collaboration among navies.

India-Japan joint exercise 'Dharma Guardian' commenced in Rajasthan

- The fifth edition of the joint military exercise **'Dharma Guardian'** between the **Indian Army and the Japanese Ground Self-Defense Forces** commenced at Mahajan Field Firing Range in Rajasthan **on 25 February 2024.**
- 'Dharma Guardian' is an annual exercise held alternately in **India and Japan.**
- The Japanese contingent was represented by soldiers of the 34th Infantry Regiment, and the Indian Army contingent was represented by a battalion of the Rajputana Rifles.

India, France, UAE conduct joint mega air exercise over Arabian Sea

- The Indian Air Force (IAF) joined forces with the French Air and Space Force (FASF) and United Arab Emirates (UAE) Air Force in Exercise "Desert Knight".
- The Indian Air Force operated from its **west coast bases,** while the French and UAE air forces operated from the **Al Dhafra air base.**
- This trilateral exercise involves India's Su-30MKI and Jaguar jets, France's Rafale fighters, and the UAE's F-16 aircraft.

India and Egypt Armies Unite for exercise Cyclone's Special Operations

- The Indian Army and the Egyptian Armed Forces united for the 2nd edition of the joint special forces exercise named **'Cyclone'.**
- The exercise was conducted at **Anshas, Egypt** from **January 22nd to February 1st, 2024.** The first edition of the exercise was conducted last year in India.
- The aim of the exercise is to acquaint both sides with each other's operating procedures in the backdrop of Special Operations in desert/semi-desert terrain.

Joint Exercise 'Sahyog Kaijin' Between Indian And Japanese Coast Guards

- The Indian and Japanese Coast Guards completed a successful cooperative exercise called **'Sahyog Kaijin' off the coast of Chennai.**
- This exercise is part of the two countries' continuous partnership under the **Memorandum of Cooperation (MoC), signed in 2006.**
- The exercise involved the **Indian Coast Guard Ship (ICGS) Shaurya and the Japan Coast Guard Ship (JCGS) Yashima,** along with other support vessels and aircraft.

NATO military exercise "Steadfast Defender 2024"

- The North Atlantic Treaty Organization **(NATO)** has commenced its largest military exercise since the Cold War, **"Steadfast Defender 2024".**
- The exercise involves approximately 90,000 troops from all **31 NATO Allies,** as well as partner Sweden.
- "Steadfast Defender 2024" is a multi-domain exercise, incorporating land, air, sea, cyber, and space operations.

Indian – Kyrgyzstan joint special forces exercise Khanjar commenced

- The **11th edition** of India-Kyrgyzstan Joint Special Forces Exercise **"Khanjar"** held at the Special Forces Training School **in Bakloh, Himachal Pradesh.**
- It aims to exchange experiences and best practices in Counter Terrorism and Special Forces Operations in Built-up Area and Mountainous Terrain.
- This exercise has been organized between the two countries since 2011.

Exercise 'Desert Cyclone' held in Rajasthan

- The collaborative military exercise **'Desert Cyclone 2024'** involving India and the UAE was held in Rajasthan **from January 2 to January 15.**
- The joint manoeuvres during 'Desert Cyclone 2024' **aim to boost interoperability** through the exchange of knowledge and best practices in urban operations.
- The first-ever India-UAE Joint Air Forces exercise took place in **September 2008 at the Al-Dhafra base** in Abu Dhabi.

IAF conducted the mega exercise 'Vayu Shakti 2024' in Jaisalmer

- The Indian Air Force conducted the extensive exercise Vayu Shakti 2024 at the Pokhran Range in Jaisalmer on 17th February 2024.
- This exercise showcased the Air Force's combat and operational capabilities, emphasizing interoperability and maneuvering.
- Various indigenous aircraft and helicopters such as Tejas, Prachand, and Dhruv was participated.

Malaysia bilateral maritime exercise 'Samudra Laksamana'

- The 3rd edition of the India-Malaysia bilateral maritime exercise, Samudra Lakshmana, was held off the coast of Visakhapatnam from February 28 to March 2, 2024.
- The exercise involved Indian Naval Ship Kiltan and Royal Malaysian Ship KD Lekir.

MoU and Deals

Defence Ministry Signs Deal with Hal for 12 Su-30mki Aircraft

- Ministry of Defence (MoD) has signed a contract with Hindustan Aeronautics Ltd (HAL) for the procurement of 12 Su-30MKI aircraft.
- The deal, valued at approximately ₹13,500 crore, includes associated equipment and is inclusive of taxes and duties.
- The Russian-origin Su-30MKI jets are procured for the Indian Air Force. These jets are now manufactured by the HAL under an intergovernmental framework.

Indian Navy received MH-60R Seahawk helicopters

- On 5th December 2024, the Indian Navy received the MH-60R Seahawk multi-role helicopters under the Foreign Military Sales (FMS) program from the United States.
- These helicopters, also known as "Romeos," are designed for anti-submarine warfare (ASW), anti-surface warfare (ASuW), search and rescue (SAR), and logistical missions.

US to Sell High Altitude Anti-Submarine Warfare Sonobuoys to India

- The United States has decided to sell High Altitude Anti-Submarine Warfare (HAASW) sonobuoys worth USD 52.8 million to India.
- These sonobuoys will improve India's

ability to perform anti-submarine warfare operations using MH-60R helicopters.

- Sonobuoys are devices that are air-launched and can detect underwater sounds, sending the information to processors.
- They are cost-effective tools used by airborne anti-submarine warfare forces.

UAE Completes Arab World's First Nuclear Plant

- The United Arab Emirates (UAE) has built the first nuclear power plant in the Arab world, called the 'Barakah Nuclear Energy Plant'.
- It is located in Al Dhafra, Abu Dhabi, about 53 km from Ruwais on the Arabian Gulf.
- The Barakah plant marks a significant achievement for the Arab world in the field of nuclear energy.

PM Modi Inaugurates India's First Private Military Aircraft Plant in Gujarat

- On 28th October 2024, Prime Minister Narendra Modi and Spanish President Pedro Sanchez inaugurated India's first private military aircraft plant in Vadodara, Gujarat.
- The plant, built by Tata-Airbus, is India's first private Final Assembly Line (FAL) for military aircraft.
- It will produce C-295 military transport aircraft for the Indian Air Force, with 40 aircraft being manufactured in India and 16 delivered from Spain.
- The first aircraft from this plant will be ready by 2026.

Defence Ministry Awards Grant to Velmenni for Li-Fi Technology

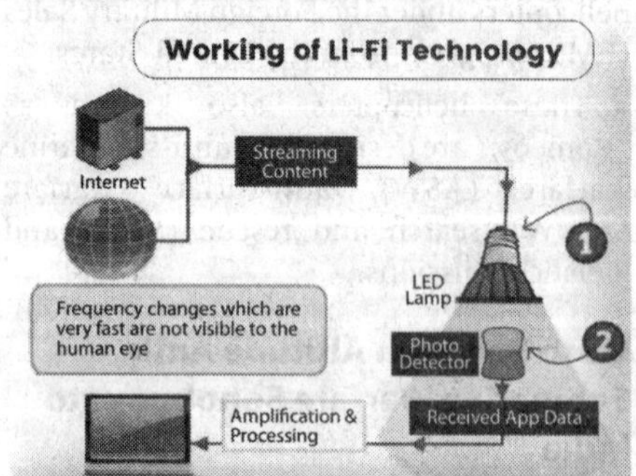

- Velmenni, a leader in light-based communication technology, received a grant from the Ministry of Defence (MoD) under the iDEX initiative for its Light Fidelity (Li-Fi) technology.
- Li-Fi uses visible light for communication instead of radio waves like Wi-Fi.
- This technology provides a highly secure and high-speed network for both outdoor and indoor use.

Defence Ministry signed 2,269 Crore Rupees contract with BEL

- On 13th February 2024, the Ministry of Defence signed a ₹2,269.54 crore contract with Bharat Electronics Limited (BEL) for the procurement of 11 Shakti Electronic Warfare Systems for the Indian Navy.
- The Shakti EW System, indigenously designed and developed, enhances the Navy's defense capabilities by accurately intercepting electronic emissions and implementing countermeasures in dense electromagnetic environments.
- The project will generate two and a half lakh man-days of employment over four years, involving over 155 industry partners, including MSMEs.

Meetings and Conferences

First Joint Commanders' Conference Begins in Lucknow

- The first Joint Commanders' Conference (JCC) began on 4th September 2024 in Lucknow.
- The theme of the conference is 'Sashakt and Surakshit Bharat: Transforming Armed Forces.'
- Defence Minister Rajnath Singh chaired the event, which focuses on preparing India's military for changing operational needs.

Army Chief Launches 'Agniastra' at Gangtok Conference

- Army Chief General Upendra Dwivedi launched 'Agniastra,' a portable multi-target detonation device, during the Army Commanders Conference in Gangtok.
- Developed by Major Rajprasad, this advanced detonation system works in wired and wireless modes with a range of 2.5 km.
- The device can selectively or simultaneously fire multiple targets, making it ideal for safe demolition operations.

India-Mongolia Joint Working Group Meeting

- The **12th Joint Working Group meeting** between the Defence Ministries of India and Mongolia concluded in **Ulaanbaatar.**
- Co-chaired by **India's Joint Secretary Amitabh Prasad and Mongolia's Brigadier General Gankhuyag Davagdorj,** the meeting reviewed bilateral defence cooperation and explored ways to enhance it.
- The Indian delegation highlighted the capabilities of India's defence industry, which was positively received by Mongolia.

Maharashtra MSME Defence Expo

- The country's largest and Maharashtra's first **'Maharashtra MSME Defense Expo'** was inaugurated by Deputy Chief Minister **Devendra Fadnavis** at International Exhibition and Convention Center at Moshi near Pune.
- Maharashtra has formulated an aerospace and defence policy **in 2017** and a fund of **1000 crores** has been created to promote this sector. 600 MSMEs have been created out of it.
- More than 1,200 small companies producing arms as well as other materials related to the defence sector will present their capabilities in the Expo.

New Weapons

China's First Type 076 Amphibious Assault Ship

- China has launched its first Type 076 amphibious assault ship, **Sichuan**, at the Hudong-Zhonghua shipyard in Shanghai.
- The ship features a **40,000-tonne** displacement, a **dual-island design**, and a full-length flight deck.
- It is equipped with an electromagnetic catapult and arresting system, allowing it to launch and recover fixed-wing aircraft, helicopters, and amphibious vehicles.

Stealth frigate 'INS Tushil' commissioned into the Indian Navy in Russia

- The Russian-built multi-role stealth-guided missile frigate 'INS Tushil' was commissioned into the Indian Navy at the Yantar Shipyard in Kaliningrad, Russia.
- INS Tushil (F70) is a Talwar-class frigate of the Indian Navy.
- It is the seventh ship of the Talwar-class frigates and the first of the third batch of the class frigates ordered by the Indian Navy.

India successfully tested K-4 nuclear-capable ballistic missile

- In November 2024, India successfully tested the K-4 nuclear-capable ballistic missile from the newly commissioned 'INS Arighaat' submarine in the Bay of Bengal.

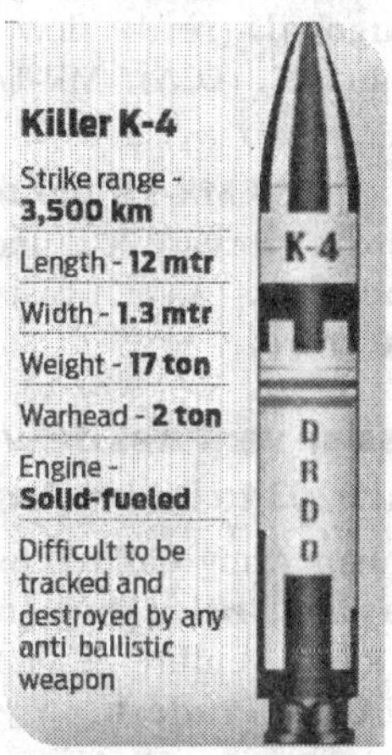

- The K-4 is a solid fuelled missile which has a striking range of 3,500 km. It was launched from a 6000-tonne submarine.
- The second Arihant-class submarine INS Arighaat was commissioned into the Indian Navy on August 29 with an aim to strengthen India's nuclear deterrence.

India Debuts New Swadeshi Kamikaze Drones

- The National Aerospace Laboratories (NAL) has developed indigenous 'Kamikaze drones' with home-built engines, capable of flying up to 1,000 km.
- These "do-and-die" unmanned aerial vehicles are designed for targeted attacks and destruction missions.
- Kamikaze drones have been widely used in the Russia-Ukraine war and the Israel-Hamas conflict in Gaza.
- In Ukraine, these drones have been extensively used to target Russian infantry and armored vehicles.

Indian Army Inducts 'Asmi' Sub-Machine Guns

- The Indian Army has inducted 550 'Asmi' 9×19 mm sub-machine guns (SMGs), manufactured by Hyderabad-based Lokesh Machines.
- The 'Asmi' machine pistol, developed by Colonel Prasad Bansod of the Indian Army in collaboration with DRDO, is a 100% Make-in-India weapon.

DRDO Unveils 'Zorawar' Tank for High-Altitude Warfare

- India has unveiled the Zorawar light tank, designed specifically for high-altitude warfare.
- It was jointly developed by DRDO and Larsen & Toubro (L&T) Limited to meet Indian Army requirements in eastern Ladakh.
- The tank is named after 19th-century Dogra General Zorawar Singh and will be inducted into the Indian Army by 2027.
- It is intended to counter Chinese deployments along the Line of Actual Control (LAC).

Indian Navy Certifies New Explosive 'SEBEX 2'

- On 1 July 2024, the Indian Navy certified SEBEX 2, a cutting-edge explosive with a TNT equivalence of 2.01, making it one of the most powerful non-nuclear explosives globally.
- Developed by Economic Explosives Limited (EEL) under the Make in India initiative, SEBEX 2 enhances the lethality of warheads, aerial bombs, and artillery shells without increasing their weight.

India Successfully Test-Fires Rudram-1 Anti-Radiation Missile

- India has successfully tested the Rudram-1, its first indigenous anti-radiation missile, developed by DRDO for the Indian Air Force (IAF).
- The missile is integrated with Sukhoi-30MKI jets as the launch platform.
- It uses INS-GPS navigation and a Passive Homing Head to accurately destroy radiation-emitting targets.

DRDO Successfully Tests Long-Range Glide Bomb 'Gaurav'

- On 13 August 2024, the DRDO conducted the maiden flight test of the Long Range Glide Bomb (LRGB) 'Gaurav', launched from an IAF Sukhoi-30MKI aircraft off the coast of Odisha.
- The bomb, weighing 1,000 kg, demonstrated pinpoint accuracy using a hybrid navigation system combining INS and GPS data.
- The bomb was designed and developed by Research Centre Imarat (RCI) in Hyderabad.

DRDO & Indian Navy Successfully Test VL-SRSAM

- On 12 September 2024, India successfully test-fired the Vertical Launch Short Range Surface-to-Air Missile (VL-SRSAM) at the Integrated Test Range (ITR) in Chandipur, Balasore district, Odisha.
- The missile, developed jointly by DRDO and the Indian Navy, is a ship-borne weapon designed to neutralize various aerial threats at close ranges, including sea-skimming targets.

Pakistan Successfully Test-Fires 'Shaheen-II' Ballistic Missile

- On 20 August 2024, Pakistan successfully conducted a training launch of the 'Shaheen-II' ballistic missile, a surface-to-surface missile with a range of 2,000 km.

- The missile is capable of carrying both nuclear and conventional warheads.
- The launch was conducted to validate various technical parameters and assess the performance of different subsystems.
- In May, Pakistan conducted a successful training launch of the Fateh-II Guided Rocket System having a range of 400 kilometres.

North Korea Conducts Longest-Ever ICBM Test

- On 30 October 2024, North Korea conducted its longest-ever intercontinental ballistic missile (ICBM) test using the 'Hwasong-19' missile.
- The missile was launched near Pyongyang, flew for 87 minutes, and reached an altitude of 7,000 km before splashing down in the sea between Japan and Russia.
- The test drew international condemnation amid rising tensions over reports of North Korea deploying troops to Russia.

Russia Developed Space-Based Anti-Satellite (ASAT) Weapon

- Russia has developed a nuclear-armed, space-based anti-satellite (ASAT) weapon.
- This system, if deployed, could pose a significant threat to satellites and space assets of other nations.

MQ-9B Drones (UAV)

- The **US State Department** has approved the sale of **MQ-9B remotely piloted aircraft** to India under the foreign military sales program.
- It covers the proposed sale of **31 Sky Guardian drones** and related equipment to India for an estimated cost of $3. 99 billion.
- It is a derivative of the MQ-9 Reaper designed for both remotely controlled and autonomous flight operations.

Indian Army gets Igla-S Air Defence Systems from Russia

- The Indian Army received the first batch of 24 Russia-made Igla-S Man Portable Air Defence Systems (MANPADS) and 100 missiles on April 8, 2024.
- These systems enhance the **Army's Very Short Range Air Defence (VSHORAD) capabilities** particularly in high mountainous terrain along the northern border.
- The Igla-S system is designed to bring down **low-flying aircraft** and can also identify and **neutralize air targets** such as cruise missiles and drones.
- It comprises the 9M342 missile, the 9P522 launching mechanism, the 9V866-2 mobile test station, and the 9F719-2 test set.

Indian Air Force Tested Bhishm Portable Hospital for Airdrop in Agra

- On 14 May 2024, the Indian Air Force conducted field tests of the **Arogya Maitri Cube- BHISHM portable hospital** by performing an airdrop in Agra, Uttar Pradesh.
- The portable hospital, **weighing 720 kg,** was air-dropped from a transport aircraft using specially designed parachutes.
- The BHISHM portable hospital is part of **"Project BHISHM"** and can treat up to 200 casualties, focusing on swift response and comprehensive care.

Indian Army Tested Anti-Tank Guided Missile at 'Super-High-Altitude' In Sikkim

- The Indian **Army's Trishakti Corps** conducted a training exercise involving the firing of anti-tank guided missiles (ATGMs) at a **"super high-altitude area of 17,000 feet"** in Sikkim.
- The ATGM system's performance in high-altitude environments reaffirms the **"Ek Missile Ek Tank" goal.**
- It highlights its accuracy and effectiveness in "super-high-altitude terrain".

India to test 130 km strike range Astra Mark-2 missile this year

- India plans to test the Astra Mark-2 air-to-air missile with a 130 km strike range in 2024.
- Developed by the Defence Research and Development Organisation (DRDO), this missile aims to enhance the Indian Air Force's aerial combat capabilities.
- The Astra Mark-2 will provide an edge in air-to-air combat and can be exported to friendly nations.
- The missile is part of the Astra series, which includes the Astra Mark-1 (90-100 km range) already in service.

India Test-Fires Manportable Anti-Tank Guided Missile

- India's Defence Research and Development Organisation (DRDO) and the Indian Army successfully test-fired the Man-Portable Anti-Tank Guided Missile (MPATGM).
- The MPATGM can strike armored vehicles at a range of 2.5 km. It features day/night and top attack capabilities with a dual mode seeker.
- The **Warhead Flight Trials** were successfully conducted at the **Pokhran Field Firing Range,** Rajasthan on 13 April, 2024.

LCA Tejas MK-1A completed maiden flight in Bengaluru

- The first **Tejas Mk-1A aircraft** made its maiden flight from a Hindustan Aeronautics Limited (HAL) facility **in Bengaluru on 28 March 2024.**
- HAL's chief test pilot **Group Captain KK Venugopal (retd)** flew the light combat aircraft (LCA) Mk-1A for **18 minutes.**
- IAF ordered **83 Mk-1A fighters** for Rs. 48,000 crore in February 2021 and **plans to buy 97 more** Mk-1As at a cost of around **Rs. 67,000 crore.**

Indo-Russian ventures delivered 27,000 AK-203 to Indian Army

- The Indian Army has received **27,000 AK-203 assault rifles** through an Indo-Russian joint venture established **at Korwa in Uttar Pradesh.**
- These rifles are part of a larger contract **signed in July 2021,** aiming to manufacture over 6. 1 lakh AK-203 rifles in India with technology transfer from Russia.
- The AK-203, a modernized version of the AK-200 series chambered for the 7.62x39mm cartridge, enhances the combat capabilities of the Indian Army.

MH 60R Seahawk helicopter

- The Indian Navy commissioned the MH-60R Seahawk multi-role helicopter, marking a pivotal moment in its defense modernization journey.
- The INAS 334 'Seahawks' naval air squadron was commissioned at a ceremony at INS Garuda in Kochi in the presence of Navy Chief Admiral R Hari Kumar.
- These helicopters, part of a 24-aircraft Foreign Military Sales contract signed with the US in February 2020, are equipped for anti-submarine warfare, anti-surface warfare, search and rescue, medical evacuation, and vertical replenishment.

Indian Navy commissions INS Jatayu at Minicoy

- The Indian Navy commissioned INS Jatayu, a strategically important naval base, on March 6, 2024, at Minicoy Island in the Lakshadweep archipelago.
- The base, named after the mythical bird from the Ramayana, was commissioned by Admiral R Hari Kumar, Chief of Naval Staff.
- It will operate under the Southern Naval Command and strengthen India's maritime presence in the Indian Ocean.

Guyana To Acquire Two HAL Made Dornier 228 Aircraft From India

- Guyana's Defence Force (GDF) acquired two Dornier 228 aircraft from India's Hindustan Aeronautics Limited (HAL).
- The deal, worth $23.27 million USD, was financed by the Export-Import Bank of India (EXIM Bank).
- The aircraft, commissioned on November 17, 2024, enhance GDF's capabilities in border security, disaster response, and medical evacuations.
- The acquisition strengthens Guyana's defense infrastructure and underscores the growing strategic partnership between Guyana and India.

India Successfully conducted 1st Flight Test Of Agni-5 Missile

- India successfully conducted the first flight test of the Agni-5 missile on March 11, 2024, under Mission Divyastra.
- The missile, equipped with Multiple Independently Targetable Re-entry Vehicle (MIRV) technology, was launched from Dr APJ Abdul Kalam Island in Odisha.
- The Agni-5, with a range of 5,000 kilometers, is classified as an intermediate-range ballistic missile (IRBM), but its actual range may exceed 5,500 kilometers.

DRDO To Test Indigenous Laser Weapon DURGA-2

- Defence Research and Development Organisation (DRDO) of India is preparing to test its indigenous laser weapon system, **DURGA-2.**
- Named Directionally Unrestricted Ray Gun Array, it's a directed energy weapon (DEW) designed to neutralize missile and drone threats.
- The 25KW laser can target ballistic missiles up to 5 km away, with plans to extend the range to 100 km.
- The DURGA-2 Is planned to be integrated with land, sea and air based platforms.

Turkish 5th-Gen Fighter KAAN Completed Maiden Flight

- Turkey's Turkish Aerospace Industries (TAI) successfully completed the maiden flight of the 5th-generation fighter jet KAAN on February 21, 2024.
- The jet, known as KAAN, was **developed by Turkish Aerospace Industries** with help from the **UK's BAE Systems.**
- The aircraft, piloted by Barbaros Demirbas, reached an altitude of 8,000 feet and a speed of 230 knots.
- The KAAN, designed to replace Turkey's aging F-16 fleet, features advanced avionics, stealth capabilities, and can undertake command roles in battle.

INS Sandhayak Commissioned in Visakhapatnam

- The Indian Navy commissioned INS Sandhayak, the first Survey Vessel Large (SVL), on February 3, 2024, at the Naval Dockyard in Visakhapatnam.
- The ship, built by Garden Reach Shipbuilders & Engineers (GRSE) in Kolkata, has over 80% indigenous content.
- It is designed for hydrographic surveys, mapping navigational channels, ports, and coastal areas.
- The ship also supports maritime operations and has a top speed of 18 knots.

Operations

Balochistan Liberation Army Launches 'Operation Herof' Against Pakistan Military

- The Baloch Liberation Army (BLA) has initiated 'Operation Herof' (Black Storm), a Fidayeen (suicide) operation conducted by its elite Majeed Brigade.
- The BLA claims this operation has inflicted heavy losses on Pakistani military forces in Balochistan, marking it as a significant military action.

IAF Conducted Bambi Bucket Operations To Combat Forest Fires In Uttarakhand

- In response to the raging forest fires in the **Pauri Garhwal sector** of Uttarakhand, the Indian Air Force (IAF) proactively deployed its **Mi17 V5 helicopters** for **Bambi Bucket operations.**
- These helicopters efficiently transported and released over **4,500 liters of water** over the affected areas, working in close coordination with the Uttarakhand government.

India Launched "Operation Indravati" To Evacuate Citizens From Violence-Hit Haiti

- On 21 March 2024, India launched **'Operation Indravati'** to evacuate its citizens from the **turmoil-stricken Haiti** to the neighboring Dominican Republic.
- Haiti, situated in the Caribbean, has **plunged into chaos with armed gangs** seizing control of the streets, resulting in the virtual disappearance of the government.

Indian Army launched large-scale counter-terror operation 'Operation Sarvashakti'

- The Indian Army launched Operation Sarvashakti on January 17, 2024, targeting terrorist activities in Jammu and Kashmir.
- The operation focuses on the Rajouri-Poonch sector, aiming to eliminate terrorists responsible for recent ambushes on Indian troops.
- Conducted by the Chinar Corps in Srinagar and the White Knight Corps in Nagrota, it involves close coordination with J&K Police, CRPF, and intelligence agencies.

EU Naval Mission 'Mission Aspides'

- **Mission Aspides** is a European Union (EU) naval mission to protect commercial vessels **in the Red Sea** from attacks by **Iran-backed Houthi rebels.**
- They claim their actions are in solidarity with Palestinians in Gaza during the Israel-Hamas conflict.
- The EU states that the mission Aspides, initially set for one year, is aimed at safeguarding civilian shipping in the Red Sea and assures that no attacks will be conducted on Yemeni soil.

Others

Mohana Singh Becomes First Woman Fighter Pilot in LCA Tejas Fleet

- On 18 September 2024, Squadron Leader Mohana Singh became the first woman fighter pilot to join the elite 18 'Flying Bullets' squadron, which operates India's indigenously made LCA Tejas fighter jets.

- Mohana Singh was one of the first three women inducted as fighter pilots in the Indian Air Force in 2016, alongside Bhawna Kanth and Avni Chaturvedi.
- She also participated in the recent 'Tarang Shakti' exercise held in Jodhpur.

Mysuru's Capt. Supreetha Becomes First Woman Officer to Deployed at Siachen Glacier

- Captain Supreetha C.T. from Mysuru has become the first woman officer from the Corps of Army Air Defence to be operationally deployed at the Siachen Glacier.
- The Siachen Glacier, located in the Eastern Karakoram range of the Himalayas, is the world's highest battlefield.
- India launched 'Operation Meghdoot' in 1984, gaining control of the glacier from Pakistan, which is of great strategic importance.

INS Shivalik Wins Naval Gunfire Support Competition at RIMPAC 2024

- INS Shivalik won the Naval Gunfire Support Competition at RIMPAC 2024, the world's largest international maritime exercise involving 29 nations.
- The stealth frigate's outstanding firepower and accuracy earned it the prestigious RODEO trophy, showcasing India's maritime strength.
- RIMPAC started in 1971 as an annual exercise with the US, Australia, and Canada but became a biennial event in 1974.
- India first participated in RIMPAC in 2014 with INS Sahyadri.

Goa Shipyard Launches India's First Pollution Control Vessel Samudra Pratap

- On 29 August 2024, the Indian Coast Guard launched its first indigenous Pollution Control Vessel (PCV), named 'Samudra Pratap', in Goa.
- The vessel, named by Smt. Neeta Seth, was built by Goa Shipyard Limited (GSL) to meet ICG's specific needs.
- It is 114.5 meters long, 16.5 meters wide, and displaces 4170 tons.
- GSL signed a contract to build two vessels for Rs 583 crores.

India's First Indigenous Combat Unmanned Aircraft FWD 200B Takes Flight

- Bengaluru-based firm Flying Wedge Defence and Aerospace (FWDA) launched India's first indigenous Unmanned Combat Aerial Vehicle (UCAV), the 'FWD 200B'.
- It is a Medium Altitude Long Endurance (MALE) UCAV with a 102 kg maximum take-off weight (MTOW) and a 30 kg payload capacity.
- The UCAV operates at a cruise altitude of 12,000 feet, reaching up to 15,000 feet, with speeds of 152–250 kmph.

Indian Navy Launches ASW Vessels Malpe and Mulki

- On 9 September 2024, the Indian Navy launched two Anti-Submarine Warfare (ASW) shallow water crafts, named 'Malpe and Mulki', at Cochin Shipyard Ltd. (CSL) in Kochi.
- These are the fourth and fifth vessels under the Eight ASW Shallow Water Craft Project, initiated by a contract signed on 30 April 2019.
- These ships have a maximum speed of 25 knots and a range of 1800 nautical miles.

US Deploys Advanced 'THAAD' Missile Defense System to Israel

- The United States deployed the Terminal High Altitude Area Defense (THAAD) missile system to Israel along with 100 troops for its operation.
- This marks the first US military deployment in Israel since the Hamas-led attacks a year ago.
- THAAD is a ground-based interceptor system designed to defend against ballistic missile threats.

North Korea Tests 'Suicide Drones' in Military Drill

- On 24 August 2024, North Korean leader Kim Jong Un unveiled new 'suicide drones' during a demonstration.
- These drones are designed to crash into targets, with Kim overseeing tests where drones destroyed mock-ups of South Korea's K-2 battle tanks.
- The drones are part of North Korea's efforts to enhance its military capabilities amid rising tensions with the U.S. and South Korea.
- The Indian Army also has inducted 'Nagastra-1', India's first indigenous suicide drone.

US Approves $52.8M Sonobuoy Deal with India

- On 24 August 2024, the U.S. approved a $52.8 million sale of anti-submarine warfare sonobuoys to India.
- This sale includes AN/SSQ-53G, AN/SSQ-62F, and AN/SSQ-36 sonobuoys, along with technical support and documentation.
- The sonobuoys will enhance India's anti-submarine capabilities, particularly for its MH-60R Seahawk helicopters.

Foundation Laid for India's Second VLF Radar Station in Vikarabad

- Defence Minister Rajnath Singh laid the foundation stone for the Indian Navy's Very Low Frequency (VLF) radar station in Vikarabad, Telangana.
- This will be India's second VLF radar, with the first one located in Tirunelveli, Tamil Nadu.
- The radar, costing Rs 3,200 crores, enhances communication with submarines submerged at depths of 20–30 meters.

India Approves New Airfields in Lakshadweep to Strengthen IOR Security

- The Indian government approved two military airfields in Lakshadweep, including one at the Minicoy naval base INS Jatayu, commissioned in March 2024.
- Minicoy's location, near Thuraakunu Island in the Maldives, enhances security in the Indian Ocean Region (IOR).

IAF and Army Execute Para-Drop of BHISHM Trauma Cube

- On 17 August 2024, the Indian Air Force and Indian Army successfully executed the para-drop of a BHISHM Trauma Care Cube from 15,000 feet.
- Developed under Project BHISHM, these cubes provide critical trauma care in remote areas.
- The operation used the IAF's C-130J Super Hercules aircraft and the Army's Para Brigade.

Indian Navy Launches Multi-Purpose Vessel Samarthak

- On 14 October 2024, the Indian Navy launched its first multi-purpose vessel (MPV), Samarthak, at L&T Shipyard, Kattupalli, Chennai.
- Built by Larsen & Toubro, this MPV is part of a two-ship project to enhance naval adaptability.
- Samarthak can tow ships, launch targets, operate uncrewed vehicles, and test new weapons.

Kaksar Bridge in Kargil Renamed Capt. Amit Bhardwaj Setu

- On 16 October 2024, the Kaksar Bridge in Kargil was renamed Capt. Amit Bhardwaj

Setu to honor his sacrifice during the Kargil War in 1999.

- Capt. Bhardwaj, of the 4 JAT Battalion, sacrificed his life while rescuing his platoon from an ambush in Kaksar.
- His bravery is remembered for showcasing unparalleled courage.

Indian Army Installed High-Altitude Tank Repair Facility In Ladakh

- The Indian Army has established two of the **world's highest tank repair facilities** in Ladakh, close to the Line of Actual Control (LAC) along China.
- These facilities, located in **Nyoma and the DBO Sector,** support over 500 tanks and infantry combat vehicles deployed following the 2020 India-China standoff.
- These repair centers play a crucial role in sustaining armored vehicle operations in this strategically important area.

Indian Army's New Tech Unit STEAG

- The Indian Army established the Signals Technology Evaluation and Adaptation Group (STEAG) on March 23, 2024.
- STEAG focuses on researching and evaluating advanced communication technologies like 6G, AI, machine learning, and quantum computing for military use.
- Its goal is to enhance military communication systems, ensuring seamless connectivity and superior information sharing during operations.

SARVATRA: Indian Army's Mobile Bridge System

- The Sarvatra Mobile Bridge System, developed by DRDO and produced by BEML, is a versatile, truck-mounted, multi-span bridging system for the Indian Army.
- It consists of five 15-meter aluminum alloy scissor bridges, each mounted on a modified Tatra T-815 8x8 chassis. The system can span up to 75 meters and deploy in less than 2.5 hours.
- It's adjustable in height from 2.5 to 6 meters and can be used in emergencies like floods and earthquakes.
- Sarvatra replaces older bridges, offering cost-effective and efficient solutions for military and disaster relief operations.

Indian Navy successfully launched LSAM 19 (Yard 129)

- The Indian Navy successfully launched LSAM 19 (Yard 129), a versatile barge equipped with ammunition, torpedoes, and missiles, on 24 January.
- It marks the completion of the fifth barge under the 11 x ACTCM Barge Project.
- The LSAM 19 was manufactured by MSME Shipyard, Suryadipta Projects Private Limited, Thane, at the SPPL launch site dedicated to the Indian Navy.

INS Cheetah, Guldar and Kumbhir decommissioned after 40 Years of Glorious Service

- Indian Navy Ships Cheetah, Guldar, and Kumbhir were decommissioned **in January 2024.**
- They were built at **Gdynia Shipyard, Poland** as Polnocny class Landing Ships and were commissioned into the Indian Navy **in 1984, 1985, and 1986** respectively.
- The decommissioning ceremony took place **at Port Blair,** where the National Flag, the Naval Ensign, and the Decommissioning Pennants of the three ships were lowered for the last time at sunset.

First Female Helicopter Pilot of Indian Navy

- Sub-Lieutenant Anamika B Rajeev made history on June 7, 2024, by becoming the first female helicopter pilot in the Indian Navy.
- She received the prestigious Golden Wings at INS Rajali in Tamil Nadu after completing a rigorous 22-week training program.
- Rajeev is now qualified to fly various helicopters, including Sea Kings, ALH Dhruvs, Chetaks, and MH-60R Seahawks.

GAME AND PUZZLE

Across

4. India's first Pollution Control Vessel
6. Indian missile to destroy enemy radars

Down

1. India-Mongolia Army peacekeeping training
2. India joined Australia's largest naval exercise
3. India-France naval exercise in the Mediterranean Sea
5. India-Thailand Army exercise in jungles

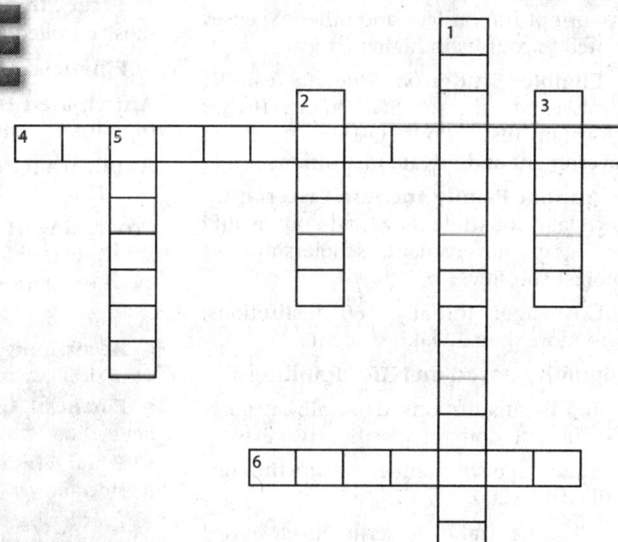

SCAN TO GET MULTIPLE CHOICE QUESTIONS

Scan Me

Answer Key (Puzzle):

1. NomadicElephant 2. Kakadu 3. VARUNA 4. SamudraPratap 5. MAITREE 6. Rudram1

PM VIDYALAXMI SCHEME

- In November 2024, the central government approved the PM-Vidyalakshmi Yojana to support meritorious students aspiring to pursue higher education in top-ranked institutions in India.
- The PM Vidyalakshmi Yojana will complement the Central Sector Interest Subsidy (CSIS) and Credit Guarantee Fund Scheme for Education Loans (CGFSEL) initiatives under the Department of Higher Education.
- **Launch Date:** 6th November 2024
- **Objective:** To provide financial assistance through collateral free, guarantor free loans from banks and financial institutions to cover the entire amount of tuition fees and other expenses related to courses in higher education.
- **Eligible Students:** Students gaining admission to the top 860 Quality Higher Education Institutions (QHEIs), including government and private institutions.
- **Annual Family Income Criteria:** Up to ₹8 lakh for students who do not qualify for other government scholarships or interest subsidies.
- **Coverage:** Initially 860 institutions, with more than 22 lakh students

Eligibility Based on NIRF Rankings:

- Top 100 institutions in overall, category-specific, and domain-specific NIRF lists.
- State government-run institutions ranked 101-200.
- All Central government-governed institutions.

Loan Amounts:

- Loans up to ₹7.5 lakh with a 75% credit guarantee.
- For loans up to ₹10 lakh, 3% interest subvention during the moratorium period.
- **Target Beneficiaries:** Every year, about 1 lakh students enroll, with a preference for those enrolled in government-run technical or professional programs.
- **Financial Outlay:** ₹3,600 crore for the period from 2024-25 to 2030-31.

Anticipated Impact: Over the course of the program, 7 lakh new students will benefit from interest subsidies.

Application Procedure: To apply for loans and interest incentives, use the PM-Vidyalaxmi portal.

Processing of Payments: Central Bank Digital Currency (CBDC) wallets and e-vouchers are supported for interest-based payments.

BENEFITS OF PM VIDYALAXMI SCHEME

- **Accessibility:** Students can obtain loans through a digital interface without having to visit a physical location or complete a lot of paperwork.
- **Financial Relief:** Credit guarantees and interest subsidies lessen the financial strain on families and students.
- **Equal Education Opportunity:** Allows students from low-income families to attend highly regarded universities.
- **Promotion of Skill Development:** Gives professional and technical education top priority, in line with India's surge in STEM sectors.
- **Future Economic Impact:** By promoting education, the program indirectly boosts the economy by creating a workforce that is better educated and skilled.

NEW SCHEMES, IMPLEMENT, PROGRAMME/PROJECTS

Top 3 States in rooftop solar installations under PM Surya Ghar scheme

- Gujarat, Maharashtra, and Uttar Pradesh have emerged as the top three states with the highest number of rooftop solar installations under the PM Surya Ghar Muft Bijli Yojana scheme.
- The PM Surya Ghar Muft Bijli Yojana, launched by Prime Minister Narendra Modi on February 15, 2024, aims to provide rooftop solar power to one crore households by March 2027.

PM Modi launches LIC's 'Bima Sakhi Yojana'

- Prime Minister Narendra Modi has launched 'Bima Sakhi Yojana' in Panipat to promote financial literacy and insurance awareness among women.
- This initiative of Life Insurance Corporation of India (LIC) is designed to empower women aged 18-70 years, who are Class X pass.
- They will receive specialized training and a stipend for the first three years to promote financial literacy and insurance awareness.

AYUSHMAN BHARAT SCHEME TO PROVIDE HEALTH COVERAGE FOR ALL SENIOR CITIZENS AGED 70 AND ABOVE

- On 29th October 2024, Prime Minister Narendra Modi announced the expansion of the Ayushman Bharat Pradhan Mantri Jan Arogya Yojana (AB-PMJAY) to include health coverage for all senior citizens aged 70 and above.
- This initiative, called the Ayushman Vaya Vandana Card, provides an additional ₹5 lakh in health coverage per year for seniors, irrespective of their income.

Government to extend UDAN Scheme for 10 more years

- On 21st October 2024, the Indian government announced the extension of the UDAN (Ude Desh ka Aam Nagrik) scheme for 10 more years.
- Initially launched in 2016, UDAN aims to enhance regional air connectivity and make flying more affordable.
- The scheme has already operationalized 601 routes and 71 airports, facilitating travel for over 1.44 crore passengers.

AYUSHMAN BHARAT PRADHAN MANTRI JAN AROGYA YOJANA (AB-PMJAY)

- AB-PMJAY was launched on 23 September 2018.
- The scheme provides secondary and tertiary care hospitalization benefits up to ₹5 lakh per family per year.
- The scheme covers around 55 crore beneficiaries, representing the bottom 40% of India's population based on the Socio-Economic Caste Census (SECC) 2011.
- It provides health coverage to over 12 crore poor and vulnerable families.
- In September 2024, the scheme was expanded to include all senior citizens aged 70 years and above, regardless of their income.
- The expansion aims to benefit around 4.5 crore families, including 6 crore senior citizens.

Centre approves ₹1 lakh crore for PM-RKVY and Krishnannati Yojana

- On 3rd October 2024, the Union Cabinet, chaired by Prime Minister Narendra Modi, approved the Pradhan Mantri Rashtriya Krishi Vikas Yojana (PM-RKVY) and Krishonnati Yojana (KY) with a combined outlay of over ₹1 lakh crore.
- The PM-RKVY aims to promote sustainable agriculture, while the KY focuses on achieving food security and agricultural self-sufficiency.

Government launches PM E-DRIVE Scheme

- On 1st October 2024, the Indian government launched the PM Electric Drive Revolution in Innovative Vehicle Enhancement (PM E-DRIVE) scheme.
- With a financial outlay of ₹10,900 crore over two years, the scheme aims to accelerate the adoption of electric vehicles (EVs), establish charging infrastructure, and build a robust EV manufacturing ecosystem.
- The scheme aims to incentivize approximately 24.79 lakh electric two-wheelers (e-2Ws).The initiative is designed to incentivize around 3.2 lakh electric three-wheelers.
- A budget of Rs. 500 crore has been allocated for deploying e-ambulances under this scheme. A fund of Rs. 500 crore has been set aside to incentivize the use of e-trucks. A total of Rs. 4,391 crore is allocated for the procurement of 14,028 electric buses by State Transport Undertakings (STUs)/public transport agencies.

Ministry of Tourism launched Paryatan Mitra and Paryatan Didi initiatives

- On World Tourism Day (27th September), the Ministry of Tourism launched the 'Paryatan Mitra and Paryatan Didi' in 50 tourist destinations initiatives to enhance tourist experiences across India.
- These programs train locals, especially women and youth, to become tourism ambassadors, focusing on hospitality, cleanliness, and sustainability.
- Training covers digital literacy and local storytelling, ensuring tourists receive high standards of hospitality and care.

UNION CABINET APPROVED PRADHAN MANTRI JANJATIYA UNNAT GRAM ABHIYAN (PMJUGA)

- On 18th September 2024, the Union Cabinet approved the Pradhan Mantri Janjatiya Unnat Gram Abhiyan (PMJUGA) with a budget of ₹79,156 crore.
- This initiative aims to uplift tribal communities in over 63,000 villages across India.
- It focuses on improving socio-economic conditions through better housing, healthcare, education, and infrastructure.

Union Finance Minister Nirmala Sitharaman launched the NPS Vatsalya scheme

- On 19th September 2024, Union Finance Minister Nirmala Sitharaman launched the 'NPS Vatsalya scheme'.
- This innovative pension scheme is designed for minors, allowing parents or guardians to open and contribute to a National Pension System (NPS) account on behalf of their children.
- The launch of NPS Vatsalya was simultaneously organised at 75 locations throughout the country, with distribution of over 250 PRAN to minor subscribers.

Cabinet approves Bio-RIDE scheme

- On 18 September 2024, the Union Cabinet approved the Bio-RIDE scheme (Biotechnology Research Innovation and Entrepreneurship Development).
- This initiative merges two existing schemes to support cutting-edge R&D in biotechnology, bio manufacturing, and bio foundry.
- The proposed outlay for the implementation of the unified scheme 'Bio-RIDE' is Rs.9197 crore during the 15th finance Commission period from 2021-22 to 2025-26.

Swachh Bharat Mission marked its 10th anniversary

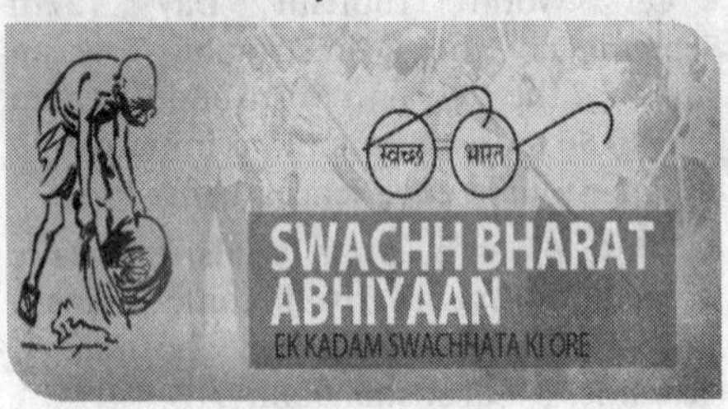

- On 02 October 2024, the Swachh Bharat Mission marked its 10th anniversary with the launch of the 'Swachhata Hi Seva' (SHS) 2024 campaign.
- Themed "Swabhav Swachhata, Sanskar Swachhata," this nationwide initiative aims to clean over 6 lakh difficult spots across India.
- During the program, the Prime Minister launched and laid the foundation stone for several projects related to sanitation and cleanliness, with a total worth exceeding Rs 9,600 crore.

Cabinet approves Rs 3,435 Crore Scheme for 38,000 Electric Buses

- On 11 September 2024, the Union Cabinet approved the PM-eBus Sewa-Payment Security Mechanism (PSM) scheme with an outlay of Rs 3,435.33 crore.
- This scheme aims to deploy over 38,000 electric buses across India from FY 2024-25 to FY 2028-29.

Union Cabinet approves ₹70,125 crore for PMGSY-IV Road Scheme

- On 11 September 2024, the Union Cabinet approved the Pradhan Mantri Gram Sadak Yojana-IV (PMGSY-IV) with a budget of ₹70,125 crore.
- This scheme, running from FY 2024-25 to 2028-29, aims to construct 62,500 km of roads and upgrade bridges, connecting 25,000 unconnected habitations.
- The central government will contribute ₹49,087.50 crore, while the states will provide ₹21,037.50 crore.

Dr. Mandaviya launched 'RESET' program for Retired Athletes

- On 29 August 2024, Dr. Mansukh Mandaviya, Union Minister of Youth Affairs & Sports, launched the Retired Sportsperson Empowerment Training' (RESET) Programme.
- This initiative, unveiled on National Sports Day, aims to equip retired athletes with skills and knowledge to enhance their employability.
- The program offers two levels of training based on educational qualifications and includes internships and placement assistance.
- Eligibility for the RESET Programme is open to retired athletes aged 20-50 years who have either won international medals, participated in international events, or gained recognition at the national or state level.

Spices Board Launches SPICED Scheme to Boost Spice Exports and Productivity

- The Spices Board of India launched the "SPICED" scheme on 22nd August 2024.
- This initiative, titled "Sustainability in Spice Sector through Progressive, Innovative and Collaborative Interventions for Export Development", aims to enhance spice exports and cardamom productivity.
- With a budget of ₹422.30 crore, the scheme focuses on value addition, innovation, and sustainability.
- The scheme will be implemented during the remaining period of the 15th Finance Commission cycle, until FY 2025-26.

Cabinet approves 'Vigyan Dhara' Scheme

- The Vigyan Dhara scheme, approved by the Union Cabinet, merges three umbrella schemes under the Department of Science and Technology (DST).
- The proposed outlay for implementing Vigyan Dhara is ₹10,579.84 crore during the 15th Finance Commission period (2021-22 to 2025-26).
- The research and development component of the scheme will be aligned in line with the Anusandhan National Research Foundation (ANRF).

Thalassemia Bal Sewa Yojana completes 500 bone marrow transplants

- On 19 August 2024, the Thalassemia Bal Sewa Yojana (TBSY) achieved a significant milestone by successfully completing 500 bone marrow transplants.
- TBSY provides financial assistance of up to ₹10 lakh per patient for treating Thalassemia Major and Aplastic Anemia.
- The program has benefited 356 underprivileged children across India, supporting families with an annual income below ₹8 lakh.

Government to launch 'Kisano Ki Baat' radio programme

- On 15 August 2024, Union Agriculture Minister Shivraj Singh Chouhan announced the launch of the 'Kisano Ki Baat' radio programme.
- Starting in September, this monthly show aims to modernize agricultural practices by providing farmers with cutting-edge scientific information.
- The programme will feature contributions from agricultural scientists, department officials, and the minister himself, offering insights into best practices and scientific advancements.

Government to include AYUSH in Ayushman Bharat scheme

- On 13th August 2024, the Indian government announced plans to integrate AYUSH (Ayurveda, Yoga, Naturopathy, Unani, Siddha, and Homeopathy) into the Ayushman Bharat Pradhan Mantri Jan Arogya Yojana (AB PM-JAY).
- This initiative aims to enhance health coverage for over 55 crore citizens by including traditional and alternative medicine treatments.

Cabinet approves Pradhan Mantri Awas Yojana-Urban 2.0

- On 9th August 2024, the Union Cabinet approved the Pradhan Mantri Awas Yojana-Urban (PMAY-U) 2.0.
- This scheme aims to provide financial assistance for constructing, purchasing, or renting affordable housing for one crore urban poor and middle-class families.
- With an investment of ₹10 lakh crore and a government subsidy of ₹2.30 lakh crore, PMAY-U 2.0 focuses on enhancing urban housing.

Cities across India set to launch Rs 5,000 crore under the AMRUT 2.0

- On 5th August 2024, cities across India are set to launch projects worth Rs 5,000 crore under the Atal Mission for Rejuvenation and Urban Transformation (AMRUT) 2.0.

- These projects will focus on enhancing water supply, sewage treatment, and the rejuvenation of water bodies and parks.
- Part of the government's 100-day agenda, AMRUT 2.0 aims to provide tap water to all households in 4,800 statutory towns by 2026.

ATAL MISSION FOR REJUVENATION AND URBAN TRANSFORMATION (AMRUT)

- AMRUT is a flagship urban development scheme launched by the Government of India in 25th June 2015.
- The mission is a Central Sponsored Scheme.
- It aims to provide basic urban infrastructure to improve the quality of life in cities and towns.
- The Mission is overseen by an Apex Committee (AC) chaired by the Secretary of Ministry of Housing and Urban Affairs (MoHUA).
- The total outlay for AMRUT was ₹50,000 crore for five years from FY 2015-16 to FY 2019-20.
- It is divided among States/UTs in an equitable formula in which 50:50 weightage.
- The Mission covers 500 cities including all cities and towns with a population of over one lakh with notified Municipalities.

NSDC launched the Women Entrepreneurship Program

- On 1st August 2024, the National Skill Development Corporation (NSDC) launched the Women Entrepreneurship Program.
- This initiative aims to empower 25 lakh women across India by providing essential skills, knowledge, and resources.
- In partnership with Britannia Industries Limited, the program offers financial grants and features participants' products on the Skill India Digital Hub.

Rs 920 Cr Namami Gange Mission 2.0 projects in UP and Bihar

- On 6th August 2024, the Indian government operationalized four major projects worth ₹920 crores under the Namami Gange Mission 2.0 in Uttar Pradesh and Bihar.
- Key projects include a ₹366 crore initiative in Munger, Bihar, with a 175 km sewerage network and a 30 MLD STP, and a ₹129 crore project in Mirzapur, Uttar Pradesh, adding two new STPs with a combined capacity of 31 MLD.

Vriksharopan Abhiyan 2024 Launch in Dhanbad

- On 25th July 2024, Union Minister of Coal and Mines G. Kishan Reddy inaugurated the Vriksharopan Abhiyan 2024 at Bharat Coking Coal Limited in Dhanbad.
- This initiative, part of the "Ek Ped Maa Ke Naam" campaign, was launched simultaneously at 300 locations across 47 districts in 11 coal/lignite-bearing states.

Government launches revised Model Skill Loan Scheme

- On 25th July 2024, the Indian government launched the revised Model Skill Loan Scheme.
- This revamped scheme aims to provide financial support for skill development courses, offering collateral-free loans up to ₹7.5 lakh.
- The scheme now includes a broader range of lenders, such as Non-Banking Financial Companies (NBFCs) and small finance banks.

Cabinet approves Pradhan Mantri Janjatiya Unnat Gram Abhiyan

- Union Cabinet approved 'Pradhan Mantri Janjatiya Unnat Gram Abhiyan' (PM-JUGA) with total outlay of Rs.79,156 crore.
- PM-JUGA is based on learnings and success of PM-JANMAN (Pradhan Mantri Janjati Adivasi Nyaya Maha Abhiyan).
- It will cover 549 districts and 2,740 blocks spread across all tribal majority villages across 30 States / UTs.

Digital India Initiative completes 9 years

- On 1st July 2024, India celebrated the successful completion of 9 years of the Digital India initiative.
- Launched in 2015, this transformative program aims to turn India into a digitally empowered society and knowledge economy.
- It covers 9 pillars of growth areas which are given in the image.

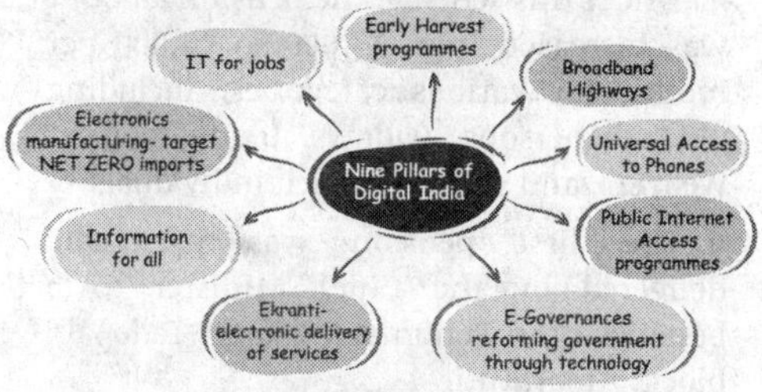

Union Minister launches the 2nd phase of KIRTI Programme

- On 19th July 2024, Union Minister for Youth Affairs & Sports and Labour & employment, Dr. Mansukh Mandaviya launched the second phase of the "KIRTI" (Khelo India Rising Talent Identification) programme at the Jawaharlal Nehru Stadium in New Delhi.
- The Government has decided to identify 1 lakh budding young athletes within 100 days under the KIRTI programme.
- Under the KIRTI programme, everyone will be given opportunities to develop their sports skills, whether they live in a village or a city, and whether they come from a poor background or otherwise.

Gujarat CM launches 'Shramik Basera' Scheme

- On 18th July 2024, Gujarat Chief Minister Bhupendra Patel launched the 'Shramik Basera' scheme in Ahmedabad.
- This initiative aims to provide temporary accommodation for construction workers at a nominal rate of ₹5 per day.
- The scheme will initially benefit 15,000 workers, with plans to expand to 3 lakh workers over the next three years.

NITI Aayog launches 'Sampoornata Abhiyan'

- NITI Aayog has launched the 'Sampoornata Abhiyan', a 3-month campaign running from July 4th to September 30th, 2024.
- The campaign aims to achieve 100% saturation of 12 key social sector indicators across all Aspirational Districts and Blocks in India.
- These indicators span themes such as Health, Nutrition, Agriculture, Social Development, and Education.

Chandrababu Naidu launched the 'NTR Bharosa pension scheme'

- On 1st July 2024, Andhra Pradesh Chief Minister Chandrababu Naidu launched the 'NTR Bharosa pension scheme'.
- Under this scheme, the pension amount was increased from ₹3,000 to ₹4,000 per month for various categories, including old age persons, widows, toddy tappers, weavers, and specially-abled individuals.
- The first pension was personally delivered by the Chief Minister to a beneficiary in Penumaka village, Tadepalli block, Amaravati.

Raksha Rajya Mantri Shri Sanjay Seth launches GAINS 2024

- On 10th July 2024, Raksha Rajya Mantri Shri Sanjay Seth inaugurated the GRSE Accelerated Innovation Nurturing Scheme (GAINS 2024) at Garden Reach Shipbuilders & Engineers Limited (GRSE) in Kolkata.
- This innovative scheme aims to address shipyard-related challenges and promote technology development through start-ups nurtured within India.
- 'GAINS' is a unique national scheme to encourage and enable MSMEs and Start-Ups to develop innovative solutions that GRSE may incorporate for further technological advancement.

ICAR to launch 'One Scientist, One Product' Scheme

- On 16th July 2024, the Indian Council of Agricultural Research (ICAR) launched the "One Scientist-One Product" program.
- This initiative aims to enhance research in agriculture and animal husbandry, encouraging each of the 5,521 ICAR scientists to develop a product, technology, model, concept, or publication annually.
- As part of the programme, ICAR announced the release of 323 new varieties of 56 crops, including cereals, oilseeds, forage crops, and sugarcane.

PM-Surya Ghar: Muft Bijli Yojana

- **The PM-Surya Ghar: Muft Bijli Yojana** is an ambitious initiative launched by the Government of India to promote the **adoption of solar energy and ensure free electricity for households** across the country.
- This scheme, part of Prime Minister Narendra Modi's broader vision for a sustainable and energy-independent India, aims to harness the abundant solar energy available in the country to meet the rising demand for electricity and reduce the reliance on fossil fuels.

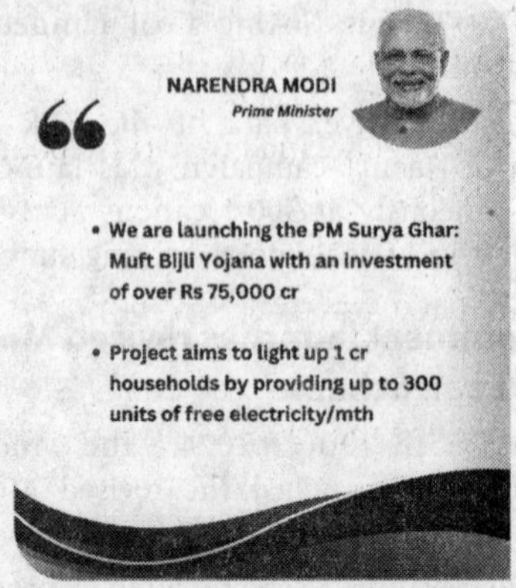

Objectives of the Scheme

The primary objectives of PM-Surya Ghar: Muft Bijli Yojana are:

- **Promote Solar Energy:** Encourage households to adopt solar energy by installing rooftop solar panels.
- **Provide Free Electricity:** Ensure free electricity for households through government-subsidized solar energy systems.
- **Sustainability:** Promote sustainable energy practices and reduce carbon footprint.
- **Economic Empowerment:** Reduce electricity bills and provide financial relief to households.

Key Features of PM-Surya Ghar

- **Rooftop Solar Panel Installation:**
  - The scheme facilitates the installation of rooftop solar panels on residential buildings.
  - The government provides financial assistance and subsidies to reduce the cost burden on households.
- **Net Metering:**
  - Households can generate their own electricity and feed surplus power back into the grid.
  - This surplus power is credited against the electricity consumed from the grid, effectively reducing electricity bills to zero.
- **Subsidies and Financial Assistance:**
  - Up to 70% of the installation cost is covered by government subsidies.
  - Low-interest loans are made available to further ease the financial burden on households.
- **Maintenance and Support:**
  - The government ensures regular maintenance and technical support for the installed solar panels.
  - Helplines and support centers are established to assist beneficiaries with any issues.
- **Awareness Campaigns:**
  - Nationwide campaigns to educate the public about the benefits of solar energy and the specifics of the scheme.
  - Workshops and seminars are conducted to train technicians and create job opportunities in the solar energy sector.

Implementation Strategy

The successful implementation of PM-Surya Ghar relies on a **well-coordinated strategy involving multiple stakeholders:**

- **Central and State Governments:**
  - The central government collaborates with state governments to implement the scheme at the grassroots level.
  - State-specific policies and incentives are introduced to complement the central scheme.
- **Public-Private Partnerships:**
  - Partnerships with private companies specializing in solar technology are established to leverage their expertise and resources.
  - Competitive bidding processes are used to ensure cost-effectiveness and quality.
- **Local Bodies and Community Organizations:**
  - Local governing bodies, such as municipal corporations and panchayats, play a crucial role in identifying eligible households and facilitating installations.
  - Community organizations help raise awareness and ensure community participation.
- **Monitoring and Evaluation:**
  - Robust monitoring systems are established to track the progress and effectiveness of the scheme.
  - Regular audits and evaluations help identify challenges and improve implementation.

Impact and Benefits

- The PM-Surya Ghar: Muft Bijli Yojana is expected to have a profound impact on various fronts.

- **Environmental Impact:**
  - Significant reduction in greenhouse gas emissions by decreasing reliance on fossil fuels.
  - Contribution to India's commitment to international climate goals, such as the Paris Agreement.
- **Economic Benefits:**
  - Reduction in electricity bills for households, leading to increased disposable income.
  - Creation of new job opportunities in the solar energy sector, boosting local economies.
- **Energy Security:**
  - Enhanced energy security by reducing dependence on imported fuels.
  - Greater energy resilience in rural and remote areas.
- **Social Impact:**
  - Improved quality of life through reliable and affordable electricity.
  - Empowerment of communities through education and job creation in the renewable energy sector.

How to Apply for PM-Surya Ghar: Muft Bijli Yojana

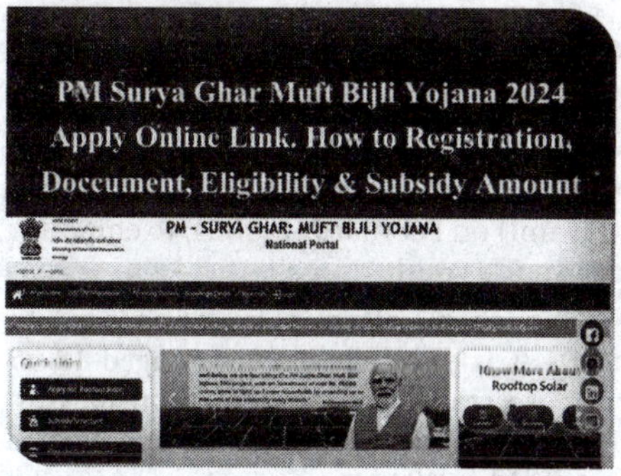

The PM-Surya Ghar: Muft Bijli Yojana is a significant government initiative aimed at promoting solar energy adoption by providing financial support and ensuring free electricity for households. **Here are the steps and necessary details on how to apply for the scheme:**

Eligibility Criteria

Before applying, make sure you meet the eligibility criteria for the scheme:

- **Residential Status:** The applicant must be a resident of India.
- **Property Ownership:** The property where the solar panels will be installed should be owned by the applicant.
- **Type of Property:** The scheme is applicable to residential properties. Commercial and industrial properties are not covered under this scheme.

Application Process

- **Online Application**
  - Go to the official website of the PM-Surya Ghar: Muft Bijli Yojana. The portal will provide all the necessary information and updates about the scheme.
- **Offline Application**
  - Visit the nearest office of the Ministry of New and Renewable Energy (MNRE) or designated government offices handling the PM-Surya Ghar: Muft Bijli Yojana.

Installation of Solar Panels

- Approved beneficiaries will be contacted by authorized vendors for the installation of solar panels.
- Schedule a convenient date and time for the installation process.
- The authorized vendor will install and commission the solar panels on your rooftop.
- A final inspection may be conducted to ensure that the installation is done correctly and is operational.

Central Financial Assistance (CFA) for Residential Rooftop Solar

PM-Surya Ghar Muft Bijli Yojana provides a CFA of 60% of the system cost for 2 kW systems and 40% of the additional system cost for systems between 2 to 3 kW capacity.

The CFA cap will be 3 kW. At current benchmark prices, this would mean a subsidy of **Rs 30,000 for a 1 kW** system, **Rs 60,000 for a 2 kW** system and **Rs 78,000 for a system of 3 kW** or above.

Households will be able to access collateral-free low-interest loan products currently at around 7% for installation of residential RTS systems up to 3 kW.

India to Host The Inaugural World Audio Visual Entertainment Summit (WAVES) 2025

- India will host the **World Audio Visual Entertainment Summit (WAVES)** from February 5-9, 2025 in **New Delhi**, for the first time.
- **Focus on Content Innovation:** It will highlight India's advancements in animation, gaming, entertainment technology, and both regional and mainstream cinema.
- **Positioning India as a Global Hub:** WAVES aims to establish India as a global hub for world-class content creation.

Chief Minister Vayoshree Yojana

- On 5th February, 2024, the Maharashtra Government announced the launch of the **'Chief Minister Vayoshree Yojana,'** expected to benefit 15 lakh senior citizens with disabilities, offering financial assistance and various other initiatives.
- Under the 'Chief Minister Vayoshree Yojana,' senior citizens **above 65 years** suffering from physical or mental disabilities will receive **Rs 3,000 after screening**.

'Neengal Nalama' scheme

- The Chief Minister of Tamil Nadu announced the launch of a **new initiative called "Neengal Nalama"** (Are you doing well) on the 6th of March 2024.
- This scheme is also called the 'Are you alright scheme'.
- The 'Neengal Nalama' (Are you fine?) scheme is a beneficiary outreach program aimed at reviewing the implementation of flagship schemes and addressing the grievances of the public.

MYUVA Scheme

- Chief Minister Yogi Adityanath launches the "Mukhyamantri Yuva Udyami Vikas Abhiyan (MYUVA)" scheme in Uttar Pradesh, aimed at nurturing entrepreneurship among the state's youth.
- This ambitious initiative reflects the government's commitment to empowering young entrepreneurs and fostering a culture of innovation and enterprise.

Central Council for Research in Ayurvedic Sciences to launched PRAGATI-2024

- The Central Council for Research in Ayurvedic Sciences (CCRAS) launched PRAGATI-2024 (Pharma Research in AyurGyan And Techno Innovation) on May 28, 2024.

- Held at the India Habitat Centre in New Delhi, the event aimed to foster collaboration between CCRAS and the Ayurveda drug industry.
- The program included technical sessions, panel discussions, and focused group discussions to identify research priorities and strengthen researcher-industry collaborations.

Department of Pharmaceuticals announced RPTUAS Scheme

- The Revamped Pharmaceuticals Technology Upgradation Assistance (RPTUAS) Scheme is announced by the Department of Pharmaceuticals on March 11, 2024.
- The scheme supports existing pharmaceutical units with an average turnover of less than ₹500 crore over the last three years to meet Revised Schedule-M and WHO-GMP standards.
- It offers incentives based on turnover, with up to 20% of eligible investment for units with a turnover less than ₹50 crore, and up to 10% for those with a turnover between ₹250 crore and ₹500 crore.

PM launches Mahtari Vandan Yojana in Chhattisgarh

- Prime Minister Narendra Modi virtually launched Chhattisgarh government's Mahtari Vandan Yojana.
- He disbursed the first installment of **655 crore rupees** to around 70 lakh women in the scheme's first phase.
- Under the Mahtari Vandan Yojana, about 70 lakh women would receive 1000 rupees monthly.

PM Modi to launch Pradhan Mantri Uchchatar Shiksha Abhiyan at Mumbai University

- Prime Minister Narendra Modi digitally launched the Pradhan Mantri Uchchatar Shiksha Abhiyan (PM-USHA) through video conferencing at a programme in Sir Kawasji Jahangir Convocation Hall of Mumbai University.
- A grant of 20 crore rupees has been approved for the infrastructure and educational development of Mumbai University.

Shri Dharmendra Pradhan Inaugurated the Rashtriya Udyamita Vikas Pariyojana

- The Union Minister of Education and Skill Development & Entrepreneurship, Shri Dharmendra Pradhan, inaugurated the Rashtriya Udyamita Vikas Pariyojana in Sambalpur, Odisha.
- The initiative was also launched virtually across 9 cities including Bhopal, Kanpur, Indore, Varanasi, Bharatpur, Shillong, Silchar, Dibrugarh, and Guwahati.
- The Rashtriya Udyamita Vikas Pariyojana will offer comprehensive entrepreneurship training over a period of 22 weeks, combining theoretical knowledge with practical exposure through experiential learning.

Government Launched 'Bharat Rice' at Subsidised Rates for Consumers

- The Government of India launched the Bharat Rice initiative on February 6, 2024, to combat rising food prices.
- Available at ₹29/kg in 5 kg and 10 kg packs, Bharat Rice is sold through Kendriya Bhandar, NAFED, and NCCF outlets.
- The scheme aims to provide affordable rice to consumers, especially those affected by a 15% increase in rice prices over the past year.

Cabinet approved "Pradhan Mantri Matsya Kisan Samridhi Sah-Yojana (PM-MKSSY)"

- The "**Pradhan Mantri Matsya Kisan Samridhi Sah-Yojana** (PM-MKSSY)" was approved by the Indian Cabinet to enhance the livelihood and income of fish farmers and fishers.
- The scheme aims to promote sustainable fish farming and **boost fish production** through financial assistance, modern technologies, and infrastructure development.
- It focuses on increasing productivity, ensuring sustainable practices, and improving the post-harvest value chain, including marketing and branding.

Rajasthan Mukhyamantri Vishwakarma Pension Yojana 2024

- Rajasthan Finance Minister Diya Kumari presented Rajasthan's budget on February 8, 2024, under Chief Minister Bhajan Lal's leadership, after nearly 22 years.
- One significant announcement is the Mukhyamantri Vishwakarma Pension Yojana, offering a monthly pension of **Rs. 2,000** to eligible laborers and street vendors aged 60 and above.
- This scheme aims to support their daily needs and promote independent living.

Haryana launched 'Van Mitra' scheme to boost green cover

- In June 2024, the Haryana government launched the Van Mitra scheme to boost green cover by involving local communities in tree plantation on non-forest lands.
- The scheme targets families with an annual income of less than ₹1.8 lakh, encouraging them to plant saplings and ensure their care.
- The scheme integrates with the "Ek Ped Maa Ke Naam" campaign and provides support through designated nurseries and the Van Mitra portal/app.

Odisha govt launched LABHA: A 100 Percent State-Funded MSP scheme

- The Odisha government has launched **LABHA Yojana,** a 100% State-funded minimum support price (MSP) scheme for minor forest produce (MFP).
- It aims to benefit the state's large tribal population, **constituting 23% of the total population**.
- Under the scheme, the State government will annually determine the MSP for MFP.

Odisha govt introduced 'Swayam' Scheme for Youth Empowerment

- The Odisha government introduced the Swayam Scheme (Swatantra Yuva Udyami) on February 12, 2024, to empower the state's youth.
- The scheme offers interest-free loans up to Rs. 1 lakh to eligible youth aged 18-35 years to start or expand small businesses. For SC/ST/PwD categories, the age limit is extended to 40 years.

Assam govt unveiled Mukhyamantri Mahila Udyamita Abhiyan

- Recently, the **Assam government** introduced the **Mukhyamantri Mahila Udyamita Abhiyaan (MMUA),** a financial support scheme aimed at empowering rural women entrepreneurs.
- The MMUA scheme is designed to foster the development of rural women who are part of self-help groups, transforming them into "rural micro-entrepreneurs" with a target annual income of **Rs 1 lakh per member**.
- The total amount earmarked by the scheme as part of the state annual **budget is ₹3,900 crore**, making it the biggest such scheme in the state.

PM launches "Pradhan Mantri Suryodaya Yojana"

- The **Pradhan Mantri Suryodaya Yojana** is a visionary initiative announced by **Prime Minister Narendra Modi** in January 2024.
- This scheme aims **to harness solar energy** and targets the installation of rooftop solar panels on one crore houses, predominantly benefiting poor and middle-class households.
- The scheme was launched to reduce the electricity bill of the poor and middle class, along with making India self-reliant in the energy sector.

NAMASTE Scheme

- The National Safai Karamcharis Finance and Development Corporation (NSKFDC) implemented the NAMASTE scheme for three years, from FY 2023-24 to FY 2025-26, with a budget allocation of 349.73 crores.
- NAMASTE scheme is a Central Sector Scheme launched in 2022.
- he scheme has replaced the Self-Employment Scheme for the Rehabilitation of Manual Scavengers (SRMS), which was started in 2007.
- It was launched as a joint initiative of the Ministry of Social Justice 'and Empowerment (MoSJE) and the Ministry of Housing and Urban Affairs (MoHUA).

Swadesh Darshan and PRASAD Scheme

- Recently, the Prime Minister dedicated and launched 52 tourism sector projects worth more than Rs 1400 crores under the Swadesh Darshan and PRASAD Scheme.
- The projects launched included three projects under the PRASHAD Scheme (Hazratbal- Srinagar, Jogulamba-Telangana, Amarkantak Madhya Pradesh) worth Rs 129.35 Cr.
- Under the Swadesh Darshan scheme, 6 projects in the States of Bihar, Meghalaya and Rajasthan amounting to ₹ 339.59 Crores were also inaugurated.

ULLAS Scheme

- Recently the Ministry of Education is set to conduct the Foundational Literacy and Numeracy Assessment Test (FLNAT) as part of the **ULLAS - Nav Bharat Saaksharta** Karyakram.
- ULLAS stands for **Understanding Lifelong Learning for All in Society.**
- The ULLAS User-Friendly Mobile Application is a digital platform that provides access to a variety of learning resources through the DIKSHA portal.

Over 3.8 crore beneficiaries enrolled under PM Matru Vandana Yojana

- As of 2024, over 3.8 crore beneficiaries have enrolled under the Pradhan Mantri Matru Vandana Yojana (PMMVY).
- This scheme provides cash incentives to pregnant women and lactating mothers to compensate for wage loss and promote better health-seeking behavior.
- The scheme offers three installments: ₹1,000 for early registration, ₹2,000 after six months of pregnancy, and ₹2,000 post childbirth.

Union Minister Rupala launched updated AHIDF Scheme

- Union Minister Parshottam Rupala launched the realigned Animal Husbandry Infrastructure Development Fund (AHIDF) Scheme on February 14, 2024.
- The scheme, initially started during the COVID-19 period, has been extended for three more years with an increased outlay of ₹29,610 crore.
- The realigned scheme subsumes the Dairy Infrastructure Development Fund, offering a 3% interest subvention and credit guarantee support.

J & K becomes first UT to implement PM Vishwakarma Yojana

- **Jammu and Kashmir** has become the **first Union Territory** in the country to implement the **PM Vishwakarma Yojana** with the start of training for the **first batch of 30 trainees.**
- The Pradhan Mantri Vishwakarma Yojana was launched by the Central government in September 2023 with an aim to recognise artisans and craftspeople through PM Vishwakarma certificates and ID cards.
- Under the scheme, the trainees are imparted a basic training of five to seven days, **advanced training of 15 or more days, a stipend of Rs 500 per day,** and a free modern toolkit worth Rs 15,000 for trained Vishwakarmas.

Cabinet approved overarching scheme "PRITHvi VIgyan (PRITHVI)"

- The Union Cabinet, chaired by **Prime Minister Narendra Modi**, has approved the implementation of the **"PRITHvi VIgyan (PRITHVI)"** scheme by the Ministry of Earth Sciences.
- The scheme will be implemented during the period from 2021-26 at a **total cost of Rs. 4,797 crore.**

Govt Launched Rs 515-Cr Solar Scheme For Electrification Of Houses In Tribal Areas

- The Central government has launched a new solar scheme for **Particularly Vulnerable Tribal Groups (PVTG)** habitations and villages.
- This scheme was launched under the **Pradhan Mantri Janjati Adivasi Nyaya Abhiyan (PM-JANMAN) programme.**
- Scheme worth **Rs 515 crore** aimed at electrification under **Pradhan Mantri Janjati Adivasi Nyaya Abhiyan (PM-JANMAN) programme.**

30 crore Ayushman Cards created under Ayushman Bharat PM Jan Arogya Yojana

- Ayushman Cards under Ayushman Bharat Pradhan Mantri Jan Arogya Yojana have saved over **₹1.25 lakh crore** in out-of-pocket expenditure for the poor and vulnerable population.
- **30 crore Ayushman Cards** have been created, aiming to provide health cover of **₹5 lakh per family per year** for secondary and tertiary care hospitalization.
- The scheme has successfully catered to 6.2 crore hospital admissions, totaling over ₹79 thousand crore in value.

Ministry of Education launched PRERANA: an experiential learning program

- Ministry of Education, Government of India has launched 'Prerana: An Experiential Learning program'.
- It aims to offer a meaningful, unique, and inspiring experience to all participants, thereby empowering them with leadership qualities.
- PRERNA focuses on nine core human values and aims to inspire students to contribute to a developed India.

Government approved E- Vehicle policy to promote India as a manufacturing destination for EVs

- The Union Government has approved a scheme to promote India as a manufacturing destination so that e-vehicles (EV) with the latest technology can be manufactured in the country.

- The policy is designed to attract investments in the e-vehicle space by reputed global EV manufacturers.
- Companies setting up manufacturing facilities for EVs to be allowed limited imports of cars at lower custom duty.

Education Minister launched SWAYAM Plus platform

- Union Minister Dharmendra Pradhan launched the SWAYAM Plus platform on February 27 in New Delhi.
- Aimed at enhancing employability and professional development, SWAYAM Plus offers high-quality, industry-relevant courses in collaboration with academia and industry partners.
- The platform supports multilingual courses and integrates with APAAR for credit recognition.

WCD Ministry Organises Poshan Pakhwada 2024

- The Ministry of Women and Child Development hosted Poshan Pakhwada nationwide from March 9 to March 23, 2024.
- The campaign aims to foster public participation and a collective movement to emphasize the significance of nutrition and advocate for healthier eating habits.
- The previous Poshan Pakhwada saw over 4 crore sensitization activities, including promoting millets and celebrating healthy children.

PM launched PM-SURAJ Portal

- Prime Minister Narendra Modi launched the **PM-SURAJ national portal**, providing credit assistance to one lakh entrepreneurs from disadvantaged communities.
- PM-SURAJ national portal for credit support to disadvantaged sections embodies the Prime Minister's commitment to prioritize the underprivileged.
- Direct Benefit Transfer of 720 crore rupees to beneficiaries was highlighted, along with efforts to ensure equitable access to essential facilities.

NCPCR launched GHAR Portal for Child Restoration and Repatriation

- The National Commission for Protection of Child Rights (NCPCR) launched the GHAR (Go Home and Re-Unite) Portal on February 2, 2024.
- The portal, under the Ministry of Women and Child Development, digitally monitors and tracks the restoration and repatriation of children in the Juvenile Justice system.
- The portal also links children with government schemes for family support and monitors progress to ensure timely repatriation.

Union Minister launched 'Smart Gram Panchayat: Revolution towards Digitization of Gram Panchayat'

- The Union Minister of Rural Development and Panchayati Raj launched the Smart Gram Panchayat: Revolution towards Digitization of Gram Panchayat initiative on February 13, 2024.
- The pilot project was launched with the aim to extend PM-WANI (Prime Minister's Wi-Fi Access Network Interface) Service in all Gram Panchayats across Begusarai District in Bihar.
- Begusarai has now become the **first District in Bihar** to equip all Gram Panchayats with Wi-Fi services under the PM-WANI Scheme.

Shri Pashupati Kumar Paras launched "SUFALAM"

- Shri Pashupati Kumar Paras launched the "SUFALAM" initiative, aiming to enhance the processing and preservation of agricultural produce.
- This scheme is designed to reduce post-harvest losses, improve the value chain, and ensure better income for farmers.
- "SUFALAM" focuses on the establishment of processing units and cold storage facilities, providing financial assistance and technical support to farmers and agribusinesses.

NHAI takes 'One Vehicle One FASTag' initiative

- **National Highways Authority of India (NHAI)** has implemented the **'One Vehicle, One FASTag'** initiative to discourage the use of a single FASTag for multiple vehicles or linking multiple FASTags to a particular vehicle.
- Users are encouraged to complete the **'Know Your Customer' (KYC)** process for their latest FASTag by updating the KYC as per RBI guidelines.
- The initiative aims **to enhance efficiency at toll plazas** and ensure seamless movement for National Highway users.

e-SAKSHI Mobile application launched for the Revised Fund Flow Procedure

- Minister of State (Independent Charge) of MoSPI, Rao Inderjit Singh, launched the MPLADS **e-SAKSHI Mobile Application** in New Delhi.
- The app supports the revised fund flow procedure under the Members of Parliament Local Area Development Scheme (MPLAD).
- It allows MPs to propose, track, and oversee development projects conveniently.

Jal Shakti Abhiyan: Catch The Rain-2024 campaign launch

- The Union Minister for Jal Shakti, launched the nationwide **'Jal Shakti Abhiyan: Catch the Rain-2024' campaign on March 9, 2024, from New Delhi.**
- **The fifth edition** of the campaign was **themed 'Nari Shakti se Jal Shakti'** to recognize the crucial role played by women in water management, conservation, and sustainability.
- The campaign run from March 9, 2024, to November 30, 2024, focusing on water conservation and rainwater harvesting in both urban and rural areas across all districts in the nation.

SUMMIT AND CONFERENCE

- The 19th G20 Summit 2024, officially known as Summit Rio 2024, was held in Rio de Janeiro, Brazil. This was the first time Brazil hosted the G20 Summit.

Host Country:	Brazil
Dates:	November 18 and 19, 2024
Host City:	Rio de Janeiro
Venue:	Museum of Modern Art (MAM)
Chairperson:	President Luiz Inácio Lula da Silva
Theme:	Building a Just World and a Sustainable Planet
Main Agenda:	Social inclusion, energy transition, sustainable development, global governance reform
Key Initiatives:	Global Alliance Against Hunger and Poverty, comprehensive reform of global institutions
Notable Attendees:	Leaders from G20 member countries, representatives from the African Union, European Union, and other invited states

Major Outcomes of G20 Summit 2024

- **Climate Finance Commitment:** Recognized the urgent need to scale up climate finance from billions to trillions. Leaders supported COP29 in Azerbaijan and called for enhanced financing to help developing nations adapt to climate change.
- **Taxation of Billionaires:** Endorsed measures to tax ultra-high-net-worth individuals. Brazil led the charge, with discussions about a global tax on the super-rich.
- **Global Hunger and Poverty Alliance:** Launched the Global Alliance Against Hunger and Poverty, aiming to mobilize resources and knowledge to reduce hunger and poverty. The initiative gained support from 82 countries and aims to help 500 million people by 2030.
- **Financial Reform and MDB Cooperation:** Reaffirmed the need to reform Multilateral Development Banks (MDBs) to better address global challenges, including climate change and poverty. Leaders agreed on strengthening cooperation within MDBs.
- **Energy Transition and Fossil Fuel Subsidies:** Highlighted the need for continued investment in renewable energy and clean technologies. However, no reaffirmation of the previous COP28 commitment to phase out fossil fuel subsidies.
- **Global Governance Reform:** Emphasized the need for more representative international institutions. The summit included discussions on global governance reform.

Prime Minister Narendra Modi at the 2024 G20 Summit in Brazil

- Prime Minister Narendra Modi attended the 2024 G20 Summit held in Rio de Janeiro, Brazil from 18th and 19th November 2024.
- This summit focused on key global issues such as social inclusion, energy transition, sustainable development, and global governance reform.

G20 Presidency

- The G20 has no permanent secretariat, with the Presidency supported by the Troika—comprising the previous, current, and incoming Presidencies.

OVERVIEW OF G20 SUMMITS

- The Group of Twenty (G20) is an international forum composed of 19 individual countries and the European Union, the African Union, the African Union, representing the world's largest economies. The G20 plays a crucial role in global economic governance, international trade, financial stability, and policy coordination.

Introduction to G20

- The G20 was established in 1999 in the aftermath of the 1997-1998 Asian financial crisis.
- Initially, it served as a forum for finance ministers and central bank governors of major industrialized and developing economies.
- After the global financial crisis of 2008, the G20 was upgraded to include heads of state or heads of government.
- By 2009, it was designated as the "premier forum for international economic cooperation".
- The summit convenes annually to discuss key issues related to the global economy, sustainable development, climate change, international trade, and other major global challenges.

Membership

- The G20 includes 19 countries: Argentina, Australia, Brazil, Canada, China, France, Germany, India, Indonesia, Italy, Japan, Mexico, Russia, Saudi Arabia, South Africa, South Korea, Turkey, the United Kingdom, and the United States.
- The European Union (EU) is the 20th member, represented by the European Commission and the European Central Bank.
- Together, these members account for around 85% of global GDP and 75% of international trade.

Annual Summits

- The G20 Summit is held annually, with the host country rotating between the members. Each summit is typically attended by the heads of state or government, as well as other key government officials.

Other Facts

- The first G20 summit was convened in Washington, D.C. in 2008, following the global financial crisis.
- The COVID-19 pandemic led to the Riyadh Summit (2020) being held virtually, focusing on health crises, economic recovery, and global vaccine distribution.

Headquarters

- The G20 does not have a permanent secretariat or headquarters. Instead, the presidency rotates annually among member countries, which host the summit and set the agenda for the year.

Year	Host Country	Venue/City	Host Leader
2008	United States	Washington, D.C.	George W. Bush
2009	United Kingdom	London	Gordon Brown
2010	Canada	Toronto, Ontario	Stephen Harper
2011	France	Cannes	Nicolas Sarkozy
2012	Mexico	Los Cabos	Felipe Calderón
2013	Russia	Saint Petersburg	Vladimir Putin
2014	Australia	Brisbane	Tony Abbott
2015	Turkey	Antalya	Recep Tayyip Erdoğan
2016	China	Hangzhou	Xi Jinping
2017	Germany	Hamburg	Angela Merkel
2018	Argentina	Buenos Aires	Mauricio Macri
2019	Japan	Osaka	Shinzo Abe
2020	Saudi Arabia	Riyadh (Virtual)	Salman bin Abdulaziz Al Saud
2021	Italy	Rome	Mario Draghi
2022	Indonesia	Nusa Dua, Bali	Joko Widodo
2023	India	New Delhi	Narendra Modi
2024	Brazil	Rio de Janeiro	Luiz Inácio Lula da Silva
2025	South Africa	Johannesburg	-
2026	United States	-	-

PRIME MINISTER'S SPEECH

- **Achievements:** Highlighted India's success in lifting 250 million people out of poverty and providing food grains to over 800 million people.
- **Women Empowerment:** Mentioned the linking of over 300 million women micro-entrepreneurs to banks with credit access.
- **Agricultural Advancements:** Discussed the development of climate-resilient crop varieties and the Digital Agriculture Mission.

Notable Statements

- **Climate Leadership:** Emphasized India's role in fulfilling Paris Agreement commitments ahead of schedule.
- **Global South:** Stressed the importance of addressing the challenges faced by the Global South, particularly in food, fuel, and fertilizer supply chains.

2023 G20 SUMMIT INDIA

- The 2023 G20 summit was held on 9 and 10 September 2023 in New Delhi, India.
- This was the first time that the G20 summit was held in India.
- The theme of the 2023 G20 summit was "One Earth, One Family, One Future".

NATIONAL AND INTERNATIONAL SUMMITS

16TH CONFERENCE OF PARTIES (COP-16)

- **Location:** Cali, Colombia
- **Date:** 21st October to 1st November 2024
- **Theme:** 'Peace With Nature'
- **Main Outcome:** Launch of the Kunming-Montreal Global Biodiversity Framework (KMGBF)
- **Key Goal:** Protect 30% of land and marine areas by 2030
- **New Fund:** Establishment of the Cali Fund for benefit-sharing from digital sequence information (DSI)
- **Inclusion:** Creation of a new subsidiary body to involve indigenous communities in biodiversity discussions
- **Other:**
  - India launched the updated National Biodiversity Strategy and Action Plan (NBSAP) at COP 16 to the CBD aligning with the Kunming-Montreal Global Biodiversity Framework (KMGBF).
  - It is the first COP since the adoption of Kunming-Montreal Global Biodiversity Framework (KMGBF).

UN Climate Change Conference COP 29

- The UN Climate Change Conference, COP 29, took place in Baku, Azerbaijan, from November 11 to 22, 2024.
- The conference brought together nearly 200 countries to discuss and negotiate actions to address the climate crisis.
- Key outcomes included a new climate finance goal to triple public finance to developing countries, reaching $300 billion annually by 2035.

Climate and Health Africa Conference (CHAC) 2024

- The Climate and Health Africa Conference (CHAC) 2024 took place in Harare, Zimbabwe from 29th to 31st October 2024.
- The conference was hosted by CeSHHAR Zimbabwe in collaboration with the Zimbabwean Ministry of Environment, Climate and Wildlife and the Ministry of Health and Child Care.
- The conference aimed to address the urgent health impacts of climate change in Africa.

Asian Organization of Supreme Audit Institutions (ASOSAI)

- President Droupadi Murmu inaugurated the 16th ASOSAI Assembly in New Delhi on September 24, 2024, focusing on how Supreme Audit Institutions (SAIs) could improve transparency and accountability in governments.
- Girish Chandra Murmu, India's Comptroller and Auditor General, took over as ASOSAI chair for the 2024-2027 term. Over 200 delegates from 42 countries participated in the event.
- The assembly included a symposium on how digital infrastructure can reduce gender gaps in public services. ASOSAI, founded in 1979, now has 48 members and continues to play a key role in global public auditing.

8th Edition of the Future Investment Initiative

- The 8th edition of the Future Investment Initiative (FII) took place from 29th October to 31st October 2024, at the King Abdulaziz International Conference Centre (KAICC) in Riyadh, Saudi Arabia.
- Under the theme "Infinite Horizons: Investing Today, Shaping Tomorrow", the conference brought together global leaders, innovators, and policymakers to discuss investment opportunities and sustainable development.

INTERNATIONAL TELECOMMUNICATION UNION (ITU)

- The International Telecommunication Union (ITU) is a specialized agency of the United Nations responsible for issues related to information and communication technology (ICT).
- The ITU was founded in 1865.
- The ITU is headquartered in Geneva, Switzerland.
- The ITU has 194 member countries and over 900 regional members.

WTSA-24 took place in New Delhi

- The World Telecommunication Standardization Assembly (WTSA-24) took place from 15th to 24th October 2024, at Bharat Mandapam in New Delhi.
- This significant event, organized by the International Telecommunication Union (ITU), is held every four years and sets the agenda for the ITU Telecommunication Standardization Sector (ITU-T) for the next study period.
- The summit adopted the Astana Declaration and approved 25 strategic agreements on energy, security, trade, finance, and information security.

17th Urban Mobility India Conference

- The 17th Urban Mobility India Conference took place from 25th to 27th October 2024, at Mahatma Mandir in Gandhinagar, Gujarat.
- The conference was organized by the Ministry of Housing and Urban Affairs.
- It brought together policymakers, industry leaders, and experts to discuss sustainable urban mobility, innovative financing, and the integration of various transport modes.

2024 edition of Pravasi Parichay

- In October 2024, the Indian Embassy in Saudi Arabia hosted the 2024 edition of Pravasi Parichay, a flagship diaspora engagement event.
- The exhibition features accomplished artists including Nilofer Fatima, Susmitha Dhruva Chitradurga, and Vini Venugopal, each bringing their unique perspective to this cultural celebration.

World Congress on Engineering Asset Management

- The World Congress on Engineering Asset Management (WCEAM) is a flagship event organized by the International Society of Engineering Asset Management (ISEAM).
- It serves as a global platform for educators, policymakers, practitioners, researchers, and trainers to engage in intellectual discourse on the development and advancement of the body of knowledge and practice of managing engineered assets.
- The first WCEAM was held in 2006 in Gold Coast, Australia. Since then, it has become an annual event, hosted in various countries around the world.

18th World Congress on Engineering Asset Management

- The 18th World Congress on Engineering Asset Management (WCEAM) took place from 23rd to 25th October 2024, at the Constitution Club of India in New Delhi.

- WCEAM was organized by the Indian Institute of Technology Kanpur (IIT Kanpur).
- Key themes included sustainable manufacturing, public infrastructure, and digital transformation in asset management. The hosting of 19th WCEAM is being planned for Chile.

Amaravati Drone Summit 2024

- The Amaravati Drone Summit 2024 took place from 22nd and 23rd October 2024, at the CK Convention Center in Mangalagiri, Andhra Pradesh.
- The summit was organized by the Andhra Pradesh Drone Corporation in collaboration with the Ministry of Civil Aviation and the Drone Federation of India.
- The event featured panel discussions, workshops, and a spectacular drone show with over 5,500 drones at Punnami Ghat in Vijayawada.

Modi attends 16th BRICS Summit in Kazan

- From 22nd to 24th October 2024, Prime Minister Narendra Modi attended the 16th BRICS Summit in Kazan, Russia.
- The summit, themed "Strengthening Multilateralism for Just Global Development and Security", provided a platform for leaders to discuss key global issues.
- Modi held bilateral meetings with several world leaders, including Russian President Vladimir Putin, Chinese President Xi Jinping, and UAE President Sheikh Mohamed bin Zayed Al Nahyan.

Chanakya Defence Dialogue 2024

- The Chanakya Defence Dialogue 2024 took place on 24th and 25th October 2024, at the Manekshaw Centre in New Delhi.
- It was organized by the Indian Army in collaboration with the Centre for Land Warfare Studies (CLAWS), the event focused on "Drivers in Nation Building: Fuelling Growth Through Comprehensive Security."

14th All India Civil Defence and Home Guards Conference

- The 14th All India Civil Defence and Home Guards Conference was held on 22nd and 23rd October 2024, at Mahatma Mandir in Gandhinagar, Gujarat.
- Union Home Minister Amit Shah inaugurated the event, which was attended by over 60 senior officials and 1,200 members from across India.
- The conference focused on modernizing civil defence and home guard forces, discussing the Draft Civil Defence Bill and Model Home Guard Bill, and exploring the role of technology in enhancing efficiency.

14th Biennial Lake Conference

- The 14th Biennial Lake Conference, themed "Lake 2024 – Wetlands for Human Well-being," took place in Moodbidri from 17th to 20th October 2024.
- The conference was organized by the Indian Institute of Science and Alva's Education Foundation.
- It emphasized the protection of ecologically sensitive panchayats and sustainable wetland use.

Asia-Pacific Ministerial Conference on Disaster Risk Reduction (APMCDRR) 2024

- The Asia-Pacific Ministerial Conference on Disaster Risk Reduction (APMCDRR) 2024 took place from October 14 to 17, 2024, at the Philippine International Convention Center in Manila.
- The conference was hosted by the Philippine government and the UN Office for Disaster Risk Reduction.
- The conference focused on enhancing disaster resilience through private sector engagement, gender-responsive governance, and urban-rural resilience.
- Key themes included science and technology, multi-stakeholder collaboration, and building back better. The event aimed to accelerate disaster risk reduction efforts in the region.

SHANGHAI COOPERATION ORGANISATION (SCO)

- Shanghai Cooperation Organisation (SCO) was created in 2001.
- SCO is a permanent intergovernmental international organisation.
- The SCO Charter was signed in 2002, and entered into force in 2003.
- In SCO Summit to be held in September 2022 in Uzbekistan, Varanasi has been selected as the SCO region's first "Tourism and Cultural Capital for 2022-23.
- India and Pakistan became members in 2017.
- Iran officially became a member in 2023.
- Members of SCO: China, India, Kazakhstan, Kyrgyzstan, Russia, Pakistan, Tajikistan, Iran, and Uzbekistan and Belarus.
- Headquarters: Beijing, China (Secretariat)
- Secretary-General: Zhang Ming
- Official languages: Russian and Chinese.

25th SCO Summit held in Islamabad

- The 25th SCO Summit was held in Islamabad, Pakistan, on 15th and 16th October 2024.
- Chaired by Prime Minister Shehbaz Sharif, the summit focused on regional security, economic cooperation, and cultural ties.
- The SCO, originally formed in 1996 as the Shanghai Five, expanded in 2001 to include more members, aiming to address regional security and economic issues.

19th International Conference of Drug Regulatory Authorities (ICDRA)

- The 19th International Conference of Drug Regulatory Authorities (ICDRA) was held in New Delhi, India, from 14th to 18th October 2024.
- It was organized by the Central Drugs Standard Control Organization (CDSCO) and the WHO. It focused on regulatory reforms, quality issues, and the safety of medical products.
- Established in 1980, ICDRA provides a platform for regulatory authorities from WHO member states to collaborate and develop international consensus on regulatory priorities.

21st ASEAN-India Summit 2024

- The 21st ASEAN-India Summit was held on 10th October 2024, in Vientiane, Laos.
- This summit marked a decade of India's Act East Policy and focused on enhancing the ASEAN-India Comprehensive Strategic Partnership.
- India's Prime Minister Narendra Modi announced a 10-point plan at the 21st ASEAN-India Summit 2024 in Vientiane, Laos.

2024 edition of the Indo-Pacific Regional Dialogue (IPRD)

- The 2024 edition of the Indo-Pacific Regional Dialogue (IPRD) took place from 3 to 5 October 2024, in New Delhi.
- Organized by the Indian Navy, this apex-level international conference focused on the theme "Resource-Geopolitics and Security in the Indo-Pacific".
- The event brought together global experts, senior officers, government officials, and scholars to discuss maritime security, resource competition, and regional stability.

17th India-Germany MCSG meeting held in Berlin

- The 17th India-Germany Military Cooperation Sub-Group (MCSG) Meeting was held in Berlin from 1 and 2 October 2024.

- Discussions focused on new initiatives to enhance bilateral military cooperation and strengthen ongoing defense engagements.
- The MCSG aims to boost defense cooperation through regular strategic and operational talks between the Headquarters, Integrated Defence Staff, and the Department of International Cooperation Armed Forces, Germany.

10th World Green Economy Summit

- On 2 October 2024, the 10th World Green Economy Summit (WGES) was launched in Dubai by HH Sheikh Ahmed bin Saeed Al Maktoum.
- The summit was organized by the Dubai Supreme Council of Energy, DEWA, and the World Green Economy Organization (WGEO).
- With the theme 'Empowering Global Action: Unlocking Opportunities and Advancing Progress', the event aims to further the UAE's leadership in global climate initiatives.

7th edition of Global Aerospace Summit

- The seventh edition of the Global Aerospace Summit took place from 25 and 26 September 2024, at the St. Regis Saadiyat Island Resort in Abu Dhabi.
- This premier event brought together leaders from the aerospace, aviation, space, and defense sectors to discuss sustainability, youth engagement, and innovation.
- Key highlights included the VISTA startup program and the NextGen Leadership Programme, aimed at fostering future industry leaders.

10th annual World Free Zones Organisation (World FZO) Congress

- The 10th annual World Free Zones Organisation (World FZO) Congress was held from 23 to 25 September 2024, in Dubai. This event attracted over 2,000 participants from 136 countries.
- Under the patronage of Sheikh Mohammed bin Rashid Al Maktoum, the congress focused on the future of free zones, artificial intelligence, and emerging technologies in global trade.
- World Free Zones Organisation (World FZO) was established in 2014. World FZO has grown to include 1,600 members from 141 countries.

National Conference on Digital Public Infrastructure

- The National Conference on Digital Public Infrastructure (DPI) was held on 25 September 2024, organized by the Union Agriculture Ministry.
- The conference aimed to advance the Digital Agriculture Mission by integrating digital technology into agriculture to enhance efficiency and service delivery.
- The event emphasized collaboration between central and state governments to streamline agricultural processes and improve outcomes for farmers.

10th Commonwealth Parliamentary Association Conference

- The 10th Commonwealth Parliamentary Association (CPA) India Region Conference was held in New Delhi on 23 and 24 September 2024.
- Chaired by Lok Sabha Speaker Om Birla, the conference focused on the theme "The role of legislative bodies in the attainment of sustainable and inclusive development".
- The event brought together presiding officers, speakers, and deputy speakers from various states and union territories.

Prime Minister attends 6th Quad Leaders' Summit in Wilmington

- Prime Minister Narendra Modi attended the 6th Quad Leaders' Summit in Wilmington, Delaware, on 21 September 2024.
- Hosted by U.S. President Joe Biden at his alma mater, Archmere Academy, the summit also included Japanese Prime Minister Fumio Kishida and Australian Prime Minister Anthony Albanese.
- The leaders discussed regional security, technology, clean energy, and health.
- They issued the "Wilmington Declaration," reaffirming their commitment to a free and open Indo-Pacific.

2nd Global Food Regulators Summit 2024

- From 20 to 21 September 2024, India hosted the 2nd Global Food Regulators Summit in New Delhi.
- The summit was organized by the Food Safety and Standards Authority of India (FSSAI) under the Union Health Ministry.
- The event aimed to enhance food safety standards and foster international collaboration.
- The summit aligns with India's vision of "One Earth, One Family, One Future".

International WASH Conference 2024

- The International WASH Conference 2024 was held from 17 to 19 September 2024, in New Delhi, as part of the 8th India Water Week.
- The conference was organized by the Department of Drinking Water and Sanitation, Ministry of Jal Shakti.
- The conference focused on the theme "Sustaining Rural Water Supply".
- It featured over 40 thematic sessions and over 180 paper presentations, addressing key challenges in water, sanitation, and hygiene (WASH) sectors.

4th Akhil Bharatiya Rajbhasha Sammelan held in New Delhi

- The 4th Akhil Bharatiya Rajbhasha Sammelan was held at Bharat Mandapam in New Delhi on 14 and 15 September 2024.
- It was organized by the Department of Official Language under the Ministry of Home Affairs.
- The event also saw the inauguration of the Bharatiya Bhasha Anubhag, aimed at promoting Indian languages alongside Hindi. Awards like Rajbhasha Gaurav and Rajbhasha Kirti were also presented.

GLOBAL BIO INDIA 2024

- Global Bio-India 2024 was a significant event in the biotechnology sector, held from September 12-14, 2024, at Pragati Maidan, New Delhi.
- The event was organized by the Department of Biotechnology (DBT) and the Biotechnology Industry Research Assistance Council (BIRAC).
- The main themes were 'Biotech Innovation' and 'Bio-manufacturing', emphasizing the importance of these areas in boosting India's bioeconomy.

79th United Nations General Assembly

- The 79th United Nations General Assembly (UNGA) took place from

10th to 30th September 2024 at the UN Headquarters in New York.

- The theme was "Leaving no one behind: acting together for the advancement of peace, sustainable development, and human dignity for present and future generations.".
- The assembly was presided over by Philemon Yang, former Prime Minister of Cameroon.

2nd Asia Pacific Ministerial Conference on Civil Aviation

- The Second Asia Pacific Ministerial Conference on Civil Aviation was held on 11 and 12 September 2024, at Bharat Mandapam, New Delhi.
- The Conference was co-hosted by the International Civil Aviation Organization (ICAO) and India's Ministry of Civil Aviation.
- The event focused on regional aviation growth, sustainability, and infrastructure development.

7th National Security Strategies Conference 2024

- On 13 September 2024, Union Home Minister Amit Shah inaugurated the two-day 7th National Security Strategies Conference in New Delhi.
- The event brought together over 750 participants, including senior police leadership, Central Armed Police Forces, and intelligence agencies.
- Shah also launched a dashboard developed by the National Crime Records Bureau to implement decisions from previous conferences.

2nd International Conference on Green Hydrogen

- The 2nd International Conference on Green Hydrogen (ICGH-2024) was held from September 11-13, 2024, at Bharat Mandapam, New Delhi.
- The conference is organized by the Union Ministry of New and Renewable Energy and the Office of the Principal Scientific Adviser to the Government of India, with associate partners including the Union Ministry of Petroleum and Natural Gas, the Department of Science and Technology, and the Department of Scientific and Industrial Research.
- The conference highlighted India's National Green Hydrogen Mission, which aims to establish a green hydrogen ecosystem in the country.

BRICS Literature Forum 2024

- The BRICS Literature Forum 2024 took place in Kazan, Russia, from September 11-14, 2024.
- This year's theme was "World literature in the new reality: Dialogue of traditions, national values, and cultures."
- The forum brought together literary figures from the BRICS nations—Brazil, Russia, India, China, and South Africa.

5th Defence Cooperation Dialogue between India and Maldives

- On 6 September 2024, India and the Maldives held their 5th Defence Cooperation Dialogue in New Delhi.
- The Indian delegation was led by Defence Secretary Giridhar Aramane, while the Maldivian side was headed by Chief of Defence Force General Ibrahim Hilmy.
- Both sides also deliberated on participation in upcoming bilateral military exercises, aiming to enhance cooperation and stability in the Indian Ocean Region.

1st ever CII India Mediterranean Business Conclave 2024

- The first ever CII India Mediterranean Business Conclave was held on September 6, 2024, at Sushma Swaraj Bhawan, New Delhi.
- The conclave was organized by the Confederation of Indian Industry (CII) in partnership with the Ministry of External Affairs, Government of India.
- The conclave aimed to enhance trade and economic cooperation between India and the Mediterranean region.
- India's total trade with Mediterranean countries doubled from US$ 48.60 billion in 2017 to US$ 83.20 billion in 2022.

India and Kenya holds 3rd Joint Defence Cooperation Committee meeting

- The third edition of Joint Defence Cooperation Committee (JDCC) meeting between India and Kenya was held in New Delhi on September 3, 2024.

- The two countries discussed a wide range of avenues for defence cooperation in areas like military cooperation, training, defence industries, R&D etc.

Colombo Security Conclave (CSC)

- In August 2024, Member states of the Colombo Security Conclave (CSC) signed the Charter and the MoU for the establishment of the CSC Secretariat in Colombo.
- CSC is a regional security grouping comprising India, Bangladesh, Sri Lanka, Maldives, and Mauritius.
- The CSC's core objective is to promote regional security by addressing transnational threats and challenges of common concern to the Member States.

5th Global Fintech Fest

- The 5th Global Fintech Fest (GFF) took place from 28th to 30th August 2024, at the Jio World Convention Centre in Mumbai, Maharashtra.
- The fest was organized by the Payments Council of India (PCI), the National Payments Corporation of India (NPCI), and the Fintech Convergence Council (FCC).
- The theme was "Blueprint for the next decade of finance: Responsible AI | Inclusive | Resilient".

2nd India-Singapore Ministerial Round Table Conference held in Singapore

- The Second India-Singapore Ministerial Roundtable (ISMR) took place in Singapore on 26 August 2024.
- The ISMR serves as a vital bilateral platform for cooperation and exchange of views on mutual interests between the two nations.

1st edition of Bharat Dalhan Seminar 2024

- The inaugural edition of Bharat Dalhan Seminar 2024 is a significant event organized by the India Pulses and Grains Association (IPGA) in New Delhi.

- The seminar focused on creating a strategic roadmap to increase indigenous pulse production and bridge the gap between the demand and supply of pulses.

19th CII India Africa Business Conclave held in New Delhi

- The 19th CII India Africa Business Conclave was held from 20th to 22nd August 2024 at Hotel Taj Palace, New Delhi.
- The conclave was organized by the Confederation of Indian Industry (CII) in partnership with the Ministry of Commerce & Industry and the Ministry of External Affairs.
- Key focus areas include agriculture, food processing, defence, digital partnership, financial services, healthcare, infrastructure, and skill development.

3rd Voice of Global South Summit

- The 3rd Voice of Global South Summit (VOGSS) was hosted by India on August 17, 2024, in a virtual format.
- The overarching theme of the summit was "An Empowered Global South for a Sustainable Future".
- India announced significant initiatives, including a USD 2.5 million fund to boost trade promotion activities and a USD 1 million fund for capacity building in trade policy and trade negotiation.

India hosted first BIMSTEC Business Summit in 2024

- From 6 to 8 August 2024, India hosted the first Bay of Bengal Initiative for Multi-Sectoral Technical and Economic Cooperation (BIMSTEC) Business Summit in New Delhi.
- The summit was organized by the Ministry of External Affairs in collaboration with the Confederation of Indian Industries (CII).
- Key topics included trade facilitation, regional connectivity, energy security, inclusive growth, and sustainable development.

5th ASEAN-India Trade in Goods Agreement Joint Committee Meeting

- From 29 July to 1 August 2024, the 5th ASEAN-India Trade in Goods Agreement (AITIGA) Joint Committee meeting was held at the ASEAN Secretariat in Jakarta.
- The meeting aimed to enhance economic cooperation between ASEAN and India.
- Delegates from all 10 ASEAN countries and India participated, discussing key areas like market access, rules of origin, and trade facilitation.

32nd International Conference of Agricultural Economists (ICAE)

- The 32nd International Conference of Agricultural Economists (ICAE) is scheduled to take place from 2nd to 7th August 2024, at the National Agricultural Science Centre (NASC) Complex in New Delhi, India.
- This triennial event was organized by the International Association of Agricultural Economists (IAAE).
- It will focus on the theme "Transformation Towards Sustainable Agri-Food Systems".

World Education Conference 2024

- On 29 July 2024, the Tech Leaders Forum of India (TELFI) was launched at the World Education Conference 2024, hosted by Federation of Economic Development Association (FEDA) at Hamdan Bin Mohammed Smart University in Dubai.

World Education Summit

- Its primary goal is to provide engineers with the resources, knowledge, and network needed to excel in their careers and drive technological advancements both in India and internationally.

9th Governing Council Meeting

- On 27 July 2024, Prime Minister Narendra Modi chaired the 9th Governing Council Meeting of NITI Aayog at the Rashtrapati Bhavan Cultural Centre in New Delhi.
- The meeting focused on the theme 'Viksit Bharat@2047', aiming to transform India into a developed nation by 2047.

United States hosted the 2024 NATO Summit

- From 9 and 11 July, 2024, the United States hosted the 2024 NATO Summit in Washington, D.C., marking the 75th anniversary of the Alliance.
- The summit brought together leaders from NATO's 32 member countries, including newly joined Sweden.
- Key discussions focused on strengthening support for Ukraine, enhancing NATO's defense posture, and addressing global security challenges.

2nd Retreat of the Foreign Ministers of BIMSTEC

- The 2nd Retreat of the Foreign Ministers of the Bay of Bengal Initiative for Multi-Sectoral Technical and Economic Cooperation (BIMSTEC) took place in New Delhi on 11 and 12 July 2024.
- Discussions covered regional cooperation within the BIMSTEC framework and potential outcomes for the 6th BIMSTEC Summit scheduled for September 2024.

46th Session of World Heritage Committee

- On 21 July 2024, Prime Minister Narendra Modi inaugurated the 46th Session of the World Heritage Committee at Bharat Mandapam in New Delhi.

- Prime Minister Modi announced a $1 million grant to the UNESCO World Heritage Centre to support capacity building, technical assistance, and conservation efforts, particularly benefiting Global South countries.
- The session saw the inscription of 24 new World Heritage Sites, including 19 cultural, 4 natural, and 1 mixed property.
- North East India's Maidam was nominated for inclusion in UNESCO's Cultural World Heritage list.

24th SCO summit held in Astana

- The 24th Shanghai Cooperation Organization (SCO) summit was held in Astana, Kazakhstan on 3rd and 4th July 2024.
- During the summit, Belarus was admitted as the 10th member state of the SCO.
- The summit adopted the Astana Declaration and approved 25 strategic agreements on energy, security, trade, finance and information security.

6th meeting of the GPAI Ministerial Council

- The 6th meeting of the GPAI Ministerial Council was held on 3rd July 2024 at Bharat Mandapam, New Delhi in a hybrid mode.
- The 2024 GPAI New Delhi meeting and the consensus reached on the future of GPAI underscores India's leadership in the global AI discourse, cementing its pivotal role in steering the ethical and inclusive development of AI.

Global IndiaAI Summit 2024

- The Global IndiaAI Summit 2024 was held on 3rd and 4th July in New Delhi, India.
- The summit was organized by the Ministry of Electronics and Information Technology (MeitY).

- The summit provided a platform for international AI experts from science, industry, civil society, governments, international organizations, and academia to share insights on key AI issues and challenges.

3rd UN Conference on Afghanistan at Doha

- The current government of Afghanistan, the Taliban, took part in the UN Conference on Afghanistan for the first time. It took place in Doha, Qatar, on 30 June and 1 July 2024.
- The conference included representatives from 25 countries and international organizations.

G-7 Italia 2024

Theme : "Building a Resilient and Inclusive Global Economy."

Event	50th G7 Summit
Host Country	Italy
Venue	Borgo Egnazia, Apulia, Italy
Dates	June 13-15, 2024
Host	Prime Minister Giorgia Meloni
Participants	Canada, France, Germany, Italy, Japan, UK, US, EU
Invited Guests	India, Saudi Arabia, Jordan, Brazil, Argentina, Turkey, UAE, Kenya, Algeria, Tunisia, Mauritania (AU), Vatican City
Key Topics	Ukraine conflict, Middle East issues, climate change, AI
Special Sessions	Outreach on AI, energy, Africa, Mediterranean
Expected Outcomes	Joint statements, policy agreements, strategic partnerships
Bilateral Meetings	PM Modi with Italian PM Meloni, among others

G7 Summit 2025

The **G7 Summit 2025** will be hosted by Canada, in Kananaskis, Alberta from June 15-17, bringing together leaders from Canada, France, Germany, Italy, Japan, the United Kingdom, the United States, and the European Union.

India to Host The Inaugural World Audio Visual Entertainment Summit (WAVES) 2025

- India will host the **World Audio Visual Entertainment Summit (WAVES)** from February 5-9, 2025 in **New Delhi**, for the first time.
- **Focus on Content Innovation:** It will highlight India's advancements in animation, gaming, entertainment technology, and both regional and mainstream cinema.
- **Positioning India as a Global Hub:** WAVES aims to establish India as a global hub for world-class content creation.

Neem Summit 2024

- The Neem Summit & Global Neem Trade fair is organized by collaboration with **ICAR-Central Agroforestry Research Institute, Jhansi** in New Delhi on 19-20 February 2024.
- The theme of this Summit is **"Neem for Sustainable Agriculture, Health, and Environment."**
- The event aims to showcase the multifaceted uses of neem in agriculture, healthcare, and environmental sustainability.

2nd LEADS Programme 2024 by INSA and NCGG

- The **Indian National Science Academy (INSA)** and the **National Centre for Good Governance (NCGG)** jointly organized the 2nd INSA-NCGG Leadership Development Program in Science and Technology (LEADS) at New Delhi from 1 to 7, April 2024.
- This pioneering programme seeks **to nurture and empower future leaders in the field of science and technology,** fostering visionary leadership and advancing scientific excellence in India.
- The National Centre for Good Governance (NCGG) is an apex institution for governance-related training, research, and consultancy.
- It aims to enhance the capabilities of individuals and organizations involved in governance and public administration in India.

UAE-India Business Summit

- India and the UAE launched the **UAE-India CEPA Council (UICC)** to encourage close partnerships and tangible cooperation across all levels of the UAE and Indian business communities
- This was launched at the **Vibrant Gujarat Global Summit 2024.**
- The business summit involving the two nations was held under the theme of **'Two Nations, One Vision'.**

Raisina Dialogue 2024

- Prime Minister Narendra Modi inaugurated the **9th edition of Raisina Dialogue** in New Delhi.
- Keynote address has been delivered by the Chief Guest Prime Minister of the Hellenic Republic (Greece), Kyriakos Mitsotakis.

- Raisina Dialogue is India's flagship conference on geopolitics and geo-economics, committed to addressing the most challenging issues facing the international community.
- Theme of 2024 edition: **"Chaturanga: Conflict, Contest, Cooperate, Create".**

2024 Vibrant Gujarat Global Summit

- The **10th Vibrant Gujarat Global Summit (VGGS)** was held from January 10 to 12, 2024, at Mahatma Mandir Convention and Exhibition Centre in **Gandhinagar, Gujarat, India.**
- The summit, organized by the Government of Gujarat in partnership with the Confederation of Indian Industry (CII) and iNDEXTb.
- The theme of this year's summit is **'Gateway to the Future'** and includes the participation of **34 partner countries** and 16 partner organizations.
- The Czech Republic is also a partner country in the 10th Summit.

9th Edition Of India International Science Festival

- Minister of State (Independent Charge) for Science and Technology Jitendra Singh inaugurated the **ninth edition of the India International Science Festival (IISF)** in Faridabad, Haryana.
- The festival focused on celebrating the achievements of Indian scientific institutions around the theme **"science and technology public outreach in Amrit Kaal".**
- The primary goal of the India International Science Festival (IISF) is to offer an inspiring platform for people from various backgrounds, including students, educators, scientists, researchers, industry professionals, entrepreneurs, and science communicators, to engage and participate.

19th Non-Aligned Movement (NAM) Summit

- The two-day 19th Non-Aligned Movement (NAM) Summit was held in **Uganda's Kampala.**
- External Affairs Minister (EAM), **Dr. S. Jaishankar** represented the Indian delegation.
- The EAM has co-chaired the 6th India-Nigeria Joint Commission Meeting (JCM) with his counterpart and meet with other leaders.

13th Ministerial Conference of the WTO

- 13th Ministerial Conference **(MC13)** of the World Trade Organization (WTO) took place from 26 to 29 February 2024 in **Abu Dhabi,** United Arab Emirates.
- The conference was chaired by **H.E. Dr Thani bin Ahmed Al Zeyoudi,** UAE's Minister of State for Foreign Trade.
- The conference aimed to build on the successes of **MC12 in Geneva in June 2022** and ensure the movement of goods and services remains free and fair for every member.

8th Asia Economic Dialogue

- Asia Economic Dialogue 2024, annual geo-economics conference, organised jointly by the Ministry of External Affairs (MEA) and Pune International Centre (PIC) was held in the city from February 29 to March 2.
- Focused on the theme, **'Geo-economic Challenges in an Era of Flux'.**

The Great Indian Board Reboot: Roadshow 2024

- The Indian Institute of Corporate Affairs (IICA), the apex think tank of the Ministry of Corporate Affairs, hosted the inaugural edition of 'The Great Indian Board Reboot: Roadshow 2024' at the NSE Headquarters in Mumbai on 31 January 2024.
- This landmark inaugural event, conducted in partnership with **National Stock Exchange - NSE India and Bombay Stock Exchange (BSE).**
- **'The Great Indian Board Reboot: Roadshow 2024'** is aimed at setting a new benchmark in discussions around corporate governance in India.

World Governments Summit 2024

- Prime Minister Modi participated in the World Governments Summit **in Dubai** as Guest of Honour. He also delivered the special keynote address on the theme of the Summit - **"Shaping the Future Governments".**
- The World Government Summit is a global platform dedicated to shaping the future of government worldwide.

7th Indian Ocean Conference

- The 7th Indian Ocean Conference took place in **Perth, Australia** from 9th to 10th February 2024, in partnership with the Department of Foreign Affairs and Trade of the Australian Government.
- The conference was also co-hosted by the S. Rajaratnam School of International Studies in Singapore and the Perth-US Asia Centre in Australia.
- Under the theme **"Towards a Stable and Sustainable Indian Ocean,"** the conference aims to foster discussions and initiatives geared towards promoting stability and sustainability in the Indian Ocean region.

16th conference of World Social Forum 2024

- The **16th World Social Forum (WSF) 2024** held in **Kathmandu,** focusing on horizontal exchange among civil society groups opposing neoliberal globalization.
- The event, themed **"Another World is Possible,"** kicked off with a Solidarity March advocating justice, peace, equality, and an end to discrimination.
- The Forum addresses pressing global issues through dialogue and action, aiming for a more equitable and just world.

Harivansh attended 148 Assembly of Inter-Parliamentary Union in Geneva

- The Indian Parliamentary Delegation, led by Deputy Chairman of Rajya Sabha, Harivansh Narayan Singh held a bilateral meeting with their Armenian counterparts on the sidelines of the Inter-Parliamentary Union (IPU) event in Geneva, Switzerland.
- The Armenian delegation was represented by the Vice President of the National Assembly, Hakob Arshakyan.
- Mr. Harivansh highlighted the rich cultural heritage of both countries and proposed enhancing focus on promoting cultural exchanges, such as art exhibitions, film festivals, and academic collaborations.

4th Shanghai Cooperation Organisation (SCO) Startup Forum

- The fourth edition of the Shanghai Cooperation Organisation (SCO) Startup Forum was organized on **19th March 2024 in New Delhi.**
- The initiative aims to enhance startup interactions among SCO Member States. It fosters innovation, supports job creation, and encourages young talent to develop innovative solutions.

'2+2' defence ministerial dialogue

- **India and Brazil** explored ways to expand cooperation in areas of energy, critical minerals, technology and counter-terrorism at their first '2+2' defence and foreign ministerial dialogue.
- It was co-chaired by additional secretary in the external affairs ministry G V Srinivas

and joint secretary in the defence ministry Vishwesh Negi.

- The Brazilian delegation was led by Director at Brazilian foreign ministry Marcelo Camara and Rear Admiral Fernando de Luca Marques de Oliviera.

Startup Mahakumbh Event 2024

- The Startup Mahakumbh was **held from March 18-20 at Bharat Mandapam** in New Delhi.
- The event is organized jointly by apex industry associations, Bootstrap Incubation & Advisory Foundation and Indian Venture and Alternate Capital Association (IVCA).
- The focus of PM's address was on the government's initiatives to enhance emerging sectors like **deeptech, agritech, biotech, medtech, and AI.**

Bharat Steam Boiler Expo 2024

- The first Bharat Steam Boiler Expo 2024 was inaugurated at **Veterinary College Field in Guwahati's Khanapara.**
- This ground breaking event is a dynamic collaboration with industry giants such as Indian Oil Corporation Limited (IOCL), Oil India Limited (OIL), Numaligarh Refinery Ltd. (NRL), Brahmaputra Cracker and Polymer Ltd. (BCPL), Assam PetroChemicals Limited and NTPC Limited.

Maiden Rainbow Tourism Conference

- **Nepal** hosts its **1st Rainbow Tourism Conference,** with Nepal presenting itself as a safe and respectable destination in South Asia for the sexual minority community.
- The one-day international conference was **organized by Mayako Pehchan Nepal,** a non-governmental organization.
- The main objective of the conference is to establish Nepal as an LGBT-friendly tourism destination.

International Humanitarian Conference

- On 15 April, 2024, the French capital, Paris, hosted an International Humanitarian Conference for Sudan and Neighbouring Countries.
- The conference was organized in response to the United Nations' funding appeal on 7 February 2024.
- The devastating conflict in Sudan has plunged the nation into a profound humanitarian crisis, prompting the international community to take swift action.
- The conference was a collaborative effort by France, Germany, and the European Union.

World Future Energy Summit 2024

- A panel discussion on "Future Growth Opportunities for Long Duration Energy Storage" took place at the World Future Energy Summit 2024 **in Abu Dhabi.**
- The World Future Energy Summit is an annual event organised in Abu Dhabi, United Arab Emirates, with the goal of advancing future energy, energy efficiency, and sustainable technology.

Tri-Service Conference 'Parivartan Chintan'

- **Parivartan Chintan,** a pioneering Tri-Service Conference aimed at generating new and fresh ideas, initiatives and reforms to propel Jointness and Integration efforts was **held in New Delhi on 8 April 2024.**
- It was first ever conference of the Heads of all Tri- Services Institutions, the Department of Military Affairs, Headquarters Integrated Defence Staff and the three Services.

Summits and Conferences 2024

Name of the Summit	Organized/Led by	Venue	Aim/Theme
World Press Freedom Conference	Chile and UNESCO	Santiago, Chile	Theme:"A Press for the Planet: Journalism in the face of the Environmental Crisis"
UN's 1st International Conference on DPI	Permanent Mission of India and the Ministry of Electronics and Information Technology	New York, USA.	Promoting international cooperation for the development of digital infrastructure globally
Cold Chain and Logistics Summit	Federation of Indian Chambers of Commerce and Industry	New Delhi	To foster collaboration and innovation in developing an integrated
Parivartan Chintan Tri-Service Conference	Headquarters Integrated Defence Staff	New Delhi	Theme:"Future Ready".
World Hepatitis Summit	WHO	Lisbon, Portugal	Theme:"Integrate, Accelerate, Eliminate"
Tiger Conservation Conference	Royal Government of Bhutan and the Tiger Conservation Coalition	Bhutan	Theme: "Sustainable Finance for Tiger Landscape.
India-Kuwait Investment Conference 2.0	Indian Embassy	Kuwait	To strengthen economic ties between the two countries.
6th Edition of the International Conference on Disaster Resilient Infrastructure	Coalition for Disaster Resilient Infrastructure	New Delhi	Theme:"Investing today for a more resilient tomorrow"
Critical minerals summit	Ministry of Mines, Government of India	New Delhi	Theme:Enhancing Beneficiation and Processing Capabilities"
International Rainbow Tourism Conference	NGO Mayako Pahichan Nepal and the Nepal Tourism Board	Kathmandu, Nepal	To promote Nepal as a safe and inclusive destination for LGBT tourists
9th Annual Shakti International Women Entrepreneurs	India SME Forum and the Ministry of MSME	New Delhi	To inspire and promote entrepreneurship among women by providing a platform for successful women entrepreneurs

Name of the Summit	Organized/Led by	Venue	Aim/Theme
54th DG-level BGB-BSF Border Conference	BSF and BGB	(BGB) headquarters in Dhaka	To enhance coordination and cooperation between the two forces.
Naval Commanders' Conference	Indian Navy	INS Vikramaditya	Served as a platform for Naval Commanders to deliberate on strategic, operational, and administrative matters concerning maritime security.
Third Summit for Democracy	South Korea	Seoul	Theme: 'Democracy for Future Generations'.
Army Commanders' Conference	Indian Army	New Delhi	Focused on critical agendas impacting the field army and veterans' welfare
(CLEA) - (CASGC) 2024	Commonwealth Attorneys and Solicitors	Vigyan Bhawan in New Delhi	Theme: "Cross-Border Challenges in Justice Delivery"
World Sustainable Development Summit (WSDS) 2024	The Energy and Resources Institute (TERI)	Habitat Centre in New Delhi	Theme: 'Leadership for Sustainable Development and Climate Justice'.
"Road to Paris 2024" Conference	National Anti-Doping Agency	New Delhi	Theme: Championing Clean Sports and Uniting for Anti-Doping
19th Annual Banking Technology Conference	Indian Banks' Association (IBA)	Trident Hotel, Nariman Point, Mumbai	"Building the AI-Enabled Bank of the Future"
60th Munich Security Conference	Munich Security Conference Foundation, a non-profit foundation	Hotel Bayerischer Hof and the Hotel Rosewood Munich	Theme: "Currency for Change: World Politics on a Budget"
National Conference on Jal Jeevan Mission (JJM)	Department of Drinking Water and Sanitation	Lucknow, Uttar Pradesh	Theme: 'Unified Approach Towards Sustainable Solutions in the Rural WASH Sector'
INDUS-X Summit	Innovations for Defence Excellence (iDEX)	New Delhi	Theme: Bilateral Cooperation Mechanism, Public–Private Partnerships
21st edition of BioAsia Summit 2024	Government of Telangana	Hyderabad, India	Theme: "Transforming Life Sciences with Data and AI,"
first-ever Future Skills Summit	Ministry of Electronics and Information Technology	Guwahati	Theme: "Catalyzing future-ready talent for India & the World"
National CSR Summit	Confederation Of Indian Industry	IIT Madras	Theme: 'Building India 2047 – Technology for Better Tomorrow',
9th edition of the Raisina Dialogue Conferenece	Observer Research Foundation	New Delhi	Theme: "Chaturanga: Conflict, Contest, Cooperate, Create"
All India Conference of Directors General and Inspectors General of Police 2023	Intelligence Bureau	Rajasthan International Centre, Jaipur	wide range of policing and internal security issues
12th General Assembly of the Asian Buddhist Conference	Asian Buddhist Conference	New Delhi	Theme:"ABCP - The Buddhist Voice of Global South".
Climate Summit 2024	Ministry of Environment, Forest and Climate Change, Government of India.	Mumbai, Maharashtra	Theme: "Decoding the Green Transition for India,"
5th International and 44th All India Criminology Conference	Union Home Minister and Minister of Cooperation, Shri Amit Shah.	Gandhinagar, Gujarat	Theme: "Behavioural Forensics: Reintegrating Expanding Contours of Criminology and Criminalistics".
National Conference on Strategic Trade Controls	Directorate General of Foreign Trade	Vigyan Bhawan, New Delhi.	To shed light on India's Strategic Trade Control system
19th NAM summit	-	Uganda	Theme: 'Deepening Cooperation for Shared Global Affluence'.

44th CISO Training Programme

- The **44th CISO Deep-Dive training programme** was organized by the National e-Governance Division (NeGD) under the **Cyber Surakshit Bharat initiative** of the Ministry of Electronics and Information Technology (MeitY).
- The program aimed to spread awareness about cyber-crime and build capacities of Chief Information Security Officers (CISOs) and frontline IT officials across all government departments.

Kazakhstan Co-Chairs Int'l conference on Nuclear Security in Vienna

- **Kazakhstan,** in collaboration with Australia, co-chaired the International Conference on Nuclear Security: Shaping the Future (ICONS 2024) **in Vienna from 20 to 24 May 2024.**
- The conference, organized under the auspices of the **International Atomic Energy Agency (IAEA),** brought together over 2,000 delegates from more than 130 countries.
- Kazakh Vice Minister of Energy, Sungat Yessimkhanov, emphasized the need to adapt nuclear security regimes to evolving technologies.

46th Antarctic Treaty meet

- India successfully concluded hosting of the **46th Antarctic Treaty Consultative Meeting (ATCM-46)** and the 26th Committee on Environmental Protection (CEP-26) from **May 20th to May 30th, 2024** in **Kochi, Kerala.**
- The ATCM-46 was held with the overarching theme of **Vasudhaiva Kutumbakam,** a Sanskrit phrase that means one Earth, one family, one future.
- The ATCM-46 and CEP-26 were hosted by the Ministry of Earth Sciences, Government of India, through the National Centre for Polar and Ocean Research (NCPOR), Goa, with support from the Antarctic Treaty Secretariat headquartered in Argentina.
- The Antarctic Treaty, **signed in 1959** and **in force since 1961,** designates Antarctica as a peaceful area for scientific research and environmental protection.

10th World Water Forum

- The 10th World Water Forum has commenced **in Bali, Indonesia,** bringing together global leaders, experts, and stakeholders to address critical water-related challenges.
- This forum serves as a platform for discussing sustainable water management, conservation, and equitable access.
- The forum aims to foster international cooperation and drive actionable initiatives toward a water-secure world.

World Hydrogen Summit 2024

- World Hydrogen Summit 2024 was held in **Rotterdam, Netherlands,** during May 13 – 15, 2024.
- For the first time, India has set up its own pavilion, at the World Hydrogen Summit 2024.
- It provides a stage for showcasing the noteworthy developments in green hydrogen made in the country.

5th Joint Group of Customs (JGC) meeting

- The 5th Joint Group of Customs (JGC) meeting **between India and Bhutan** was held on 6th-7th May, 2024 in Leh, Ladakh.
- The 5th JGC meeting discussed issues such as opening of new Land Customs Stations and notifying new trade routes, development of infrastructure, automation and digitisation of transit processes, prevention of smuggling, coordinated cross-border management, pre-arrival exchange of Customs data, bilateral agreement on Customs cooperation and movement of transit cargo under electronic cargo system.
- There are 10 Land Customs Stations along the India-Bhuan Border in the States of West Bengal (6) and Assam (4).

Nuclear Energy Summit 2024 Held in Brussels

- The first-ever Nuclear Energy Summit was **held in Brussels, Belgium,** emphasizing the role of nuclear energy in reducing fossil fuel use and enhancing energy security.
- The summit, **attended by over 30 countries,** highlighted the need to triple nuclear power capacity **by 2050** to meet climate goals.
- The event was co-hosted by the **International Atomic Energy Agency (IAEA)** and Belgium, with key discussions focusing on financing, workforce development, and international cooperation.

14th Counter-Terrorism Dialogue

- On 7 May 2024, in New Delhi, the **European Union and India** convened their 14th Counter-Terrorism Dialogue.
- The discussion provided a chance to maintain and strengthen collaboration on this crucial pillar of the EU-India Strategic Partnership.

- The European Union and India have vehemently denounced terrorism in all of its forms and manifestations and have underscored the necessity of bolstering global collaboration to address counterterrorism obstacles.

Commonwealth Attorneys and Solicitors General Conference (CASGC) 2024

- PM Modi inaugurated the Commonwealth Legal Education Association (CLEA) - Commonwealth Attorneys and Solicitors General Conference (CASGC) 2024 at **Vigyan Bhawan, New Delhi.**
- The theme of the conference is **"Cross-Border Challenges in Justice Delivery".**
- It witnessed the participation of Attorney Generals and Solicitors from the Commonwealth nations spanning the Asia-Pacific, Africa, and the Caribbean along with various international delegations.

37th African Union Summit

- 37th African Union Summit was **held in Ethiopia** in February 2024.
- The African Union theme of the year 2024 is **"Educate and Skill Africa for the 21st Century".**
- The Africa Club was launched at the 37th African Union Summit **in Addis Ababa, Ethiopia.**

International Big Cat Alliance

- The Union Cabinet approved the establishment of International Big Cat Alliance (IBCA).
- During the Global Tiger Day event in 2019, PM Modi urged global leaders **to unite against poaching in Asia.**
- So far, 16 countries have given their written consent to be part of the IBCA.

46th session of the World Heritage Committee

- India has been selected for the **first time to chair and host** the 46th session of the UNESCO World Heritage Committee.
- The 46th session of the UNESCO World Heritage Committee held in New Delhi between 21 and 31 July 2024.
- The World Heritage Committee currently consists of 21 countries.

Indus Food 2024 Exhibition

- Union Minister of Commerce & Industry, **Consumer Affairs, Food & Public Distribution and Textiles,** Shri Piyush Goyal inaugurated the 'Indus Food 2024', exhibition to showcase India's vibrant and diverse food ecosystem, being held in India Exposition Mart, Greater Noida.
- The Minister highlighted that India's agricultural exports stood at an aggregate of about US$ 53 Billion.

Launch of "Alliance for Global Good-Gender Equity and Equality"

- India has unveiled the "Alliance for Global Good-Gender Equity and Equality."
- The Ministry of Women & Child Development launched the **logo and the website** for the Alliance for Global Good – Gender Equity and Equality.
- **Launched in Davos 2024** (54th annual World Economic Forum), it is a testament to India's unwavering commitment to the cause of women-led development.

National Conference on APAAR: One Nation One Student ID Card

- Dharmendra Pradhan, Union Minister of education graced the National Conference on **APAAR: One Nation One Student ID Card** in New Delhi.
- The APAAR ID is a unique and aspirational document for Indian students, which is intended to have global recognition. This ID is linked to the **Academic Bank of Credits (ABC)** of the respective student.
- The Indian government is introducing a new identification system called the **Automated Permanent Academic Account Registry (APAAR),** also known as 'One Nation, One Student ID,' as part of the National Education Policy of 2020. **APAAR is an 'EduLocker.'**

MEGHAYAN 2024

- As part of the World Meteorological Day celebrations, a METOC (Meteorological and Oceanographic) seminar 'Meghayan-24' was conducted by School of Naval Oceanology & Meteorology (SNOM) and Indian Naval Meteorological Analysis Centre (INMAC) at **Southern Naval Command** on 28 Mar 24.
- On this occasion an indigenous mobile application INDRA (Indian Naval Dynamic Resource for Weather Analysis) to disseminate weather related information and forecasts empowering optimal & quick decision making was also launched.

Seventy-seventh World Health Assembly (WHA77)

- The Seventy-seventh World Health Assembly was **held in Geneva, Switzerland,** on 27 May – 1 June 2024.
- The theme of this year's Health Assembly is: **All for Health, Health for All.**
- The World Health Assembly is the decision-making body of WHO.

KAZA Summit 2024

- In May 2024, Heads of State Summit for the **Kavango-Zambezi Trans-Frontier Conservation Area (KAZA-TFCA)** took place in Livingstone, **Zambia.**
- KAZA-TFCA spans across five southern African nations namely, **Angola, Botswana, Namibia, Zambia, and Zimbabwe** along the Okavango and Zambezi river basins.
- The main focus of Summit was the **ban on ivory and wildlife product** trade affects conservation funding, as revenue from sales could aid wildlife management.

WTO Ministerial Conference MC13 Held in Abu Dhabi

- The 13th WTO Ministerial Conference (MC13) was held in Abu Dhabi from February 26 to 29, 2024. It **focused on crucial trade issues and future agendas for the WTO.**
- **Comoros and Timor-Leste** were officially welcomed as the **165th and 166th members of the WTO** during the conference.
- India called for a permanent solution to public stockholding for food security, emphasized the restoration of the Appellate Body, and opposed the Investment Facilitation Development Agreement (IFD).

SCAN TO GET MULTIPLE CHOICE QUESTIONS

Scan Me

ENVIRONMENT AND ECOLOGY

THE STATE OF THE WORLD'S MANGROVES 2024

Key Points

- **Report title:** "The State of the World's Mangroves 2024"
- **Released by:** Global Mangrove Alliance (GMA)
- **Release date:** World Mangrove Day (26 July 2024)
- **GMA:** An alliance of 100+ members focused on mangrove conservation and restoration

DRIVERS OF MANGROVE LOSS

- Climate change (sea-level rise, increased storm intensity).
- Expansion of industrial shrimp aquaculture (Andhra Pradesh, West Bengal, Gujarat).
- Conversion to oil palm plantations, rice cultivation (43% loss between 2000- 2020).

Highlights of Report

- Southeast Asia has almost about one-third of all mangroves globally (Indonesia alone has 21% of world's mangroves), followed by West and Central Africa.
- Half of world's mangrove provinces are considered threatened (IUCN Red List of Mangrove Ecosystems).
- Mangroves in Lakshadweep archipelago and on coast of Tamil Nadu are critically endangered.
- It maps 147,256 km² of mangroves in 2020, adding data for six new territories.
- Southeast Asia holds about one-third of the world's mangroves, with Indonesia alone accounting for 21%.

MANGROVES

Diverse group of salt-tolerant plant communities found in the (tropical/subtropical) coastal intertidal zone

CHARACTERISTICS

- Survive under hostile environments (high salt, low oxygen)
- Their roots (pneumatophores) absorb oxygen from atmosphere
- Thick succulent leaves to store fresh water

MANGROVE COVER

- **Global:** Asia> Africa> North and Central America > South America
- **India (ISFR 2021):** West Bengal > Gujarat > A&N Islands > Andhra Pradesh > Maharashtra

SIGNIFICANCE

- **Stabilise the coastline** and reduce soil erosion
- **Protection** against cyclones
- **Improve water quality** by absorbing nutrients. Important **carbon sink**

THREATS

- Commercialisation of coastal areas
- Emergence of shrimp farms
- Temperature fluctuations (Mangroves can't survive freezing temperatures)

CONSERVATION MEASURES

Sunderbans - World's largest single patch of Mangrove forests

Global

- Inclusion of Mangroves in Biosphere Reserves and UNESCO Global Geoparks
- Mangroves for the Future Initiative (IUCN & UNDP)
- Mangrove Alliance for Climate (UNFCCC COP27)

India

- National Mangrove Committee (1976)
- Mangrove Initiative for Shoreline Habitats & Tangible Incomes (MISHTI) (Union Budget 2023-24)

International day for conservation of the mangrove ecosystem - July 26 (UNESCO)

Initiatives for Mangroves

India

- Mangrove Initiative for Shoreline Habitats & Tangible Incomes (MISHTI).
- Sustainable Aquaculture in Mangrove Ecosystem (SAIME).

Global

- Mangrove Breakthrough by GMA.
- Mangrove Alliance for Climate, headed by UAE in partnership with Indonesia.

Benefits of Mangroves

- Support variety of plants and animals e.g. Over 5,700 plant/animal species have been recorded in Indian mangroves.
- Acts as carbon sinks i.e. store an average of 394 tonnes of carbon per hectare.
- Protect coastal regions from disasters i.e. Reduce flood depths by 15- 20%, and over 70% in some areas.
- Fish and seafood sourced from mangrove ecosystems are often rich in essential nutrients like protein, omega-3 fatty acids, vitamins (e.g. vitamins D and B12), and minerals (e.g., iron, zinc).
- Improves water quality through filtering pollutants and trapping sediments.

MANGROVE STATUS IN INDIA

- The report reveals that large swathes of mangrove forests along India's southern coast are critically endangered.
- In particular, mangroves in the Lakshadweep archipelago and along the coast of Tamil Nadu face rising sea levels due to global warming.
- On India's western seaboard, extending from Gujarat to Kerala, mangroves are vulnerable to collapse.
- The GMA attributes these vulnerabilities to a combination of natural threats, such as tropical storms, and human activities like shrimp aquaculture.

MANGROVES IN INDIA

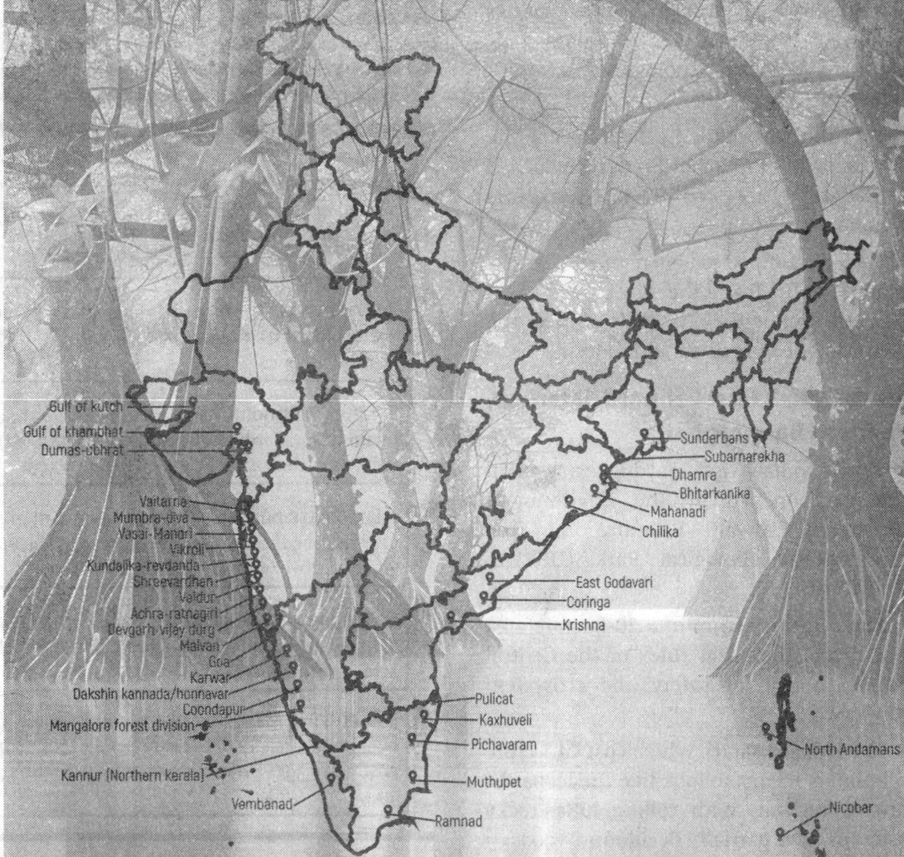

FACTS

- UNESCO observes July 26 as the International Day for the Conservation of the Mangrove Ecosystem.
- As per ISFR 2021, the mangrove cover in India is 4,992 sq km, which is 0.15% of the country's total geographical area.
- West Bengal>Gujarat>A&N Islands>Andhra Pradesh>Maharashtra, have the largest Mangrove cover in India (ISFR 2021).
- In India, mangroves are protected by the Environmental (Protection) Act 1986 and Coastal Zone Regulations.
- Sunderbans, a UNESCO World Heritage Site, is the world's largest single patch of Mangrove Forests.
- Sundarbans is the first Mangrove forest in the world, which was brought under scientific management, as early as in 1892.
- The emergence of shrimp farms is responsible for at least 35% of the overall loss of mangrove forests.

ENVIRONMENT AND ECOLOGY

Odisha Villages Recognised as Tsunami Ready by UNESCO

- In November 2024, 24 coastal villages in Odisha were recognised as tsunami ready based on validation by the National Tsunami Preparedness Recognition Board (NTRB) during the 2nd Global Tsunami Symposium in Indonesia.
- NTRB implements the Tsunami Preparedness Identification Programme, involving scientists from the Indian National Centre for Ocean Information Services (INCOIS) and officials from the National Disaster Management Authority (NDMA).
- UNESCO targeted 24 tsunami-prone coastal villages falling under six coastal districts of Odisha: Balasore, Bhadrak, Kendrapara, Jagatsinghpur, Puri and Ganjam.

Neelakurinji Added to IUCN Red List as Vulnerable Species

- The Neelakurinji *(Strobilanthes kunthiana)* has been classified as Vulnerable on the IUCN Red List of Threatened Species.
- *Strobilanthes kunthiana* is a three-meter-tall endemic shrub found only in the high-altitude shola grassland habitats of five mountain ranges in southwest India, at elevations ranging from 1,340 to 2,600 meters.
- The Neelakurinji gets its scientific name from the Kunthi River in Kerala's Silent Valley National Park, where it can be found in abundance.

New Horned Frog Species Discovered in Northeast India

- Xenophrys apatani is a new species of horned frog that was just named by scientists from the Zoological Survey of India (ZSI).
- The find was made in the Tale Wildlife Sanctuary in Arunachal Pradesh, which is in the heavily forested northeastern parts of India.
- The new species is named for the Apatani tribe from the Lower Subansiri Valley to honor their work to protect the environment in Arunachal Pradesh.

South India's First Leopard Safari Opens at Bannerghatta

- South India's first and biggest leopard tour was opened by the Environment Minister, Eshwar Khandre at the Bannerghatta Biological Park (BBP) – Bengaluru.
- The safari is set up in a 20-hectare area that meets the strict rules of the Central Zoo Authority for safety and ecosystem mimicry.
- The leopard safari, which cost ₹4.5 crore to build, is meant to look like the leopards' natural habitat, with rolling hills, rocky outcrops, and partially deciduous woods.

Nitin Gadkari inaugurates Oxygen Bird Park in Nagpur, Maharashtra

- Union Minister of Road Transport and Highways Sh. Nitin Gadkari inaugurated Oxygen Bird Park (Amrit Mahotsav Park) along the Nagpur-Hyderabad National Highway-44 in Nagpur, Maharashtra.
- It has a total area of 8.23 hectares, of which 2.5 hectares is dedicated to social forestry.
- The project, which integrates environmental sustainability and recreational facilities, was formally approved in March 2023 with a development cost of ₹14.31 crores.

WHY MANGROVES MATTER

Mangroves consist of a variety of salt-tolerant trees and shrubs that thrive in shallow and muddy saltwater. Mangrove forests can be found in mostly tropical and subtropical coastal regions. There are about 80 species of mangroves globally, 3 of which occur in Belize, and they take up to 15 years to reach maturity.

MANGROVES PROVIDE A VARIETY OF BENEFITS INCLUDING:

1. **Biodiversity Hotspots:** Mangroves are home to an incredible array of species, providing habitat for fish, sharks, rays, sea turtles, and birds. An estimated 80% of the global fish catch relies on mangrove forests either directly or indirectly
2. **Livelihoods:** The fisher communities we work with depend on their natural environment to provide for their families. Healthy mangrove ecosystems mean healthy fisheries
3. **Water Filtration:** Mangroves are vital to maintain seawater quality. They retain flowing sediments, and can trap pollutants, protecting connected habitats such as coral reefs and seagrass beds.
4. **Landmass builders:** The dense network of roots and surrounding vegetation which trap sediment prevents erosion and can buildup coastlines and cayes over time.
5. **Fighting climate change:** Mangroves extract carbon from the atmosphere at a higher rate than tropical forests, and can store up to 5 times more carbon per acre in their soils.
6. **Economy:** Many coastal communities rely on mangroves for their economic benefits, especially in the fisheries and tourism sectors. Mangroves also reduce costly damages from hurricanes by providing protection against wave action and storm surges.

Mangrove roots promote water clarity and provide protection for juvenile fishes.

Juvenile lemon sharks are almost exclusively found in mangrove habitats.

INDIA'S 56TH TIGER RESERVE

Aspect	Details
Tiger Reserve Name	Guru Ghasidas-Tamor Pingla Tiger Reserve
State	Chhattisgarh
Notification	Declared as the 56th Tiger Reserve in India (October 2021)
Area	Total: 2,829.38 sq. km – Core Area: 2,049.2 sq. km – Buffer Area: 780.15 sq. km
Components	– Guru Ghasidas National Park – Tamor Pingla Wildlife Sanctuary
Geographical Location	– Located in Chota Nagpur Plateau & partly in Baghelkhand Plateau – Spread across Manendragarh, Chirmiri, Bharatpur, Korea, Surajpur, Balrampur
Rank in Size	3rd largest Tiger Reserve in India after Nagarjunasagar-Srisailam (Andhra Pradesh) & Manas (Assam)
Chhattisgarh's Tiger Reserves	Chhattisgarh now has 4 Tiger Reserves, contributing greatly to tiger conservation

World's Oldest Termite Mounds Discovered in Namaqualand

- Recently, Scientists have discovered the world's oldest, inhabited termite mounds along the Buffels River in Namaqualand.
- These mounds, dating back a staggering 34,000 years, are rewriting our understanding of prehistoric life, climate and carbon storage.

German Scientists Discover Plastic-Eating Fungi for Waste Reduction

- Scientists in Germany have found fungi that can eat plastic, which could help tackle the global problem of plastic pollution.
- The study identified 18 fungal strains, with four showing a strong ability to degrade plastics, especially polyurethane.
- In 2011, Pestalotiopsis microspora was found in the Amazon rainforest and was noted for its ability to degrade plastic even in low-oxygen environments.

IndusInd Bank Partners with UNICEF for Climate Action

- IndusInd Bank has partnered with UNICEF to tackle climate risks, which aims to enhance community resilience in five Indian districts.
- The partnership will focus on five districts:
  - Dharashiv, Maharashtra
  - Begusarai, Bihar
  - Virudhunagar, Tamil Nadu
  - Baran, Rajasthan
  - Bahraich, Uttar Pradesh

New Frog Species Discovered in Meghalaya

- A team of scientists from SACON (The Sálim Ali Centre for Ornithology and Natural History) in Anaikatti, has discovered a new frog species during a two-year study in Meghalaya.
- They called the species *'Raorchestes asakgrensis'* after the discovery site, the Eman Asakgre Community Reserve in Meghalaya's Garo Hills.
- The research team conducted nocturnal surveys across 13 sites in the Garo and Khasi Hills between October 2020 and January 2022 to locate and study bush frogs.

- This discovery took place over two years, from October 2020 to January 2022.
- The research team surveyed various locations in the Garo and Khasi Hills, which were published in the journal Herpetozoa on November 18.

India Ranks 10th in Climate Change Index 2025

- India has been evaluated in the Climate Change Performance Index (CCPI) 2025 and ranks 10th among over 60 countries.
- This evaluation assesses efforts to combat climate change and the report was released during the UN climate conference in Baku.
- The top three spots in the report are vacant, followed by Denmark and the Netherlands, while the two biggest emitters, China and the US, are ranked 55th and 57th respectively.

Lucknow's First Night Safari Project Unveiled

- The Uttar Pradesh government is developing India's inaugural night safari in Lucknow. Construction commenced recently, with a projected completion date of June 26, 2026, which will open its doors to visitors in December 2026.
- The night safari will span a 900-acre area within the Kukrail forest, which is designed in the shape of a maple leaf. The safari will be the fifth of its kind globally.
- The concept of a night safari originated in Singapore in 1994.

Unique Mineral Chimneys Discovered in the Dead Sea Floor

- Researchers have discovered unique mineral chimneys on the Dead Sea floor, which are a result of highly salty groundwater.
- The chimneys can reach heights of up to 7 meters, that can grow several centimeters daily. Their widths range from 2 to 3 meters.

Cyclone Dana

- Cyclonic Storm Dana was a tropical cyclone which affected the states of West Bengal and Odisha in India.
- Dana's name was suggested by Qatar, which means generosity.
- The third cyclonic storm and second severe cyclonic storm of the 2024 North Indian Ocean cyclone season, Dana formed from a low pressure area that the Indian Meteorological Department first monitored on October 20.

Typhoon Yagi

- In early September 2024, Typhoon Yagi became the strongest storm of the year in Asia, hitting several countries like Myanmar, Vietnam, Laos, and Thailand.
- Yagi, which means goat or the constellation of Capricornus in Japanese, was the eleventh named storm, the first violent typhoon of the season, and the first super typhoon of the annual typhoon season.

ZSI and Odisha Forest Department Launch Project to Tag Horseshoe Crabs

- Recently, the Zoological Survey of India (ZSI) and the Odisha Forest Department have launched a project to tag horseshoe crabs.
- India has two species of horseshoe crabs: Tachypleus gigas, found on the Odisha coast, and Carcinoscorpius rotundicauda, found in the Sundarbans mangroves of West Bengal.
- Both species are protected under India's Wildlife Protection Act of 1972.

INDIA'S 57TH TIGER RESERVE

Aspect	Details
Tiger Reserve Name	Ratapani Tiger Reserve
State	Madhya Pradesh (8th Tiger Reserve)
Ecological Significance	- Home to teak forests, significant wildlife, and Bhimbetka Rock Shelters (UNESCO World Heritage Site). - Includes historical and religious sites like Ginnourgarh Fort, POW camp, Keri Mahadeo, Ratapani Dam, etc.
Area Breakdown	Core Area: 763.8 sq km, Buffer Area: 507.6 sq km, Total area: 1,271.4 sq km
Legal & Administrative Aspects	- Declared under Section 38V of Wildlife Protection Act, 1972. - Protection of the tiger population and the fragile ecosystem.
Future Developments	- Madhav National Park to be declared a tiger reserve soon, further expanding MP's tiger reserve network.

Tawa Reservoir - 83rd Ramsar Site

Designation: Notified as the 2547th Ramsar Site of India.
Location: Narmadapuram District, Madhya Pradesh.
Area: 20,050 ha.
Creation: Man-made wetland created by constructing Tawa Dam for irrigation.
Significance: Located within the Satpura Tiger Reserve, Central Indian Highlands.
Ecological role: Supports 57 fish species, 21 mammals, and over 280 migratory bird species.
Notable Fauna: Habitat for the Indian giant squirrel (*Ratufa indica*) and state fish tor mahseer (*Tor tor*), revered by local communities.

Nanjarayan Bird Sanctuary - 84th Ramsar Site

Designation: Notified as the 2549th Ramsar Site of India.
Location: Tiruppur District, Tamil Nadu.
Area: 125.9 ha.
Creation: Freshwater lake constructed 400 years ago by King Nanjarayan.
Significance: Habitat for 191 bird species, 87 butterflies, and other aquatic and terrestrial species.
Notable Fauna: Nesting habitat for Indian darter (Anhinga melanogaster) and Indian flapshell turtle (Lissemys punctata).

Kazhuveli Bird Sanctuary -85th Ramsar Site

Designation: Notified as the 2548th Ramsar Site of India.
Location: Tamil Nadu.
Area: 5,151.6 ha.
Creation: Second largest brackish lake in Peninsular India, connected to the Bay of Bengal.
Significance: Habitat for 229 bird species, 85 fish, and other diverse fauna.
Notable Fauna: Nesting site for spot-billed pelicans (*Pelecanus philippensis*) and feeding grounds for spotted eagle (*Aquila clanga*). Recognized as a Bird Sanctuary in 2021.

Points to Remember

- India is one of the parties to Ramsar Convention, which was framed in Ramsar, Iran, in 1971.
- India became a signatory to the convention on February 1, 1982.
- Between 1982 and 2013, India added a total of 26 sites to the list of Ramsar sites; since 2014 , the country has added 59 new wetlands to the list of Ramsar sites.
- Tamil Nadu has the maximum number of Ramsar Sites (18 sites) followed by Uttar Pradesh (10 sites).

LIST OF RAMSAR SITES

S.No	Ramsar Site	State/UT	Designated Date	Area (Hectares)
1	**Nanjarayan Bird Sanctuary**	**Tamil Nadu**	**16 January 2024**	**125.865**
2	**Kazhuveli Bird Sanctuary**	**Tamil Nadu**	**16 January 2024**	**5151.6**
3	**Tawa Reservoir**	**Madhya Pradesh**	**08 January 2024**	**20050**
4	**Nagi Bird Sanctuary**	**Bihar (Jamui)**	**07 June 2024**	**205.8**
5	**Nakti Bird Sanctuary**	**Bihar**	**07 June 2024**	**332.6**
6	Kolleru Lake	Andhra Pradesh	19 August 2002	90100
7	Deepor Beel	Assam	19 August 2002	4000
8	Kanwar Taal or Kabar Taal Lake	Bihar	21 July 2020	2620
9	Nalsarovar	Gujarat	24 September 2012	12000
10	Wadhvana Wetland	Gujarat	05 April 2021	630
11	Thol Lake	Gujarat	05 April 2021	699
12	Khijadia Wildlife Sanctuary	Gujarat	02 February 2022	512
13	Nanda Lake	Goa	8 June 2022	42
14	Sultanpur National Park	Haryana	25 May 2021	143
15	Bhindawas Wildlife Sanctuary	Haryana	25 May 2021	412
16	Pong Dam Lake	Himachal Pradesh	19 August 2002	15662
17	Chandertal Wetland	Himachal Pradesh	8 November 2005	49
18	Renuka Wetland	Himachal Pradesh	8 November 2005	20
19	Wular Lake	Jammu and Kashmir	23 March 1990	18900
20	Surinsar-Mansar Lakes	Jammu and Kashmir	8 November 2005	350
21	Hokera Wetland	Jammu and Kashmir	8 November 2005	1375
22	Hygam Wetland Conservation Reserve	Jammu and Kashmir	8 November 2022	802
23	Shallbugh Wetland Conservation Reserve	Jammu and Kashmir	8 November 2022	1675
24	Ranganathittu Bird Sanctuary	Karnataka	15 February 2022	518
25	Ankasamudra Bird Conservation Reserve	Karnataka	26 April 2023	98.76
26	Aghanashini Estuary	Karnataka	26 April 2023	4801
27	Magadi Kere Conservation Reserve	Karnataka	26 April 2023	54.38
28	Asthamudi Wetland	Kerala	19 August 2002	6140
29	Sasthamkotta Lake	Kerala	19 August 2002	373
30	VembanadKol Wetland	Kerala	19 August 2002	151250
31	Tso Kar Wetland Complex	Ladakh	17 November 2020	9577
32	Tsomoriri Lake	Ladakh	19 August 2002	12000
33	Bhoj Wetlands	Madhya Pradesh	19 August 2002	3201
34	Sirpur Wetland	Madhya Pradesh	26 February 2022	161
35	Sakhya Sagar	Madhya Pradesh	26 February 2022	248
36	Yashwant Sagar	Madhya Pradesh	26 February 2022	823
37	Nandur Madhameshwar	Maharashtra	21 June 2019	1437
38	Lonar Lake	Maharashtra	22 July 2020	427
39	Thane Creek	Maharashtra	14 September 2022	6521
40	Loktak Lake	Manipur	23 March 1990	26600
41	Pala Wetland	Mizoram	28 April 2021	1850
42	Chilka Lake	Odisha	1 October 1981	116500
43	Bhitarkanika Mangroves	Odisha	19 August 2002	65000
44	Satkosia Gorge	Odisha	24 August 2021	98197
45	Tampara Lake	Odisha	24 August 2021	300
46	Hirakud Reservoir	Odisha	24 August 2021	65400
47	Ansupa Lake	Odisha	24 August 2021	231
48	Harike Lake	Punjab	23 March 1990	4100
49	Kanjli Lake	Punjab	22 January 2002	183
50	Ropar Lake	Punjab	22 January 2002	1365
51	Beas Conservation Reserve	Punjab	26 September 2019	6429
52	Keshopur – Miani Community Reserve	Punjab	26 September 2019	344
53	Nangal Wildlife Sanctuary	Punjab	26 September 2019	116
54	Keoladeo Ghana National Park	Rajasthan	1 October 1981	2873
55	Sambhar Lake	Rajasthan	23 March 1990	24000
56	Point Calimere Wildlife and Bird Sanctuary	Tamil Nadu	19 August 2002	38500

S.No	Ramsar Site	State/UT	Designated Date	Area (Hectares)
57	Koonthankulam Bird Sanctuary	Tamil Nadu	8 April 2021	72
58	Chitrangudi Bird Sanctuary	Tamil Nadu	8 April 2021	260
59	Karikili Bird Sanctuary	Tamil Nadu	13 June 2022	58
60	Pichavaram Mangrove	Tamil Nadu	13 June 2022	1479
61	Pallikaranai Marsh Reserve Forest	Tamil Nadu	13 June 2022	1248
62	Gulf of Mannar Marine Biosphere Reserve	Tamil Nadu	13 June 2022	52672
63	Vembannur Wetland Complex	Tamil Nadu	13 June 2022	20
64	Vellode Bird Sanctuary	Tamil Nadu	13 June 2022	77
65	Udhayamarthandapuram Bird Sanctuary	Tamil Nadu	13 June 2022	44
66	Vedanthangal Bird Sanctuary	Tamil Nadu	13 June 2022	40
67	Suchindram Theroor Wetland Complex	Tamil Nadu	13 June 2022	94
68	Vaduvur Bird Sanctuary	Tamil Nadu	13 June 2022	113
69	Kanjirankulam Bird Sanctuary	Tamil Nadu	13 June 2022	97
70	Karaivetti Bird Sanctuary	Tamil Nadu	13 February 2023	453.72
71	Longwood Shola Reserve Forest	Tamil Nadu	13 February 2023	116.007
72	Rudrasagar Lake	Tripura	8 November 2005	240
73	Upper Ganga River	Uttar Pradesh	8 November 2005	26590
74	Nawabganj Bird Sanctuary	Uttar Pradesh	19 September 2019	225
75	Parvati Arga Bird Sanctuary	Uttar Pradesh	2 December 2019	722
76	Saman Bird Sanctuary	Uttar Pradesh	2 December 2019	526
77	Samaspur Bird Sanctuary	Uttar Pradesh	3 October 2019	799
78	Sandi Bird Sanctuary	Uttar Pradesh	26 September 2019	309
79	Sarsai Nawar Jheel	Uttar Pradesh	19 September 2019	161
80	Sur Sarovar	Uttar Pradesh	21 August 2020	431
81	Haiderpur Wetland	Uttar Pradesh	13 April 2021	6908
82	Bakhira Wildlife Sanctuary	Uttar Pradesh	2 February 2022	2894
83	Asan Conservation Reserve	Uttarakhand	21 July 2020	444
84	East Calcutta Wetlands	West Bengal	19 August 2002	12500
85	Sunderbans Wetland	West Bengal	30 January 2019	423000

Novel Hydrogel Removes Microplastics From Water

- To combat microplastics pollutant, researchers at the **Indian Institute of Science (IISc)** have designed a sustainable hydrogel to remove microplastics from water.
- The material has a unique intertwined polymer network that can bind the contaminants and degrade them **using UV light irradiation.**
- The novel hydrogel developed by the team consists of three different polymer layers – **chitosan, polyvinyl alcohol and polyaniline** – intertwined together, making an Interpenetrating Polymer Network (IPN) architecture.

Global Forest Watch (GFW)

- The latest data from the Global Forest Watch (GFW) monitoring project has revealed that India has lost **2.33 million hectares** of tree cover since the year 2000.
- The GFW data reveals that India lost a staggering **4,14,000 hectares** of humid primary forest (approximately 4.1% of the total tree cover) between 2002 and 2023.
- A striking 95% of the tree cover loss in India between 2013 and 2023 occurred within natural forests.
- Assam experienced the highest tree cover loss at 324,000 hectares (compared to an average of 66,600 hectares).

Himalayan Wolf Listed As 'Vulnerable' In IUCN

- The Himalayan Wolf (Canis lupus chanco) has been assessed for the first time in the International Union for Conservation of Nature **(IUCN)'s Red List.**
- The animal has been categorised as **'Vulnerable'** on the IUCN Red List.

Fourth Biodiversity Heritage Site In Odisha

- **Gupteswar forest,** located near the Gupteswar Shiva temple within the **Dhondrakhol reserve forest** of the Jeypore forest division in Odisha's Koraput district, has been officially recognized as the **state's fourth** Biodiversity Heritage Site (BHS).

Denmark Announces Alliance On Green Fuels In India

- Denmark has announced its **Green Fuels Alliance India (GFAI)** initiative to boost collaborative efforts between the two countries in the sustainable energy solutions sector and advance their joint global goal towards carbon neutrality.
- GFAI's primary objective is to promote sustainable energy growth in India by establishing an ecosystem that encourages collaboration among businesses, government entities, research institutions, and financial stakeholders from both the Indian and Danish sectors.

Rising acidity threatens Antarctic Shelf Ecosystems

- A new study has raised concerns about the **rising acidity levels** of the continental shelves in Antarctic Marine Protected Areas (MPA) under high levels of greenhouse gas emissions.
- Carbon emissions from human activities may be vertically mixed with ocean waters in coastal regions, resulting in severe acidification at all water levels.

Union Cabinet approved ₹8,500 Crore VGF for Coal Gasification

- The Union Cabinet, led by Prime Minister Narendra Modi, has approved the Ministry of Coal's proposal to launch the **coal and lignite gasification program.**

- The program entails a Viability Gap Funding (VGF) of **₹8,500 crore** to be extended to both public and private sectors.
- A provision of ₹4,050 crore will be exclusively available for government Public Sector Undertakings (PSUs).
- In coal gasification, coal is chemically transformed into syngas using steam and controlled oxygen.

Tamil Nadu Endangered Species Conservation Fund (TNESCF)

- The Tamil Nadu Government has announced the establishment of a first-of-its-kind Tamil Nadu Endangered Species Conservation Fund **(TNESCF) of ₹50 crore.**
- The fund will aid in the conservation of species, particularly those native to the state.

SIDBI secures first green climate fund project worth $120 million

- **SIDBI** has secured approval from the Green Climate Fund (GCF) for its first anchored project, **Avaana Sustainability Fund (ASF),** valued at USD 120 million.
- The closure was announced at the 38th board meeting of the GCF, which will invest USD 24.5 million in the fund, in Kigali, Rwanda, on March 5, SIDBI, an accredited entity of GCF.
- The primary aim of the ASF project is to invest in early-stage companies harnessing technology-led innovation to spur climate solutions and sustainability in the country.

National Action Plan for Prevention and Control of Snakebite Envenoming in India

- Shri Apurva Chandra, Union Health Secretary launched a National Action Plan for Prevention and Control of Snakebite Envenoming (NAP-SE) in India.
- With a vision to reduce snakebite deaths by halve by 2030, NAPSE provides a broad framework for states to develop their own action plan for management, prevention and control of snakebites through the **'One Health'** approach.
- **Snakebite envenoming** is a significant health issue in India, causing around 50,000 deaths annually.

Bhutan hosts summit targeting $1 billion USD for the conservation of tiger landscapes

- On Earth Day 2024, the Royal Government of Bhutan hosted the **Sustainable Finance for Tiger Landscapes Conference** under the patronage of her majesty the Queen, Jetsun Pema Wangchuck.
- The Conference launches the ambition to mobilise $1 billion USD in new funding over ten years for the **preservation of tiger landscapes.**

Scientists discover Leaf Litter Frog that emits ultrasonic sounds

- Researchers have discovered that the **Leaf Litter Frog** makes noises that are too low for people to hear, yet they have the ability to frighten off predators.
- It lives on forest edges and main and secondary forests. Usually, one can find it on the **leaves of low plants** within the forest or in the leaf litter on the forest floor.
- This particular species of frog is exclusive to the **Atlantic rainforest in Brazil.**

G7 commits to Net Zero Emissions by 2050

- The Group of Seven (G7), consisting of **Canada, France, Germany, Italy, Japan, the United Kingdom, and the United States,** has taken a significant step toward combating climate change.
- The G7 nations recognize the importance of aligning official international financing with **global net zero goals** and have called on all countries, especially major emitting economies, to join this effort.

Venezuela first country to loose all its glaciers

- **Venezuela** has become the **first Andean country** to lose all of its glaciers.
- **The Humboldt Glacier,** also known as **La Corona,** located in the Sierra Nevada, has now been reclassified as an ice field due to significant shrinkage.
- This reclassification marks a grim milestone, making Venezuela the first country in the Americas and the first globally to lose all its glaciers.

Global Report on Internal Displacement 2024 (GRID-2024)

- The **2024 Global Report on Internal Displacement (GRID)** presents data and analysis on the **75.9 million people** living in internal displacement as of the end of 2023.
- This **ninth edition** of the GRID provides global and regional insights into the risk, scale, and impacts of internal displacement.
- Notably, there were **46.9 million internal displacements** recorded during 2023 across 151 countries and territories. These movements occurred due to both conflict and disaster events.

GAIL (India) Limited first Green Hydrogen Plant

- GAIL (India) Limited has taken a significant step towards sustainable energy by installing its **first Green Hydrogen Plant at GAIL Vijaipur** in Madhya Pradesh.
- The plant utilizes **10MW PEM** (Proton Exchange Membrane) Electrolyzer units to produce **4.3 TPD (tonnes per day)** of hydrogen through the electrolysis of water using renewable power.

First Global Mangrove Assessment

- The First Global Mangrove Assessment is a groundbreaking initiative that evaluates the health and risks faced by mangrove ecosystems worldwide.
- Conducted using the **IUCN Red List of Ecosystems,** this assessment sheds light on the urgent need for coordinated conservation efforts.
- Mangroves, covering approximately 150,000 km^2 along tropical and sub-tropical coasts, play a crucial role in biodiversity conservation, climate change mitigation, and supporting local communities.

Greening India's Wastelands with Agroforestry

- **NITI Aayog** launched the Greening and Restoration of Wasteland with Agroforestry (GROW) report and portal.
- The GROW initiative aims to restore **26 million hectares** of degraded land by 2030.
- Agroforestry covers 8.65% of India's total geographical area, approximately 28.42 million hectares.

Eurasian Otter In The Chinnar Wildlife Sanctuary

- A team of researchers have discovered **Eurasian otter** in the Chinnar Wildlife Sanctuary in **Kerala.**
- Otters are mammals of the family Mustelidae consisting of 13 species.
- They are found in every continent except **Australia and Antarctica.**
- The Eurasian otter covers the largest range of any **Palearctic mammal.**

Peninsular Hill Trout

- Scientists have decoded for the first time the **mitochondrial genome** of Peninsular Hill Trout.
- It is known locally as **'Brahmanakenda'.**
- It is a unique **freshwater fish species** of the Western Ghats.
- It is known to occur only inside **Kerala's Periyar Tiger Reserve.**

Vulture Restaurant In Jharkhand

- A 'Vulture Restaurant' has been established in **Koderma of Jharkhand** to conserve the declining vulture population.
- It is an undisturbed area where non-toxic, poison-free meat and carcasses are provided for vultures and other scavengers.
- The initiative aims to address the adverse impact of livestock drugs, particularly diclofenac, on vultures.

Status Report Of Snow Leopards In India

- India's first nationwide report, **'Status Report of Snow Leopards in India'**, was released by the Government of India recently.
- The assessment estimates **718 snow leopards in India** based on systematic surveys covering over 70% of their potential habitat from 2019-2023.

Melanistic Tiger (Black Tiger)

- Odisha is going to set up a **melanistic tiger safari,** a first of its kind in the world near **Similipal Tiger Reserve (STR).**
- The Safari will give a chance to the tourists to see "the rare and majestic" melanistic tiger species found only in Odisha and to create awareness about the need for their conservation.
- Simlipal has the world's highest rate of **black tiger** sightings in the world.

Wetland City Accreditation Scheme

- India has nominated **Indore, Bhopal and Udaipur** for the Wetland City Accreditation (WCA) scheme under the Ramsar Convention.
- These are the first three Indian cities nominated for WCA based on the proposals received from state wetlands authorities in collaboration with municipal corporations.
- This will provide an opportunity for cities that value their natural or human-made wetlands to gain international recognition.

Cameroon Adopted Nagoya Protocol

- Cameroon, located in central Africa and boasting a rich biodiversity with around 11,000 species of plants, animals, and microorganisms, has recently adopted the **Nagoya Protocol** on Access and Benefit Sharing, an agreement under the United Nations Convention on Biological Diversity (UNCBD).
- The Nagoya Protocol aims to promote the fair and equitable sharing of benefits arising from the utilization of genetic resources.

Dusted Apollo sighted in Himachal Pradesh

- **Dusted Apollo** has been sighted and photographed for the first time in **Himachal Pradesh.**
- This species is extremely rare and was **discovered in 1890.**
- The distribution range of Dusted Apollo extends from **Ladakh to West Nepal,** and it flies between 3,500 and 4,800 meters in the inner Himalayas.

First Successful Embryo Transfer In White Rhinos

- Scientists performed the first successful embryo transfer in white rhinos with the help of **In-vitro fertilization (IVF).**
- Scientists in Berlin announced the first successful embryo transfer in a white rhinoceros using a method that offers hope for saving the critically endangered northern white rhino subspecies from extinction.
- The white rhinoceros includes two distinct subspecies, **northern and southern.**

Sea Slug Named After President Of India Droupadi Murmu

- Zoological Survey of India named a new marine species of **head-shield sea** slug after President of India **Droupadi Murmu.**
- The Zoological Survey of India (ZSI) has identified this species of marine head-shield sea slug discovered along the **West Bengal and Odisha coasts.**
- **Melanochlamys droupadi** is a small invertebrate, measuring up to **7 mm** in length, with a brownish-black coloration.

Survey Of Golden Langurs

- A recent survey conducted by a collaboration of wildlife research and conservation organizations, including the Primate Research Centre NE India (PRCNE), Assam Forest Department, Bodoland Territorial Council, Salim Ali Centre for Ornithology and Natural History (SACON), and Conservation Himalayas, has estimated the **population of golden langurs in India at 7,396 individuals.**
- This endangered primate, **Trachypithecusgeei**, is found exclusively in the **Manas Biosphere Reserve** and fragmented forests in **western Assam.**

Ministry Of Petroleum Has Launched 'ethanol 100'

- Ministry of Petroleum has launched **'ETHANOL 100'**, an automotive fuel, at the **IndianOil Retail Outlet.**
- Customers can avail ETHANOL 100 at select **183 retail outlets** across five states – **Maharashtra, Karnataka, Uttar Pradesh, New Delhi, and Tamil Nadu.**
- ETHANOL 100, touted as a cleaner and greener substitute for gasoline, boasts significantly lower emissions of greenhouse gases and pollutants.

Largest River Dolphin remain of 'Pebanista Yacuruna' Found

- Scientists have discovered the **16-million-year-old remains** of the "largest river dolphin ever found" after unearthing a huge fossilised skull in the Amazon.
- Named **Pebanista yacuruna,** researchers at the **University of Zurich** found the new species in the Peruvian Amazon region.

IIT-Roorkee Researchers Found Vasuki Indicus

- Researchers at the department of earth sciences in **IIT-Roorkee** have claimed to have discovered fossils of "one of the largest snakes to have lived on earth" around 47 million years ago,measuring **11-15m.**
- Vasuki refers to the mythical snake often depicted around the neck of the Hindu god Shiva.
- The reptile **existed 47 million years ago** during a period called the **Middle Eocene,** when Africa, India and South America were one, conjoined landmass.
- It likely had a broad and cylindrical body, hinting at a robust and powerful build and was as big as **Titanoboa,** a massive snake that once roamed the earth and is reportedly the longest ever known.
- Much like present-day pythons and anaconda, **Vasuki Indicus** killed its prey by suffocation.

Extinction Of A West African Red Colobus Monkey

- Recently, it has been noticed that the **Red colobus monkeys** are threatened by poachers in Africa.
- Red colobus monkeys are found only in **sub-Saharan Africa,** ranging from Senegal in the west to the Zanzibar Archipelago in the east.
- These monkeys inhabit a diversity of forests, including rainforest, riparian forest, or mangrove swamp.
- IUCN Red List assessments indicate that every form of red colobus monkey is threatened with extinction, and **14 of the 18 taxa** are listed as Critically Endangered or Endangered.

Sea Anemone Bleaching Off Agatti Island

- **Sea anemone bleaching** has been observed for the first time in the **Lakshadweep islands,** which is a cause for concern for the local ecological system.
- Bleaching is making sea anemones more susceptible to diseases and increasing mortality.
- Sea anemones are predatory marine invertebrates belonging to the order **Actiniaria.** These aquatic animals are known for their soft bodies and stinging capabilities, which they use for capturing prey and defense.

World Wildlife Crime Report 2024

- The United Nations Office on Drugs and Crime has released the World Wildlife Crime Report 2024.
- The market for rhino horn (29 percent) constituted the biggest chunk among animal species.
- It was followed by the market for pangolin scales at 28 percent, followed by the market for elephant ivory at 15 percent.

Baobab Forests Of Madagascar

- Madagascar's baobab forests are being restored with the help of **Artificial Intelligence (AI)** using satellite footage, algorithms and remote sensings.
- The Madagascar Baobab is a tree species known for its impressive characteristics, including giant trunks and an extended lifespan. It is worth mentioning that **six out of the world's eight** baobab species are native to Madagascar.
- The IUCN Red List of Threatened Species categorizes the Madagascar Baobab as **"Least Concern."**

New Plant Species Emblica Chakrabartyi

- Recently, a new plant species **Emblica chakrabartyi** has been discovered in the **Edamalayar forest range** of Kerala.
- This new plant is the **16th new plant species** discovered from Ernakulam district within a span of 12 years.
- **55 species** of the **Genus** Emblica have been recorded all around the world. Emblica chakrabartyi is the **eleventh from India.**

India's First Biosphere Within A Tiger Reserve

- Environmentalists Jai Dhar Gupta and Vijay Dhasmana have established India's first biosphere within a tiger reserve. Named the Rajaji Raghati Biosphere (RRB), it is located in the Rajaji National Park in Uttarakhand.
- The Rajaji Raghati Biosphere (RRB), situated within the Rajaji National Park in Uttarakhand, spans a 35-acre private forest initiative.
- This biosphere focuses on identifying and reviving rare and endangered species of native trees, transforming previously barren and degraded land by removing non-native eucalyptus trees and implementing water retention, erosion prevention, and groundwater recharge techniques.

Wartsila Launches World's First Large-Scale 100% Hydrogen-Ready Engine Power Plant

- Wartsila has launched the world's first large-scale 100% hydrogen-ready engine power plant.
- This plant can operate on natural gas and blends containing up to 25% hydrogen, showcasing significant advancements in clean energy technology.
- It ensures energy security through fuel flexibility, enabling seamless transition between natural gas and hydrogen blends.

LEARN THROUGH MAP

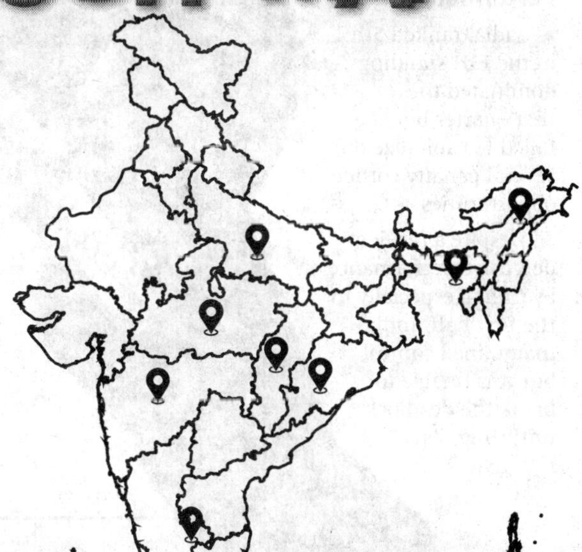

Mark the States/Regions/Initiative in above Map

1. Guru Ghasidas-Tamor Pingla Tiger Reserve is located in which Indian state?
2. Where was the frog species Raorchestes asakgrensis discovered?
3. Which Indian state houses the Tale Wildlife Sanctuary, where the new horned frog species Xenophrys apatani was found?
4. In which city is South India's first leopard safari located?
5. The Oxygen Bird Park inaugurated by Nitin Gadkari is in which Indian state?
6. India's first night safari, currently under construction, is being developed in which city?
7. UNESCO has recognized tsunami-ready villages in which Indian state?
8. Ratapani Tiger Reserve, declared as India's 57th Tiger Reserve, is located in which state?

Scan Me

SCAN TO GET MULTIPLE CHOICE QUESTIONS

Answer Key (Map):

1. Chhattisgarh 2. Meghalaya 3. Arunachal Pradesh 4. Bengaluru, Karnataka 5. Maharashtra 6. Lucknow, Uttar Pradesh 7. Odisha 8. Madhya Pradesh

Hero

SPORTS AND GAMES

ASIAN CHAMPIONS TROPHY

MOQI, CHINA 2024

Indian men's hockey team won the Asian Champions Trophy 2024 in China by defeating China 1-0 in the final.

Edition: 5th

Host Nation: Moqi, China

Third Place: Pakistan defeated South Korea 5-2 to claim the bronze medal.

Participating Teams:

- India
- Pakistan
- China
- Japan
- South Korea
- Malaysia

Match Highlights

- Jugraj Singh scored the lone goal of the match, securing India's victory in a tense fourth-quarter battle.
- India, the defending champions, claimed their 5th title in this prestigious tournament, with previous wins in 2011, 2016, 2018 (shared with Pakistan), 2023, and now 2024.
- The final marked India's sixth appearance in the tournament's final, while China made its maiden final appearance.

Tournament Performance

- India, ranked 5th in the FIH standings, dominated the first quarter but failed to capitalize on several penalty corner opportunities.
- Despite a resilient defensive performance by China, especially in the first half, India maintained control but was unable to break the deadlock until Jugraj's late goal.

- Harmanpreet Singh, who assisted Jugraj's goal in the finals, finished the tournament as India's top scorer and second overall with seven goals, including two field goals and five penalty corners.
- Harmanpreet was named Player of the Tournament.

Individual Awards

Yang Jihun (Korea) was the **Top Goal Scorer** with **nine** goals.

Kim Jaehan (Korea) was awarded **Promising Goalkeeper of the Tournament.**

Wang Caiyu (China) was named **Best Goalkeeper.**

Hanan Shahid (Pakistan) earned the **Rising Star of the Tournament award.**

ASIAN MEN'S HOCKEY CHAMPIONS TROPHY WINNER LIST

Year	Winner	Runner-up
2024	India	China
2023	India	Malaysia
2021	South Korea	Japan
2018	India and Pakistan (joint winners)	-
2016	India	Pakistan
2013	Pakistan	Japan
2012	Pakistan	India
2011	India	Pakistan

Notable Facts

The Asian Champions Trophy is an annual competition organized by the Asian Hockey Federation (AHF) since 2011, with participation from 6 Asian nations.

India won the inaugural edition in 2011 by defeating Pakistan in a penalty shootout, and has since become the most successful team in the tournament's history.

ASIAN HOCKEY FEDERATION

EVER ONWARDS

CRICKET

Cricketer Ravichandran Ashwin retires from International Cricket

- India off-spinner Ravichandran Ashwin has retired from international cricket.
- The 38-year-old, the seventh-highest wicket-taker in Test history, made the announcement after the drawn third Test against Australia in Brisbane.
- With 765 wickets in his credit, Ashwin is the second-highest wicket-taker from India after Anil Kumble.
- Ashwin started his first-class career for Tamil Nadu in a Ranji Trophy Match against Haryana in Chennai in December 2006.

Shaheen Afridi Becomes First Pakistan Bowler To Take 100 Wickets In Each Format

- Pakistan pacer Shaheen Afridi becomes country first bowler to take 100 wickets in each format of international cricket.
- Shaheen Afridi got to the milestone in the first T20I against South Africa.The hosts defeated Pakistan by 11 runs in the match.
- Shaheen also became the youngest to achieve the feat and joined the ranks of New Zealand's Tim Southee, Bangladesh's Shakib Al Hasan, and Sri Lanka's Lasith Malinga.

India Wins inaugural U-19 Women's Asia Cup champion

- India beat Bangladesh by 41 runs in the final to clinch the inaugural Women's U-19 Asia Cup at the Bayuemas Oval in Kuala Lumpur.
- Gongadi Trisha top-scored with 52 runs, while Aayyushi Shukla claimed 3 wickets.

ICC Honours 6 Nations with ICC Development Award for Associate Cricket

- The International Cricket Council (ICC) awarded six nations with the ICC Development Award for 2023, recognizing their contributions to associate cricket.
- The honourees include Mexico, Oman, Netherlands, UAE, Nepal, and Scotland.
- The award celebrates the impactful work these countries have done to grow the sport globally, both on and off the field.

India Champions Win World Championship of Legends 2024

- India Champions, led by Yuvraj Singh, defeated Pakistan Champions by five wickets in the 2024 World Championship of Legends final in Birmingham.
- India successfully chased down a target of 157 runs in 19.1 overs to claim the title.

Women's T20 World Cup 2024 Moved to UAE

- On 20 August 2024, the ICC announced the Women's T20 World Cup 2024 would be moved from Bangladesh to the UAE.
- The move was due to civil unrest in Bangladesh.
- The tournament was held from 3 to 20 October 2024 in Dubai and Sharjah.
- The ICC thanked the Emirates Cricket Board and confirmed Bangladesh would host a future ICC event.

ICC WOMEN'S T20 WORLD CUP 2024
Whatever It Takes

Dates	3 – 20 October 2024
Administrator(s)	International Cricket Council
Cricket format	Twenty20 International
Tournament format(s)	Group stage and Knockout stage
Host(s)	United Arab Emirates
Champions	New Zealand (1st title)
Runners-up	South Africa
Participants	10
Matches	23
Player of the series	Amelia Kerr
Most runs	Laura Wolvaardt (223)
Most wickets	Amelia Kerr (15)

ICC Introduces Equal Prize Money for Men's and Women's Cricket World Cups

- On 17 September 2024, the ICC announced equal prize money for the men's and women's World Cups.
- The winners of the 2024 Women's T20 World Cup receive $2.34 million, equal to the men's prize money.

First Pakistani woman nominated as International Cricket Umpire

- On 15 September 2024, Saleema Imtiaz became the first Pakistani woman to be nominated to the ICC International Panel of Development Umpires.
- This nomination allows her to officiate in women's bilateral international matches and ICC women's events.
- Imtiaz, who began her umpiring career in 2008, has previously officiated in several Asian Cricket Council tournaments.

Australian wicketkeeper Matthew Wade retires from International Cricket

- On 28th October 2024, Matthew Wade announced his retirement from international cricket.
- The Australian wicketkeeper-batter played 36 Test matches, 97 One-Day Internationals, and 92 T20 Internationals over a 13-year career.
- Wade was instrumental in Australia's 2021 T20 World Cup victory, and his career-best Test score of 117 came against England in 2019.

SLC announces Sanath Jayasuriya as men's team head coach

- On 7 October 2024, Sri Lanka Cricket (SLC) announced the appointment of former captain Sanath Jayasuriya as the head coach of the Sri Lanka men's cricket team.
- His appointment, effective from 1 October 2024, follows his successful interim tenure after the T20 World Cup 2024.
- Jayasuriya's contract will last until 31 March 2026.

New Zealand Wins First Women's T20 World Cup

- On 20 October 2024, New Zealand won their first Women's T20 World Cup.
- They beat South Africa by 32 runs in the final in Dubai.
- Amelia Kerr scored 43 runs and took 3 wickets for 24 runs.
- Brooke Halliday contributed 38 runs.
- This was New Zealand's first major ICC title since the 2000 Women's Cricket World Cup.

Darius Visser Breaks Yuvraj Singh's T20I Record

- Samoa's Darius Visser set a new world record by hitting 39 runs in a single over, breaking Yuvraj Singh's 2007 record.
- Visser achieved this feat in a match against Vanuatu at the T20 World Cup East Asia-Pacific Qualifier in Apia.
- He scored 132 runs in total, becoming the first Samoan player to score a T20I century.

Mumbai Wins 62nd Irani Cup 2024

- Mumbai won their first Irani Cup title in 27 years, defeating Rest of India by taking the first-innings lead.
- This year's Irani Cup was played in Ekana Cricket Stadium in Lucknow. In total, Mumbai has won 15 Irani Cup titles, Rest Of India 30 titles.
- Mumbai are the 42-time Ranji Trophy champions.

Dinesh Karthik Joins Paarl Royals as First Indian Player in SA20

- Former Indian wicketkeeper-batter Dinesh Karthik became the first Indian player to sign up for the South African T20 league, SA20.
- Karthik, who has played 180 international matches, will serve as a mentor and batting coach for Paarl Royals.

TATA IPL 2024

- The 2024 Indian Premier League was the **17th edition** of the Indian Premier League.
- The tournament featured ten teams competing in 74 matches from 22 March to 26 May 2024.
- It was held across 13 cities in India, with Chennai hosting the opening ceremony and the final.

TATA IPL 2024 Champion

- Kolkata Knight Riders (KKR) clinched the TATA Indian Premier League (IPL) 2024 title with a dominating all-round performance against Sunrisers Hyderabad (SRH) in the final at the MA Chidambaram Stadium in Chennai.
- At the same ground in 2012, KKR had clinched their maiden title, and on 26 May 2024, they scripted an encore to lift their third trophy.
- Shreyas Iyer became only the second KKR captain to win the IPL title after **Gautam Gambhir (2012 and 2014).**
- In the final, KKR bowlers restricted the dangerous SRH batting line-up to 113, which was chased down in only 10.3 overs with eight wickets in hand.
- Sunil Narine played a crucial role in KKR's success, delivering a swashbuckling knock of 81 (39) against Lucknow Super Giants and contributing significantly in the final.

IPL 2024 Facts

- For the first time in history, the IPL auction moved out of the borders of India and took place on December 19, 2023, at the Coca-Cola Arena in Dubai, UAE.
- A staggering sum of Rs 230 crore was spent on 72 players during the 2024 IPL auction, out of which 30 were overseas players.
- Creating a new record, **Mitchell Starc** became the most expensive player in IPL history, as Kolkata Knight Riders bought him **for ₹24.75 crore (US$3.1 million).**

- Virat Kohli became the first player in IPL history to score **1000+ runs against 3 different opponents – DC, CSK and PBKS.**
- Virat Kohli became the first player to **play 250 matches from the same team,** he achieved this feat with Royal Challengers Bangalore.
- SRH is the first team in IPL history to chase 160+ runs within 10 overs and score 100+ runs twice in the powerplay.

ICC T20 World Cup 2024

- India beat South Africa in the T20 World Cup 2024 final by seven runs in Barbados on 29 June 2024.

- The ICC T20 World Cup 2024 was the 9th edition of the ICC Men's T20 World Cup.
- It was co-hosted by the West Indies and the United States from 1 to 29 June 2024.
- The teams played 55 matches, with three cities in the United States hosting 12 matches and the rest hosted by six venues in the Caribbean.
- The 2024 ICC T20 World Cup featured 20 teams, an increase from previous editions.

Intresting Facts/Records @ T20 World Cup 2024

- Indian cricket team became the first team to win the ICC Men's T20 World Cup without losing a match.
- India became the third team to win the Men's T20 World Cup for the second time, having won the inaugural edition title in 2007 for the first time.
- The ICC Men's T20 World Cup trophy is made of rhodium and silver; it weighs over 7 kg and stands at 51 cm in height. The trophy was manufactured by Links of London - a British company.
- Legendary Jamaican athlete Usain Bolt was named as a brand ambassador for the 2024 Men's ICC T20 World Cup, alongside former cricketers Shahid Afridi, Yuvraj Singh and Chris Gayle.
- Uganda and Canada made their debut at the ICC Men's T20 World Cup in 2024, by virtue of qualification. On the other hand, the USA was also a first-time participant by virtue of being a co-host.
- The opening match was played with co-hosts United States facing Canada in the first ever T20I match at Grand Prairie Stadium on 1 June.

Virat Kohli, Rohit Sharma & Ravindra Jadeja Announced Retirement From International T20 cricket

- Virat Kohli and Rohit Sharma announced their retirements from T20Is following India's seven-run victory against South Africa in the final of the 2024 Men's T20 World Cup.
- Rohit, who made his T20I debut in the inaugural T20 World Cup played 159 matches for India, scoring 4231 runs to end his career as the highest run-getter in the format for his country.
- Kohli, who made his T20I debut in June 2010, featured in 125 games for India in the format and scored 4188 runs, which included one century and 38 half-centuries.

Dinesh Kartik Announced Retirement from IPL

- Dinesh Karthik, wicket-keeper batter of Royal Challengers Bengaluru (RCB), concluded his illustrious Indian Premier League (IPL).
- Karthik made his IPL debut 16 years ago and featured for six franchises over his career.
- He ends with 4,842 runs in 257 matches, including 22 fifties.

Amul Appointed As 'Official Sponsor' Of Sri Lanka Men's Team For Icc Men's T20 World Cup 2024

- Amul, an Indian dairy producer, has been named the "Official Sponsor" of the Sri Lanka Men's Team for the 2024 ICC Men's T20 World Cup, according to a statement released by Sri Lanka Cricket.
- Amul has been associated with the Sri Lankan team most recently in the 2023 ICC Cricket World Cup.

New Zealand's Colin Munro Retires From International Cricket

- Colin Munro has retired from international cricket after missing out on a spot in the Black Caps' T20 World Cup squad.
- Making his T20I debut against South Africa in 2012, Munro played 122 white ball matches for New Zealand and a solitary test against the Proteas in 2013.

Indian women completed 5-0 series sweep against Bangladesh in Women's T20 Cricket

- In Women's T-20 Cricket, India completed a **5-0 series sweep** after a 21-run win in the fifth and final match against Bangladesh in Sylhet on 9 may 2024.
- Chasing a target of 157 runs, Bangladesh made 135 runs for 6 in the stipulated 20 overs.
- Radha Yadav was awarded Player of the Series.

Mumbai won the Ranji Trophy 2024 after beating Vidarbha

- Mumbai won the Ranji Trophy 2024 after beating Vidarbha by 169 runs at the Wankhede Stadium in Mumbai.
- It also happened to be their **42nd title for Mumbai.**
- Rahane became the 26th Mumbai captain to win the Ranji Trophy.

Neil Wagner announced retirement from International Cricket

- New Zealand pacer Neil Wagner has announced his retirement from Test cricket ahead of the two-Test series against Australia.
- With 64 Tests and 260 wickets to his name, Wagner leaves behind a distinguished career as one of New Zealand's most prolific wicket takers.

T20 World Cup 2024 Award Winners List

Award Name	Recipient	Prize Amount (USD)	Prize Amount (INR)
Player of the Tournament	Jasprit Bumrah	$15,000	INR 12,30,000
Player of the Match (Final)	Virat Kohli	$5,000	INR 4,10,000
Smart Catch of the Match	Suryakumar Yadav	$3,000	INR 2,46,000

Note: T20 World Cup winners 2024 India were given ₹20.37 crore and runners-up South Africa ₹10.64 crore as prizes

Ravichandran Ashwin joins elite 500 test wicket club

- Indian off-spinner Ravichandran Ashwin claimed his 500th Test wicket in the first innings of the third Test match against England at the Niranjan Shah Stadium in Rajkot.
- The 37-year-old achieved this monumental feat in his 98th Test Match.
- Achieving this feat during the, Ashwin became only the third Indian and the [specific rank globally] bowler to achieve this landmark.

Jacintha Kalyan became India's first female pitch curator

- Jacintha Kalyan has become India's first female pitch curator. She has been associated with the Karnataka State Cricket Association (KSCA) for more than 30 years.

Ravichandran Ashwin becomes 14th player to play 100 Tests for India

- Ravichandran Ashwin became just the **14th player to reach the milestone of 100 Tests for India** during the fifth Test against England at the Himachal Pradesh Cricket Association stadium in Dharamsala.
- Ashwin, who made his Test debut against the West Indies in New Delhi in 2011, is also the first player from Tamil Nadu to breach the 100-Test milestone.
- He is also the oldest Indian to reach the landmark at 37 years old.

Royal Challengers Bangalore beat Delhi Capitals by 8 wickets to lift Women's Premier League title

- In the Women's Premier League (WPL) Cricket final, **Royal Challengers Bangalore (RCB)** defeated Delhi Capitals by 8 wickets at Arun Jaitley Stadium in New Delhi.
- RCB chased down a target of 114 runs, scoring 115/2 in 19.3 overs.

England will host the 2027 World Test Championship (WTC) final

- The International Cricket Council (ICC) has officially declared that **England will host the 2027 World Test Championship (WTC) final** in June 2024.
- This marks the fourth consecutive time that England will host the WTC final, having previously staged the events in 2021, 2023, and the upcoming 2025 final at Lord's.

Virat Kohli crowned ICC Men's ODI Cricketer of the year 2023

- Virat Kohli was named the ICC Men's ODI Cricketer of the Year 2023. This marks the fourth time that Kohli has been honored with this award.
- In 2023, Kohli had an exceptional year in the 50-over format. He scored 1377 runs, took 1 wicket, and made 12 catches in 27 matches.
- He was also the Player of the Tournament at the ICC Men's Cricket World Cup 2023.

Australian batter David Warner announces retirement from One Day International cricket

- Australian batter David Warner has announced his retirement from One Day Internationals (ODIs).
- Warner is Australia's sixth-highest run scorer in the ODI format and is only second to former captain Ricky Ponting's tally for most Centuries for Australia in ODIs.

Chamari Athapaththu ICC Women's ODI Cricketer of the year

- Sri Lankan cricketer Chamari Athapaththu has been named the **ICC Women's ODI Cricketer of the Year for 2023.**
- She had an exceptional year with the bat in ODIs, scoring 415 runs in 8 matches.

Lockie Ferguson Bowl 4 Maiden Overs In A Match

- Lockie Ferguson of New Zealand made history by becoming the first bowler to deliver four consecutive maiden overs in the T20 World Cup, with an impressive spell of 4-4-0-3 against Papua New Guinea.
- Ferguson's exceptional bowling performance, which included 24 dot balls and three wickets, played a crucial role in dismissing Papua New Guinea for just 78 runs in the ICC Men's T20 World Cup 2024 match held in Trinidad.

Trent Boult Announces Retirement From International Cricket

- New Zealand's left-arm fast bowler Trent Boult has announced his retirement from International Cricket after the 2024 T20 ICC Cricket World Cup.
- Trent Boult had an illustrious 13-year international career, making his debut in 2011 and representing New Zealand in all formats of the game.

FOOTBALL

Brazilian Vinicius Junior wins FIFA Best Male Awards 2024

- Brazillian and Real Madrid football player Vinicius Junior won the "2024 FIFA Best Male Footballer" of the Year award.
- Aitana Bonmati won the "Best FIFA Female Award" for the second consecutive time. She was part of the Spanish team which won the 2023 FIFA Women's World Cup.
- The 2024 FIFA Awards winners were announced and felicitated at a function held in Doha, Qatar. FIFA President Gianni Infantino presented the awards to the winners.

FIFA Awards 2024

- **Best FIFA Women's Goalkeeper** – Alyssa Naeher of the United States of America
- **Best FIFA Men's Goalkeeper** – Emiliano Martinez of Argentina and English club Aston Villa.
- **Best FIFA Women's Coach** – Emma Hayes, coach of the United States women's team.
- **Best FIFA Men's Coach** – Carlo Ancelotti, coach of the Real Madrid football club of Spain.
- **1st Marta Award** – Marta of Brazil.
- **Puskas Award** – Alejandro Garnacho of English football club Manchester United.
- **FIFA Fair Play Award-** Thiago Maia of Brazil.

FIFA Confirms Saudi Arabia As 2034 World Cup Host

- FIFA has confirmed that Saudi Arabia will host the 2034 World Cup.
- At the same time, a virtual Congress of world football's governing body confirmed that Morocco, Spain and Portugal will be joint hosts of the 2030 World Cup, in which three games will also be played in South America.

Cristiano Ronaldo Scores 900th Career Goal Against Croatia

- Cristiano Ronaldo became the first footballer in history to score 900 career goals.
- His 900th goal came during Portugal's Nations League match against Croatia, marking his 131st international goal.
- The remaining 769 goals were scored at the club level. Ronaldo is a five-time Ballon d'Or winner.

Thomas Müller Retires from International Football

- On July 15, 2024, German footballer Thomas Müller officially retired from international football after 131 appearances.
- His farewell came after Germany's Euro 2024 quarter-final loss to Spain.
- Müller was part of Germany's 2014 World Cup-winning squad and won the Golden Boot at the 2010 World Cup.

Bala Devi became 1st Indian woman to score 50 international goals

- On 17th October 2024, Bala Devi became the first Indian woman to score 50 international goals during the SAFF Women's Championship in Nepal.
- She achieved this milestone in a match against Pakistan, scoring her historic goal in the 35th minute.
- Bala Devi, often referred to as the "goal machine" of Indian women's football, dedicated her achievement to her late father, expressing her gratitude and emotional connection to the milestone.

Lallianzuala Chhangte and Indumathi Kathiresan Win AIFF Player of the Year Awards

- Lallianzuala Chhangte was named AIFF Men's Player of the Year for the second consecutive time.
- Chhangte, a winger for Mumbai City FC, secured the award for his stellar performance in the 2024 season.
- Indumathi Kathiresan became the first player from Tamil Nadu to win the AIFF Women's Player of the Year award.

Brazil will host FIFA Women's World Cup 2027

- Brazil has been confirmed as the host of the 2027 FIFA Women's World Cup.
- This decision was made at the FIFA Congress in Bangkok, where Brazil received 119 votes, surpassing the joint bid from Belgium, Germany, and the Netherlands.
- The 2027 World Cup will be the **tenth edition of the tournament,** with 32 nations competing.

Manchester City won their fourth consecutive Premier League title

- Manchester City has made history by becoming the **first team to win four consecutive Premier League titles.**
- This historic achievement was sealed with a 3-1 victory over West Ham United at the Etihad Stadium.
- This is the sixth time in seven seasons that Manchester City has won the Premier League.

Australia to host AFC Women's Asian Cup 2026

- The Asian Football Confederation (AFC) has officially announced **that Australia will host the 2026 Women's Asian Cup.**
- The Women's Asian Cup is a quadrennial international football tournament competed by the women's national teams in the Asian Football Confederation.
- The 2026 edition will be the **21st edition of the AFC** Women's Asian Cup.

Sunil Chhetri announced retirement from International Football

- Sunil Chhetri, the iconic Indian footballer and national team captain, **announced his retirement from international football** on 6 June, 2024.
- His illustrious career spanned 19 years, during which he **played 145 matches for the national team** and scored an impressive 93 goals.
- He holds the record of being the **fourth**-highest scorer of international goals.

Ronaldo tops forbes' list of highest-paid athletes again

- Cristiano Ronaldo has **topped Forbes' list of highest-paid athletes** for the fourth time, with estimated earnings of around $260 million.
- **Spanish golfer Jon Rahm moved up to second place** following his switch to Saudi-backed LIV Golf.
- Ronaldo's move to Saudi Arabian side Al-Nassr contributed significantly to his earnings, marking an all-time high for a football player.

Real Madrid has clinched their 36th La Liga title

- Real Madrid secured the title on 4 May 2024, after a combination of their own victory and a loss by their closest rivals.
- The title was clinched following Real Madrid's win against Cádiz, with the team achieving a 3-0 victory at the Santiago Bernabeu stadium.

CHESS

D Gukesh Becomes Youngest World Chess Champion

- Indian Grandmaster Gukesh Dommaraju became the youngest world chess champion by winning against Ding Liren in the 14th game of the World Chess Championship match in Singapore.
- He is only 18 years old. Gukesh is the second Indian to win the classical chess world championship, after Viswanathan Anand.
- He broke the previous record held by Garry Kasparov, who became the youngest world chess champion at 22 years old in 1985.

India Wins Historic Gold at Chess Olympiad 2024

- On 22 September 2024, India won double gold in both the Open and Women's sections at the Chess Olympiad in Budapest.
- The men's team beat Slovenia, and the women's team defeated Azerbaijan.

Shubhi Gupta wins gold and bronze at Commonwealth Chess Championships

- On 10 September 2024, Shubhi Gupta won gold in the U-16 category and bronze in the U-20 category at the Commonwealth Chess Championships in Kalutara, Sri Lanka.
- A Women FIDE Master and reigning U-19 national champion, Shubhi secured seven wins and two draws in the U-16 category.

Vaishali Ramesh Babu Awarded Grandmaster Title By FIDE

- Vaishali Ramesh Babu has been officially awarded the title of Grandmaster by FIDE, making her **the third Indian Female Grandmaster after Koneru Humpy and Harika Dronavalli.**
- Notably, Vaishali and her brother, Rameshbabu Praggnanandhaa, are the world's first Grandmaster brother-sister duo.
- Vaishali achieved the required 2500 ELO points at the Llobregat Open tournament in Spain last year, and the title was conferred during the FIDE Council meeting in Toronto.

Praggnanandhaa topples world no. 1 Magnus Carlsen for first time

- Indian Grandmaster R. Praggnanandhaa achieved a remarkable milestone by defeating world number one Magnus Carlsen in a classical game during the Norway Chess tournament.
- This victory marks Praggnanandhaa's maiden classical win against Carlsen, who is renowned for his chess prowess.

India's 17-Year-Old D Gukesh Wins Candidates Chess Tournament

- The 17-year-old Grandmaster D Gukesh Dommaraju from India has made history by winning the 2024 FIDE Candidates Tournament. **This victory makes him the youngest player in history to win a Candidates Tournament.**
- After 14 rounds Gukesh's draw against Grandmaster Hikaru Nakamura was enough to secure his advancement.

Rameshbabu Praggnanandhaa surpasses Viswanathan Anand to become India's number-one Chess player

- India Chess Wizard Rameshbabu Praggnanandhaa defeated World Chess Champion Ding Liren in the Tata Steel Masters in Wijk aan Zee, in the Netherlands.
- As a result of this victory, Praggnanandhaa became only the second Indian after Vishwanathan Anand to defeat a reigning champion.

8-year-old Indian-origin boy Ashwath Kaushik beats Polish Grandmaster

- Ashwath Kaushik, an 8-year-old Indian-origin boy from Singapore, has made history by becoming the youngest player ever to defeat a Chess grandmaster.
- Ashwath defeated Polish chess grandmaster Jacek Stopa at the Burgdorfer Stadthaus Open in Switzerland.
- With this feat, he became the youngest ever player to beat a grandmaster in the classical version of the game.

Divya Deshmukh Wins World Junior Girls' Chess Championship

- In chess, India's Divya Deshmukh won the World Junior Girls' Chess Championship after beating Bulgaria's Beloslava Krasteva in the final round at the Gift City Club in Gandhinagar, Gujarat.
- She finished unbeaten in the championship by winning nine of her games while drawing the other two.

Koneru Humpy Becomes Second Woman to Win World Rapid Chess Title Twice

- Indian Grandmaster Koneru Humpy won the **FIDE Women's World Rapid Champion 2024** title in New York.

- She had won the same title in 2019, and became only the **second woman** ever after China's Ju Wenjun to clinch it twice.
- **Volodar Murzin**, from **Russia**, won the open category World Rapid Chess Champion.
- The World Rapid Chess Championship 2024 was the 2024 edition of the annual World Rapid Chess Championship held by FIDE to determine the world champions in chess played under rapid time controls.
- The tournament was held in New York City from 26 to 28 December 2024.

TENNIS

137th WIMBLEDON TENNIS CHAMPIONSHIPS 2024

The 2024 Wimbledon Tennis Championships took place from 1 July to 14 July at the All England Lawn Tennis Club in London.

The winner's list

Category	Winner(s)	Runner(s)-up
Men's Singles	Carlos Alcaraz	Novak Djokovic
Women's Singles	Barbora Krejčíková	Jasmine Paolini
Mixed Doubles	Hsieh Su-Wei & Jan Zielinski	Santiago Gonzalez & Giuliana Olmos
Women's Doubles	Taylor Townsend & Katerina Siniakova	Gabriela Dabrowski & Erin Routliffe
Men's Doubles	Harri Heliövaara and Henry Patten	Max Purcell & Jordan Thompson

144th US OPEN TENNIS CHAMPIONSHIPS 2024

The 2024 US Open Tennis Championships took place from 26 August to 8 September 2024, at the USTA Billie Jean King National Tennis Center in New York.

Event	Winner(s)
Men's Singles	Jannik Sinner
Women's Singles	Aryna Sabalenka
Men's Doubles	Max Purcell / Jordan Thompson
Women's Doubles	Kichenok/Ostapenko
Mixed Doubles	Errani/Vavassori

Tennis Player Rafael Nadal announced his retirement

- On 10th October 2024, Rafael Nadal announced his retirement from professional tennis.
- The 38-year-old Spaniard revealed his decision in a video message, stating that the Davis Cup Finals in Malaga, scheduled for November 2024, will be his final event.

2024 China Open Championship

- The 2024 China Open took place from September 25 to October 6, 2024, at the National Tennis Center in Beijing.

- In the men's singles final, Carlos Alcaraz defeated Jannik Sinner in a thrilling match, 6–7 (6–8), 6–4, 7–6 (7–3).
- In the women's singles final, Coco Gauff triumphed over Karolina Muchova in straight sets, 6-1, 6-3.

Sinner and Sabalenka claim Cincinnati Open Titles

- On 19 August 2024, Jannik Sinner and Aryna Sabalenka won the Cincinnati Open singles category respectively.
- Sinner defeated Frances Tiafoe with a score of 7-6 (7-4), 6-2 in the men's singles final.
- In the women's singles final, Sabalenka triumphed over Jessica Pegula with a score of 6-3, 7-5, demonstrating her resilience and strategic play.

French Open 2024

- Carlos Alcaraz of Spain won his first French Open men's singles title, while world No. 1 Iga Swiatek of Poland secured her fourth French Open women's singles title.
- The 123rd edition of the French Open, also known as Roland Garros, took place at Stade Roland Garros in Paris, France, and is the second Grand Slam event of the year following the Australian Open.

The French Open is played on clay courts, with the finals held on the Philippe Chatrier Court at Stade Roland Garros, which features multiple courts for the tournament.

Novak Djokovic breaks Roger Federer's record, becomes oldest World No. 1 in ATP rankings history

- Novak Djokovic officially became the oldest World No. 1 in ATP Rankings history, a record previously held by one of his greatest rivals in Roger Federer.
- Serbia's Djokovic, the most decorated male tennis player in the Open era with 24 Majors, is 36 years and 321 days old.

Australian Open 2024

- The Australian Open 2024 was a Grand Slam level tennis tournament held at Melbourne Park, from 14–28 January 2024.
- It was the 112th edition of the Australian Open, the 56th in the Open Era, and the first major of the year.

Here are the winners of the Australian Open 2024

Event	Winner	Runner-Up
Men's Singles	Jannik Sinner (Italy)	Daniil Medvedev (Russia)
Women's Singles	Aryna Sabalenka (Belarus)	Zheng Qinwen (China)
Men's Doubles	Rohan Bopanna (India) & Matthew Ebden (Australia)	Simone Bolelli and Andrea Vavassori (Italy)
Women's Doubles	Hsieh Su-Wei (Taiwan) & Elise Mertens (Belgium)	Jelena Ostapenko (Latvia) and Lyudmyla Kichenok (Ukraine)
Mixed Doubles	Hsieh Su-wei (Taiwan) & Jan Zielinski (Poland)	Desirae Krawczyk (USA) & Neal Skupski (Britain)

India's Rohan Bopanna becomes oldest player to hold number one spot in men's doubles tennis

- Indian tennis sensation Rohan Bopanna became the **oldest player to hold the No. 1 men's doubles ranking.**
- The 43-year-old Ace player, alongside Australia's Matthew Ebden, defeated the Argentine pair Máximo González and Andrés Molteni in straight sets 6-4, 7-6 in the 2024 Australian Open quarter-finals.

Russian Tennis player Daniil Savelev Suspended for 2 years for doping

- Russian tennis player Daniil Savelev has been banned for two years for breaking anti-doping rules.
- The International Tennis Integrity Agency (ITIA) tested positive for the banned substance 'Meldonium' in July 2024.
- He has been suspended since August 2024, and his suspension will end in August 2026.

ATHLETICS

Delhi to Host 2025 Para Athletics World Championships

- India is set to host the 2025 Para Athletics World Championships.
- The competition is scheduled to take place between September 26 and October 5, 2025, at the Jawaharlal Nehru Stadium in New Delhi.
- This event will be the 12th edition of the Para Athletics World Championships and the fourth time it is being held in Asia.

India to host ISSF Junior World Cup 2025

- India has been chosen to host the 2025 International Shooting Sport Federation (ISSF) Junior World Cup for Rifle/Pistol/Shotgun.
- Launched in 2016 by the ISSF, Junior World Cups are premier annual shooting events for under-21 athletes.
- This will mark India's third major ISSF competition in three years, after Bhopal's 2023 senior ISSF World Cup and New Delhi's 2024 World Cup Final.

Neeraj Chopra Finishes Second at Lausanne Diamond League 2024

- Olympic silver medalist Neeraj Chopra took second place in the men's javelin throw at the Lausanne Diamond League in Switzerland.
- He achieved his season-best throw of 89.49 metres, finishing behind Grenada's Peters Anderson, who threw 90.61 metres.

Sabeera Haris Wins Bronze at ISSF Junior World Cup

- Indian shooter Sabeera Haris won a bronze medal in the women's trap category at the ISSF Junior World Cup in Porpetto, Italy.
- Carey Garrison from the USA took the gold with a perfect score of 40, while Sofia Gori of Italy won the silver with 39 hits.

Indian women won overall 2nd place at U20 World Wrestling Championship

- On 8 September 2024, the Indian women's team secured overall second place at the U20 World Wrestling Championships in Pontevedra, Spain.
- The team won one gold, one silver, and five bronze medals.
- Jyoti Berwal clinched gold in the women's 76kg category, while Neha and Nikita earned bronze in the 57kg and 62kg categories, respectively.

ISSF Junior World Shooting Championship 2024

- The 2024 ISSF Junior World Shooting Championships took place from 27 September to 6 October 2024, at the Las Palmas Shooting Range in Lima, Peru.

- India topped the medal tally with 13 gold, 3 silver, and 8 bronze medals.
- Italy finished in second place, while Norway took the third spot.

Dipa Karmakar clinched India's first-ever gold medal in Women's Vault at Asian Championships

- Dipa Karmakar won the first-ever gold medal for India in the Asian Championships in **Tashkent, Uzbekistan.**
- The 30-year-old Olympian finished the women's Vault final with an average score of 13.566.

India's Deepthi Jeevanji smashes world record in women's 400-meter event

- At the World Para Athletics Championships **in Kobe, Japan,** Deepthi Jeevanji broke the world record in the women's 400m T20, clocking 55.07 seconds to win gold.
- Aysel Onder of Turkey and Lizanshela Angulo of Ecuador took silver and bronze, respectively.

Next Generation of Squash Players inducted in TOPS

- The Ministry of Youth Affairs and Sports' Mission Olympics Cell (MOC) has inducted squash players Anahat Singh, Abhay Singh, and Velavan Senthilkumar into the Development Group of the Target Olympic Podium Scheme (TOPS), focusing on the **2028 Los Angeles Olympics** where squash will debut.
- This move aims to build on the legacy of Indian squash champions Saurav Ghosal, Dipika Pallikal, and Joshna Chinappa.

Abha Khatua sets national record winning gold in women's shot put

- Abha Khatua achieved a national record and secured a gold medal in Women's Shot Put by throwing an impressive distance of 18.41 meters at the National Federation Cup Athletics Competition in Bhubaneswar.
- Representing Maharashtra, she previously shared the record of 18.06 meters with Manpreet Kaur.

Ethiopia's Sisay Lemma wins first Boston Marathon title

- Ethiopia's Sisay Lemma won his first Boston Marathon title, finishing with a time of 2:06:17 in the men's race, while Hellen Obiri of Kenya retained her 2023 title in the women's race.
- Obiri, 34, is the first woman to win back-to-back Boston Marathons since Catherine Ndereba accomplished the feat in 2004 and 2005.

Vinay wins gold at para powerlifting World Cup in Egypt

- Vinay has secured victory at the Para Powerlifting World Cup held in Egypt.
- The 18-year-old athlete showcased his prowess by claiming the gold medal in the 59kg youth category, lifting an impressive 120kg weight.

India makes new guinness world record in Kabaddi with participation of 128 players

- India made history by making a Guinness World record with participation of 128 players on the World Kabaddi Day.
- The history was written at Tau Devi Lal Indoor Stadium of Panchkula in Haryana.

Indian sailor Vishnu Saravanan clinches gold medal at Europa Cup in Spain

- Indian sailor Vishnu Saravanan won the gold medal in the ILCA 7 category at the Europa Cup 2024 in Mallorca, Spain.
- He topped the 91-boat race with 17 net points, becoming the first Indian to win gold in this category.

India loses to Japan; Fails to qualify for Paris 2024 Olympics

- Indian Women's hockey team failed to qualify for the Olympics for the first time since 2016 after falling to a 1-0 loss against Japan in the third-place playoff match at the **FIH Women's Hockey Olympic Qualifiers in Ranchi.**

Yogesh Singh wins gold in men's 25m standard pistol event at Asian Shooting Championships, Jakarta

- In Shooting, India's Yogesh Singh won a gold medal in the men's 25m standard pistol event at the Asian Shooting Championships 2024 in Jakarta, Indonesia.

PM Modi inaugurated 6th Khelo India Youth Games 2023 in Chennai

- Prime Minister Narendra Modi inaugurated the 6th Khelo India Youth Games in Chennai to be held from January 19 to 31.
- The games were held from 19 to 31 January at the Jawaharlal Nehru Stadium in Chennai.
- The logo for the games incorporates the figure of poet **Thiruvalluvar.** On the other hand, **'Veera Mangai'** is the mascot for the games.

World Champion Neeraj Chopra Wins Gold

- Olympic and World Champion Neeraj Chopra has won the Gold medal in the men's javelin throw competition at the World Athletics Continental Gold Tour at the Paavo Nurmi Stadium in Turku, Finland.
- He topped an eight-man field with a best effort of 85.97 meters.

OLYMPIC AND PARALYMPIC GAMES

IOC Announces Olympic Esports Games in Saudi Arabia for 2025

- The International Olympic Committee (IOC) has partnered with the Saudi Olympic and Paralympic Committee to host the first Olympic Esports Games in 2025.
- The event will be held in Saudi Arabia, with a 12-year partnership between the IOC and the Saudi National Olympic Committee.
- The Olympic Esports Games will be held regularly starting in 2025.

India completes Paris Olympics 2024 with 6 Medals

- India concluded its campaign at the Paris Olympics 2024 with a total of six medals, including one silver and five bronze.
- The event held from 26 July to 11 August 2024.

Randhir Singh Elected as First Indian President of Olympic Council of Asia

- Former shooter and sports administrator Raja Randhir Singh has been elected as the first Indian president of the Olympic Council of Asia (OCA).
- A five-time Olympian, Randhir Singh, aged 77, will serve as president from 2024 to 2028.
- The OCA is the governing body for Asian sports and is recognized by the International Olympic Committee (IOC).

Gagan Narang Appointed Chef-de-Mission for Paris 2024 Olympics

- Olympic bronze medalist and shooter Gagan Narang has been named Chef-de-Mission for the Indian team at the Paris 2024 Olympics.

PARIS OLYMPICS 2024 HIGHLIGHTS

PARIS 2024

Particular	Details
Official Name	Games of the XXXIII Olympiad
Edition	33rd Summer Olympics
Official Mascots	 "Les Phryges"
Opening Ceremony	July 26, 2024
Closing Ceremony	August 11, 2024
Slogan	Games Wide Open
Total events	329 events
Number of Sports	32 sports (including the 4 additional sports)
Paricipated Athletes	10,714
Nations	204 (including the AIN and EOR teams)
Host City	Paris, France
Flag bearer for India (Opening Ceremony)	PV Sindhu & Sharath Kamal
Flag bearer for India (Closing Ceremony)	PR Sreejesh & Manu Bhaker
India's Participation	117 athletes

- Narang replaced MC Mary Kom, who stepped down for personal reasons, and will represent and oversee the Indian contingent at the Games.

Adani Group became Principal Sponsor for Indian Team at 2024 Paris Olympics

- The Adani Group was announced as the principal sponsor for the Indian team at the 2024 Paris Olympics.
- The partnership aimed to support India's athletes as they competed in the Olympics from July 26 to August 11, 2024.

Lt Col Kabilan Sai Ashok became India's Youngest Boxing Referee at Paris Olympics

- Lieutenant Colonel Kabilan Sai Ashok became India's youngest Olympic boxing referee at the Paris Olympics 2024.
- At 32, he was the fourth Indian to officiate at the Olympics since 1904.
- He is the Joint Secretary at the Services Sports Control Board.

Preethi Pal Becomes First Indian Track and Field Athlete to Win Two Paralympic Medals

- Preethi Pal made history as the first Indian woman to win two track and field medals at the Paralympic Games.
- She secured bronze in both the 100m and 200m T35 events.

PARIS PARALYMPIC GAMES 2024 AT A GLANCE

- **Date**: August 28 – September 8, 2024
- **Location**: Paris, France
- **Sports Disciplines**: 22 sports, including new additions like para-cycling, para-rowing, and blind judo
- **Mascot**: The Paralympic Phryge, symbolizing liberty and freedom, inspired by the Phrygian cap
- **Countries Participating**: Athletes from over 160 nations
- **Indian Flag bearers (opening)**: Bhagyashree Jadhav & Sumit Antil
- **Indian Flag bearers (closing)**: Preethi Pal & Harvinder Singh
- **Performance Highlights**:
- **Top Performers**: China finished at the top with 94 golds, followed by Great Britain (49 golds) and the United States (36 golds)
- **India's Performance**:
  - **Total Medals**: 29 (7 Gold, 9 Silver, 13 Bronze)
  - **Rank**: 18th overall
  - **Significant Achievements**: India won its first-ever gold in men's javelin throw F41 (Navdeep Singh) and crossed 50 medals in Paralympic history.
  - **Athletes**: India sent 84 para-athletes across 12 disciplines, a notable increase from previous Paralympic Games (9 disciplines in Tokyo 2021).
  - **Note: Avani Lekhara** won India's first gold medal in the women's 10 m air rifle event.
    Harvinder Singh won India's first Paralympic gold medal in archery.

- Preethi is only the second Indian woman to win two medals at the same Paralympic Games, following Avani Lekhara's gold and bronze in Tokyo 2020.

TABLE OF THE WINNERS

Olympian	Sport	Event	Medal
Neeraj Chopra	Athletics	Men's Javelin Throw	Silver
Manu Bhaker	Shooting	Women's 10m Air Pistol	Bronze
Manu Bhaker & Sarabjot Singh	Shooting	Mixed 10m Air Pistol	Bronze
Swapnil Kusale	Shooting	Men's 50m 3 Positions	Bronze
Indian Men's Hockey Team	Hockey	Men's Event	Bronze
Aman Sehrawat	Wrestling	Men's 57kg Freestyle	Bronze

PARIS 2024 OLYMPIC MEDAL TABLE

Teams	Medals			
	Gold	Silver	Bronze	Total
United States	40	44	42	126
China	40	27	24	91
Japan	20	12	13	45
Australia	18	19	16	53
India	0	1	5	6

MISCELLANEOUS

Indian Hockey team won Women's Junior Asia Cup title at Muscat

- Indian women's junior hockey team successfully defended their Women's Junior Asia Cup title in Muscat, Oman, by defeating China 3-2 in the final.
- India, the previous 2023 edition winner, won the 10th Women's Junior Asia Cup,3-2 in the penalty shoot-out in the final played at Muscat.
- The top five finishers at the 2024 Women's Junior Asia Cup -India, China, Japan, South Korea and Malaysia qualified for the 2025 FIH Women's Junior World Cup in Chile.
- The 10th Women's Junior Asia Cup was held in Muscat, Oman, from 7 to 15 December 2024.

India women's hockey team Wins Asian Champions Trophy

- On 20th November 2024, the India women's hockey team won the Asian Champions Trophy by defeating China 1-0 in the final held in Rajgir, Bihar.
- This victory marked India's third title in the tournament, equalling South Korea as the most successful team in the competition's history.
- Deepika Sehrawat scored the decisive goal, finishing as the tournament's top scorer with 11 goals. The team's dominant performance included five clean sheets and a total of 29 goals scored in the tournament.

Ladakh to host Khelo India Winter Games from Jan 23

- Union Territory of Ladakh will host the ice events from January 23 to 27, 2025 while the UT of Jammu & Kashmir will host the snow events from February 22 to 25, 2025.
- The 2024 edition of KIWG witnessed over 1,200 participants, including more than 700 athletes, 141 support staff, 113 technical officials, and over 250 volunteers. A total of 136 medals were contested.
- For the first time in 2024, the Ministry of Youth Affairs and Sports, Government of India, along with the Sports Authority of India, managed the technical aspects of the Games in collaboration with the National Sports Federations and the Indian Olympic Association (IOA).

Bihar to host Khelo India Youth Games and Para Games in April 2025

- Bihar was announced as the host city for the Khelo India Youth Games and Para Games 2025 in April.
- For the first time, the Khelo India Para Games will also be held in Bihar, following the Youth Games with a 10-15 Day gap.
- The first edition of the Para Games was held in Delhi last year.
- Bihar just hosted the women's Asian Champions Trophy hockey championship in Rajgir. In the same championship, India defeated Paris Olympics silver medalists China to retain the continental title.

Salman Khan Named Brand Ambassador for Kho Kho World Cup

- The Kho Kho Federation of India (KKFI) has named Bollywood superstar Salman Khan as the brand ambassador for the inaugural Kho Kho World Cup that is set to take place in New Delhi from January 13 to January 19, 2025.
- The Kho Kho World Cup 2025 will feature 21 men's teams and 20 women's teams.

38th National Games Uttarakhand Unveils Mascot, Logo, Anthem, and Tagline

- Uttarakhand Chief Minister Pushkar Singh Dhami launched the mascot, logo, jersey, torch, anthem and the tag line of the 38th National Games to be held in the state from January 28 to February 14, 2025.
- The mascot for the 38th National Games is named "Mauli," Inspired by the Himalayan Monal (Uttarakhand's state bird).
- The official tagline of the 38th National Games is "Sankalp Se Shikhar Tak" (From Resolve to Zenith).

Sania Mirza, Mary Kom, and Rannvijay Singha Become Play Sports Brand Ambassadors

- Six-time Grand Slam champion Sania Mirza, Olympic bronze medalist Mary Kom, and TV host Rannvijay Singha were named brand ambassadors for Play Sports.
- Their role involves improving sports infrastructure, running academies, scouting new talent, and promoting sports nationwide.

Scindia Inaugurates Shooting Range Named After Double Olympic Medalist Manu Bhaker

- Union Communications Minister Jyotiraditya Scindia inaugurated a shooting range named after Manu Bhaker, the double bronze medalist from the 2024 Paris Olympics.
- Bhaker and her partner Sarabjot Singh won bronze in the 10m Air Pistol Mixed Team event at the Paris Olympics.

- Bhaker became the first athlete from post-independence India to win two medals in a single edition of the Paris Olympics.

Glasgow Confirmed as Hosts for the 2026 Commonwealth Games

- The Commonwealth Games Federation (CGF) officially confirmed Glasgow as the host city for the 2026 Commonwealth Games.
- Glasgow was chosen after Victoria, Australia, withdrew its bid due to logistical issues.
- The 2026 Games will be held after the Birmingham 2022 Commonwealth Games.

OSCAR PIASTRI WINS MAIDEN F1 TITLE AT HUNGARIAN GRAND PRIX

- On July 21, 2024, Australian driver Oscar Piastri claimed his first Formula 1 victory at the Hungarian Grand Prix.
- Despite finishing second, Lando Norris followed team orders, allowing Piastri to take the chequered flag.
- Piastri becomes the fifth Australian to win an F1 Grand Prix, joining legends like Jack Brabham, Alan Jones, Mark Webber, and Daniel Ricciardo.

Argentina Wins 2nd Consecutive Copa America Title

- On July 15, 2024, Argentina defeated Colombia 1-0 to win their second straight Copa America championship.
- This victory marks Argentina's third major title in a row, following their 2021 Copa America and 2022 World Cup triumphs, equaling Spain's record.

Spain Wins Euro 2024 Title

- Spain won their fourth UEFA European Championship title on 14 July 2024.
- They defeated England 2-1 in the final at Berlin's Olympiastadion.
- This victory added to Spain's previous wins in 1964, 2008, and 2012.

PR Sreejesh Named Head Coach of India Junior Men's Hockey Team

- On 9 August 2024, Hockey India announced PR Sreejesh as the head coach of the India Junior Men's Hockey Team.
- Sreejesh retired after India's bronze medal win at the Paris Olympics 2024.
- His first assignment as head coach was the Sultan of Johor Cup in October 2024.

Haryana Launches First-Ever Global Women's Kabaddi League

- The first-ever Global Women's Kabaddi League was launched in September 2024.
- Organized by HIPSA and World Kabaddi, it featured female athletes from over 15 countries.
- The tournament aimed to promote and develop women's kabaddi globally.

Odisha Naval Tata Wins Women's Title in Junior Hockey

- On 12 August 2024, Odisha Naval Tata Hockey High-Performance Centre won the women's title at the Hockey India Junior Academy Championship.
- They defeated Roundglass Punjab Hockey Club Academy 5-3 in a penalty shootout after a 2-2 draw in regular time.
- Prabhjot Kaur and Surekha Bahala scored for Odisha, while Rubby and Ribka scored for Punjab.

Para shuttler Pramod Bhagat suspended for violating anti-doping rules

- On 13 August 2024, Indian para shuttler Pramod Bhagat was suspended for 18 months for breaching anti-doping regulations.
- The suspension, effective immediately, results from three whereabouts failures within a 12-month period.
- Bhagat's appeal to the Court of Arbitration for Sport (CAS) was dismissed, confirming the suspension.

Jeevan-Vijay Pair Clinches Hangzhou Open 2024 Title

- On 24 September 2024, Jeevan Nedunchezhiyan and Vijay Sundar Prashanth won the men's doubles title at the Hangzhou Open.
- They defeated Germany's Constantin Frantzen and Hendrik Jebens 4-6, 7-6, [10-7] in the final.
- This was Jeevan's second ATP Tour title and Vijay's first.

Nazira Banoo Wins Gold Medal in Taekwondo at Khelo India Women's League

- In September 2024, Nazira Banoo won a gold medal in the individual Poomsae under-30 category at the Khelo India Women's Taekwondo League in Vadodara.
- Nazira's victory qualified her for the Khelo India Women's League Nationals Phase-III in Bhubaneswar.

Anuya Prasad Wins Gold at World Deaf Shooting Championship

- In September 2024, Anuya Prasad won the women's air pistol gold at the World Deaf Shooting Championship in Hannover, Germany.
- She won with a score of 232.2 points, narrowly beating Sofia Olenych by 0.1 point.

Hockey Punjab Wins 14th Hockey India Junior Men's National Championship 2024

- On 19 September 2024, Hockey Punjab won the 14th Hockey India Junior Men's National Championship in Jalandhar, Punjab.
- They defeated Uttar Pradesh Hockey 4-3 in a penalty shootout.

Kho Kho World Cup to Debut in India in 2025

- On 2 October 2024, the Kho Kho Federation of India (KKFI), in association with the International Kho Kho Federation, announced that India will host the first-ever Kho Kho World Cup in 2025.
- This historic event will feature 16 men's and 16 women's teams from 24 countries across six continents.

Indian gymnast Dipa Karmakar announces retirement

- On 7 October 2024, celebrated Indian gymnast Dipa Karmakar announced her retirement from competitive gymnastics.
- Dipa is the first Indian female gymnast to qualify for the Olympics (2016 Rio Olympics).
- She won a bronze medal at the 2014 Glasgow Commonwealth Games and a gold medal at the FIG World Challenge Cup in 2018.

2024 Asian Youth Archery Championship

- The 2024 Asian Youth Archery Championship was held from 27 September to 3 October 2024, in Taipei City, Chinese Taipei.

- The event featured two age categories (U18 and U21) and two disciplines (compound and recurve).
- India's Vaishnavi Pawar played in the recurve U-18 women's team category, helping the team secure a silver medal.

Hockey India League 2024-25 begins in Rourkela, Odisha

- The Hockey India League (HIL) 2024-25 begins at the Birsa Munda Hockey Stadium in Rourkela, Odisha from 28 December 2024.
- The league is being held in two phases. Phase One runs from December 28 to January 18, followed by Phase Two, which starts on January 19.
- The final match of the league is scheduled for the 1st of February, 2025.

India Concludes Asian Youth and Junior Weightlifting Championships 2024 with 33 Medals

- The young Indian weightlifters finished their campaign at the 2024 Asian Youth and Junior Weightlifting Championships with a total of 33 medals.
- They won seven Gold medals, sixteen Silver medals, and ten Bronze medals.
- The championship was organised by the Asian Weightlifting Federation in Doha, Qatar from 19-25 December 2024.
- 16-year-old Jyoshna Sabar of Uttar Pradesh bagged three Gold medals.

M Raghu & Devika Sihag crowned 2024 Sr. National Badminton Champion

- Karnataka's M.Raghu and Haryana's Devika Sihag won the men's and women's singles title respectively, at the 86th Senior National Badminton Championships 2024.
- In the final M Raghu defeated former champion Mithun Manjunath of Karnataka 14-21, 21-14, 24-22 to win his first senior national championship.
- 19-year-old Devika Sihag of Haryana won her first senior National Badminton Championships by defeating Telangana's Shriyanshi Valishetty 21-15, 21-16.
- The 86th Senior National Badminton Championships was organised by the Badminton Association of India and hosted by Karnataka Badminton Association in Bengaluru, Karnataka from 20-24 December 2024.

Nikhat Zareen and Meenakshi won gold in Elorda Cup 2024

- Indian boxers Nikhat Zareen and Minakshi clinched gold medals at the Elorda Cup 2024 in Astana, Kazakhstan.
- Nikhat Zareen triumphed in the women's 52 kg category, defeating Zhazira Urakbayeva of Kazakhstan with a 5-0 scoreline.
- Minakshi won in the women's 48 kg category, beating Uzbekistan's Rahmonova Saidahon 4-1.

Haryana won the title in Boxing Sub Junior National Championship

- Haryana clinched the team titles in both the boys and girls categories with an impressive combined haul of 19 medals at the boxing Sub Junior National Championship.
- Haryana, the reigning champions in the girls section, finished on top of the table with 64 points.
- They won 10 medals including seven gold, one silver and two bronze.

Hardik Singh And Salima Tete Win Hockey India Player Awards

- **Hardik Singh** was named Player of the Year for 2023 in the **men's category.**
- Salima Tete named Player of the Year for 2023 in the **women's category,** announced at the **sixth annual Hockey India Awards.**
- Hockey India announces the revival of Hockey India League (HIL). HIL to return in January 2025 after hiatus since 2017.

Japan won the 30th Sultan Azlan Shah Trophy

- Japan won its maiden Sultan Azlan Shah Hockey trophy by defeating Pakistan 4-1 in the penalty shoot-out in the final.
- The final was played **at the Azlan Shah Stadium in Ipoh, Malaysia,** on 11 May 2024.

Harendra Singh appointed as Coach of Indian Women's Hockey team until 2028 Olympics

- Dronacharya awardee Harendra Singh has been reappointed as the coach of the Indian women's hockey team.
- He previously coached the team from 2017 to 2018.
- Harendra's focus will be on preparing the team for the 2028 Los Angeles Olympics.

India to host BWF World Junior Badminton Championships 2025

- India will host the BWF World Junior Championships 2025 at the National Centre of Excellence in Guwahati, the **Badminton World Federation (BWF)** announced on 30 April.
- The **2025 edition in India** will mark the return of the BWF Junior World Championships to the country for the first time since 2008 when Pune hosted the event.

Satwiksairaj Rankireddy And Chirag Shetty Win Doubles Title At French Open Badminton Tournament

- Satwiksairaj Rankireddy and Chirag Shetty secured their second French Open Men's doubles Badminton title with a straight games victory over Yang Po-han and Lee Jhe-huei of Taiwan in the final, winning 21-11, 21-17.
- The Indian pair, who were top seeds, had previously claimed the title in 2022.

Indian Shuttler B Sai Praneeth Announced Retirement From International Badminton

- Indian shuttler B Sai Praneeth has announced his retirement from international badminton due to nagging injuries since the Tokyo Olympics.
- In his 24-year-long career, he won a World Championships bronze medal and represented India at the Tokyo 2020 Olympics.

BWF Para Badminton World Championships 2024

- The 2024 BWF Para-Badminton World Championships, officially known as NSDF Royal Beach Cliff BWF Para Badminton World Championships 2024, was held from February 20 to 25, 2024, **in Pattaya, Thailand.**
- In the Men's Singles SH6 category, **Krishna Nagar won** the gold medal.
- In the Women's Singles WH2 category, **Liu Yutong won** the gold medal.
- India performed well, securing 3 gold, 4 silver, and 11 bronze medals.

Badminton Asia Team Championships 2024

- The Indian women's badminton team, led by **PV Sindhu and Anmol Kharb, won a historic gold medal at the Badminton Asia Team Championships 2024,** which was held in Shah Alam, Malaysia from February 13 to 18.
- This was India's first-ever gold medal at the Badminton Asia Team Championships.

Sharath Kamal named flagbearer of Paris Olympics 2024

- Ace table tennis player Sharath Kamal will be the Indian team's flagbearer for the upcoming Paris 2024 Olympics, while Olympic bronze medalist MC Mary Kom has been named as the chef de mission for the Summer Games, the Indian Olympic Association (IOA) announced.
- Kamal has won the national table tennis championship a record 10 times.

Charles Leclerc creates F1 history with win in Monaco

- Charles Leclerc, the talented Monegasque driver, etched his name in Formula One history by securing a breakthrough victory at the Monaco Grand Prix.

Max Verstappen wins F1 at Japanese Grand Prix

- Max Verstappen, the reigning world champion, reclaimed his winning form by securing his third consecutive pole-to-flag victory at the Japanese Formula One Grand Prix.
- Racing at the Suzuka Circuit, Verstappen led his Red Bull teammate, Sergio Perez, to a dominant one-two finish.

Max Verstappen wins the Saudi Arabian Grand Prix

- Red Bull's Max Verstappen won from pole position at the Saudi Arabian Grand Prix, giving the team their second consecutive first-second place finish in the Formula One season.
- Mexican Sergio Perez secured the runner-up spot.

Asian Wrestling Championship

- Indian wrestler **Udit secured a silver medal** after losing 4-5 to Kento Yumiya of Japan in the men's freestyle 57kg final at the senior Asian Championship.
- Additionally, India won two bronze medals: Abhimanyu won in the men's 70kg freestyle category by defeating Begijon Kuldashev of Uzbekistan 6-5, and Vicky secured a bronze in the men's 97kg category by defeating home favorite Andrey Romanovitch Aronov 10-1.

Naveen Malik won National Wrestling Championship in 74kg category

- Naveen Malik, **Commonwealth Games gold medallist,** emerged victorious in the men's freestyle 74kg category at the National wrestling championships.
- Malik faced a tough challenge from Yash Tushir, a former World junior bronze medallist, but managed to secure a narrow 5-4 victory.

AWARDS AND HONOURS

NOBEL PRIZE 2024

Physiology or Medicine

- **Winners in 2024**: Victor Ambros (United States) and Gary Ruvkun (United States)
- **Awarded For**: Discovery of microRNA
- **Winners in 2023**: Katalin Kariko and Drew Weissman
- **Awarded For**: mRNA Vaccines

Physics

- **Winners in 2024**: John J. Hopfield (United States) and Geoffrey E. Hinton (Canada/UK)
- **Awarded For**: Discoveries and inventions that enable machine learning with artificial neural networks.
- **Winners in 2023**: Pierre Agostini, Ferenc Krausz and Anne L'Huillier
- **Awarded For**: Electron dynamics in matter

Chemistry

- **Winners in 2024**: David Baker (United States), Demis Hassabis (United Kingdom), and John M. Jumper (United States)
- **Awarded For**: Protein structure prediction
- **Winners in 2023**: Moungi Bawendi, Louis Brus and Alexei Ekimov
- **Awarded For**: Discovery and synthesis of quantum dots

Literature

- **Winners in 2024**: Han Kang (South Korea)
- **Awarded For**: Poetic prose that confronts historical traumas and exposes the fragility of human life
- **Winners in 2023**: Jon Fosse
- **Awarded For**: His innovative plays and prose which give voice to the unsayable".

Peace

- **Winners in 2024**: Nihon Hidankyo (Japan)
- **Awarded For**: Efforts to achieve a nuclear weapons-free world
- **Winners in 2023**: Narges Mohammadi
- **Research Area**: Fight against women's oppression in Iran

Economic Sciences

- **Winners in 2024**: Daron Acemoglu (Turkey/United States), Simon Johnson (United Kingdom/United States), and James A. Robinson (United Kingdom/United States)
- **Awarded For**: Studies of how institutions are formed and affect prosperity
- **Winners in 2023**: Claudia Goldin
- **Awarded For**: Gender Gap in labour market

THE NOBEL PRIZES ARE AWARDED IN SIX CATEGORIES

✎ **Four Physiology or Medicine:** Awarded by the Karolinska Institute for groundbreaking work in medical research.

✎ **Physics:** Selected by the Royal Swedish Academy of Sciences for revolutionary discoveries in physics.

✎ **Chemistry:** Chosen by the Royal Swedish Academy of Sciences, honoring advances in chemistry.

✎ **Literature:** Awarded by the Swedish Academy for literary works of outstanding merit.

✎ **Peace:** Awarded by the Norwegian Nobel Committee to individuals or groups advancing peace.

✎ **Economic Sciences:** Established later in 1968 and selected by the Royal Swedish Academy of Sciences.

About Nobel Prize

- **Origin:** The Nobel Prize was established by the will of Alfred Nobel, the inventor of dynamite.
- First awarded in 1901 on the 5th anniversary of the death of Alfred Nobel.
- In 1968, a sixth prize was introduced in Economic Sciences (Sveriges Riksbank Prize in Economic Sciences) but is not officially called a Nobel Prize.
- **Venue:** The prizes are awarded by the Nobel Foundation in Stockholm, Sweden.
- The Peace Prize is awarded in Oslo, Norway.
- **Eligibility:** It can only be awarded to individuals except for the peace prize that can be conferred on individuals or institutions.
- A maximum of 3 individuals can share a prize.

Nobel Prize and India

- Rabindranath Tagore was the first non-European and Indian to receive a Nobel Prize in 1913 for Literature.
- He was honoured for his poetry collection Geetanjali.
- India's first Nobel Prize in Physics was awarded to Sir Chandrasekhara Venkata Raman in 1930 for his work on the scattering of light and the discovery of the Raman Effect.

THE LIST OF INDIAN NOBEL LAUREATES

Indian Citizenship

Nobel Winner	Field	Year
Rabindranath Tagore	Literature	1913
C. V Raman	Physics	1930
Mother Teresa	Peace	1979
Amartya Sen	Economic Sciences	1998
Kailash Satyarthi	Peace	2014

Born in India but different Citizenship

Nobel Winner	Field	Year	Nationality
Har Gobind Khorana	Physiology/Medicine	1968	United States
Subrahmanyam Chandrasekhar	Physics	1983	United States
Venkatraman Ramakrishnan	Chemistry	2009	United Kingdom
Abhijit Banerjee	Economic Sciences	2019	United States

Indian Residents at the time of being awarded & Non-Indian Citizenship

Nobel Winner	Field	Year	Nationality
Ronald Ross	Physiology/Medicine	1902	United Kingdom
Rudyard Kipling	Literature	1907	United Kingdom
Tenzing Gyatso (14th Dalai Lama)	Peace	1989	Tibet

ALFRED NOBEL

✎ Alfred Nobel (1833-1896) was a Swedish chemist, engineer, inventor, and businessman best known for inventing dynamite.

✎ Born on October 21, 1833, in Stockholm, Sweden, Nobel held 355 patents in his lifetime.

✎ Nobel's most famous invention, dynamite, was patented in 1867.

✎ He also invented gelignite and ballistite.

✎ Upon his death on December 10, 1896, in San Remo, Italy, Nobel bequeathed his fortune to establish the Nobel Prizes, which annually recognize individuals and organizations that have conferred the greatest benefit to humankind.

NATIONAL AWARDS 2024

70TH NATIONAL FILM AWARDS 2024

- The 70th National Film Awards were announced on 16 August 2024, celebrating the best of Indian cinema from 2022. The awards were presented by the National Film Development Corporation of India.

Category	Winner	Film/Language
Best Feature Film	Aattam	Malayalam
Best Actor	Rishab Shetty	Kantara
Best Actress	Nithya Menen, Mansi Parekh	Thiruchitrambalam, Kutch Express
Best Director	Sooraj Barjatya	Uunchai
Best Popular Film Providing Wholesome Entertainment	Kantara	Kannada
Best Film in AVGC (Animation, Visual Effects, Gaming & Comic)	Brahmastra: Part One – Shiva	Hindi
Best Debut Film of a Director	Fouja	Haryanvi

IIFA 2024 AWARDS

- The 24th International Indian Film Academy (IIFA) Awards took place from 27 to 29 September 2024, at Yas Island, Abu Dhabi.
- Established in 2000, the IIFA Awards aim to promote Indian cinema globally.

List of Major Award Winners

Sr. No.	Category	Winner
1.	Best Film	Animal
2.	Best Director	Vidhu Vinod Chopra – (12th Fail)
3.	Best Actor	Shah Rukh Khan – (Jawan)
4.	Best Actress	Rani Mukerji – (Mrs. Chatterjee vs Norway)
5.	Best Supporting Actor	Anil Kapoor – (Animal)
6.	Best Supporting Actress	Shabana Azmi – (Rocky Aur Rani Kii Prem Kahaani)
7.	Best Performance in a Negative Role	Bobby Deol – (Animal)
8.	Best Music	Animal
9.	Best Male Singer	Bhupinder Babbal – "Arjan Vailly" – (Animal)
10.	Best Female Singer	Shilpa Rao – "Chaleya" – (Jawan)
11.	Best Story	Rocky Aur Rani Ki Prem Kahaani

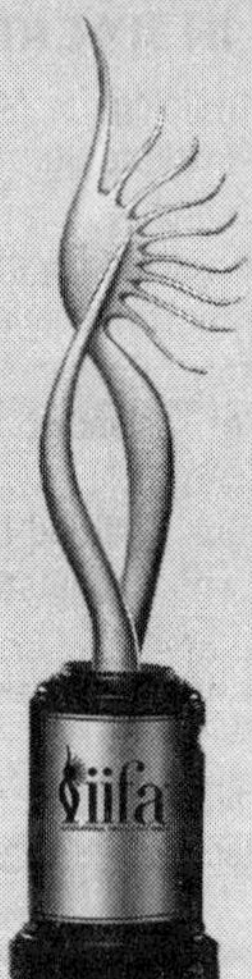

Kiran Mazumdar gets 'Jamsetji Tata Award' for biosciences movement in India

- Biocon Group Chairperson Kiran Mazumdar-Shaw was conferred the prestigious Jamsetji Tata Award by the Indian Society for Quality (ISQ) for pioneering the biosciences movement in India.
- The Jamsetji Tata Award, instituted in 2004 by ISQ recognises business leaders who have made significant contributions to Indian society.
- Mazumdar-Shaw received the award from Janak Kumar Mehta, President of ISQ and Chairman and Managing Director, TQM International.

Gagan Gill wins Sahitya Akademi Awards for Hindi

- Gagan Gill (Hindi) and Easterine Kire (English) are among 21 winners of the Sahitya Akademi Awards 2024.
- Easterine Kire from Nagaland won the Sahitya Akademi Award 2024 for her novel Spirit Nights.
- Hindi poet Gagan Gill received the award for her poetry book Main Jab Tak Aai Bahar.
- The award honors outstanding books in 24 Indian languages, initiated in 1954, with the first awards given in 1955.

Indira Gandhi Prize for Peace, Disarmament, and Development

- Former Chilean President Michelle Bachelet was awarded with 2024 Indira Gandhi Prize for Peace, Disarmament, and Development.
- The award was announced by the international jury of the Indira Gandhi Memorial Trust, chaired by former Foreign Secretary and National Security Advisor Shivshankar Menon.
- The prize consists of a monetary award of 25 lakh rupees along with a citation.

SAHITYA AKADEMI AWARDS 2024

Category	Language	Winner	Work Title
Poetry	Hindi	Gagan Gill	Main Jab Tak Aai Bahar
	Punjabi	Paul Kaur	Sun Gunvanta Sun Budhivanta: Itihaasnama Punjab
	Malayalam	K Jayakumar	-
	Manipuri	Haobam Satyabati Devi	-
	Gujarati	Dileep Jhaveri	-
	Assamese	Sameer Tanti	-
	Rajasthani	Mukut Maniraj	-
	Sanskrit	Dipak Kumar Sharma	-
Novel	English	Easterine Kire	Spirit Nights
	Kashmiri	Sohan Kaul	Psychiatric Ward
	Bodo	Aron Raja	Swrni Thakhai
Short Stories	Nepali	Yuva Baral	Chhichimira
	Sindhi	Hundraj Balwani	Purzo
Essay	Konkani	Mukesh Thali	-
	Maithili	Mahendra Malangia	-
	Odia	Baishnab Charan Samai	-
Play	Santali	Maheshwar Sorn	Seched Sawnta Ren Andha Manmi
Research	Tamil	AR Venkatachalapathy	-
Literary Criticism	Kannada	KV Narayana	-
	Marathi	Sudhir Rasal	-
	Telugu	Penugonda Lakshminarayana	-

Ustad Bismillah Khan Yuva Puraskar for the Years 2022 and 2023

- The Ustad Bismillah Khan Yuva Puraskar for the years 2022 and 2023 was awarded to a total of 82 young artists.
- The award ceremony took place on 22nd November 2024, at the Dr. Ambedkar International Centre in New Delhi.
- Each Awardee Received Twenty Five Thousand Rupees.
- This prestigious award, instituted in 2006 by Sangeet Natak Akademi, recognizes outstanding young artists under the age of 40 in the fields of music, dance, drama, folk and tribal arts, and puppetry.

Manoj Bajpayee's film "The Fable" won the Best Film award

- On 15th November 2024, Manoj Bajpayee's film "The Fable" won the Best Film award at the 38th Leeds International Film Festival.
- The film was directed by Raam Reddy. It's the first Indian film to achieve this honour.
- The film, which premiered at the Berlinale Film Festival 2024, also won the Special Jury Prize at the 2024 MAMI Mumbai Film Festival.

President Droupadi Murmu conferred the National Florence Nightingale Awards 2024

- On 11 September 2024, President Droupadi Murmu conferred the National Florence Nightingale Awards 2024 to 15 Nurses at Rashtrapati Bhavan in New Delhi.
- Each award consists of a Certificate of Merit, Cash Award of Rs.1,00,000/- and a medal.
- This award is given as a mark of recognition for the meritorious services rendered by the nurses and nursing professionals to society.
- The National Florence Nightingale Award was instituted by the Ministry of Health and Family Welfare in the year 1973.

President Droupadi Murmu confers National Geoscience Awards for 2023

- On 20 August 2024, President Droupadi Murmu conferred the National Geoscience Awards (NGA) for 2023 to 21 geoscientists, including academicians and professionals from across the country.
- The awards, totalling 12, recognised outstanding achievements in geosciences, mineral exploration, and natural hazard investigations.
- The awardees were honoured in three categories: National Geoscience Award for Lifetime Achievement, National Geoscience Award, and National Young Geoscientist Award.

Gallantry Awards 2024

- On 15 August 2024, during the 78th Independence Day celebrations, President Droupadi Murmu presented the Gallantry Awards to honor the bravery and sacrifice of the armed forces and police personnel.
- A total of 103 Gallantry awards were conferred, including 4 Kirti Chakras (3 posthumous), 18 Shaurya Chakras (4 posthumous), 1 Bar to Sena Medal (Gallantry), 63 Sena Medals (Gallantry) (2 posthumous), 11 Nao Sena Medals (Gallantry), and 6 Vayu Sena Medals (Gallantry).
- Additionally, 213 Police Medals for Gallantry were awarded.

RASHTRIYA VIGYAN PURASKAR 2024

- On 7 August 2024, the Rashtriya Vigyan Puraskar 2024 were announced.
- These awards, reinstated to honor excellence in science, technology, and innovation, will be presented on 23 August 2024, coinciding with National Space Day.
- The awards are categorized into four: Vigyan Ratna for lifetime achievements, Vigyan Shri for distinguished contributions, Vigyan Yuva for young scientists under 45, and Vigyan Team for collaborative research.

Central Electronics Limited Awarded Mini RATNA Status

- Central Electronics Limited (CEL), during its Golden Jubilee celebration, achieved the prestigious "Mini RATNA" status (Category-1).
- To qualify for this recognition, an organization must demonstrate consistent profitability over the last three years, with a pre-tax profit of ₹30 crores or more in at least one of those years, along with a positive net worth.
- As of October 2024, there are 14 Maharatna, 24 Navratna, 51 Miniratna I and 11 Miniratna II companies in India.

Rbi Bags 'Risk Manager of The Year Award 2024'

- In 2024, the Reserve Bank of India (RBI) received the prestigious "Risk Manager of the Year Award" from Central Banking, headquartered in London, United Kingdom.
- The award recognizes RBI's efforts in enhancing risk culture and awareness, crucial for ensuring India's financial stability.

SASTRA Ramanujan Prize 2024

- The 2024 SASTRA Ramanujan Prize has been awarded to Dr. Alexander Dunn from Georgia Tech for his outstanding contributions to analytic number theory.
- Announced on 30 September 2024, the $10,000 prize was presented at the International Conference on Number Theory from 20 to 22 December 2024, at SASTRA University in Kumbakonam.It was established in 2005 and given by the Shanmugha Arts, Science, Technology & Research Academy (SASTRA) University, Tamil Nadu.

Best Heritage Tourism Village of 2024

- Manipur's Andro village was awarded the Best Heritage Tourism Village of 2024 along with Hafeshwar village-Gujarat, Mawphlang village -Meghalaya, Keeladi village - Tamil Nadu, Pura Mahadev village -Uttar Pradesh on 27 September 2024.
- The award, presented during the World Tourism Day celebrations at Vigyan Bhawan, New Delhi, recognizes Andro's rich cultural heritage, including the ancient Panam Ningthou Temple and traditional fire worship practices.

32nd Ekalabya Puraskar for 2024

- On 22 September 2024, swimmer Pratyasa Ray was awarded the 32nd Ekalabya Puraskar.
- This award, instituted by IMPaCT (Indian Metals Public Charitable Trust) in 1993 and managed by IMFA, recognizes her outstanding achievements in swimming.
- Pratyasa received a cash prize of Rs 7 lakh, an increase from the previous Rs 5 lakh.

Swachh Vayu Survekshan Awards 2024

- On 7 September 2024, the Swachh Vayu Survekshan Awards were presented in Jaipur to recognize cities excelling in air quality improvement under the National Clean Air Programme (NCAP).
- The awards were categorized based on population: Category-1 (over 10 lakhs) winners were Surat, Jabalpur, and Agra; Category-2 (3-10 lakhs) winners were Firozabad, Amravati, and Jhansi; and Category-3 (under 3 lakhs) winners were Raebareli, Nalgonda, and Nalagarh.

Kerala Tourism clinches PATA Gold Award 2024

- Kerala Tourism was awarded the prestigious Pacific Asia Travel Association (PATA) Gold Award 2024 for its innovative 'Holiday Heist' campaign in the Digital Marketing Campaign category.
- The award ceremony took place on 28 August 2024, at the Queen Sirikit National Convention Center in Bangkok.

Rajbhasha Gaurav Samman 2023-24 award Ceremony

- The Rajbhasha Gaurav Samman 2023-24 award ceremony was held on 26 July 2024.
- Hosted by NTPC and chaired by Atul Bhatt, Chairman of the Town Official Language Implementation Committee (TOLIC), the event recognized Public Sector Undertakings (PSUs) in Visakhapatnam for their exemplary performance in promoting Hindi.
- Awards were given in three categories, with HPCL-Visakha Refinery, GAIL, and MSTC winning first prizes in their respective groups.

Nagaland wins Best State in Horticulture Award 2024

- Nagaland emerged as the "Best State in Horticulture" at the Agriculture Leadership Awards 2024.
- Minister for Women Resource Development & Horticulture, Salhoutuonuo Kruse, accepted the award in New Delhi, highlighting the state's clever horticulture projects.
- The state has achieved geographical indication (GI) registration of three horticultural crops — Naga Mircha, Naga Tree Tomato and Naga Sweet Cucumber.

P. Geetha receives inaugural K. Saraswathi Amma Award

- On 3 July 2024, writer, critic, and feminist activist P. Geetha was honoured with the inaugural K. Saraswathi Amma Award by WINGS (Women's Integration and Growth Through Sports) Kerala.
- This prestigious award recognizes her outstanding work in feminist studies. Geetha's thought-provoking work titled "Aan Thachukal" (which translates to "Male Creations") delves into the scripts renowned author M.T. Vasudevan Nair.

INTERNATIONAL AWARDS 2024

55TH INTERNATIONAL FILM FESTIVAL OF INDIA

- The 55th International Film Festival of India (IFFI) concluded in Goa on 28th November 2024. The festival showcased 270 films from 81 countries, including 15 International Premieres.

List of Winners

Award	Winner	Film/Project	Country
Golden Peacock (Best Film)	Saule Bliuvaite	Toxic	Lithuania
Silver Peacock (Best Director)	Bogdan Muresanu	The New Year That Never Came	Romania
Silver Peacock (Best Actor – Male)	Clément Faveau	Holy Cow	France
Silver Peacock (Best Actor – Female)	Vesta Matulyte, Ieva Rupeikaite	Toxic	Lithuania
Best Debut Feature Film	Sarah Friedland	Familiar Touch	USA
Best Debut Director of Indian Film	Navjyot Bandiwadekar	Gharat Ganpati	India
ICFT-UNESCO Gandhi Medal	Levan Akin	Crossing	Georgia
Best Web Series (OTT)	Nipun Dharmadhikari	Lampan	India
Indian Film Personality of the Year	Vikrant Massey	—	India
Special Jury Award	Louise Courvoisier	Holy Cow	France

PM Modi Receives Kuwait's Highest Honour

- Prime Minister Narendra Modi received Kuwait's highest honour, "The Order of Mubarak Al Kabeer," in December 2024.
- He received the honour from Kuwait's Amir Sheikh Meshal Al-Ahmad Al-Jaber Al-Sabah.This is the 20th international honour given to PM Modi by a country
- The Order of Mubarak Al Kabeer is a knighthood order of Kuwait.

Arun Kapur Receives Bhutan's Highest Honour

- Renowned Indian educationist Arun Kapur conferred with the 'Bura Marp' (red scarf) and 'Patang' (ceremonial sword) by Bhutan's King Jigme Khesar Namgyel at the 117th Bhutanese National Day.
- Along with these awards, he was granted the honorary title 'Dasho', typically reserved for senior officials in Bhutan.
- In 2019, Mr Kapur was awarded the 'Druk Thuksey' for his work in setting up the Royal Academy school and developing the Bhutan Baccalaureate educational system.

Ram Temple project Gets UK Honour

- The 'Ram Temple project' of the Shri Ram Janmaboomi Temple in Ayodhya has been awarded the 'Sword of Honour' by the British Safety Council.
- This award was one of the highest recognitions in safety management.
- Larsen & Toubro, the construction company for the temple, previously received the 'Golden Trophy' from the National Safety Council.

Ecologist Madhav Gadgil honoured with 'Champions of Earth Award'

- India's veteran ecologist, Madhav Gadgil has been named as one of the six 'Champions of the Earth' by the United Nations Environment Programme (UNEP) for 2024.
- He has been honoured in the "Lifetime Achievement" category.
- Other awardees include Brazil's Sonia Guajajara, Amy Bowers Cordalis from the United States, Gabriel Paun from Romania, Lu Qi from China and SEKEM, a sustainable agriculture initiative.
- The 'Champions of the Earth award is considered the United Nation's highest environmental honour.

Nepal Army Chief Conferred Honorary Rank By President Murmu

- President Droupadi Murmu conferred the honorary rank of 'General of Indian Army' on Nepal's Army chief General Suprabal Janasewashree General Ashok Raj Sigdel in New Delhi.
- He was honoured for his commendable military prowess and immeasurable contribution to further fostering Nepal's long and friendly association with India.
- Since 1950, the army chiefs of Nepal and India have had a unique tradition of being conferred the title of Honorary General.

Abathsahayeswarar Temple & BJPCI Project bag UNESCO Heritage Award

- Two Indian heritage conservation projects, Abathsahayeswarar Temple Conservation Project in Thukkatchi, Tamil Nadu, and the BJPCI Conservation Project of Mumbai, Maharashtra have won UNESCO's Asia-Pacific Awards for Cultural Heritage Conservation 2024.
- UNESCO announced the award winners at its regional office in Bangkok, Thailand, on 6 December 2024.
- The Abathsahayeswarar Temple Conservation Project won the 'Award of Distinction' in the UNESCO's Award category.
- BJPCI (Sir Byramjee Jeejeebhoy Parsee Charitable Institution) Conservation project bagged the 'Merit Award' of UNESCO's Asia-Pacific Awards for Cultural Heritage Conservation 2024.

Tom Cruise Honoured with US Navy's top Civilian Award

- Hollywood star Tom Cruise felicitated with the US Navy's top civilian honour, the Distinguished Public Service Award.
- Cruise was awarded the Navy's top civilian honor for "outstanding contributions to the Navy and Marine Corps" through his work in Movie 'Top Gun', A Few Good Men, and Mission Impossible franchises.

Samantha Harvey won the Booker Prize

- In November 2024, British author Samantha Harvey won the Booker Prize for Fiction with her novel "Orbital".
- Harvey is the first woman to win the prize since 2019.
- The book, set in space, follows six astronauts observing Earth from the International Space Station over 24 hours.
- Harvey was previously longlisted for the Booker prize in 2009 for her debut novel, The Wilderness.Last year, Irish writer Paul Lynch won award for his dystopian novel 'Prophet Song'.

PM Modi Received honours from Guyana and Dominica

- On 21st November 2024, Prime Minister Narendra Modi received the Order of Excellence from Guyana and the Dominica Award of Honour from Dominica.

- These awards recognize his leadership during the COVID-19 pandemic and his efforts to strengthen bilateral ties.

PM Honoured with "Grand Commander of the Order of Niger"

- On 17th November 2024, Prime Minister Narendra Modi was honoured with Nigeria's second-highest national award, the "Grand Commander of the Order of the Niger" (GCON), by President Bola Ahmed Tinubu.

- Prime Minister Shri Narendra Modi is the first foreign leader to be conferred with this award after Queen Elizabeth II since 1969, recognizes Modi's significant contributions to strengthening India-Nigeria relations.

Coal India Ltd honoured with Green World Environment Award 2024

- In November 2024, Coal India Limited (CIL) received the 'Green World Environment Award' 2024 in the Corporate Social Responsibility (CSR) category at Kensington Palace, London.
- The award, given by The Green Organization, recognized CIL's Thalassemia Bal Sewa Yojna, which provides curative treatment for over 600 Thalassemia patients through Bone Marrow Transplants.
- CIL was also honoured with the title of 'Green World Ambassador' for its environmental initiatives, including expanding green cover and providing mine water to villagers.

ICC HONORED WITH THE 2024 OPCW-THE HAGUE AWARD

✎ On 25th November 2024, the Indian Chemical Council (ICC) was honored with the 2024 OPCW-The Hague Award during the 29th Session of the Conference of the States Parties (CSP) of the Organisation for the Prohibition of Chemical Weapons (OPCW) in The Hague.

✎ This prestigious award, established in 2014, recognizes ICC's efforts in promoting chemical safety, compliance with the Chemical Weapons Convention (CWC), and enhancing industry-wide security practices.

Dr. Usha Thakur Receives Prestigious 12th Vishwa Hindi Samman

- Dr. Usha Thakur, a prominent figure in Hindi literature and culture, was honored with the 12th Vishwa Hindi Samman. The award ceremony took place at Tribhuvan University in Kathmandu.
- Dr. Thakur's remarkable efforts include translating over 40 literary works into Hindi and Nepali, emphasizing the importance of Hindi as a widespread contact language for tourists and locals in Nepal.

Australian Filmmaker Phillip Noyce honoured with the Satyajit Ray Lifetime Achievement Award

- In November 2024, veteran Australian filmmaker Phillip Noyce was honoured with the Satyajit Ray Lifetime Achievement Award at the 55th International Film Festival of India (IFFI) in Goa.
- Noyce, known for films like "Salt" and "Patriot Games", received the award for his outstanding contribution to world cinema.
- The festival, themed "Young Filmmakers - The Future is Now," featured over 180 films from 81 countries.

Sanjana Thakur wins 2024 Commonwealth Short Story Prize

- Sanjana Thakur, a 26-year-old writer from Mumbai, emerged as the overall winner of the 2024 Commonwealth Short Story Prize.
- Her captivating story, titled "Aishwarya Rai," stood out among 7,359 entrants worldwide and earned her a £5,000 prize.
- In this poignant tale, Avni, a young woman in Mumbai, grapples with choosing a mother from a local shelter.

Arundhati Roy honoured with Prestigious Pen Pinter Prize 2024

- Arundhati Roy, the acclaimed Indian writer known for her fearless and impactful writing, has been awarded the PEN Pinter Prize 2024.
- The award ceremony was co-hosted by the British Library.
- The prize, established in 2009 by the charity English PEN, defends freedom of expression and celebrates literature in memory of Nobel-Laureate playwright Harold Pinter.

'The Golden Thread' bags Golden Conch award at 18th MIFF 2024

- The Indian documentary "The Golden Thread," directed by Nistha Jain, received the prestigious Golden Conch award for Best Documentary at the 18th Mumbai International Film Festival (MIFF) 2024.
- The award includes a Golden Conch, a certificate, and a cash prize of Rs. 10 lakhs.

Filmmaker Vinod Ganatra honoured with Nelson Mandela Lifetime Achievement Award

- Vinod Ganatra, an eminent children's filmmaker, has made history as the first Indian to receive the prestigious 'Nelson Mandela Lifetime Achievement Award' from South Africa.
- He was conferred with the award at the 7th Nelson Mandela Children's Film Festival for his outstanding contribution to children's cinema.Nelson Mandela is perhaps the most famous personality in South Africa who has the distinction of being the first black President of South Africa.

IPBES wins 2024 Blue Planet Prize for environmental leadership

- The Intergovernmental Platform on Biodiversity and Ecosystem Services (IPBES) has been honoured with the '2024 Blue Planet Prize' for its exceptional efforts in biodiversity and ecosystem services.
- This prestigious award recognizes IPBES as "the leading global authority on the state of knowledge and science about biodiversity, ecosystem services, and nature's contributions to people."
- It is awarded by the Asahi Glass Foundation headquartered in Tokyo, Japan.

Kalash Gupta, IIT Delhi Student won World's Largest Coding Competition

- Kalash Gupta, a third-year computer science student at IIT Delhi, secured the coveted title of "World's Best Coder" in the TCS CodeVita Season 10.
- CodeVita holds the Guinness World Records title as the world's largest computer programming competition.
- The first and second runner ups of the contest were from Chile and Taiwan respectively.
- This prestigious global programming competition, organized annually by Tata Consultancy Services, witnessed participation from over 1 lakh coders across 87 countries.

NIMHANS awarded Nelson Mandela Award for Health Promotion

- The National Institute of Mental Health and Neuro Sciences (NIMHANS) in Bengaluru has been awarded the 2024 Nelson Mandela Award for Health Promotion by the World Health Organization (WHO).

- Recognized for its remarkable contributions to health promotion, NIMHANS is an Institute of National Importance under the Ministry of Health and Family Welfare.
- The award, established by WHO in 2019, honors outstanding contributions to health promotion.

Sanya Malhotra clinches best actress award at New York Indian Film Festival

- Sanya Malhotra has won the Best Actress award at the prestigious New York Indian Film Festival 2024 for her role in the film 'Mrs'.
- Directed by Arati Kadav, 'Mrs' is said to be the Hindi adaptation of the acclaimed Malayalam movie, 'The Great Indian Kitchen'.
- 'Mrs.' is produced by Jyoti Deshpande, Pammi Baweja and Harman Baweja's Baweja Movies.

Emmy Awards 2024

- On 15 September 2024, the 76th Primetime Emmy Awards were held at the Peacock Theater in Los Angeles.
- "Shogun" won Best Drama Series and earned 18 awards overall.
- "Hacks" won Best Comedy Series, while "Baby Reindeer" took Best Limited Series.
- Notable acting winners included Hiroyuki Sanada and Anna Sawai for "Shogun," and Jeremy Allen White for "The Bear".

JAMIE LEE CURTIS WON CREATIVE ARTS EMMY AWARD FOR GUEST ACTRESS

✎ On 8 September 2024, Jamie Lee Curtis won the Creative Arts Emmy Award for Outstanding Guest Actress in a Comedy Series for her role as Donna Berzatto in "The Bear".

✎ This marks her first Emmy win, where she competed against notable actresses like Olivia Colman and Maya Rudolph.

NTPC Talcher Kaniha wins 2024 Energy Management Insight Award

- On 7 September 2024, NTPC Talcher Kaniha was honored with the prestigious 2024 Energy Management Insight Award by the Clean Energy Ministerial (CEM).
- This global recognition was awarded for the station's high-quality case study on ISO 50001 energy management, showcasing its sustainable practices and energy efficiency.
- CEM is a global forum consisting of 29 member govts and 21 participating countries.

24th International Mother Teresa Awards

- The 24th International Mother Teresa Awards Ceremony took place on 26 August 2024, at the Millennium Plaza Dubai.
- This event, organized by the All-India Minority and Weaker Sections Council, commemorated the 114th birth anniversary of Mother Teresa.
- The awards recognized exceptional contributions in various fields such as education, science, culture, sports, social work, medicine, industry, and politics.

Shah Rukh Khan Honoured at 77th Locarno Film Festival

- On 10 August 2024, Shah Rukh Khan was honoured with the 'Pardo alla Carriera' award at the 77th Locarno Film Festival.
- This prestigious lifetime achievement award recognizes his remarkable contributions to cinema.

SHAH RUKH KHAN HONOURED WITH GOLD COINS

✎ Shah Rukh Khan was honoured with customized gold coins by the Grévin Museum in Paris on 24 July 2024.

✎ This makes him the first Indian actor to receive such an honor. The coins feature his likeness and celebrate his contributions to global cinema.

Abhinav Bindra Awarded prestigious olympic order by IOC

- Abhinav Bindra was awarded the prestigious Olympic Order by the International Olympic Committee (IOC) on 22 July 2024.
- This honor recognizes his outstanding contributions to the Olympic Movement.
- Bindra, India's first individual Olympic gold medallist, has been a member of the IOC Athletes Commission since 2018.

Chhangte, Indumathi Win Top Male and Female Awards at Aiff Awards 2024

- Lallianzuala Chhangte and Indumathi Kathiresan were honoured as the AIFF Best Men's and Women's Players of the Year 2023-24 at the AIFF Award on 19 July 2024.
- The awards were given at a function organised by the national football federation.
- The most Promising Player of Year award went to David Lahlansanga of I-League-winning club Mohammedan Sporting.
- The proven Khalid Jamil of Jamshedpur FC won the Best Male Coach of the Year award, while former India player Shukla Dutta bagged the honour in the women's section.

Nobel Laureate Rigoberta Menchú Tum receives prestigious Gandhi Mandela Award 2020

- Nobel Peace Prize laureate Rigoberta Menchú Tum received the Gandhi Mandela Award 2020 on Nelson Mandela's 106th birth anniversary for promoting the values of Gandhi and Mandela, including community service and social development.
- Her autobiography, "I, Rigoberta Menchú," published in 1983, garnered international attention and highlighted her remarkable life and struggles.

PM Modi receives Russia's highest civilian honour for "outstanding service"

- On 9 July 2024, Russian President Vladimir Putin officially bestowed Indian Prime Minister Narendra Modi with Russia's highest civilian honour, "The Order of St. Andrew the Apostle".
- The Order of St. Andrew, established in 1698 by Tsar Peter the Great, holds deep historical and cultural significance. It features a golden cross with blue enamel, adorned with a crucified Saint Andrew the Apostle.

Sopna Kallingal wins Spice Award 2024

- Sopna Kallingal, an agriculturist from Kallingal Plantation in Thrissur, Kerala, received the 'Spice Award 2024'.
- The award ceremony took place on 3 July 2024, in Kozhikode.
- This prestigious award was instituted by the ICAR-Indian Institute of Spices Research. Sopna Kallingal was recognized for her outstanding work in business diversification and integrated crop management.

Kaamya Karthikeyan Became Youngest Female to Climb Highest Peaks of Each Continent

- **Kaamya Karthikeyan**, a Class 12 student from Mumbai, became the **youngest female to climb the highest peaks on all seven continents.**
- She completed the Seven Summits Challenge by scaling Mount Vinson in Antarctica on December 24, accompanied by her father, Cdr S Karthikeyan.
- She had previously climbed **Mt Kilimanjaro** (Africa), **Mt Elbrus** (Europe), **Mt Kosciuszko** (Australia), **Mt Aconcagua** (South America), **Mt Denali** (North America), and **Mt Everest** (Asia).

Ashwini Vaishnaw confers '69th Ati Vishisht Rail Seva Award 2024'

- Union Minister of Railways, Information and Broadcasting, Electronics and IT, Shri Ashwini Vaishnaw, awarded the "69th Ati Vishisht Rail Seva Puraskar" to 101 railway officials.
- He also presented 22 Shields to the best-performing Zones in different categories.
- Indian Railways confers 'Ati Vishisht Rail Seva Puraskar' to its employees every year.
- These awards are given into two categories, the individual awards, as well as Shields presented to the best-performing Railway Zones.

President of India Presents 'Pradhan Mantri Rashtriya Bal Puraskar' 2023

- The President of India, Smt Droupadi Murmu conferred the "Pradhan Mantri Rashtriya Bal Puraskar" on 17 children, in seven categories, for their exceptional achievements.
- The winner of the Pradhan Mantri Rashtriya Bal Puraskar is awarded a Medal, a Certificate, and a Cash prize of Rs. One Lakh.
- The children will also participate in the Republic Day parade on 26th January, 2024.
- The award was announced and conferred on the occasion of the Veer Baal Diwas.

Maheshwari Chauhan and Anantjeet Singh win 'Skeet Mixed Team National' Title

- Paris Olympians Maheshwari Chauhan and Anantjeet Singh Naruka won gold for Rajasthan in the 'Skeet Mixed Team event'.
- They achieved this at the '67th National Shooting Championship' in New Delhi.
- The duo achieved a victory with a score of 44-43 against the Uttar Pradesh team of Mairaj Ahmad Khan and Areeba Khan.
- Punjab's Ganemat Sekhon and Abhay Singh Sekhon won the bronze medal in the event.

RINL wins Gold award at the AP State Energy Conservation Award-2024

- RINL (Rashtriya Ispat Nigam Limited) has been honoured with the prestigious "Gold Award" in the State Energy Conservation Award 2024 competition.
- RINL is the corporate entity of Visakhapatnam Steel Plant, India's first shore-based integrated steel plant.
- RINL received a prestigious Gold award for implementing energy conservation measures and harnessing waste energy over the past three years.

Jaishankar Honoured with 'Sri Chandrasekarendra Saraswathi National Eminence Award'

- External Affairs Minister S. Jaishankar recently received the "Sri Chandrasekarendra Saraswathi National Eminence Award" for Public Leadership from the South Indian Education Society (SIES).
- The award is named in honour of Sri Chandrasekarendra Saraswathi, a revered spiritual leader and the 68th Shankaracharya of the Kanchi Kamakoti Peetham, known for his wisdom and service to humanity.

Bharat Ratna 2024

- In 2024, the Bharat Ratna was awarded to five distinguished individuals, surpassing the traditional limit of three awards per year.
- The central government announced on January 23, 2024, that the late Karpoori Thakur, a socialist icon and former Chief Minister of Bihar, would be the 49th recipient and the 15th posthumous awardee of this honor.
- Prime Minister Narendra Modi conferred the Bharat Ratna to senior BJP leader L. K. Advani on March 3, 2024, in recognition of his 50 years in Indian politics.

KARPOORI THAKUR

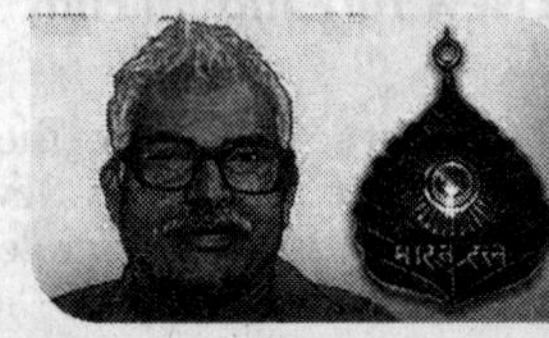

- **Born:** January 24, 1924, in Samastipur, Bihar
- **Known for:** Champion of the poor, Gandhian socialist leader
- **Political Achievements:** 11th Chief Minister of Bihar (served twice: from 1970-71 and 1977-79)
- **Died:** February 17, 1988, in Patna, Bihar

LAL KRISHNA ADVANI

- **Born:** November 8, 1927, in Karachi (now in Pakistan)
- **Known for:** Leading the Ram Janmabhoomi movement and the 1990 Rath Yatra from Somnath to Ayodhya for the construction of the Ram Temple.
- **Political Achievements:** Served as a Member of Parliament eleven times, Home Minister (1998-2004), and Deputy Prime Minister (2002-2004)

CHAUDHARY CHARAN SINGH

- **Born:** December 23, 1902, in Hapur, United Provinces (now Uttar Pradesh)
- **Died:** May 29, 1987, in Delhi
- **Known for:** Freedom fighter, farmers' leader, and Prime Minister of India
- **Political Achievements:** 5th Prime Minister of India (July 28 to August 20, 1979), Union Home Minister (1977-1978), and Finance Minister (1979). Served in the Uttar Pradesh Legislative Assembly and Parliament.

Awards and Honours

Bruhat Soma Wins 2024 Scripps National Spelling Bee

- **Bruhat Soma,** a seventh-grader, won the US National Spelling Bee champion title along with a Scripps Cup trophy and a USD 50,000 check after acing a 90-second spell-off against the second runner-up, 12-year-old Faizan Zaki from Texas.
- Bruhat spelled 29 words correctly in the tiebreaker, surpassing Zaki by nine, to win the title on Thursday night.
- His winning word was "abseil," referring to a descent in mountaineering using a rope looped over a projection above."

RBI Wins Risk Manager Of The Year Award 2024

- The Reserve Bank of India (RBI) has been awarded the **"Risk Manager of the Year Award 2024"** by Central Banking, a renowned publication headquartered in London.
- The award was accepted by then RBI's Executive Director, Manoranjan Mishra, in London, UK.
- The RBI established a regulatory sandbox for fintech experimentation, enabling risk assessment of new financial products.

First Indian Honoured With 'Nelson Mandela Lifetime Achievement Award'

- Globally acclaimed film-maker Vinod Ganatra has become the first Indian to be conferred the prestigious 'Nelson Mandela Lifetime Achievement Award' of South Africa for his contribution to films.
- He was honoured with the coveted award at the ongoing 7th Nelson Mandela Children's Film Festival, for his immense contributions to the world of cinema for kids.

Top PSUs Honoured At Outlook Planet Sustainability Summit 2024

- **The Outlook Planet Sustainability Summit & Awards 2024** recognized outstanding sustainability initiatives by **Central Public Sector Enterprises (CPSEs).**
- The event, held in Goa on 27 May, celebrated pioneers across various categories.
- **Notably, REC Limited received the prestigious "Sustainability Champion—Editor's Choice Award",** while **Power Finance Corporation (PFC) Limited was honoured with the Corporate Social Responsibility award** in the Non-Fossil Fuel sub-category.

Payal Kapadia Wins Grand Prix At Cannes Film Festival

- Payal Kapadia, the talented Indian filmmaker, has scripted history by becoming **the first Indian director to win the Grand Prix award at the 77th Cannes Film Festival.**
- Her remarkable achievement is attributed to her film **"All We Imagine as Light",** which bagged this prestigious honour.
- The Grand Prix is the second-most prestigious prize at Cannes, following the iconic Palme d'Or.

Jenny Erpenbeck's 'Kairos' won International Booker Prize

- **"Kairos" by Jenny Erpenbeck,** translated by **Michael Hofmann,** has **won the International Booker Prize 2024.**
- This novel, **originally written in German,** follows a destructive affair between a young woman and an older man in 1980s East Berlin.
- It intertwines the personal and the political as the two lovers seemingly embody East Germany's crushed idealism.

Srinivas R. Kulkarni Honoured With Shaw Prize In Astronomy

- Srinivas R. Kulkarni, an Indian-origin American scientist and the George Ellery Hale Professor of Astronomy and Planetary Science at the California Institute of Technology (Caltech), has been awarded the prestigious **Shaw Prize in Astronomy for 2024.**
- He has been recognized for his groundbreaking discoveries about millisecond pulsars, gamma-ray bursts, supernovae, and other transient astronomical phenomena.
- The Shaw Prize, often referred to as the **'Nobel of the East',** carries a monetary prize of $1.2 million and is awarded annually in three categories: **astronomy, life science and medicine, and mathematical sciences.**

Ruskin Bond Awarded Sahitya Akademi Fellowship

- Renowned British-Indian author Ruskin Bond has been awarded the prestigious Sahitya Akademi Fellowship for his exceptional contributions to literature.
- The honour was **presented to him at his home in Mussoorie on 11 May 2024.**

President Presents Padma Awards At Rashtrapati Bhavan

- President Droupadi Murmu presented the Padma Awards at Rashtrapati Bhavan during the second Civil Investiture Ceremony.
- The Padma Awards are among the country's **highest civilian honours,** conferred in three categories: **Padma Vibhushan, Padma Bhushan,** and **Padma Shri,** across various fields such as art, social work, science, literature, sports, and civil service.

2024 Pulitzer Prize Winners

- The Pulitzer Prizes, **administered by Columbia University,** have gained attention this year amidst student demonstrations against the war in Gaza.
- These awards **celebrate excellence in journalism and literary works.**
- Among the winners are publications like The New York Times and ProPublica, as well as authors such as **Jayne Anne Phillips** and **Jonathan Eig.**

Shabana Azmi Received Freedom Of City Of London Award

- Veteran Indian actress Shabana Azmi honoured with the City of London Corporation's "Freedom of City of London Award" on 10 May **in the UK capital's Guildhall.**
- This recognition is for her significant contributions to Indian cinema and her advocacy for women's rights.

UNESCO Guillermo Cano Prize Awarded To Gaza Journalists

- The 2024 UNESCO/Guillermo Cano World Press Freedom Prize was awarded to Palestinian journalists covering the crisis in Gaza.
- The award ceremony took place on May 2, 2024, **during the World Press Freedom Conference in Santiago, Chile.**
- The **prize recognized the unique suffering and fearless reporting of Gaza's journalists.**

Purnima Devi Barman Wins Whitley Gold Award

- Dr. Purnima Devi Barman, **a wildlife biologist from Assam,** has been awarded the prestigious Whitley Gold Award **by the Whitley Fund for Nature (WFN) in the UK.**
- She received GBP 100,000 for her conservation efforts focused on the endangered Greater Adjutant Stork and its wetland habitat.
- Whitley gold award is also known as **'Green Oscar'.**

Dr. Bina Modi Honored For Corporate Social Responsibility

- Dr. Bina Modi was honoured by the esteemed Vice President of India, Jagdeep Dhankar, **for her 'Outstanding Contribution to the cause of Corporate Social Responsibility (CSR)'.**
- The felicitation took place during the inauguration of the new building for the Society of Indian Law Firms (SILF).

Alok Shukla Wins Goldman Environmental Prize For Asia

- Alok Shukla, the **convenor of the Chhattisgarh Bachao Andolan** and a founding **member of the Hasdeo Aranya Bachao Sangharsh Samiti,** has been honored with the 2024 Goldman Prize for Asia.
- His relentless efforts to preserve the forests of Hasdeo Aranya in Chhattisgarh have earned him this prestigious recognition.

Meryl Streep Received Honorary Palme D'or At Cannes

- Meryl Streep, **an acclaimed performer,** presented with an honorary Palme d'Or **during the 77th Cannes Film Festival's opening ceremony** on 14 May 2024.
- Meryl has **a record 21 Oscar nominations, three wins,** and is one of the most beloved actors in Hollywood history.

Ratan Tata Receives KISS Humanitarian Award

- Renowned industrialist and philanthropist Ratan Tata, was honoured with the prestigious KISS Humanitarian Award 2021.
- The award ceremony was held at his residence in Mumbai, marking a significant recognition of his commitment to social development and exemplary corporate leadership.
- The **award was presented by the founder of KIIT and KISS Achyuta Samanta.**

MATTER Wins Clarivate South Asia Innovation Award

- **MATTER, a pioneering force in India's Electric mobility and energy landscape,** proudly announced winning the Clarivate South Asia Innovation Awards 2024 **in the Automotive category.**
- This esteemed accolade celebrates MATTER's relentless commitment to innovation and technological excellence in the realm of clean energy & mobility solutions.
- In the fiscal year 2023-2024, MATTER's intellectual property achievements have been remarkable, with 15 granted patents and 62 published patents.

Indian Students Win NASA Rover Challenge Awards

- Two Indian students' teams from the New Delhi area and Mumbai have won awards from NASA for the Human Exploration Rover Challenge.
- **The KIET Group of Institutions, Delhi-NCR** has won the award in the **"Crash and Burn" category of the annual Human Exploration Rover Challenge (HERC)** award, the National Aeronautics and Space Administration (NASA) announced on 22 March 2024.
- **The Kanakia International School** from Mumbai was given the **"Rookie of the Year" award.**

Mohammed Salem Wins World Press Photo Of The Year

- Reuters photographer Mohammed Salem won the prestigious 2024 World Press Photo of the Year award for his **image of a Palestinian woman cradling the body of her five-year-old niece in the Gaza Strip.**

Pavuluri Subba Rao Wins Aryabhatta Award

- Ananth Technologies Founder, CEO and Chairman Pavuluri Subba Rao has been conferred with the **'Aryabhatta Award'** instituted by the Aeronautical Society of India (ASI).
- He was also presented with ASI's **'Distinguished Fellow'** title.

Navalnaya Wins Freedom Prize Of The Media

- Kremlin critic **Yulia Navalnaya and her husband Alexei Navalny,** who died a in a Russian prison, received this year's "Freedom Prize of the Media".
- The award ceremony is took place on **19 April** at the **Ludwig Erhard Summit,** named after the former German chancellor, at Bavaria's Tegernsee lake.

Amitabh Bachchan Receives Lata Deenanath Mangeshkar Award

- Bollywood Megastar Amitabh Bachchan honoured with the prestigious **third Lata Dinanath Mangeshkar award** for his remarkable dedication to the nation, its people, and society.
- Previous recipients of this esteemed award include Prime Minister **Narendra Modi** and popular **singer Asha Bhosale.**
- Lata Dinanath Mangeshkar award was established in memory of the late Bharat Ratna awardee and legendary singer Lata Mangeshkar.

Adwaita Nayar Named Young Global Leader By WEF

- **Adwaita Nayar, the co-founder of Nykaa and CEO of Nykaa Fashion,** has been inducted into the esteemed World Economic Forum's Young Global Leaders Community as part of the Class of 2024.
- **Comprising 90 remarkable individuals, this group of change makers** is at the forefront of shaping the future and fostering positive change through their innovative endeavors.

Mamta G Sagar won International Literature Prize

- **Kannada poet, playwright and academic, Mamta G Sagar,** was awarded the World Literary Prize for her contribution to literature **by the World Organization of Writers (WOW)** on 6 April 2024.
- The event was a collaboration between ANA and Pan African Writers Association (PAWA).

REC won SKOCH ESG Award

- REC Limited, **a Maharatna Central Public Sector Enterprise** under the Ministry of Power and a leading NBFC has been bestowed with the SKOCH ESG Award 2024 in the **'Renewable Energy Financing' category.**
- The award underscores REC's dedication to sustainable financing, paving the way for a greener future and accelerating the transition to renewable energy.
- REC has emerged as a significant player in India's clean energy transition, actively contributing to the nation's sustainable future.

Lokesh Muni Receives American President's Volunteer Award

- Jain Acharya Lokesh Muni has become the **first Indian monk to receive the American President's Gold Volunteer Service Award.**
- Instituted in 2003 during George Bush's presidency, this award recognizes outstanding volunteerism.

Michel Talagrand was Awarded 2024 Abel Prize

- **The Norwegian Academy of Science and Letters** has decided to award the

Abel Prize for 2024 to Michel Talagrand of the French National Center for Scientific Research (CNRS), Paris, France.

- Michel Talagrand receives the prize **for his work in probability theory and stochastic processes.**

ISRO Receives Aviation Week Laureates Award For Chandrayaan-3

- The Indian Space Research Organisation (ISRO) has been honoured with the prestigious Aviation Week Laureates Award for its achievements with the historic Chandrayaan-3 mission.
- The award was received on behalf of Isro by Sripriya Ranganathan, Deputy Ambassador at the Indian Embassy in the US.
- The Aviation Week Laureates Award is renowned **for recognising extraordinary accomplishments within the aerospace industry,** and this year, it celebrated ISRO's groundbreaking mission, Chandrayaan-3.

PM Modi Awarded Bhutan's 'Order Of The Druk Gyalpo'

- On 22 March 2024, the King of Bhutan conferred the Order of the Druk Gyalpo on Prime Minister **Narendra Modi,** who became **the first foreign head of government to receive Bhutan's highest civilian honour.**
- The Order of the Druk Gyalpo holds immense significance within Bhutan's honour system, symbolising a lifetime of **outstanding achievements and contributions to society.**
- The announcement for the honour was made by the King of Bhutan during the 114th National Day celebrations on December 17, 2021.

Chameli Devi Jain Award 2024 For Outstanding Woman Media Person

- **The Indian Express's Chief of National Bureau (govt) Ritika Chopra** and independent journalist **Greeshma Kuthar** have been jointly awarded the Chameli Devi Jain Award 2024 for Outstanding Woman Media Person of the Year.
- The winners were chosen from more than 65 entries of women journalists.

President Murmu Confers Sangeet Natak Akademi Awards

- President Droupadi Murmu awarded the **Sangeet Natak Akademi Awards for 2022 and 2023 to ninety-four artists** in New Delhi, recognizing their excellence in various performing arts fields.
- **Seven artists were also honoured with the prestigious Sangeet Natak Akademi Fellowship.**
- Recipients of the Fellowship included Vinayak Khedekar, R Visweswaran, Nitu Kumari Nootan, Shailesh Shrivastava, and Maddali Usha Gayatri.

Oscar Awards

- Hollywood's **96th Oscars** took place at the Dolby Theatre in Los Angeles, California.
- **Emma Stone won Best Actress** for her role in "Poor Things".
- **"Oppenheimer" dominated with six awards,** including Best Actor for Cillian Murphy and Best Director for Christopher Nolan.

Here's a table summarizing the winners in some major categories:

Category	Winner
Best Picture	Oppenheimer
Best Director	Christopher Nolan (Oppenheimer)
Best Actor	Cillian Murphy (Oppenheimer)
Best Actress	Jennifer Lame (Oppenheimer)
Best Supporting Actor	Robert Downey Jr. (Oppenheimer)
Best Supporting Actress	Thelma Schoonmaker (Killers of the Flower Moon)
Best Animated Feature	Spider-Man: Across the Spider-Verse

Krystyna Pyszkova Crowned Miss World 2024

- **Krystyna Pyszková from the Czech Republic** was crowned the **71st Miss World in Mumbai,** competing against contestants from 115 countries.
- Last year's winner, Karolina Bielawska of Poland, crowned her.
- Yasmina Zaytoun of Lebanon was named the First Runner-Up.

Riken Yamamoto Wins 2024 Pritzker Prize

- **Riken Yamamoto,** a Japanese architect born in Beijing, China in 1945, has been announced as the **2024 Laureate of the Pritzker Architecture Prize.**
- This award is widely recognized as the **highest honor in the field of architecture** internationally.

Prabha Varma Receives Saraswati Samman for 2023

- Renowned **poet Prabha Varma has been honored with the prestigious Saraswati Samman for the year 2023** for his exceptional contributions to Malayalam literature.
- His work "Roudra Sathwikam" has been particularly acknowledged, along with his overall literary contributions from 2013 to 2022.
- **"Roudra Sathwikam,"** published in 2022, is **a poetic masterpiece in Malayalam** that delves into the intricate dynamics of power and politics, the individual's struggle against the state, and the interplay between art and authority in a distinctive manner.

Suresh Wadkar Receives Lata Mangeshkar Award

- Veteran **playback singer Suresh Wadkar** has been honoured with the **Gansamragini Lata Mangeshkar Award.**
- Wadkar is known for his playback singing in Hindi and Marathi.

Underwater Photographer Of The Year 2024

- **Swedish photographer Alex Dawson** has been named as Underwater Photographer of the Year 2024 for his image **'Whale Bones'.** The photo shows a diver beneath the Greenland ice sheet exploring the skeleton of a minke whale.

Grammy Awards Of 2024

- The esteemed Grammy Awards of 2024 witnessed the triumph of the fusion ensemble Shakti, comprising eminent Indian musicians **Shankar Mahadevan and Zakir Hussain,** in the coveted **Best Global Music Album category for their latest opus, "This Moment."**
- Notably, **Rakesh Chaurasia,** a venerable exponent of Indian classical flute, achieved the distinction of a dual Grammy triumph for his collaborative endeavor titled **"As We Speak,"** recognized in both the **Best Contemporary Instrumental and Best Global Music Performance categories.**

Vice-President Dhankhar Presents Assam's Highest Civilian Awards

- Vice-President Jagdeep Dhankhar visited Guwahati in Assam on a day-long tour to present the Assam government's highest civilian awards - Assam Baibhav, Assam Saurabh, and Assam Gaurav to the winners.
- The state government had decided to confer the awards to **22 individuals selected from diverse sectors for their outstanding contributions** in their respective fields.

- **Ranjan Gogoi,** Member of Parliament and former Chief Justice of India, was **honored with the Assam Baibhav, the state's premier civilian honor.**

K.P.P. Nambiar Award For ISRO Chairman S. Somanath

- The field of space exploration and technology in India witnessed a momentous occasion as the **IEEE Kerala Section announced the recipient** of the prestigious K.P.P. Nambiar Award.
- The conferment of the K.P.P. Nambiar Award to S. Somanath serves as an inspiration to technologists and innovators across the state and beyond.

Swachh Survekshan Awards 2023

- The President of India conferred **Swachh Survekshan Awards 2023 at Bharat Mandapam, New Delhi** hosted by the Ministry of Housing and Urban Affairs **(MoHUA).**

TOP 10 CITIES
1 Indore, Madhya Pradesh
1 Surat, Gujarat
3 Navi Mumbai, Maharashtra
4 Visakhapatnam, Andhra Pradesh
5 Bhopal, Madhya Pradesh
6 Vijaywada, Andhra Pradesh
7 New Delhi (NDMC), Delhi
8 Tirupati, Andhra Pradesh
9 Greater Hyderabad, Telangana
10 Pune, Maharashtra

BOTTOM 3 CITIES
1 Kolkata, West Bengal
2 Asansol, West Bengal
3 Haora, West Bengal

TOP STATES
1 Maharashtra 411
2 Madhya Pradesh 378
3 Chhattisgarh 169

THE MOST IMPROVED CITIES	
PANAJI, GOA Fastest moving city with population of over 100,000	NOWROZABAD, MP Fastest moving city with population less than 100,000

- It is an annual survey of cleanliness, hygiene and sanitation in cities and towns across India, launched as part of the **Swachh Bharat Abhiyan (specifically under SBA-Urban).**
- This was for the **seventh year in a row that Indore has been ranked** as the cleanest city in India.
- The theme for the Cleanliness Survey 2024 is **"Reduce, Reuse, and Recycle."**

India Wins The 9th GovTech Prize For Ai Road Safety

- India won the annual award instituted **by the UAE government for 'AI-Powered Government Services'.**
- The accolade acknowledges the **Ministry for Road Transport & Highways,** Government of India, for its innovative project, iRASTE, which integrates AI technology to revolutionize road safety.

Gulzar And Jagadguru Rambhadracharya Win 58th Jnanpith Award

- Renowned **Urdu poet Gulzar and Sanskrit scholar Jagadguru Rambhadracharya** have been chosen as the recipients of the **58th Jnanpith Award.**
- Gulzar, a renowned Hindi filmmaker and Urdu poet, will be honoured alongside Jagadguru Rambhadracharya, the founder of Tulsi Peeth in Chitrakoot.

Adani Energy Wins Sustainability Award 2023

- **Adani Energy Solutions Limited** was awarded the **'Global Sustainability Leadership Award 2023' in the 'Best Overall Sustainable Performance' category by the World Sustainability Congress in Mauritius.**
- The award recognized AESL's sustainable practices and its contributions as an innovator in the power sector.

'Nritya Kalanidhi' Award Conferred On Vasanthalakshmi

- **Vasanthalakshmi Narasimhachari** was awarded the **'Nritya Kalanidhi'** award at the **17th Dance Festival of the Music Academy in Chennai.**
- 'Nritya Kalanidhi' award is presented in the **field of dance** every year by the **Madras Music Academy.**

'Rashtriya Khel Protsahan Puruskar' 2023 Announced

- The **Ministry of Youth Affairs and Sports** has announced the **Rashtriya Khel Protsahan Puruskar 2023.**
- Odisha Mining Corporate Limited has received an award for **"Encouragement to Sports through Corporate Social Responsibility."**
- **The Rashtriya Khel Protsahan Puruskar** is given to **corporate entities, Sports Control Boards, NGOs, and sports bodies** at both the State and National level for their role in sports promotion and development.

Emmy Awards 2024 Winners

- **The Emmy Awards, the highest honours in television, were handed out at a live ceremony in Los Angeles.**
- **"Succession" and "The Bear" won the best drama series and best comedy** at the Emmy Awards respectively.
- Quinta Brunson made an emotional and historic win for **"Abbott Elementary"**
- Matthew Perry was honoured in the In Memoriam segment along with other late stars
- **"Beef" won best-limited series,** with Steven Yeun and Ali Wong making history as the first Asian Americans to win in their categories
- Niecy Nash-Betts won best supporting actress in a limited series for **"Dahmer – Monster: The Jeffrey Dahmer Story"**

Wings India Awards 2024

- Wings India Awards 2024 **presented by Union Civil Aviation Minister** Jyotiraditya M Scindia (Former).
- **Bangalore and Delhi Airports jointly won the Best Airport award.**
- Vistara received the Best Airline of the Year award.
- Air India recognized for International Connectivity.
- Alliance Air acknowledged for Regional Connectivity.

81st Golden Globe Award Winners

- **Christopher Nolan's** epic biographical thriller **Oppenheimer and Jesse Armstrong's satirical drama series Succession earned top honours at the 81st Golden Globes,** marking Hollywood's star-studded kickoff to its annual awards season.

WINNER HIGHLIGHTS

1. **Best Motion Picture** – Drama: (Oppenheimer)
2. **Best Motion Picture** – Musical or Comedy: (Poor Things)
3. **Best Motion Picture** – Animated: (The Boy and the Heron)
4. **Cinematic and Box Office Achievement:** (Barbie)
5. **Best Motion Picture** – Non-English Language: (Anatomy of a Fall, France)
6. **Best Performance by a Male Actor in a Motion Picture** – Drama: (Cillian Murphy, Oppenheimer)
7. **Best Performance by a Female Actor in a Motion Picture** – Drama: (Lily Gladstone, Killers of the Flower Moon)

8. **Best Performance by a Female Actor in a Motion Picture** – Musical or Comedy: (Emma Stone, Poor Things)
9. **Best Performance by a Female Actor in a Supporting Role in Any Motion Picture:** (Da'Vine Joy Randolph, The Holdovers)
10. **Best Director** – Motion Picture: (Christopher Nolan, Oppenheimer)
11. **Best Original Song** – Motion Picture: ("What Was I Made For?" Barbie, Music and lyrics by Billie Eilish, Finneas)
12. **Best Television Series** – Drama: (Succession)

Padma Awards 2024

- For the year 2024, the President has approved conferment of **132 Padma Awards** including 2 duo cases (in a duo case, the Award is counted as one) as per list below.
- The list comprises **5 Padma Vibhushan, 17 Padma Bhushan and 110 Padma Shri Awards.** 30 of the awardees are women and the list also includes 8 persons from the category of Foreigners / NRI / PIO / OCI and 9 Posthumous awardees.
- These Awards are conferred by the President of India at ceremonial functions which are held at Rashtrapati Bhawan usually around March/April every year.

Padma Vibhushan (5)

Sr. No.	Name	Field	State/Region/Country
1.	Ms. Vyjayantimala Bali	Art	Tamil Nadu
2.	Shri Konidela Chiranjeevi	Art	Andhra Pradesh
3.	Shri M Venkaiah Naidu	Public Affairs	Andhra Pradesh
4.	Shri Bindeshwar Pathak **Posthumous)**	Social Work	Bihar
5.	Ms. Padma Subrahmanyam	Art	Tamil Nadu

Padma Bhushan (17)

Sr. No.	Name	Field	State/Region/Country
1.	Ms. M Fathima Beevi (Posthumous)	Justice	Kerala
2.	Shri Hormusji N Cama	Literature & Education - Journalism	Maharashtra
3.	Shri Mithun Chakraborty	Art	West Bengal
4.	Shri Sitaram Jindal	Trade & Industry	Karnataka
5.	Shri Young Liu	Trade & Industry	Taiwan
6.	Shri Ashwin Balachand Mehta	Medicine	Maharashtra
7.	Shri Satyabrata Mookherjee **(Posthumous)**	Public Affairs	West Bengal
8.	Shri Ram Naik	Public Affairs	Maharashtra
9.	Shri Tejas Madhusudan Patel	Medicine	Gujarat
10.	Shri Olanchery Rajagopal	Public Affairs	Kerala
11.	Shri Dattatray Ambadas Mayaloo alias Rajdutt	Art	Maharashtra
12.	Shri Togdan Rinpoche **(Posthumous)**	Others - Spiritualism	Ladakh
13.	Shri Pyarelal Sharma	Art	Maharashtra
14.	Shri Chandreshwar Prasad Thakur	Medicine	Bihar
15.	Ms. Usha Uthup	Art	West Bengal
16.	Shri Vijaykanth **(Posthumous)**	Art	Tamil Nadu
17.	Shri Kundan Vyas	Literature & Education - Journalism	Maharashtra

MATCHING GAME

Person/Organization/Event	Achievement/Award
1. Manoj Bajpayee'S 'The Fable'	A. Best Heritage Tourism Village of 2024
2. Samantha Harvey	B. Booker Prize for Fiction 2024
3. Dr. Usha Thakur	C. Best Film award at the 38th Leeds International Film Festival
4. Kalash Gupta	D. World's Best Coder in TCS CodeVita Season 10
5. Garden Reach Shipbuilders & Engineers (GRSE)	E. Sustainable Governance Champion Award 2024
6. Manipur's Andro	F. 12th Vishwa Hindi Samman

SCAN TO GET MULTIPLE CHOICE QUESTIONS

Scan Me

Answer Key: 1 → C, 2 → B, 3 → F, 4 → D, 5 → E, 6 → A

APPOINTMENTS AND RESIGNATION

Sanjiv Khanna
(51st Chief Justice of India)

- **Head of Supreme Court**
  - **Appointment**: Justice Sanjiv Khanna was appointed as the **51st Chief Justice of India (CJI)** on **November 11, 2024**, succeeding Justice D.Y. Chandrachud.
  - **Tenure**: His tenure as CJI will last until **May 13, 2025**.

- **Background**:
  - Born: **May 14, 1960**.
  - Enrolled as an Advocate in 1983; practiced in **Tis Hazari District Courts** and **Delhi High Court**.
  - Appointed as a judge of **Delhi High Court** in 2005, became permanent in 2006, and appointed to the **Supreme Court in 2019**.

Notable Cases

- Contributed to landmark judgments on the **RTI Act**, **hate speech regulation**, **Central Vista project**, and **Article 370 (Jammu & Kashmir)**.
- Part of the bench that validated **EVMs** and struck down the **electoral bond scheme**.

Appointment Process for CJI

- **Constitutional Framework**: According to **Article 124(2)** of the Constitution, Supreme Court judges, including the CJI, are appointed by the **President of India**.
- **Seniority Principle**: The most senior judge of the Supreme Court is conventionally appointed as the CJI based on length of service.
- **Collegium System**: The **CJI** and the **four most senior judges of the Supreme Court** form the collegium, which recommends the appointment of judges.
- **Process**: When the incumbent CJI's term is ending, the current CJI recommends the name of the most senior judge to the **President** for the new appointment.
- The **President** formally appoints the recommended judge as the new CJI.

CJI's Removal

- The CJI can only be **removed by the President** after an **address by Parliament**, supported by a **special majority** (majority of total members and at least two-thirds of those present and voting).

CJI's Administrative Role

- **Supervising Court Operations**:
  - Oversees the day-to-day functioning of the **Supreme Court**.
  - Ensures smooth operation and timely disposal of cases.
- **Appointments and Transfers**:
  - CJI leads the **collegium**, responsible for recommending the appointment and transfer of **Supreme Court** and **High Court judges**.
  - The collegium ensures the **independence** of the judiciary by collectively deciding on judicial appointments, free from executive influence.
- **Judicial Reforms**:
  - CJI plays a crucial role in **reforming judicial processes** to improve **efficiency, citizens' access to justice**, and the **delivery of legal services**.
  - Involved in discussions with the **government**, **lawyers**, and **civil society** for judicial reforms.

Key Responsibilities and Role of the CJI

- **Judicial Leadership**:
  - **Chairs Supreme Court sittings** and **manages the court's functioning**.
  - Directs **important constitutional benches** that decide significant national cases.
- **Master of the Roster**:
  - The CJI has the authority to **assign specific cases** to different benches and manage the scheduling of hearings.

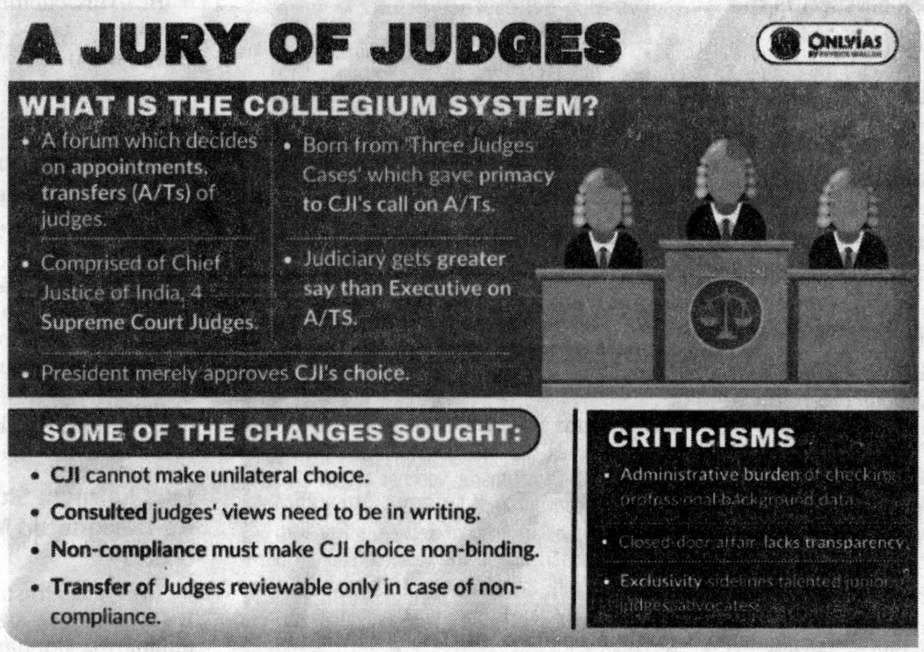

NATIONAL APPOINTMENTS

RBL Bank Reappoints R Subramaniakumar as MD & CEO for 3 Years

- RBL Bank's Board of Directors has approved the reappointment of R Subramaniakumar as the Managing Director and Chief Executive Officer (MD & CEO) for a further period of three years, effective June 23, 2025.
- The reappointment is subject to approval from the Reserve Bank of India (RBI).
- Subramaniakumar, who was initially appointed as MD & CEO in June 2022, became the second public sector banker after Prashant Kumar to head a private sector bank.

Rahul Narwekar of BJP re-elected Speaker of 15th Maharashtra Assembly

- Rahul Narwekar of the ruling Bharatiya Janata Party was re-elected as the 15th Maharashtra Legislative Assembly Speaker.
- Rahul Narwekar, who was the Speaker for two and a half years in the previous 14th Legislative Assembly, was elected unopposed.
- Rahul Narwekar is the second person after Balasaheb Bharde to be re-elected as the Speaker of the Maharashtra Legislative Assembly.

Former Assam Cricketer Devajit Saikia appointed as BCCI's acting Secretary after Jay Shah

- Former Assam cricketer Devajit Saikia has been named as the acting secretary of the Board of Control for Cricket in India (BCCI).
- He replaced BCCI president Jay Shah who recently took over the reigns as ICC chairman.
- Board president Roger Binny used his constitutional powers for the appointment. Saikia worked as a joint secretary at BCCI earlier.

Govt appoints Ram Mohan Rao Amara as MD of SBI

- The Union government has approved the appointment of Rama Mohan Rao Amara for the position of managing director of the State Bank of India (SBI).
- Amara, Deputy Managing Director, State Bank of India, has been appointed Managing Director for three years.
- Amara takes over the position previously held by CS Setty, who assumed charge as Chairman of SBI in August.

AIR MARSHAL AMAR PREET SINGH APPOINTED NEXT CHIEF OF THE AIR STAFF

- On 21 September 2024, the Indian government appointed Air Marshal Amar Preet Singh as the next Chief of the Air Staff.
- Previously serving as the Vice Chief of the Air Staff, he succeeded Air Chief Marshal Vivek Ram Chaudhari on 30 September 2024. He is the current and 28th Chief of the Air Staff.
- With nearly 40 years of service, Singh has held numerous key positions, including Air Officer Commanding-in-Chief of Central Air Command and Project Director for the MIG-29 upgrade.

Bibhuti Bhusan Nayak elected as the President of ICMAI

- Bibhuti Bhusan Nayak has been unanimously elected as the 67th President of the Institute of Cost Accountants of India (ICMAI) for the 2024-25 term.
- He succeeded Ashwin Dalwadi, who was the president for the 2023-24 period.
- TCA Srinivasa Prasad has been elected as the vice president of the Institute of Cost Accountants of India for 2024-25.

Alok Ranjan appointed NCRB Chief

- Senior IPS officer Alok Ranjan has been appointed as the Director of the National Crime Records Bureau (NCRB) on 21 September 2024.
- He succeeded Vivek Gogia. Ranjan will serve until his superannuation on 30 June 2026.
- About NCRB:
- Formed- 11 March 1986
- Headquarters- Delhi
- Parent department- Ministry of Home Affairs

Anurag Garg appointed as Narcotics Control Bureau Director General

- On 17 September 2024, Anurag Garg, a 1993-batch IPS officer from the Himachal Pradesh cadre, was appointed as the Director General of the Narcotics Control Bureau (NCB).
- Previously serving as Additional DG in the Border Security Force (BSF), Garg's appointment was approved by the Appointments Committee of the Cabinet.
- He succeeded current CRPF Director General Anish Dayal Singh, who held the post in an additional capacity. Garg's tenure as NCB DG will last until May 23, 2026, or until further orders.

K V Subramanian appointed as MD & CEO of Federal Bank for three years

- Krishnan Venkat Subramanian, formerly the Joint Managing Director of Kotak Mahindra Bank Limited, has been appointed as the Managing Director & Chief Executive Officer of Federal Bank.
- The Reserve Bank of India (RBI) approved his appointment for a three-year term starting from 23 September 2024.

Manolo Marquez appointed head coach of Indian Men's Football Team

- Manolo Marquez, the current head coach of FC Goa, has been appointed as the new Indian men's senior team coach.
- The decision was made by the All India Football Federation (AIFF) during their Executive Committee meeting on July 20, 2024.

- Marquez will continue to coach both FC Goa and the national team concurrently throughout the 2024-25 season before focusing solely on the national side.

GOVERNMENT APPOINTS ROBERT J RAVI AS NEW CMD OF BSNL

- The Indian government has appointed Robert Jerard Ravi as the new Chairman and Managing Director (CMD) of Bharat Sanchar Nigam Limited (BSNL), effective from 15 July 2024.
- Ravi, an Indian Telecom Service officer with 34 years of experience in the telecom sector, most recently held the position of Deputy Director General at the Department of Telecommunications (DoT).

Dr. B.N. Gangadhar appointed as Chairperson of the National Medical Commission

- On 3 July 2024, Dr. B.N. Gangadhar has been appointed as the Chairperson of the National Medical Commission under Section 4 of the NMC Act, 2019.
- His tenure will last for 4 years or until he reaches the age of 70, whichever comes first.
- The decision was made by the Appointment Committee of the Cabinet (ACC). Dr. Gangadhar was previously serving as the President of the Medical Assessment and Rating Board.

Ex-R&AW Chief Rajinder Khanna appointed new additional NSA

- Rajinder Khanna, former Research and Analysis Wing (R&AW) chief, has been appointed as the Additional National Security Advisor (NSA).
- This significant upgrade reflects the government's emphasis on continuity in the national security apparatus during the Narendra Modi 3.0 regime.
- Additionally, T. V. Ravichandran and Pavan Kapoor have also been appointed as Deputy NSAs.

SBI General Insurance names Naveen Chandra Jha as New MD & CEO

- SBI General Insurance Company has appointed Shri Naveen Chandra Jha as its new Managing Director and Chief Executive Officer.
- He was nominated by the parent company, State Bank of India (SBI), for this position.
- Jha succeeded Shri Kishore Kumar Poludasu.

Sujata Saunik appointed Maharashtra's first Woman Chief Secretary

- Sujata Saunik, a senior IAS officer from the 1987 batch, has made history by becoming Maharashtra's first woman Chief Secretary. She assumed the position on 30 June 2024, succeeding Nitin Kareer.
- Saunik has over 30 years of experience in governance, public policy, and disaster management.

LIC Chairman Siddhartha Mohanty Re-Designated Managing Director & CEO

- The Life Insurance Corporation of India (LIC) re-designated its chairman, Siddhartha Mohanty, as the Managing Director (MD) and Chief Executive Officer (CEO) with effect from 30 June 2024.
- Life Insurance Corporation of India is a statutory Corporation established under Section 3 of LIC Act, 1956. It came into existence on 1st September, 1956

Justice Bidyut Ranjan Sarangi Appointed Chief Justice of Jharkhand HC

- Justice Bidyut Ranjan Sarangi took oath as the 15th Chief Justice of the Jharkhand High Court on July 5, 2024. Governor C.P. Radhakrishnan administered the oath of office to Justice Sarangi at the Raj Bhavan in Ranchi.
- Chief Minister Hemant Soren and Speaker Rabindra Nath Mahato attended the swearing-in ceremony, besides several judges and senior government officials.

NASSCOM appointed SAP Labs India MD Sindhu Gangadharan as Chairperson

- On 26 August 2024, National Association of Software and Service

Companies (NASSCOM) appointed Sindhu Gangadharan, Managing Director of SAP Labs India, as its new Chairperson.

- Gangadharan, the first woman to lead SAP Labs India, succeeded Rajesh Nambiar.
- She has been a prominent figure in the Indian tech industry, holding additional roles such as the head of customer innovation services at SAP and serving on the boards of Siemens India and Titan Company.

Sanjeev Raina appointed ITBP Additional Director General

- Sanjeev Raina was appointed as the Additional Director General (ADG) of the Indo-Tibetan Border Police (ITBP) on 25 August 2024.
- With over three decades of experience in various capacities within the ITBP, Raina has been recognized for his strategic acumen and leadership skills.

Deepti Gaur Mukherjee assumes charge as MCA Secretary

- On 22 August 2024, Deepti Gaur Mukherjee, a 1993 batch IAS officer of the Madhya Pradesh cadre, assumed charge as Secretary to the Ministry of Corporate Affairs (MCA).
- She succeeded Manoj Govil, who recently took over as the Expenditure Secretary. Prior to this appointment, Mukherjee served as the Chief Executive Officer (CEO) of the National Health Authority.
- As the new MCA Secretary, she will oversee key legislations and reforms, including framing the draft Digital Competition Bill, ushering in IBC 2.0, and enhancing the capacity of NCLTs.

Rajesh Nambiar appointed as NASSCOM President-Designate

- On 22 August 2024, the National Association of Software and Service Companies (NASSCOM) announced the appointment of Rajesh Nambiar as its President-Designate.
- Nambiar, a seasoned industry veteran, previously served as the Chairman and Managing Director of Cognizant India.
- He succeeded Debjani Ghosh, who completes her tenure in November 2024. Nambiar's leadership and strategic initiatives have been instrumental in positioning India's tech sector as a global leader.

Govind Mohan took charge as Union Home Secretary

- On 22 August 2024, Govind Mohan, a seasoned 1989-batch IAS officer of the Sikkim cadre, assumed the position of Union Home Secretary.
- He succeeded Ajay Kumar Bhalla, who completed his five-year tenure. Mohan, previously serving as the Union Culture Secretary, has extensive experience in both Sikkim and central governments.

OTHER RECENT APPOINTMENT 2024

Designation	Name
Acting Director of the United States Secret Service	Ronald L. Rowe Jr.
Group Chief Executive of HSBC Holdings plc	Georges Elhedery
President of Mumbai Cricket Association	Ajinkya Naik
Judges of the Supreme Court	Justice Nongmeikapam Kotiswar Singh & Justice R. Mahadevan
Chief Justice of Punjab and Haryana High Court	Justice Sheel Nagu
Executive Director of RBI	Charulatha S Kar
Principal Spokesperson of the Government	Dhirendra K Ojha
Assistant Coach of Afghanistan Cricket Team	Ramakrishnan Sridhar
Secretary, Department for Promotion of Industry and Internal Trade (DPIIT)	Amardeep Singh Bhatia
Indian Ambassador to the United States	Vinay Mohan Kwatra
Vice-Chair of IPEF Supply Chain Council	India (no individual name)
Chief Justice of Jharkhand High Court	Justice M.S. Ramachandra Rao
Board Member at Stability AI	James Cameron
Indian Ambassador to the Netherlands	Kumar Tuhin
Indian Ambassador to Algeria	Dr. Swati Vijay Kulkarni
Managing Director of NAFED	Deepak Agarwal
Director General of Police (DGP), Jharkhand	Ajay Kumar Singh
President of Indian Chamber of Commerce	Abhyuday Jindal
CEO of ACKO Life	Sandip Goenka
CEO of GeM Portal	L Satya Srinivas
MD & CEO of NSDL	Vijay Chandok
Indian Ambassador to Brazil	Dinesh Bhatia
Chief Secretary of Mizoram	Khilli Ram Meena
Chief Justice of Manipur High Court	Justice D. Krishnakumar
Brand Ambassador of ALT EFF	Jackie Shroff
President of IMSA	Nandan Kumar Jha
Mentor for ACA Women's Cricket Operations	Mithali Raj
Ambassadors for Dubai Sports Council	Harbhajan Singh & Sania Mirza
Brand Ambassador and Honorary Tourism Advisor for Thailand	Sonu Sood
Defence Secretary	Rajesh Kumar Singh
Chairman of India Yamaha Motor	Itaru Otani

Ashutosh Gowariker appointed honorary chairman for Ajanta-Ellora FF.

- Filmmaker Ashutosh Gowariker has been appointed as the honorary chairman for the 10th Ajanta-Ellora International Film Festival (AIFF).
- The festival will be held from 15 to 19 January 2025 in Chhatrapati Sambhajinagar (formerly Aurangabad).
- Ashutosh Gowariker is well known for his films like 'Lagaan', 'Swades' and 'Jodhaa Akbar'.

RS Sharma appointed as the Non-Executive Chairperson of ONDC

- RS Sharma, former TRAI chief and NHA CEO, was appointed as the Non-Executive Chairperson of the Open Network for Digital Commerce (ONDC) on 10 September 2024.
- Sharma, an expert in digital public infrastructure, played a pivotal role in projects like Aadhaar and CoWIN.
- His leadership is expected to drive ONDC's next phase of innovation and expansion.

Amit Shah re-elected as Chairperson of Parliamentary Committee on Official Language

- On 9 September 2024, Union Home Minister Amit Shah was unanimously re-elected as the Chairperson of the Parliamentary Committee on Official Language.
- Shah emphasized the importance of Hindi in national integration and its role as a friend to all regional languages.
- The Parliamentary Committee on Official Language was established under Section 4 of the Official Languages Act, 1963, in 1976.
- It comprises 30 members from both the Lok Sabha and the Rajya Sabha.

IAS officer Tuhin Kanta Pandey appointed as Finance Secretary

- On 7 September 2024, Tuhin Kanta Pandey, a 1987 batch IAS officer from the Odisha cadre, was appointed as India's new Finance Secretary.
- He succeeded T.V. Somanathan, who was appointed as Cabinet Secretary.
- Previously the Secretary of the Department of Investment and Public Asset Management (DIPAM), Pandey is known for his role in the sale of Air India and the listing of Life Insurance Corporation.

Air Marshal Tejinder Singh takes over as Deputy Chief of the Air Staff

- On 1 September 2024, Air Marshal Tejinder Singh assumed the role of Deputy Chief of the Air Staff at Air Headquarters (Vayu Bhawan), New Delhi.
- Air Marshal Tejinder was commissioned in the fighter stream of the IAF on 13 June 1987.
- He was also awarded the Vayu Sena Medal in 2007 and Ati Vishisht Seva Medal in 2022.

Vipin Kumar assumed the role of Chairman of AAI

- On 28th October 2024, Vipin Kumar, an IAS officer from the 1996 Bihar cadre, assumed the role of Chairman of the Airports Authority of India (AAI).
- Prior to this, he served as Additional Secretary in the Department of School Education & Literacy, Ministry of Education, overseeing key initiatives like the Samagra Shiksha Scheme and the National Education Policy-2020.

FSIB recommends Ashok Chandra as next MD and CEO of PNB

- Financial Services Institutions Bureau (FSIB) has recommended Ashok Chandra as the next Managing Director (MD) and Chief Executive Officer (CEO) of Punjab National Bank (PNB).
- Recently he was serving as Executive Director at Canara Bank since November 2022.
- FSIB serves as an autonomous body responsible for recommending candidates for high-level appointments in public sector banks.

Vikram Dev Dutt takes charge as Coal Secretary

- On 21st October 2024, Vikram Dev Dutt assumed charge as the Secretary of the Ministry of Coal. Prior to this, VL Kantha Rao (Secretary of the Ministry of Mines) was handling the additional charge.
- Indian government plans to increase coal production to over 1 billion tonnes and add 80 gigawatts of coal-fired capacity by 2032.

Vijaya Kishore Rahatkar appointed as Chairperson of NCW

- On 19th October 2024, Vijaya Kishore Rahatkar was appointed as the new Chairperson of the National Commission for Women (NCW).

- She succeeded Rekha Sharma and will serve a tenure of three years or until she reaches the age of 65, whichever comes first.
- The appointment made under Section 3 of the National Commission for Women Act, 1990. She is the ninth chairperson of the National Commission for Women

Sourav Ganguly appointed as the Director of Cricket for JSW Sports

- On 17th October 2024, Sourav Ganguly was appointed as the Director of Cricket for JSW Sports, overseeing all cricketing properties, including the Delhi Capitals' IPL and WPL teams, as well as the Pretoria Capitals in the SA20 League.
- Ganguly, who joined Delhi Capitals in 2019 as an advisor and later served as Director of Cricket.
- He is the formar captain of the Indian national cricket team.

IRFC welcomes Manoj Kumar Dubey as New CMD and CEO

- On 10th October 2024, Manoj Kumar Dubey assumed the role of Chairman & Managing Director (CMD) and Chief Executive Officer (CEO) of the Indian Railway Finance Corporation (IRFC).

- A 1993-batch Indian Railway Accounts Service (IRAS) officer, Dubey previously served as Director (Finance) and Chief Financial Officer of Container Corporation of India (CONCOR).

PARTHA PRATIM SENGUPTA APPOINTED AS MD & CEO OF BANDHAN BANK

- On 10th October 2024, the Reserve Bank of India (RBI) approved the appointment of Partha Pratim Sengupta as the Managing Director (MD) and Chief Executive Officer (CEO) of Bandhan Bank for a three-year term.
- Sengupta, with four decades of banking experience, previously served as MD & CEO of Indian Overseas Bank (IOB) and held senior roles at State Bank of India (SBI).
- He replaces Bandhan's founder Chandra Shekhar Ghosh, who announced his retirement in July 2024.

RBI Deputy Governor M. Rajeshwar Rao's tenure extended for 1 year

- In 9th October 2024, the Appointments Committee of the Cabinet approved a one-year extension for RBI Deputy Governor M. Rajeshwar Rao, effective immediately.
- This is his second one-year extension, initially appointed in October 2020 for three years.
- Rao will continue overseeing key departments, including Regulation, Communication, Enforcement, Legal, and Risk Monitoring.

FSIB recommended Binod Kumar as MD & CEO of Indian Bank

- In November 2024, the Financial Services Institutions Bureau (FSIB) recommended Binod Kumar as the Managing Director and Chief Executive Officer (MD & CEO) of Indian Bank.
- Kumar, previously working as the Executive Director of Punjab National Bank (PNB), replaced S L Jain upon his superannuation on 31st December 2024.

G. Balasubramanian appointed as India's High Commissioner to Maldives

- On 25th November 2024, G. Balasubramanian, a seasoned diplomat from the 1998 Indian Foreign Service (IFS) batch, was appointed as India's High Commissioner to the Maldives.
- Recently served as the High Commissioner to Nigeria, Balasubramanian has held key roles in Moscow, Washington DC, and Bangkok, including Deputy Chief of Mission and Deputy Permanent Representative to UNESCAP.

Government appoints K Sanjay Murthy as Next CAG

- On 18th November 2024, the Government of India appointed K Sanjay Murthy as the new Comptroller and Auditor General (CAG) of India.
- Murthy, a 1989-batch IAS officer from the Himachal Pradesh cadre, succeeded Girish Chandra Murmu, who retired on November 20, 2024.
- Before this appointment, Murthy served as the Secretary of the Department of Higher Education.

Arvinder Singh Sahney appointed as new Chairman of IOC

- In November 2024, Arvinder Singh Sahney was appointed as the new Chairman of the Indian Oil Corporation (IOC).
- He previously headed IOC's petrochemical division and played a key role in commissioning the 15 MMTPA Paradip Refinery.

New Leadership for the Indian Army

"Lt. General Upendra Dwivedi Appointed As The 30th Chief Of Army Staff"

- Lieutenant General Upendra Dwivedi has officially taken over as the 30th Chief of Army Staff (COAS) of India. He succeeds General Manoj Pande, who retired on June 30, 2024, after a one-month extension from his original retirement date of May 31, 2024.

Background

- **Birthdate:** July 01, 1964
- **Commission:** Commissioned into the Infantry (Jammu & Kashmir Rifles) on December 15, 1984
- **Current Position:** Vice Chief of the Army Staff
- **Early Education:** Alumnus of Sainik School, Rewa, Madhya Pradesh
- **Military Career:**
  - Commissioned in 1984 into the 18th Jammu and Kashmir Rifles
  - Commanded the same unit later in his career
  - Served as Sector Commander and Inspector General of Assam Rifles
  - Held the position of Director General of Infantry
  - General Officer Commanding in Chief, Northern Command (2022-2024)
  - Vice Chief of the Army Staff

Recognitions

- Awards:
  - Param Vishisht Seva Medal
  - Ati Vishisht Seva Medal
  - Three GOC-in-C Commendation Cards

New Commandant of NDA Assumes Position

- Vice Admiral Gurcharan Singh assumed the appointment of Commandant, National Defence Academy from Vice Admiral Ajay Kocchar in Pune on 25 May 2024.
- An alumnus of the National Defence Academy (Khadakwasla), he was commissioned into the Indian Navy on 1st July 1990.

PESB Recommends New Director (Personnel) Of SJVN

- Ajay Kumar Sharma assumed charge as Director (Personnel) of SJVN in September 2024.
- The Public Enterprises Selection Board (PESB) had recommended his name for the post of Director (Personnel) of SJVN,
- Shri Sharma was previously serving as General Manager in Corporate Human Resources department, SJVN.

Sony Appoints New India CEO

- Sony Pictures Networks India (SPNI) has appointed Gaurav Banerjee as its new chief executive officer (CEO).
- Banerjee, a former executive from Walt Disney, will lead Sony's television and media businesses in India.

New MD & CEO Appointed For IndiaFirst Life Insurance

- Rushabh Gandhi, currently the Deputy CEO of IndiaFirst Life Insurance, has been promoted to the position of Managing Director (MD) and Chief Executive Officer (CEO).

• With over 25 years of experience in both national and international markets, Rushabh is a prodigious financial services leader.

• His strategic vision and innovative approach have significantly contributed to IndiaFirst Life's growth. Notably, he has implemented a successful Bancassurance business and a Multichannel Distribution strategy.

New President Elected For Supreme Court Bar Association

• Senior Advocate Kapil Sibal has been elected as the President of the Supreme Court Bar Association (SCBA) for the fourth time.

• He secured 1,066 votes, defeating his nearest rival, Senior Advocate Pradeep Rai.

• Sibal, a Rajya Sabha MP and former Union minister, has held the SCBA presidency three times between 1995 and 2002.

• He announced his candidature for the post on 8 May 2024. The election results were declared on 19 May 2024.

RBI Approves New Director At IDFC First Bank

• The Reserve Bank of India (RBI) has approved the appointment of Pradeep Natarajan as the Whole Time Director of IDFC FIRST Bank.

• The appointment is for a period of three years. This decision follows an earlier notification from the bank dated December 30, 2023.

• This is a significant development for IDFC FIRST Bank and reflects the bank's commitment to strong governance and leadership.

CII Elects New President For 2024-25

• Sanjiv Puri, Chairman and Managing Director of ITC Limited, has assumed office as the President of the Confederation of Indian Industry (CII) for 2024-25.

• He takes over from R Dinesh, Chairman of TVS Supply Chain Solutions.

• Puri heads ITC Ltd, a conglomerate with businesses in FMCG, hotels, paperboards & packaging, agribusiness, and IT.

• Rajiv Memani, Chairman of EY India, becomes President-Designate of CII for 2024-25.

New Additional Directors Appointed In CBI

• Senior IPS officers A.Y.V. Krishna and N. Venu Gopal have been appointed as Additional Directors in the Central Bureau of Investigation (CBI).

• Krishna, a 1995-batch Indian Police Service officer of Assam-Meghalaya cadre, is currently working as Inspector General in the Central Reserve Police Force (CRPF).

• He has been inducted as the additional director of CBI for a tenure up to 6 August 2028.

• Venu Gopal, Krishna's batchmate from the Himachal Pradesh cadre, is presently working as joint director in the CBI.

• He has been appointed as additional director, CBI for a tenure up to 24 May 2027.

Ujjivan Small Finance Bank Names New MD & CEO

• Sanjeev Nautiyal has been appointed as the Managing Director (MD) and Chief Executive Officer (CEO) of Ujjivan Small Finance Bank.

• The Reserve Bank of India (RBI) approved Sanjeev Nautiyal's appointment as MD & CEO from 1 July 2024, for a period of three years.

• Sanjeev Nautiyal is a seasoned banker with over three decades of experience.

Meghalaya Appoints First Woman Police Chief

• Idashisha Nongrang has made history as the first woman to be appointed as the Director General of Police (DGP) in Meghalaya.

• She is a senior IPS officer who will take over from LR Bishnoi, who is set to retire on 19 May 2024.

HPCL Names New Govt. Director

• Hindustan Petroleum Corporation (HPCL) has appointed Vinod Seshan as a Government Director on its board, replacing Sujata Sharma.

• Seshan, a Director from the Ministry of Petroleum & Natural Gas, will serve for three years on a co-terminus basis, effective immediately.

Tata Electronics Appoints New Chairman

• N. Chandrasekaran was appointed Chairman of Tata Electronics on May 14, 2024. He replaced Banmali Agrawala, who transitioned into an advisory role.

• Chandrasekaran, who also chairs Tata Sons, brings a wealth of experience from his 30-year career at Tata Consultancy Services (TCS).

• His appointment underscores Tata Electronics' strategic focus on semiconductor manufacturing and expanding its electronics manufacturing footprint.

RBI Appoints New Executive Director

• The Reserve Bank of India (RBI) has appointed R. Lakshmi Kanth Rao as Executive Director (ED) with effect from 10 May 2024.

• Prior to this, Rao served as Chief General Manager-in-Charge in the Department of Regulation.

• With over three decades of experience at the RBI, Rao has worked in the regulation of banks and NBFCs, supervision of banks, and consumer protection.

• He has also served as Banking Ombudsman in Chennai and Regional Director in Uttar Pradesh.

New Chief Of Personnel Named For Indian Navy

• Vice Admiral Sanjay Bhalla has taken over as the Chief of Personnel of the Indian Navy, having joined the Navy in January 1989.

• With 35 years of experience, he has served in various roles at sea and on land, including commanding INS Nishank, INS Taragiri, INS Beas, and the Eastern Fleet.

• He has received accolades such as the Ati Vishisht Seva Medal, Nao Sena Medal, and commendations from senior naval officials for his outstanding service.

Ministry Of Ayush Appoints New Director

• Subodh Kumar, an IAS officer of the 2010 batch from the Tamil Nadu cadre, has been appointed as the Director of the Ministry of Ayush.

• He was Additional Secretary in the Ministry of Steel and Director General of the National Testing Agency (NTA).

Visa Names New India Country Manager

• Visa, the global digital payments platform, has appointed Sujai Raina as the new Country Manager for India.

• Chhabra previously served as VP and Head of Merchant Services & Acquiring for India and South Asia at Visa.

• He has also held leadership roles at Fiserv, First Data Corp, PayPal, JP Morgan, ABN AMRO, and General Electric.

Ujjivan Small Finance Bank Appoints New MD & CEO

- Sanjeev Nautiyal was appointed as the Managing Director & CEO of Ujjivan Small Finance Bank on July 1, 2024, for a three-year term approved by the Reserve Bank of India.
- He also served as MD & CEO of SBI Life Insurance and held significant roles at SBI, including Deputy Managing Director for Financial Inclusion & Micro Markets.

HDFC Bank Re-Appoints Chairman

- The Reserve Bank of India (RBI) has approved the re-appointment of Atanu Chakraborty as the Part Time Chairman of HDFC Bank for a three-year term starting from 5 May 2024.
- The bank's Board of Directors has also approved his re-appointment as Part Time Chairman and Independent Director for the same duration.
- Shareholders' approval for these re-appointments is being sought through a postal ballot notice.

New President Appointed For GSTAT

- Sanjaya Kumar Mishra was appointed as the President of the GST Appellate Tribunal (GSTAT) on May 6, 2024.
- A former Chief Justice of the Jharkhand High Court, Mishra was selected by a Search-cum-Selection Committee headed by the Chief Justice of India.
- The tribunal includes a Principal Bench in New Delhi and 31 State Benches nationwide.

Department Of Land Resources Appoints New Director

- Sarvadanand Barnwal, a 2010 Indian Statistical Service (ISS) officer, has been appointed as the Director of the Department of Land Resources in Delhi for a five-year tenure.
- His selection under the Central Staffing Scheme (CSS) reflects his expertise and potential to contribute to national-level statistical and programmatic efforts, facilitated by the Ministry of Statistics & Programme Implementation.

Akashvani News Appoints New DG

- On 1 May, 2024, Maushumi Chakravarty, a senior Indian Information Service officer, took over as director general of Akashvani News.
- Ms. Chakravarty, an IIS officer from the 1991 batch, has extensive experience working for the I&B Ministry's Press Information Bureau and Central Bureau of Communication, among other media organizations.

Axis Bank Re-Appoints MD & CEO

- The Board of Axis Bank has approved the re-appointment of Amitabh Chaudhry as Managing Director & CEO of the Bank, for another three-year term, effective 1 January 2025.
- Chaudhry, age 59 years, has been serving Axis Bank as MD & CEO since January 1, 2019, after working with HDFC Standard Life Insurance Company Limited (HDFC Life) for nine years.

New CVO For Cotton Corporation Of India

- The Central Government has approved the appointment of Nidhi S Jain (IA&AS) as Chief Vigilance Officer (CVO) of Cotton Corporation of India Limited (CCI).
- Nidhi is an Indian Audit and Accounts Service (IA&AS) service officer of 2009-batch.
- Presently, she is posted as Director of Audit (Environment & Scientific Departments), Branch office, Mumbai.

First Woman Vice Chancellor Of Aligarh Muslim University

- The central government has appointed Naima Khatoon as the Vice Chancellor of the Aligarh Muslim University (AMU), making her the first woman to hold the top post in over 100 years.
- The appointment was approved by President Droupadi Murmu and the Election Commission of India (ECI) because of the Model Code of Conduct (MCC) being in place.
- Naima Khatoon, Principal, Women's College, has been appointed as the Vice Chancellor of AMU for a period of five years.

New Railway Adviser In High Commission Of India, Bangladesh

- Government of India has approved the appointment of Narpat Singh (IRTS) to the post of Railway Adviser in the High Commission of India & Dhaka, Bangladesh.
- Singh is an Indian Railway Traffic Service (IRTS) of 2009-batch. Previously, he was posted as Director (Traffic Transpiration) in the Railway Board.

New Chief Of NSG Appointed

- Senior IPS officer Nalin Prabhat has been appointed as the Director-General of National Security Guard (NSG), the country's counter-terrorism force.
- Prabhat, a 1992 batch IPS officer of Andhra Pradesh cadre, is presently working as Additional Director General in CRPF.
- The Appointments Committee of the Cabinet (ACC) has approved his appointment as the Director General, NSG for a period up to August 31, 2028 i.e. the date of his superannuation.

New Chief Of The Naval Staff Appointed

- Admiral Dinesh K Tripathi took over as the new Chief of the Naval Staff on April 30, 2024.
- He succeeded Admiral R Hari Kumar and was previously the Vice Chief of Naval Staff.
- He has served on frontline warships, held various operational and staff appointments, and commanded warships like INS Vinash, INS Kirch, and INS Trishul.

BharatPe Appoints New CEO

- BharatPe, one of India's leading players in the fintech sector, announced the elevation of Nalin Negi as its Chief Executive Officer (CEO).
- Under his leadership, BharatPe recorded 182% increase in revenue from operations in FY23 and clocked October'23 as the first EBITDA positive month.
- Nalin Negi joined BharatPe in 2022, with over 28 years of experience in building and scaling businesses in the fintech and banking domains.

Senior IPS Officer As Joint Director Of CBI

- Senior IPS officer Anurag Kumar was appointed to the post of Joint Director, Central Bureau of Investigation (CBI) on 12 April 2024.
- Kumar, a 2004 batch Indian Police Service (IPS) officer of Assam-Meghalaya cadre, is currently working in the Bureau of Police Research and Development (BPR&D).

JSW One Platforms Appoints Independent Director

- JSW One Platforms announced the appointment of Ranjan Pai as independent director on its board.
- The company is the e-commerce venture of the $23 billion JSW Group. It operates B2B tech-enabled marketplace JSW One MSME, to service the building material needs of Industrial & Construction MSMEs in India.
- As part of his role, Pai will provide strategic guidance to shape the company's future and create long-term value for stakeholders.

NDDB Chief Elected As NCDFI Chairman

- Dr. Meenesh Shah has been unanimously elected as the Chairman of the National Cooperative Dairy Federation of India Ltd. (NCDFI) in its Board elections.

- The election process was overseen by Praveen Chaudhary, IAS, District Collector of Anand, who served as the Returning Officer.
- NCDFI is a national-level apex dairy cooperative established on December 7, 1970, and is governed under the provisions of the Multi-State Cooperative Societies (Amendment) Act, 2023.

New Principal Director General Of PIB Takes Charge

- Ms Sheyphali B. Sharan assumed charge as the Principal Director General, Press Information Bureau upon superannuation of Shri Manish Desai on April 1, 2024.
- Ms. Sharan is an officer of the 1990 batch of Indian Information Service.
- She has also served as the Spokesperson for Election Commission of India.

New President Appointed For ASSOCHAM

- Sanjay Nayar, Chairman of Sorin Investment Fund, has assumed the role of President of Assocham for the term 2024-25, succeeding Ajay Singh, the Chairman and MD of SpiceJet.
- Nayar brings over four decades of experience in global financial and capital markets, including 25 years at Citi and nearly 14 years at KKR, where he established KKR India operations in 2009.
- At KKR, Nayar led investments totaling around USD 14 billion in private equity, real estate, and infrastructure, with private equity alone reaching approximately USD 10 billion in valuation.

IIT-Kanpur Alumnus Elected FISME President

- Sandeep Jain, an auto-component manufacturer and graduate of IIT-Kanpur, has been elected as the President of the Federation of Indian Micro and Small & Medium Enterprises (FISME) for the term 2024-25.
- FISME follows a system where one-third of its CEC members are elected each year, and the newly formed body chooses the President for the upcoming year.
- Sandeep Jain succeeds Prashant Patel, a manufacturer of dyes and chemicals based in Ahmedabad and Surat, who previously held the position of Vice President within FISME.

New MD & CEO Appointed For Bank Of Maharashtra

- Nidhu Saxena was appointed as the Managing Director & Chief Executive Officer (MD & CEO) of Bank of Maharashtra on March 27, 2024.
- He replaced AS Rajeev, who became Vigilance Commissioner in the Central Vigilance Commission (CVC).
- Saxena, an Executive Director at Union Bank of India, brings over 26 years of banking experience.
- He started his career at Bank of Baroda and has held key positions at UCO Bank and Union Bank of India.

New Director General Appointed For NIA, New Chiefs For NDRF And BPR&D

- Maharashtra Anti-Terrorism Squad chief Sadanand Vasant Date has been appointed as the Director General of the National Investigation Agency (NIA).
- Date is a 1990-batch Indian Police Service (IPS) officer of Maharashtra cadre.
- The ACC also appointed Rajeev Kumar Sharma, a 1990-batch IPS officer of Rajasthan cadre, as the Director General of the Bureau of Police Research & Development.

New Judicial Member Sworn In For Lokpal Of India

- Justice Ritu Raj Awasthi sworn in as judicial member, Lokpal. The oath was administered by Justice A. M. Khanwilkar, Chairperson, Lokpal of India.
- Shri Pankaj Kumar and Shri Ajay Tirkey took oath as member, Lokpal. The oath ceremony was organised today at the Lokpal of India office in New Delhi.
- Shri Justice Ritu Raj Awasthi, before joining as Judicial Member, Lokpal of India, was serving as the Chairperson of 22nd Law Commission of India. Before that, he was Chief Justice of Karnataka High Court.
- Shri Pankaj Kumar is a 1986 batch IAS officer from Gujarat cadre. Before joining as Member of Lokpal of India, he was serving as Chief Secretary of Gujarat.

New Appointment For Director In UPSC

- Hansha Mishra, an officer of the Indian Audit and Accounts Service (IA&AS) from the 2010 batch, has been appointed as Director in the Union Public Service Commission (UPSC), Delhi.
- Her appointment comes after she was recommended for central deputation by the Comptroller and Auditor General (CAG) of India.
- Her appointment under the Central Staffing Scheme is for five years.

FIEO Elects New President

- Mr Ashwani Kumar, Partner, Victor Forgings, Jalandhar has been unanimously elected as the New President of the Federation of Indian Export Organisations (FIEO) on March 11, 2024.
- Mr Ashwani Kumar is a well known and popular business entrepreneur and exporter from Jalandhar (Punjab), representing the engineering sector of exports.

Indian Steel Association's New President Assumes Office

- Naveen Jindal, chairman, Jindal Steel and Power, took charge as president of Indian Steel Association (ISA), the apex body for steel producers.
- He succeeds Dilip Oommen, CEO of ArcelorMittal Nippon Steel India.
- For India to realise its development goals, steel along with its upstream and downstream manufacturing value chains have to grow in tandem.

Indian Banks' Association Elects New Chairman

- Indian Banks Association (IBA) has a new Chairman in M V Rao, Managing Director and CEO, Central Bank of India.
- Rao was elected as IBA Chairman for the term 2023-24 at a meeting of the Managing Committee of IBA held.
- Three Deputy Chairmen for IBA would be Dinesh Kumar Khara, Chairman, State Bank of India (SBI); S L Jain, MD and CEO, Indian Bank and N Kamakodi, Managing Director and CEO, City Union Bank.

New Director General Appointed For NSG

- Daljit Singh Chaudhary, a 1990 batch IPS officer, has been appointed as the Director General (DG) of the National Security Guard (NSG), marking a significant change in India's security apparatus.
- Chaudhary, who presently serves as the DG of Sashastra Seema Bal (SSB), will now lead the NSG, commonly referred to as the "black cats".

PayU Appoints New Chairperson And Independent Director

- Renu Sud Karnad, the former Managing Director of Housing Development Finance Corporation Ltd. (HDFC) until June 30, 2023, has been appointed as the Independent Director and Board Chairperson of PayU Payments.
- Karnad, who currently serves as the President of the International Union of Housing Finance (IUHF), brings over four decades of industry experience to her new role. She has also been a Non-Executive Director on the HDFC Bank Board.

New Director Of Operations Takes Charge At NTPC

- Ravindra Kumar has been appointed to a post by the Appointments Committee of the Cabinet, effective February 26. He has over 34 years of experience, primarily with NTPC Limited.
- He has worked at the NTPC Kahalgaon Project and the Corporate Centre, providing technical support to the Director (Technical).

Justice Ajay Manikrao appointed New Chairperson of Lokpal

- Justice Ajay Manikrao Khanwilkar was sworn in as the Chairperson of Lokpal on March 10, 2024.
- Khanwilkar served as Chief Justice of the Himachal Pradesh and Madhya Pradesh High Courts before being elevated to the Supreme Court of India in 2016.
- He also chaired the Mahanadi Water Disputes Tribunal and the News Broadcasters Federation.

New Rajya Sabha Member Takes Oath

- Philanthropist Sudha Murty was sworn in as a member of the Rajya Sabha.
- Rajya Sabha Chairman Jagdeep Dhankhar administered the oath to Sudha Murty in the Parliament House.
- Infosys founder Narayan Murty and Leader of the Rajya Sabha Piyush Goyal were present at the ceremony. Sudha Murty was nominated to the Rajya Sabha by President Droupadi Murmu.

Rahul Singh appointed new chairperson of CBSE

- Senior bureaucrat Rahul Singh, a 1996-batch Indian Administrative Service (IAS) officer of the Bihar cadre, has been appointed as the new chairperson of the Central Board of Secondary Education (CBSE).
- He succeeds Nidhi Chhibber in this role. The appointment comes as part of a senior-level bureaucratic reshuffle announced by the Centre.
- Currently serving as the Additional Secretary in the Department of Personnel and Training (DoPT).

New Governor Takes Charge In Telangana

- C.P. Radhakrishnan has assumed office as the Governor of Telangana, succeeding the previous governor.
- The oath of office was administered by Telangana High Court Chief Justice Alok Aradhe at a ceremony held at Raj Bhavan in Hyderabad.
- The event was attended by Chief Minister A. Revanth Reddy, ministers, public representatives, and senior officials.

Infosys CEO Joins USISPF Board

- Salil Parekh, the CEO and Managing Director of Infosys, has joined the Board of Directors of the US-India Strategic Partnership Forum (USISPF).
- Parekh, an industry veteran with nearly three decades in the IT services industry, is recognized for his adeptness in executing business transformations and overseeing fruitful acquisitions.
- The USISPF is an independent institution dedicated to strengthening the partnership between the United States and India.

AS Rajeev Appointed New Vigilance Commissioner

- A S Rajeev, the former Chief Executive of Bank of Maharashtra, has been appointed as the Vigilance Commissioner in the Central Vigilance Commission (CVC) by President Droupadi Murmu.
- Prior to this appointment, A S Rajeev was the Managing Director & CEO of Bank of Maharashtra, a public sector bank.
- The Central Vigilance Commission became a three-member body, with the Central Vigilance Commissioner and two Vigilance Commissioners.
- While Praveen Kumar Srivastava has been Central Vigilance Commissioner since May 2023, Arvinda Kumar has been a Vigilance Commissioner since August 2022.

TRAI Appoints New Chairman

- Anil Kumar Lahoti has been appointed as the new Chairman of the Telecom Regulatory Authority of India (TRAI).
- He is a retired Indian Railway Service of Engineers (IRSE) officer from the 1984 batch and former Chairman and CEO of the Railway Board under the Ministry of Railways, Government of India.

Tata Digital Appoints New CEO

- Tata Digital, the superapp under Tata Sons, appointed Naveen Tahilyani as its new CEO and MD.
- Tahilyani replaces Pratik Pal, who led the company since Tata's entry into digital commerce and the creation of the Tata Neu superapp. Currently serving as the CEO and MD of Tata AIA Life Insurance Company.

NPCI Appoints New Non-Executive Chairman

- Ajay Kumar Choudhary has been appointed as the new non-executive chairman and independent director of the National Payments Corporation of India (NPCI), with effect from February 8, 2024.
- With a distinguished career spanning over three decades at the Reserve Bank of India (RBI), Mr. Choudhary brings a wealth of experience and expertise as a central banker to this significant role.

Tata AIA Life Appoints New MD And CEO

- Venkatachalam H. was appointed as the new Managing Director & CEO of Tata AIA Life Insurance on February 6, 2024. He succeeds Naveen Tahilyani.
- Venkatachalam, known as Venky, brings over 27 years of experience in life insurance, asset management, and custodial services.
- He previously served as President and Chief Distribution Officer at Tata AIA, leading several initiatives in marketing, strategy, and digital business.

ICAI Elects New President And Vice President

- Ranjeet Kumar Agarwal has been elected as the new President of the Institute of Chartered Accountants of India (ICAI), succeeding Aniket S. Talati.
- He is the 72nd President of ICAI and has been a practicing Chartered Accountant for 24 years, holding additional qualifications as a Company Secretary and DISA from ICAI.
- Charanjot Singh Nanda has been elected as the Vice President for the Year 2024-25. Nanda, a graduate of M L N College, is a rank holder in CA Inter examination and completed his Chartered Accountancy in 1991.

SBICAPS Appoints New MD And CEO

- Virendra Bansal has been named as the new Managing Director and Chief Executive Officer of SBI Capital Markets (SBICAPS), succeeding Rajay Kumar Sinha. Sinha has been appointed as the Whole Time Member (Finance and Investment) of IRDAI.
- Prior to his new role, Bansal served as Country Head for SBI's US Operations and held various positions within the bank, including CEO of SBI's New York office and Vice-Chairman of SBI (California).

FAITH tourism association appoints new head

- The Federation of Associations in Indian Tourism & Hospitality (FAITH) has appointed Puneet Chhatwal, managing director and CEO of Indian Hotels Company Limited, as its new chairperson.
- He takes over from ITC executive director Nakul Anand, who retired this week.
- Chhatwal will also continue as president of HAI, a position he was re-elected to in 2022.

New Vice Chief of the Naval Staff Appointed

- Vice-Admiral Dinesh K. Tripathi took over as the Vice-Chief of the Naval Staff (VCNS).
- He has become the senior-most Naval officer after Admiral R. Hari Kumar steps down on April 30.
- Vice-Admiral Sanjay Jasjit Singh took over from him as the Flag Officer Commanding-in-Chief (FOCINC), Western Naval Command.
- Vice-Admiral V. Srinivas has become the 30th FOCINC of the Southern Naval Command, succeeding Vice-Admiral M. A. Hampiholi.

Maharashtra's First Woman Director General Of Police Appointed

- The Maharashtra government appointed 1988 batch Indian Police Service (IPS) officer Rashmi Shukla as the Director General of Police.
- Ms. Shukla became the first woman police officer to hold the top police post in the State.
- Before this role, she was on central deputation heading the Sashastra Seema Bal (SSB) and had also served as the Additional Director-General of the Central Reserve Police Force (CRPF).

New president elected for AIRIA

- Shashi Singh has been elected as the president of the All India Rubber Industries Association (AIRIA), the apex body for rubber industries in India.
- The elections took place during the Annual General Meeting held on December 23, 2023, in Mumbai.
- Mr. Zafar Ahmed, the Managing Director of New India Rubber Works Pvt. Ltd., has been elected as the Senior Vice-President of AIRIA for the year 2023-24.

RBI clears appointment of whole-time director by Bandhan Bank

- Bandhan Bank has received approval from the Reserve Bank of India (RBI) to appoint Rajinder Kumar Babbar as whole-time director.
- Babbar, currently the Group Head – Transportation, Infrastructure, and Tractor Finance Group at HDFC Bank, has 35 years of experience in the banking sector in various leadership roles.
- His previous roles include building and managing the Rural Banking Group for HDFC Bank, as well as positions at Centurion Bank, Bank of Punjab, and Central Bank of India.

PepsiCo India appoints new CEO

- Jagrut Kotecha has been appointed as the next CEO of PepsiCo India, succeeding Ahmed El Sheikh.
- Kotecha currently serves as the Senior Vice President and Chief Commercial Officer for AMESA.
- He joined PepsiCo in 1994 and held various sales and marketing roles, including Regional Sales Manager and Marketing Manager for Western Snack.

Ajit Doval Reappointed As National Security Adviser

- Ajit Doval will continue serving as the National Security Advisor (NSA) in the Narendra Modi-led NDA government.
- The Appointments Committee of the Cabinet approved his reappointment, effective from June 10, 2024.
- Doval, a 1968 batch IPS officer and a renowned counter-terrorism expert, has been serving as NSA since May 2014.
- The Appointments Committee of the Cabinet has reappointed P.K. Mishra as the Principal Secretary to Prime Minister Narendra Modi. Additionally, Amit Khare and Tarun Kapoor, both retired IAS officers, have been appointed as advisers to the Prime Minister.

Ajith Kumar Appointed New MD and CEO of Dhanlaxmi Bank

- Ajith Kumar KK has been appointed as the Managing Director (MD) and CEO of Dhanlaxmi Bank, with his tenure beginning on June 20, 2024, for a period of three years.
- Ajith Kumar KK brings over 36 years of experience in various aspects of banking, including credit, human resources, business, and branch banking, having served at Federal Bank where he is currently the Chief Human Resources Officer.

Sandeep Batra as ICICI Prudential Board chairman

- The Insurance Regulatory and Development Authority of India (IRDAI) has approved the appointment of Sandeep Batra as the Chairman of the Board of Directors of ICICI Prudential.
- Batra's appointment will be effective from June 30, 2024.
- Batra has been associated with the ICICI Group since September 2000 and is currently an Executive Director on the board of ICICI Bank since July 2018, in charge of corporate centre.

President Appoints Pro Tem Speaker Of Lok Sabha

- President Droupadi Murmu on 20th June appointed Member of Parliament and BJP leader Bhartruhari Mahtab as Pro Tem Speaker of Lok Sabha.
- Bhartruhari Mahtab, a seven-time MP from Cuttack and son of Odisha's former Chief Minister Harekrushna Mahtab, moved to the Bharatiya Janata Party ahead of the Lok Sabha polls ending his long association with Naveen Patnaik's Biju Janata Dal.

V. Ramasubramanian Appointed as New Chairperson of NHRC

- President Droupadi Murmu appointed former Supreme Court judge V Ramasubramanian as the chairperson of the National Human Rights Commission (NHRC).
- The post of NHRC chairperson was vacant since Justice (retd.) Arun Kumar Mishra completed his tenure on June 1, 2024.
- Ramasubramanian is a former Supreme Court judge, who also served as chief justice of the Himachal Pradesh High Court in 2019.
- The President also appointed Priyank Kanoongo and Justice (retd.) Bidyut Ranjan Sarangi as members of the rights panel.

IAS officer Arunish Chawla appointed as new Revenue Secretary

- Arunish Chawla, an IAS officer of the Bihar cadre has been appointed as the new Revenue Secretary in the Ministry of Finance.
- Previously he has served as the Secretary in the Department of Pharmaceuticals in the Ministry of Chemicals and Fertilisers since November 1, 2023.
- The post of Revenue Secretary had fallen vacant after Sanjay Malhotra was appointed the RBI Governor to replace Shaktikanta Das.

President Appoints New Governors for Five States

- President Draupadi Murmu made a major reshuffle in the Governors of five states.
- Former Union Home Secretary Ajay Kumar Bhalla has been appointed as the new Governor of Manipur.
- Arif Mohammed Khan has been reassigned from Kerala to Bihar.

- Hari Babu Kambhampati, previously the Governor of Mizoram, has been moved to Odisha.
- General (Dr.) Vijay Kumar Singh, a retired military officer, has been appointed as the new Governor of Mizoram.
- Rajendra Vishwanath Arlekar, the former Governor of Bihar, has been reassigned to Kerala.

Dr. Sandip Shah Appointed as the Chairperson of NABL-QCI

- Dr. Sandip Shah has been appointed as the Chairperson of the National Accreditation Board for Testing and Calibration Laboratories (NABL), a constituent board of the Quality Council of India (QCI).
- He succeeds Prof. Subbanna Ayyappan in this role. The Quality Council of India (QCI) is a premier autonomous body set up by the Government of India.
- The National Accreditation Board for Testing and Calibration Laboratories (NABL) operates accreditation programs for laboratories, ensuring reliability and accuracy in testing and calibration.

INTERNATIONAL APPOINTMENTS

Justice Madan B. Lokur Appointed Chairperson of UN Internal Justice Council

- Former Supreme Court Justice Madan B Lokur was appointed as a Chairperson of the UN Internal Justice Council ('the Council') for a term of four years, ending on 12-11-2028.
- The Internal Justice Council comprises five members appointed by the Secretary-General. The other four members on the list are Carmen Artigas (Uruguay), Rosalie Balkin (Australia), Stefan Brezina (Austria) and Jay Pozenal (United States of America).

Google appoints Preeti Lobana as India Head

- Tech giant Google has appointed Preeti Lobana as its new Country Manager and Vice President for India.
- Preeti has replaced interim head Roma Datta Chobey and is succeeding Sanjay Gupta, who was elevated earlier this year to the position of President of the Asia-Pacific region.
- Google was founded on September 4, 1998, by American computer scientists Larry Page and Sergey Brin.

Emmanuel Macron announces Francois Bayrou as the new PM of France

- French President Emmanuel Macron named Francois Bayrou as the new Prime Minister of France.
- Centrist Bayrou marks the country's fourth prime minister this year after Barnier resigned on Dec. 5 in the wake of a historic no-confidence vote.
- Francois Bayrou led France's centre-right Democratic Movement since he founded it in 2007 and is a longtime ally of Macron.

Mikheil Kavelashvili Elected as the President of Georgia

- Mikheil Kavelashvili, a former Manchester City footballer and MP with the Georgian Dream party has become Georgia's next president.
- Kavelashvili joined George Weah of Liberia as only the second former footballer to serve as a head of state.
- Georgia is a parliamentary democracy with the president the head of state, and the prime minister the head of Parliament.

Mohammad al-Bashir appointed Interim Prime Minister of Syria

- The Hayat Tahrir al-Sham, or HTS rebels in Syria, appointed Mohammad al-Bashir as Interim Prime Minister of Syria after Bashar al-Assad's government fell.
- Mohammad al-Bashir will remain the head of the transitional government in Syria until 1st March 2025.
- Syrian Ex-President Bashar al-Assad recently fled from the country.

Nita Ambani unanimously reelected as IOCM

- Nita Ambani, the founder and chairperson of Reliance Foundation, has been unanimously re-elected as a member of the International Olympic Committee (IOC) for the Paris Olympics 2024.
- Under her guidance, Reliance Foundation has reached over 22 million children and youth through initiatives promoting multi-sport participation.
- Nita Ambani was first appointed to join the prestigious body in 2016, at the Rio de Janeiro Olympic Games. Since then, as India's first woman to join the IOC.

Vinay Mohan Kwatra appointed as New Ambassador of India to Us

- On 19 July 2024, Vinay Mohan Kwatra, a retired Indian Foreign Service diplomat and former Foreign Secretary, was appointed as India's next Ambassador to the United States.
- He succeeded Taranjit Singh Sandhu on 13th August 2024, who retired in January 2024.
- Kwatra's extensive expertise in dealing with India's neighborhood, the US, China, and Europe positions him well for this crucial diplomatic role.
- Previously, he served as the Ambassador of India to France and Nepal.

JAY SHAH REPLACES GREG BARCLAY AS ICC CHAIRMAN

- Jay Shah, the former secretary of the Board of Control for Cricket in India (BCCI), officially assumed the role of International Cricket Council (ICC) Chair on December 1, 2024 succeeding Greg Barclay.
- He became the 4th Chairman of the International Cricket Council.
- He is the third Indian to become Chair of the International Cricket Council, after N. Srinivasan and Shashank Manohar.

Nepal President Appoints KP Oli as new Prime Minister

- Nepal's President Ram Chandra Paudel has appointed KP Sharma Oli as the new Prime Minister.
- Oli, the chairman of the Communist Party of Nepal-Unified Marxist Leninist (CPN-UML), will lead the government for the next 18 months. He is serving as the 38th prime minister of Nepal.

Satya Prakash Sangwan named Chef de Mission for Paris 2024 Paralympics

- On 20 August 2024, Satya Prakash Sangwan was appointed as the Chef de Mission for the Indian contingent at the Paris 2024 Paralympic Games.
- As Vice President of the Paralympic Committee of India (PCI), Sangwan led India's largest-ever contingent of 84 para-athletes competing across 12 sports disciplines.

Kagame sworn in for 4th term as Rwandan President

- On 11 August 2024, Paul Kagame was sworn in for his fourth term as Rwandan President. He secured over 99% of the vote in the July elections.
- The inauguration ceremony took place at the 45,000-seat Amahoro National Stadium in Kigali, attended by numerous African leaders.
- Kagame, who has been in power since the end of the 1994 genocide, pledged to preserve peace and national unity.

Janet Yang re-elected Film Academy's President

- On 1 August 2024, Janet Yang was re-elected as the president of the Academy of Motion Picture Arts and Sciences.

- This marks her third term in this role, having first been elected in August 2022.
- Yang is an Emmy-winning producer known for films like "The Joy Luck Club" and "The People vs. Larry Flynt."

Lt Gen Muhammad Asim Malik appointed new ISI chief

- Lieutenant General Muhammad Asim Malik has been appointed as the new Director General of Pakistan's Inter-Services Intelligence (ISI), succeeding Lt Gen Nadeem Anjum.
- Malik, previously serving as Adjutant General at the General Headquarters in Rawalpindi, assumed his new role on 30 September 2024.
- Known for his administrative expertise and military command experience in Balochistan and South Waziristan, Malik's appointment comes at a critical time for Pakistan's national security landscape.

R. Ravindra appointed as India's Ambassador to Iceland

- R. Ravindra, an Indian Foreign Service officer from the 1999 batch, was appointed as India's Ambassador to Iceland in September 2024.
- R Ravindra took charge in November 2024.
- Before that, he served as the Ambassador and Deputy Permanent Representative of India to the United Nations in New York.

> **MICHEL BARNIER IS NEW FRENCH PRIME MINISTER**
>
> ✎ French President Emmanuel Macron has appointed François Bayrou as the new Prime Minister of France amidst a worsening political crisis on 13th December 2024.
>
> ✎ The appointment follows a vote of no-confidence that ousted Michel Barnier's minority government, leaving France in political instability, rising borrowing costs, and a European leadership vacuum.

Hezbollah announces Naim Qassem as new leader

- In October 2024, Hezbollah announced Naim Qassem as its new chief, succeeding Hassan Nasrallah, who was killed in an Israeli airstrike.
- Qassem, previously the deputy leader, has been a key figure in Hezbollah since its formation in the early 1980s.

Prakash Man Singh Raut appointed new Chief Justice of Nepal

- On 6 October 2024, Prakash Man Singh Raut was appointed as the new Chief Justice of Nepal by President Ramchandra Paudel.
- Raut, the senior-most justice of the Supreme Court, was recommended for the role by the Constitutional Council on 16 September.
- He succeeded Bishowambhar Prasad Shrestha, who retired upon reaching the mandatory retirement age of 65.

Claudia Sheinbaum becomes Mexico's first female President

- On 1 October 2024, Claudia Sheinbaum was sworn in as Mexico's first female president. Sheinbaum replaced Andrés Manuel López Obrador.

- The 62-year-old scientist and former mayor of Mexico City took the oath of office in a historic ceremony at Mexico's Congress.

Karoline Leavitt as youngest White House press secretary

- On 15th November 2024, President-elect Donald Trump announced Karoline Leavitt as the next White House press secretary. At 27 years of age, she will be the youngest in U.S. history.
- Leavitt, who served as Trump's campaign press secretary, has a background in communications and political science from Saint Anselm College.
- She previously worked in the Trump administration and ran for Congress in 2022.

The First Woman Chief Justice of Lahore Takes Oath

- Justice Aalia Neelum made history by becoming the first woman Chief Justice of the Lahore High Court (LHC).
- On 11 July 2024, Pakistan's Punjab Governor Saleem Haider Khan administered the oath to her at the Governor House.
- The Judicial Commission of Pakistan unanimously approved her elevation, and President Asif Ali Zardari officially notified her appointment.

Mexico's first woman president

- Climate scientist and former mayor of Mexico City, Claudia Sheinbaum, has been elected as the first woman to be elected as President of Mexico.
- She will also be the first Jewish leader of Jewish heritage to hold the office.
- Sheinbaum (61) received nearly 58 per cent of the vote.

Allamaye Halina appointed Chad's new Prime Minister

- Allamaye Halina was appointed as Chad's new Prime Minister on May 23, 2024.

- Previously Chad's ambassador to China, Halina's appointment followed the inauguration of President Mahamat Idriss Deby.
- Halina's predecessor, Succès Masra, resigned after losing the presidential election.

NASA Appoints New Chief AI Officer

- NASA appointed David Salvagnini as its first Chief Artificial Intelligence Officer (CAIO) on May 13, 2024.
- Salvagnini, who also serves as NASA's Chief Data Officer, brings over 20 years of experience in technology leadership from his time in the intelligence community.
- He previously worked as Director of the Architecture and Integration Group and Chief Architect at the Office of the Director of National Intelligence.

Iran Appoints New Acting President

- Iran's Supreme Leader Ayatollah Ali Khamenei has appointed Vice President Mohammad Mokhber as acting president after Ebrahim Raisi's death in a helicopter crash.
- Khamenei also declared five days of national mourning for Raisi.
- Mokhber, now interim president, must organize new elections within 50 days.

Taiwan's President-Elect Takes Oath

- President-elect Lai Ching-te of Taiwan took the oath of office on May 20, 2024.
- Lai, also known as William Lai, served as Vice President for the past four years during incumbent President Tsai Ing-wen's second term.
- In his inaugural address, Lai urged China to stop its military and political threats, and emphasized that peace is the only choice.

Scotland's New First Minister Sworn In

- SNP leader John Swinney has been sworn in as the seventh first minister of Scotland.
- Swinney, 60, succeeds Humza Yousaf, who formally resigned from the role earlier on 7 May after his announcement last week.
- Swinney, who has 16 years of cabinet experience, previously led the Scottish National Party (SNP) from 2000 to 2004.

Papua New Guinea Appoints First Defense Adviser To India

- Papua New Guinea has appointed Col Edison Napyo as its first Defence Advisor to India.
- His appointment aims to enhance defence cooperation between the two countries, following Prime Minister Narendra Modi's visit to PNG in May 2023.

India's Gita Sabharwal Appointed To Top UN Post In Indonesia

- United Nations Secretary-General António Guterres has appointed Gita Sabharwal of India as the United Nations Resident Coordinator (designate) in Indonesia.
- Previously she served as UN Resident Coordinator in Thailand and as Peacebuilding and Development Advisor at the United Nations in Sri Lanka.

Former Pakistan PM Elected Senate Chairman

- Yusuf Raza Gilani, former Prime Minister and Pakistan Peoples Party (PPP) leader, has been elected as the chairman of the senate, Pakistan's upper house of parliament.
- Gilani, who served as Prime Minister from 2008 to 2012, aims to build bridges and enable dialogue within parliamentary norms.
- His election followed a boycott by lawmakers from Imran Khan's party, PTI.

UN Appoints New Assistant Secretary-General

- In March 2024, Kamal Kishore of India was appointed as the new Assistant Secretary-General and Special Representative of the Secretary-General for Disaster Risk Reduction by the United Nations.
- Kishore brings nearly three decades of experience in disaster risk reduction, climate action, and sustainable development.
- As part of India's G20 presidency, he led the G20 Working Group on Disaster Risk Reduction and contributed to the Coalition for Disaster Resilient Infrastructure.

Luis Montenegro Appointed New PM Of Portugal

- After eight years of Socialist rule in Portugal, Luis Montenegro, leader of the centre-right Democratic Alliance (AD), has been appointed as the new prime minister.
- Montenegro's appointment marks the return of a centre-right leader to the prime minister's office after more than eight years.
- Despite his party's victory in the recent election, the AD falls short of a majority in the parliament, with only 80 out of 230 seats.
- Montenegro's rejection of a coalition with the far-right Chega party leaves his government in a fragile position, necessitating negotiations with other parties for legislative support.

Finland's New President Sworn In

- A former Prime Minister and Foreign Minister Alexander Stubb was sworn in as Finland's new President on March 1, 2024.
- He emphasized Finland's new era as a NATO member and plans to inspect NATO military drills in Norway.
- He took his oath in Finnish and Swedish, becoming Finland's 13th president since its independence from Russia in 1917.

Shehbaz Sharif elected Pakistan PM for second term

- Shehbaz Sharif, a leader of the Pakistan Muslim League-Nawaz (PML-N), has been elected as the Prime Minister of Pakistan, securing 201 votes in the National Assembly.
- His rival, Omer Ayub Khan, backed by Imran Khan's PTI, received 92 votes amid widespread uproar during the voting session. PTI-backed lawmakers demanded Imran Khan's release and accused Sharif of winning through electoral rigging.
- After his election, Sharif thanked his brother Nawaz and allies for their trust. The general elections were marked by allegations of mass vote rigging, with PTI claiming victory for candidates despite others securing more votes.

Asif Ali Zardari Takes Oath As Pakistan's 14th President

- Asif Ali Zardari was sworn in as Pakistan's 14th President, following his overwhelming election as the next head of state.
- Chief Justice of Pakistan Qazi Faez Isa administered the oath to the 68-year-old Zardari at Aiwan-e-Sadr, the Presidential Palace.
- Zardari succeeded Dr. Arif Alvi, who remained in office for an additional five months despite completing his five-year term in September last year.

Palestine Appoints New Prime Minister

- Palestinian President Mahmoud Abbas appointed Mohammad Mustafa as the new Prime Minister of Palestine in March 2024.
- Mustafa is a political independent and economist educated in the United States, serving as an economic advisor to Abbas.
- He will lead a technocratic government in the Israeli-occupied West Bank.

World Bank's GEF Appoints First Woman Director

- Geeta Batra, an Indian economist, has been named as the new Director at the Independent Evaluation Office of the World Bank's Global Environment Facility (GEF), making her the first-ever woman from a developing country to hold the coveted post.
- Her name was unanimously recommended for the coveted position at the 66th GEF Council Meeting held in Washington on 9 February and was announced last week.

Lebanese Judge Elected As ICJ's New President

- Lebanese Judge Nawaf Salam has been elected as the new President of the International Court of Justice (ICJ) for a three-year term.
- Additionally, Ugandan Judge Julia Sebutinde has been elected as the Vice President of the ICJ for the same term.
- The International Court of Justice (ICJ) consists of 15 judges who serve nine-year terms, elected by the UN General Assembly and the Security Council.

New BIMSTEC Secretary General Assumes Charge

- Indra Mani Pandey, a seasoned Indian diplomat, has assumed charge as the new secretary general of BIMSTEC.
- Pandey, a 1990-batch Indian Foreign Service (IFS) official, previously served as India's permanent representative to the United Nations and other international organisations in Geneva.
- Pandey assumed the charge as the fourth secretary general of BIMSTEC at its secretariat in Dhaka.

Gabriel Attal Becomes France's Youngest Prime Minister

- Emmanuel Macron appointed 34-year-old Gabriel Attal as the new prime minister of France, signaling a desire for new momentum in his presidency ahead of European parliament elections.
- Attal, a close ally of Macron and former government spokesman during the COVID pandemic, will replace outgoing Prime Minister Elisabeth Borne.
- Attal is recognized as a savvy minister and a popular figure in recent opinion polls, known for his ease in media appearances and parliament.

Masato Kanda Elected as ADB President

- The Asian Development Bank (ADB) Board of Governors has unanimously elected Masato Kanda as ADB's 11th President.
- Mr. Kanda, 59, currently serves as Special Advisor to Japan's Prime Minister and Minister of Finance.
- He will assume office on 24 February 2025, succeeding Masatsugu Asakawa, who will leave office on 23 February 2025.
- Mr. Kanda will complete the unexpired term of President Asakawa, which ends on 23 November 2026.

Trump appoints Indian American Krishnan as senior policy advisor on AI

- US President-elect Donald Trump appointed Indian-American entrepreneur and venture capitalist Sriram Krishnan as the senior White House policy adviser on Artificial Intelligence (AI).
- Krishnan, who has previously led product teams at Microsoft, Twitter, Yahoo!, Facebook and Snap, will work along with David O. Sacks who will be the White House AI & Crypto Czar.
- Sriram started his career at Microsoft as a founding member of Windows Azure.

Indian-American Kash Patel Nominated as FBI Director By Donald Trump

- US President-elect Donald Trump has nominated Indian-American Pentagon official Kashyap "Kash" Patel as Director of Federal Bureau of Investigation (FBI).
- He will replace Current FBI Director Christopher Wray, who was appointed in 2017.
- Kashyap Pramod Vinod Patel is an American lawyer and former federal prosecutor at the U.S. Department of Justice.
- The FBI director is appointed for a single 10-year term by the president of the United States and confirmed by the Senate.

Tonga elects 'Aisake Valu Eke' as new Prime Minister

- The Pacific Island nation of Tonga has elected veteran politician Aisake Valu Eke as its new Prime Minister.
- Aisake Valu Eke will succeed the former Prime Minister Siaosi Sovaleni who resigned two weeks ago after a no-confidence motion was moved against him in the Parliament.
- Aisake Valu Eke will be formally sworn in as the new Prime Minister of the country in February 2025.

Maia Sandu Sworn in as President of Moldova for 2nd Term

- Ms Maia Sandu was sworn in as the President of the European country of Moldova for her second term of four years on 24 December 2024.
- The presidential election was held in Moldova on 20 October 2024
- Ms Maia Sandu first became the President of Moldova in 2020.
- She is the first woman to become the President of the country after it gained Independence in 1991, following the collapse of the Soviet Union.

Resignation

UPSC CHAIRMAN MANOJ SONI RESIGNS

- Dr. Manoj Soni, the former Chairman of the Union Public Service Commission (UPSC), resigned from his position five years before his term was set to end in 2029.
- His tenure at the UPSC began in 2017, and he took the oath as chairperson on 16 May 2023.

JAPAN'S PRIME MINISTER FUMIO KISHIDA RESIGNED

- On 13 August 2024, Japanese Prime Minister Fumio Kishida announced his resignation as the leader of the Liberal Democratic Party (LDP). He effectively stepped down as Prime Minister on 1st October 2024.
- His decision follows a series of political scandals and plummeting approval ratings.
- Shigeru Ishiba took over as Japan's new prime minister on October 1st, 2024
- Kishida's tenure, which began in 2021, was marked by efforts to recover from these controversies and maintain party unity.

Prestige Estates CEO Resigns

- Venkata has served as CEO of Prestige Estates since August 2017, with a total of 20 years at the company.
- He has resigned from his CEO position and from board committees, effective 10 May 2024.

Reliance Jio MD Steps Down

- Sanjay Mashruwala, one of the two managing directors at Reliance Jio has decided to step down. Mashruwala has been the MD of the company since 2013.
- Mashruwala will leave Reliance Jio effective from June 9, the company said.
- Mashruwala, a Jio veteran, has been a key executive with Reliance since founder Dhirubhai Ambani's times and has been involved with several of its projects and business initiatives.

Wipro CEO Resigns

- Thierry Delaporte, the CEO and MD of Wipro, has resigned from his position. Srinivas Pallia was announced as his successor in a regulatory filing to stock exchanges on April 6.
- Srinivas Pallia, former CEO of Wipro's America region, will step into the roles of CEO and MD from April 7, 2024, for a five-year term.

Paytm Payments Bank CEO Resigns

- Surinder Chawla, the managing director and CEO of Paytm Payments Bank, has resigned from the company, as announced in a regulatory filing by Paytm's parent company, One97 Communications, on April 9.
- Chawla's decision to resign comes at a time when Paytm Payments Bank is facing regulatory action from the Reserve Bank of India (RBI).

President Accepts Resignation, Assigns Additional Charge To Kiren Rijiju

- President Droupadi Murmu accepted the resignation of Union Minister Pashupati Kumar Paras on March 20, 2024.
- Paras, from the Rashtriya Lok Janshakti Party (RLJP), resigned due to disagreements over seat-sharing for the 2024 Lok Sabha elections.
- Kiren Rijiju, the Minister of Earth Sciences, was assigned the additional charge of the Ministry of Food Processing Industries.

Punjab Governor Banwarilal Purohit Resigns

- Banwarilal Purohit resigned as Punjab Governor and Administrator of Chandigarh on February 3, 2024, citing personal reasons and other commitments.
- Appointed in August 2021, Purohit previously served as Governor of Tamil Nadu (2017-2021) and Assam (2016-2017).

OBITUARIES

AFFAIRS

(28 Dec 1937 - 09 Oct 2024)

Ratan Tata
(Philanthropy and Social Welfare)

- **Role & Leadership**
  - **Position**: Former Emeritus Chairman, Tata Group
  - **Key Contribution**: Transformed Tata Group into a global conglomerate.
  - **Approach**: Focus on innovation, growth, and philanthropy.

RATAN TATA'S LEADERSHIP AND LEGACY

- **Journey Begins**
- **1961**: Began career on the shop floor at Tata Steel, Jamshedpur.

Vision & Impact

- Visionary leadership in creating global brands, advancing innovation, and contributing to social causes through philanthropy.

Key Achievements

- **Tata Motors**
  - **Tata Indica (1998)**: First indigenously designed Indian passenger car.
  - **Tata Nano (2008)**: World's cheapest car at Rs 1 lakh, aimed at making cars affordable for middle-class India.
- **Global Expansion & Acquisitions**
  - **Tetley Tea**: Acquired British tea brand.
  - **Jaguar Land Rover**: Acquired iconic British automotive brands.
  - **Corus Steel**: Acquired major UK steel company.
  - **Starbucks (2012)**: Strategic partnership in India.

Ratan Tata's Social Work & Philanthropy

- **Commitment to Social Welfare:** Ratan Tata directed a significant portion of Tata Group's profits towards charitable causes, making philanthropy an integral part of his leadership.
- **Tata Trusts:** Under his leadership, **Tata Trusts** allocated **65% of Tata Group's profits** to support initiatives in **education**, **healthcare**, and **rural development**.
- **Covid-19 Relief: Rs 500 crore donation (2021)** to support India's fight against the **Covid-19 pandemic**.
- **Global Philanthropy: USD 50 million donation** to **Harvard Business School** to establish an executive centre, demonstrating his commitment to **education** and **leadership development**.
- **Healthcare Initiatives:** Instrumental in the establishment of the **Tata Medical Center** in **Kolkata**, a world-class cancer care facility serving underprivileged communities.
- **Mumbai Terror Attacks Relief:** Following the 2008 **Mumbai terrorist attacks**, he founded the **Taj Public Service Welfare Trust** to aid victims and their families.

Animal Welfare

- Lifelong advocate for **animal welfare**:
  - Ensured stray animals at **Bombay House** had access to shelters.

  - Opened a **state-of-the-art animal hospital** in Mumbai in **2024**, providing **24/7 emergency care** for animals.

Year	Award	Awarding Body
2023	Honorary Officer of the Order of Australia	King Charles III
2023	Maharashtra Udyog Ratna	Government of Maharashtra
2008	Honorary Citizen Award	Government of Singapore
2008	**Padma Vibhushan**	Government of India
2007	Carnegie Medal of Philanthropy	Carnegie Endowment for International Peace
2000	**Padma Bhushan**	Government of India

"Philanthropy in its true sense is not personal; it is humanity-based. It's about the sensitivity you have to all the hardships that people face."

— Ratan Tata, Chairman, Tata Trusts

NATIONAL AND INTERNATIONAL OBITUARIES

Legendary Tabla Maestro Zakir Hussain Passes Away at 73

- Legendary tabla maestro Zakir Hussain passed away at the age of 73.
- He was an Indian tabla player, composer, percussionist, music producer, and film actor.
- He was the eldest son of tabla player Alla Rakha, Who won four Grammy Awards.
- Hussain won five Grammy Awards, including three at the 66th Grammy Awards earlier this year.
- Hussain received the Padma Shri, one of the country's highest civilian honours, in 1988, the Padma Bhushan in 2002, and the Padma Vibhushan in 2023.

Former Haryana Chief Minister Om Prakash Chautala Passes Away at 89

- Former Haryana Chief Minister and Indian National Lok Dal (INLD) leader Om Prakash Chautala has passed away at the age of 89.
- He was the five-time chief minister of Haryana
- On December 2, 1989, he became the CM for the first time after Devi Lal vacated the chair and went to Parliament.

Former Karnataka CM SM Krishna Passes Away at 92

- Former Karnataka Chief Minister and Union Minister SM Krishna passed away at the age of 92.
- Krishna served as the chief minister of Karnataka from October 11, 1999, to May 20, 2004.
- Following his tenure as CM, he was appointed as the governor of Maharashtra, serving from December 6, 2004, to March 8, 2008.

Iconic Classical Dancer Yamini Krishnamurthy Passes Away

- Renowned classical dancer Yamini Krishnamurthy passed away on 3 August 2024, at the age of 83.
- A pioneer in Bharatanatyam and Kuchipudi, she also mastered Odissi.
- Born on 20 December 1940, in Andhra Pradesh, she began her dance journey at Kalakshetra under **Rukmini Devi Arundale.**
- Krishnamurthy received numerous accolades, including the **Padma Shri** (1968), **Padma Bhushan** (2001), and **Padma Vibhushan** (2016).

Renowned Physicist and Gender Equity Proponent Rohini Godbole Passed Away at 71

- Rohini Godbole, a distinguished Indian physicist and advocate for gender equity in science, passed away on 25th October 2024, at age 71.
- She received numerous prestigious awards, including the **Padma Shri** (2019), **France's Ordre national du Mérite** (2021), and the Lifetime Achievement award given by the Karnataka science and technology department.

Vasant Anant Gadgil Passed Away at 94

- Sanskrit scholar Vasant Anant Gadgil passed away on October 18, 2024, at the age of 94 in Pune.
- Gadgil founded the Sharda Gyan Peetham in Pune and **promoted Sanskrit globally**, including in the US and Africa.
- He was known for his work on ancient Sanskrit texts like the Vedas and Upanishads, and published a Sanskrit biography of Dr. Bhimrao Ambedkar.
- Gadgil was also felicitated by then Gujarat Chief Minister Narendra Modi in 2012 and received the **Mahakavi Kalidas Sanskrit-Vrati National Award.**

Eminent Agriculturist Padma Shri Kamala Pujari Passes Away

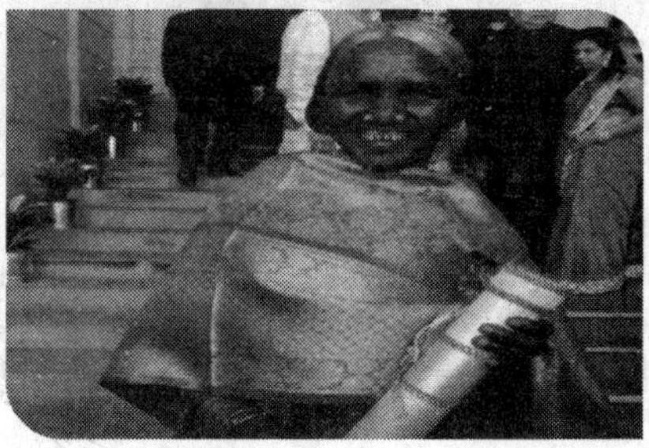

- On 20 July 2024, the **renowned organic farmer and Padma Shri awardee,** Kamala Pujari, passed away in Cuttack at the age of 74.
- Kamala Pujari was celebrated for her remarkable efforts in conserving rare and endangered seeds, promoting organic farming, and empowering women farmers.

Former CSIR Director-General Girish Sahni Passes Away at 68

- On 19 August 2024, Dr. Girish Sahni, the esteemed former Director General of the Council of Scientific and Industrial Research (CSIR), passed away at the age of 68.
- Dr. Sahni played a pivotal role in translating science into world-class biotechnology, including the development of life-saving protein drugs like streptokinase.
- About CSIR:
- Works under: Ministry of Science and Technology
- Established: 26 September 1942
- Director General: N. Kalaiselvi

Former Army Chief General Sundararajan Padmanabhan Passes Away at 83

- On 19 August 2024, former Indian Army Chief General Sundararajan Padmanabhan passed away at the age of 83 in Chennai.
- Known affectionately as "**Paddy,**" he served as the **20th Chief of Army Staff** from October 2000 to December 2002.

• Rtd. General Padmanabhan led the Indian Army during **Operation Parakram**, a significant military mobilization following the 2001 Parliament attack.

Israel Defense Forces killed Hamas leader Yahya Sinwar

• On 16th October 2024, the Israel Defense Forces (IDF) killed Hamas leader Yahya Sinwar during a routine patrol in Rafah, Gaza Strip.

• Sinwar, who masterminded the October 7, 2023, attack on Israel, was identified posthumously through DNA testing. His death marks a significant blow to Hamas, which now faces a leadership vacuum.

Brazilian Music icon Sergio Mendes Passed Away at 83

• On 5 September 2024, Brazilian music icon Sérgio Mendes passed away at the age of 83 in Los Angeles.

• He was best known for hits like "Mas Que Nada" and "The Look of Love".

• Mendes recorded over 35 albums, many achieving gold or platinum status.

Albania's World-Renowned Novelist Ismail Kadare Died at 88

• On 1 July 2024, the celebrated Albanian novelist and poet, Ismail Kadare, passed away in Tirana at the age of 88.

• Kadare's novel "The General of the Dead Army" remains a powerful exploration of war's futility, resonating across borders and generations.

Dal Khalsa Founder Gajinder Singh Khalsa Dies in Pakistan

• On 3 July 2024, Pro-Khalistan leader Gajinder Singh, was one of the most-wanted persons in the record of the Ministry of Home Affairs (MHA), passed away at the age of 73.

• Gajinder Singh was one of five members of the previously banned organization, Dal Khalsa, who hijacked Indian Airlines flight IC-423 on 29 September 1981.

Former Lebanese Prime Minister Salim Al-Hoss Passed Away at 94

• On 25 August 2024, Salim Hoss, a five-time former Lebanese Prime Minister, passed away at the age of 94.

• Hoss served during some of Lebanon's most tumultuous years, including the 15-year civil war from 1975 to 1990.

• Widely respected as a rare statesman in a country marked by political and sectarian divisions, he was often described as a technocrat. His final term in office was from 1998 to 2000.

Former Prime Minister Manmohan Singh Passes Away at 92

• Former Indian prime minister Manmohan Singh has died at the age of 92.

• He was widely regarded as the architect of India's economic reform program.

• A state of mourning has been declared for seven days until January 1, 2025. During the mourning period, the National Flag will be flown at half-mast throughout Bharat and at all Indian Missions and High Commissions abroad.

World's Oldest Person Maria Branyas Morera Passed Away

• On 19 August 2024, Maria Branyas Morera, the world's oldest verified living person, passed away at the age of 117 years and 168 days.

• Born in California in 1907, she later settled in Catalonia, Spain. Maria lived through two world wars, the Spanish Civil War, the 1918 flu pandemic, and the COVID-19 pandemic.

Veteran Director Shyam Benegal Passes Away

• Veteran film director, Shyam Benegal passed away at the age of 90 years.

• He was honoured with India's highest film award DadaSaheb Phalke Award in

KNOW ABOUT MANMOHAN SINGH

GOVERNMENT AND ECONOMIC ROLES

- **Economic Adviser:** Ministry of Foreign Trade, 1971
- **Chief Economic Adviser:** Ministry of Finance, 1972-1976
- **Secretary, Department of Economic Affairs:** November 1976 to April 1980
- **Member Secretary, Planning Commission:** April 1980 to September 1982
- **Governor of Reserve Bank of India:** September 1982 to January 1985 (15th)
- **Deputy Chairman of the Planning Commission:** 15 January 1985-31 August 1987

POLITICAL LEADERSHIP

Finance Minister of India: 1991-1996

Prime Minister of India:

- **First Term:** May 22, 2004, to May 2009 (14th Prime Minister)
- **Second Term:** May 2009 to 2014 (14th Prime Minister)

AWARDS AND HONOURS

- **Padma Vibhushan:** India's second-highest civilian honor, 1987
- **Jawaharlal Nehru Birth Centenary Award:** Indian Science Congress, 1995
- **Asia Money Award:** Finance Minister of the Year, 1993 & 1994
- **Euro Money Award:** Finance Minister of the Year, 1993
- **Adam Smith Prize:** University of Cambridge, 1956

AWARDS & HONORS

2005. He also received 18 National Film Awards.

- He was honoured with India's third-highest civilian award Padma Bhushan in 1991.
- He was honoured with India's fourth highest civilian award Padma Shri in 1976.

Osamu Suzuki, Man behind Maruti 800 Success, Dies at 94

- Osamu Suzuki, founder and former chairman of the Japanese company Suzuki Motor Corporation has died in Japan.
- He was 94 years old and was suffering from Lymphoma(a type of blood cancer).
- Osamu Suzuki was also the Director and honourary chairman of Maruti Suzuki India Limited.
- Osamu Suzuki led Suzuki Motor Limited for over 40 years, turning it into a global car company and bringing the affordable Maruti 800 to millions in India.
- The government of India conferred Osamu Suzuki with India's third-highest civilian award Padma Bhushan in 2007.

Death of Iran's President Ebrahim Raisi

- Iran's President Ebrahim Raisi and Foreign Minister Hossein Amirabdollahian were confirmed dead on May 20, 2024, following a helicopter crash in the East Azerbaijan province of Iran.

- The helicopter, a decades-old Bell 212 manufactured in the United States, went down in dense fog, killing all eight people on board, including the crew.
- Ebrahim Raisi's deputy Mohammad Mokhber has been appointed as the acting President.
- Ayatollah Khamenei has confirmed that Vice President Mohammad Mokhber has been appointed as the acting President in accordance with Article 131 of Iran's Constitution.

Veteran congress leader and former governor Kamla Beniwal passed away at 97

- Veteran Congress leader and **former governor of Gujarat**, Kamla Beniwal, passed away at the age of 97 on 15 May, 2024.
- Beniwal had a distinguished political career, serving as a **seven-time MLA,** the **deputy chief minister of Rajasthan,** and the governor of Gujarat, Tripura, and Mizoram.

Banking Icon N Vaghul passed away at 88

- Narayanan Vaghul, a renowned banker and **former Chairman of ICICI Bank,** passed away at the age of 88 in Chennai.
- Known as the **architect of modern banking in India,** Vaghul played a key role in transformation of ICICI into the second largest commercial bank in the country.
- He introduced the **concept of credit rating** in India and established CRISIL (Credit Rating Information Services of India Ltd).

Sushil Kumar Modi passed away at New Delhi

- On 13 May 2024, Senior Bharatiya Janata Party **(BJP) leader** and **former Bihar Deputy Chief Minister** Sushil Kumar Modi died in New Delhi at the age of 72 years.
- He served as the Deputy Chief Minister of Bihar from **2005 to 2013** and again from **2017 to 2020.**

Yakshagana exponent Subrahmanya Dhareshwar passed away at 67

- Yakshagana thespian Subrahmanya Dhareshwar, who had earned the fame of **'Bhagavata Shrestha'** for his scintillating voice, passed away at the age of 67 in Bengaluru.
- Subrahmanya Dhareshwar had served for 46 years in the field of Yakshagana and had served as the main singer for 28 years in **Perdoor Mela alone.**

Indian Air Force's oldest pilot Dalip Singh Majithia passes away at 103

- The oldest living pilot of the Indian Air Force, **Squadron Leader Dalip Singh Majithia,** died at the age of 103 in Uttarakhand.
- Squadron Leader Majithia joined the Indian Air Force (IAF) volunteer reserve **in 1940 during World War-II.**

Renowned Rabindra Sangeet Singer Sadi Mohammad passed away at 70

- In Bangladesh, a legendary Rabindra Sangeet singer Sadi Mohammad passed away at the age of 70.
- Sadi served as the director of the cultural organisation **Rabi Raag.**

Former Navy Chief Admiral Ramdas passed away at 90

- Former navy chief and war hero **Admiral Laxminarayan Ramdas** passed away at 90 in Secunderabad.
- He was known for promoting gender equality and peace.
- Ramdas was the **navy chief** during 1990-93.

Padma Shri Awardee Arun Sharma passed away at 91

- Padma Shri awardee **Arun Kumar Sharma,** a distinguished archaeologist and key witness in the Ram Janmabhoomi case, passed away at 91 in Raipur.
- He was instrumental in providing archaeological evidence for a Hindu temple at **Ayodhya's disputed site.**

Ghazal legend Pankaj Udhas passed away at 72

- **Veteran singer Pankaj Udhas** passed away at the age of 72 on 26 February 2024 following prolonged illness.
- Pankaj Udhas is best known for lending his voice to memorable tracks like **Chitthi Aayi Hai, Chandi Jaisa Rang Hai, Aaj Phir Tumpe, Jeeye to Jeeye Kaise,** and **Chhupana Bhi Nahi Aata** etc.

Jain muni Acharya Vidyasagar Maharaj passed away at 77

- Prominent Jain muni Acharya **Vidyasagar Maharaj** passed away at Chandragiri Teerth in Chhattisgarh's Dongargarh. He was 77.
- Acharya Vidyasagar Maharaj attained Samadhi through 'Sallekhna' at Chandragiri teerth.
- **Sallekhna** is a Jain religious practice involving voluntary fasting unto death for spiritual purification.

India's oldest MP and Samajwadi party leader Shafiqur Rahman Barq passed away at 94

- Samajwadi Party **MP Shafiqur Rahman Barq** died in Uttar Pradesh's Moradabad at the age of 94 after prolonged illness.
- He started his political career with farmer leader and former Prime Minister of India Bharat Ratna Chaudhary Charan Singh.
- He was the oldest MP in 17th Lok Sabha.

Former Chief Minister of Maharashtra, Shri Manohar Joshi passed away

- Former Maharashtra Chief Minister **Manohar Joshi** passed away on 23 February at the age of 86.
- Joshi was the Chief Minister of Maharashtra **from 1995 to 1999** and **Speaker of the Lok Sabha from 2002 to 2004.**
- He was also a **Member of Rajya Sabha from 2006 to 2012,** and Minister of Heavy Industries and Public Enterprises from 1999 to 2002.

Eminent Hindi and Maithili litterateur Usha Kiran Khan passed away at 82

- Renowned **Hindi and Maithili author Usha Kiran Khan** passed away at the age of 82 after battling a prolonged illness in Patna.
- She was awarded the Padma Shree, the fourth highest civilian honor in India.
- Usha Kiran Khan also received various literary awards, including the esteemed Sahitya Academy and Bharat Bharati awards.

Dattajirao Gaekwad, Nation's oldest test cricketer, passed away at 95

- **Dattajirao Gaekwad,** India's oldest Test cricketer and former captain, passed away at 95 due to age-related ailments.
- He played 11 Tests for India and led the team on their 1959 England tour.

Rana Talwar, first Asian to head a global bank, passes away at 76

- Rana Talwar, the **first person from Asia to head a global bank** (Standard Chartered) passed away at the age of 76.
- Besides DLF, he served on the boards of various companies including Asahi India Glass Limited and Great Eastern Energy Corporation Limited.

Dr Nitya Anand, man who discovered India's first oral contraceptive pill 'Saheli', passed away

- Dr Nitya Anand, who developed **India's first oral contraceptive pill 'Saheli',** passed away at Lucknow.
- From 1974 to 1984, Anand served as the Central Drug Research Institute's **(CDRI) former director.**

Padma Bhushan awardee Prof Ved Prakash Nanda passed away

- **Professor Ved Prakash Nanda,** a distinguished Indian-American academic and Padma Bhushan awardee, passed away on January 2, 2024.
- He was honored with the **Padma Bhushan award in 2018** in the field of Literature and Education.

Urdu poet Munawwar Rana passed away

- Renowned Urdu poet **Munawwar Rana** passed away at Lucknow.
- Mr. Munawwar Rana was awarded the Gyanpeeth Award in 2014.
- Mr. Munawwar Rana's poem Maa, which is considered one of his most famous works, has a special place in the world of Urdu literature.
- In 2014, he was honoured with the Sahitya Akademi Award for his poem, 'Shahdaba'.

Music maestro Ustad Rashid Khan passed away

- The celebrated **music maestro** Ustad Rashid Khan passed away in Kolkata.
- Rashid Khan was an exponent of the **Rampur-Sahaswan gayaki** (style of singing) which is closely related to the **Gwalior gharana.**
- The vocalist won several awards including Padma Shri and the Sangeet Natak Akademi Award in 2006. In 2022, he was honoured with the Padma Bhushan, the third-highest civilian award of the country.

Malawi Vice President Saulos Klaus Chilima Killed In Plane Crash

- Malawi's Vice President Saulos Klaus Chilima and nine others on board a military aircraft that went missing were killed in a plane crash.
- The plane, a military aircraft, disappeared from airport radars.

Legendary Disney Songwriter Richard M. Sherman Passed Away At 95

- **Richard M. Sherman,** the legendary Disney songwriter, passed away at the age of 95.
- Richard was a prolific **composer-lyricist** in the history of family entertainment.
- Together, they penned beloved songs for Disney films such as "Mary Poppins," "The Jungle Book," and "Chitty Chitty Bang Bang."

Bette Nash, world's longest-serving flight attendant passed away at 88

- Bette Nash, the **world's longest-serving flight attendant,** passed away on 17 May 2024, at the age of 88.
- She held the Guinness World Record for her remarkable **67-year career** as a flight attendant, surpassing any other in history.

Nobel Prize-winning author Alice Munro dies at 92

- **Alice Munro** passed away at the age of 92 at her home in Port Hope, Ontario.
- The **Nobel Prize-winning Canadian author** Munro known for her mastery of the short story.
- Awarded the International Booker Prize for her body of work in 2009, and the Nobel Prize in Literature in 2013.

Bernard Hill Has Passed Away At The Age Of 79

- **Bernard Hill,** the renowned British actor known for his roles in **'Titanic' and 'The Lord of the Rings,'** has passed away at the age of 79.
- Bernard Hill was best known for his roles as Captain Edward Smith in the 1997 Oscar-winning film 'Titanic' and as King Théoden in 'The Lord of the Rings' trilogy.

England Spin Great Derek Underwood Dies Aged 78

- Derek Underwood, the **most successful spin bowler** in England's Test cricket history, has died at the age of 78.
- Underwood bagged **297 wickets** in 86 Test matches between 1966 and 1982.

British Physicist Peter Higgs Passed Away at The Age Of 94

- Renowned British theoretical physicist Peter Higgs, aged 94, passed away on April 8th.
- Higgs famously predicted the existence of the **Higgs boson particle** in the 1960s, a prediction that was confirmed with the discovery of the particle in 2012.
- He also won Nobel prize for Physics in 2013.

World's Oldest Man, Juan Vicente Perez Mora from Venezuela dies at 114

- Venezuelan Juan Vicente Perez Mora, certified in 2022 by Guinness World Records as the oldest man in the world, died at the age of 114.
- Juan Vicente Pérez, a Venezuelan man, lived an exceptionally long life, born on 27 May 1909, in El Cobre, Venezuela.

Namibia's President Hage Geingob dies at 82

- Namibian President **Hage Geingob,** aged 82, passed away at the capital Windhoek.
- Geingob, the country's third President, had been in office since 2015 and was serving his second term.
- He also held the position of Namibia's first Prime Minister from 1990 to 2002, following Namibia's independence from South Africa.

German football legend Franz Beckenbauer (Der Kaiser) passed away

- German football legend Franz Beckenbauer has passed away at the age of 78.
- He **captained West Germany** to the World Cup title in 1974. He also coached the national side that **won the 1990 World Cup final** against Argentina.
- Nicknamed **"Der Kaiser",** he won numerous other honours, including a hat-trick of European Cups with Bayern Munich in the 1970s.

Mario Zagallo, Brazil's World Cup Winning Player And Coach Passed Away

- **Mario Zagallo,** a legendary figure in Brazilian football, passed away at the age of 92 due to multiple-organ failure and comorbidities.
- He was the **first person to win the World Cup both as a player and a manager,** an achievement that was later matched by Franz Beckenbauer and Didier Deschamps.
- He played a key role in **Brazil's first World Cup victory in 1958.**
- As a coach, he led Brazil to victory in the 1970 World Cup and served as an assistant coach in the 1994 and 2006 World Cup wins.

IMPORTANT DAYS

23 August

NATIONAL SPACE DAY

Touching lives while touching the Moon: India's Space Saga

Key Facts

- **First Celebration:** The first National Space Day was celebrated on 23rd August 2024.
- **Theme for 2024:** The theme for National Space Day 2024 is "Touching Lives while Touching the Moon: India's Space Saga".
- **Significance:** The day highlights India's space exploration capabilities and aims to inspire future generations to pursue careers in science, technology, engineering, and mathematics (STEM).

National Space Day 2024

- India celebrated its first National Space Day on 23rd August 2024. This day was declared by Prime Minister Narendra Modi.
- It is celebrated to mark the safe and soft landing of Vikram Lander of Chandrayaan-3 mission, on the lunar surface on 23rd August 2023.
- India became the fourth country to achieve a soft landing on the Moon and the first to reach its southern polar region.

Chandrayaan-3

- Chandrayaan-3 Mission represents India's second endeavor, following Chandrayaan-2, to showcase its expertise in safe lunar landing and surface exploration.
- On August 23, 2023, the Lander Module of Chandrayaan-3, carrying both the Lander named Vikram and the Rover named Pragyan, achieved a historic soft landing on the Lunar South Pole.
- This achievement solidified India's position as the first nation to softly land on the Lunar South Pole and the fourth globally to accomplish a soft lunar landing.
- The Indian Space Research Organisation initiated the Chandrayaan-3 Mission on July 14, 2023, employing the Geosynchronous Satellite Launch Vehicle Mark III (LVM3) from Sriharikota.

Important Person Associated with this Mission

- **ISRO Chairman:** S Somanath
- **Chandrayaan-3 project director:** P Veeramuthuvel
- **Mission Director:** Mohana Kumar
- **Vikram Sarabhai Space Centre (VSSC) Director:** S Unnikrishnan Nair
- **U R Rao Satellite Centre (URSC) Director:** M Sankaran
- **Launch Authorisation Board (LAB) chief:** A Rajarajan
- **Lifespan of the Mission:** 1 Lunar Day (14 Earth days)
- **Budget of Mission:** Approx. ₹615 crore

Timeline of the Chandrayaan 3 Mission

- **Launched:** July 14, 2023
- **Inserted into Lunar Orbit:** August 05, 2023
- **Separation of the Lander Module from the Propulsion Module:** August 17, 2023
- **Soft landing on Moon:** August 23, 2023
- **Rover started its exploration:** August 24, 2023
- **Shiv Shakti Point:** The spot where Vikram Lander made the soft landing
- **Tiranga Point:** Where the Chandrayaan-2 lander crash- landed on the Moon's surface in 2019
- **National Space Day:** August 23 (The day the Chandrayaan-3 lander touched down on the lunar surface)

India's Achievements in Space Exploration

- India's journey in space exploration began in 1962 with the establishment of the Indian National Committee for Space Research (INCOSPAR) under the leadership of Dr. Vikram Sarabhai.

- This committee laid the foundation for the Indian Space Research Organisation (ISRO), which was formally established in 1969.
- **Aryabhata (1975):** India's first satellite, named after the ancient Indian mathematician, was launched by the Soviet Union. It marked India's entry into space technology and provided valuable data on X-ray astronomy and solar physics.
- **SLV-3 (1980):** The first Satellite Launch Vehicle (SLV-3) was successfully launched, marking a significant milestone in India's space capabilities.
- **INSAT Series (1983 onwards):** The Indian National Satellite (INSAT) series revolutionized communication in India, providing services like television broadcasting, telecommunication, and weather forecasting.
- **Chandrayaan-1 (2008):** India's first lunar probe, which discovered water molecules on the Moon, was a major scientific achievement.
- **Mars Orbiter Mission (Mangalyaan) (2014):** India became the first country to reach Mars on its first attempt, making it the fourth space agency to reach Mars and the first to do so in a maiden mission.
- **Chandrayaan-2 (2019):** Although the lander Vikram faced a hard landing, the orbiter continues to provide valuable data about the Moon.
- **Chandrayaan-3 (2023):** India achieved a historic soft landing near the Moon's south pole, making it the fourth country to do so and the first to reach the lunar south pole.
- **Recent Developments**
  - **Aditya-L1 (2023):** India's first solar mission aimed at studying the Sun's corona and its impact on space weather.
  - **Xposat (2024):** A mission focused on uncovering mysteries of the universe through advanced space research.
  - **International Collaborations:** India has actively participated in international space missions, including collaborations with the European Space Agency (ESA) and NASA.
  - **Gaganyaan TV-D1 Test:** ISRO conducted its Flight Test Vehicle Abort Mission-1 (TV-D1), using a modified L-40 Vikas engine for the Gaganyaan human spaceflight mission.
- **Future Plans**
  - **Indian Space Station (2035):** Plans to establish an independent space station, which will be known as "Bharatiya Antriksh Station", by 2035.
  - **Crewed Lunar Mission (2040):** Aiming to send astronauts to the Moon by 2040.
  - **Enhanced Private Sector Participation:** Encouraging private companies to participate in space missions through entities like NewSpace India Limited (NSIL) and the Indian National Space Promotion and Authorization Center (IN-SPACe).

INDIAN SPACE RESEARCH ORGANISATION

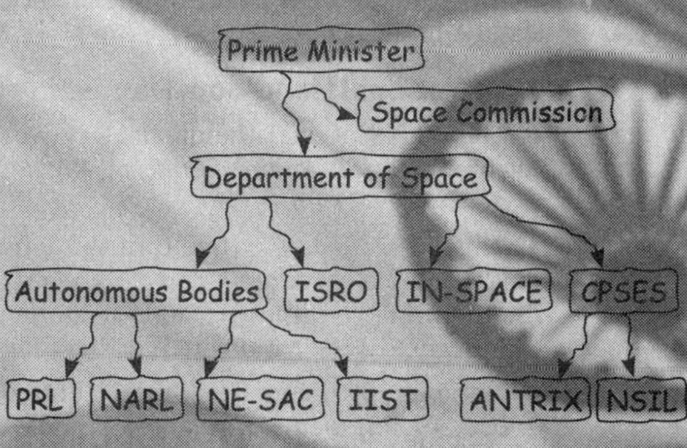

Department: Department of Space

Genesis: Indian National Committee for Space Research (INCOSPAR) was set up by in 1962.

- ISRO was formed in 1969 superseding INCOSPAR.
- Brought under DOS in 1972.

Mandate: As National Space Agency, development and application of space technology for various national needs.

Composition: Headed by Chairman, who is secretary of DOS and Chairman of Space commission the apex body that formulates the policies and overseas the implementation of Indian Space Programme

NATIONAL DAYS 2024

Mahaparinirvan Diwas 2024

- Mahaparinirvan Diwas is observed every year on December 6 to commemorate the death anniversary of Dr. Bhimrao Ramji Ambedkar, who was the architect of modern India and a staunch advocate for social justice.
- This year Mahaparinirvan Diwas marks the 69th death anniversary of Dr. BR Ambedkar.
- The word "Mahaparinirvan" is deciphered from the Buddhist Philosophy which represents the state of nirvana which is achieved after death.

National Milk Day

- National Milk Day is celebrated annually on 26th November in India.
- This day commemorates the birth anniversary of Dr. Verghese Kurien, known as the "Father of the White Revolution".
- The day highlights the importance of milk as a vital source of nutrition and its role in the economic growth of rural India.

Samvidhan Diwas

- Samvidhan Diwas, also known as Constitution Day, is celebrated in India on 26th November each year.
- Instituted in 2015, Samvidhan Diwas honours the vision and efforts of Dr. Bhim Rao Ambedkar, the principal architect of the Constitution.
- This day commemorates the adoption of the Indian Constitution by the Constituent Assembly on 26th November 1949.

National Press Day

- National Press Day is observed annually on 16th November in India.
- This day celebrates the essential role of the press in a democratic society and commemorates the establishment of the Press Council of India (PCI) on this date in 1966.
- The theme for 2024 is "Changing Nature of the Press", reflecting on the evolving dynamics of media in the digital age.

National Unity Day

- National Unity Day, also known as Rashtriya Ekta Diwas, is celebrated in India on 31st October each year.
- Introduced by the Government of India in 2014, this day commemorates the birth anniversary of Sardar Vallabhbhai Patel, the first Deputy Prime Minister and Home Minister of India.
- Known as the "Iron Man of India," Patel played a crucial role in the political integration of over 560 princely states into a united India.

National Postal Day

- National Postal Day is celebrated annually on 10th October in India.
- This day commemorates the establishment of the Indian Postal Service on 10th October 1854.
- National Postal Day also coincides with World Post Day, a global event established by the Universal Postal Union (UPU) to celebrate the formation of the UPU in 1874.

Ayurveda Day

- Ayurveda Day is celebrated annually on Dhanteras, a date that varies but typically falls in October or November. This year Ayurveda Day 2024 is celebrated on 29 October.
- Established by the Indian Ministry of AYUSH in 2016, the day honors Lord Dhanvantari, the God of Ayurveda.
- The theme for 2024 is "Ayurveda Innovations for Global Health", highlighting Ayurveda's holistic approach to health and well-being.

National Sports Day

- National Sports Day is celebrated annually on 29 August in India.
- The day is celebrated to commemorate the birth anniversary of Major Dhyan Chand, one of the greatest hockey players of the country.
- Major Dhyan Chand, known as "The Wizard," brought India international recognition with his exceptional hockey skills, leading the Indian team to win three Olympic gold medals (1928, 1932, 1936).

Antyodaya Diwas

- Antyodaya Diwas is observed annually on 25 September to commemorate the birth anniversary of Pandit Deendayal Upadhyaya.
- Born in 1916 in Mathura, Uttar Pradesh, Upadhyaya was a prominent Indian political leader and thinker.
- The term "Antyodaya" means "upliftment of the last person," reflecting Upadhyaya's mission to address the needs of the most disadvantaged individuals in society.
- The day was announced in 2014 by Prime Minister Narendra Modi.

Hindi Diwas

- Hindi Diwas 2024 is celebrated every year on 14 September.
- On 14 September 1949, the Constituent Assembly of India made a landmark decision to adopt Hindi, written in the Devanagari script, as one of the official languages of the newly independent nation.
- Jawaharlal Nehru, India's first Prime Minister, recognized the importance of this decision and proposed the observance of September 14th as Hindi Diwas.

National Mountain Climbing Day

- National Mountain Climbing Day is celebrated annually on 1 August.
- This day honors the achievements of mountain climbers and promotes the sport of mountain climbing, which combines physical endurance, mental toughness, and a love for nature.
- National Mountain Climbing Day was founded in 2015 to celebrate Bobby Matthews and Josh Madigan, who successfully climbed all 46 Adirondack peaks.

10th National Handloom Day

- The 10th National Handloom Day was celebrated on 7 August 2024, at Vigyan Bhawan, New Delhi.
- This day honors the contributions of handloom workers and highlights the cultural, traditional, and economic significance of the handloom industry.
- National Handloom Day, first celebrated in 2015, commemorates the Swadeshi Movement of 1905, promoting indigenous crafts and empowering local artisans.

Kargil Vijay Diwas

- Kargil Vijay Diwas is observed annually on 26 July every year.
- Kargil Vijay Diwas commemorates India's victory in the Kargil War of 1999.
- In 2024, Prime Minister Narendra Modi visited Drass in Ladakh to honor the 25th anniversary of Kargil Vijay Diwas.

National Income Tax Day

- National Income Tax Day is observed annually on 24 July.
- The day commemorates the introduction of income tax in India.
- On this day in 1860, Sir James Wilson imposed income tax for the first time in the country.

National Doctor's Day

- National Doctor's Day is observed on 1 July each year in India.
- The theme for 2024 is "Healing Hands, Caring Hearts," emphasizing doctors' dedication, compassion, and empathy in their medical practice.
- The day was established to commemorate the birth and death anniversary of Dr. Bidhan Chandra Roy.

World Football Day 2024

World Football Day: Celebrating the Global Game

- World Football Day, **established by the United Nations General Assembly** in May 2024, is a day dedicated to celebrating the immense popularity and positive influence of football (also known as soccer in some regions) around the world.
- In a momentous decision that celebrates the universal language of football, the United Nations General Assembly has unanimously proclaimed 25th May as World Football Day.

Upcoming FIFA Football Events

Event	Date(s)	Location(s)
2025 FIFA Club World Cup	June 2025	USA
2025 FIFA U-20 World Cup	May - June 2025	Indonesia
2025 FIFA U-17 World Cup	October - November 2025	Qatar
2026 FIFA World Cup	June - July 2026	USA, Canada, Mexico
2028 Summer Olympics Football	July - August 2028	Los Angeles, USA

Hindi Journalism Day 2024

- Hindi Journalism Day **(Hindi Patrakarita Diwas)** is celebrated on 30 May 2024.
- The journey of Hindi journalism began on 30 May 1826, with the publication of the first Hindi newspaper, 'Udant Martand,' started by Pt. Jugal Kishore Shukla.

Indian Commonwealth Day 2024

- Indian Commonwealth Day is commemorated every year on **24th May.**
- This day, also known as Empire Day, celebrates the formation of the British Empire in India and other colonies of Britain.

National Endangered Species Day 2024

- National Endangered Species Day is observed annually on the **third Friday in May** to promote awareness about wildlife conservation and restoration efforts for imperiled species.
- In 2024, it was celebrated on 17th May.

National Technology Day, 2024

- National Technology Day is celebrated annually on **11 May** to commemorate India's achievements in science and technology.
- The theme for National Technology Day 2024 is **"School to Startups-Igniting Young Minds to Innovate".**

National Panchayati Raj Day 2024

- National Panchayati Raj Day is celebrated every year on **24 April** in India.
- This day honours the establishment of the Panchayati Raj System, a devolved form of governance in the country, which was **introduced in 1993 by the 73rd Constitutional Amendment Act.**

National Civil Service Day 2024

- **21 April** is observed as the National Civil Service Day by the Government of India every year.
- This day is celebrated with the aim of acknowledging the exemplary work done by civil servants across the country.

National Library Day 2024

- National Library Day is observed annually on **April 6th** to honour the significance of libraries and librarians in society.
- It serves as a day of celebration and reflection on the importance of reading and ensuring access to books for all individuals.

Indian Newspaper Day 2024

- Indian Newspaper Day is observed on **28th January** each year.
- It marks the inception of newspapers in India, a historic moment when James Augustus Hicky introduced the first printed newspaper, Hicky's Bengal Gazette, **in 1780.**

National Tourism Day 2024

- National Tourism Day is celebrated every year **on 25 January.**
- The theme for National Tourism Day 2024 is **'Sustainable Journeys, Timeless Memories'.**

National Voters' Day 2024

- The 14th National Voters' Day was celebrated on **January 25, 2024.**
- The main purpose of the National Voters' Day celebration is to create electoral awareness amongst citizens and encourage them to participate in the electoral process.
- The theme for National Voters' Day 2024 was **'Nothing Like Voting, I Vote For sure'.**

Indian Army Day 2024

- The 76th Indian Army Day was celebrated on **January 15, 2024.** This day is dedicated to honour the soldiers of the Indian Army and their sacrifices for the nation.
- The theme for Indian Army Day 2024 was **"In Service of the Nation".**

National Startup Day 2024

- In India, National Startup Day is celebrated on **16th January** every year.
- National Startup Day aims to recognize the significant growth and contributions of the startup community to the Indian economy.

INTERNATIONAL DAYS 2024

UNGA declares December 21 as World Meditation Day

- The United Nations General Assembly has unanimously adopted a resolution declaring December 21 as World Meditation Day.
- India, along with Liechtenstein, Sri Lanka, Nepal, Mexico, and Andorra, played a leading role as part of the core group that guided the adoption of the resolution titled World Meditation Day in the 193-member UNGA.
- It occurs six months after June 21, which is celebrated as the International Day of Yoga, coinciding with the Summer Solstice.

International Migrants Day

- International Migrants Day is observed annually on 18th December.
- Its objective is to raise awareness about the issues faced by migrants, including their rights, integration challenges, and contributions to host communities.
- Theme 2024 – Honouring the contributions of migrants and respecting their rights.

World Human Rights Day

- World Human Rights Day is observed annually on December 10.
- This day also empowers people and communities across the world to build a better future.
- Theme for 2024 is 'Our Rights, Our Future'
- World Human Rights Day was established in 1948 when the United Nations General Assembly adopted the Universal Declaration of Human Rights (UDHR). It is the first global enunciation of human rights.

World AIDS Day

- World AIDS Day is observed annually on 1st December.
- First established in 1988 by the World Health Organization (WHO), this day aims to raise awareness about HIV/AIDS and honor those who have lost their lives to the disease.
- The theme for 2024 is "Take the Rights Path: My Health, My Right!".

World Polio Day

- World Polio Day is observed annually on 24th October.
- The day was established by Rotary International in 1988 to honor Dr. Jonas Salk, who developed the first effective polio vaccine.
- This day raises awareness about polio, a crippling and potentially fatal infectious disease.
- The theme for 2024 is "A Global Mission to Reach Every Child".

United Nations Day

- United Nations Day is celebrated annually on 24th October, marking the anniversary of the UN Charter's entry into force in 1945.
- Established to promote peace, security, and international cooperation, the United Nations works on a wide range of global issues, including human rights, development, and humanitarian aid.
- Theme: A symbol of hope for global unity

World Statistics Day

- World Statistics Day is an international celebration held every five years. In 2024, The day is celebrated on 20th October.
- Established by the United Nations Statistical Commission in 2010, this global event occurs every five years to emphasize the crucial role of reliable data and statistics in policy-making, governance, and global progress.
- Theme: "Connecting the world with data we can trust."

World Food Day

- World Food Day is celebrated annually on 16th October, marking the founding of the Food and Agriculture Organization (FAO) of the United Nations in 1945.
- The day highlights global efforts to combat hunger, ensure food security, and promote sustainable agriculture.
- The theme for 2024 is "Sustainable Agriculture for a Food-Secure World".

International Day for Disaster Risk Reduction

- The International Day for Disaster Risk Reduction (IDDR) is observed annually on 13th October.
- This day, established by the United Nations General Assembly in 1989, aims to promote a global culture of risk-awareness and disaster reduction.
- The theme for 2024 is "Empowering the Next Generation for a Resilient Future."

World Migratory Bird Day

- World Migratory Bird Day is celebrated annually on 12th October.
- This year's theme is "Protect Insects, Protect Birds".
- The campaign, organized by a network of global partners, emphasizes the critical role insects play in the life cycle of migratory birds and the alarming global decline in insect populations.
- World Migratory Bird Day Unveils 2025 Conservation Theme: Creating Bird-Friendly Cities & Communities.

World Cotton Day

- World Cotton Day is celebrated annually on 7 October.
- This day was first proposed in 2019 by the Cotton Four (Benin, Burkina Faso, Chad, and Mali) at the World Trade Organization.
- It aims to raise awareness about the importance of cotton and its significant role in the global economy.
- The official theme of World Cotton Day is, 'Cotton for Good'.

World Habitat Day

- World Habitat Day is observed annually on the first Monday of October.
- First celebrated in 1986, it was established by the United Nations General Assembly in 1985 to reflect on the state of towns and cities, and to promote the right to adequate shelter.
- The theme for 2024 is "Engaging Youth to Create a Better Urban Future."

World Animal Day

- World Animal Day is celebrated annually on 4 October.
- First observed in 1925 by German cynologist Heinrich Zimmermann, the day was initially held on 24 March but was later moved to October 4 to align with the Feast Day of St. Francis of Assisi.

World Heart Day

- World Heart Day is observed annually on 29 September.
- The day was established by the World Heart Federation in 2000.
- It aims to raise awareness about cardiovascular diseases (CVDs), which are the leading cause of death globally.
- The 2024 theme, "Use Heart for Action," emphasizes proactive measures for heart health.

World Rabies Day

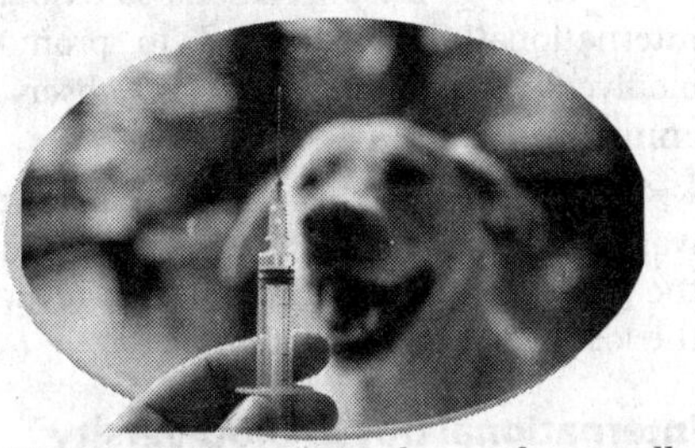

- World Rabies Day is observed annually on 28 September.
- The day was established in 2007 by the Global Alliance for Rabies Control.
- It commemorates the death of Louis Pasteur, who developed the first rabies vaccine.
- The 2024 theme, "Breaking Rabies Boundaries," emphasizes the need for innovative strategies and cross-sector collaboration to eliminate rabies.

World Environmental Health Day

- World Environmental Health Day is observed annually on 26 September.
- The day was established by the International Federation of Environmental Health (IFEH) in 2011.
- The 2024 theme, "Creating Resilient Communities Through Disaster Risk Reduction and Climate Change Mitigation and Adaptation."

World Tourism Day

- World Tourism Day is celebrated annually on 27 September.
- Established by the United Nations World Tourism Organization (UNWTO) in 1980, it commemorates the adoption of the UNWTO statutes in 1975.
- The official theme of World Tourism Day is "Tourism and Peace."

World Rhino Day

- World Rhino Day is celebrated annually on 22 September to raise awareness about the conservation of the world's five rhino species.
- Initiated in 2011 by the World Wildlife Fund (WWF), the day unites conservationists, wildlife enthusiasts, and governments globally.
- The theme for 2024 is "Collaboration is Key."

International Day of Peace

- The International Day of Peace is observed annually on 21 September.
- The day was established by the United Nations in 1981, it promotes global peace and non-violence.
- The 2024 theme, "Cultivating a Culture of Peace," emphasizes understanding and cooperation.

World Water Week 2024

- World Water Week 2024 is an annual event hosted by the Stockholm International Water Institute. The week was organized from 25 to 29 August 2024.
- This year's theme is "Bridging Borders: Water for a Peaceful and Sustainable Future."
- The focus is on water cooperation, emphasizing regional and global interconnectivity among communities and nations.
- World Water Week is the leading conference on global water issues, held every year since 1991.

International Day of Remembrance and Tribute to the Victims of Terrorism

- The International Day of Remembrance and Tribute to the Victims of Terrorism is observed annually on 21st August.
- The day serves as a solemn reminder of the ongoing global challenge posed by terrorism.
- This day aims to honour and support the victims and survivors of terrorist acts while promoting the protection of their human rights and fundamental freedoms.

World Humanitarian Day

- World Humanitarian Day, observed annually on 19 August.
- The year 2023 marked the deadliest year on record for aid workers, and 2024 threatens to surpass this grim milestone.
- The International Day was established through UN General Assembly Resolution 72/165 in 2017.

World Sanskrit Day

- World Sanskrit Day, also known as Vishva-Samskrita-Dinam, is celebrated annually on Shraavana Poornima, the full moon day of the Shraavana month in the Hindu calendar.
- This year, it was observed on 19 August 2024.
- The day aims to promote and preserve the ancient Indian language of Sanskrit through various activities such as lectures, cultural events, and educational programs.

World Elephant Day

- World Elephant Day 2024 was observed on 12 August, under the theme "Personifying Prehistoric Beauty, Theological Relevance, and Environmental Importance".

- This annual event aims to raise awareness about the urgent threats facing elephants and to support efforts to ensure their survival and well-being.

World Organ Donation Day

- World Organ Donation Day 2024 was observed on 13 August, under the theme "Be the Reason for Someone's Smile Today!".
- This day aims to raise awareness about the critical need for organ donors and to encourage individuals to register as organ donors.

International Youth Day

- International Youth Day 2024 was celebrated on 12 August.
- The theme for International Youth Day 2024 is "From Clicks to Progress: Youth Digital Pathways for Sustainable Development".
- The day serves as a reminder of the potential of youth in driving digital transformation and sustainable development.

Hiroshima Day

- Hiroshima Day is observed annually on 6 August to commemorate the atomic bombing of Hiroshima, Japan, by the United States in 1945.
- In 2024, it marks the 79th anniversary of this tragic event.
- The bombing resulted in the immediate deaths of approximately 70,000-80,000 people, with tens of thousands more succumbing to injuries and radiation exposure later.

International Tiger Day

- International Tiger Day, also known as Global Tiger Day, is observed annually on 29 July.
- It was established in 2010 during the Saint Petersburg Tiger Summit in Russia.
- The theme of the 2024 International Tiger Day is Call for Action.
- The day aims to raise awareness about tiger conservation and the urgent need to protect these majestic creatures.

World Hepatitis Day

- World Hepatitis Day is observed globally on 28 July every year.
- This year's theme is: "It's time for action".
- This date honors Nobel Laureate Dr. Baruch Samuel Blumberg, who discovered the hepatitis B virus and developed the first hepatitis B vaccine.

World Mangrove Day

- 26 July is International Day for Conservation of Mangrove Ecosystems.
- The day was declared by UNESCO to raise awareness and promote sustainable management of mangroves, vital for coastal protection, storm mitigation, and carbon sequestration.
- It was established by UNESCO in 2015.

International Chess Day

- International Chess Day is celebrated annually on 20 July.
- The day is a worldwide commemoration that honours the ancient game of chess.
- This date holds special importance in the chess world, as it commemorates the founding of the International Chess Federation (FIDE) on July 20, 1924, in Paris, France.

Nelson Mandela International Day

- Nelson Mandela International Day is observed every year on 18 July
- The day serves not only as a commemoration but also as a call to action on a global scale, encouraging individuals and communities around the world to embrace Mandela's spirit of service and dedication to social justice.
- He was first black president of South Africa.
- Mandela became the first democratically elected president of the country on May 10, 1994, and he is referred to as the 'Father of the Nation' in South Africa.

World Population Day

- World Population Day is celebrated every year on 11 July.
- The day was established by the United Nations in 1989.
- The theme for World Population Day 2024, "Leave no one behind, count everyone."

World Youth Skills Day

- World Youth Skills Day is observed annually on 15 July.
- The day was established by the United Nations General Assembly in 2014.
- 2024 Theme: "Youth Skills for Peace and Development".
- It serves as a global platform to highlight the importance of equipping young people with skills essential for employment, decent work, and entrepreneurship.

International Plastic Bag Free Day

- International Plastic Bag Free Day is observed every year on 3 July.
- It aims to raise awareness about the harmful effects of plastic bags on our environment.
- The day aligns with the Break Free from Plastic Movement, seeking solutions to the plastic pollution crisis for a safer planet.

World Hunger Day 2024

- World Hunger Day is observed annually on **28 May.**
- The day is a global initiative to raise awareness about the critical issue of hunger and malnutrition.
- The theme for World Hunger Day 2024 is **– Thriving Mothers. Thriving world.**

International Day for Biological Diversity 2024

- The International Day for Biological Diversity (also known as World Biodiversity Day) is a United Nations-sanctioned international day dedicated to promote biodiversity awareness. It is observed annually **on 22 May.**
- The theme for this year's celebration was **"Be part of the Plan"**, emphasizing the global commitment to halt and reverse the loss of nature by 2050.

International Day of Biodiversity

- The International Day for Biodiversity is observed every year **on 22 May.**
- It highlights the significance of biodiversity as a primary source of water, food, medicine, clothing, fuel, shelter, and energy for humans.
- The theme for this year's international day was **"Be Part of the Plan"**.

World AIDS Vaccine Day 2024

- World AIDS Vaccine Day, also known as HIV Vaccine Awareness Day, is observed annually on **18 May.**
- On this day, HIV vaccine advocates emphasize the urgent need for a vaccine to prevent HIV infection and AIDS.

World Hypertension Day 2024

- World Hypertension Day is observed annually **on May 17th** to raise awareness about hypertension (high blood pressure) and promote its prevention, detection, and treatment.
- The day aims to encourage global action to combat this "silent killer," which significantly increases the risk of heart disease, stroke, and kidney failure.

World Telecommunication Day 2024

- World Telecommunication and Information Society Day (WTISD) is observed annually **on 17 May** to commemorate the establishment of the International Telecommunication Union (ITU) on 17 May 1969.

Anti-Terrorism Day 2024

- Anti-Terrorism Day is observed across the country on the death anniversary of former Prime Minister Rajiv Gandhi who was assassinated on May 21, 1991.
- The day aims to educate people about the negative effects of terrorism and violence on society and the nation.

World Red Cross Day 2024

- World Red Cross Day is an annual celebration of the principles of the International Red Cross and Red Crescent Movement, which is celebrated **on 8 May** each year.
- This year, the theme for World Red Cross and Red Crescent Day is: **"Keeping Humanity Alive"**.

International Nurses Day, 2024

- International Nurses Day is celebrated every year on **11 May.**
- International Nurses Day is celebrated across the world on the birth anniversary of Florence Nightingale to mark the contributions of nurses towards society.
- International Council of Nurses has declared the theme for 2024 as 'Our Nurses Our Future, The Economic Power of Care'.

World Athletics Day 2024

- World Athletics Day is celebrated annually **on May 7th** to promote the importance of athletics in schools and encourage young people to engage in sports.
- The day aims to inspire and develop the next generation of athletes.

World Press Freedom Day 2024

- World Press Freedom Day, observed annually **on 3 May,** honours and upholds the principles of press freedom globally.
- **The 31st World Press Freedom Day Conference was hosted by the Government of Chile and UNESCO in Santiago.**
- In 2024, World Press Freedom Day theme was **"A Press for the Planet: Journalism in the Face of the Environmental Crisis."**

World Veterinary Day 2024

- World Veterinary Day is celebrated every year on the last Saturday of April. In 2024, it was celebrated on April 27, 2024.
- The theme for World Veterinary Day 2024 was **"Veterinarians are essential health workers".**

World Malaria Day 2024

- World Malaria Day is celebrated **on 25 April every year.**
- The theme for World Malaria Day 2024 is **"Accelerating the fight against malaria for a more equitable world".**
- World Malaria Day is observed to spread awareness about the disease, its symptoms, and precautions.

World Earth Day 2024

- The annual event of World Earth Day falls **on 22 April.**
- The theme for World Earth Day 2024 is **Planet vs Plastics.**

World Liver Day 2024

- World Liver Day is celebrated every year on **19th April.**
- The day is an initiative dedicated to shedding light on the importance of liver health and promoting preventive measures against liver diseases.
- Theme for the 2024 is **"Keep your liver healthy and disease-free."**

World Heritage Day 2024

- World Heritage Day is also known as International Day for Monuments and Sites.
- The day is celebrated annually **on April 18** to honour and preserve our heritage.
- World Heritage Day brings together individuals, organisations, societies and governments to unite to raise awareness about the importance of historical sites and to promote their protection.
- The theme for World Heritage Day 2024 is **'Discover and Experience Diversity.'**

World Hemophilia Day 2024

- World Hemophilia Day is an annual observance held on **April 17th** to raise awareness about hemophilia, a rare and inherited bleeding disorder.
- This year, the theme for World Hemophilia Day 2024 is **"Equitable access for all: recognizing all bleeding disorders."**

World Art Day 2024

- Every year on **April 15th,** people around the globe celebrate World Art Day.
- The day is a tribute to the enduring impact of art across various cultures and societies.
- The theme for World Art Day 2024 is **"A Garden of Expression: Cultivating Community Through Art."**

International Day of Sport for Development and Peace 2024

- **April 6th** is celebrated annually as the International Day of Sport for Development and Peace (IDSDP) worldwide.
- It aims to recognize the positive impact of sports and physical activity on individuals' lives and communities globally.
- The theme for International Day of Sport for Development and Peace 2024 is **"Sport for the Promotion of Peaceful and Inclusive Societies,"** highlighting the role of sports in uniting people, fostering social change, and contributing to sustainable development and lasting peace.

International Day of Human Space Flight

- On 12 April 2011, the UN General Assembly declared the International Day of Human Space Flight to honor Yuri Gagarin's first human spaceflight in 1961.
- This day marks the start of humanity's space era and emphasizes the role of space science in sustainable development and promoting peaceful use of outer space.

World Tuberculosis Day 2024

- World Tuberculosis Day is observed annually **on March 24th** to raise awareness about the global epidemic of tuberculosis (TB) and efforts to eliminate the disease.
- It commemorates the date in 1882 when Dr. Robert Koch announced his discovery of Mycobacterium tuberculosis, the bacteria that causes TB.

World Meteorological Day 2024

- World Meteorological Day is observed annually on 23 March.
- It's celebrated annually to commemorate the founding of the World Meteorological Organization (WMO) in 1950.
- The theme for World Meteorological Day 2024 was **"At the Frontline of Climate Action".**

World Water Day 2024

- World Water Day is observed annually **on 22 March.**
- Theme for 2024 is **"Leveraging Water for Peace".**
- The 2024 edition of this flagship report, titled "Water for Prosperity and Peace," explores this theme in detail.

World Poetry Day 2024

- World Poetry Day is celebrated annually on 21 March.
- It was established by the United Nations Educational, Scientific and Cultural Organization (UNESCO) in 1999.
- The theme for 2024 was **"Standing on the Shoulders of Giants."**

World Sparrow Day 2024

- World Sparrow Day is observed annually **on March 20th** to raise awareness about the conservation of sparrows and their declining populations worldwide.
- The day was first celebrated in 2010, initiated by the Nature Forever Society of India in collaboration with the Eco-Sys Action Foundation of France.

World Wildlife Day 2024

- World Wildlife Day, celebrated annually **on March 3rd,** promotes awareness of biodiversity conservation and wildlife protection.
- This year's theme is **"Connecting People and Planet: Exploring Digital Innovation in Wildlife Conservation."**

International Women's Day 2024

- International Women's Day is celebrated annually **on March 8th.**
- It commemorates the achievements of women in various spheres and advocates for gender equality.
- The theme for International Women's Day 2024 is **'Invest in Women: Accelerate Progress.'**

No Smoking Day 2024

- No Smoking Day is observed annually **on 13 March** to raise awareness about the harmful effects of smoking and promote a smoke-free environment.
- No Smoking Day is crucial in addressing the global tobacco epidemic, which kills over 8 million people annually.
- The theme for No Smoking Day 2024 is **'Protecting children from tobacco industry interference.'**

International Day for the Elimination of Racial Discrimination 2024

- The International Day for the Elimination of Racial Discrimination, observed annually **on March 21,** calls on people worldwide to speak out against racial discrimination, slavery, and colonialism.
- The theme for 2024 is **"A Decade of Recognition, Justice, and Development: Implementation of the International Decade for People of African Descent."**

World NGO Day 2024

- World NGO Day is celebrated every year on **27 February.**
- The theme for World NGO Day 2024 is **"Building a Sustainable Future: The Role of NGOs in Achieving the Sustainable Development Goals (SDGs)".**

World Pulses Day 2024

- World Pulses Day is celebrated every year on 10 February.
- The theme for the year 2024 was **"Pulses: Nourishing Soils and People".**

World Wetlands Day 2024

- World Wetlands Day is observed on 2 February, every year.
- The theme for 2024 was "Wetlands and Human Wellbeing."
- It is an international day dedicated to promoting the conservation and sustainable management of wetlands.

World Cancer Day 2024

- World Cancer Day is observed annually on **4th February.**
- The Day aims to save millions of preventable deaths each year through education, raising awareness and pressing governments and individuals across the world to take action against the deadly disease.
- The theme for 2022-2024 was **"Close the Care Gap,"** focusing on equity in cancer care.

International Day of Women and Girls in Science 2024

- The International Day of Women and Girls in Science is celebrated **on 11 February** each year.
- It aims to promote gender equality and encourage women and girls to pursue careers in science, technology, engineering, and mathematics (STEM).

World Radio Day 2024

- World Radio Day, observed annually on **February 13th,** was established by UNESCO in 2011 and later adopted by the United Nations General Assembly in 2012.
- This year's theme was **"Radio: A Century informing, entertaining, and educating."**

International Mother Language Day 2024

- International Mother Language Day is a worldwide annual observance held on **February 21st** to promote awareness of linguistic and cultural diversity and to promote multilingualism.
- **Theme for 2024:** Multilingual education is a pillar of intergenerational learning.

World Day of Social Justice 2024

- World Day of Social Justice is observed annually **on 20 February.**
- It is established to promote social justice, solidarity, and the elimination of poverty, gender and racial discrimination, and other social injustices around the world.
- Theme for 2024: **"Bridging Gaps, Building Alliances".**

World Human Spirit Day 2024

- World Human Spirit Day is observed annually **on February 17th.**
- It is a day dedicated to celebrate the power and resilience of the human spirit and encouraging individuals to reflect on their inner strength, positivity, and potential for personal growth and transformation.

World Anthropology Day 2024

- World Anthropology Day is an annual event celebrated on the **third Thursday of February.**
- It is a day dedicated to highlight the contributions of anthropology to understanding human diversity, culture, and society.
- In 2024, it was celebrated on February 15.

World Braille Day 2024

- World Braille Day is celebrated across the world **on 4 January** every year.
- This day holds special importance as it marks the birthday of Louis Braille, the visionary inventor of the Braille script, born in France in 1809.

World Hindi Day 2024

- Every year, World Hindi Day is celebrated on **10 January.**
- Its objective is to create awareness for the promotion of Hindi in the world and to present Hindi as an international language.

World Environment Day 2024

- World Environment Day is observed on June 5th.
- Theme for World Environment Day 2024 is "land restoration, desertification and drought resilience".

International Day of Yoga 2024

- International Yoga Day is a worldwide celebration of yoga, an ancient Indian practice that promotes physical, mental, and spiritual well-being.
- Observed annually on June 21st, this special day brings together millions of people across the globe for yoga classes, workshops, and talks.
- This year marks the 10th International Day of Yoga with the theme "Yoga for Self and Society."

International Olympic Day 2024

- Every year on June 23, the world celebrates International Olympic Day, a commemoration of the modern Olympic Games and an opportunity to promote the values of sports across the globe.
- The theme for International Olympic Day 2024 is "Let's Move and Celebrate."

Important Days From January 2024 to June 2024

Important Day	Date	Theme 2024	Launch Year
World Braille Day	January 4	Bridging the Digital Divide for Braille Users	2019
International Day of Education	January 24	To Invest in People, Prioritize Education	2018
World Cancer Day	February 4	Close the Care Gap	2000
International Day of Women and Girls in Science	February 11	Innovate. Demonstrate. Elevate. Advance.	2015
World Radio Day	February 13	Radio and Peace	2011
International Mother Language Day	February 21	Multilingual education – a necessity to transform education	2000
World Wildlife Day	March 3	Partnerships for Wildlife Conservation	2013
International Women's Day	March 8	Gender Equality: Realizing Women's Rights	1911
World Kidney Day	March 14	Kidney Health for All	2006
International Day of Happiness	March 20	Happier Together	2012
World Water Day	March 22	Accelerating Change	1993
World Tuberculosis Day	March 24	Yes! We can end TB!	1982
World Health Day	April 7	Health for All	1950
Earth Day	April 22	Invest in Our Planet	1970
International Workers' Day	May 1	Protecting Workers' Rights	1889
World Press Freedom Day	May 3	Shaping a Future of Rights: Freedom of expression as a driver for all other human rights	1993
World Environment Day	June 5	Beat Plastic Pollution	1974
World Oceans Day	June 8	Planet Ocean: Tides are Changing	2008
World Blood Donor Day	June 14	Give blood, give plasma, share life, share often	2004
International Day of Yoga	June 21	Yoga for Humanity	2015
World Refugee Day	June 20	Hope away from home	2001

Mother Mary Comes to Me: Arundhati Roy's First Memoir

- "Mother Mary Comes to Me" is the first memoir by Booker Prize-winning author Arundhati Roy, set to be published in September 2025 by Penguin India.
- This deeply personal Memoir explores Roy's complex relationship with her mother, Mary Roy, whom she describes as "my shelter and my storm".

Historical Background

- The memoir was written in response to Mary Roy's death in September 2022.
- Arundhati Roy began the memoir to process her emotions and make sense of her feelings about the mother she ran from at age 18, not out of lack of love, but to continue loving her.

Themes and Content

- The memoir delves into Roy's life from childhood to the present, from Kerala to Delhi.
- It is a poignant exploration of love, freedom, and grace, filled with heart, humor, and pathos.
- Roy reflects on her personal and political awakening, offering an intimate and inspiring glimpse into her journey as a writer and individual.

Who is Arundhati Roy?

- Arundhati Roy is an Indian author, essayist, and political activist, best known for her novel "The God of Small Things" and her outspoken advocacy on various political and social issues.

Literary Breakthrough: The God of Small Things (1997)

- Arundhati Roy's debut novel, The God of Small Things, published in 1997, catapulted her to international fame.
- The novel won the prestigious Man Booker Prize for Fiction in 1997, making Roy the first Indian woman to win the award.

- The God of Small Things became a bestseller worldwide, translated into over 40 languages.

Some of Her Most Notable Works of Non-Fiction Include

"The End of Imagination" (1998)
"The Greater Common Good" (1999)
"Power Politics" (2001)
"War Talk" (2003)
"Walking with the Comrades" (2011)
"Capitalism: A Ghost Story" (2014)

AWARDS AND HONORS

- **Man Booker Prize** for Fiction (1997) for **The God of Small Things.**
- **Norman Mailer Prize** for Distinguished Writing (2011).
- **Sydney Peace Prize** (2004) for her work in social campaigns and advocacy for non-violence.
- **Lannan Cultural Freedom Prize** (2002) for her advocacy of human rights.
- Time Magazine's 100 Most Influential People in the World (2004).
- **Ambassador of Conscience Award** from Amnesty International (2002).

IMPORTANT BOOKS IN 2024

Book Titled: "Beyond the Higgs Boson"

- On November 26, 2024, HarperCollins published "Beyond the Higgs Boson: The W Boson and Dr. Ashutosh Kotwal's Quest for the Unknown," written by Manik Kotwal and translated by Jerry Pinto.
- The book details the life of Dr. Ashutosh Kotwal, a renowned particle physicist, from his childhood in India to his significant contributions to the discovery of the Higgs boson and W boson.
- It was Originally published in Marathi as 'Putra Vhava Aisa to critical acclaim.

Book Titled: BRING IT ON: The Incredible Story of My Life'

- Harper Collins India has announced the upcoming publication of 'BRING IT ON: The Incredible Story of My Life', a memoir by India's most celebrated para-athlete, Dr. Deepa Malik.
- She is India's first-ever female Paralympic medalist, winning a silver medal in shot put at the 2016 Rio Paralympics.

Book Titled: "Why Bharat Matters"

- In November 2024, External Affairs Minister Dr S. Jaishankar launched his new book, "Why Bharat Matters", at the Mohammed Bin Rashid Library in Dubai, UAE.
- Why Bharat Matters is a 2024 non-fictional book published by Rupa Publications.
- The book discusses India's rising global stature, strategic priorities, and its evolving role in shaping a multipolar world.

Book Titled: Ratan Tata: A Life

- HarperCollins India recently published a book titled "Ratan Tata: A Life" written by Thomas Mathew.
- This biography meticulously traces Ratan Tata's journey from his lonely childhood to his role as the head of Tata Trusts, India's largest philanthropic enterprise.
- Ratan Tata has received numerous awards and honors, including the Padma Bhushan in 2000, the Padma Vibhushan in 2008, and the Honorary Knight Grand Cross of the Order of the British Empire in 2014.

Book Titled: Mountain Mammals of the World

- "Mountain Mammals of the World" by M.K. Ranjitsinh was launched on 11th October 2024.
- This comprehensive guide features 58 species and 119 taxa of large mammals found in mountain ranges globally.
- It is published by Penguin Random House.
- This Book was launched by former politician-author Padma Vibhushan Dr Karan Singh at WWF in New Delhi.

Book Titled: WAR

- Newly Launched Book "WAR" by Bob Woodward was launched on October 15, 2024 and published by Simon & Schuster.
- This investigative book delves into three major conflicts: the war in Ukraine, the Middle East conflict, and the political struggle for the American presidency.
- Bob Woodward is the best-known International journalist and Pulitzer Prize winner.

Book Titled: Sri Rama in Tamilagam – An inseparable bond

- On 14 September 2024, Tamil Nadu Governor R.N. Ravi released the book "Sri Rama in Tamilagam – An Inseparable Bond" by Dr. D.K. Hari and Dr. D.K. Hema Hari.
- The authors emphasize that Lord Rama's connection to Tamilagam goes beyond the famous Sethu Bandha (Adam's Bridge).
- Tamilagam stands as a living heritage museum of Ramayana with different temples depicting scenes connected with Ramayana, right from His birth to His departure from earth.

Book Titled: ISRO: Exploring New Frontiers

- On 5 September 2024, ISRO Chairman S. Somanath launched a coffee-table book titled "ISRO: Exploring New Frontiers - To The Moon, The Sun & Beyond", published by The Hindu Group.

- Curated by T.S. Subramanian, the book documents India's space journey from the 1960s to recent missions like Chandrayaan-3 and Aditya L-1.

Book Titled: The Scientist Entrepreneur: Empowering Millions of Women

- On 21 August 2024, Dr. Soumya Swaminathan, Chairperson of the M.S. Swaminathan Research Foundation and former WHO chief scientist, released "The Scientist Entrepreneur: Empowering Millions of Women".
- This autobiography, written by activist Kalpana Sankar, sheds light on the impact of Hand in Hand India, an international non-profit organization co-founded by Dr. Kalpana.
- The book captures lessons from successfully managing micro-finance initiatives, emphasizing the vital role of NGOs in bridging the gap between government and communities.

Book Titled: Power Within: The Leadership Legacy of Narendra Modi

- Book titled "Power Within: The Leadership Legacy of Narendra Modi" is authored by renowned author and development activist Dr. R Balasubramaniam.
- The book, "Power Within" : The Leadership Legacy of Narendra Modi, is inspired by the 'exercise of leadership'.
- It examines this practice by presenting the civilizational wisdom of Bharat through the lived experiences of Prime Minister Narendra Modi.

Book Titled: Modi's Governance Triumph

- Tarun Chugh, BJP General Secretary, unveiled his book titled "Modi's Governance Triumph: Reshaping India's Path to Prosperity" on 17 August 2024, in New Delhi.
- The book highlights visionary initiatives, including 'Make in India' and the implementation of the Goods and Services Tax (GST).

Book Titled: Jamsetji Tata: Powerful Learnings for Corporate Success

- Book "Jamsetji Tata: Powerful Learnings for Corporate Success" is authored by Harish Bhat and R. Gopalakrishnan.

- It highlights the entrepreneurial principles of Jamsetji Tata, the visionary who pioneered modern Indian industry.
- Jamsetji Tata was an Indian philanthropist and entrepreneur who founded the Tata Group.

Book Titled: 75 Great Revolutionaries of India

- On 11 August 2024, Rajya Sabha Deputy Chairman Harivansh Narayan Singh attended the launch of the book "75 Great Revolutionaries of India" by MP Bhim Singh.
- The book highlights the contributions of lesser-known 75 freedom fighters who played crucial roles in India's independence.
- The book aims to recognize and honor the sacrifices of these unsung heroes, serving as a source of inspiration for building a developed India.

Book Titled: Breaking Rocks and Barriers

- "Breaking Rocks and Barriers: The Adventurous Life of Sudipta Sengupta" is a memoir by Sudipta Sengupta, released on 24 July 2024.
- The book chronicles her remarkable journey as a pioneering geologist and mountaineer.
- Sengupta, one of the first Indian women to set foot on Antarctica, shares her experiences of fieldwork in remote areas, from encounters with snakes in Bihar's mines to trekking across a 'black glacier' in Norway.

Book Titled: The Prisoner of Bhopal

- Tim Walker, an award-winning designer-turned-author, has released a historical fiction novel titled "The Prisoner of Bhopal."
- It is aimed at young readers to commemorate the 40th anniversary of the Bhopal gas tragedy.
- The Bhopal disaster, also known as the Bhopal gas tragedy, was a chemical accident that occurred on the night of December 2–3, 1984, at the Union Carbide India Limited pesticide plant in Bhopal, Madhya Pradesh, India.

Book Titled: Kargil War: The Turning Point

- On 3 July 2024, the Governor of Arunachal Pradesh, Lt. General KT Parnaik (Retd.), launched a book titled "Kargil War: The Turning Point" at the Rajendra Singhji Army Officers Institute (RSAOI) in Bengaluru.
- Authored by the late Col M B Ravindranath, Vir Chakra (VrC), this book provides detailed insights into the actions and operations of the 2nd battalion of Rajputana Rifles (2 RAJ RIF) during Operation Vijay in 1999.

OTHER IMPORTANT BOOKS

Name of the Author	Name of the book
Dr I.V. Subba Rao	"Celebrating Bharat – The Mission and Message of Shri M Venkaiah Naidu as 13th Vice–President of India"
Sanjay Kishore	"Mahaneta – Life and Journey of Shri M. Venkaiah Naidu"
Alia Bhatt	"The Adventures of Ed-a-Mamma: Ed Finds a Home"
R. Ashwin and Sidharth Monga	"I Have the Streets: A Kutti Cricket Story"
Alpana Killawala	"A Fly on the RBI Wall: An Insider's View of the Central Bank"

The Idea of Democracy: Sam Pitroda's New Book

- Sam Pitroda's latest book, **"The Idea of Democracy,"** is a compelling exploration of democratic principles and practices in the contemporary world.
- In this book, Pitroda delves into the fundamental tenets of democracy, examining its evolution, current challenges, and future prospects.

Themes and Concepts

- **"The Idea of Democracy"** covers a broad range of themes, including the historical evolution of democracy, the role of technology in democratic governance, the importance of inclusive and participatory decision-making, and the impact of globalization on democratic institutions.
- Pitroda emphasizes the need for transparency, accountability, and citizen engagement in ensuring the robustness and resilience of democratic systems.

EAM Jaishankar Received Copy Of Book 'India's Nuclear Titans'

- External Affairs Minister S. Jaishankar received a copy of the book **'India's Nuclear Titans,'** edited by Soumya Awasthi and Shrabana Barua.
- 'India's Nuclear Titans' traces the evolution of India into a nuclear state while highlighting the pivotal roles played by renowned figures like **Homi Bhabha, Vikram Sarabhai, Abdul Kalam, and K. Subrahmanyam,** among others.

Harinder Sikka Pens New Novel 'Gobind'

- Harinder Sikka has released a new novel titled "Gobind"
- It's a gripping story about a man named Gobind, born into an impoverished Sikh family in Bihar.
- Harinder Sikka's book "Calling Sehmat" was made into the 2018 film "Raazi," starring Alia Bhatt.

Anuradha Mascarenhas authored a book 'At The Wheel of Research'

- Anuradha Mascarenhas has authored a new book titled **"At The Wheel of Research: An Exclusive Biography of Dr. Soumya Swaminathan".**
- The book provides insights into Swaminathan's life, drawing upon interviews with family members, close friends, and eminent scientists.

A new book, 'India — the Road to Renaissance: A Vision and an Agenda' by Bhimeswara Chall

- Bhimeshwar Challa's book, **"India - The Road to Renaissance:** A Vision and an Agenda" was released at the Administrative Staff College of India (ASCI) campus in Hyderabad.
- This book is a "passionate plea for a new, resurgent India" – a call to action for all those who refuse to accept the status quo and demand a brighter future for the country.

A new book "The Law and Spirituality: Reconnecting the Bond" by Prof. Raman Mittal and Dr. Seema Singh

- "The Law and Spirituality: Reconnecting the Bond" by Prof. Raman Mittal and Dr. Seema Singh explores the intersection of law and spirituality.
- The authors argue that spirituality is the foundation of ethics and morality, which in turn shape legal systems.
- The book aims to unearth spiritual jurisprudence and highlight its relevance in contemporary legal contexts, fostering consensus and fraternity.

Salman Rushdie releases 'Knife' memoir recounting stabbing

- "Knife: Meditations After an Attempted Murder" by Salman Rushdie, published in April 2024, recounts the August 2022 stabbing attack on him during a lecture in New York.
- The book has received positive reviews and hit number one on the Sunday Times Bestsellers List.
- He gained international fame with his second novel, "Midnight's Children" (1981), which won the Booker Prize and was later named the "Best of the Booker".

Siddharth Rajsekar unveils 'I Can Coach' Volumes 2 & 3

- Bestselling author and digital coaching leader Siddharth Rajsekar announced the release of volumes 2 and 3 of his transformative book series, **'I Can Coach'.**
- The books were launched at the Freedom Business Retreat 2024, a two-day event at the Leela Palace, Chennai.
- It showcase inspiring stories of commitment and aspiration within the digital coaching revolution.

Parshottam Rupala release book on Sagar Parikrama at Rajkot

- Union Minister for Fisheries, Animal Husbandry, and Dairying, Shri Parshottam Rupala, release a book and video titled **"Sagar Parikrama"** at the Engineering Association in Rajkot, Gujarat.
- The book aims to chronicle the Sagar Parikrama Yatra, encompassing diverse elements such as the maritime route, cultural and geographical explorations, and notable impacts from all 12 phases of the journey.

Sri Lanka ex-President Gotabaya Rajapaksa launched a book

- Recently, former Sri Lankan President Gotabaya Rajapaksa launched a book named **'The Conspiracy to oust me from the Presidency',** two years after he was dramatically removed from office by a popular mass movement.
- In this book he attributes the political collapse to a "conspiracy" involving foreign and local parties.

A book title "Basic Structure and Republic" Released by Governor P. S. Sreedharan Pillai

- "Basic Structure and Republic" by P. S. Sreedharan Pillai, released on February 27, 2024, explores the evolution of India's constitutional framework.
- The book is based on the Golden Jubilee speeches and focuses on the landmark Kesavananda Bharati vs. State of Kerala case, which was decided by a 13-judge bench after 66 days of hearings.
- Pillai emphasizes the importance of the basic structure doctrine in maintaining the integrity of the Constitution.

A book on Indian modern art "The Gems of Indian Art" launched

- "The Gems of Indian Art" is a comprehensive book on Indian modern art, launched in New Delhi in February 2024.
- The book, nearly 300 pages long, documents the late Harish Khullar's collection of 20th-century Indian modern and contemporary art.
- The book offers a detailed exploration of Khullar's impressive collection, showcasing the richness and diversity of Indian modern art.

Book titled "Dabbling in Diplomacy" by Prof. S.D. Muni

- "Dabbling in Diplomacy: Authorised & Otherwise, Recollections of a Non-Career Diplomat" is a fascinating book authored by **Prof. S.D. Muni,** a well-known South Asian expert.

- The book offers insights into South Asian geopolitical affairs from an academic and diplomatic standpoint.

A New book titled "Sculpted Stones: Mysteries of Mamallapuram" authored by Ashwin Prabhu

- "Sculpted Stones: Mysteries of Mamallapuram" by Ashwin Prabhu, published by Tulika Books.
- It takes readers on a journey through the UNESCO World Heritage site of Mamallapuram (Mahabalipuram) on Tamil Nadu's coast.
- The book showcases the town's stunning sculptural art, including relief panels, cave temples, and monoliths.

CDS Anil Chauhan reveals book "AI and National Security"

- Chief of Defence Staff General Anil Chauhan unveiled the book "Artificial Intelligence and National Security" at the Defence Literature Festival "Kalam and Kavach" in Pune.
- The book marks a significant milestone in integrating India's rich cultural heritage with modern national security strategies.

Jagdeep Dhankhar released "9 Incredible Years of Haryana Government".

- **Vice President Jagdeep Dhankhar** released a book titled "9 Incredible Years of Haryana Government: Emergence of a New and Vibrant Haryana."
- The book chronicles the state's transformation, detailing achievements and reforms across good governance, agriculture, sports, and defense services.

"Maha Swaapnikudu" book launched by Chandrababu Naidu

- "Maha Swaapnikudu" (A Great Visionary) by N. Chandrababu Naidu was launched on February 11, 2024.
- The book, released by former Supreme Court judge V. Gopala Gowda, delves into Naidu's vision for governance and societal development.
- The launch event highlighted Naidu's commitment to education and literature, making the book a valuable resource for aspirants preparing for government exams.

'Ek Samandar, Mere Andar' book written by Sanjeev Joshi

- National Security Advisor Ajit Doval and Chief of Defence Staff General Anil Chauhan launched the book **'Ek Samandar, Mere Andar'**, written by BrahMos Aerospace Deputy CEO Sanjeev Joshi.
- 'Ek Samandar, Mere Andar' is a **collection of 75 poems** penned by BrahMos Aerospace Deputy CEO Sanjeev Joshi.
- This book reflects the confluence of creative expression and defence expertise.

Romesh Bhattacharji authored "KASHMIR: Travels in Paradise on Earth"

- "KASHMIR: Travels in Paradise on Earth" by Romesh Bhattacharji, published by HarperCollins India on January 29, 2024.
- Bhattacharji, who began trekking in Kashmir in the 1960s, shares his deep love for the region through detailed descriptions and hand-drawn maps.
- The book captures the splendor of Kashmir's lakes, meadows, valleys, and peaks, offering an eloquent and absorbing account of his adventures.

Smita Das Jain co-authored a chapter "Cracking the Rich Code: Vol 12"

- "Cracking the Rich Code: Vol 12" features a chapter by Smita Das Jain, titled "Destiny by Design: The Empower Yourself Blueprint to Success".
- Published on February 21, 2024, this volume is curated by Jim Britt and endorsed by Tony Robbins.
- Jain's chapter shares her journey from corporate uncertainty to global recognition as an executive and life coach.

A book "Gandhi A Life in Three Campaigns" launched by M.J. Akbar

- Renowned author M.J. Akbar, along with co-author K. Natwar Singh, launched a new book titled **"Gandhi: A Life in Three Campaigns."**
- This book throws light on the life and struggles of **Mahatma Gandhi,** particularly focusing on three important mass campaigns **(Non-Cooperation Movement (1920), Salt Satyagraha (1930), Quit India Movement (1942)** led by him.

"Conversations with Aurangzeb" translated in English by Nandini Krishna.

- **"Conversations with Aurangzeb"** is a novel written by the Tamil author **Charu Nivedita** and translated into **English by Nandini Krishnan.** The book is a part historical novel and part satire.
- The book touches upon a variety of topics, from marketing strategies for emperors to mutiny, from Marxism to Sunny Leone.
- The book is published by HarperCollins India.

'Fertilising the Future: Bharat's March Towards Fertilizer Self-Sufficiency' written by Dr. Mansukh Mandaviya

- "Fertilising the Future: Bharat's March Towards Fertilizer Self-Sufficiency" by Dr. Mansukh Mandaviya was published by Rupa Publications.
- The book details India's progress towards self-reliance in the fertilizer sector under the leadership of Prime Minister Narendra Modi.
- The book highlights the successful commercial production of nano urea and nano DAP, making India the first country to achieve this milestone.
- The Hindi version of the book is titled **'Urvarak-Atmanirbharta ki Raah.'**

Union Minister Amit Shah Launches A Book "Assam's Braveheart Lachit Barphukan"

- The Book **"Assam's Braveheart Lachit Barphukan"** written by **Arup Kumar Dutta** at the Srimanta Sankardeva International Auditorium in Guwahati in the presence of Chief Minister, Himanta Biswa Sarma launched.
- The book "Assam's Braveheart Lachit Barphukan" has been published by the State government in English language and translated into **24 Scheduled Indian languages.**

1000+ CURRENT AFFAIRS BLASTER

1. Which state's woman police station recently achieved the ISO 9001:2015 certification in July 2024? **-Itanagar (Arunachal Pradesh)**
2. Which word has been declared by Oxford University Press as the 'Oxford Word of the Year 2024'? **-'Brain rot'**
3. Where has Uber launched Shikara ride booking under Asia's first water transport service? **-Dal Lake (Srinagar)**
4. Which city hosted the World Maritime Conference 2024? **-Chennai**
5. In July 2024, India became the world's ___ largest domestic aviation market. **-3rd**
6. Which Indian state's Chief Minister launched the "Mukhya Mantri Kisan Samman Nidhi" in July 2024? **-Rajasthan**
7. In July 2024, Union Minister Shri G Kishan Reddy launched which portal to reward mains aspirants of the National Civil Services Examination? **-NIRMAN Portal**
8. In July 2024, the Indian government signed a $170 million loan agreement with which international financial body to strengthen pandemic preparedness? **-Asian Development Bank (ADB)**
9. Which country has become the first in the world to prepare a checklist of its entire fauna, covering 104,561 species, positioning itself as a global leader in biodiversity documentation? **-India**
10. In July 2024, which Indian state's government extended the age limit for the Mukhyamantri Majhi Ladki Bahin Yojana to 65 years? **-Maharashtra**
11. Which country recently introduced new 3D holographic banknotes in July 2024? **-Japan**
12. Which international organization did Belarus join as its 10th member in July 2024? **-Shanghai Cooperation Organisation (SCO)**
13. In July 2024, which country hosted the NATO summit in Washington, DC? **- USA.**
14. In July 2024, which country was welcomed as the fifth member of the Colombo Security Conclave? **- Bangladesh**
15. In November 2024, which bank raised ₹10,000 crore through an infrastructure bond issuance? **-State Bank of India (SBI)**
16. Which Indian bank launched the 'Union Premier' branches for high value customers in rural and semi urban markets in July 2024? **-Union Bank of India**
17. In July 2024, which financial service company partnered with HDFC ERGO to unveil fraud insurance? **-Truecaller**
18. In July 2024, who was appointed as the new Chairperson of the National Medical Commission? **-B.N. Gangadhar**
19. In July 2024, who was appointed as the Managing Director and CEO of IndiaFirst Life Insurance? **-Rushabh Gandhi**
20. Who was appointed as the new Principal Advisor to the Union Health Ministry in July 2024? **-Soumya Swaminathan**
21. Who became the first woman Chief Secretary of Maharashtra in July 2024? **-Sujata Saunik**
22. Who was appointed Chairman of the Central Board of Direct Taxes (CBDT) in July 2024? **-Ravi Agrawal**
23. Which Indian naval ship participated in the Rim of the Pacific (RIMPAC) naval exercise in Pearl Harbor in July 2024? **- INS Shivalik**
24. Which indigenous light tank was unveiled by DRDO in July 2024? **-Zorawar**
25. In July 2024, India conducted a joint military exercise with which country's army in Meghalaya? **-Mongolia (Nomadic Elephant)**
26. Which defence manufacturing company signed a pact with Thales to produce 70mm rockets in India in July 2024? **-Adani Defence & Aerospace**
27. Who won the Women's Singles title at Wimbledon 2024? **-Barbora Krejcíkova**
28. Who won the 2024 Grand Prix of Spain in wrestling? **-Vinesh Phogat**
29. Which Indian shooter won a bronze medal at the Shotgun Junior World Cup in July 2024? **-Sabeera Haris**
30. Which Formula 1 driver ended a 3 year drought by winning the British Grand Prix in July 2024? **-Lewis Hamilton**
31. Which three books did PM Modi release in July 2024? **-"Venkaiah Naidu – Life in Service" by S Nagesh Kumar, "Celebrating Bharat – The Mission and Message of M. Venkaiah Naidu as 13th Vice President of India" compiled by I. V. Subba Rao, and "Mahaneta – Life and Journey of M. Venkaiah Naidu" by Sanjay Kishore.**
32. What is the theme of World Population Day on July 11, 2024? **-Leave No One Behind, Count Everyone**
33. What is the theme of World Youth Skills Day on July 15, 2024? **-Youth Skills for Peace and Development**
34. Who was the former Indian midfielder who passed away in July 2024? **-Bhupinder Singh Rawat**
35. Who was the Oscar winning producer of "Titanic" and "Avatar" who passed away in July 2024? **-Jon Landau**
36. Which portal was recently integrated with Ayushman Bharat Digital by the Uttarakhand government? **-eSwasthya Dham**
37. Which companies recently collaborated to revolutionize mango cultivation in Karnataka? **-Coca Cola India and Gram Unnati**
38. Which new digital initiative was launched by Jayant Chaudhary recently to ensure transparent scheme access? **-Skill India Digital Hub**
39. Where was Asia's first pre clinical network facility recently inaugurated? **-Faridabad**
40. Which new portal and mobile app did Jyotiraditya Scindia launch recently for farmers in the northeast? **-NE-RACE portal and mobile app**
41. Which scheme was recently launched by the Maharashtra government to boost youth employability? **-Mukhyamantri Yuva Karya Prashikshan Yojana**
42. Which upskilling program was launched recently by the National Film Development Corporation (NFDC) in partnership with Netflix? **-"The Voicebox"**
43. Which organizations recently partnered to launch advanced drone training programmes? **-Drone Destination and National Small Industries Corporation (NSIC)**
44. Who was recently honoured with the COSPAR Harrie Massey Award for 2024? **-Prahlad Chandra Agrawal**
45. Who topped the celebrity brand valuation in 2023? **-Virat Kohli**
46. Which organization recently signed an MoU with the Rajasthan government to develop a greenfield airport at Kota? **-AAI (Airports Authority of India)**
47. What major change did the BJP government recently make to the Odisha Rajya Krida Samman Award? **-It was renamed from Biju Patnaik Sports Award**
48. Where was the 46th World Heritage Committee session of UNESCO hosted recently? **-New Delhi**
49. The "Rajiv Gandhi Civils Abhayahastam" scheme was launched by the Chief Minister of ________ to provide assistance to civil services aspirants. **-Telangana**
50. Which organization recently signed an MoU with the Indian Institute of Science, Bengaluru, to promote standardization? **-BIS (Bureau of Indian Standards)**
51. Which state recently topped the PM SVANidhi Scheme as the best performing state? **-Madhya Pradesh (MP)**
52. Which company recently announced plans to launch retail shops to distribute energy efficient products in India? **-Energy Efficiency Services Ltd (EESL)**

53. Where was the 'International Centre for Audit of Local Governance' inaugurated recently? -Rajkot
54. Which aviation company plans to launch India's first 'Made in India' H 125 helicopter in 2026? -Airbus
55. What theme did Jyotiraditya M. Scindia announce for the 2024 India Mobile Congress? -'The Future is Now'
56. Which Indian site was recently nominated for UNESCO World Heritage status? -Assam's Charaideo Maidam
57. Which two organizations signed a Letter of Intent to build joint innovation programs in the global south recently? -Atal Innovation Mission and WIPO
58. Which country recently launched the world's first high speed carbon fiber train? -China
59. Who recently launched his brand in partnership with FanCode Shop? -Hardik Pandya
60. Which prominent Non-Banking Financial Company launched a savings product called "Savings+" recently? -Bajaj Finserv AMC
61. Which organization raised India's growth forecast to 7% for 2024 25 in July 2024? -IMF
62. Which bank launched the Amrit Vrishti 444 Day Term Deposit with a 25% interest rate recently? -SBI
63. Which major international organization approved loans worth $240.5 million for rooftop solar systems in India? -ADB (Asian Development Bank)
64. Which insurance company partnered with IDFC First Bank recently to boost bancassurance in India? -LIC
65. Who was recently re elected for a fourth term as President of Rwanda? -Paul Kagame
66. Who was recently appointed as the next Indian Ambassador to the US? -Vinay Mohan Kwatra
67. Which South Asian Paralympic representative was appointed recently by the Asian Paralympic Committee? -Deepa Malik
68. Which South Indian Bank recently appointed Dolphy Jose as its Whole time Director? -South Indian Bank
69. Which bank received RBI approval for the reappointment of K Paul Thomas as MD & CEO? -ESAF Small Finance Bank.
70. Which renowned scientist from CSIR Indian Institute of Chemical Technology was inducted as a Fellow of the Royal Society of Chemistry? -S. Sridhar.
71. Which country will host the 2030 Winter Olympics and Paralympic Games? -France
72. Which famous football club became the first in the world to report €1 billion in revenue? -Real Madrid
73. Who won the maiden Women's Asia Cup title recently in cricket? -Sri Lanka
74. Who became the first Indian rider to participate in the World Superbike Championships recently? -Kavin Quintal
75. Which Indian tennis players were recently inducted into the International Tennis Hall of Fame? - Leander Paes and Vijay Amritraj
76. Who won the bronze medal in the 2024 Paris Olympics in shooting, making history for India? -Manu Bhaker
77. What international recognition did Abhinav Bindra receive recently? -The Olympic Order by the IOC.
78. What was the theme for World Ranger Day 2024? -30 by 30.
79. Who received the Oxford Bookstore Art Book Prize 2024 for her book 'Tantra on the Edge'? -Madhu Khanna
80. Who was the youngest and fastest female para swimmer to swim solo across the English Channel? -Jiya Rai
81. Which notable event related to the Paris Olympics 2024 recently took place on the River Seine? -The 2024 Paris Olympics Opening Parade.
82. Which country will host the T20 Asia Cup 2025, and which format will be used for the 2027 edition? -India, ODI format.
83. Which renowned tennis player, who is considered a legend, recently announced his retirement after the Davis Cup Finals 2024? -Rafael Nadal
84. What significant day was recently observed on 22nd July, with a focus on the brain? -World Brain Day 2024
85. Which team won the Women's Asia Cup 2024, defeating India in the final? -Sri Lanka's women's cricket team.
86. Which international cricket star was recently honoured with customized gold coins by Paris' Grevin Museum? -Shah Rukh Khan.
87. What was the theme for World Drowning Prevention Day 2024, observed on 25th July? -"Anyone can drown, no one should"
88. Which country's coal mines were recently included in the World's top 10 largest coal mines list? -India's Gevra & Kusmunda coal mines
89. What was the theme for World Listening Day 2024, celebrated on 18th July? -Listening to the Weave of Time
90. What was the theme of International Moon Day 2024, observed on 20th July? -Illuminating the Shadows
91. Which Indian cricketer recently joined MotoGP India as the brand ambassador? -Shikhar Dhawan.
92. Who recently represented India at the 4th Annual BIMSTEC Security Chiefs Meeting held in Naypyitaw? -Ajit Doval
93. Which tele consultancy services did the Indian Army launch for veterans recently? -E SeHAT Tele Consultancy
94. Which program did the Education Minister launch in August 2024, with Rs. 100 crore in stipends? -NATS 2.0
95. When and where is the 32nd International Conference of Agricultural Economists being held? -2nd to 7th August 2024 in New Delhi
96. What position has India taken in the Indo Pacific Economic Framework for Prosperity (IPEF)? -Vice Chair of the Supply Chain Council
97. What special status was granted to KIIT DU by the UN ECOSOC? -Special Consultative Status.
98. Where did India rank in the Travel & Tourism Development Index 2024? -39th
99. Which new app did Zomato launch to target the 'going out' market? -District
100. What position did India retain in global agriculture exports in 2023 according to the WTO? -Eighth position
101. Which ministry and organization signed a donor agreement recently? -Ayush Ministry and WHO
102. Which countries are collaborating to preserve maritime history in Lothal? -India and Vietnam
103. Which state is home to Tata Group's ₹27,000 crore semiconductor facility? -Assam.
104. Which digital initiative did Amit Shah launch in August 2024? -e Sakshya, Nyaya Setu, Nyaya Shruti, and e Summon App.
105. What exhibition did the Textile Ministry kickstart for the 10th National Handloom Day? -VIRAASAT exhibition
106. Which country did India sign a $500 million agreement with for the Green National Highway Corridor project? -World Bank
107. Which country's commemorative stamps were released for the 33rd Paris Olympics? -India
108. Which bank became the first private sector lender to merge UPI and NCMC in RuPay credit cards? -RBL Bank
109. Which state introduced a new disaster risk management solution in collaboration with SBI General Insurance? -Nagaland
110. Which company acquired the French software firm Zeenea for €24 million? -HCLTech
111. Who became the new MD & CEO of Unity Small Finance Bank? -Inderjit Camotra
112. Who was sworn in as the new Governor of Jharkhand? -Santosh Kumar Gangwar
113. Who has been appointed as the new MD of National Housing Bank? -Sanjay Shukla
114. Who has been appointed as the new High Commissioner of India to Rwanda? -Mridu Pawan Das
115. Who became the first woman DG of Medical Services (Army)? -Lt Gen Sadhna Saxena Nair
116. Who took charge as the new Director General of BSF in August 2024? -Daljit Singh Chawdhary
117. Who has been appointed as the new CEO of Boeing? -Kelly Ortberg.
118. Who was appointed as the ambassador for the SA20 league? -Dinesh Karthik.
119. Who was appointed as the next Director of ICAR Central Marine Fisheries Research Institute (CMFRI)? -Grinson George
120. Who became the new DG of Assam Rifles in August 2024? -Lieutenant General Vikas Lakhera

121. Who was appointed as the new Member in the Central Electricity Regulatory Commission in August 2024? -Harish Dudani

122. Who became the Chief Adviser of Interim Government of Bangladesh?-Muhammad Yunus

123. Who was appointed as Additional Secretary in the PM's Office in October 2024? -Subhasish Panda

124. Who was appointed as the new Chairman of SBI? -Challa Sreenivasulu Setty

125. Who will step down as the CEO of DBS Bank India in March 2025? -Piyush Gupta

126. Who was sworn in as the 25th Lieutenant Governor of Puducherry? -K. Kailashnathan

127. Who was appointed as the new head coach of the Indian junior men's hockey team? -PR Sreejesh

128. Who is the current caretaker PM of Bulgariaas of December 2024? -Dimitar Glavchev

129. Who was recently appointed as the new Cabinet Secretary for India for 2 years? -T V Somanathan

130. Who is the current Chairman & Managing Director of NHPC Ltd? -Raj Kumar Chaudhary

131. Who was sworn in as the 18th Governor of Sikkim? -Om Prakash Mathur

132. Who was appointed as the new MD of SBI? -Rana AK Singh

133. Who took charge as Secretary of the Ministry of Steel? -Sandeep Poundrik

134. Which Indian company won the Global Water Tech Award for its environmental initiatives? -DMRC (Delhi Metro Rail Corporation)

135. Who won the V Venkayya Epigraphy Award 2024? -V. Vedachalam

136. Which Indian leader was conferred the "Companion of the Order of Fiji"? -President Droupadi Murmu

137. Which Indian wrestler was disqualified from the Paris Olympics in August 2024? -Vinesh Phogat

138. Which Indian athlete became the first to qualify for the 3000m steeplechase final in the Olympics? -Avinash Sable

139. Who became the flag bearer for India at the Paris Olympics Closing Ceremony? -Manu Bhaker and PR Sreejesh

140. Who became India's youngest boxing referee at the Olympics? -Lt Col Kabilan Sai Ashok

141. Which international day is observed on 9th August to protect indigenous peoples' rights? -International Day of the World's Indigenous Peoples.

142. Which anniversary of its Independence Day was celebrated by India on 15 August 2024? -78th Independence Day

143. Which former YouTube CEO passed away recently? -Susan Wojcicki.

144. Which three Ramsar wetland sites were recently added to India, taking the total to 85 in August 2024? -Nanjarayan Bird Sanctuary, Kazhuveli Bird Sanctuary, and Tawa Reservoir.

145. Which airport in India became the first to receive the 'Net Zero Carbon Emission' status in August 2024? -Delhi Airport.

146. Which app did the Jal Shakti Minister launch in August 2024 to enhance flood monitoring? -FloodWatch India App (version 2.0).

147. Which scheme did the Uttar Pradesh government launch in August 2024 to promote youth entrepreneurship? Mukhyamantri Yuva Udyami Vikas Abhiyan

148. Who won the gold medal for India in the individual event of SL3 category of Paralympic badminton at Paris 2024 Paralympics? -Nitesh Kumar

149. Who is the first Indian female athlete to win two medals in track and field events in Paralympics? -Preeti Pal

150. How many crores of rupees has been approved by the Union Cabinet for the Digital Agriculture Mission in September 2024? -2,817 crores

151. In which event did Sumit Antil win the gold medal in Paris Paralympics 2024? -Javelin Throw F64 class

152. Recently which state assembly passed the anti rape 'Aparajita' bill? -West Bengal

153. In which city of UP the three day Armed Forces Festival is organized? -Lucknow

154. Which country will host the ICC World Test Championship final in the year 2025? -England

155. Who has been appointed by Hero MotoCorp as the Executive Vice President of the company? -Sanjay Bhan

156. The World Bank has raised India's growth forecast for FY25 to _____ in October 2024. -7.0%

157. Who has become the first Indian PM to make an official bilateral visit to Brunei ? -Narendra Modi

158. For which discovery Victor Ambrose and Gary Ruvkun were awarded the Nobel Prize in Medicine for the year 2024? -Discovery of microRNA

159. In which state did PM Modi inaugurate the Banjara Heritage Museum? -Maharashtra

160. Who was awarded the Nobel Prize for Medicine for the year 2024? -Victor Ambrose and Gary Ruvkun

161. Who launched the logo, website and app of the upcoming Maha Kumbh Mela 2025? -Yogi Adityanath

162. Who has been appointed by BCCI as the new chairman of its Anti Corruption Unit? -Sharad Kumar

163. Recently which state government launched 'Nijut Moina' scheme for female students? -Assam

164. Who was awarded the Nobel Prize for Chemistry for the year 2024? -David Baker, Demis Hassabis and John M. Jumper

165. Who has been recently appointed as the next Ambassador of India to France? -Sanjeev Kumar Singla

166. When is World Postal Day celebrated every year? -09 October

167. Who was awarded the Nobel Prize in Physics for the year 2024? -John Hopfield and Geoffrey Hinton

168. Who has been chosen as the new MD of Nestle India? -Manish Tiwary

169. Who has recently been appointed the head coach of the Sri Lankan cricket team? -Sanath Jayasuriya

170. Who has been awarded the Nobel Prize for Literature for the year 2024? Han Kang

171. Which country won the bronze medal in Asian Table Tennis Women's Championship 2024? -India

172. Where did PM Modi recently inaugurate the Indian Institute of Skills? -Mumbai

173. Han Kang, who was awarded the Nobel Prize for Literature this year, is a citizen of which country? -South Korea

174. Which organization was awarded the Nobel Peace Prize in the year 2024? -Nihon Hidankyo Organization

175. Who has been appointed as the new chairman of Tata Trust in October 2024? -Noel Tata

176. In which district of Bihar will the state's second tiger reserve be established? -Kaimur

177. Which Indian state's Postal Circle issued a commemorative cover in honor of Ratan Naval Tata's contributions? -Bihar

178. The 2024 Nobel Prize in Economics was awarded to Daron Acemoglu, Simon Johnson and James A. Robinson for the study of -"How institutions are formed and affect prosperity"

179. Who was recently appointed as the additional CEO of Government e Marketplace (GeM)? -L Satya Srinivas

180. Harmanpreet Kaur set a national record in which weight category in the National Weightlifting Championships 2024? -76 kg senior women's category

181. Who was recently appointed as MD and CEO of Bandhan Bank? -Partha Pratim Sengupta

182. Who took oath as the new Chief Minister of Jammu and Kashmir in October 2024? -Omar Abdullah

183. Who was crowned as ICC Male Player of the Month for September 2024? -Kamindu Mendis

184. Who built the Indian Navy's new ship 'Sampark'? -L&T Shipyard

185. Who was crowned as ICC Female Player of the Month for September 2024? -Tammy Beaumont

186. Who has been appointed as the Deputy Chief Minister (DCM) of Jammu and Kashmir? -Surinder Kumar Choudhary

187. Who is the second Indian women's cricketer inducted into the ICC Hall of Fame? -Neetu David

188. Which country hosted the 23rd SCO meeting in October 2024? -Pakistan

189. Who has taken oath as the new Chief Minister of Haryana -Nayab Singh Saini

190. Where was India's first airport based self operated indoor air quality monitoring facility launched? -Thiruvananthapuram

191. Who has been appointed as the national brand ambassador of the Indian Cyber Crime Coordination Centre (I4C)? -Rashmika Mandanna
192. Recently, India signed a drone deal worth $3.5 billion with which country? -USA
193. Indian Navy's 1st Training Squadron (1TS) completed long distance training deployment in -Manama, Bahrain
194. Who was recently appointed as the Director of Cricket at JSW Sports? -Sourav Ganguly
195. Recently which state government has been preparing to declare Sanskrit as a compulsory subject? -Uttarakhand
196. The Ministry of Rural Development has recently tied up with how many banks for personal financing for high scale enterprises? -10
197. Which Indian batsman completed his 9000 runs in Test Matches in October 2024? -Virat Kohli
198. Who has been appointed as the new chairperson of National Commission for Women? -Vijaya Kishor Rahatkar
199. Which bowler recently achieved the milestone of taking 300 wickets in the fewest number of balls in Test cricket? -Kagiso Rabada
200. The Indian Army organized the 'Swavlamban Shakti Exercise' in which state? -Jhansi, Uttar Pradesh
201. Which corps unit of Indian Army participated in the 'Swavalamban Shakti Exercise' of Indian Army? -Sudarshan Chakra Corps
202. Who has been appointed as the new President of Indian Chamber of Commerce in October 2024? -Abhyuday Jindal
203. Which country hosted the BRICS Summit 2024? -Russia
204. Many sports have been excluded from the 2026 edition of the Commonwealth Games, where will it be held? -Glasgow
205. The National Para Swimming Championship 2024 was organized in ____ -Panaji
206. How many years has the central government recently extended the regional flight scheme? -10 years
207. In which district of UP a new airport was inaugurated under the Udan scheme? -Saharanpur
208. Which country has named the cyclonic storm 'Dana' that arose in the Bay of Bengal? Qatar
209. Who represented India in BRICS Summit 2024? -PM Narendra Modi
210. When was 'National Learning Week' or 'Karmayogi Saptah' organized? -19 to 25 October
211. Who launched the new logo of Bharat Sanchar Nigam Limited (BSNL)? -Jyotiraditya Scindia
212. Luong Cuong has been elected as the new President of which country? -Vietnam
213. Which player scored the fastest double century in List A cricket? -Chad Bowes
214. Which country was recently declared malaria free by the World Health Organization? -Egypt
215. The Pravasi Parichay 2024 program was organized in the Indian Embassy of which country? -Saudi Arabia
216. Two railway projects have been approved recently to connect how many districts of Andhra Pradesh, Telangana and Bihar with the rail network? -8 districts
217. Who has been recently appointed as the CEO of JP Morgan Chase India? -Pranav Chawda
218. Who was recently awarded the Global Anti Racism Championship Award 2024? -Urmila Chaudhary
219. The Leadership Summit 2024 was held at the ______. -IIT Guwahati
220. When is World Development Information Day celebrated every year? -24 October
221. Which bank was recently declared the best bank of India for 2024 by Global Finance Magazine? -State Bank of India
222. Barda Wildlife Sanctuary was inaugurated in which state? -Gujarat
223. In which state was India's first private military aircraft factory inaugurated? -Gujarat
224. The Under 23 Wrestling World Championship 2024 was organized in ____. -Tirana, Albania
225. Which state government has recently announced the creation of a 'Special Education Zone' in the state? -Uttar Pradesh
226. "Special Education Zones were created in how many districts of Uttar Pradesh?" -6 districts
227. Who inaugurated and laid the foundation stone of health care projects worth about Rs 13,000 crore on the occasion of Dhanvantari Jayanti and 9th Ayurveda Day? -Prime Minister Narendra Modi
228. Who flagged off the 'Run for Unity' organized in New Delhi as part of National Unity Day 2024? -Amit Shah
229. Who won the Ballon d'Or 2024 Men's Player of the Year award? -Rodri
230. What are the names of the two Indigenous patrol vessels recently launched by the Indian Coast Guard? -'Adamya' and 'Akshar'
231. In which state was the country's first 'Writers Village' inaugurated? -Dehradun, Uttarakhand
232. Who was recently appointed as the Chairman of Airport Authority of India? -Vipin Kumar
233. What is India's rank in the World Justice Project's 2024 Rule of Law Index? -79
234. What is the rank of Nepal in the World Justice Project's 2024 Rule of Law Index? -69
235. In October 2024, who has been recommended for the position of managing director (MD) & chief executive officer (CEO) of Punjab National Bank by Financial Services Institutions Bureau (FSIB)? -Ashok Chandra
236. Which female footballer won the Women's Ballon d'Or Award in 2024? -Aitana Bonmati
237. When is National Ayurveda Day celebrated every year? -On Dhanvantari Jayanti
238. Matthew Wade has recently announced his retirement from cricket, he is a player of which country? -Australia
239. In which city of Himachal Pradesh was the state's first digital library inaugurated -Bilaspur
240. Who took over the appointment as Air Officer in Charge Maintenance of the Indian Air Force? -Air Marshal Ajay Kumar Arora
241. India's first analog space mission has been launched at ________. -Leh, Ladakh
242. Recently Bibek Debroy passed away, he was a famous person in which field? -Economics
243. What is the current total gold reserve held by the Reserve Bank of India (RBI) as of September 2024? -854.73 metric tons
244. Who among the following recently took charge as Defense Secretary? -Rajesh Kumar Singh
245. Who recently unveiled the Ayushman Vaya Vandana Card, free healthcare for all senior citizens above 70 years of age? -PM Narendra Modi
246. Who has been elected as the President of International Solar Alliance for two-year term? -India
247. Where was the annual meeting of the International Solar Alliance organized in November 2024? -New Delhi
248. Which medal did Atanu Das win in Swiss Open 2024 archery Championship? -Bronze
249. Duma Boko has been elected President of which country? Botswana
250. Where was the first Asian Buddhist Summit held? -New Delhi
251. With which country did India sign a Memorandum of Understanding (MoU) for bilateral defense relations in November 2024? -Algeria
252. The joint military exercise 'Vinbax' is organized between India and which country? -Vietnam
253. Which country has fined Meta nearly $15 million over a collection of user data? -South Korea
254. Recently, the Punjab government has increased the dearness allowance (DA) for government employees by what percentage? -4%
255. In which category did Kannada short film 'Sunflowers Were the First Ones to Know' secure a place in Oscars 2025? -Best Live Action Short Film category
256. Where was the International Ancient Arts Festival 2024 organized? -New Delhi
257. Which country's tourism department has appointed actor Sonu Sood as a brand ambassador for tourism? -Thailand
258. Who was elected as the President of International Hockey Federation in November 2024? -Tayyab Ikram
259. When is National Education Day celebrated every year? -11 November
260. In which city of Uttar Pradesh the state's first double decker electric bus service was launched? -Lucknow
261. Who has been sworn in as the 51st Chief Justice of India? -Justice Sanjiv Khanna

262. Who has been replaced by Justice Sanjeev Khanna, the new Chief Justice of India? -DY Chandrachud
263. Where has INSV Tarini reached for the first phase of Navika Sagar Parikrama II campaign? -Fremantle, Australia
264. Who has been chosen by the newly elected President of USA Donald Trump as the secretary of defense? -Pete Hegseth
265. Where is the United Nations Climate Change Conference (COP29) was organized -Baku (Azerbaijan)
266. Who is the Foreign Secretary to whom the government has given extension in November 2024? -Vikram Misri
267. The Union Home Ministry has approved the creation of the first all women battalion in which security force? -CISF
268. In which Indian city the Russian Business Center was inaugurated? -New Delhi
269. Who has been appointed as the new Chairman of Indian Oil Corporation? -Arvindar Singh Sahney
270. Recently Vistara Airlines has been merged with ______. -Air India
271. In which city of Bihar did Prime Minister Narendra Modi laid the foundation stone of AIIMS recently? -Darbhanga
272. Who has been chosen by the newly elected President of USA Donald Trump as the Secretary of State? -Marco Rubio
273. Recently 'Garuda Shakti' exercise was organized between India and which country? -Indonesia
274. Which edition of the Pan-India Coastal Defence Exercise Sea Vigil 24 concluded recently successfully on 21 Nov. 2024? -4th
275. Sukhna Lake, which was in the news recently, is in which city? -Chandigarh
276. When is World Diabetes Day celebrated every year? -14 November
277. Who has been awarded the Booker Prize 2024 for the novel "Orbital" based on the International Space Station? -Samantha Harvey
278. The State of the Climate Report 2024 has been recently released by? -CSIRO and the Bureau of Meteorology
279. Who inaugurated the India International Trade Fair in New Delhi? -Piyush Goyal
280. Who has been appointed as the new brand ambassador of Madhya Pradesh Tourism Department recently? -Pankaj Tripathi
281. Recently, which state government has announced 100% exemption on road and registration taxes for electric vehicles? -Telangana
282. Recently, coastal villages of which state have been recognized as 'Tsunami Ready' by UNESCO? -Odisha
283. Nugu Wildlife Sanctuary, which was in the news recently, is located in which state? -Karnataka
284. Which country has recently launched the 'Global Energy Efficiency Alliance'? -UAE
285. Who has been recently elected as the new Secretary General of Interpol? -Valdecy Urquiza
286. Who has been appointed as the new brand ambassador of Dubai Sports Council? -Sania Mirza and Harbhajan Singh
287. The G20 Summit 2024 was organized in ______. -Rio de Janeiro (Brazil)
288. Who has been appointed as the new Comptroller and Auditor General (CAG) of the country recently? -Sanjay Murthy
289. Which has become 56th tiger reserve of India? -Guru Ghasidas Tamor Pingla Tiger Reserve
290. Which committee recommended the introduction of Grievance Redressal Assessment and Index (GRAI)? -Parliamentary Standing Committee
291. Recently which communication satellite of India was launched by SpaceX's Falcon 9 rocket? -GSAT N2 (GSAT 20)
292. Who won the Tata Steel Chess Blitz title in November 2024? -Magnus Carlsen
293. Which country has recently approved a new constitution through a referendum? -Gabon
294. ______ became the winner of the 14th Hockey India Senior National Championship 2024. -Odisha
295. Which state won the title of the 4th National Finswimming Championship? -West Bengal
296. Guru Ghasidas Tamor Pingla Tiger Reserve is located in which state? -Chhattisgarh
297. Who has recently resigned from the post of MD and CEO of Zee Entertainment? -Punit Goenka
298. Which country will host the first 'Kho Kho' World Cup in 2025? -India
299. The 'Global Alliance Against Hunger and Poverty' was recently released during which conference? -G20
300. With which countries has India agreed to use digital public infrastructure and AI to reduce global inequality? -Brazil, South Africa
301. Who won the double title of Maharashtra State Open Badminton Tournament 2024? -Harshit Mahimkar and Prisha Shah
302. Recently the United Nations has named Bastar village of which state as a tourist destination? -Chhattisgarh
303. India's first night safari park is being developed in which city? -Lucknow
304. In which state was the joint military exercise 'Purvi Prahar' organized in November 2024? -Arunachal Pradesh
305. Who won the title of Women's Asian Hockey Champions Trophy 2024? -India
306. SECI has signed MoU with which organization to promote Green Hydrogen initiative? -H2 Global
307. ADB has recently approved a loan of €89.47 million ($100 million equivalent) to which country to boost sustainability, climate resilience -Sri Lanka
308. Who launched India's first Artificial Intelligence (AI) data bank? -Dr Jitendra Singh
309. Which OTT platform was launched by India's public broadcaster Prasar Bharati? -Waves
310. Recently, which country has become the 104th member of the International Solar Alliance (ISA)? -Armenia
311. Who has been appointed as the Chief Election Commissioner of Bangladesh recently? -AMM Nasir Uddin
312. Which state will host the Khelo India Youth Games and Khelo India Para Games (KIPG) in 2025? -Bihar
313. Recently ISRO has signed an agreement with which country's space agency for 'Gaganyaan' mission? -Australia
314. When will the IPL 2025 season start? -14 March 2025
315. Recently how many artists have been awarded with Ustad Bismillah Khan Yuva Puraskar for the Years 2022 and 2023? -82
316. "Ab Koi Bahana Nahi" campaign has been launched in collaboration with ______. -UN Women
317. Recently Dinesh Bhatia was appointed as the next Ambassador of India to which country? -Brazil
318. Who is the youngest player to be sold in IPL auction history? -Vaibhav Suryavanshi (13 Years)
319. Who has become the most expensive player in IPL auction history? -Rishabh Pant (27 Crore)
320. When is Constitution Day celebrated every year in India? -26 November
321. Which team bought Rishabh Pant, the most expensive player in IPL auction history? -Lucknow Super Giants
322. Recently the famous writer Breyten Breytenbach passed away, he belonged to which country? -South Africa
323. Who has taken oath as the Chief Minister of Jharkhand in November 2024? -Hemant Soren
324. With which country India has recently started bilateral exercise "Agniwarrior 2024"? -Singapore
325. Where has Indian Coast Guard's National Maritime Search and Rescue Exercise and Workshop (SAREX 24) been conducted? -Kochi, Kerala
326. Which Union Minister recently launched the national campaign "Child Marriage Free India"? -Annapurna Devi
327. Who has been recently appointed as the new Chief of Brahmos Aerospace? -Dr Jaiteerth R Joshi
328. Where was India's first green hydrogen fuel station inaugurated? -Leh
329. Who won the title of the recently held Las Vegas Grand Prix? -Max Verstappen
330. What is India's rank in the Network Readiness Index 2024? -49th

331. Who has been nominated by the newly elected US President Donald Trump as special envoy for Russia and Ukraine? **-Keith Kellogg**

332. Recently Amiya Kumar Bagchi passed away, he was a famous person in which field? **-Economics**

333. Where was the International Tourism Mart organized recently -Kaziranga National Park

334. Which film won the Golden Peacock Award for Best Film at the 55th International Film Festival of India? **-Toxic**

335. When will the anniversary of 'Pran Pratishtha' of Ayodhya Ram Temple be celebrated next year? **-11 January 2025**

336. Which scheme was launched by Maharashtra on the occasion of Raksha Bandhan in August 2024 for the benefits of women across the state? **-Mukhyamantri Majhi Ladki Bahin Yojana.**

337. India and which country joined forces to create a new water technology centre at IIT Madras in August 2024? **-Israel**

338. Which company was ranked as the world's strongest food brand in Brand Finance Food & Drink 2024 Report? **-Amul**

339. India recently approved an additional 251 MW of power exports from which country in August 2024? **-Nepal**

340. Which foundation signed an MoU with the India Meteorological Department (IMD) to strengthen weather information in August 2024? **-Reliance Foundation**

341. Which commission partnered with the Department of Posts to accelerate PMEGP unit verification in August 2024? **-Khadi and Village Industries Commission**

342. Which electric vehicle manufacturer became the only EV maker to secure PLI certification for four electric scooters in August 2024? **-Ola Electric**

343. Which organization partnered with Hindustan Zinc Ltd. to scale up indigenous Zn ion battery technologies in August 2024? **-JNCASR**

344. Which university established India's first Constitution Museum to commemorate the 75th anniversary of the Constitution? **-OP Jindal Global University, Sonipat**

345. Which country recently announced visa free access to Indians and nationals from 34 other countries from October 31, 2024? **-Sri Lanka**

346. Which country joined the BRICS partners for the launch of the Centre for Industrial Competences in August 2024? **-UAE**

347. Which fintech company collaborated with Karnataka Bank to introduce a credit line on UPI in August 2024? **-Navi Technologies**

348. Which financial institution launched an AI powered face match feature for secure banking transactions? **-Airtel Payments Bank**

349. Who was appointed as the new Home Secretary of India in August 2024? **-Govind Mohan**

350. Who has been appointed as the Permanent Representative of India to the United Nations? **-Shri Parvathaneni Harish**

351. Who has been appointed as the full time Chief of Enforcement Directorate (ED)? **-Rahul Navin**

352. Who has been appointed as the new CEO of NASSCOM in August 2024? **-Sindhu Gangadharan**

353. Which Indian state won the best airport award for the third consecutive year in 2024? **-RGIA Hyderabad**

354. Who ranked as the top central banker globally for the second consecutive year in 2024? **-RBI Governor Shaktikanta Das**

355. Who presented the National Geoscience Awards 2023 in August 2024? **-President Droupadi Murmu**

356. Which Indian athlete won silver medal at the Lausanne Diamond League 2024 Championship? **-Neeraj Chopra**

357. Who has become First Indian female Racer to win National Car Racing Championship? **-Diana Pundole**

358. Who has won the F1 Dutch Grand Prix 2024? **-Lando Norris.**

359. Which country launched the world's first mobile launched hybrid rocket, RHUMI I, in August 2024? **-India**

360. Which renowned DRDO scientist passed away at the age of 83 in August 2024? **-Ram Narain Agarwal ('Father of Agni Missiles')**

361. Which veteran Congress leader passed away in August 2024? **-Vasantrao Chavan**

362. Which former Prime Minister of Lebanon passed away at the age of 94 in August 2024? **-Salim al Hoss.**

363. In which State 'Subhadra Scheme' has been launched by Prime Minister Shri Narendra Modi in September 2024? **-Odisha**

364. Which chatbox, developed by Eastern Railway, aims to provide easier access to railway rules in August 2024? **-Prabodh**

365. Which Indian state government plans to convert the Samanatham Tank into a bird sanctuary? **-Tamil Nadu**

366. Which project was initiated to boost science and technology ecosystems by the Indian government in August 2024? **-Vigyan Dhara Scheme**

367. Prime Minister Narendra Modi presented BHISHM Cubes to which country during his first visit to Kyiv in August 2024? **-Ukraine**

368. Which country launched a new suicide drone, named "Kamikaze" in August 2024, marking a significant military development? **-North Korea**

369. Which bank announced the launch of its 'Avni Saving Account for Women' in August 2024? **-Bandhan Bank**

370. Which financial institution is the first to launch the Unified Lending Interface (ULI) to facilitate credit for small, rural borrowers? **-RBI**

371. Who was appointed as the Chairman and CEO of the Railway Board in August 2024? **-Satish Kumar**

372. Who was appointed as the new Director General of the NSG (National Security Guard)? **-B Srinivasan**

373. Which country appointed Fatemeh Mohajerani as its first female government spokesperson in August 2024? **-Iran**

374. Who has taken over as the youngest president of ICC? **-Jai Shah**

375. With which country does India organize the joint military exercise 'Harimau Shakti'? **-Malaysia**

376. When is National Pollution Control Day celebrated every year? **-02 December**

377. Which state launched Mission 'Arun Himveer' recently to enhance market linkages for local agricultural and horticultural producers? **-Arunachal Pradesh**

378. With which company did GAIL sign a long-term charter contract for LNG ship in November 2024? **-"K" Line**

379. Arjun Erigasi becomes ________Indian player to achieve 2800 Elo rating in classical chess. **-Second**

380. Who has been nominated by newly elected US President Donald Trump as FBI Director? **-Kash Patel**

381. Who laid the foundation stone of a modern head post office in Ashoknagar, Madhya Pradesh **-Union Minister Jyotiraditya Scindia**

382. Ratapani Wildlife Sanctuary has been declared the eighth Tiger Reserve of which state Recently? **-Madhya Pradesh**

383. Which Indian state has recently been declared as the top destination for heritage tourism by UNESCO? **-West Bengal**

384. Recently USA provided military aid worth of how many million dollars to Ukraine? **-725 million dollars**

385. Bihar Pavilion was awarded which award in the 43rd Indian International Trade Fair? **-Gold Award**

386. GST on products like cigarettes and tobacco is expected to be increased to what percentage? **-35%**

387. Who won the bronze medal in e-football at the 2024 Asian Esports Games? **-Pavan Kampelli**

388. When did India Post Payments Bank (IPPB) recently celebrate its 7th Foundation Day? **-September 1, 2024**

389. What motto is inscribed on the new insignia of the Supreme Court of India? **-"Yato Dharmastato Jayah"**

390. What semiconductor unit was approved by the Union Cabinet in September 2024, and where is it located? **-Kaynes Semicon, Gujarat (Sanand)**

391. What is India's target for global alcoholic beverage exports as of September 2024? **-Rs. 8,000 crore**

392. What new fashion forecasting initiative was launched recently by India's Textile Ministry? **-'VisioNxt'**

393. When and where was th.e Khel Utsav 2024 organized recently? -August 27-30, New Delhi

394. 'Brindavan Gram' model villages scheme was launched by which state government recently? -Madhya Pradesh

395. What was the focus of the "Vishanu Yuddh Abhyas" conducted recently in Rajasthan? -Pandemic preparedness

396. Who approved the constitution of the 23rd Law Commission of India, recently? -President Draupadi Murmu

397. Who recently inaugurated IIT Delhi's campus in Abu Dhabi? -Sheikh Khaled bin Mohamed bin Zayed Al Nahyan

398. Which powerful storm hit Southeast Asia in September 2024? -Typhoon Yagi

399. Who assumed the role of AOC-In-C, Central Air Command on September 1, 2024? -Air Marshal Ashutosh Dixit

400. Who is currently working as Union Minister of Parliamentary Affairs and Minority Affairs? -Kiren Rijiju

401. Who is the newly appointed Managing Director of Philips India as of September 2024? Bharath Sesha

402. Which Bollywood actress was recently named L'Oreal Paris Global Ambassador? -Alia Bhatt

403. Who was recently appointed as a member of Indian men's cricket team Selection Committee? -Ajay Ratra

404. What was India's GST collection in August 2024? -₹1.75 lakh crore

405. Which company recently became India's first to surpass ₹10 lakh crore in revenue? -Reliance Industries Limited

406. What new insurance policies did Star Health introduce recently for the visually impaired? -Braille

407. Where was the first Joint Commander's Conference of the Indian Armed Forces recently held? -Lucknow

408. What fund was recently launched by Union Agriculture Minister Shivraj Singh Chouhan for agricultural start-ups? -₹750 crore

409. When was the Agni-4 IRBM successfully tested recently? -September 6, 2024

410. Which Japanese animator received the Ramon Magsaysay Award in 2024? -Hayao Miyazaki

411. Which ministry recently won the e-Governance Gold Award for the Poshan Tracker initiative? -Ministry of Women and Child Development

412. Which athlete becomes India's First Female Pistol Para-Shooting Medallist after winning Bronze medal in Women's 10m Air Pistol SH1 event at the Paris Paralympics 2024? -Rubina Francis

413. Who became the first Indian woman to win two Paralympic medals in athletics? -Preethi Pal

414. Which Indian athlete won silver in the men's T47 high jump at the Paris Paralympics 2024? -Nishad Kumar

415. Where will the ICC World Test Championship Final be held in 2025? -Lord's Cricket Ground

416. Which team recently won their first Durand Cup title? -NorthEast United FC

417. Which athlete won Gold medal in the women's air pistol event at the World Deaf Shooting Championship in Hannover, Germany? -Anuya Prasad

418. Who won India's first-ever Paralympic gold medal in archery at the Paris 2024 Paralympics? -Harvinder Singh

419. What medal did Sachin Sarjerao Khilari win in the men's F46 shot put event at the Paris 2024 Paralympics? -Silver

420. Which athletes won gold and silver in the men's F51 club throw event at the Paris 2024 Paralympics? -Dharambir (gold) and Pranav Soorma (silver)

421. Who won India's first Paralympic judo medal? -Kapil Parmar (Bronze)

422. What medal did Hokato Hotozhe Sema win at the Paris 2024 Paralympics? -Bronze

423. Who won Gold medal in men's high jump T64 at the Paris Paralympics 2024? -Praveen Kumar

424. Who secured Bronze medal in mixed team compound archery event at the Paris 2024 Paralympics? -Sheetal Devi and Rakesh Kumar

425. Which Indian badminton player won silver in the men's singles SL4 category at the Paris 2024 Paralympics? -Suhas Yathiraj

426. Who won gold Medal in men's javelin throw F64 at the Paris 2024 Paralympics? -Sumit Antil

427. When is National Nutrition Week observed? -September 1 to 7

428. When is the International Day of Police Cooperation observed? -7 September

429. Who made a historic debut at the Gama International Fighting Championship 2024? -Sangram Singh

430. Who won the title of Miss India Worldwide 2024? -Dhruvi Patel

431. Who received the ICC Lifetime Achievement Award 2023? -Deepak C Mehta

432. Who was appointed as the Director General of the Aeronautical Development Agency with effect from September 11, 2024? -Jitendra J Jadhav

433. Who has been elected as the President of the National Rifle Association of India? -Kalikesh Singh Deo

434. What was celebrated on September 24 to recognize the influence of Indian cinema? -World Bollywood Day

435. Who inaugurated the 16th ASOSAI Assembly in India? -President Droupadi Murmu

436. Which country celebrated the ninth anniversary of its Constitution declaration in September 2024? -Nepal

437. What initiative did the Delhi government launch to support local communities in tourism? -Paryatan Mitra and Paryatan Didi Initiative

438. Who took charge as the MD and CEO of Federal Bank? -KVS Manian

439. Who was appointed as the first director of the UN's Loss and Damage Fund? -Ibrahima Cheikh Diong

440. Which Indian cricketer joined the elite club with 400 international wickets in September 2024? -Jasprit Bumrah

441. Which award did Odisha swimmer Pratyasa Ray receive for her achievements in swimming? -32nd Ekalabya Puraskar

442. Who was appointed as the Chief of the National Crime Records Bureau? -Alok Ranjan

443. Where was the Confederation of Indian Industry (CII) Partnership Summit 2024 held? -New Delhi

444. Netumbo Nandi-Ndaitwah has been elected as the first female president of which country? -Namibia

445. Which organization was officially recognized as an awarding body by NCVET in the space sector? -Indian National Space Promotion and Authorization Center (IN-SPACe)

446. Where was the Confederation of Indian Industry (CII) Partnership Summit 2024 held? -New Delhi

447. What is the name of the innovative water purification technology launched at the National Zoological Park, Delhi? -Nano Bubble Technology

448. Netumbo Nandi-Ndaitwah has been elected as the first female president of which country? -Namibia

449. Which word has been selected as Oxford Word of the Year 2024? -Brain Rot

450. What is the name of portal developed by Department of Consumer Affairs for fair trade and consumer protection? -National Legal Metrology Portal (eMaap)

451. Which state/UT is the host of International Gita Mahotsav-2024? -Haryana

452. Which country won the Men's Hockey Junior Asia Cup 2024 title in Muscat, Oman? -India

453. Which day is observed as Mahaparinirvan Diwas every year? -December 6

454. What is the name of the Public Distribution System (PDS) Supply Chain optimization tool launched by government of India? -Anna Chakra

455. What is the primary objective of Global Strategy for Resilient Drylands (GSRD) initiative launched at UNCCD COP16? -Enhance food security, conserve biodiversity, and build resilient livelihoods in drylands

456. Which country has been chosen to Chair the 68th Session of the Commission on Narcotic Drugs (CND)? -India

457. Rimtalba Jean Emmanuel Ouedraogo has been appointed as the Prime Minister of which country? -Burkina Faso

458. Where was the Rising Rajasthan Global Investment Summit 2024 organized? -Jaipur

459. What is the theme of India Internet Governance Forum (IIGF) 2024? -Innovating Internet Governance for India

460. Which day is observed as International Anti-Corruption Day every year? -December 9
461. Which state government recently launched the Urajveer Scheme to promote the energy efficient appliances? -Andhra Pradesh
462. Which Indian temple was selected by UNESCO for the 2023 Award of Distinction for its conservation? -Abathsahayeswarar Temple
463. Which organization has launched an AI model for weather prediction called GenCast? -Google
464. Pradhan Mantri Poshan Shakti Nirman (PM POSHAN) Scheme is an initiative of which ministry? -Ministry of Education
465. Pilibhit Tiger Reserve is located in which state? -Uttar Pradesh
466. Which country has developed the world's first carbon-14 diamond battery? -United Kingdom
467. Which Indian ecologist won the Champions of the Earth award 2024? -Madhav Gadgil
468. What is the name of the AI-powered platform developed by IIIT-Delhi for discovering molecules to slow down ageing? -AgeXtend
469. Which state government has launched the Indira Gandhi Sukh Shiksha Yojana? -Himachal Pradesh
470. Which ministry organized the India Maritime Heritage Conclave 2024 (IMHC 2024)? -Ministry of Ports, Shipping and Waterways
471. Yuva Sahakar Scheme has been implemented by which organization? -National Cooperative Development Corporation (NCDC)
472. Which organization has launched a quantum computing chip called Willow? -Google
473. What is the name of the chatbot launched by the Prime Minister to assist devotees during Mahakumbh Mela 2025? -Kumbh Sahayak
474. Who chaired India's fourth 'National Conference of Chief Secretaries' in 2024? -Prime Minister of India
475. Francois Bayrou has been appointed as the new prime minister of which country? -France
476. India's first diabetes biobank has been established in which city? -Chennai
477. Which country won the Women's Hockey Junior Asia Cup 2024? -India
478. Kaleshwaram Lift Irrigation Scheme (KLIS) is associated with which state? -Telangana
479. Mikheil Kavelashvili was elected as the new President of which country? -Georgia
480. What is the name of scheme launched by government to facilitate credit assess for farmers through e-NWRs? -Credit Guarantee Scheme
481. Where was Gujarat's first Outsourced Semiconductor Assembly and Testing (OSAT) plant inaugurated? -Surat
482. What is the theme of the 10th International Forest Fair organized by Madhya Pradesh? -Women Empowerment through Minor Forest Produce
483. Which Indian temple won 'Sword of Honour' award for safety excellence? -Ram Temple, Ayodhya
484. What is the name of India's first anti-pesticide bodysuit launched by Ministry of Science and Technology? -Kisan Kavach
485. Which day is celebrated as Minority Rights Day? -December 18
486. Which country has joined the International Solar Alliance (ISA) by signing the ISA Framework Agreement in December 2024? -Moldova
487. The Indian army has launched the "Artificial Intelligence Incubation Centre" in which city? -Bengaluru
488. Who has become the world's youngest world chess champion? -D Gukesh
489. With whom has BMW Group signed an agreement with the aim to transform the educational landscape in rural India? -UNESCO
490. President Draupadi Murmu conferred the honorary rank of 'General of the Indian Army' to the Army Chief of which country? -Nepal
491. In which city of Uttar Pradesh, PM Modi launched major development projects worth ₹5,500 crore? -Prayagraj
492. Who has been appointed as the new Executive Director of Yes Bank? -Manish Jain
493. Who was awarded the ICC Player of the Month award for November 2024? -Haris Rauf
494. Who has become the first female cricketer to score 4 ODI centuries in a calendar year? -Smriti Mandhana
495. Who will be honored with the Lifetime Achievement Award at the Directors Guild of America Awards? -Ang Lee
496. What position did India secure in the Asian Women's Handball Championship 2024? -Sixth
497. What is the full form of UCC? -Uniform Civil Code
498. Which award was conferred upon Tom Cruise by the US Navy? -Distinguished Public Service Award
499. Which team won the 2024 FIFA Intercontinental Cup? -Real Madrid
500. What is the name of the affordable housing scheme launched by West Bengal Chief Minister Mamata Banerjee? -Banglar Bari
501. What is the duration of the Good Governance Week 2024? -December 19 to December 24, 2024
502. What is the mascot for the 38th National Games 2025? -Mauli
503. Where was the Indian Army AI Incubation Centre (IAAIIC) launched? -Bengaluru
504. Which Women cricketer has scored the fastest test century in Test International? -Nat Sciver-Brunt
505. Which of the following is India's first indigenous anti-pesticide bodysuit? -Kisan Kavach
506. The Ram temple project in Ayodhya has been awarded which prestigious safety award? -Sword of Honour
507. The Gadhimai Festival is held in which country? -Nepal
508. Who was awarded the prestigious Jamsetji Tata Award by the Indian Society for Quality (ISQ)? -Kiran Mazumdar-Shaw
509. Which ministry launched a scheme to promote international cooperation for AYUSH systems worldwide? -Ministry of AYUSH
510. In which city was Uber's 'Moto Women' pilot program launched? -Bengaluru
511. What is the theme for International Migrants Day in 2024? -"Honouring the contributions of migrants and respecting their rights"
512. Who won The Best FIFA Men's Player award in 2024? -Vinicius Jr.
513. Which organization primarily uses the SARAT tool? -Indian Coast Guard
514. The eighth edition of the India International Science Festival (IISF) will be held in which city? -Bhopal
515. Which of the following country will host an International Conference "Standing with the Ukrainian People"? -France
516. Which airline has been awarded the 'Safety Performer of the Year' award by GMR Delhi Airport Awards for being the top performer among the self-handling airlines? -SpiceJet
517. Who has become the third cricketer in history to score 10000 Test runs and also takes 50 test wicket recently? -Joe Root
518. The 6th Edition of Indo – Kazakhstan joint training exercise "KAZIND-22" is conducted at Umroi, ________. -Meghalaya
519. Which country recently passed a law to completely end tobacco smoking by banning youth from buying cigarettes for life? -Italy
520. Which IIT has signed an MoU with Army Training Command to set up centre of excellence? -IIT Ropar
521. India plans to commission 20 nuclear power plants by ________. -2031
522. In which state was the foundation stone of ISRO's second spaceport laid? -Tamil Nadu (Kulasekharapattinam)
523. Who has been appointed by the World Gold Council as its new CEO for India? -Sachin Jain
524. When was 'Annual Financial Literacy' week organized by RBI in 2024? -February 26 - March 1
525. Whom did President Draupadi Murmu appoint as the Chairman of Lokpal in February 2024? - Ajay Manikrao Khanwilkar
526. With which country did the Ministry of AYUSH sign an agreement to promote Ayurveda in February 2024? -Thailand
527. With whom did the Election Commission start the 'Mera Pehla Vote Desh Ke Liye' campaign in February 2024? -Ministry of Education
528. What is the theme of National Science Day 2024? -"Indigenous Technologies for Viksit Bharat"

529. How many astronauts were nominated for the Gaganyaan mission in February 2024? **-4**

530. When is World NGO Day celebrated every year? **-27 February**

531. Where was a new regional office of the Central Board of Film Certification established in February 2024? **-Chandigarh**

532. In which Indian state was the world's first Vedic clock established in February 2024? **-Madhya Pradesh (Ujjain)**

533. Which New Zealand's fast bowler retired from international cricket in February 2024? **-Neil Wagner,**

534. Who made the record of the fastest century in T20 International cricket history in February 2024? **-Estonia's Sahil Chauhan**

535. In which country was the Mobile World Congress 2024 organized in February 2024? **-Spain**

536. How many railway stations were redeveloped under the Amrit Bharat Station Scheme as announced in February 2024? **-553**

537. Which is India's longest cable-stayed bridge, inaugurated by PM Modi in February 2024? **-Sudarshan Setu (Gujarat)**

538. Who inaugurated the global textile event 'Bharat Tex 2024' in February 2024? **-PM Narendra Modi**

539. Between which countries was the joint military exercise 'Dharma Guardian' organized in February 2024? **-India and Japan**

540. Who won the Best Male Actor Award at the Screen Actors Guild Awards in February 2024? **-Cillian Murphy**

541. In which country was the SAFF Under-16 Women's Championship organized in February 2024? **-Nepal**

542. Where was the global textile event 'Bharat Tex 2024' organized? **-New Delhi**

543. With whom did the Bihar state government sign an agreement to promote the startup ecosystem in February 2024? **-SIDBI**

544. Who laid the foundation stone of the first railway station of Sikkim state in February 2024? **-PM Narendra Modi**

545. When was the first match of IPL 2024 played between Chennai Super Kings and Royal Challenger Bangalore? **-22 March 2024**

546. Who was appointed as the new Vigilance Commissioner in the Central Vigilance Commission in February 2024? **-Shri AS Rajeev**

547. Where was the three-day International Geeta Mahotsav organized in February 2024? **-Colombo**

548. Former Speaker of Lok Sabha Manohar Joshi passed away in February 2024, he was also the former Chief Minister of which state? **-Maharashtra**

549. Who became the first Indian bowler to take 100 wickets against England in Test cricket in February 2024? **-Ravichandran Ashwin**

550. Which IIT launched India's largest drone pilot training facility in February 2024? **-IIT Guwahati**

551. Where were the Khelo India Youth Games 2024 held from 19 January to 31 January 2024? **-Tamil Nadu (Chennai, Madurai, Trichy and Coimbatore)**

552. What campaign did the Indian government launch in February 2024 to promote and monitor flagship central schemes? **-Viksit Bharat Sankalp Yatra**

553. Which heritage corridor project was unveiled by the Odisha CM in February 2024 around Puri's Jagannath Temple? **-"Shree Mandir Parikrama Prakalpa"**

554. Where did the Wings India 2024 event commence in February 2024? **-Begumpet Airport in Hyderabad**

555. Where was the 12th General Assembly of the Asian Buddhist Conference for Peace (ABCP) held in February 2024? **-New Delhi, India**

556. Who won The Best FIFA Men's Player Award in February 2024? **-Lionel Messi**

557. According to NITI Aayog, how many people lifted themselves out of poverty in the last nine years as of February 2024? **-Around 25 crore**

558. Where did the 54th World Economic Forum Summit begin in February 2024? **-Davos, Switzerland**

559. What significant ritual began for the consecration of Ram Lala Virajman in February 2024? **-Pran Pratishtha**

560. Who became the new King of Denmark in February 2024? **-Frederik X**

561. Who lost in the men's doubles final at the Malaysia Open Super 1000 in February 2024? **-Satwiksairaj Rankireddy and Chirag Shetty**

562. Who recently took oath as a judicial member of Lokpal? **-Ritu Raj Awasthi**

563. Who has been appointed by Microsoft as the new head of both Windows and Surface in March 2024? **-Pawan Davuluri**

564. Which Indian has been appointed by the UN Secretary General as his Special Representative for Disaster Risk Reduction in March 2024? **-Kamal Kishore**

565. Who has Rajasthan Royals included in the team as a replacement for Prasidh Krishna in March 2024? **-Keshav Maharaj**

566. Who is the first umpire from Bangladesh to be included in the ICC Elite Panel of Umpires in March 2024? **-Sharafuddaulah Ibne Shahid**

567. In which country is the Popocatepetl volcano, which was in discussion in March 2024, located? **-Mexico**

568. In which country is the Baltimore Bridge, which was in the news in March 2024, located? **-USA**

569. According to Brand Finance Insurance 100 2024 report, which is the strongest insurance brand? **-Life Insurance Corporation of India**

570. In which state was a 900-year-old Kannada inscription of the Kalyana Chalukya dynasty found in March 2024? **-Telangana**

571. Which team made the biggest team score in IPL history in March 2024? **-Sunrisers Hyderabad**

572. Who was appointed as Additional Judge of Jammu and Kashmir and Ladakh High Court in March 2024? **-Justice Mohammad Yusuf Wani**

573. 'Nimmu-Padam-Darcha' road connects which two states, as mentioned in March 2024? **-Ladakh and Himachal Pradesh**

574. Which Gulf country will participate in the Miss Universe pageant for the first time in March 2024? **-Saudi Arabia**

575. Who has been named as the new Ambassador of India to Myanmar in March 2024? **-Abhay Thakur**

576. Who has acquired Lanco Amarkantak Power Limited, as approved by CCI in March 2024? **-Adani Power Limited**

577. Who led the Indian delegation to the 148th meeting of the Inter-Parliamentary Union in Geneva in March 2024? **-Harivansh Narayan Singh**

578. Who won the gold medal in the 59 kg youth category in the recent Para Powerlifting World Cup in March 2024? **-Vinay**

579. Who has been appointed the head of the National Investigation Agency in March 2024? **-Sadanand Vasant Date**

580. Which app has been launched to make the election process easier for the disabled in March 2024? **-'Saksham'**

581. Chandrayaan-3 landing site was recognized by the International Astronomical Union, what was it named in March 2024? **-Statio 'Shiv Shakti'**

582. In which city will the Cinevistar International Film Festival be organized in March 2024? **-Chandigarh**

583. Who won two gold medals in the Indian Masters National Badminton Championship 2024 in March 2024? **-Naheed Divecha**

584. Which team won the title of Boxing Sub Junior National Championship in March 2024? **-Haryana**

585. TRAI has issued recommendations on 'Use of Embedded SIM for Machine-to-Machine Communication' in March 2024, when was TRAI established? **-1997**

586. Who has been selected as the flag bearer for India at Paris Olympics 2024 in March 2024? **-Sharath Kamal**

587. ISRO successfully tested the landing mission of the reusable launch vehicle in March 2024, what is it called? **-'Pushpak'**

588. Who has been appointed as the new President of the Federation of Indian Export Organization in March 2024? **-Ashwini Kumar**

589. Who has been appointed as the new Commissioner of Mumbai Municipal Corporation in March 2024? **-Bhushan Gagrani**

590. Where was the 4th Shanghai Cooperation Organization Startup Forum organized in March 2024? **-New Delhi**

591. Who has recently been appointed as the new Director General of Police of West Bengal in March 2024? **-Sanjay Mukherjee**

592. Who has recently been nominated for the prestigious Saraswati Samman-2023 in March 2024? -Prabha Verma
593. Who has taken charge as the President of Indian Steel Association in March 2024? -Naveen Jindal
594. Leo Varadkar, who recently resigned, was the Prime Minister of which country in March 2024? -Ireland
595. When is World Forestry Day celebrated every year? -21 March
596. Where was the fourth edition of the Shanghai Cooperation Organization Startup Forum held in March 2024? -New Delhi
597. Who has been selected as the new Election Commissioner in March 2024? -Sukhbir Sandhu and Gyanesh Kumar
598. The recently discussed 'Mahtari Vandan Yojana' was started by which state government in March 2024? -Chhattisgarh
599. Who launched Prasar Bharati's new service PB-'Shabd' in March 2024? -Anurag Thakur
600. Who has been honored with the award of Outstanding Male Cricketer of the Year for New Zealand in March 2024? -Rachin Ravindra
601. Who is the chairman of the committee formed on 'One Nation One Election' that submitted its report in March 2024? -Ramnath Kovind
602. India's first automobile in-plant railway siding project was inaugurated in which state in March 2024? -Gujarat
603. Which Union Minister launched the credit assistance program for Jan Aushadhi Kendras in March 2024? -Dr. Mansukh Mandaviya
604. With whom has SBI partnered for its transaction banking platform in March 2024? -Aurionpro
605. India recently signed an agreement with which country to establish a Joint Economic and Trade Committee in March 2024? -Dominican Republic
606. According to SIPRI report, which country is the world's top arms importer between 2019-2023? -India
607. Where did PM Modi lay the foundation stone of India's first commercial semiconductor fabrication service in March 2024? -Gujarat (Dholera)
608. Who recently inaugurated the regional airline service Fly91 in March 2024? -Jyotiraditya Scindia
609. Where did Prime Minister Narendra Modi inaugurate the Kochrab Ashram in March 2024? -Gujarat
610. Who has been elected as the new Chief Minister of Haryana in March 2024? -Naib Saini
611. Who won the ICC Men's Player of the Month award for the month of February 2024? -Yashasvi Jaiswal
612. Exercise Cutlass Express 2024 was organized in which country in March 2024? -Seychelles
613. Who launched "Subhash Abhinandan", a digital exhibition based on the life of Subhash Chandra Bose in March 2024? -Arjun Ram Meghwal
614. Which missile was successfully tested with MIRV technology recently in March 2024? -Agni-V intercontinental ballistic missile
615. Who inaugurated India's first elevated 8-lane expressway in March 2024? -Narendra Modi
616. Who won the Best Actor Award at the Academy Awards 2024 (Oscars)? -Cillian Murphy
617. Kristina Pijkova, who won the 71st Miss World title in March 2024, belongs to which country? -Czech Republic
618. Who took oath as the 14th President of Pakistan in March 2024? -Asif Ali Zardari
619. Union Minister Narayan Rane recently laid the foundation stone of MSME-Technology Center in which state in March 2024? -Maharashtra
620. In which state of India was the world's longest twin-lane tunnel inaugurated in March 2024? -Arunachal Pradesh
621. Who was honored with the 'Miss World Humanitarian Award' in March 2024? -Nita Ambani
622. Which country has become a new member of the military alliance NATO in March 2024? -Sweden
623. With whom has the Reserve Bank of India signed an agreement to promote the use of local currencies in March 2024? -Bank Indonesia
624. With which country will the Indian Coast Guard organize 'Sea Defenders-2024' in March 2024? -USA
625. Where will 'Bharat-Shakti', the joint exercise of the three armies of India, be organized in March 2024? -Pokhran, Rajasthan
626. Which country has become 99th member of the International Solar Alliance in May 2024? -Spain
627. Whom did President Draupadi Murmu recently nominate to Rajya Sabha in March 2024? -Sudha Murthy
628. When is International Women's Day celebrated every year? -08 March
629. Which Union Minister launched NITI Aayog's platform 'Niti for States' in March 2024? -Ashwini Vaishnaw
630. Who has become the 14th player to play 100 test matches for India in March 2024? -Ravichandran Ashwin
631. Which country has recently devalued its currency in March 2024? -Egypt
632. With whom has NPCI joined hands for cooperation in the field of Blockchain and Artificial Intelligence in March 2024? -IISc, Bangalore
633. Who won the first prize in the National Youth Parliament Festival, 2024? -Yatin Bhaskar Duggal (Haryana)
634. On which island of Lakshadweep has the Indian Navy established its new base in March 2024? -Minicoy Island
635. With whose collaboration has NITI Aayog launched 'Frontier Technology Labs' in March 2024? -Meta
636. In which state did PM Modi inaugurate India's first underwater metro in March 2024? -West Bengal
637. Sansad Khel Mahakumbh 3.0, recently seen in the news, is organised in which state? -Himachal Pradesh (Bilaspur)
638. In which state was India's first small scale LNG unit inaugurated in March 2024? -Madhya Pradesh
639. With whom has NLC India Green Energy Limited signed an agreement for a solar power project in March 2024? -Gujarat Urja Vikas Nigam Limited (GUVNL)
640. Which state government recently approved the Green Hydrogen Policy in March 2024? -Uttar Pradesh
641. In which state has the Widow Remarriage Promotion Scheme been launched recently in March 2024? -Jharkhand
642. Where was India's first green hydrogen plant established in the stainless steel sector in March 2024? -Hisar
643. Where is the Asian River Rafting Championship organized in March 2024? -Shimla
644. Who has Sunrisers Hyderabad appointed as its new captain before IPL 2024? -Pat Cummins
645. Who took oath as the 24th Prime Minister of Pakistan in March 2024? -Shahbaz Sharif
646. 'Risa' is a tribal costume of which state, which was recently granted GI tag in March 2024? -Tripura
647. Who has been appointed as the new Chief Electoral Officer of Maharashtra in March 2024? -S. Chokalingam
648. Who has become the first woman sniper of Border Security Force (BSF)? -Suman Kumari
649. 'Melanochlamys Draupadi' which was in discussion recently in March 2024 is related to which of the following? -Sea slug
650. Who recently inaugurated the ASTDS tug named 'Ocean Grace' in March 2024? -Shri Sarbananda Sonowal
651. Union Minister Dr. Mansukh Mandaviya launched the AYUSH-ICMR Advanced Centre in which city in March 2024? -New Delhi
652. Exercise 'Samudra Laksamana' was conducted between India and which country in March 2024? -Malaysia
653. Global Resources Outlook Report 2024 is released by? -UNEP
654. 'Aditi Scheme' is related to which of the following areas, launched in March 2024? -Defense sector
655. How many crore rupees has the Union Cabinet approved for the International Big Cat Alliance in March 2024? -150 crores
656. In which state was the country's first semiconductor fab established in March 2024? -Gujarat

657. National Birth Defect Awareness Month 2024 was launched by whom in March 2024? **-V K Paul (NITI Aayog)**

658. When is World Civil Defense Day celebrated every year? **-1 March**

659. Who has recently been nominated for the prestigious Saraswati Samman-2023 in March 2024? **-Prabha Verma**

660. Who has recently been appointed as Joint Director in CBI in April 2024? **-Anurag Kumar**

661. What is India's rank in the recently released World Cyber Crime Index as of April 2024? **-10**

662. Who was the CEO of Byju's India who resigned from his post in April 2024? **-Arjun Mohan**

663. Who has been appointed the new director of the National Judicial Academy, Bhopal in April 2024? **-Justice Aniruddha Bose**

664. Who was recently named South Asian Person of the Year by Harvard University? **-Avantika Vandanapu**

665. When is World Art Day celebrated every year, as noted in April 2024? **-15 April**

666. With whom has KABIL signed an agreement for technical cooperation for minerals in April 2024? **-CSIR-IMMT**

667. Where was the first steel cutting ceremony of Fleet Support Ships for the Indian Navy held in April 2024? **-Visakhapatnam**

668. Who has become the eighth Indian to score 7,000 or more runs in T20 cricket as of April 2024? **-Surya Kumar Yadav**

669. Who has been appointed the head of the US-India Tax Forum in April 2024? **-Tarun Bajaj**

670. In which country is the Asian Wrestling Championship 2024 being organized in April 2024? **-Kyrgyzstan**

671. Who has been recently elected as the Chairman of the Senate, the upper house of the Pakistani Parliament in April 2024? **-Yusuf Raza Gilani**

672. When is the International Human Space Flight Day observed every year, as mentioned in April 2024? **-12 April**

673. Who has been appointed as the full-time member of the Sixteenth Finance Commission in April 2024? **-Manoj Panda**

674. Who has been sworn in as the new Prime Minister of Ireland in April 2024? **-Simon Harris**

675. Who has been elected as the next Prime Minister of Iceland in April 2024? **-Bjarni Benediktsson**

676. For which mission was the ISRO team awarded the prestigious 'John L. 'Jack' Swigert Jr.' Award in April 2024? **-Chandrayaan-3 mission**

677. Who has Air India recently appointed as the head of its global airport operations? **-Jayaraj Shanmugam**

678. How many US dollars was World Athletics award to the gold medal winners in athletics at the Paris Olympics, as announced in April 2024? **-US $ 50,000**

679. When is World Homeopathy Day celebrated every year, as noted in April 2024? **-10 April**

680. In which country was the Clean Energy Investor Forum organized by IPEF in April 2024? **-Singapore**

681. Which organisation organized 'Shakti - Festival of Music and Dance' in April 2024? **-Sangeet Natak Academy**

682. Who has been recently appointed as the CEO and MD of the company by Wipro? **-Srini Pallia**

683. In which city was the National Women's Hockey League inaugurated in April 2024? **-Ranchi**

684. Who has launched India's first private sub-meter resolution surveillance satellite in April 2024? **-Tata Advanced Systems Limited**

685. India has acquired the right to operate the overseas Sittwe port, in which country, as of April 2024? **-Myanmar**

686. In which city was the Indian Navy Half Marathon organized in November 2024? **-New Delhi**

687. Which country has changed its employment visa program in April 2024? **-New Zealand**

688. The city of Miraj, which has been granted a GI tag for its art of making musical instruments Sitars and tanpuras, is located in which state, as mentioned in April 2024? **-Maharashtra**

689. When is World Health Day celebrated every year, as noted in April 2024? **-07 April**

690. Where was the 'Sagar Kavach' exercise organized in April 2024? **-Lakshadweep**

691. At what rate has RBI maintained the repo rate for the seventh time in a row as of April 2024? **-6.50**

692. Which Mini Ratna company was honored with the 15th CIDC Vishwakarma Award 2024 in April 2024? **-SJVN Limited**

693. How many billion euros is NATO preparing to fund to support Ukraine in its war with Russia, as mentioned in April 2024? **-100 billion Euros**

694. Who has been appointed as a member of the Economic Advisory Panel by the World Bank Group in April 2024? **-Rakesh Mohan**

695. Who won the title of CCI Snooker Classic in April 2024? **-Pankaj Advani**

696. When is National Maritime Day celebrated every year, as noted in April 2024? **-05 April**

697. When is International Mine Awareness Day observed every year, as mentioned in April 2024? **-04 April**

698. Where was India's first domestic gene therapy for cancer launched in April 2024? **-IIT Bombay**

699. Which ballistic missile was successfully tested by DRDO in April 2024? **-Missile Agni-Prime**

700. Who has been appointed as the new Managing Director of Tata International in April 2024? **-Rajiv Singhal**

701. Kathia wheat, which has recently been given a GI tag, belongs to which state? **-Uttar Pradesh**

702. Who has taken charge as the President of ASSOCHAM in April 2024? **-Sanjay Nayar**

703. Which has become India's largest port in terms of cargo volume as of June 2024? **-Paradip Port**

704. Recently Abdel-Fattah Al-Sisi has been sworn in as the President of which country? **-Egypt**

705. Who has become India's top-ranked chess player as of April 2024? **-Arjun Erigaisi**

706. Hindustan Aeronautics Limited has handed over two Dornier 228 aircraft to which country in April 2024? **-Guyana**

707. 'Operation Sankalp', which was in the news in April 2024, is related to which of the following? **-Maritime security**

708. Who won the National Kho Kho Championship 2023-24 Men's Title in April 2024? **-Maharashtra Team**

709. Who won the men's singles title of Miami Open 2024 in April 2024? **-Jannik Sinner**

710. Who took charge as the 33rd Director General of Electronics and Mechanical Engineers in April 2024? **-Lieutenant General JS Sidana**

711. Which pair won the men's doubles title of Miami Open 2024 in April 2024? **-Matt Ebden- Rohan Bopanna**

712. Who has been appointed as the first woman Prime Minister of Congo in April 2024? **-Judith Suminwa Tuluka**

713. Who has become the first Indian wicketkeeper to score 7,000 runs in T20 cricket as of April 2024? **-MS Dhoni**

714. Who has taken charge as the Principal Director General of PIB in April 2024? **-Sheyphali B Sharan**

715. Who has taken charge as the National President of FICCI Ladies Organization in April 2024? **-Joyshree Das Verma**

716. DRDO recently successfully tested RudraM-II missile, what type of missile is it? **-Air to surface**

717. In which country is the multi-national military exercise 'Red Flag 24' being organized in May 2024? **-USA**

718. Where was the Antarctic Treaty Consultative Meeting held in May 2024? **-Kochi**

719. Which ministry has launched the Mass Communication Internship Programme in May 2024? **-Ministry of Water Power**

720. When is Hindi Journalism Day celebrated every year in May 2024? **-30 May**

721. When is World No Tobacco Day observed every year in May 2024? **-31 May**

722. The cyclone 'Remal' has been named by which country which occur in May 2024? **-Oman**

723. Which state government has imposed a one-year ban on gutkha and pan masala in May 2024? **-Telangana**

724. Where was the International Conference on Nuclear Security (ICONS-2024) held? **-Vienna**

725. With whom has the Indian Army signed an agreement for hydrogen fuel cell bus in May 2024? **-IOCL**

726. Who is the chairman of DRDO whose tenure has been extended by one year in May 2024? **-Dr. Sameer V Kamat**

727. When is World Hunger Day observed every year? **-28 May**

728. Which country host the 2026 AFC Women's Asia Cupin May 2024? **-Australia**

729. Who is the oldest Indian woman to conquer Mount Everest recently in May 2024? -Jyoti Ratre
730. Which Indian-origin professor was recently awarded the prestigious Shaw Prize in Astronomy? -Srinivas R. Kulkarni
731. General Tu Lam was elected as the new President of which country in May 2024? -Vietnam
732. The President of the United Arab Emirates presented the First Class Independence Medal to the Ambassador of which country in May 2024? -Paraguay
733. Travel and Tourism Development Index 2024 was recently released by which organization? -World Economic Forum
734. Which European country has recently granted country status to Palestine? -Slovenia
735. Which medal did Deepti Jeevanji of India win in the World Para Athletics Championship in May 2024? -Gold
736. When is the International Biodiversity Day celebrated every year? -22 May
737. Which institute has recently presented a research report on 'Air pollution and health effects in North India'? -IIT Delhi
738. With whom has the Department of Animal Husbandry and Dairying, Government of India signed an agreement for vaccine cold chain management? -UNDP
739. Which female tennis player won the Italian Open title in May 2024? -Iga Swiatek
740. Who has taken charge as the President of Confederation of Indian Industry? -Sanjeev Puri
741. Ibrahim Raisi was the President of which country who recently died in a helicopter crash in May 2024? -Iran
742. On which date World Refugee Day is observed across the world? -20 June
743. When is the National Anti-Terrorism Day observed every year? -21 May
744. Neeraj Chopra won the gold medal in Federation Cup 2024, where was it organized in May 2024? -Bhubaneshwar
745. Indian Pavilion inaugurated at Cannes Film Festival 2024, where was it held in May 2024? -France
746. Which famous Indian footballer has announced his retirement from international football in May 2024? -Sunil Chhetri
747. In which country has PhonePe launched UPI services in May 2024? -Sri Lanka
748. Where did the Indian Air Force airdrop-test indigenous mobile hospital 'Bhishma' Cube in May 2024? -Agra
749. Who has recently become the 85th Grandmaster of India? -P Shaymanikhil
750. Which Organisation has appointed Davide Salvagnini as its first Chief AI Officer In May 2024? -NASA
751. Who has been appointed as the captain of the team by Bangladesh for T20 World Cup 2024? -Nazmul Hussain Shanto
752. Who has been recently elected as the Chairman of IFFCO? -Dileep Sanghani
753. Which day has been declared by the United Nations General Assembly as World Football Day? -25 May
754. Which team becomes second team to qualify for the IPL 2024 playoffs? -Rajasthan Royals
755. In which country is the World Hydrogen Summit 2024 organized? -Netherlands
756. Chabahar Port, which was in the news recently, is located in which country? -Iran
757. Which England cricketer announced his retirement from international cricket in May 2024? -James Anderson
758. Who has become the first Indian male wrestler to secure quota for Paris Olympics 2024? -Aman Sehrawat
759. In which state 7th edition of the India-France joint military exercise 'Shakti' organized in May 2024? -Meghalaya
760. Where was the Senior Nationals Sailing Championship 2024 organized in May 2024? -Mumbai
761. Who has made the record of climbing the world's highest peak Mount Everest the most number of times in May 2024? -Kami Rita Sherpa
762. Where was the 46th Antarctic Treaty Consultative Meeting held in May 2024? -Kochi
763. Which Indian wrestler has been banned by the global governing body of wrestling in May 2024? -Bajrang Punia
764. Who has been appointed as the Chairman of HDFC Life in May 2024? -Keki Mistry
765. India has withdrawn its military personnel from which country in May 2024? -Maldives
766. The Shinku-La Pass, which was in the news in May 2024, is located in which state? -Himachal Pradesh
767. Who has been appointed by the global digital payments platform Visa as the new Country Manager in India? -Sujai Raina
768. In which state was the 'School on Wheels' initiative launched in May 2024? -Manipur
769. Who has been appointed as the MD and CEO of Ujjivan Small Finance Bank in May 2024? -Sanjeev Nautiyal
770. When is International Thalassemia Day observed every year? -08 May
771. Sunita Williams again fly into space, how many times has she traveled to space before? -Twice
772. When is the birth anniversary of former President of India Giani Zail Singh celebrated? -5 May
773. India has invited election management bodies of how many countries under the International Election Visitors Programme in May 2024? -23
774. In which country will the ICC Women's T20 World Cup 2024 be organized in Oct, 2024? -Bangladesh
775. Which Bollywood actress has been appointed as the National Brand Ambassador of UNICEF India? -Kareena Kapoor Khan
776. Jeremiah Manele has recently been appointed as the Prime Minister of which country? -Solomon Islands
777. Which country has recently issued its new currency 'ZiG'? -Zimbabwe
778. NPCI International Payments Limited has signed an agreement with which African country for UPI-like services recently? -Namibia
779. Who has been named as the brand ambassador of ICC Men's T20 World Cup 2024? -Yuvraj Singh
780. When is World Press Freedom Day celebrated every year? -03 May
781. Who was recently awarded the 84th title of Grandmaster by the International Chess Federation in May 2024? -Vaishali Rameshbabu
782. Which IIT was awarded a patent by the Government of India on an indigenously developed compact inverter? -IIT Patna
783. Who has been appointed as the new director of DPIIT? -Pratima Singh
784. India test fired a smart anti-submarine missile developed by whom in May 2024? -DRDO
785. Who has taken over as the Vice Chief of the Indian Navy in May 2024? -Vice Admiral Krishna Swaminathan AVSM
786. How many crore Indians set a new world record by voting in the 2024 Lok Sabha elections? -64.2 Crores
787. Who was India's first female permanent representative to the United Nations who has recently retired? -Ruchira Kamboj
788. When is World Bicycle Day observed every year? -3rd June
789. Which state recently received central approval to establish an IIM? -Assam
790. Which country will host the next annual general meeting of the International Air Transport Association? -India
791. Which country recently sent the Chang'e-6 mission to the Moon? -China
792. The Ministry of Defense has partnered with which ministry to set up a dedicated Tele Manas cell for the armed forces? -Union Ministry of Health and Family Welfare
793. Which country has recently officially launched its space agency? -South Korea
794. When is World Environment Day observed every year? -5 June
795. Claudia Sheinbaum has become the first woman elected president of which country? -Mexico
796. Recently, a new species of blue ant was discovered in which state? -Arunachal Pradesh
797. Recently, which country has banned the entry of Israeli passport holders? -Maldives
798. The mobile app 'Sarathi 2.0' was recently launched by which organization? -SEBI
799. Who has become the first batsman in the world to hit 600 sixes in international cricket? -Rohit Sharma

800. In which seat were more than 2 lakh votes cast on NOTA in the 2024 Lok Sabha elections? **-Indore (Madhya Pradesh)**

801. 'Sparsh' service, seen recently in the news, is related to which ministry? **-Defence Ministry**

802. Recently in June 2024, which state has signed an agreement with the World Bank to tackle air pollution? **-Haryana**

803. Who has been appointed as the new Crown Prince by the Emir of Kuwait? **Sheikh Sabah Khalid Al Sabah**

804. Who has been chosen as the leader of the National Democratic Alliance (NDA)? **-Narendra Modi**

805. Recently, on World Environment Day 2024, two wetlands of which state have been included in the list of 'Ramsar sites'? **-Bihar**

806. When is World Food Safety Day observed every year? **-7 June**

807. In which state was a plastic waste management and recycling plant inaugurated recently? **-Sikkim**

808. Who has been given the additional charge of Director General of Employees State Insurance Corporation? **-Shri Kamal Kishore Soan**

809. At what rate has the Monetary Policy Committee kept the repo rate unchanged for the eighth consecutive time? **-6.50%**

810. Bharat Heavy Electricals Limited has secured an order for a thermal power project from which company? **-Adani Power Limited**

811. Narendra Modi has taken oath as the PM of India for the third consecutive time; he won from which Lok Sabha constituency? **-Varanasi**

812. How many former chief ministers are included in the Modi cabinet this time? **-7**

813. Which country has recently been added by the UN to the global list of criminals committing crimes against children? **-Israel**

814. Iga Swiatek, who won the French Open 2024 women's title, is a player of which country? **-Poland**

815. Who has been given the Ministry of Road Transport in the Modi Cabinet 2024? **-Nitin Gadkari**

816. Which ministries have been given to former Haryana Chief Minister Manohar Lal Khattar in the Modi Cabinet 2024? **-Ministry of Power and Ministry of Housing and Urban Affairs**

817. Who holds the Ministry of Personnel, Public Grievances, and Pensions in the Union Cabinet 2024? **-PM Narendra Modi**

818. Who has been named as the next Chief of the Indian Army? **-Lieutenant General Upendra Dwivedi**

819. Who has been sworn in as the new Chief Minister of Odisha? **-Mohan Charan Majhi**

820. Who has taken oath as the new Chief Minister of Andhra Pradesh? **-Chandrababu Naidu**

821. Suhelwa Wildlife Sanctuary is seen in the news recently; it is in which state? **-Uttar Pradesh**

822. In which country will the FIH Hockey Men's Junior World Cup 2025 be organized? **-India**

823. Carlos Alcaraz is a player of which country who won the title of French Open 2024? **-Spain**

824. Who has taken oath as the Deputy Chief Minister of Andhra Pradesh? **-Pawan Kalyan**

825. Who has taken oath as the Deputy Chief Minister of Odisha? **-KV Singh Deo and Pravati Parida**

826. What is India's rank in the Global Gender Gap Index 2024? **-129**

827. Where was the G7 summit organized? **-Italy**

828. Recently, the Container Port Performance Index 2024 was released by? **-The World Bank and S&P Global Market Intelligence**

829. After whom did the International Astronomical Union named a Lal Crater on Mars? **-Professor Devendra Lal**

830. NASA is working with which IIT in India to research multidrug-resistant pathogens? **-IIT Madras**

831. Pema Khandu has taken oath as the Chief Minister of which state? **-Arunachal Pradesh**

832. Which country has achieved the first rank in the Global Gender Gap Index 2024? **-Iceland**

833. When is World Blood Donor Day observed every year? **-14 June**

834. With whom has the Indira Gandhi National Center for the Arts signed an agreement to promote Indian art and culture? **-Sansad TV**

835. India has sent humanitarian aid worth how many million US dollars to disaster-hit Papua New Guinea? **-USD 1 million**

836. Who has been selected as the next MD of 'Dedicated Freight Corridor Corporation of India' Limited? **-Praveen Kumar**

837. Who has recently been re-appointed as the Principal Secretary to Prime Minister Narendra Modi? **-Dr. Pramod Kumar Mishra**

838. Ajit Doval is the longest-serving person in which post? **-National Security Advisor**

839. In which state did the Kanchanjunga Express train accident occur? **-West Bengal**

840. The Indian Railways completed the first trial run on the world's highest railway bridge, over which river? **-Chenab**

841. Who deployed the MI17 helicopter to control the forest fire in Binsar Wildlife Sanctuary? **-Indian Air Force**

842. Gandhi Sagar Wildlife Sanctuary was recently in the news; in which state is it located? **-Madhya Pradesh**

843. Recently, which service was inaugurated by Madhya Pradesh Chief Minister Dr. Mohan Yadav? **-PM Shri Tourism Air Service**

844. Who was re-elected as the President of South Africa by the South African Parliament? **-Cyril Ramaphosa**

845. Which edition of the JIMEX exercise was held in 2024? **-Eighth**

846. Where was the second edition of Exercise 'Red Flag 2024' held in the US? **-Eielson Air Force Base, Alaska**

847. Who has recently taken charge as the Controller of Warship Production and Procurement in the Navy? **-Vice Admiral B Sivakumar**

848. In which state will India's first submarine tourism start? **-Gujarat**

849. Who has been appointed as the new Managing Director by the skincare brand 'Nivea India'? **-Geetika Mehta**

850. Who has recently assumed the charge of 'Chief of Material' in the Navy? **-Vice Admiral Kiran Deshmukh**

851. In which city of UP did Defense Minister Rajnath Singh inaugurate the first Sainik School for girls? **-Vrindavan**

852. Who has been appointed as the Director General of Fire Services, Civil Defense, and Home Guards? **-Vivek Srivastava**

853. Who has been appointed by the Central Government as the Chairman of the 16th Finance Commission? **-Arvind Panagariya**

854. Who inaugurated the Kochi-Lakshadweep Islands Submarine Optical Fiber Connectionin Kavaratti, Lakshadweep? **-PM Narendra Modi**

855. Joint military exercise 'Desert Cyclone' is conducted between India and which country? **-United Arab Emirates**

856. For how many years has India started its tenure as a member of the United Nations Statistical Commission? **-4 years**

857. Who has been recently appointed as the new Chief Secretary of Rajasthan? **-Sudhansh Pant**

858. Who has been appointed as the new Chairman and Managing Director of Power Grid Corporation? **-Ravindra Kumar Tyagi**

859. Who recently took command of 'Chetak Corps' as General Officer Commanding? **-Lieutenant General Nagendra Singh**

860. Who recently received the M.S. Swaminathan Award? **-B.R. Kamboj**

861. Who was the chief guest of the Vibrant Gujarat Global Summit? **-Mohammed bin Zayed Al Nahyan**

862. Which two Indians have been included by the ICC in the list of match officials for the upcoming Under-19 Men's World Cup? **-KNA Padmanabhan and Narayanan Kutty**

863. When is World Hindi Day celebrated every year? **-January 10**

864. Who has Indian Fintech 'PhonePe' recently appointed as the CEO of its International Payment Business? **-Ritesh Pai**

865. Footballer Franz Beckenbauer has passed away recently; he was a legendary footballer of which country? **-Germany**

866. In which neighbouring country will the new campus of IIT Madras be started? **-Sri Lanka**

867. Who has been named as the new Prime Minister of France? **-Gabriel Attal**

868. In which city was the 27th National Youth Festival organized? **-Nashik**

869. How many players, including Mohammed Shami, were honored with the Arjuna Award for 2023? **-26**

870. Which country will chair the UNESCO World Heritage Committee in July this year? **-India**

871. 'Chandubi Mahotsav' was recently celebrated in which state? **-Assam**

872. When is 'Pravasi Bharatiya Diwas' celebrated every year? -09 January

873. In which state was the 'College Phagthansi Mission' started recently? -Manipur

874. Elisabeth Borne was the Prime Minister of which country who has recently resigned? -France

875. Which two badminton players were awarded the Major Dhyan Chand Khel Ratna Award this year? -Chirag Shetty and Satwik Sairaj Rankireddy

876. Which team won the gold medal in the men's 10-meter air pistol team event in the Asian Olympic Qualifier? -India

877. Who won the Best Director-Motion Picture Award at the Golden Globes 2024? -Christopher Nolan

878. Tata Power recently announced an investment of ₹70,000 crore in which state? -Tamil Nadu

879. On which lake was the training program organized under the Amrit Dharohar Capacity Building Scheme? -Chilika Lake

880. Who has been appointed as the new CEO of 'Adani Ports'? -Mr. Ashwani Gupta

881. Who inaugurated the 'Indus Food 2024' exhibition? -Shri Piyush Goyal

882. Who received the Best Actor Award for Best Performance in a Motion Picture, Drama Category at the Golden Globes 2024? -'Cillian Murphy'

883. Krishna Godavari Basin Deep Sea Project in the Bay of Bengal is being operated by? -ONGC

884. Which film received the Best Film (Drama) Award at the Golden Globes 2024? -Oppenheimer

885. Who inaugurated the 'NCC Republic Day Camp' 2024? -Vice President Jagdeep Dhankhar

886. What amount of fund has been allocated by the central government for the 'Prithvi Vigyan scheme'? -RS. 4,797 crores

887. Where did Union Sports Minister Anurag Thakur inaugurate the 'Beach Games'? -Ghoghla Beach (Diu)

888. 'Kadiyal Sarees' belong to which state which recently got a GI tag? -West Bengal

889. Who has been appointed as the Managing Director of 'National Asset Reconstruction Company'? -P Santosh

890. Who was awarded 'Rashtriya Khel Protsahan Puruskar' 2023 for Corporate Social Responsibility? -Odisha Mining Corporate Limited

891. The Board of Control for Cricket in India has banned which Odisha cricketer for two years? -Sumit Sharma

892. Defense Ministry has signed a contract worth what amount of fund for the purchase of military equipment? -Rs. 802 crores

893. Where was Aatmnirbhar Bharat Utsav 2024 organized? -Bharat Mandapam, New Delhi

894. In which city did the Chief Minister of Himachal Pradesh inaugurate the five-day winter carnival? -Manali

895. Which wildlife sanctuary was recently included in the Swadesh Darshan 2.0 scheme? -Debrigarh Wildlife Sanctuary

896. In which state was 'Rahat Vani Kendra' inaugurated for early disaster warning? -Uttar Pradesh

897. Which company has become the first tyre company to achieve ISCC-Plus certification? -JK Tyre's Chennai Plant

898. Who has recently been appointed Chairman of the Supreme Court Legal Services Committee? -Justice BR Gavai

899. Who won the men's singles title at the French Open 2024? -Carlos Alcaraz

900. Who did Carlos Alcaraz defeat in the men's singles final at the French Open 2024? -Alexander Zverev

901. Which player did Iga Swiatek defeat in the women's singles final at the French Open 2024? -Jasmine Paolini

902. Who was defeated by Carlos Alcaraz in the men's singles final at the French Open 2024? -Marcelo Arevalo & Mate Pavić

903. Who won the women's doubles title at the French Open 2024? -Coco Gauff & Katerina Siniakova

904. Who won the mixed doubles title at the French Open 2024? -Laura Siegemund and Edouard Roger-Vasselin

905. Which country remained the most peaceful in the Global Peace Index 2024? -Iceland

906. Which country was ranked the least peaceful in the Global Peace Index 2024? -Yemen

907. According to the latest Global Peace Index 2024, released by the Institute for Economics and Peace (IEP), what was the economic impact of violence on the global economy in 2023? -$19.1 trillion

908. The MotoGP event in India will be hosted by Greater Noida, specifically at the Buddh International Circuit (BIC), from 2025 until 2029 annually? -Greater Noida

909. Which Indian state has established two specialized cells to address the concerns of Non-Resident Indians (NRIs)? -Haryana

910. Who won the Norway Chess Tournament in 2024? -Magnus Carlsen and Ju Wenjun

911. Who claimed the victory at the Canadian Grand Prix 2024? -Max Verstappen

912. Who was the ICC Men's Player of the Month for May 2024? -Gudakesh Motie

913. Who was the ICC Women's Player of the Month for May 2024? -Chamari Athapaththu

914. Who clinched the FIDE Under-20 Girl's World Chess Championship title in 2024? -Divya Deshmukh

915. In June 2024, Indian Army launched a new Internet of Things (IoT)-enabled integrated generator tracking, protection, and control system. What is the name of this initiative? -Vidyut Rakshak

916. Who became the first Indian rider to win a three-star Grand Prix event? -Shruti Vora

917. What is the title of Bill Gates' memoir, released on February 4, 2025? -"Source Code: My Beginnings"

918. Which Indian city achieved the 19th position in the Container Port Performance Index 2023? -Visakhapatnam Port

919. Who was named the new Chairman of the Cellular Operators' Association of India (COAI) for the 2024-25 term? -Abhijit Kishore

920. Which Indian athlete won the Heilbronn Neckarcup 2024 ATP Challenger Tennis tournament? -Sumit Nagal

921. With which ministry, Ministry of Agriculture and Farmers' Welfare has recently signed an MoU for the Krishi Sakhi Certification Program? - Ministry of Rural Development

922. With which bank has the Ministry of External Affairs recently signed an MoU for e-Migrate? -SBI

923. David Weese has recently announced his retirement from international cricket. He played for which country? -Namibia

924. What is the rank of India in the recently released Environmental Performance Index 2024? -176

925. Which country will host the first multinational air exercise 'Taranga Shakti'? -India

926. Which New Zealand cricketer recently made history in the 2024 T20 World Cup by bowling four consecutive maiden overs and taking three wickets in a match against Papua New Guinea? -Lockie Ferguson

927. The Reserve Bank of India canceled the license of which cooperative bank in June 2024? -Purvanchal Cooperative Bank

928. Where did PM Modi recently release the 17th installment of PM Kisan Samman Nidhi Yojana? -Varanasi

929. Which state government has announced to soon recruit Van Mitras under the Van Mitra Yojana? -Haryana

930. Who inaugurated the newly constructed Prerna Sthal at the Parliament House Complex? -Vice President Jagdeep Dhankar

931. Why did the RBI recently cancel the license of Purvanchal Co-op Bank? -Due to insufficient capital

932. Which golfer recently secured a sixth-place tie at the Ladies Italian Open Golf? -Diksha Dagar

933. Where did India recently clinch their first medal at the BRICS Games? -Kazan, Russia

934. What is the primary purpose of India and the United States (US) jointly launching the NASA-ISRO Synthetic Aperture Radar? -to combat climate change

935. Which Indian state secretariat recently became the first eco-friendly state government headquarters? -Assam Secretariat

936. Which company recently became the world's most valuable? -Nvidia

937. Under which initiative was the recently seen Digital Health Incentive Scheme launched? -Ayushman Bharat Digital Mission

938. What is 'Planet Nine,' recently seen in the news? -A hypothetical planet in the outer region of our solar system

939. The "Joint Communiqué on a Peace Framework" was recently in the news regarding which two countries? **-Russia and Ukraine**

940. Which Indian state-owned aerospace and defense company was recently given a unique contract worth about Rs 50,000 crore by the UK Ministry of Defence? **-Hindustan Aeronautics Limited (HAL)**

941. Which Indian Naval ship is recently participating in the India Japan Maritime Naval Exercise Jimex 24? **-INS Shivalik**

942. Which country recently abstained from voting on the UN Security Council resolution calling for an 'immediate, full and complete ceasefire' in Gaza Strip? **-Russia**

943. Name the Vice President of Malawi, whose plane was recently missing after takeoff from its capital Lilongwe. **-Saulos Chilima**

944. Where was the BRICS transport ministers' meet held in June 2024? **-Saint Petersburg, Russia**

945. Who has been recently allotted the Railway Ministry for a second term? **-Ashwini Vaishnaw**

946. Prem Singh Tamang, who recently began his second term as Chief Minister of Sikkim, belongs to which polictical party? **-Sikkim Krantikari Morcha (SKM)**

947. How many women ministers are recently included in the newly formed cabinet of the Modi government? **-7**

948. Who is the President of France, who recently dissolved the Parliament on June 9th, 2024? **-Emmanuel Macron**

949. Where did the 10th edition of the Khelo India women's league recently kick off with the South Zone wushu league? **-Bagalkot, Karnataka**

950. The United Nations celebrates World Oceans Day every year on 8 June. What was its theme for the year 2024? **-Awaken New Depths**

951. Mette Frederiksen, recently in the news, is the Prime Minister of which country? **-Denmark**

952. Name the Indian football player who retired from international games in May 2024. **-Sunil Chhetri**

953. Where was the sea-borne pandemic that recently wiped out sea urchin populations in 2023 first observed? **-Gulf of Aqaba**

954. Which country did the delegates of the Toy Association of India (TAI) recently visit to promote the Indian toy industry in terms of manufacturing and export? **-United Arab Emirates (UAE)**

955. What is the theme of the 46th Antarctic Treaty Consultative Meeting (ATCM-46) recently held in Kochi? **-Vasudhaiva Kutumbakam (one Earth, one family, one future)**

956. Where did Prime Minister Shri Narendra Modi inaugurate the new campus of Nalanda University recently? **-Rajgir, Bihar**

957. Where did the Karnataka Governor inaugurate the first National Yoga Olympiad recently? **-Mysuru**

958. In which state will the Vadhavan port be built? **-Maharashtra**

959. What is the theme of International Yoga Day 2024? **-Yoga for Self and Society**

960. Who became the second fastest bowler to take 100 wickets in T20 International? **-Sandeep Lamichhane**

961. Which famous historian and writer recently passed away? **-P. Thankappan Nair**

962. Who has been appointed as the Delhi MCD Commissioner recently? **-Ashwini Kumar**

963. In which state did Prime Minister Narendra Modi inaugurate the Nalanda University New campus? **-Bihar**

964. For which crops has the Union Cabinet recently increased the MSP? **-Kharif**

965. Who won the gold medal in the men's javelin event at the Paavo Nurmi Games 2024 Athletics Meet? **-Neeraj Chopra**

966. Who has been appointed as the Protem Speaker of Lok Sabha recently? **-Bhartruhari Mahtab**

967. When is World Refugee Day celebrated every year? **-20 June**

968. Which United Nations organization appointed British actor Theo James as Global Goodwill Ambassador? **-UNHCR**

969. When is World Music Day celebrated every year? **-21 June**

970. With whom has the Government of India signed a loan agreement to improve the health sector? **-Asian Development Bank**

971. In which city did PM Narendra Modi participate in the program under International Yoga Day 2024? **-Srinagar**

972. What is the theme of World Refugee Day 2024? **-For a World Where Refugees Are Welcomed**

973. Who took oath as the Protem Speaker of the 18th Lok Sabha? **-Bhartruhari Mahtab**

974. Who inaugurated the 'Fast Track Immigration - Trusted Traveller Facility' at Indira Gandhi International Airport? **-Home Minister Amit Shah**

975. India recently announced to start e-medical visa facility for the citizens of which country? **-Bangladesh**

976. In which state will the world's first conservation center for red-headed vultures be established? **-Uttar Pradesh**

977. Who has been appointed the leader of the House in Rajya Sabha? **-Jagat Prakash Nadda**

978. Which city in Kerala has been officially declared India's first UNESCO City of Literature? **-Kozhikode**

979. Who has been appointed MD and CEO of HDFC ERGO General Insurance? **-Anuj Tyagi**

980. Lake Natron, which was in the news recently, is located in which country? **-Tanzania**

981. Which city has been awarded the tag of World Crafts City by the World Crafts Council? **-Srinagar**

982. Who recently released the World Investment Report 2024? **-UNCTAD**

983. Who launched the National Stop Diarrhea Campaign 2024? **-JP Nadda**

984. Which four teams have reached the semi-finals of T20 World Cup 2024? **-India, Afghanistan, England, and South Africa**

985. Who has been elected as the Speaker of the 18th Lok Sabha? **-Om Birla**

986. What is the target of tree plantation set by the Air Quality Management Commission in NCR? **-4.5 crore**

987. Where was the India Olympic Research and Education Center launched? **-Gujarat**

988. Who qualified for Paris Olympics 2024 through Universality Quota in Swimming? **-Srihari Nataraj and Dhanidhi Desinghu**

989. How many medals did India win in the Under-17 Asian Wrestling Championship? **-11**

990. Which state recently announced to establish 'Prime Minister Excellence College' in every district? **-Madhya Pradesh**

991. How many medals has India won in the BRICS Games 2024? **-29**

992. Speaker of the 18th Lok Sabha, Om Birla is a member from which Lok Sabha constituency? **-Kota (Rajasthan)**

993. Who has recently become the 100th full member of the International Solar Alliance? **-Paraguay**

994. The Privilege Committee of Rajya Sabha announced to cancel the suspension of which Rajya Sabha MP? **-Sanjay Singh**

995. Who has been appointed as the next Secretary General of NATO? **-Mark Rutte**

996. The United States recently named which country as its major non-NATO ally? **-Kenya**

997. Which mobile application has been launched by Director General of Railway Protection Force Manoj Yadav? **-Sangyan App**

998. Which is the first team to reach the final of T20 World Cup 2024 by defeating Afghanistan? **-South Africa**

999. When is International Day against Drug Abuse and Illicit Trafficking celebrated every year? **-26 June**

1000. DRDO recently handed over the medium range microwave obscurant chaff rocket to whom? **-Indian Navy**

1001. Who has been honored with the PEN Pinter Award 2024 established in the memory of playwright Harold Pinter? **-Arundhati Roy**

1002. Where did the Two-Day India-IORA Cruise Tourism Conference conclude in June 2024? **-New Delhi**

1003. Which ministry recently signed an MoU with SBI to enhance digital payment services for eMigrate portal users? **-External Affairs Ministry**

1004. Who inaugurated Prerna Sthal to honor Indian icons? **-VP Dhankhar**

1005. Which state police launched 'Mission Nishchay'? **-Punjab**

1006. Which app did the National Crime Records Bureau launch in June 2024? **-NCRB Sankalan Of Criminal Laws**

1007. How much is IFC investing in Brookfield's Bikaner Solar Power project? **-$105 million**

Office	Officer Holder's Name
President	Draupadi Murmu
Vice President & Rajya Sabha Chairman	Jagdeep Dhankhar
Prime Minister	Narendra Modi
Chief Justice of India	Justice Sanjiv Khanna
Speaker of the Lok Sabha	Om Birla
Chief Election Commissioner	Rajiv Kumar
Chief Information Commissioner	Heeralal Samariya
Chairman of Union Public Service Commission (UPSC)	Preeti Sudan
Comptroller and Auditor General of India	Shri K Sanjay Murthy
Chairman of CBSE	Rahul Singh
Chairman of NCERT	Dr. Dinesh Prasad Saklani
Attorney General of India	R. Venkataramani
Home Minister	Amit Shah
Finance Minister	Niramala Sitharaman
Defence Minister	Rajnath Singh
Railway Minister	Ashwini Vaishnaw
External Affairs Minister	Dr. Subrahmanyam Jaishankar
Education Minister	Dharmendra Pradhan
Agriculture Minister	Shivraj Singh Chouhan
Law & Justice Minister	Arjun Ram Meghwal (MoS- Independent Charge)
Information & Broadcasting Minister	Ashwini Vaishnaw
Cabinet Secretary of India	Dr. T.V. Somanathan
Principal Secretary to Prime Minister	Pramod Kumar Mishra
Advisors to Prime Minister	Amit Khare, Tarun Kapoor
Secretary General of the Lok Sabha	Utpal Kumar Singh
Secretary General of the Rajya Sabha	Pramod Chandra Mody
Railway Board CEO	Satish Kumar
Home Secretary	Govind Mohan
Finance Secretary	Tuhin Kanta Pandey
Defence Secretary	Rajesh Kumar Singh
Foreign Secretary	Vikram Misri
Solicitor General of India	Tushar Mehta
Chief Economic Adviser	V Anantha Nageswaran

Office	Officer Holder's Name
Chairman, National Human Rights Commission	Vijaya Bharathi Sayani
Chairman, National Commission for Minorities	Iqbal Singh Lalpura
Chairman of National Commission for Scheduled Caste	Kishore Makwana
Chairman of National Commission for Scheduled Tribes	Antar Singh Arya
Chairman of National Commission for Backward Classes	Hansraj Gangaram Ahir
Chairman, National Commission for Women	Vijaya Kishore Rahatkar
Chairman, Central Administrative Tribunal	Justice Ranjit More
Chairman, Central Vigilance Commission	Praveen Kumar Srivastava
Chairman, Atomic Energy Commission of India	Dr. Ajit Kumar Mohanty
Chairman, Department of Space	Dr. S. Somanath
Chairman, University Grants Commission (UGC)	Mamidala Jagadesh Kumar
Chairman, Central Water Commission	Kushvinder Vohra
Director, Space Application Centre	Nilesh M Desai
Chairman, National Forest Commission	Bhupinder Nath Kirpal
Chairman, Competition Commission of India	Ravneet Kaur
Chairman, 16th Finance Commission of India	Arvind Panagariya
Chairman, SEBI	Madhabi Puri Buch
Chairman, IRDAI	Debasish Panda
Chairman, 7th Pay Commission	Ashok Kumar Mathur
Chairman, SIDBI	Manoj Mittal
Chairman, Company Law Board	Mahesh Mittal Kumar
Chairman, Exim Bank	Harsha Bangari
CEO, National Housing Bank	Sanjay Shukla
Chairman, NABARD	Shaji KV
Chairman, SBI	Challa Sreenivasulu Setty
MD & CEO, IFCI Ltd.	Rahul Bhave
Chairman, National Stock Exchange	Mr. Ashishkumar Chauhan (Managing Director & CEO)
Chairman, Bombay Stock Exchange	Subhasis Chaudhuri
Chairman, LIC	Siddhartha Mohanty
President, Federation of Indian Chambers of Commerce & Industry (FICCI)	Harsha Vardhan Agarwal
Pension Fund Regulatory and Development Authority (PFRDA) Chairman	Dr. Deepak Mohanty
Chairman, Telecom Regulatory Authority of India (TRAI)	Anil Kumar Lahoti
Chairman, Press Information Bureau (PIB)	Dhirendra K Ojha
Chairman, Banks Board Bureau	Bhanu Pratap Sharma
MD & CEO, SBI Life Insurance	Amit Jhingran
President, Confederation of Indian Industry (CII)	Sanjiv Puri
President, Associated Chambers of Commerce and Industry of India (ASSOCHAM)	Sanjay Nayar
Chairman, National Statistical Commission	Rajeeva Laxman Karandikar
Director-General, Archaeological Survey of India	Yadubir Singh Rawat
Director, Enforcement Directorate	Rahul Navin
Chairman & CEO, ONGC	Arun Kumar Singh
Chairman & MD, GAIL	Sandeep Kumar Gupta
Chairman, IOCL	Arvindar Singh Sahney

Office	Officer Holder's Name
Chairman, Oil India Limited	Dr. Ranjit Rath
Chief of the Army Staff	General Upendra Dwivedi
Chief of the Naval Staff	Admiral Dinesh K Tripathi
Chief of the Air Staff	Air Chief Marshal Amar Preet Singh
Director, Intelligence Bureau	Tapan Deka
Director, CBI	Praveen Sood
Director-General, BSF	Daljit Singh Chaudhary
Director-General, CRPF	Anish Dayal Singh
Director-General, CISF	Rajwinder Singh Bhatti
Director-General, ITBP	Rahul Rasgotra
Director-General, NSG	B.Srinivasan
Director-General, NIA	Sadanand Vasant Date
Director-General, NDRF	Piyush Anand
Chief, R&AW	Ravi Sinha
Chairperson, National Testing Agency (NTA)	Pradeep Kumar Joshi
National Security Adviser	Ajit Doval
Governor, Reserve Bank of India	Sanjay Malhotra

LIST OF CHIEF MINISTERS & GOVERNORS OF INDIA

State	Capital	Chief Minister	Governor
Andhra Pradesh	Amaravati	Nara Chandrababu Naidu	Shri Justice (Retd.) S. Abdul Nazeer
Arunachal Pradesh	Itanagar	Pema Khandu	Lt. General Kaiwalya Trivikram Parnaik
Assam	Dispur	Himanta Biswa Sarma	Shri Lakshman Prasad Acharya
Bihar	Patna	Nitish Kumar	Shri Rajendra Vishwanath Arlekar
Chhattisgarh	Raipur	Vishnu Deo Sai	Shri Ramen Deka
Goa	Panaji	Pramod Sawant	Shri P.S. Sreedharan Pillai
Gujarat	Gandhinagar	Vishnu Deo Sai	Shri Acharya Devvrat
Haryana	Chandigarh	Nayab Singh Saini	Shri Bandaru Dattatreya
Himachal Pradesh	Shimla	Sukhvinder Singh Sukhu	Shri Shiv Pratap Shukla
Jharkhand	Ranchi	Hemant Soren	Shri Santosh Kumar Gangwar
Karnataka	Bengaluru	Siddaramaiah	Shri Thawar Chand Gehlot
Kerala	Thiruvananthapuram	Pinarayi Vijayan	Shri Arif Mohammed Khan
Madhya Pradesh	Bhopal	Mohan Yadav	Shri Mangubhai Chhaganbhai Patel
Maharashtra	Mumbai	Devendra Fadnavis	Shri C.P. Radhakrishnan
Manipur	Imphal	N. Biren Singh	Shri Lakshman Prasad Acharya (Additional Charge)
Meghalaya	Shillong	Conrad Kongkal Sangma	Shri C H Vijayashankar
Mizoram	Aizawl	Lalduhoma	Shri Kambhampati Hari Babu
Nagaland	Kohima	Neiphiu Rio	Shri La. Ganesan
Odisha	Bhubaneswar	Mohan Charan Majhi	Shri Raghubar Das
Punjab	Chandigarh	Bhagwant Mann	Shri Gulab Chand Kataria
Rajasthan	Jaipur	Bhajan Lal Sharma	Shri Haribhau Kisanrao Bagde
Sikkim	Gangtok	Prem Singh Tamang	Shri Om Prakash Mathur
Tamil Nadu	Chennai	M. K. Stalin	Shri R. N. Ravi
Telangana	Hyderabad	Revanth Reddy	Shri Jishnu Dev Varma
Tripura	Agartala	Manik Saha	Shri Nallu Indrasena Reddy
Uttar Pradesh	Lucknow	Yogi Adityanath	Smt. Anandiben Patel
Uttarakhand	Dehradun	Pushkar Singh Dhami	Lt. Gen. Gurmit Singh
West Bengal	Kolkata	Mamata Banerjee	Dr. C.V. Ananda Bose

PAST YEAR CURRENT AFFAIRS

IBPS PO MAINS 2024

1. Who is the director of the Oscar entry film "Lapata Ladies" from India?
   (a) Kiran Rao
   (b) Zoya Akhtar
   (c) Gauri Shinde
   (d) Ashwiny Iyer Tiwari
   (e) Meghna Gulzar

2. In October 2024, the Reserve Bank of India (RBI) imposed restrictions on four non-banking finance companies (NBFCs) from sanctioning and disbursing new loans. Which of the following non-banking finance companies has been fined?
   (a) Navi Finserv
   (b) Asirvad Microfinance
   (c) Arohan Financial Services
   (d) DMI Finance
   (e) All of the above

3. What is the maximum limit for UPI123 Pay and UPI Lite Wallet?
   (a) ₹1,0000 and ₹5,000
   (b) ₹2,000 and ₹1,000
   (c) ₹5,000 and ₹2,000
   (d) ₹10,000 and ₹1,000
   (e) ₹2,000 and ₹5,000

4. Which small finance bank recently merged with North East Small Finance Bank?
   (a) Jana Small Finance Bank
   (b) Ujjivan Small Finance Bank
   (c) Moneytap
   (d) Slice
   (e) AU Small Finance Bank

5. What is the maximum interest rate for the Sukanya Samriddhi Yojana scheme?
   (a) 7.5% (b) 7.8% (c) 8.0% (d) 8.2%
   (e) 8.5%

6. In which year is ISRO's Orbital Venus Mission expected to launch?
   (a) 2025 (b) 2026
   (c) 2027 (d) 2028
   (e) 2030

7. Which bank recently opened a branch in Singapore?
   (a) Bank of Baroda
   (b) State Bank of India
   (c) ICICI Bank
   (d) Kotak Mahindra Bank
   (e) Indian Overseas Bank

8. Which Australian university has opened a campus in GIFT City?
   (a) University of Melbourne
   (b) University of Sydney
   (c) University of New South Wales (UNSW)
   (d) Monash University
   (e) Deakin University

9. What is the target for Small Finance Bank's PSL (Priority Sector Lending) as per recent guidelines?
   (a) 40% of ANBC (b) 50% of ANBC
   (c) 60% of ANBC (d) 75% of ANBC
   (e) 100% of ANBC

10. Which bank is associated with the "Lakh Pati Didi" scheme?
    (a) State Bank of India
    (b) Indian Bank
    (c) Bank of Baroda
    (d) Punjab National Bank
    (e) Canara Bank

11. Which list is India's biodiversity conservation in the top 5 countries for?
    (a) Global Environmental Performance Index
    (b) World Conservation Ranking
    (c) United Nations Biodiversity Index
    (d) Red List of Endangered Species Recovery
    (e) National Park Protection Coverage

12. 2024 Asian Women's Handball Championship held in:
    (a) Maharashtra (b) Bihar
    (c) Jharkhand (d) Assam
    (e) Sikkim

13. What is ISRO's Pushpak mission related to?
    (a) Moon exploration
    (b) Solar energy collection
    (c) Interplanetary cargo transport
    (d) Space debris cleanup
    (e) Satellite-based communication

14. What is the maximum loan limit for SC/ST individuals under the TReDS scheme?
    (a) ₹10 lakh (b) ₹25 lakh
    (c) ₹50 lakh (d) ₹75 lakh
    (e) ₹1 crore

15. Which company manufactures the Vande Bharat train in India?
    (a) Hindustan Aeronautics Limited
    (b) Bharat Heavy Electricals Limited
    (c) Integral Coach Factory (ICF)
    (d) Tata Advanced Systems
    (e) Larsen & Toubro

16. What is the minimum CRAR set by RBI for banks?
    (a) 8% (b) 9% (c) 10% (d) 11%
    (e) 12%

17. What is the minimum holding period for KYC compliance in India?
    (a) 1 year (b) 2 years
    (c) 3 years (d) 5 years
    (e) 7 years

18. What is the National Mission for Hydrogen (NMH) targeted towards?
    (a) Reducing fossil fuel usage
    (b) Developing green hydrogen technology
    (c) Promoting solar energy
    (d) Enhancing biofuel adoption
    (e) Increasing hydropower generation

19. In September 2024, the Union Cabinet chaired by Prime Minister, Shri Narendra Modi, approved seven schemes to improve farmers' lives and increase their incomes at a total outlay of:
    (a) Rs 12,500 crore (b) Rs 14,235 crore
    (c) Rs 15,000 crore (d) Rs 13,000 crore
    (e) Rs 11,500 crore

20. What is the collaboration amount between IFC and Axis Bank for Blue Finance?
    (a) $200 million (b) $300 million
    (c) $400 million (d) $500 million
    (e) $600 million

21. Which bank sold its Oman operations to Bank Dhofar?
    (a) Bank of Baroda
    (b) State Bank of India
    (c) ICICI Bank
    (d) HDFC Bank
    (e) Axis Bank

22. Which countries are participating in Project Nexus, where RBI is a member?
    (a) India, Malaysia, Philippines, Singapore, Thailand
    (b) India, Indonesia, Malaysia, Philippines, Thailand
    (c) India, Malaysia, Singapore, Thailand, Vietnam
    (d) India, Malaysia, Philippines, Singapore, Indonesia
    (e) India, Malaysia, Philippines, Singapore, China

23. Which law university topped the NIRF (National Institutional Ranking Framework)?
    (a) National Law University, Delhi
    (b) National Law University, Bangalore
    (c) National Law University, Jodhpur
    (d) National Law University, Hyderabad
    (e) National Law University, Kolkata

24. Who was re-elected as an International Olympic Committee (IOC) member from India in July 2024?
    (a) Nita Ambani (b) Anil Khanna
    (c) Narinder Batra (d) Abhay Chautala
    (e) Randhir Singh

25. The Reserve Bank of India has increased the limit of funds transfer under the Indo-Nepal Remittance Facility Scheme from Rs 50,000 per transaction to:
    (a) Rs 1 lakh per transaction
    (b) Rs 1.5 lakh per transaction
    (c) Rs 2 lakh per transaction
    (d) Rs 2.5 lakh per transaction
    (e) Rs 5 lakh per transaction

26. Which of the following organizations has launched an online tool Daava Soochak for depositors to track their claim status in September 2024?
(a) Reserve Bank of India
(b) NABARD
(c) Life Insurance Corporation of India
(d) Deposit Insurance and Credit Guarantee Corporation
(e) None of the above

27. On October 5, 2024, the Life Insurance Corporation of India (LIC) increased its stake in Bank of Maharashtra from 4.05% to:
(a) 5.50% (b) 5.90% (c) 6.70% (d) 7.10%
(e) 7.80%

28. Which of the following IPO got listed on the National Stock Exchange (NSE) in November 2024 at Rs 78.14?
(a) Apex Ecotech
(b) Niva Bupa Health Insurance
(c) Agarwal Toughened Glass India
(d) Ganesh Infraworld
(e) Abha Power and Steel

29. Who among the following is the current Chairman of Telecom Regulatory Authority of India (TRAI)?
(a) Ranjan Bose
(b) Anil Kumar Lahoti
(c) Neelkanth Mishra
(d) Atul Kumar Chaudhary
(e) Abhay Shanker Verma

30. Which of the following banks sponsored the Chennai Open ATP Challenger 100 Men's International Tennis Championship 2024?
(a) Bank of Maharashtra
(b) Canara Bank
(c) Indian Bank
(d) Axis Bank
(e) Yes Bank

31. How many central ministries have been integrated in the PM Gati Shakti National Master Plan (NMP) for multi-modal connectivity, launched on October 13, 2021?
(a) 35 (b) 39 (c) 42 (d) 44
(e) 48

32. Which university topped the NIRF (National Institutional Ranking Framework) ranking for 2024?
(a) National Law University, Delhi
(b) Indian Institute of Science, Bangalore
(c) Jawaharlal Nehru University, New Delhi
(d) Banaras Hindu University, Varanasi
(e) University of Calcutta, Kolkata

33. What is the maximum amount a resident individual can remit under the Liberalised Remittance Scheme (LRS) per financial year?
(a) USD 100,000 (b) USD 150,000
(c) USD 200,000 (d) USD 250,000
(e) USD 300,000

34. What is the primary objective of Project Nexus launched by the Bank for International Settlements (BIS)?
(a) To enhance cross-border trade
(b) To improve international payment systems
(c) To boost foreign direct investment
(d) To develop regional payment connectivity
(e) To support cryptocurrency transactions

35. What is the minimum Capital to Risk Weighted Assets Ratio (CRAR) that Tier 1 Urban Cooperative Banks (UCBs) must maintain according to RBI guidelines?
(a) 7% (b) 8% (c) 9% (d) 10%
(e) 11%

36. PP Sengupta has been appointed as the Managing Director and Chief Executive Officer of Bandhan Bank in November 2024. Earlier, he was the MD and CEO of which bank?
(a) HDFC Bank
(b) ICICI Bank
(c) Axis Bank
(d) Indian Overseas Bank
(e) Karnataka Bank

SBI PO MAINS 2024

37. Arjuna Award winner Ayhika Mukherjee is associated with which of the following sports?
(a) Badminton (b) Squash
(c) Table Tennis (d) Hockey
(e) Lawn Tennis

38. Which tiger reserve has been recognized as India's first Dark Sky Park and the fifth in Asia, aimed at preserving the night sky and preventing light pollution, appealing to astronomy enthusiasts?
(a) Bandipur Tiger Reserve
(b) Pench Tiger Reserve
(c) Kanha Tiger Reserve
(d) Ranthambhore Tiger Reserve
(e) Sariska Tiger Reserve

39. The Union Government has extended the term of the CBDT Chairperson Nitin Gupta by ______.
(a) 3 months (b) 6 months
(c) 9 months (d) 12 months
(e) 18 months

40. Government has launched PM JANMAN (PM-Janjati Adivasi Nyaya Maha Abhiyan) which is aimed at comprehensive development of 75 Particularly Vulnerable Tribal Groups (PVTGs) residing in _______ and 1 UT who continue to lag behind in socio economic indicators of educational, health and livelihood with a total outlay of Rs.24,104 crore.
(a) 10 states (b) 12 states
(c) 15 states (d) 18 states
(e) 22 states

41. Govt launched the MPLADS e-SAKSHI Mobile Application for revised fund flow procedure under MPLAD Scheme. What amount of funds each year MPs receive under MPLAD Scheme?
(a) Rs. 2 crore (b) Rs. 3 crore
(c) Rs. 4 crore (d) Rs. 5 crore
(e) Rs. 7 crore

42. The Pension Fund Regulatory and Development Authority (PFRDA) has notified the National Pension System Trust (Second Amendment) Regulations 2023 and Pension Fund (Amendment) Regulations 2023 that simplify the provisions related to appointment of Trustees, their terms and conditions, holding of meetings of Board of Trustees and appointment of CEO - NPS Trust. Amendments to Pension Fund Regulations simplify the provisions related to governance of Pension Funds in line with______.
(a) Companies Act, 2013
(b) Limited Liability Partnership Act 2008
(c) Prevention of Money-Laundering Act, 2002
(d) Banking Regulation Acts 1949
(e) Pension Reforms Act (PFRDAAct, 2013)

43. The Ram Mandir in Ayodhya is designed in which style of architecture?
(a) Dravida (b) Vesara
(c) Nagara (d) Western
(e) Rajput

44. Recently, ISRO's third lunar mission Chandrayaan-3 landed on the moon while the first moon mission was launched by NASA. So far, how many times has the NASA mission landed on the moon?
(a) 7 (b) 8
(c) 9 (d) 10
(e) 12

45. In collaboration with which bank and the Reserve Bank Innovation Hub (RBIH) the DLabs at the Indian School of Business (ISB) launched 'Build for Billions' a startup accelerator program to focus on promoting financial inclusion for the informal economy?
(a) Canara Bank
(b) Indian Bank
(c) Bank of India
(d) Union Bank of India
(e) State Bank of India

46. According to the annual survey on International Trade in Banking Services (ITBS, 2022-23, Indian banks expanded their global presence through _____.
(a) branch route
(b) subsidiaries route
(c) join venture route
(d) Both A and B
(e) None of the above

47. Which of the following pairs of types of banks and their numbers is not correctly matched?
(a) Public sector banks -12
(b) Regional Rural Banks – 43
(c) Local Area Banks - 4
(d) Small Finance Bank -12
(e) Payments Bank – 6

48. Which of the following types of banks can not extend MUDRA loan?
(a) Regional Rural Banks
(b) Payments Bank
(c) Small Finance Bank
(d) NBFCs
(e) MFIs

49. Which of the following union territories have the Regional Rural Banks (RRBs)?
(a) Ladakh
(b) Puducherry
(c) Andaman and Nicobar

(d) Lakshadweep
(e) Dadra and Nagar Haveli

50. As per RBI guidelines, a savings account will be treated as inoperative / dormant if there are no transactions in the account for over a period of ______.
(a) six month (b) one year
(c) two years (d) three years
(e) None of the above

51. The Reserve Bank of India (RBI) has included how many nonbanking finance companies (NBFCs) in the upper layer under scale based regulation for NBFCs for the year 2023-24?
(a) 10 (b) 12 (c) 15 (d) 18
(e) 20

52. Which fintech company has signed an agreement with the NPCI International Payments to expand the scope of Unified Payments Interface (UPI) payments outside India?
(a) PhonePe (b) Google Pay
(c) Paytm (d) Mobikwik
(e) Amazon Pay

53. State Bank of India (SBI) has raised what amount through its second Basel III compliant Additional Tier 1 bond issuance for the current financial year at a coupon rate of 8.34%?
(a) ₹3,000 crore (b) ₹4,000 crore
(c) ₹5,000 crore (d) ₹6,000 crore
(e) ₹8,000 crore

54. Which of the following banks is looking to open its first branch in Singapore?
(a) ICICI Bank (b) Yes Bank
(c) HDFC Bank (d) IndusInd Bank
(e) Kotak Mahindra Bank

55. What amount of penalty should be imposed on the first breach of Guidelines for Regulation of Coaching Center 2024 as per the new guidelines for the operation of coaching centres in the country issued by the Ministry of Education?
(a) ₹ 10, 000 (b) ₹ 25, 000
(c) ₹ 50, 000 (d) ₹ 75, 000
(e) ₹ 1,00,000

56. What is the upper limit of annual household income for a collateral free Microfinance loan?
(a) ₹ 1,00,000 (b) ₹ 1,50,000
(c) ₹ 2,00,000 (d) ₹ 2,50,000
(e) ₹ 3,00,000

57. Which of the following entities became the top arranger for Indian offshore loans in 2023?
(a) HSBC Holdings Plc
(b) BNP Paribas
(c) Mizuho Financial Group Inc
(d) Citi Bank
(e) Barclays Bank

58. The Reserve Bank of India has proposed enhancing the limit for UPI payments to hospitals and educational institutions from Rs 1 lakh to Rs 5 lakh per transaction. What is the transaction limit for UPI payments for retail direct schemes and for IPO subscriptions?
(a) Rs 1 lakh (b) Rs 2 lakh
(c) Rs 3 lakh (d) Rs 4 lakh
(e) Rs 5 lakh

59. Which portal has been launched by the Reserve Bank of India for the search of unclaimed deposits across multiple banks at one place?
(a) UDGAM (b) MANI
(c) DAMINI (d) SCORES
(e) YUKTI

60. According to GST regulations, any person registered under GST who initiates the transportation of goods with a consignment value exceeding ________must provide details of these goods in an E-way bill before the goods begin their journey.
(a) ₹ 25,000 (b) ₹ 50,000
(c) ₹ 75,000 (d) ₹ 100,000
(e) ₹ 200,000

61. The government hiked windfall tax on domestically produced crude oil to ₹3,300 per tonne from ₹3,200 per tonne. The tax is levied in the form of a _____.
(a) Value Added Tax
(b) Special Additional Excise Duty
(c) Special Additional custom duty
(d) Ad-Valorem Tax
(e) Special Goods and Service Tax

62. Who among the following do not hold the post of G20 sherpa?
(a) Girish Chandara Murmu
(b) Amitabh Kant
(c) Suresh Prabhu
(d) Shaktikanta Das
(e) Montek Singh Ahluwalia

63. How many numbers of unicorns were added in 2022 and 2021 respectively?
(a) 20 and 44 (b) 21 and 40
(c) 22 and 45 (d) 25 and 52
(e) 26 and 56

64. The Reserve Bank of India (RBI) has expanded the trade receivables discounting system (TReDS) by allowing insurance companies to participate. Which of the following is not a participant of TReDS platform?
(a) MSME sellers
(b) Corporate and other buyer
(c) PSUs
(d) NBFC Factors
(e) Import Agents

65. REC Limited, a Maharatna Central Public Sector Enterprise (CPSE) under the Ministry of Power, has achieved a significant milestone by issuing its inaugural Japanese Yen (JPY) 61.1 billion (approximately Rs 3,500 crore) green bonds for how many years?
(a) 2 years (b) 3 years
(c) 5 years (d) 7 years
(e) 8 years

66. Which Indian petrochemical company has become the first ISO 27001:2022 certified petrochemical organization in India, certified by British Standards Institution (BSI)?
(a) Haldia Petrochemicals Ltd (HPL)
(b) Reliance Petroleum
(c) Finolex Ind
(d) National Organic Chemical Industry Limited
(e) IG Petrochemicals Limited

67. In the BrandZ study, conducted by WPP and Kantar, Tata Consultancy Services (TCS) retained its top position as India's most valuable brand for the second consecutive year with a brand value of _______.
(a) $36 billion (b) $41 billion
(c) $43 billion (d) $48 billion
(e) $52 billion

68. As per the 'Responsible Lending Conducts' issued by the Reserve Bank of India, banks and NBFCs have to release original movable, immovable property documents within _____ days of full repayments of loan.
(a) 15 days (b) 30 days
(c) 45 days (d) 60 days
(e) 90 days

69. A false or misleading claim made by an organization about the positive impact that a company, product or service has on the environment is known as ______.
(a) Greenwashing
(b) Greentrading
(c) Greenmarketing
(d) Greenwarming
(e) None of the above

70. Which of the following entities is not regulated by SEBI?
(a) Merchants Brokers
(b) Stock Brokers
(c) Clearing Corporation of India
(d) Portfolio managers
(e) Debenture trustees

71. Which financing agency has unveiled a groundbreaking seven-year USD 100 million Plastic Waste Reduction-Linked Bond, an innovative financial instrument that ties investor returns to Plastic Waste Collection Credits, Plastic Waste Recycling Credits, and Voluntary Carbon Units expected to be generated by projects in Ghana and Indonesia?
(a) World Economic Forum
(b) World Bank
(c) International Monetary Funds
(d) Asian Development Bank
(e) New Development Bank

72. Indian Renewable Energy Development Agency (IREDA) and which bank has signed a Memorandum of Understanding (MoU) aimed at advancing renewable energy initiatives across the nation?
(a) Punjab National Bank
(b) Union Bank of India
(c) Canara Bank
(d) Indian Bank
(e) Bank of Baroda

73. Video, Audio, and images edited and manipulated using Artificial Intelligence (AI) is known as ______.
(a) Deepfake Technology
(b) AI-enhanced Media Editing
(c) Synthetic Media Production
(d) Neural Network Editing
(e) Machine Learning Manipulation

74. Which of the following languages are not part of the classical languages list of national education policy NEP?

(a) Pali (b) Prakrit
(c) Persian (d) Bengali
(e) Malayalam

75. The National Quantum mission has been launched for how many years?
(a) 3 years (b) 4 years
(c) 6 years (d) 8 years
(e) 10 years

76. What is the name of the DRDO multi-barrel rocket launchers (MBRL) system?
(a) Pinaka (b) Dhanush
(c) Akash (d) Gandiv
(e) Vijay

77. Which of the following is not included for the Liberelised Remittance Scheme (LRS)?
(a) Diversification of investment
(b) Overseas education
(c) Gift and Donation
(d) Medical Treatment
(e) All of the above

78. In the ICC World Cup tournament 2023 the Netherlands won the match defeating which of the following countries?
(a) Australia (b) Bangladesh
(c) England (d) New Zealand
(e) India

79. What is the tenure of the Board of Directors of the Reserve Bank of India?
(a) 2 years (b) 3 years
(c) 4 years (d) 5 years
(e) 6 years

80. As per the Report on Trend and Progress of Banking in India 2021- 22 published by the Reserve Bank of India (RBI), the Gross Non-Performing Assets (GNPA) ratio of Scheduled Commercial Banks (SCBs) has declined to ___ in September 2022 from 9% in 2017-18.
(a) 4% (b) 5% (c) 6% (d) 7%
(e) 8%

81. Name the Argentina's state-owned enterprise with which the Khanij Bidesh India Ltd. (KABIL) has signed an MoU to acquire five lithium blocks in Argentina for exploration and development?
(a) CAMYEN (b) ENERGIA
(c) ENPGAS (d) INDAUTOR
(e) EDESA

82. Which of the following is not a category of 'States' startup ranking 2022 recently released by the Department for Promotion of Industry and Internal Trade (DPIIT)?
(a) Beginners
(b) Leaders
(c) Best Performers
(d) Top Performers
(e) Aspiring Leaders

83. According to the United Nations Population Fund (UNFPA), how much percentage of Indian population come under 15-64 working as a group?
(a) 52 percent (b) 54 percent
(c) 57 percent (d) 65 percent
(e) 68 percent

84. India's first Dark Sky Reserve Hanle, is located in which state/UTs?
(a) Puducherry (b) Maharashtra
(c) Goa (d) Ladakh
(e) Jammu and Kashmir

85. Who headed the Kovid-19 stress committee constituted in August 2020 by the Reserve Bank of India?
(a) KV Kamath (b) Diwakar Gupta
(c) TN Manoharan (d) Ashvin Parekh
(e) Sunil Mehta

86. Which of the following are Domestically systematic insurers (D-SIIs)?
(i) Life Insurance Corporation (LIC)
(ii) New India Assurance
(iii) General Insurance Corporation (GIC Re)
(a) Only 1 and 2 (b) Only 2 and 3
(c) Only 1 and 3 (d) Only 3
(e) Only 1, 2 and 3

SSC CGL 2024

87. Who is Union Minister of State (Independent Charge) for Science and Technology as of July 2023?
(a) Dharmendra Pradhan
(b) Jitendra Singh
(c) Ashwini Vaishnaw
(d) Ramesh Pokhriyal

88. Who is the Chief Minister of Tamil Nadu as of July 2023?
(a) KN Nehru
(b) Pinarayi Vijayan
(c) M Yedurappa
(d) MK Stalin

89. The inaugural match of the Women Premier League 2023 cricket was played in which of the following venues?
(a) Chennai (b) Kolkata
(c) Delhi (d) Mumbai

90. The government of which of the following states created a draft policy in 2022 for senior citizens on the basis of article 41, which aims to form a directorate for the welfare of senior citizens?
(a) Karnataka (b) Kerala
(c) Telangana (d) Tamil Nadu

91. When was the High Court and Supreme Court Judges (Salaries and Conditions of Service) Amendment Bill, 2021 introduced in Lok Sabha?
(a) 30 November 2021
(b) 27 September 2021
(c) 29 March 2021
(d) 28 April 2021

92. In which year was the 'Naye Bharat Ke Sapne' campaign launched by Meta and the Ministry of Women?
(a) 2022 (b) 2021
(c) 2023 (d) 2020

93. Which government honoured a distinguished percussionist named Pandit Anindo Chatterjee with the Banga Vibhushan Award in 2022?
(a) Jharkhand (b) West Bengal
(c) Tripura (d) Assam

94. Who was appointed as India's 28th Controller General of Accounts (CGA) in March 2023?
(a) Praveen Sharma (b) SS Dubey
(c) Vikram Devdutt (d) Arun Goel

95. Which of the following was the mascot of the FIH men's Hockey World Cup - 2023?
(a) Asha (b) Bheema
(c) Jitu (d) Olly

96. How many awards were presented at the National Sports and Adventure Awards-2022 ceremony held at Rashtrapati Bhavan on 30 November 2022?
(a) 44 (b) 52 (c) 28 (d) 32

97. As of March 2023, how many High Courts are there in India?
(a) 20 (b) 35 (c) 25 (d) 30

98. According to the Agricultural and Processed food products Export Development Authority (APEDA) 2020-2021, which state of India has the first rank in grapes production?
(a) Bihar (b) Uttar Pradesh
(c) Kamataka (d) Maharashtra

99. How many medals did India win in International Shooting Sport Federation (ISSF) World Cup 2022, which was held in Cairo, Egypt?
(a) 9 (b) 7
(c) 6 (d) 8

100. As of 2021, which is the world's largest drainage basin with an area of about 70,00,000 km2?
(a) Amazon basin (b) Congo basin
(c) Amur basin (d) Nile basin

101. Which of the following States has declared a social security scheme for registered newspaper hawkers in the State in 2021 considering the losses they faced during the pandemic and that they are a part of the unorganised sector?
(a) Maharashtra (b) Gujarat
(c) Tamil Nadu (d) Odisha

102. What is the aim of the PM Ujjwala 2.0 Yojna launched in August 2021?
(a) Free gas stove for BPL Households:
(b) 20 million LPG connections will be provided to the beneficiaries
(c) Free LPG connections for commercial use
(d) 10 million LPG connections will be provided to the beneficiaries

103. As for the year 2020-21, which of the following states had the lowest unemployment rate among persons aged 15 years and above?
(a) Gujarat (b) Sikkim
(c) Madhya Pradesh (d) Chhattisgarh

104. Madhuri Barthwal, a folk singer and Padma Shri 2022 awardee, belongs to which of the following states of India?
(a) Maharashtra (b) Himachal Pradesh
(c) Uttarakhand (d) Uttar Pradesh

105. Which of the following types of direct tax collection increased as of 10 February 2023 budget?
(a) Octroi duties
(b) Personal income tax

(c) Commercial tax
(d) Corporate tax

106. Which Ghazal singer was conferred with the prestigious Deenanath Mangeshkar Award in April 2023?
(a) Ghazal Srinivas (b) Pankaj Ughas
(c) Bhupinder Singh (d) Talat Aziz

107. Who has written the book 'Fearless Governance', published in January 2021, describing her stint as Governor?
(a) Draupadi Murmu (b) Kiran Bedi
(c) Anandi ben Patel (d) Baby Rani Maurya

108. Tabla player, Ustad Zakir Hussain was awarded which of the following awards by the Government of India in 2023?
(a) Padma Bhushan (b) Bharat Ratna
(c) Padma Vibhushan (d) Padma Shri

109. Which of the following famous indian athletes won the Zurich Diamond League final 2022 in September 2022?
(a) Bajrang Punia (b) PT Usha
(c) Neera Chopra (d) Mirabai Chanu

110. As in July 2021, The NIPUN Bharat Scheme was launched by which of the following Ministries?
(a) Ministry of Agriculture and Farmers
(b) Ministry of Education
(c) Ministry of Health and Family Welfare
(d) Ministry of Corporate Affairs

111. As per the report of the NITI Aayog in 2023, which among the following states in india has the lowest percentage of the total population that is multidimensionally poor?
(a) Uttarakhand (b) Sikkim
(c) Kerala (d) Goa

112. Which of the following Indian states has the least number of operational airports as of 2022?
(a) Kamataka (b) Mizoram
(c) Maharashtra (d) Bihar

113. In May 2022, Then President Ram Nath Kovind appointed ________ as the Lieutenant Governor of Delhi.
(a) Vijai Kapoor
(b) Vinai Kumar Saxena
(c) Anil Baijal
(d) Kiran Bedi

114. In 2022, which of the following railway stations has been selected for the 'One Station One Product' scheme launched by Indian Railways, which identifies Kanchipuram sarees as the chosen product?
(a) Patna Jn (b) Visakhapatnam
(c) Chennal Central (d) Howrah

115. In August 2022, the Ministry of Social Justice and Empowerment launched the scheme, with an aim to provide comprehensive rehabilitation services to people engaged in begging in 75 municipalities.
(a) SMILE-75 (b) BEAM-75
(c) TWINKLE-75 (d) RISE-75

116. Which of the following is NOT an amendment made to the Airport Economic Regulatory Authority (AERA) Amendment Act, 2021?
(a) The government can call any airport a major airport just by notification.
(b) A major airport is one which has an annual traffic of minimum 35 lakh passengers
(c) The government will club together profit-making and loss-making airports.
(d) The government can offer airports as a package in PPP mode to the prospective bidders.

117. Who among the following was selected as the Sherpa for India's G20 hosted in 2022- 237
(a) Amitabh Kant
(b) Piyush Goyal
(c) Ashwini Vaishnav
(d) Shaktikanta Das

118. Hindustani singer Pandit Venkatesh Kumar was honoured with "Kalidas Samman-2022 by which state government?
(a) Maharashtra (b) Madhya Pradesh
(c) Gujarat (d) Uttar Pradesh

119. Who is the world's most popular leader as per Global Leader Approval Ratings released by US-based Morning Consult in February 2023?
(a) Xi Jinping (b) Vladimir Putin
(c) Joe Biden (d) Narendra Modi

120. Which of the following nations won the seven times women's Asia Cup cricket Championship?
(a) Pakistan (b) Bangladesh
(c) India (d) Sri Lanka

121. As of 31 May 2021, only 47% of total routes and 39% of airports (unserved and underserved) have been operationalised under UDAN, according to ICRA. What is the full form of UDAN?
(a) Udtha Desh Ka Aam Nayak
(b) Ude Desh Ka Aam Naagrik
(c) Unnath Desh Ka Aam Naagrik
(d) Ujwal Desh Ka Aam Naagrik

122. Tabla maestro, Bickram Ghosh, was awarded with which of the following awards in 2023 in the Contemporary Category?
(a) Padma Shri
(b) Padma Bhushan
(c) Sangeet Natak Akademi
(d) Sangeet Kalanidhi

123. Which team won the T20 cricket event, Syed Mushtaq Ali Trophy 2022-2023?
(a) Vidarbha
(b) Himanchal Pradesh
(c) Mumbai
(d) Punjab

124. Who among the following famous Indian women cricketers announced retirement in June 2022?
(a) Smriti Mandhana (b) Mithali Raj
(c) Anjum Chopra (d) Jhulan Goswami

125. Who won the paralympic bronze medal in archery for India at Tokyo in 2020?
(a) Deepika Kumari (b) Harvinder Singh
(c) Atanu Das (d) Pravin Jadhav

126. For which of the following states was the Constitution (Scheduled Castes and Scheduled Tribes) Orders (Second Amendment) Bill, 2022, introduced in the Parliament?
(a) Bihar (b) Uttar Pradesh
(c) Odisha (d) Madhya Pradesh

127. Which of the following nations won the ICC World Test Championship, defeating India, in 2023?
(a) Australia (b) England
(c) South Africa (d) New Zealand

128. Who among the following is appointed as the new Chairman of Pension Fund Regulatory and Development Authority (PFRDA) in March 20237
(a) Mamta Shankar
(b) Supratim Bandopadhyay
(c) Shasikanta Das
(d) Deepak Moharity

129. Which Bill was passed by the Parliament, in July 2021, to help in the availability of working capital for the micro, small and medium enterprises sector?
(a) The Factoring Regulation (Amendment) Bill, 2021
(b) The Minerals Laws (Amendment) Bill, 2020
(c) The Insolvency and Bankruptcy Code (Amendment) Bill, 2021
(d) The Essential Commodities (Amendment) Bil, 2020

130. In which of the following years will India host the World Badminton Championship?
(a) 2025 (b) 2027
(c) 2026 (d) 2028

131. Who was the player of the match in the semi-final of the T20 Women's World Cup 2023 played between India and Australia?
(a) Meg Lanning
(b) Ashleigh Gardner
(c) Harmanpreet kaur
(d) Deepti Sharma

132. Who among the following won a Gold Medal at the 2021 World Cadet Wrestling Championship held in Budapest, Hungary?
(a) Vinesh Phogat (b) Priya Malik
(c) Geeta Phogat (d) Pooja Dhanda

133. Which of the following schemes was launched for the welfare of the unorganised sector workers and labourers on 26 August 2021?
(a) e-Shram Portal
(b) PM Daksh Yojana
(c) Gram Ujala Scheme
(d) PM Mentoring Yuva Scheme

134. Prabha Atre, who received the Padma Vibhushan Award 2022, belongs to which Gharana?
(a) Agra gharana (b) Mewati gharana
(c) Kirana gharana (d) Indore gharana

135. Who among the following sports persons is designated as brand ambassador for Nikshay Mitra, an initiative under Pradhan Mantri TB Mukt Bharat Abhiyaan by Ministry of Health and Family welfare of GOI in November 2022?
(a) Deepa Malik (b) Abhinav Bindra
(c) Pullela Gopichand (d) Mary Kom

136. Which of the following was the mascot of the Khelo India University Games 2022?
(a) Moga (b) Bheema
(c) Jitu (d) Saavaj

137. On 29th October 2020, the Ministry of Science and Technology launched the SERB- POWER Scheme. What is the objective of the scheme?
(a) To strengthen the solar programme of india with France
(b) To mitigate gender disparity in science and engineering research funding in various academic programmes and laboratories
(c) To allow reservation for women in the Parliament and Judiciary
(d) To allow reservation for women in the Ministry of Science and Technology

138. Indira PP Bora is a Padma Shri Awardee 2020 for her contribution to which Indian classical dance?
(a) Bharatanatyam (b) Kathak
(c) Kuchipudi (d) Sattriya

139. Which Lavani singer got Padma Shri 2022 by the President of India?
(a) Sulochana Chavan (b) Vaishali Samant
(c) Bela Shende (d) Devaki Pandit

140. Who among the following was appointed as the Governor of Jharkhand in February 2023?
(a) T Gahlot
(b) RN Ravi
(c) Ramesh Bais
(d) CP Radhakrishnan

141. What is the amount of financial assistance provided per month to girl students studying in government schools under the 'Tamil Nadu Pudhumai Penn Scheme' launched by the Government of Tamil Nadu in 2023?
(a) ₹2,000 per month (b) ₹500 per month
(c) 23,000 per month (d) ₹1,000 per month

142. When was the Rajiv Gandhi Khel Ratna Award renamed as Major Dhyan Chand Khel Ratna Award?
(a) 6th August 2021 (b) 6th August 2022
(c) 5th January 2022 (d) 5th January 2021

143. According to the Ministry of Road Transport and which position does India have in terms of road networks in Annual report (2020-2021),
(a) Third (b) First
(c) Second (d) Fourth

144. Who among the following is one of the Deputy Chief Ministers of Uttar Pradesh as of July 2023?
(a) Keshav Prasad Maurya
(b) Manoj Sinha
(c) Narottam Mishra
(d) Yogi Adityanath

145. The Parliament passed the Essential Defence Services Bill, 2021 in August 2021. Which of the following is an objective behind passing it?
(a) To prohibit strikes, lockouts and layoffs in units engaged in essential defence services
(b) To appoint more women in defence services
(c) To encourage more FDI in defence services
(d) To implement one rank one pension

146. Who among the following was the Former Secretary (HRD), Information and Broadcasting (I&B) and has been appointed as the advisor to the Prime Minister of India in October 2021?
(a) Amit Khare
(b) PK Sinha
(c) Amarjeet Sinha
(d) Shri Apurva Chandra

147. Indian classical violinist Annavarapu Rama Swamy was awarded with the in 2021.
(a) Sangeet Natak Akademi
(b) Padma Vibhushan
(c) Padma Bhushan
(d) Padma Shri

148. The Epidemic Diseases (Amendment) Ordinance, 2020 amended which of the following Acts?
(a) The Epidemic Diseases Act, 1890
(b) The Epidemic Diseases Act, 1892
(c) The Epidemic Diseases Act, 1895
(d) The Epidemic Diseases Act, 1897

149. Under the 'Mera Rukh Mero Santati' initiative launched by the Sikkim Chief Minister Prem Singh Tamang in 2023, how many trees will be planted for every child born in Sikkim ?
(a) 100 (b) 150 (c) 200 (d) 50

150. Which Indian musician from Maharashtra received the Padma Vibhushan 2023?
(a) Zakir Hussain (b) Milind Date
(c) Ramdas Palsule (d) Bharat Kamat

151. Three Indians were featured in Time Magazine's list of '100 most influential people of 2021'. Whose name was NOT included in the list?
(a) Mamata Banerjee
(b) Amitabh Bachchan
(c) Narendra Modi
(d) Adar Poonawalla

152. In which year did the Central Government launch the National Air Sports Policy?
(a) 2022 (b) 2021 (c) 2023 (d) 2020

153. As of 14 October 2021, which Indian footballer was in the news for breaking Pele's 77 international goals?
(a) Bhaichung Bhutia
(b) Sunil Chhetri
(c) Gurpreet Singh Saridhu
(d) Sandesh Jhingan

154. As per a report of the Ministry of Labour and Employment, what was the rate of unemployment in Maharashtra for the year 2021-22?
(a) 3.5% (b) 3.01% (c) 4.2% (d) 4.4%

155. Who among the following was one of the recipients of the inaugural 'Prof CR Rao Centenary Gold Medal' award in 2021?
(a) Raghuram Rajan (b) Surjit Bhalla
(c) Amartya Sen (d) Jagdish Bhagwali

156. Which state Chief Minister launched the 'Kaushalya Matritva Yojana in 2022, which provides financial assistance of ₹5,000 to women giving birth to a second girl child for safe motherhood?
(a) Gujarat (b) Uttar Pradesh
(c) Rajasthan (d) Chhattisgarh

157. What is the disinvestment target of the Finance Ministry for the year 2023-24?
(a) ₹54,000 crore (b) 253,000 crore
(c) ₹50,000 crore (d) 51,000 crore

158. Pandwani singer Usha Barle was conferred with which of the following awards by the Government of India in 2023?
(a) Padma Vibhushan (b) Bharat Ratna
(c) Padma Bhushan (d) Padma Shin

159. Mulayam Singh Yadav, who passed away in October 2022, served as the Chief Minister of which state?
(a) Madhya Pradesh (b) Gujarat
(c) Uttar Pradesh (d) Bihar

160. Which of the following State governments has launched a scheme 'Ankur' in May 2021 to promote planting of trees in public, wherein people will be awarded for planting and taking care of the saplings?
(a) Bihar (b) West Bengal
(c) Uttarakhand (d) Madhya Pradesh

161. In 2022, who has been appointed as new Attorney General of India?
(a) KK Venugopal (b) Niren De
(c) Mukul Rohatgi (d) R Venkatramani

162. Coir conductor Coomi Nariman Wadia was awarded with which of the following awards by the Government of India in 2023?
(a) Padma Bhushan
(b) Padma Vibhushan
(c) Bharat Ratna
(d) Padma Shri

163. Who assumed charge as the new Vice Chief of the Indian Navy on 31 July 2021?
(a) Karambir Singh (b) Ravneet Singh
(c) SN Ghormade (d) Dinesh K Tripathi

164. Who among the following Indian cricketers were named the Wisden's cricketer of the year in the 2022 edition of the Almanack?
(a) Surya Kumar Yadav and Axar Patel
(b) Virat Kohli and Bhuvneshwar Kumar
(c) Rohit Sharma and Jasprit Bumrah
(d) Rohit Sharma and Virat Kohli

165. Which of the following countries will host the ICC men's Cricket World Cup in the year 2031?
(a) India, Bangladesh
(b) India, Sri Lanka
(c) Sri Lanka and Pakistan
(d) Sri Lanka and Bangladesh

166. Who among the following is the first Indian to win gold at Junior World Weightlifting Championship in May 2022?
(a) Sathish Sivalingam
(b) Mirabai Chanu
(c) Santoshi Matsa
(d) Harshada Sharad Garud

167. Which of the following States have enacted the Cattle Preservation Act, 2021 in July-August 2021 to regulate slaughter and transport of cattle and proposed an amendment in December

2021 to allow inter-district transportation of cattle for agricultural and animal husbandry except in districts sharing international border?
(a) Tripura (b) Sikkim
(c) Arunachal Pradesh (d) Assam

168. N. Rangasamy sworn in as the Chief Minister of Puducherry in May 2021. What is the name of the party he formed?
(a) Naam Tamilar Katchi
(b) All India NR Congress
(c) Amma Makkal Munnetra Kazagam
(d) Viduthalai Chiruthaigal Katchi

169. The final match of IPL 2023 was hosted by which of the following cities?
(a) Bengaluru (b) Chennai
(c) Mumbai (d) Ahmedabad

170. Who among the following famous badminton players won Swiss Open 2022?
(a) Jwala Gutta (b) Apama Popat
(c) Saina Nehwal (d) PV Sindhu

171. In 2022, Vinay Mohan Kwatra took charge as the Foreign Secretary of India. Prior to this, he served as the ambassador to which of the following countries?
(a) Bhutan (b) Sri Lanka
(c) Nepal (d) Maldives

172. According to the Tea Board of India's report (2021-22), which group of states in India is the largest tea producer?
(a) Andhra Pradesh and Kerala
(b) Himachal Pradesh and Uttarakhand
(c) West Bengal und Assem
(d) Tamil Nadu and Kerala

173. In January 2023, Koneru Humpy won India's first-ever silver medal at the ________ held in Almaty, Kazakhstan.
(a) FIDE World Chess Championship
(b) World Blitz Chess Championship
(c) World Correspondence Chess Championship
(d) World Rapid Chess Championship

174. In November 2021, the government declared November 15 as 'Janjatiya Gaurav Divas'. It happens to be the birth anniversary of which of the following freedom fighters?
(a) Birsa Munda
(b) Kanhu Murmu
(c) Arjun Munda
(d) Veer Narayan Singh

175. India finished on which of the following positions in overall medals tally at Commonwealth games 2022?
(a) 3rd (b) 4th (c) 1st (d) 2nd

176. Who among the following famous badminton players won Singapore Open 2022?
(a) Aparna Popat (b) Saina Nehwal
(c) Jwala Gutta (d) PV Sindhu

177. What is the cost of the 'Nand Baba Milk Mission' scheme launched by the Uttar Pradesh state government in 2023 to provide milk producers the facility of selling their milk at a reasonable price in villages through dairy co-operative societies?
(a) ₹500 crore (b) 21,500 crore
(c) 12,000 crore (d) 21,000 crore

178. At the 36th National Games, Hashika Ramchandra won six gold medals in which of the following sports?
(a) Boxing (b) Wrestling
(c) Swimming (d) Badminton

179. As per the UNDP, the rank of Sri Lanka in the Human Development Index (2022) is:
(a) 74/189 (b) 73/189
(c) 75/189 (d) 72/189

180. In February 2023, BVR Subrahmanyam was appointed as the:
(a) Chief Vigilance Commissioner
(b) Comptroller Generall Of India
(c) CEO NITI Ayog
(d) Chief Election Commissioner

181. Which of the following is a key focus area of the 'Amrit Dharohar' scheme launched by the Prime Minister Narendra Modi on World Environment Day, 2023?
(a) Preservation of ancient Indian heritage sites
(b) Development of rural infrastructure
(c) To promate values of local communities in conserving wetland ecosyatern
(d) Promobon of organic farmning

SSC MTS 2024

182. The Pharmacy (Amendment) Bill, 2023 was introduced in Lok Sabha on 3 August 2023, which amends the:
(a) Pharmacy Act, 1950
(b) Pharmacy Act, 1949
(c) Pharmacy Act, 1947
(d) Pharmacy Act, 1948

183. As of 31st October 2023, the senior-most member (in terms of age) in the 17th Lok Sabha, Shafiqur Rahman Barq represents which political party?
(a) Bharatiya Janata Party
(b) Indian National Congress
(c) Samajwadi Party
(d) Rashtriya Janata Dal

184. Who was the captain of Royal Challengers Bangalore in the Women's Premier League event 2023?
(a) Harmanpreet Kaur (b) Deepti Sharma
(c) Shafali Verma (d) Smriti Mandhana

185. How many cities have been sellected to be developed as sustainable and responsible destinations as per the Swadesh Darshan 2.0 scheme launched by the Union Ministry of Tourism in January 2023?
(a) 67 (b) 21 (c) 45 (d) 30

186. In September 2023, after the retirement of Incumbent Sanjay Kumar Mishra, who was appointed as In-charge Director of ED?
(a) Tushar Mehta (b) Rahul Navin
(c) Samant Goel (d) TV Somanathan

187. R Muthukannammal, who was awarded the Padma Shri in 2022, is a dancer.
(a) Garba (b) Sadir
(c) Rouf (d) Chhau

188. Which country won the 4th Asian Kho-Kho Championship 2023 event in the Men's category?
(a) Iran (b) Indonesia
(c) South Korea (d) India

189. Where was Global Technology Summit 2022 held?
(a) New Delhi (b) Jaipur
(c) Varanasi (d) Bengaluru

190. On 27th october 2019, Dushyant Chautala took an oath as Deputy Chief Minister of which of the following states?
(a) Himachal Pradesh (b) Haryana
(c) Punjab (d) Madhya Pradesh

191. Which of the following states of india marked the lowest in National Multi-dimensional Poverty Index: A Progress Review 2023?
(a) Goa (b) Kerala
(c) Sikkim (d) Tamil Nadu

192. Who among the following personalities was the recipient of the Lata Mangeshkar Award for Music 2021, presented by the Madhya Pradesh government?
(a) Kumar Sanu (b) Udit Narayan
(c) Shaan (d) Darshan Raval

193. At the Sansad Ratna Awards 2023, who among the following received the Dr. APJ Abdul Kalam Lifetime Achievement Award?
(a) Nagendra Singh
(b) HD Deve Gowda
(c) Laxminarayan Yadav
(d) TK Rangarajan

194. When was National Judicial Commission Bãll, which is a private member bill to regulate the appointment of judges through the National Judicial Commission, introduced in Rajya Sabha?
(a) August 2023 (b) July 2023
(c) March 2022 (d) December 2022

195. Which of the following Kathak dancers received the Padma Shri of 2022?
(a) Shakti and Mukti Mohan
(b) Sunayana Hazarlal Agrawal
(c) Shovana Narayan
(d) Kamalini and Nalini Asthana

196. Who was the Indian match referee in the ICC T20 World Cup 2021 tournament?
(a) Rahul Dravid (b) Venkatesh Prasad
(c) Sunil Gavaskar (d) Javagal Srinath

197. According to the National Multidimensional Poverty Index 2021, which Union Territory has the lowest proportion of poor?
(a) Delhi (b) Lakshadweep
(c) Chandigarh (d) Puducherry

198. What is the name of Formula E's first ever race in India, which was hosted in collaboration with the Telangana government?
(a) The 2023 Mahindra Mumbai E-Prix
(b) The 2023 Greenko Hyderabad E-Prix
(c) The 2023 Mahindra Bangalore E-Prix
(d) The 2023 Greenko Buddha Circuit E-Prix

199. Who among the following led the Parliamentary delegation to participate in the 9th BRICS Parliamentary Forum in September 2023?
(a) Harivansh Narayan Singh
(b) Nitin Gadkari
(c) Jagdeep Dhankar
(d) Om Birla

200. In October 2023, Maharashtra government planned which of the following schemes to overhaul its medical system after the death of 38 patients in Nanded?
(a) Ayushman Maharashtra
(b) Vision 2035
(c) Sahakar Mitra
(d) Arogya Mission

201. Which edition of the Intercontinental Cup event was played in India in 2023?
(a) 10th (b) 1st (c) 3rd (d) 5th

202. Which team won the Women's Asian Hockey Champions Trophy in 2023?
(a) Malaysia (b) India
(c) Japan (d) South Korea

203. S Abdul Nazeer was appointed as the Governor of ______ in February 2023.
(a) Kerala (b) Maharashtra
(c) Andhra Pradesh (d) Goa

204. Which Tamil superstar founded the Tamilaga Vettri Kazhagam (TVK) political party in Tamil Nadu and Puducherry on 2 February 2024 with the slogan 'Pirappokkum Ellaa Uyirkkum' (All are equal by birth)?
(a) Vijay (b) Kamal Haasan
(c) Rajinikanth (d) Dhanush

205. Who among the following is the ex-officio Chairperson of the Rajya Sabha as on 10 October 2023?
(a) Virendra Kumar (b) Piyush Goyal
(c) Prakash Javadekar (d) Jagdeep Dhankar

206. As on February 2024, Yanthungo Patton is the Deputy Chief Minister of which of the following states?
(a) Sikkim (b) Meghalaya
(c) Assam (d) Nagaland

207. Purushottam Dadheech, a renowned Kathak dancer who had been honoured with Padma Shri award for 2020, is associated with which of the following places?
(a) Uttar Pradesh (b) Bihar
(c) Madhya Pradesh (d) Haryana

208. In its 279th report released in April 2023, the Law Commission of India has recommended the provision of which law to be retained?
(a) Labour Law (b) Revenue Law
(c) Contract Law (d) Sedition Law

209. What was the amount earned by BCCI from the sale of five teams in the inaugural Women's Indian Premier League (WPL) in January 2023?
(a) ₹4,669.99 crore (b) ₹7,245.89 crore
(c) ₹951.25 crore (d) ₹1,289.50 crore

210. According to Labour and Employment Statistics 2022, match the states in the first column with their rate of unemployment in the year 2020-21 given in the second column.

States	Rates
(i) Kerala	(a) 6.3%
(ii) Goa	(b) 10.1%
(iii) Haryana	(c) 6.9%
(iv) Uttarakhand	(d) 10.5%

(a) (i) a, (ii) c, (iii) d, (iv) b
(b) (i) d, (ii) b, (iii) c, (iv) a
(c) (i) d, (ii) c, (iii) b, (iv) a
(d) (i) b, (ii) d, (iii) a, (iv) c

211. What was the percentage increase in the disbursal of 'Pradhan Mantri Mudra Yojana' (PMMY) loans in the first quarter of FY 2023-24 compared to the same quarter in the previous year, if the disbursal reached ₹81,597 crore, up from ₹62,650 crore?
(a) 23% (b) 27% (c) 15% (d) 20%

212. Samrat Choudhary and Vijay Kumar Sinha became the Deputy Chief Minister of ______________ on 28 January 2024.
(a) Odisha (b) West Bengal
3. Bihar (d) Jharkhand

213. Sonu Nigam was awarded the Padma Shri in 2022 for which of the following fields?
(a) Sports (b) Civil Service
(c) Public Affairs (d) Art

214. Bharatanatyam Guru __________ received the Nrithya Seva Ratna award from Indian Fine Arts Akademi, San Diego in 2023.
(a) Sailaja
(b) Ratikanth Mohapatra
(c) Vidhya Subramanian
(d) Hema Rajagopalan

215. As of 2023, what is the number of major public seaports in India?
(a) 12 (b) 10 (c) 16 (d) 13

216. As of July 2023, 137 unique products under 'One District, One Product' scheme has been notified from how many districts?
(a) 713 2. 256
(c) 538 (d) 657

217. How much money was allotted by the Gujarat government in August 2023 for the One District, One Product (ODOP) Programme to promote its indigenous products at the international level?
(a) ₹58 crore (b) ₹10 crore
(c) ₹100 crore (d) ₹25 crore

218. From 13 September 2023, DMK MP Tiruchi Siva has been appointed the chairperson of the Committee on ______________.
(a) Home
(b) Information Technology
(c) Transport
(d) Industry

219. As per HDI 2021, which of the following neighbouring countries of India had the highest female life expectancy at birth?
(a) Bangladesh (b) Maldives
(c) Sri Lanka (d) Bhutan

220. According to the Ministry of Agriculture and Farmers Welfare 2022-23, which state of India is the largest producer of sugarcane?
(a) Karnataka (b) Uttar Pradesh
(c) Andhra Pradesh (d) Bihar

221. How many components are there in the New India Literacy Program (NILP) scheme launched by the Union Ministry of Education in March 2023?
(a) Seven (b) Three (c) Nine (d) Five

222. In June 2023, which country conferred the 'Order of the Nile' award on Narendra Modi?
(a) Lebanon (b) Turkey
(c) Egypt (d) Singapore

223. According to National Multidimensional Poverty Index 2023 (A Progress Review), what was the proportion of population in multidimensional poverty (Headcount Ratio) in urban India in 2019-2021?
(a) 2.12% (b) 11.32% (c) 5.27% (d) 6.96%

224. Which edition of the Pro Kabaddi League was started in December 2023?
(a) 12th (b) 11th (c) 10th (d) 8th

225. Where was the Intercontinental Football Cup 2023 organised?
(a) Chandigarh (b) Bhubaneswar
(c) Jalpaiguri (d) Dispur

226. According to National Multidimensional Poverty Index 2023 (A Progress Review), which state has the highest proportion of multidimensionally poor people (Headcount Ratio)?
(a) Rajasthan (b) Bihar
(c) Odisha (d) Jharkhand

227. According to Economic Survey 2023-24, which of the following states is the largest wheat producing state of India?
(a) Assam (b) Uttar Pradesh
(c) West Bengal (d) Bihar

228. Odissi Guru, ________, received the first Utkal Pratibha Samman 2023 at Bhubaneswar.
(a) Ratikant Mohapatra
(b) Hema Rajagopalan
(c) Vidhya Subramanian
(d) Sailaja

229. To mark the 75 years of Indo-Lanka Diplomatic Relations, External Affairs Minister Jaishankar inaugurated the 'Geoffrey Bawa: It is Essential To be There' Exhibition in March 2023. Who was Geoffrey Bawa?
(a) Sri Lankan Architect
(b) Indian Poet
(c) Sri Lankan Poet
(d) Indian Architect

230. In 2023, Congress MP Shashi Tharoor has been named as the chairperson of the Parliamentary Committee on ________.
(a) Chemicals and Fertilisers
(b) Housing and Urban Affairs
(c) Finance and Health
(d) External Affairs

231. What is the maximum amount of home loan the eligible beneficiaries can get under the 'Mo Ghara' scheme launched by the Government of Odisha in May 2023?
(a) Upto ₹2 lakh (b) Upto ₹5.5 lakh
(c) Upto ₹3 lakh (d) Upto ₹4 lakh

232. In December 2022, the Parliament passed the Energy Conservation (Amendment) Bill, 2022. This bill aims to make use of ______
(a) non-fossil fuels
(b) tungsten filament bulbs in houses
(c) subsidy on petrol vehicles
(d) electric vehicles

233. As of February 2024, who among the following is the Deputy Chairman of Rajya Sabha?
(a) Jagat Prakash Nadda
(b) Dharmendra Pradhan
(c) Harivansh Narayan Singh
(d) Prakash Javadekar

234. In October 2023, Indrasena Reddy Nallu has been appointed the Governor of which of the following states in India?
(a) Goa (b) Tripura
(c) Assam (d) Kerala

235. In 2022, Arjun Singh Dhurve was honoured with the Padma Shri Award for his contribution in which of the following Indian folk-dance forms?
(a) Baiga (b) Laho
(c) Bihu (d) Chhau

236. In July 2023, Tribhuvaneshwar Saran Singh Deo was appointed as Deputy Chief Minister of which of the following states?
(a) West Bengal (b) Jharkhand
(c) Chhattisgarh (d) Odisha

237. In February 2023, there have been protests in Punjab to release a group of Sikh prisoners who have been in jail for more than 30 years since militancy was wiped out in Punjab in the 1990s. What are these prisoners called?
(a) Bandi Singhs (b) Babbar Bandis
(c) Khalsa Tigers (d) Qaidi Sikhs

238. Who became the first folk artist from India to walk the Cannes red carpet in 2022?
(a) Mame Khan (b) Swaroop Khan
(c) Sartaj Khan (d) Sarwar Khan

239. The union list from the Seventh Schedule of the Indian Constitution consists of how many subjects as of May 2024?
(a) Ninety three (b) Ninety five
(c) Ninety nine (d) Hundred

240. In November 2023, who was re-appointed as the Chairman of the Armed Forces Tribunal?
(a) Justice Rajendra Menon
(b) Justice Sharad Arvind Bobde
(c) Justice RF Nariman
(d) Justice NV Ramana

241. Who among the following dancers won the prestigious Padma Shree award in the year 2021, for her contribution to folk dance?
(a) Matha B Manjamma Jogathi
(b) Amubi Singh
(c) Kumudini Lakhia
(d) Teejan Bai

242. According to Global Multidimensional Poverty Index 2022, what was the population of the poor in India in 2020?
(a) 128.9 million (b) 328.9 million
(c) 228.9 million (d) 428.9 million

243. Who became the first woman to win two gold medals in a single Para Asian Games event in 2023?
(a) Sheetal Devi (b) Neema Rani
(c) Sarita Devi (d) Disha Dhayal

244. Which of the following white papers, released by NITI Aayog, is related to Public Health Surveillance in India?
(a) Vision 2035
(b) Mission Karmayogi
(c) Dhruv Mission
(d) Arogya Mission

245. The strength of Supreme Court has increased to how many judges as of 13 Feb 2023?
(a) 26 (b) 28 (c) 34 (d) 30

246. Which state received the Sportstar ACES Best State for the Promotion of Sport award in 2024?
(a) Tamil Nadu (b) Haryana
(c) Odisha (d) Punjab

247. In February 2023, who was appointed as the new Governor of Himachal Pradesh?
(a) Satyadev Narayan Arya
(b) Kalraj Mishra
(c) Bandaru Dattatreya
(d) Shiv Pratap Shukla

248. In 2023, which repository is proposed to be set up in a digital epigraphy museum, with digitisation of one lakh ancient inscriptions in the first stage?
(a) Bharat Shared Repository of Inscriptions
(b) Progressive Repository of Indigenous Folklore
(c) Amrit Repository of Numismatic Collection
(d) Indian Repository of Classical Coins

249. Who is the author of the novel 'Life and Death of Sambhaji' published in the year 2021?
(a) Amish Tripathi
(b) Chitra Banerjee Divakaruni
(c) Medha Deshmukh Bhaskaran
(d) Rita Banerji

250. Which of the following awards was conferred upon the Chhau dancer Siba Prasad Das in 2022?
(a) Sangeet Natak Akademi Fellowship
(b) Padma Shri
(c) Ustad Bismillah Khan Yuva Puraskar
(d) Sangeet Natak Akademi Amrit Award

251. In June 2023, who was appointed as the new Research and Analysis Wing (RAW) chief?
(a) Ravi Sinha (b) Samant Goel
(c) Rajiv Kumar (d) Arun Kant

252. On May 23, 2023, who assumed the position of Chairperson at the Competition Commission of India?
(a) Subhash Chandra Garg
(b) Neha Bhatia
(c) NK Singh
(d) Ravneet Kaur

253. Where did the IBA Women's World Boxing Championships 2023 take place in India?
(a) Mumbai (b) New Delhi
(c) Kolkata (d) Bengaluru

254. As of July 2023, how many products were notified under the 'One District, One Product' scheme as per the information provided by the Ministry of Food Processing Industries, Government of India?
(a) 132 (b) 125 (c) 135 (d) 137

255. In which year did India host the FIFA U-17 Women's Football World Cup?
(a) 2021 (b) 2020 (c) 2022 (d) 2019

256. The Government of India in collaboration with ______ has launched the Skills on Wheels mission in Oct 2023 for equipping rural youth with employable skills.
(a) IndusInd Bank (b) NABARD
(c) ICICI Bank (d) HDFC Bank

257. How many artists are selected for the one-time Sangeet Natak Akademi Amrit Award, 2022?
(a) 100 (b) 75 (c) 86 (d) 60

258. Which Indian state's cabinet approved the proposal for recommending the inclusion of the Kui language in the eighth schedule in July 2023?
(a) Karnataka (b) West Bengal
(c) Odisha (d) Tamil Nadu

259. An Indian Parliamentary delegation led by Minister of Parliamentary Affairs, Coal and Mines ______________ visited Brazil from 11 to 13 June 2023.
(a) Virendra Kumar (b) Narayan Rane
(c) Prahlad Joshi (d) Arjun Munda

260. Which of the following Indian cities was the host of the ICC Men's World Cup final cricket match in 2023?
(a) Mumbai (b) Chennai
(c) New Delhi (d) Ahmedabad

261. In January 2023, the Chief Minister's Residential Land Rights Scheme (Mukhyamantri Awasiy Bhu Adhikar Yojana) was launched in which Indian state?
(a) Madhya Pradesh (b) Haryana
(c) Punjab (d) Uttar Pradesh

SSC CHSL 2024

262. As of March 2024, who among the following is the Chairperson of the National Green Tribunal?
(a) Lokeshwar Singh Panta
(b) Swatanter Kumar
(c) Prakash Shrivastava
(d) Ajay Narayan Jha

263. Former minister of the state and former president of BJP alliance partner IPFT __________ received the Padma Shri award (posthumously) in 2023.
(a) Narendra Chandra Debbarma
(b) Prabhat Choudhury
(c) Rebati Mohan Das
(d) Pinaki Das Chowdhury

264. Who was the chief coordinator for the G20 summit which held in India in 2023?
(a) Vijay Gokhale
(b) Harsh Vardhan Shringla

(c) S Jaishankar
(d) Vinay Kwatra

265. In year 2023, the Government of India launched which of the following schemes to bring Indian-origin researchers to higher educational institutions in the country?
(a) VAIBHAV (b) SEEKHO
(c) AMANTRAN (d) VAPSI

266. ICC World Cup (cricket) 2023 was hosted by ______.
(a) India and Bangladesh
(b) India, Sri Lanka and Bangladesh
(c) India and Sri Lanka
(d) India

267. Who among the followings won gold at the International Shooting Sport Federation (ISSF) junior world cup 2023?
(a) Rajkanwar Singh Sandhu
(b) Dhanush Srikanth
(c) Umamahesh Maddineni
(d) Mahesh Pasupathy Anandakumar

268. According to Global Multidimensional Poverty Index (2022), which of the following groups of states is Included in top 10 poorest states of India?
(a) Manipur and Nagaland
(b) Karnataka and Tamil Nadu
(c) Punjab and Gujarat
(d) Meghalaya and Madhya Pradesh

269. ________ was sworn in as Central Vigilance Commissioner on 29 May 2023.
(a) Praveen Kumar Srivastava
(b) Arti C Srivastava
(c) Sarvan Kumar
(d) Uday Veer Singh

270. Which of the following states launched the first Migration Monitoring System in the year 2022?
(a) Maharashtra (b) Goa
(c) Kerala (d) Karnataka

271. In which event at the 2023 U-20 Asian Athletics Championships did Siddharth Choudhary win a gold medal for India?
(a) Triple jump (b) Discus throw
(c) Hammer throw (d) Shot put

272. Which organisation launched the Indian Customs Compliance Information Portal (CIP) for providing free access to information on all Customs procedures and regulatory compliance for nearly 12,000 Customs Tariff items in the year 2021?
(a) Central Board for Direct Taxes
(b) Income Tax Settlement Commission
(c) Central Board for Indirect Taxes & Customs
(d) Directorate of Enforcement

273. April 2023, the Maharashtra government has approved how much percentage of reservation for Divyang employees in promotions?
(a) 2% (b) 4% (c) 5% (d) 3%

274. In January 2023, Captain Shiva Chouhan was in the news for being the first woman officer to be deployed at which battlefield?
(a) Leh (b) Siachen
(c) Kargil (d) Dras

275. Who among the following was appointed to the UN tax committee in July 2021, as a member for the 2021 to 2025 term?
(a) TV Somanathan (b) Rasmi Ranjan Das
(c) Vipul Bansal (d) Vivek Singh

276. What is the name of the centrally sponsored scheme related to literacy that was launched by the Government of India in March 2023?
(a) Bharat Padhega
(b) National Literacy Programme
(c) New India Literacy Programme
(d) India Literacy Programme

277. In 2023, Gulab Chand Kataria became the Governor of which of the following states?
(a) Assam (b) Odisha
(c) Himachal Pradesh (d) Tamil Nadu

278. How many times has India won the South Asian Football Federation (SAFF) Championship as of December 2023?
(a) 9 times (b) 5 times
(c) 6 times (d) 7 times

279. In April 2023, Government of India launched Vibrant Village Programme from Kibithoo village which is located in ________.
(a) Arunachal Pradesh (b) Assam
(c) Bihar (d) Meghalaya

280. The fifth edition of the Khelo India Youth Games were organised in Bhopal city in which year?
(a) 2020 (b) 2022 (c) 2023 (d) 2021

281. Which of the following was NOT a venue for the 66th National School Games 2022-23?
(a) Gwalior (b) Delhi
(c) Ludhiana (d) Bhopal

282. In September 2022 the book 'Ambedkar and Modi: Reformer's Ideas Performer's Implementation' has been written by which of the following personalities?
(a) APJ Abdul Kalam
(b) Ram Nath Kovind
(c) Pratibha Patil
(d) Sarvepalli Radhakrishnan

283. In July 2021, which state government passed a resolution supporting an ad hoc committee report that favoured the creation of a legislative council?
(a) Bihar (b) Odisha
(c) Telangana (d) West Bengal

284. Which of the following state is the best governed state in the large states category as per the Public Affairs Index, 2020, which was released by the Public Affairs Centre, a non-profit organisation?
(a) Uttar Pradesh (b) Kerala
(c) Odisha (d) Bihar

285. In April 2023, Wing Commander Deepika Misra received which of the following awards?
(a) Uttam Yudh Seva Medal
(b) Vayu Sena Medal
(c) Shaurya Chakra
(d) Vir Chakra

286. To enhance the interoperability between the Indian and Russian Armies, a joint training exercise called _________ commenced at Prudboy Ranges, Volgograd in the year 2021.
(a) INDRA 2021 (b) VARUNA 2021
(c) SHAKTI 2021 (d) SURYA KIRAN 2021

287. In April 2023, India's External Affairs Minister S Jaishankar launched the project for restoration of which of the following ghats?
(a) Tulsi Ghat (b) Assi Ghat
(c) Cheer Ghat (d) Manikarnika Ghat

288. On 9 August 2021, the Parliament had passed the Limited Liability Partnership (Amendment) Bill, 2021. It amended the:
(a) Limited Liability Partnership Act, 2008
(b) Limited Liability Partnership Act, 2004
(c) Limited Liability Partnership Act, 2016
(d) Limited Liability Partnership Act, 2012

289. Which state introduced India's first 'Right to Health Care Act, 2022'?
(a) Rajasthan (b) Chhattisgarh
(c) Kerala (d) Assam

290. Which from the following unemployment scheme was extended by the government of India for a period of two years from July 2022 to June 2024?
(a) Atal Beemit Vyakti Kalyan Yojana
(b) Aatmanirbhar Bharat Rojgar Yojana
(c) Pradhan Mantri Berojgari Bhatta Yojana
(d) Grameen Udyami Yojana

291. In May 2023, the Supreme Court of India issued a set of directions to strengthen the POSH Act. To which of the following is this Act related?
(a) Sexual harassment of women at workplace
(b) Child trafficking
(c) Food security
(d) Amenities in jails

292. Indian athlete Shaili Singh won bronze medal in women's long jump at the Golden Grand Prix 2023 athletics meet held at ______.
(a) Singapore (b) Malaysia
(c) Japan (d) South Korea

293. Kiran Nadar was conferred with the highest civilian award of which country in April 2023?
(a) France (b) Egypt
(c) Poland (d) Germany

294. The Ultimate Kho-Kho League was started in which year?
(a) 2021 (b) 2023
(c) 2020 (d) 2022

295. Who was appointed as the Chief Economic Advisor to the Government of India in the year 2022?
(a) S Somanath
(b) V Anantha Nageswaran
(c) R Rangarajan
(d) Krishnamurthy Subramanian

296. The Maritime Anti-Piracy Act, 2022, received the assent of the President on ______.
(a) 31 December 2022 (b) 31 March 2023
(c) 30 April 2023 (d) 31 January 2023

297. In January 2022, which evacuation mission did the government of India launch to evacuate the Indians stranded in Ukraine?

(a) Operation Safe Homecoming
(b) Operation Raahat
(c) Operation Vande Bharat
(d) Operation Ganga

298. Who among the following cabinet ministers was appointed as the Governor of Karnataka in July 2021?
(a) Hari Babu Kambhampati
(b) Thawarchand Gehlot
(c) Rajendra Vishwanath
(d) Arjun Munda

299. According to Ministry of Agriculture and Farmers Welfare, what was the total food grain production of India in the year 2022-23?
(a) 2266.23 lakh tonnes
(b) 2876.17 lakh tonnes
(c) 2491.58 lakh tonnes
(d) 3296.87 lakh tonnes

300. Dinesh K Tripathi was appointed as _______ in January, 2024.
(a) Rear Admiral
(b) Vice Chief of Naval Staff
(c) Chief of Personnel
(d) Chief of Naval Staff

301. Which of the following teams won the IPL 2023 championship?
(a) Gujarat Titans
(b) Chennai Super Kings
(c) Lucknow SuperGiants
(d) Mumbai Indians

302. According to Global Multidimensional Poverty Index (2022), On the basis of four indicators - nutrition, cooking fuel, sanitation and housing, how much poor people live in India?
(a) 54.4 million (b) 44.4 million
(c) 34.4 million (d) 24.4 million

303. On 7 November 2022, the Supreme Court of India upheld the reservations for the weaker sections (EWS). Which of the following amendments brought this reservation in the first place?
(a) 101st Amendment of the Constitution
(b) 104th Amendment of the Constitution
(c) 102nd Amendment of the Constitution
(d) 103rd Amendment of the Constitution

304. In February 2023, Shiv Pratap Shukla was appointed governor of which state?
(a) Bihar (b) Tamil Nadu
(c) Himachal Pradesh (d) Haryana

305. What is the name of the scheme aimed at conservation of wetlands, which was announced in the Union Budget 2023-24?
(a) Amrit Dharohar
(b) Paryavaran Suraksha
(c) Dharohar
(d) Paryavaran Prahari

306. Ajit Kumar Mohanty took over the charge of Chairman, ______, in May 2023.
(a) National Commission for Backward Classes
(b) Atomic Energy Commission
(c) National Human Rights Commission of India
(d) Bhabha Atomic Research Centre

UPSC CDS II 2024

307. Which of the following are the major missions of Indian Space Research Organization in 2023?
1. Chandrayaan-3
2. Solar Mission Aditya-L1
3. Liquid fuel powered rockets
4. Solar powered rockets

Select the answer using the code given below:
(a) 1 and 2 only (b) 1, 2 and 3
(c) 3 and 4 only (d) 1, 2, 3 and 4

308. 'Bharat Parv' was organized by the Government of India during which of the following programmes?
1. Republic Day 2024
2. National Film Festival 2024
3. Cannes Film Festival 2024

(a) 1 and 2 only (b) 2 and 3 only
(c) 1 and 3 only (d) 1, 2 and 3

309. India's women's badminton team recently won the Badminton Asia Team Championship, 2024. Who among the following players was not a part of the team?
(a) P.V. Sindhu (b) Treesa Jolly
(c) Anmol Kharb (d) Saina Nehwal

310. Arrange the BRICS countries in ascending order of their rank in the Human Development Report 2023-24, released by the UNDP:
1. China 2. India
3. Russia 4. Brazil
4. South Africa

Select the answer using the code given below:
(a) 2, 5, 4, 1, 3 (b) 2, 4, 5, 3, 1
(c) 5, 4, 2, 3, 1 (d) 4, 5, 2, 1, 3

311. In June 2024, India signed a Memorandum of Understanding (MoU) with USA for supporting Indian Railways to achieve Mission Net Zero Carbon Emission by the year:
(a) 2030 (b) 2040
(c) 2050 (d) 2070

312. Which of the following statements is not correct?
(a) SAGAR-SETU is a mobile app, which aims to improve the Ease of Doing Business.
(b) Harit Sagar aims at achieving Zero Carbon Emission Goal.
(c) Sagar Manthan is a mission launched by Ministry of Ports, Shipping and Waterways, Government of India, to increase fish production.
(d) Costa Serena is the first international cruise liner in India.

313. ISRO, in its studies, has revealed that there is a 178% increase in the size of the Ghepang Ghat Glacial Lake. In which of the following States/UTs is this lake located?
(a) Jammu & Kashmir (b) Ladakh
(c) Himachal Pradesh (d) Uttarakhand

314. Which of the following State/s is/are common to Bru-Reang Agreement, NLFT (SD) Agreement and Tripartite Agreement with TIPRA?
(a) Tripura
(b) Assam and Tripura
(c) Tripura and Mizoram
(d) Manipur and Mizoram

315. Which of the following movies won the 96th Academy Award 2024 in the Best Picture category?
(a) Anatomy of a Fall
(b) Oppenheimer
(c) Barbie
(d) Killers of the Flower Moon

316. India's first dedicated OPD for the Transgenders was opened at which one among the following hospitals?
(a) AIIMS, New Delhi
(b) PGIMER, Chandigarh
(c) KGMU, Lucknow
(d) RML Hospital, New Delhi

317. Which one of the following statements about 'INS Tarmugli' is not correct?
(a) It is a fast attack craft commissioned by the Indian Navy.
(b) It was commissioned at Naval Dockyard, Visakhapatnam.
(c) It was given by the Government of India to Sri Lankan Naval Force in 2006 and returned to the Indian Navy in May 2023.
(d) It is supposed to be used for coastal surveillance.

318. Which one of the following resolutions in the final agreement reached at COP28 is associated with the target of achieving 'Net Zero by 2050'?
(a) Fossil fuel phase-out
(b) Methane emission cuts
(c) Global goal on adaptation
(d) Climate resilience

UPSC NDA II 2024

319. Consider the following statements:
I. Kozhikode has been included in UNESCO's creative cities network as the 'City of Music'.
II. Garba of Gujarat has been declared by UNESCO as an intangible cultural heritage.
III. Gwalior has been included in UNESCO's creative cities network as the 'City of Literature'.
IV. None

How many of the above statements is/are correct?
(a) None (b) 1 (c) 2 (d) 3

320. ASEAN-India Millet Festival-2023, organized by Indian Mission to ASEAN, was held in which one of the following countries?
(a) India (b) Indonesia
(c) Malaysia (d) Thailand

321. Consider the following statements:
I. First Indian Military Heritage festival was inaugurated in October 2023 in Pune.
II. First Green Hydrogen Fuel Cell Bus was flagged off in India in Bangalore.

III. South Africa chaired the 15th BRICS Summit held in 2023.
IV. Viksit Bharat Sankalp Yatra was flagged off in 2023 from Jharkhand.
How many of the above statements is/are correct?
(a) 1 (b) 2 (c) 3 (d) 4

322. Which of the following statements about 'ULLAS' scheme is/are NOT correct?
I. It's a Centrally Sponsored scheme which aims at securing childhood for street children.
II. It's a scheme aligned with National Education Policy-2020 which aims at empowering adults aged 15 or above who could not get due schooling.
Select the answer using the code given below:
(a) I only (b) II only
(c) Both I and II (d) Neither I nor II

323. In January 2024, India has entered into a bilateral agreement through which it will provide grant assistance to a country to construct a 20 feet Bailey bridge. Identify the country.
(a) Nepal (b) Bangladesh
(c) Bhutan (d) Myanmar

324. Consider the following statements:
i. India has secured 10th rank in the International Shipment category in World Bank's Logistics Performance Index Report-2023.
ii. Global Maritime India Summit-2023 was held in Vishakhapatnam.
iii. 'Maritime Amrit Kaal Vision 2047' was launched during Global Maritime India Summit-2023.
iv. None
How many of the above statements is/are correct?
(a) 4 (b) 1 (c) 2 (d) 3

AFCAT II 2024

325. Who among the following became the new Prime Minister of Nepal in July 2024?
(a) Raj Sharma
(b) Ram Chandra
(c) Sher Bahadur Deuba
(d) KP Sharma Oli

326. Recently added to the Ramsar List, the Nagi and Nakti Bird sanctuaries are situated in
(a) Uttar Pradesh (b) Bihar
(c) Rajasthan (d) Haryana

327. The 46th Antarctic Treaty Consultative Meeting (ATCM) was organised in which of the following countries?
(a) Greenland (b) Norway
(c) India (d) Switzerland

328. Which Indian state will be the first to adopt a 10-year road safety action plan aimed at reducing road accidents by 50% by 2030, and what technological measure will be implemented as part of this plan?
(a) Maharashtra (b) Tamil Nadu
(c) Rajasthan (d) Kerala

329. What is the name of the Chinese navigation satellite system that provides global positioning services?
(a) GPS (b) GLONASS
(c) Galileo (d) BeiDou

330. When was Kareena Kapoor Khan appointed as the National Ambassador of UNICEF India?
(a) March 2023 (b) May 2024
(c) January 2022 (d) July 2021

331. The Rampage missile, a recent addition to the Indian Air Force (IAF) and Indian Navy, is characterized as which of the following?
(a) A long-range, subsonic, air-to-air missile
(b) A medium-range, supersonic, anti-ship missile
(c) A long-range, supersonic, air-to-ground missile
(d) A short-range, supersonic, surface-to-air missile

SBI CLERK MAINS 2024

332. Arjuna Award winner Ayhika Mukherjee is associated with which of the following sports?
(a) Badminton (b) Squash
(c) Table Tennis (d) Hockey
(e) Lawn Tennis

333. Which tiger reserve has been recognized as India's first Dark Sky Park and the fifth in Asia, aimed at preserving the night sky and preventing light pollution, appealing to astronomy enthusiasts?
(a) Bandipur Tiger Reserve
(b) Pench Tiger Reserve
(c) Kanha Tiger Reserve
(d) Ranthambhore Tiger Reserve
(e) Sariska Tiger Reserve

334. The Union Government has extended the term of the CBDT Chairperson Nitin Gupta by ______.
(a) 3 months (b) 6 months
(c) 9 months (d) 12 months
(e) 18 months

335. Government has launched PM JANMAN (PM-Janjati Adivasi Nyaya Maha Abhiyan) which is aimed at comprehensive development of 75 Particularly Vulnerable Tribal Groups (PVTGs)
(a) 10 states (b) 12 states
(c) 15 states (d) 18 states
(e) 22 states

336. Govt launched the MPLADS e-SAKSHI Mobile Application for revised fund flow procedure under MPLAD Scheme. What amount of funds each year MPs receive under MPLAD Scheme?
(a) Rs. 2 crore (b) Rs. 3 crore
(c) Rs. 4 crore (d) Rs. 5 crore
(e) Rs. 7 crore

337. The Pension Fund Regulatory and Development Authority (PFRDA) has notified the National Pension System Trust (Second Amendment) Regulations 2023 and Pension Fund (Amendment) Regulations 2023 that simplify the provisions related to appointment of Trustees, their terms and conditions, holding of meetings of Board of Trustees and appointment of CEO - NPS Trust. Amendments to Pension Fund Regulations simplify the provisions related to governance of Pension Funds in line with ______
(a) Companies Act, 2013
(b) Limited Liability Partnership Act 2008
(c) Prevention of Money-Laundering Act, 2002
(d) Banking Regulation Acts 1949
(e) Pension Reforms Act (PFRDAAct, 2013)

338. The Ram Mandir in Ayodhya is designed in which style of architecture?
(a) Dravida (b) Vesara
(c) Nagara (d) Western
(e) Rajput

339. Recently, ISRO's third lunar mission Chandrayaan-3 landed on the moon while the first moon mission was launched by NASA. So far, how many times has the NASA mission landed on the moon?
(a) 7 (b) 8 (c) 9 (d) 10
(e) 12

340. In collaboration with which bank and the Reserve Bank Innovation Hub (RBIH) the DLabs at the Indian School of Business (ISB) launched 'Build for Billions' a startup accelerator program to focus on promoting financial inclusion for the informal economy?
(a) Canara Bank
(b) Indian Bank
(c) Bank of India
(d) Union Bank of India
(e) State Bank of India

341. According to the annual survey on International Trade in Banking Services (ITBS, 2022-23, Indian banks expanded their global presence through ______
(a) branch route (b) subsidiaries route
(c) join venture route (d) Both A and B
(e) None of the above

342. Which of the following pairs of types of banks and their numbers is not correctly matched?
(a) Public sector banks -12
(b) Regional Rural Banks – 43
(c) Local Area Banks - 4
(d) Small Finance Bank -11
(e) Payments Bank – 6

343. Which of the following types of banks can not extend MUDRA loan?
(a) Regional Rural Banks
(b) Payments Bank

(c) Small Finance Bank
(d) NBFCs
(e) MFIs

344. Which of the following union territories have the Regional Rural Banks (RRBs)?
(a) Ladakh
(b) Puducherry
(c) Andaman and Nicobar
(d) Lakshadweep
(e) Dadra and Nagar Haveli

345. As per RBI guidelines, a savings account will be treated as inoperative / dormant if there are no transactions in the account for over a period of ______.
(a) six month (b) one year
(c) two years (d) three years
(e) None of the above

346. The Reserve Bank of India (RBI) has included how many nonbanking finance companies (NBFCs) in the upper layer under scale based regulation for NBFCs for the year 2023-24?
(a) 10 (b) 12 (c) 15 (d) 18
(e) 20

347. Which fintech company has signed an agreement with the NPCI International Payments to expand the scope of Unified Payments Interface (UPI) payments outside India?
(a) PhonePe (b) Google Pay
(c) Paytm (d) Mobikwik
(e) Amazon Pay

348. State Bank of India (SBI) has raised what amount through its second Basel III compliant Additional Tier 1 bond issuance for the current financial year at a coupon rate of 8.34%?
(a) ₹3,000 crore (b) ₹4,000 crore
(c) ₹5,000 crore (d) ₹6,000 crore
(e) ₹8,000 crore

349. Which of the following banks is looking to open its first branch in Singapore?
(a) ICICI Bank (b) Yes Bank
(c) HDFC Bank (d) IndusInd Bank
(e) Kotak Mahindra Bank

350. What amount of penalty should be imposed on the first breach of Guidelines for Regulation of Coaching Center 2024 as per the new guidelines for the operation of coaching centres in the country issued by the Ministry of Education?
(a) Rs. 10, 000 (b) Rs. 25, 000
(c) Rs. 50, 000 (d) Rs. 75, 000
(e) Rs. 1,00, 000

351. What is the upper limit of annual household income for a collateral free Microfinance loan?
(a) Rs. 1,00,000 (b) Rs. 1,50,000
(c) Rs. 2,00,000 (d) Rs. 2,50,000
(e) Rs. 3,00,000

352. Which of the following entities became the top arranger for Indian offshore loans in 2023?
(a) HSBC Holdings Plc
(b) BNP Paribas
(c) Mizuho Financial Group Inc
(d) Citi Bank
(e) Barclays Bank

353. The Reserve Bank of India has proposed enhancing the limit for UPI payments to hospitals and educational institutions from Rs 1 lakh to Rs 5 lakh per transaction. What is the transaction limit for UPI payments for retail direct schemes and for IPO subscriptions?
(a) Rs 1 lakh (b) Rs 2 lakh
(c) Rs 3 lakh (d) Rs 4 lakh
(e) Rs 5 lakh

354. Which portal has been launched by the Reserve Bank of India for the search of unclaimed deposits across multiple banks at one place?
(a) UDGAM (b) MANI
(c) DAMINI (d) SCORES
(e) YUKTI

355. According to GST regulations, any person registered under GST who initiates the transportation of goods with a consignment value exceeding ______ must provide details of these goods in an E-way bill before the goods begin their journey.
(a) Rs. 25,000 (b) Rs. 50,000
(c) Rs. 75,000 (d) Rs. 100,000
(e) Rs. 200,000

356. The government hiked windfall tax on domestically produced crude oil to ₹3,300 per tonne from ₹3,200 per tonne. The tax is levied in the form of a ______.
(a) Value Added Tax
(b) Special Additional Excise Duty
(c) Special Additional custom duty
(d) Ad-Valorem Tax
(e) Special Goods and Service Tax

357. Who among the following do not hold the post of G20 sherpa?
(a) Girish Chandara Murmu
(b) Amitabh Kant
(c) Suresh Prabhu
(d) Shaktikanta Das
(e) Montek Singh Ahluwalia

358. How many numbers of unicorns were added in 2022 and 2021 respectively?
(a) 20 and 44 (b) 21 and 40
(c) 22 and 45 (d) 25 and 52
(e) 26 and 56

359. The Reserve Bank of India (RBI) has expanded the trade receivables discounting system (TReDS) by allowing insurance companies to participate. Which of the following is not a participant of TReDS platform?
(a) MSME sellers
(b) Corporate and other buyer
(c) PSUs
(d) NBFC Factors
(e) Import Agents

360. REC Limited, a Maharatna Central Public Sector Enterprise (CPSE) under the Ministry of Power, has achieved a significant milestone by issuing its inaugural Japanese Yen (JPY) 61.1 billion (approximately Rs 3,500 crore) green bonds for how many years?
(a) 2 years (b) 3 years
(c) 5 years (d) 7 years
(e) 8 years

361. Which Indian petrochemical company has become the first ISO 27001:2022 certified petrochemical organization in India, certified by British Standards Institution (BSI)?
(a) Haldia Petrochemicals Ltd (HPL)
(b) Reliance Petroleum
(c) Finolex Ind
(d) National Organic Chemical Industry Limited
(e) IG Petrochemicals Limited

362. In the BrandZ study, conducted by WPP and Kantar, Tata Consultancy Services (TCS) retained its top position as India's most valuable brand for the second consecutive year with a brand value of ______.
(a) \$36 billion (b) \$41 billion
(c) \$43 billion (d) \$48 billion
(e) \$52 billion

363. As per the 'Responsible Lending Conducts' issued by the Reserve Bank of India, banks and NBFCs have to release original movable, immovable property documents within ______ days of full repayments of loan.
(a) 15 days (b) 30 days
(c) 45 days (d) 60 days
(e) 90 days

364. A false or misleading claim made by an organization about the positive impact that a company, product or service has on the environment is known as ______.
(a) Greenwashing (b) Greentrading
(c) Greenmarketing (d) Greenwarming
(e) None of the above

365. Which of the following entities is not regulated by SEBI?
(a) Merchants Brokers
(b) Stock Brokers
(c) Clearing Corporation of India
(d) Portfolio managers
(e) Debenture trustees

366. Which financing agency has unveiled a groundbreaking seven-year USD 100 million Plastic Waste Reduction-Linked Bond, an innovative financial instrument that ties investor returns to Plastic Waste Collection Credits, Plastic Waste Recycling Credits, and Voluntary Carbon Units expected to be generated by projects in Ghana and Indonesia?
(a) World Economic Forum
(b) World Bank
(c) International Monetary Funds
(d) Asian Development Bank
(e) New Development Bank

367. Indian Renewable Energy Development Agency (IREDA) and which bank has signed a Memorandum of Understanding (MoU) aimed

at advancing renewable energy initiatives across the nation?
(a) Punjab National Bank
(b) Union Bank of India
(c) Canara Bank
(d) Indian Bank
(e) Bank of Baroda

368. Video, Audio, and images edited and manipulated using Artificial Intelligence (AI) is known as ______.
(a) Deepfake Technology
(b) AI-enhanced Media Editing
(c) Synthetic Media Production
(d) Neural Network Editing
(e) Machine Learning Manipulation

369. Which of the following languages are not part of the classical languages list of national education policy NEP?
(a) Pali (b) Prakrit
(c) Persian (d) Bengali
(e) Malayalam

370. The National Quantum mission has been launched for how many years?
(a) 3 years (b) 4 years
(c) 6 years (d) 8 years
(e) 10 years

371. What is the name of the DRDO multi-barrel rocket launchers (MBRL) system?
(a) Pinaka (b) Dhanush
(c) Akash (d) Gandiv
(e) Vijay

372. Which of the following is not included for the Liberelised Remittance Scheme (LRS)?
(a) Diversification of investment
(b) Overseas education
(c) Gift and Donation
(d) Medical Treatment
(e) All of the above

373. In the ICC World Cup tournament 2023 the Netherlands won the match defeating which of the following countries?
(a) Australia (b) Bangladesh
(c) England (d) New Zealand
(e) India

374. What is the tenure of the Board of Directors of the Reserve Bank of India?
(a) 2 years (b) 3 years
(c) 4 years (d) 5 years
(e) 6 years

375. As per the Report on Trend and Progress of Banking in India 2021- 22 published by the Reserve Bank of India (RBI), the Gross Non-Performing Assets (GNPA) ratio of Scheduled Commercial Banks (SCBs) has declined to ______ in September 2022 from 9% in 2017-18.
(a) 4% (b) 5%
(c) 6% (d) 7%
(e) 8%

376. Name the Argentina's state-owned enterprise with which the Khanij Bidesh India Ltd. (KABIL) has signed an MoU to acquire five lithium blocks in Argentina for exploration and development?
(a) CAMYEN (b) ENERGIA
(c) ENPGAS (d) INDAUTOR
(e) EDESA

377. Which of the following is not a category of 'States' startup ranking 2022 recently released by the Department for Promotion of Industry and Internal Trade (DPIIT)?
(a) Beginners (b) Leaders
(c) Best Performers (d) Top Performers
(e) Aspiring Leaders

378. According to the United Nations Population Fund (UNFPA), how much percentage of Indian population come under 15-64 working as a group?
(a) 52 percent (b) 54 percent
(c) 57 percent (d) 65 percent
(e) 68 percent

379. India's first Dark Sky Reserve Hanle, is located in which state/UTs?
(a) Puducherry (b) Maharashtra
(c) Goa (d) Ladakh
(e) Jammu and Kashmir

380. Who headed the Covid-19 stress committee constituted in August 2020 by the Reserve Bank of India?
(a) KV Kamath (b) Diwakar Gupta
(c) TN Manoharan (d) Ashvin Parekh
(e) Sunil Mehta

381. Which of the following are Domestically systematic insurers (D-SIIs)?
(i) Life Insurance Corporation (LIC)
(ii) New India Assurance
(iii) General Insurance Corporation (GIC Re)
(a) Only 1 and 2 (b) Only 2 and 3
(c) Only 1 and 3 (d) Only 3
(e) Only 1, 2 and 3

CDS - I 2024

382. Which of the following were objectives of the G20 Summit, 2023 under India's Presidency?
(i) Green development
(ii) Accelerating progress on SDGs
(iii) Women-led development
Select the correct answer using the code given below.
(a) (i) and (ii) only (b) (ii) and (iii) only
(c) (i), (ii) and (iii) (d) (i) and (iii) only

383. Which one of the following statements is true for James Webb Space Telescope launched in December 2021?
(a) It orbits the Sun, about 15 lakh km away from the Earth.
(b) It orbits the Earth, about 15 lakh km away.
(c) It is stationary in space nearly 10 lakh km away from the Earth.
(d) It revolves around the Moon nearly 3.5 lakh km away from the Earth.

384. Consider the following statements regarding instruments of monetary policy :
(i) Standing deposit facility (SDF) rate was introduced in April 2022.
(ii) SDF rate replaced fixed reverse repo rate as the floor of the LAF corridor.
Which of the above statements is/are correct?
(a) (i) only (b) (ii) only
(c) Both (i) and (ii) (d) Neither (i) nor (ii)

385. Who among the following is the author of the book Four Stars of Destiny : An Autobiography?
(a) Sam Manekshaw
(b) K. J. S. Dhillon
(c) Bipin Rawat
(d) Manoj Mukund Naravane

386. Which of the following cities were conferred with the cleanest city award under Swachh Survekshan Awards, 2023?
(a) Varanasi and Prayagraj
(b) Indore and Surat
(c) Prayagraj and Indore
(d) Surat and Varanasi

387. With which one among the following sports is Yogesh Singh, who won a Gold Medal in an Asian Championship in 2024 , associated?
(a) Badminton (b) Shooting
(c) Archery (d) Wrestling

388. Renowned classical singer Prabha Atre, who passed away recently, was an exponent of which one of the following Gharanas?
(a) Kirana Gharana (b) Patiala Gharana
(c) Gwalior Gharana (d) Agra Gharana

389. Which one of the following is an 'end-to-end secure mobile ecosystem' developed recently by the Indian Army?
(a) SANCHAR (b) VAIBHAV
(c) SAMPARK (d) SAMBHAV

390. Recently the Government of India entered into an agreement for a lithium exploration and mining project with which one among the following countries?
(a) Brazil (b) Australia
(c) Argentina (d) Chile

391. Which of the following statements about the ICC under-19 Men's Cricket World Cup, 2024 is/are correct?
(i) Australia won this title for the 4th time.
(ii) It was organised in South Africa.
Select the correct answer using the code given below.
(a) (i) only
(b) (ii) only
(c) Both (i) and (ii)
(d) Neither (i) nor (ii)

NDA -I 2024

392. Which of the following statements about India's rank in the Global Innovation Index-2023, published by the World Intellectual Property Organisation, is/are correct?
(i) India has been placed at 40th rank.
(ii) India has been on a rising trajectory over the period 2015-2023.
Select the correct answer using the code given below.
(a) (i) only (b) (ii) only
(c) Both (i) and (ii) (d) Neither (i) nor (ii)

393. Which of the following statements regarding 'aurora' is/are correct?
(i) The solar wind upon reaching the Earth's atmosphere is directed towards two magnetic poles and a colourful display of lights is seen in the night sky.
(ii) The particles interact with the different gases of the atmosphere and each gas glows with a particular colour.
(iii) In April 2023, aurora was captured in the night sky in India by the Indian Astronomical Observatory at Hanle, Ladakh.
Select the answer using the code given below:
(a) (i) only (b) (ii) and (iii) only
(c) (i) and (iii) only (d) (i), (ii) and (iii)

394. Recently the Ministry of Environment, Forest and Climate Change has submitted three nominations from India for Wetland City Accreditation (WCA) under the Ramsar Convention on Wetlands.
Which one among the following cities is not one among them?
(a) Indore (b) Bhopal
(c) Udaipur (d) Jodhpur

395. Which of the following statements is/are correct?
(i) In India, 12th March is celebrated as the National Youth Day.
(ii) National Youth Day is celebrated to commemorate the birth anniversary of Swami Vivekananda.
Select the answer using the code given below:
(a) (i) only (b) (ii) only
(c) Both (i) and (ii) (d) Neither (i) nor (ii)

396. Consider the following statements about INS Sagardhwani:
(i) It is an oceanographic research vessel of Naval Physical and Oceanographic Laboratory (NPOL) of DRDO.
(ii) Recently it embarked on the Sagar Maitri Mission-4 to establish long-term scientific partnerships with Indian Ocean Rim countries in Ocean Research and Development.
Which of the statements given above is/are correct?
(a) (i) only
(b) (ii) only
(c) Both (i) and (ii)
(d) Neither (i) nor (ii)

397. Who among the following is the Chairman of the Committee constituted by the Government of India to examine the issue of holding simultaneous elections in the country and to make recommendations thereon?
(a) Union Home Minister Shri Amit Shah
(b) Chief Justice of India Shri Dhananjaya Yeshwant Chandrachud
(c) Former President of India Shri Ram Nath Kovind
(d) Chief Election Commissioner of India Shri Rajiv Kumar

398. In January 2024, India's first all-girls' Sainik School was inaugurated at:
(a) Bhopal (b) Kohima
(c) Vrindavan (d) Namsai

399. In February 2024, Government of India has decided to scrap the Free Movement Regime (FMR) between India and:
(a) Myanmar (b) Bhutan
(c) Bangladesh (d) Nepal

400. Who among the following is the author of the book "Why Bharat Matters"?
(a) L.K. Advani
(b) S. Jaishankar
(c) Mohan Bhagwat
(d) Pranab Mukherjee

SSC GD CONSTABLE 2024

401. Which former SC judge has been appointed as the Governor of Andhra Pradesh?
(a) Sanjay Kishan Kaul
(b) S Abdul Nazeer
(c) Sanjiv khanna
(d) Bhushan Ramkrishna Gavai

402. Who has been appointed as the second Chief of Defence Staff (CDS) in India?
(a) Admiral R Hari Kumar
(b) General Manoj Pande
(c) General Manoj Mukund Naravane
(d) Lt General Anil Chauhan

403. In May 2023, Praveen Sood, the Director General of Police in Karnataka, has been appointed as the next director of the ______.
(a) World Bank
(b) Central Bureau of Investigation (CBI)
(c) CRPF
(d) FBI

404. Which of the following state's government launches Bhagwan Birsa Munda Jodaraste Scheme to Connect Tribal Villages with Main Roads?
(a) Haryana (b) Bihar
(c) Maharashtra (d) West Bengal

405. ____ has announced his new political party 'Democratic Azad Party' and also released his party flag. (September 2022)
(a) Rahul Gandhi
(b) Ghulam Nabi Azad
(c) Mallikarjun Kharge
(d) Adhir Ranjan Chowdhury

406. _____ unveiled a 12 feet high statue of the father of the nation Mahatma Gandhi and a 'Gandhi Vatika' at Gandhi Darshan in New Delhi in September 2023.
(a) Prime Minister of India
(b) President of India
(c) Home Minister of India
(d) Defense Minister of India

407. In June 2023, The Ministry of ______ recently announced that the Gandhi Peace Prize for 2021 will be conferred upon Gita Press Gorakhpur.
(a) Finance (b) Tourism
(c) Education (d) Culture

408. Which country hosts the Sultan Azlan Shah Cup?
(a) Malaysia (b) Singapore
(c) Thailand (d) Myanmar

409. The state of ______ has launched 'Chavath e Bazaar' initiative in the month of September 2023.
(a) Bihar (b) Jharkhand
(c) Madhya Pradesh (d) Goa

410. Which former Prime Minister of India has been conferred Lifetime Achievement Honour in UK?
(a) Atal Bihari Vajpayee
(b) Inder Kumar Gujral
(c) Dr. Manmohan Singh
(d) Haradanahalli Doddegowda Deve Gowda

411. Who has been recently appointed as the Vice Chief of the Indian Air Force in January 2023?
(a) Harjit Singh Arora
(b) Sandeep Singh
(c) Anil Khosla
(d) Amar Preet Singh

ANSWER KEYS

1. (a)	2. (e)	3. (a)	4. (d)	5. (d)	6. (d)	7. (c)	8. (e)	9. (d)	10. (a)
11. (c)	12. (b)	13. (c)	14. (a)	15. (c)	16. (b)	17. (d)	18. (b)	19. (b)	20. (d)
21. (a)	22. (a)	23. (b)	24. (a)	25. (c)	26. (d)	27. (d)	28. (b)	29. (b)	30. (c)
31. (d)	32. (b)	33. (d)	34. (d)	35. (c)	36. (d)	37. (c)	38. (b)	39. (c)	40. (d)
41. (d)	42. (a)	43. (c)	44. (d)	45. (d)	46. (b)	47. (c)	48. (b)	49. (b)	50. (c)
51. (c)	52. (b)	53. (c)	54. (c)	55. (b)	56. (e)	57. (a)	58. (e)	59. (a)	60. (b)
61. (b)	62. (a)	63. (c)	64. (e)	65. (c)	66. (a)	67. (c)	68. (b)	69. (a)	70. (c)
71. (b)	72. (a)	73. (a)	74. (d)	75. (d)	76. (a)	77. (e)	78. (b)	79. (c)	80. (b)
81. (a)	82. (a)	83. (e)	84. (d)	85. (a)	86. (e)	87. (b)	88. (d)	89. (d)	90. (d)
91. (a)	92. (c)	93. (b)	94. (b)	95. (d)	96. (a)	97. (c)	98. (d)	99. (b)	100. (a)
101. (d)	102. (d)	103. (a)	104. (c)	105. (b)	106. (b)	107. (b)	108. (c)	109. (c)	110. (b)
111. (c)	112. (b)	113. (b)	114. (c)	115. (a)	116. (b)	117. (a)	118. (b)	119. (d)	120. (c)
121. (b)	122. (b)	123. (c)	124. (b)	125. (b)	126. (b)	127. (a)	128. (d)	129. (a)	130. (c)
131. (b)	132. (b)	133. (a)	134. (c)	135. (a)	136. (c)	137. (b)	138. (d)	139. (a)	140. (d)
141. (d)	142. (a)	143. (c)	144. (a)	145. (a)	146. (a)	147. (d)	148. (d)	149. (a)	150. (a)
151. (b)	152. (a)	153. (b)	154. (a)	155. (d)	156. (d)	157. (d)	158. (d)	159. (c)	160. (d)
161. (d)	162. (d)	163. (c)	164. (c)	165. (a)	166. (d)	167. (d)	168. (b)	169. (d)	170. (d)
171. (c)	172. (c)	173. (b)	174. (a)	175. (b)	176. (d)	177. (d)	178. (c)	179. (b)	180. (c)
181. (c)	182. (d)	183. (c)	184. (d)	185. (d)	186. (b)	187. (b)	188. (d)	189. (a)	190. (b)
191. (b)	192. (a)	193. (d)	194. (d)	195. (d)	196. (d)	197. (d)	198. (b)	199. (a)	200. (b)
201. (c)	202. (b)	203. (c)	204. (a)	205. (d)	206. (d)	207. (c)	208. (d)	209. (a)	210. (d)
211. (a)	212. (c)	213. (d)	214. (d)	215. (a)	216. (a)	217. (a)	218. (d)	219. (b)	220. (b)
221. (d)	222. (c)	223. (c)	224. (c)	225. (b)	226. (b)	227. (b)	228. (a)	229. (a)	230. (a)
231. (c)	232. (a)	233. (c)	234. (b)	235. (a)	236. (c)	237. (a)	238. (a)	239. (d)	240. (a)
241. (a)	242. (c)	243. (a)	244. (a)	245. (c)	246. (a)	247. (d)	248. (a)	249. (c)	250. (d)
251. (a)	252. (d)	253. (b)	254. (d)	255. (c)	256. (a)	257. (c)	258. (c)	259. (c)	260. (d)
261. (a)	262. (c)	263. (a)	264. (b)	265. (a)	266. (d)	267. (b)	268. (d)	269. (a)	270. (a)
271. (d)	272. (c)	273. (b)	274. (b)	275. (b)	276. (c)	277. (a)	278. (a)	279. (a)	280. (c)
281. (c)	282. (b)	283. (d)	284. (a)	285. (b)	286. (a)	287. (a)	288. (a)	289. (a)	290. (a)
291. (a)	292. (c)	293. (a)	294. (d)	295. (b)	296. (d)	297. (d)	298. (b)	299. (d)	300. (b)
301. (b)	302. (c)	303. (d)	304. (c)	305. (a)	306. (b)	307. (a)	308. (c)	309. (c)	310. (a)
311. (a)	312. (c)	313. (c)	314. (a)	315. (b)	316. (d)	317. (c)	318. (a)	319. (b)	320. (b)
321. (b)	322. (a)	323. (d)	324. (b)	325. (d)	326. (b)	327. (c)	328. (c)	329. (d)	330. (b)
331. (c)	332. (c)	333. (b)	334. (c)	335. (d)	336. (d)	337. (a)	338. (c)	339. (d)	340. (d)
341. (b)	342. (c)	343. (b)	344. (b)	345. (c)	346. (c)	347. (b)	348. (c)	349. (c)	350. (b)
351. (e)	352. (a)	353. (e)	354. (a)	355. (b)	356. (b)	357. (a)	358. (c)	359. (e)	360. (c)
361. (a)	362. (c)	363. (b)	364. (a)	365. (c)	366. (b)	367. (a)	368. (a)	369. (d)	370. (d)
371. (a)	372. (e)	373. (b)	374. (c)	375. (b)	376. (a)	377. (a)	378. (e)	379. (d)	380. (a)
381. (e)	382. (c)	383. (a)	384. (c)	385. (d)	386. (b)	387. (b)	388. (a)	389. (d)	390. (c)
391. (c)	392. (c)	393. (d)	394. (d)	395. (b)	396. (c)	397. (c)	398. (c)	399. (a)	400. (b)
401. (b)	402. (d)	403. (b)	404. (c)	405. (b)	406. (b)	407. (d)	408. (d)	409. (d)	410. (c)
411. (d)									